WHISPERING DEATH

WHISPERING DEATH

MARK JOHNSTON

ALLEN&UNWIN

First published in 2011

Allen & Unwin
Sydney, Melbourne, Auckland, London

83 Alexander Street
Crows Nest NSW 2065
Australia
Phone: (61 2) 8425 0100
Fax: (61 2) 9906 2218
Email: info@allenandunwin.com
Web: www.allenandunwin.com

Cataloguing-in-Publication details are available from the National Library of Australia
www.trove.nla.gov.au

ISBN 978 1 74175 901 3

Maps/illustrations by Ian Faulkner
Set in 11.5/14.5 pt Bembo by Midland Typesetters, Australia
Printed and bound in Australia by Pegasus Media & Logistics

35 34 33 32 31 30

MIX
Paper | Supporting responsible forestry
FSC® C008194
www.fsc.org

The paper in this book is FSC® certified. FSC® promotes environmentally responsible, socially beneficial and economically viable management of the world's forests.

EU Authorised Representative: Easy Access System Europe, Mustamäe tee 50, 10621 Tallinn, Estonia, gpsr.requests@easproject.com

Contents

List of maps

Development of Advanced Operational Bases, November 1939 to December 1941

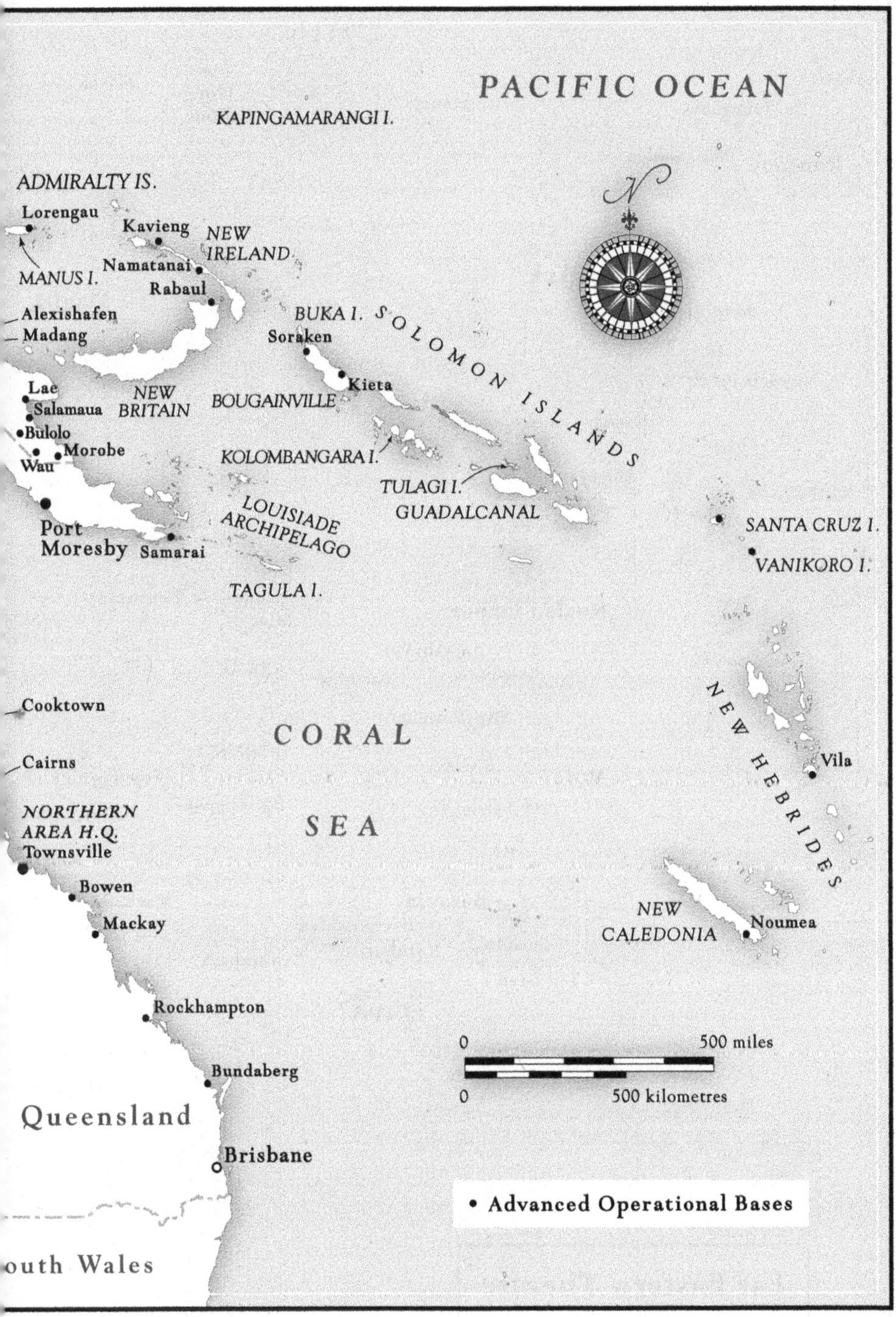
PACIFIC OCEAN
KAPINGAMARANGI I.
ADMIRALTY IS.
Lorengau
MANUS I.
Kavieng
NEW IRELAND
Namatanai
Rabaul
Alexishafen
Madang
NEW BRITAIN
Lae
Salamaua
Bulolo
Morobe
Wau
Port Moresby
Samarai
BUKA I.
Soraken
Kieta
BOUGAINVILLE
SOLOMON ISLANDS
KOLOMBANGARA I.
TULAGI I.
GUADALCANAL
LOUISIADE ARCHIPELAGO
TAGULA I.
SANTA CRUZ I.
VANIKORO I.
NEW HEBRIDES
Vila
NEW CALEDONIA
Noumea
CORAL SEA
Cooktown
Cairns
NORTHERN AREA H.Q.
Townsville
Bowen
Mackay
Rockhampton
Bundaberg
Queensland
Brisbane
outh Wales
0
500 miles
0
500 kilometres
• Advanced Operational Bases

Far Eastern Theatre

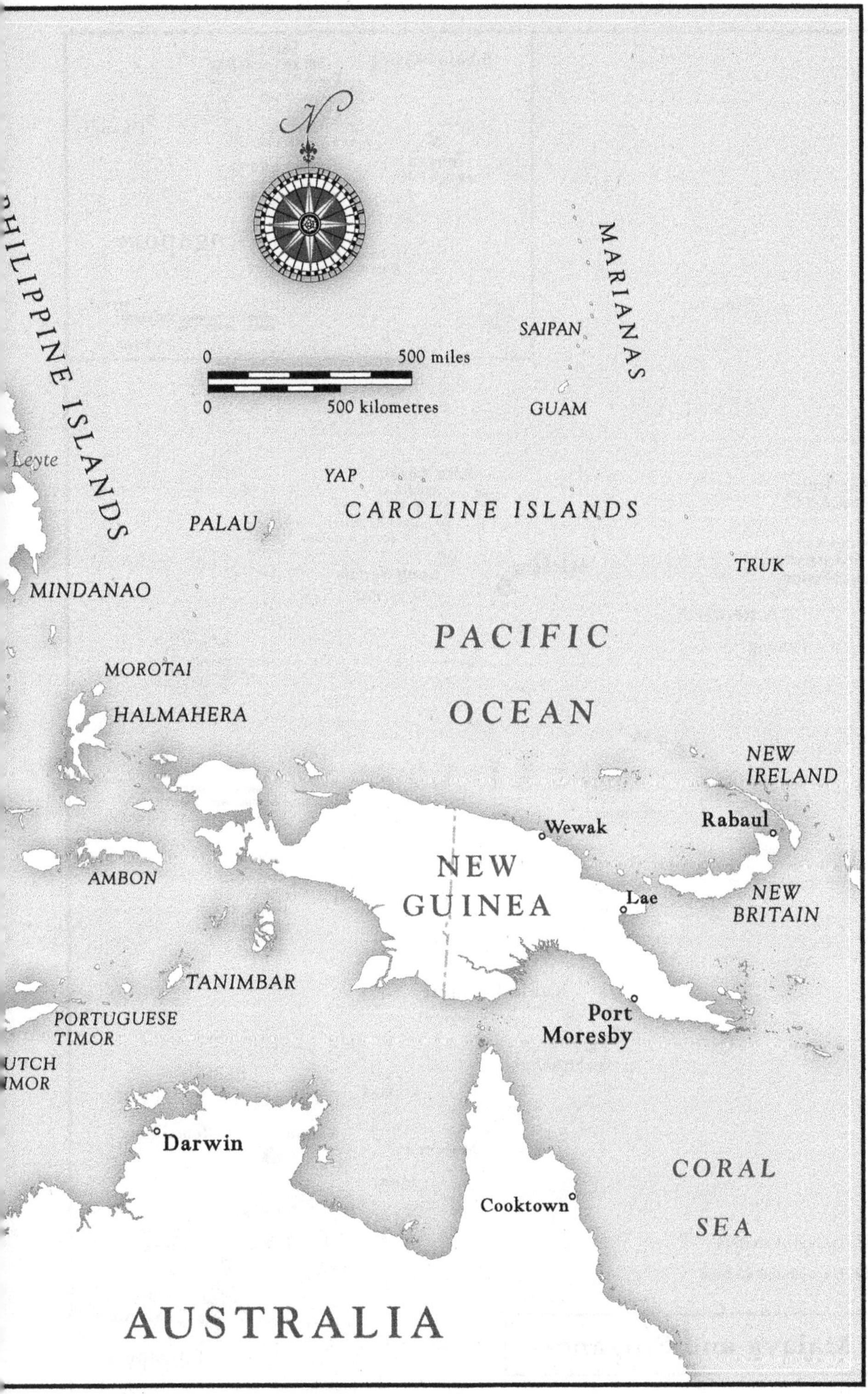

N
0
500 miles
0
500 kilometres
PHILIPPINE ISLANDS
Leyte
MINDANAO
MARIANAS
SAIPAN
GUAM
YAP
PALAU
CAROLINE ISLANDS
TRUK
PACIFIC
OCEAN
MOROTAI
HALMAHERA
NEW
IRELAND
Rabaul
Wewak
NEW
GUINEA
AMBON
Lae
NEW
BRITAIN
TANIMBAR
PORTUGUESE
TIMOR
Port
Moresby
UTCH
IMOR
Darwin
CORAL
SEA
Cooktown
AUSTRALIA

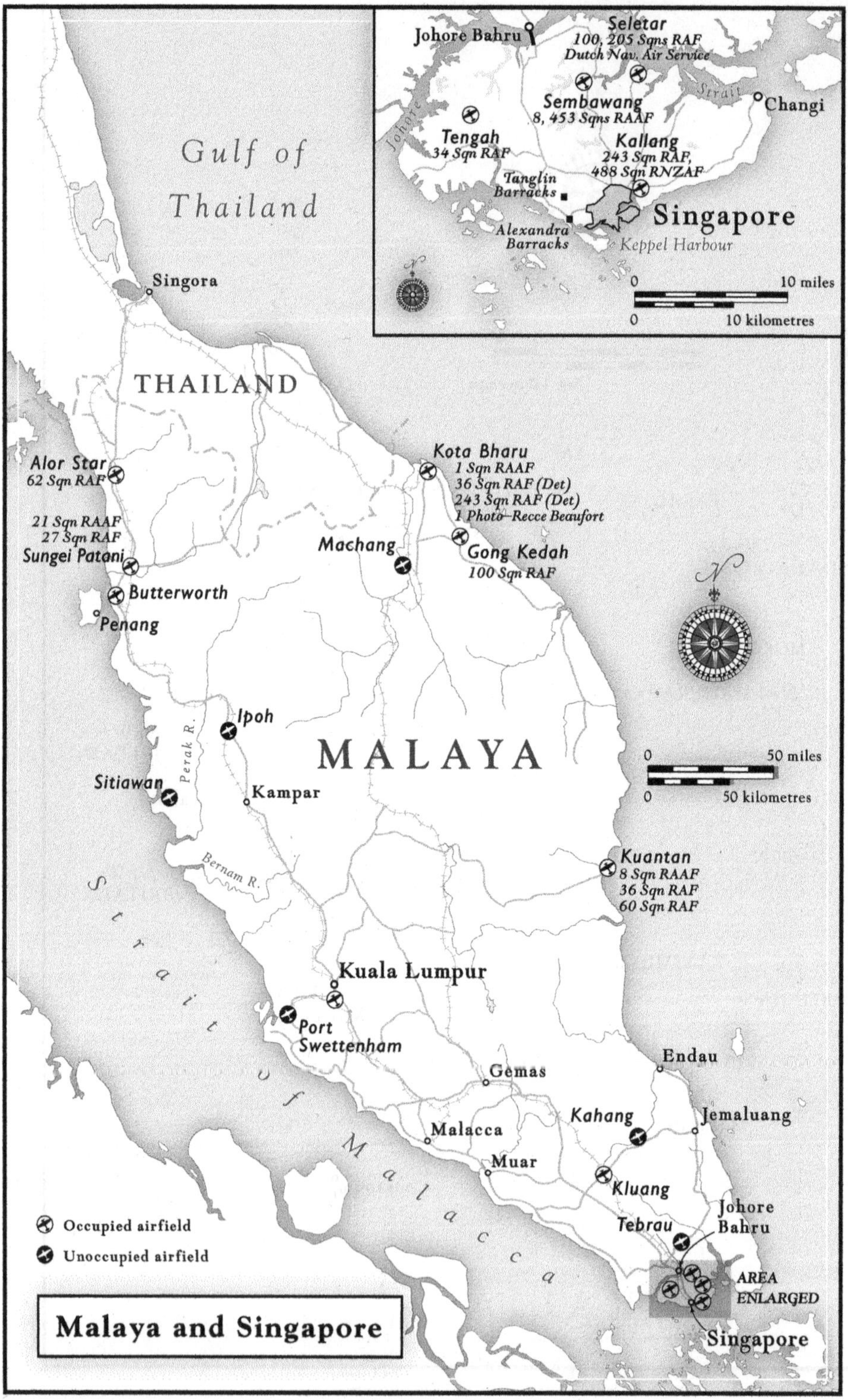

Johore Bahru
Seletar
100, 205 Sqns RAF
Dutch Nav. Air Service
Johore Strait
Changi
Sembawang
8, 453 Sqns RAAF
Tengah
34 Sqn RAF
Kallang
243 Sqn RAF,
488 Sqn RNZAF
Tanglin Barracks
Alexandra Barracks
Singapore
Keppel Harbour
0 10 miles
0 10 kilometres
Gulf of Thailand
Singora
THAILAND
Alor Star
62 Sqn RAF
21 Sqn RAAF
27 Sqn RAF
Sungei Patani
Butterworth
Penang
Kota Bharu
1 Sqn RAAF
36 Sqn RAF (Det)
243 Sqn RAF (Det)
1 Photo-Recce Beaufort
Machang
Gong Kedah
100 Sqn RAF
Ipoh
Perak R.
MALAYA
Sitiawan
Kampar
0 50 miles
0 50 kilometres
Bernam R.
Kuantan
8 Sqn RAAF
36 Sqn RAF
60 Sqn RAF
Strait of Malacca
Kuala Lumpur
Port Swettenham
Endau
Gemas
Kahang
Jemaluang
Malacca
Muar
Kluang
Johore Bahru
Tebrau
AREA ENLARGED
Singapore
Occupied airfield
Unoccupied airfield
Malaya and Singapore

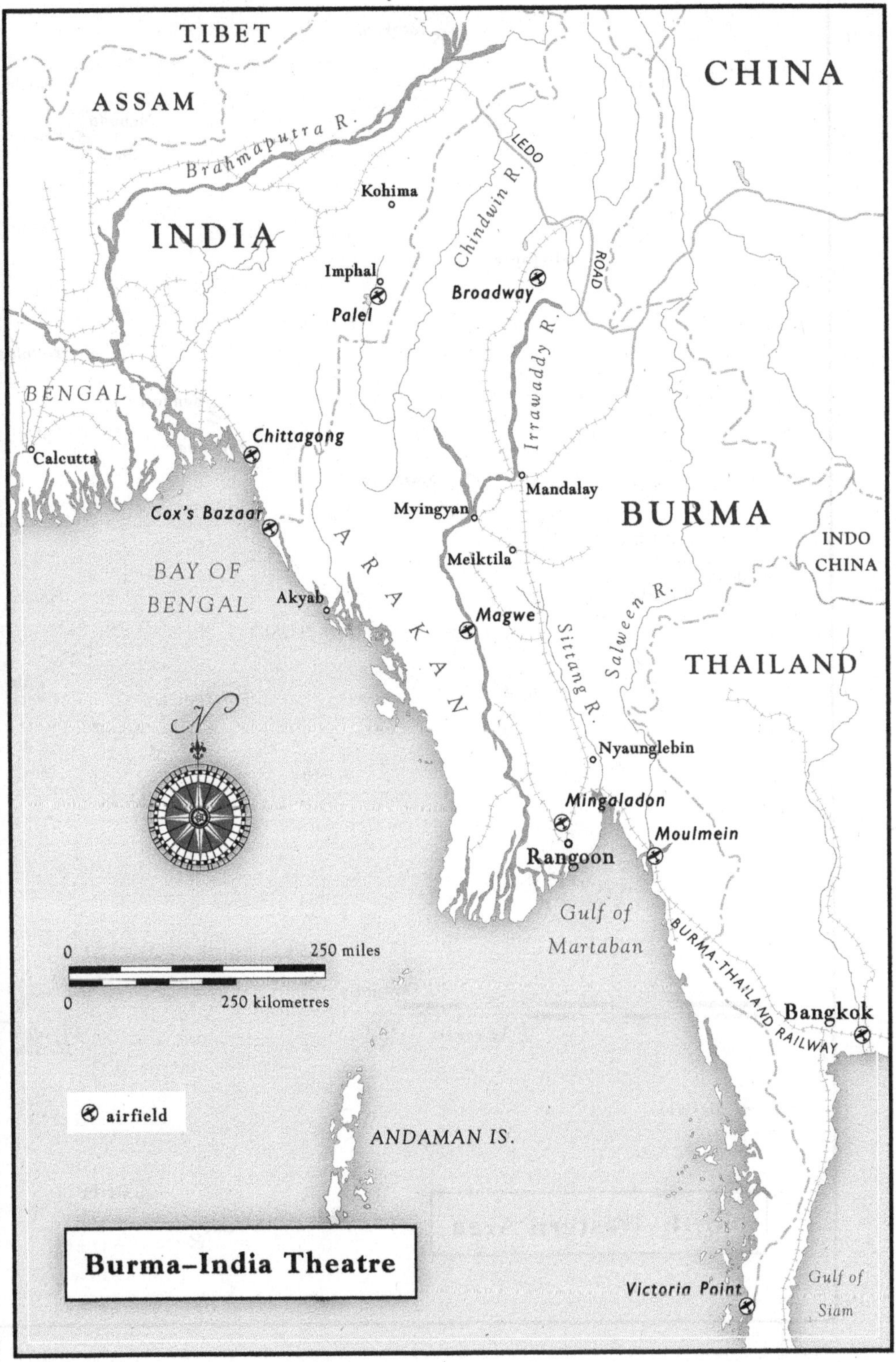

Burma–India Theatre

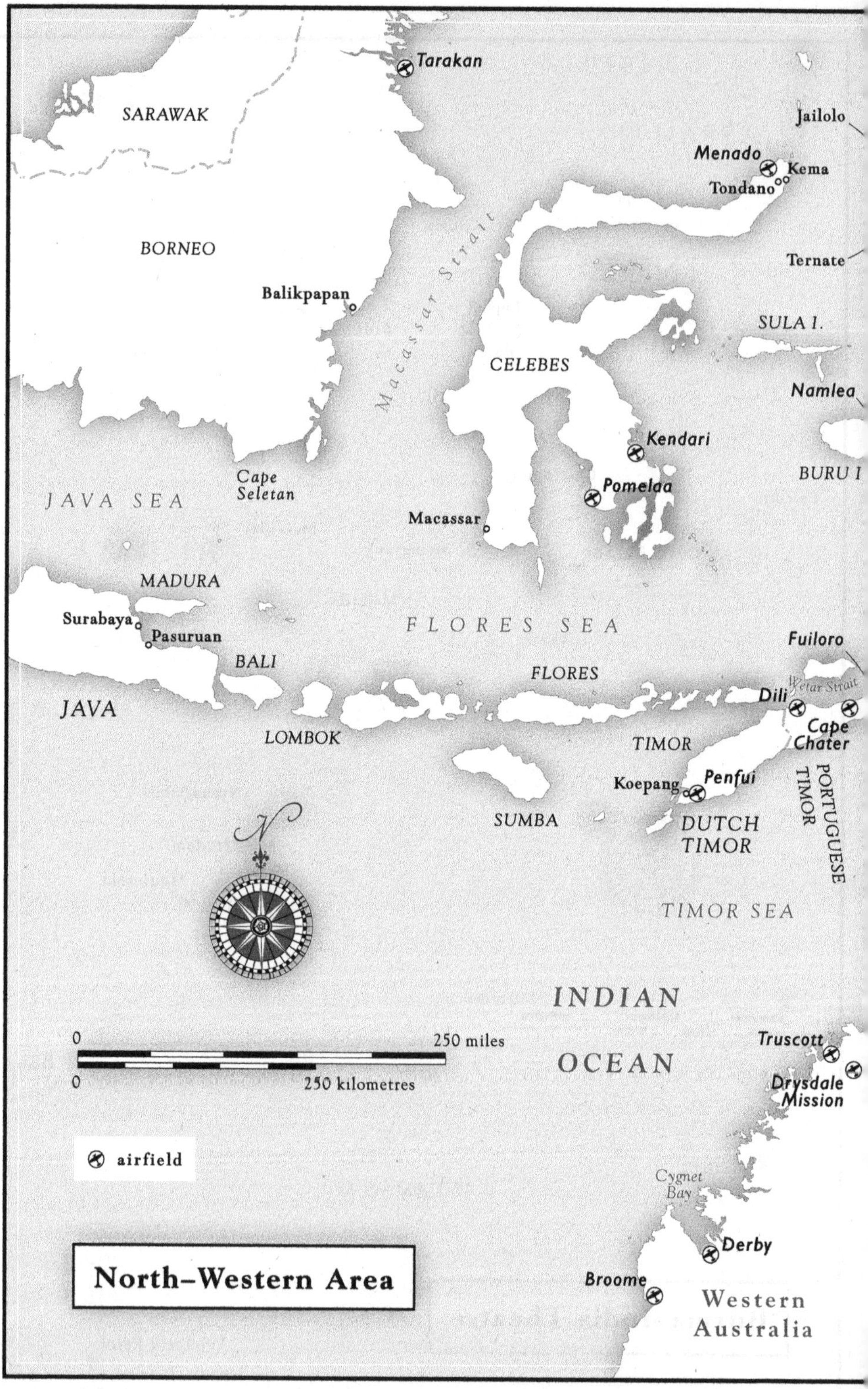

Tarakan
SARAWAK
Jailolo
Menado
Kema
Tondano
BORNEO
Ternate
Balikpapan
Macassar Strait
SULA I.
CELEBES
Namlea
Kendari
BURU I
Cape Seletan
Pomelaa
JAVA SEA
Macassar
MADURA
Surabaya
Pasuruan
FLORES SEA
Fuiloro
BALI
FLORES
Wetar Strait
Dili
JAVA
Cape Chater
LOMBOK
TIMOR
Koepang
Penfui
PORTUGUESE TIMOR
SUMBA
DUTCH TIMOR
N
TIMOR SEA
INDIAN OCEAN
0
250 miles
0
250 kilometres
Truscott
Drysdale Mission
airfield
Cygnet Bay
Derby
Broome
Western Australia
North–Western Area

TOBI I.
PACIFIC OCEAN
MOROTAI
Wama
HALMAHERA
MAPIA I.
SCHOUTEN I.
Cape Sansapor
Manokwari
BIAK
Samate
Sorong
Vogelkop Peninsula
JAPEN I.
Wakde
Sarmi
Hollandia
ROEMBERPON I.
Aitape
Wewak
Macclear Gulf
Babo
CERAM
Kokas
DUTCH NEW GUINEA
Kaimana
NORTH EAST NEW GUINEA
Haruku Strait
Timuka
BON
BANDA IS.
BANDA SEA
Dobo
NEW GUINEA
Kai Keri
ARU I.
Taberfane
PAPUA
Selaru
Cape Valsch
Merauke
SELARU I.
Torres Strait
ARAFURA SEA
THURSDAY I.
HORN I.
MELVILLE I.
HURST I.
Gove
Cape York Peninsula
Millingimbi
Darwin
Strauss
Sattler
Hughes
Livingstone
Coomalie
Batchelor
Pell
Gulf of Carpentaria
McDonald
Fenton
Katherine
Manbulloo
Tindal
Venn
Birdum
Daly Waters
Wyndham
AUSTRALIA
Tennant Creek
Rabbit Flat
Northern Territory
Queensland

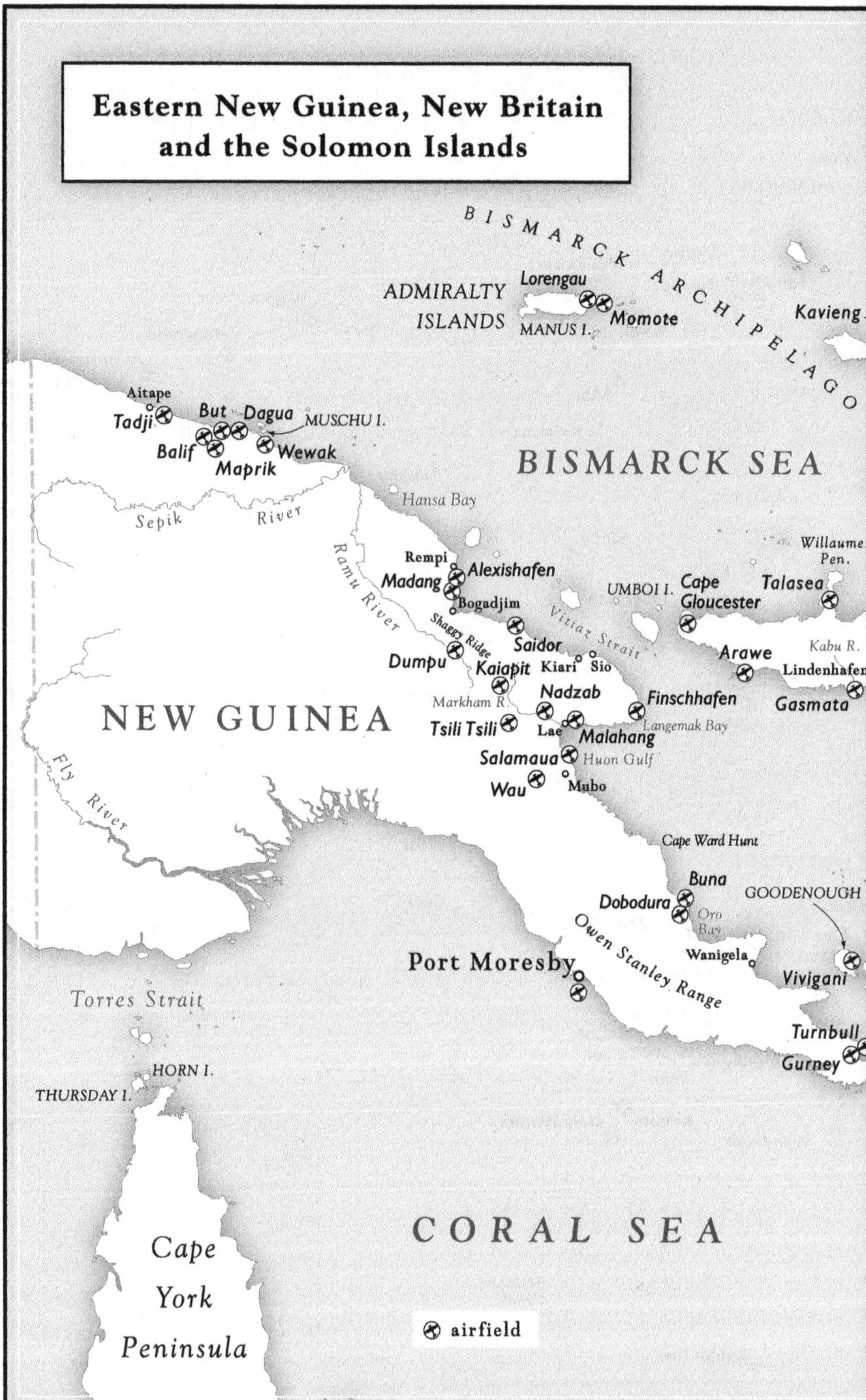

Eastern New Guinea, New Britain and the Solomon Islands
BISMARCK ARCHIPELAGO
ADMIRALTY ISLANDS
Lorengau
Momote
MANUS I.
Kavieng
Aitape
Tadji
But
Dagua
MUSCHU I.
Balif
Maprik
Wewak
BISMARCK SEA
Hansa Bay
Sepik River
Ramu River
Rempi
Alexishafen
Madang
Bogadjim
Willaumez Pen.
UMBOI I.
Cape Gloucester
Talasea
Vitiaz Strait
Shaggy Ridge
Saidor
Dumpu
Kaiapit
Kiari
Sio
Arawe
Kabu R.
Lindenhafen
Gasmata
Markham R.
Nadzab
Finschhafen
NEW GUINEA
Tsili Tsili
Lae
Malahang
Langemak Bay
Salamaua
Huon Gulf
Wau
Mubo
Fly River
Cape Ward Hunt
Buna
Dobodura
Oro Bay
GOODENOUGH I.
Owen Stanley Range
Wanigela
Port Moresby
Vivigani
Torres Strait
Turnbull
Gurney
HORN I.
THURSDAY I.
CORAL SEA
Cape York Peninsula
airfield

PACIFIC
OCEAN
WATOM I.
Tawui Point
0
5 miles
5 kilometres
Talili Bay
Rabaul
Sulphur Ck
DUKE OF YORK I.
Malaguna
Simpson Hbr
Lakunai
Praed Point
Vulcan Crater
MATUPI I.
Blanche Bay
Keravia Bay
Keravat
Ralum
Lesson Point
Vunakanau
Vunapope
Rapopo
airfield
Tobera
Gazelle Peninsula
NEW IRELAND
AREA
NLARGED
Rabaul
Cape St George
Wide Bay
BOUGAINVILLE
Jacquinot Bay
EW BRITAIN
SOLOMON ISLANDS
Torokina
Empress Augusta Bay
Buin
SHORTLAND I.
Ballale
SOLOMON SEA
Vila
NEW GEORGIA
Munda
ROBRIAND I.
KITAVA I.
WOODLARK I.
SAVO I.
Henderson Field
GUADALCANAL
0
250 miles
250 kilometres

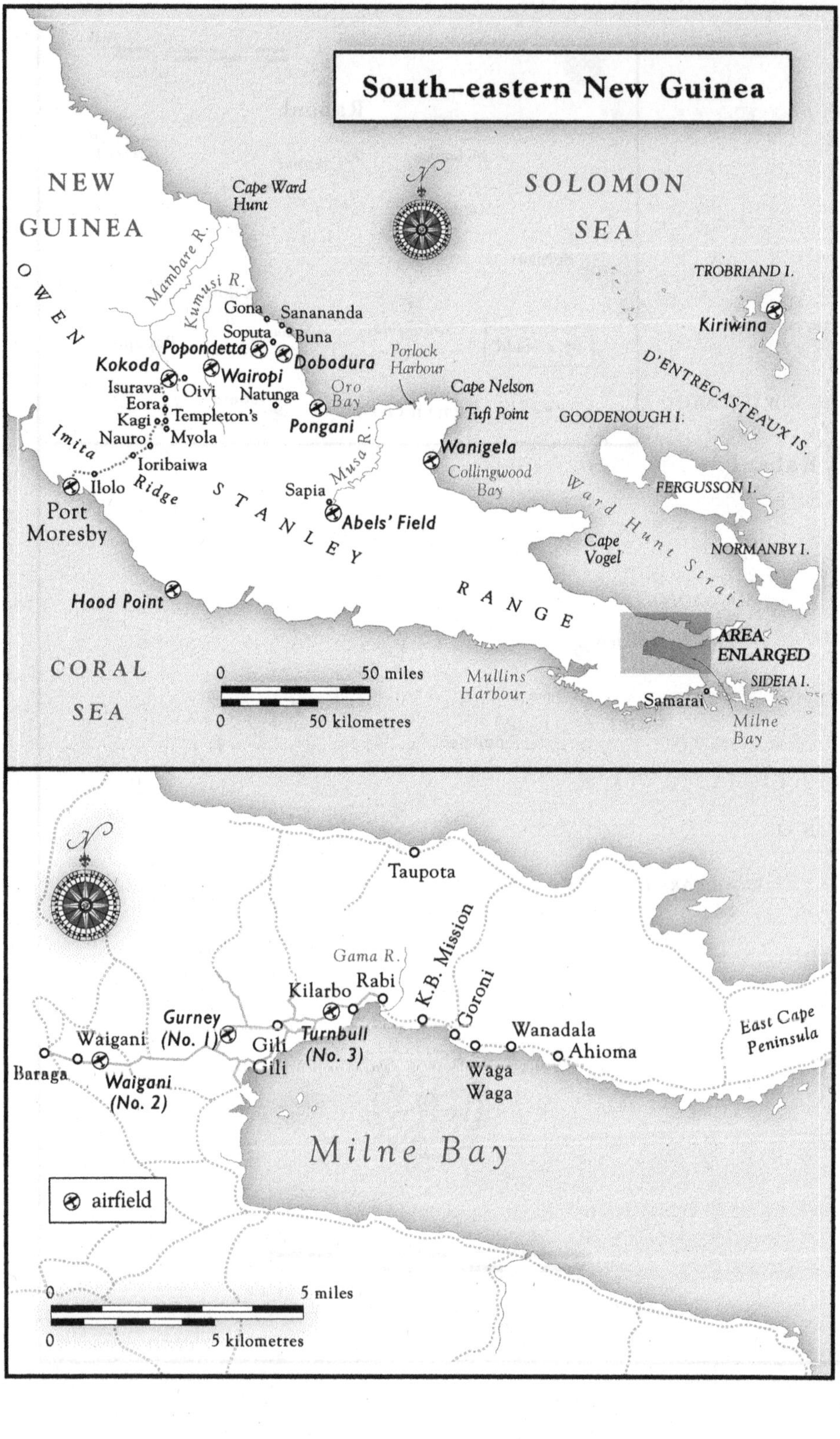
South–eastern New Guinea
NEW GUINEA
SOLOMON SEA
CORAL SEA
OWEN STANLEY RANGE
Cape Ward Hunt
Mambare R.
Kumusi R.
Gona
Sananada
Soputa
Buna
Popondetta
Dobodura
Kokoda
Wairopi
Isurava
Oivi
Natunga
Eora
Templeton's
Kagi
Nauro
Myola
Ioribaiwa
Imita Ridge
Ilolo
Port Moresby
Hood Point
Porlock Harbour
Oro Bay
Pongani
Musa R.
Sapia
Abels' Field
Cape Nelson
Tufi Point
Wanigela
Collingwood Bay
Cape Vogel
Ward Hunt Strait
TROBRIAND I.
Kiriwina
D'ENTRECASTEAUX IS.
GOODENOUGH I.
FERGUSSON I.
NORMANBY I.
AREA ENLARGED
SIDEIA I.
Samarai
Milne Bay
Mullins Harbour
0 50 miles
0 50 kilometres
Taupota
K.B. Mission
Gama R.
Rabi
Kilarbo
Goroni
Gurney (No. 1)
Turnbull (No. 3)
Gili Gili
Waigani
Baraga
Waigani (No. 2)
Wanadala
Ahioma
Waga Waga
East Cape Peninsula
Milne Bay
airfield
0 5 miles
0 5 kilometres

List of tables

Note on measurements and ranks

Measurements in this book are generally given in metric, but in line with continuing aviation practice, altitudes are given in feet. In order to save space and avoid repetition, I have also not given ranks except where this has a bearing on the story. Table 1 shows the RAAF ranks and their Army equivalents.

TABLE 1 RAAF RANKS 1939–45

RAAF	Army equivalent
Other ranks	
Aircraftman	Private
Leading Aircraftman	
Non-commissioned officers	
Corporal	Corporal
Sergeant	Sergeant
Flight Sergeant	
Warrant officers	
Warrant Officer	Warrant Officer Class I
Commissioned officers	
Pilot Officer	Second Lieutenant
Flying Officer	Lieutenant
Flight Lieutenant	Captain
Squadron Leader	Major
Wing Commander	Lieutenant-Colonel
Group Captain	Colonel
Air Commodore	Brigadier
Air Vice-Marshal	Major-General
Air Marshal	Lieutenant-General
Air Chief Marshal	General

Acknowledgements

The author of a book as big as this and on a topic so huge depends on many others. For the fact that I was given the opportunity to write this book I am very grateful to my good friend Dr Peter Stanley, who suggested my name to Allen & Unwin. At that publisher, Ian Bowring put faith in my ability to complete the task, and gave me excellent advice in the process. My thanks to the entire team who worked on the book at Allen & Unwin, especially Angela Handley, Katri Hilden and Ian Faulkner. Professor Hank Nelson, a great authority on the Pacific War and on the RAAF, was significant in the genesis of this book.

The Australian War Memorial is the first stopping point for any Australian military historian, and I have used its online resources virtually every day during the two years in which I wrote this book. The staff were also very helpful on my visits to Canberra. So too were the staff of the Office of Air Force History. I benefited enormously from the assistance I received from the RAAF Historian Dr Chris Clark, and Steve Allan of the OAFH, who enabled me to examine thousands of pages of invaluable documents. Staff at the RAAF Museum at Point Cook and the Australian National Aviation Museum also gave me assistance and inspiration.

Other individuals whom I wish to thank for their help on the many aspects of this project include Phillip Bradley, Dick Briggs, Jacqueline

Crock (nee Bladin), Brian Farrell, Judy Foster, Robert Garing, Ian Gould, Patricia and Arthur Jackson, Ken James, John May, Paul Mishura, Marnie O'Bryan, Neville Parnell, Loredana Pufulete, Alan Reed, Sherril Schultz, Joanne Smedley, Michael Taper, Craig Tibbitts and Peter Trumble.

I was fortunate indeed to be able to speak to veteran airmen John Kessey, Herb Plenty, Charles Roe and Jack Shaw. Their insights were invaluable.

My debt to other historians of the RAAF, including Alan Stephens, Lex McAulay, David Wilson, George Dick, and especially the official historians Douglas Gillison and George Odgers, will be obvious in the following pages.

Two people deserve special thanks for their expert assistance. Kristen Alexander, the author of several excellent aviation histories, read substantial parts of the text and gave me much valuable advice. Peter Hunter, whose father Bob was a 76 Squadron pilot and who is himself a present-day Qantas pilot, helped me tremendously. He generously sent me copies of his own painstakingly collected materials relating to 76 Squadron, gave me much invaluable technical advice while I was writing the book, and commented on the entire manuscript once it was finished.

Naturally I am responsible for any errors that remain.

My family, and especially my dear wife Deborah, gave me unstinting support in this unusually demanding project.

Introduction

This is the inspiring and disturbing story of Australian airmen and aircraft in the Pacific War. It is above all a rousing tale—of skill, bravery, sacrifice and ultimate triumph. Yet it is troubling, too, for sacrifice took the form of violent death. Airmen often died horribly: by burning, plummeting from great heights, drowning, or at the hands of brutal and vindictive captors. But the story is also disturbing for other reasons, mostly connected to the fact that Australia was a junior partner in an alliance with Britain and America. In matters as fundamental as the number and types of aircraft Australia had, the war fronts to which its trainees were allocated, who led its air force, and where and how the air force fought Japan, the key decisions fell to its allies. One painful consequence was that in the last two years of the Pacific War, the Royal Australian Air Force (RAAF) was relegated to a role so subordinate to the American air forces that many Australian airmen came to see their labours as a waste of time and life.

On the other hand, Australia's British and particularly its American allies brought great benefits to the nation's aerial war effort, the Americans not least by helping to contain Japan's damage to the Australian continent. Moreover, the RAAF's rapid expansion within this alliance was a mighty achievement, despite the marked defects also developed. By war's end the RAAF was reportedly the world's fourth largest, behind only those of the USA, USSR and Great Britain. It was for some time not only more numerous, but also more efficient and deadly than the once invincible Japanese air forces in its region.

The Australian airmen who are the main players in this book operated over a huge area, stretching from India to Bougainville, from the Philippines to Bass Strait. Much of that airspace was above water or jungle, where 'ditching' often meant death. Just navigating the vast distances and negotiating the threatening weather conditions of the Pacific War left few veterans without at least one near-death experience. Add to that the efforts of a determined and skilful enemy with aircraft that in 1941 took the world by surprise and you have the ingredients of a great story.

This is also a book about machines. Of the armed forces, the air force is the most dependent on technology. By war's end the RAAF was operating some 70 types of aircraft. These were a mixed assortment, and with a few notable exceptions did not represent the best technology of the day. This makes the achievements of the Australian aircrews who fought, who too often died, and who ultimately triumphed in them all the more admirable. Of course Japanese aircraft are an important part of the story too. Their Japanese names were complicated and confusing to Westerners. Their meanings were striking, including 'Heavenly Thunder', 'Dragon Killer' and 'Heavenly Mountain'. Understandably, though, the American air force developed codenames for them, giving male first names to fighters and female names to other types. Like the RAAF, I have followed their example, with the exception of the fighter the Americans officially called the 'Zeke' or, in a later version, the 'Hamp'. In this book it is usually called 'Zero', the name most Allied airmen applied to this most significant fighter. Line drawings of all the major aircraft types mentioned in the text appear in Appendix A.

Flying in a World War II aircraft was infinitely rougher, noisier and smellier than travelling as a passenger in a modern jet. Even discounting the perils of aerial combat, it was also much more dangerous, with sudden death always perched on one's shoulder in the form of a 'gremlin'—a potential mechanical failure. The guts required to fly a 1940s aircraft, be it a Boomerang or a Zero, a Beaufort or a Betty, will be obvious in the pages that follow.

Air power was critical to the Pacific War: indeed, as one leading American war correspondent wrote, 'essentially, the Pacific was an air war'.[1] The horrible events identified with its beginning, at Pearl Harbor, and its conclusion, at Hiroshima and Nagasaki, centred around aircraft. Yet essential though aircraft were, the great air battles in which Australians participated were generally fought by only a few airmen, as in the pivotal Battle of Britain. It was unusual for 100 aircraft to be in the air at once in the South and South-West Pacific, for example. Like the British, Australians owe much to an elite bunch of airmen.

In the latter part of the war, members of the RAAF became especially annoyed at the tendency of the media to exaggerate and overly glamorise what they were doing. I have tried to be true to their desire not to gild the lily, even though embellishing the truth for the purpose of pulling others' legs is an accepted part of RAAF tradition and sometimes makes it hard to separate truth from fiction. If I have done my job properly, the true stories should inspire awe at least as effectively as exaggerated ones.

Most members of the RAAF were not aircrew, but ground staff and 'rear echelon people', as their wartime commander described them.[2] The Americans worked on the principle that for every aircraft in the air there were ten personnel on the ground. Books about wartime aviation usually concentrate on aircrew, for they took the most risks, displayed the most courage and fought the decisive battles. Yet without the 'erks' of the ground staff, including drivers, armourers, fitters, riggers, cooks, intelligence and medical staff and general hands, the aircraft could not fly. While this book focuses on aircrew, the voices of many others, particularly ground staff, will be heard too.

The front-line units at the centre of this story are the squadrons. A list of the squadrons, and of their aircraft types, casualties and victories, can be found in Appendix B. These were subdivided into 'flights', and combined to form 'wings'. Squadrons usually comprised between 12 and 24 aircraft—though in operations sometimes far fewer than 12—and 300 to 450 airmen (aircrew and others). One squadron historian argues persuasively that these units did not have the same strong bonds of *esprit de corps* as army battalions.[3] For although, like the battalions, they were often nominally associated with a location—for example No. 22 was the City of Sydney Squadron—their personnel were from all states, and there was more turnover of members thanks to service tours, or 'tours of duty', which could be as short as six months. Most of the pilots who figure prominently in the following pages served with more than one squadron. Nevertheless squadrons did inspire loyalty.

What chiefly impelled many Australians to join the air force was a desire to fulfil a dream of flying powerful aircraft. This had a profound influence on the type of person who predominates in the chapters that follow. A sense of duty was a strong motive too, and that is poignantly expressed in Vincent Hunt's first diary entry after joining the RAAF in 1943. 'Good Bye ... my wife and two children,' he wrote, 'God how I hate saying good bye to them, their [sic] good soldiers, better than I am.' One can imagine him pulling his shoulders back and taking a deep breath as he finished the entry with these words: 'Well the rest lies before me.'[4]

1 A difficult childhood: Australian air power to 1939

Darwin, Thursday 19 February 1942. A showery hot night gave way to what an air force officer called a 'clear, steamy, brilliant' day.[1] Yet 'clear' was not the best word, for from its morning skies came something new and shocking for Darwin, and indeed for the whole of Australia.

RAAF Sergeant Albert Fletcher, a veteran of recent fighting in the Netherlands East Indies, was lying in bed sleepily glancing at a magazine when at about 10 a.m. he heard some of Darwin's anti-aircraft guns firing. After putting on his helmet and buckling on his gunbelt and pistol, he woke some fellow airmen who had just returned from a long flight, then dashed outside.

> And hell! [he wrote in his diary] The sky was packed with formation after formation. All Jap planes and all with a bellyful of hate and sudden death.
>
> Hundreds of men rising that day to just another day of tropical sunshine were to die before the sun had set. Some quickly and mercifully and some only in the agony that could be produced by an ocean of burning oil.
>
> One by one the dive bombers were peeling off over the harbour and town and the sound of the detonations was now accompanied by ever increasing billowing clouds of smoke.

> The familiar crackle, fascinating and deadly, of the Zero sent us crouching in our trench. From . . . about three hundred yds from the hangars, we saw the bombers screaming down to within a hundred feet of the same hangars, releasing a single black bomb and then twisting away.

Fletcher watched a Japanese fighter pursue one of the few American air force fighter planes at Darwin. Smoke was trailing from the doomed American's P-40 aircraft.

Eventually the Japanese aircraft departed, leaving 'the crackle of exploding ammunition and the bursting of oil and petrol drums and vast clouds of smoke everywhere.'[2]

In this raid and another later in the early afternoon, more than 240 Japanese aircraft bombed and strafed, killing 243 people, and sinking ten ships. Not one Australian aircraft rose to meet the attackers. An Australian air force existed, but had no battleworthy planes to meet the Japanese in Darwin, even though that port had long been identified as the back door to Australia. To add to this embarrassment for the RAAF, some of its personnel in Darwin ran away in ignominious retreat. In the words of one of the air force's leading historians, 19 February 1942 was 'the low point in RAAF history'.[3] This book tells why, despite the best efforts of air force leaders and the great courage of individual airmen, this nadir was reached. It also tells the story of how in the months and years after 19 February the RAAF contributed to victory over Japan.

Australia's air war in the Pacific was profoundly affected by two events in the first five years of the 20th century. One, in 1903, was the Wright brothers' pioneering flight, which inspired countless young men to fly. Kitty Hawk, the town in North Carolina where they made that flight, would in the 1940s be a household name in Australia. The second event, in 1905, was the Japanese victory in the Russo–Japanese war. This triumph, the first ever by an Asian power over a European one, signified that Japan would henceforth be a major force in the eastern hemisphere, and caused anxiety in Australia. The potential for a showdown with Japan was an important factor in the creation of the RAAF in 1921, and also encouraged its subsequent development.

Australian air power existed before 1921. In September 1912, just five months after Britain established its Royal Flying Corps (RFC), the Australian government also approved 'a flying school and corps', and the

Army established a flight of four aeroplanes and 43 men. Its personnel were chiefly part-time militiamen. A Central Flying School was located on flat coastal land at Point Cook, south-west of Melbourne, and in August 1914 began producing home-grown Australian military airmen. Not surprisingly, crashes were frequent, given that the aircraft were so flimsy they could not fly in strong adverse winds. The first recruit to land his fragile wire and fabric Bristol Boxkite in a 50-metre diameter circle and thereby qualify for his pilot's licence was Lieutenant Richard Williams. This was appropriate, for Williams would become the 'Father of the RAAF' and the most significant airman in Australian military history.

Although military air services received less than 1 per cent of Australian government military spending in the period 1911–1914, a foundation was laid for involvement in a great war. Once that war began, the first Australian airmen to see action were sent to Iraq, or 'Mesopotamia' as it was then known, just weeks after Anzac troops landed at Gallipoli. The Mesopotamian Half-Flight, as the Australian unit was called, was deployed to support British forces against the Turks. In primitive and decrepit aircraft, unable to exceed 80 kilometres per hour, they undertook valuable reconnaissance work. Though without guns, the pilots dropped bombs by hand or from a rack or hole in the floor. The Half-Flight expanded to become 30 Squadron RFC. Its Australian mechanics included George Mackinolty, who in the Pacific air war would be the RAAF's key logistics officer. The Half-Flight's campaign in Mesopotamia was in some ways similar to Gallipoli, for though ending with the defeat of the British ground forces at Kut in 1916, it was a creditable baptism of fire for Australian airmen, who regularly displayed initiative, skill and courage.

In the meantime, Point Cook recruited and trained sufficient airmen to man four 'Australian Flying Corps' (AFC) squadrons. No. 1 Squadron sailed for the Middle East, and Nos 2, 3 and 4 Squadrons to the Western Front. All were undertrained and ill-equipped.

From April 1916 No. 1 Squadron AFC operated over Sinai and the Suez Canal. It benefited from the initiative of Lieutenant Lawrence Wackett, who invented a gun-mounting to put on the top centre-section of bombers. Later, on the Western Front, he developed a device for dropping ammunition in parachutes to advancing machine-gunners at Hamel. Wackett would still be innovating to improve Australian air power in the next war.

No. 1 Squadron contributed to every major battle of the Palestine campaign and produced several aces—men who had shot down at least five aircraft—including Adrian Cole and Ross Smith. Smith's bravery impressed Lawrence of Arabia, and especially the Arab troops under his command. On being attached to the Arab force, Smith proceeded almost on arrival to shoot down a German bomber whose attentions had been dispiriting them. Lieutenant Frank McNamara earned the AFC's only Victoria Cross when, although seriously wounded, he landed his aircraft to rescue a downed pilot from threatening Turkish cavalry.

Richard 'Dicky' Williams, the first graduate at Point Cook, showed outstanding leadership in this campaign. By 1918, aged 27, he commanded one of two Royal Air Force (RAF) wings in Palestine. By then, the Allied aircraft enjoyed air supremacy. In 1918 British General Allenby eulogised the squadron's contribution to Allied victory, while the commander of the RAF in the Middle East, Major-General Salmond, considered No. 1 Squadron one of the RAF's best.

Nos 2, 3 and 4 Squadrons reached the Western Front in late 1917. Their aircraft patrolled, spotted for artillery, strafed, bombed and fought for air supremacy. The Australian squadrons lost a total of just 60 planes to enemy action, while No. 2 shot down 185 aircraft, and No. 4 199. Notable among the pilots was Harry Cobby, the 'Elsternwick Boy Hero' of No. 4 Squadron, who by war's end had shot down 29 planes and 13 balloons. He received the Distinguished Service Order (DSO), and the Distinguished Flying Cross (DFC) with two bars. This superb airman would play an important—though controversial—role in the Pacific War. Other outstanding Australian pilots would not survive to play such a part, including Australia's top two aces of the war, Robert Little and Stan Dallas. However, the Great War was a formative influence for several future RAAF leaders in the Pacific. Like Little and Dallas, Bill Bostock served with British forces, while George Jones rose from air mechanic, second class in No. 4 Squadron to become an air ace with a DFC and the rank of captain.

Australian airmen cut dashing figures. Cobby once landed his aircraft in the Australian lines, joined and won a horse race, and then returned to his aircraft and resumed his patrol. The motto 'Eat, drink and be merry, for tomorrow we die' was for these daring young men a practical byword rather than a boastful gesture. Men carried no parachutes, and flew aircraft that would readily burn. The physical dangers of occupying open cockpits at altitude during winter were shocking.

Primitive though air power remained in some respects, the Great War revolutionised it. Aerial doctrine included roles vital in the next war: winning air superiority, strategic bombing, reconnaissance, cooperation with ground and naval forces, and attacks on enemy shipping. In 1914, France, Britain and Germany had mustered a total of just 471 aircraft. By 1918 the figure had swelled to 10,304. Moreover, whereas in 1914 aircraft were unarmed and largely at the whim of the winds, by 1918 powerful fighters and bombers ruled the skies. The AFC had mirrored this development in miniature, growing from no squadrons in 1914 to eight by war's end, and creating a cadre of experienced airmen and a set of traditions for Australian airmen to emulate. The AFC trained 158 pilots, a figure dwarfed by the 10,998 the RAAF produced in World War II—yet to leaders of the RAAF, including Cobby, Jones, Bostock, Mackinolty and others, these times past were formative.

Air power was now a permanent element of thinking about future wars. However, the possibility of further armed conflict was not one many civilians now wanted to consider, and as we will see, for many repatriated military aviators peace was not going to be easy.

The 'Third Brother': the RAAF

On Anzac Day 1919, while Australian troops marched through London in a special parade, aircraft of the three AFC squadrons in Europe flew overhead. It was no simple flypast, for the 60 pilots rolled, spun and looped their borrowed RAF aircraft. Harry Cobby flew under wires strung between buildings along the crowded Strand. Fortunately neither airmen nor onlookers were hurt. 'All's well that ends well,' concluded Lieutenant-Colonel 'Dicky' Williams, Staff Officer for Aviation at Australian Imperial Force (AIF) Headquarters in London.[4] Cobby's assessment of that day's flying antics as the most foolish act of his life may have been closer to the truth, and this finale to the AFC's time in Europe was indicative of issues to come. Cavalier Australian flying would haunt Williams on the eve of the Pacific War, but he now had to consider the more pressing question of the future of Australian air power. When the AFC was disbanded on returning to Australia in early 1919, this very future was literally 'up in the air'.

In 1917, the South African soldier-statesman Jan Christian Smuts presented the British government with a report it had commissioned on air organisation. Smuts warned that in future wars, aerial operations might take precedence over land and naval ones. To maintain its air superiority, he asserted, Britain should amalgamate its two air forces, the RFC and Royal Naval Air Service. Against opposition from those forces, his suggestion prevailed and the Royal Air Force was established in April 1918.

This decision had implications for Australia. Its governments traditionally followed British defence policy, sometimes without much attention to the consequences of applying it to a sparsely populated nation on the other side of the world, but generally with good reason. While Japan and the US—the two powers destined to dominate the Pacific air war—were maintaining separate army and naval air forces, the British precedent of creating a new service was fundamental to the Australian decision to do the same in 1921.

Before the war ended, Japan's future military aviation intentions were already occupying the minds of Australian defence personnel. In June 1918 the Australian Naval Board called for a naval aviation service, and the Board's aviation adviser, Commander Maguire, stated that although Japan currently had no sizeable air force, it undoubtedly was planning a very large one. The potential threat posed by Japan was the unspoken danger too when the Army's Chief of the General Staff, Major-General Legge, urged the creation of a 200-aeroplane air force. Japan's opposition at the Versailles Peace Conference in 1919 to the Australian mandate over Germany's former holdings in New Guinea only increased concern about her intentions. Australia's strident opposition to Japan's desire for a declaration of racial equality in the Covenant of the new League of Nations did nothing to soften those intentions.

While Army and Navy leaders recognised the value of air power in support of their own operations, neither wanted Australian aircraft within an independent force. A third service would threaten their own strength, especially if airmen could persuade the Australian government of the value of 'strategic bombing', based on the theory of the Italian general Giulio Douhet and others that air power alone could win wars.

In 1918 the Australian Cabinet allocated £3 million to an 'aviation program' over the following three years, and in 1919 the British government generously offered her Dominions surplus aircraft to help them form their own air forces. Australia accepted this 'imperial gift', and in 1920–21 received 19,000 crates of material, containing 128 aircraft, hundreds of vehicles such as trucks, as well as engines, machine guns, bombs, radio sets, flying clothing, aerodrome equipment and even hangars.

The Australian population, recovering from the bloodiest war in history and intent on reconstruction, shared an international revulsion against the idea of military expansion. Nevertheless, many were excited by the peacetime exploits of aviators. Captain Ross Smith and his brother Keith became national heroes after flying from England to Australia in late 1919. Their skill, bravery and endurance over the 135 hours and 55 minutes of flying earned them knighthoods and a £10,000 prize. To help the winners fly safely from Darwin to Sydney by surveying landing fields, two other AFC veterans, Captain Henry Wrigley and Sergeant Arthur 'Spud' Murphy, made an epic first crossing of Australia from south to north. Both men would have distinguished careers in the RAAF, Murphy as an engineer, Wrigley as a pioneering commentator on air power.

These flights enthused not only the general populace, but also politicians such as Prime Minister Billy Hughes, who in a speech in Parliament in 1920 styled himself 'a fanatic' for aviation. More significantly, he said in this speech that the government was allocating funds for creating 'an efficient air force'.[5] This was done with the prospect of future conflict with Japan in mind, for that same year a group of experienced Australian military commanders reported to the government that Japan was 'the only potential and probable enemy.'[6] Defence Minister George Pearce, the politician most responsible for the beginning of military aviation in 1912, backed Hughes energetically, and on 9 November 1920 the Air Board was formed. That same day, new air force ranks were introduced to replace army ones, and applied to three of the board's four members: Wing Commander Richard 'Dicky' Williams and Wing Commander 'Jimmy' Goble, as well as Squadron Leader Percy McBain (an equipment specialist). The fourth member was the civilian Finance Member, A.C. Joyce.

At the board's first meeting, Williams produced a long memorandum on the future structure of the Australian Air Force, and on 31 March 1921 the 'Australian Air Force' came into existence with 164 aircraft—most of them still in packing crates—and 151 personnel. The first airman enlisted was Arthur 'Spud' Murphy. From August 1921 the new force was called the Royal Australian Air Force (RAAF).

With the 'imperial gift' aircraft and ancillary materials, as well as its independence, the RAAF was apparently starting in a healthy state. Point Cook would continue through the 1920s and 1930s to produce well trained and increasing numbers of pilots. From 1926, under an agreement with the RAF, some of these graduates were sent to England for valuable further experience. In 30-year-old Wing Commander Williams the RAAF had a fine leader. Thanks to the Prime Minister's insistence that the new force's leaders be Australian, in October 1922 Williams was the first to receive the newly created title Chief of Air Staff (CAS). However, the inter-service rivalry that had threatened the creation of the air force was to complicate his job. His was an army background, while that of Goble, the second member of the Air Board, was naval: he had become a wartime ace flying with the Royal Naval Air Service. It was probably for this reason that the government insisted the two men alternate as chairman of the Air Board and CAS. This decision was divisive, and the two former friends developed a virulent antagonism that would 'poison the senior levels of the RAAF for the next 20 years'.[7] It also established what historian Alan Stephens called 'a disgraceful tradition'.[8] Each had risked his life heroically as an aviator during the Great War and had been decorated for bravery. Each had a vision for Australian aviation, but their dreams were incompatible, as were their egos.

In his first turn as CAS, in 1922, Goble sought to create a separate naval air force, a 'fleet air arm', but Williams suspended this in 1925 as a danger to the RAAF's identity. Threats from the 'big brother' Army and Navy services preoccupied the RAAF, and especially Williams. He could be puritanical and nitpicking, but did this job skilfully. He also scrutinised even minor details of RAAF organisation. It was Williams, for example, who chose the dark blue uniforms that made RAAF personnel stand out among fellow airmen everywhere. Yet he himself acknowledged that the RAAF was lucky to be established when it was. If not for Senator Pearce's determined efforts immediately after the war and Britain's imperial gift, the financial recession that followed soon afterwards would have scotched the whole scheme. The Washington Disarmament Conference of November 1922 also discouraged military expansion.

Allocations for the RAAF were halved in the 1922–23 budget to just 5.4 per cent of defence spending. Not until 1925 were the first two RAAF squadrons, Nos 1 and 3, created at Point Cook. No. 3 soon moved to Richmond, a new airbase west of Sydney. Only then were most of the imperial gift aircraft removed from their crates and allocated to the squadrons. To reduce costs, much use was made of part-time Citizen Air Force personnel, who had only 25 days' training per year and constituted two-thirds of both squadrons.

Great aviation feats continued to excite the Australian public in the late 1920s: for example, in 1928, 'Hustling' Bert Hinkler flew from England to Australia in just 16 days, and Charles Kingsford Smith flew from San Francisco to Brisbane. Among those watching both landings was an eight-year-old boy, Arthur Tucker, whom they inspired and whose wartime experiences are important to this book.

The government was aware of its air force's inadequacies and the need to spend heavily to improve it, so in 1928 it invited RAF Air Chief Marshal Sir John Salmond to Australia to make recommendations. Though sympathetic, Salmond—who had praised the Australians in the Middle East during the Great War—declared the air force unfit for war operations. He recommended a modest nine-year program to expand the force. The Bruce government decided against expansion, partly because of financial circumstances, and partly because it saw the Navy as its first line of defence. (Australia relied on the British naval strategy of protecting British Commonwealth interests in the Far East through the base at Singapore.)

Salmond recommended the closure of an RAAF Experimental Section, which had produced several home-grown aircraft and parts. As Bruce explained, Australia did not yet have the means to manufacture engines for motor cars, let alone aircraft. At a time when the great powers were spending millions of pounds on developing aviation, Australia could not match, let alone surpass, them. The Section closed in 1930, though its chief designer, the talented and self-assured Lawrence Wackett, would resurface in private industry as an important figure in Australia's air war against Japan.

In 1929 the Scullin Labor government took office. Labor had consistently advocated a strong air force, but the onset of the Great Depression jeopardised all military spending. Salmond's report was shelved. The Army and Navy advised the government to end the RAAF's status as a separate service and give them their own air arms. The government announced an investigation into the issue. Williams attended a Council of Defence meeting on the matter where all six representatives of the Navy and Army spoke against the RAAF's continued existence. Williams spoke up for his service as offering much more than just support to ground and naval forces, and the government decided to take no action for the time being. Nevertheless, the threat remained hovering above the RAAF.

Between 1921 and 1931, expenditure on the RAAF never exceeded 9 per cent of the defence budget, and until 1936 the RAAF had an average of only 83 officers. George Jones called it 'an intimate club', all well known to each other. Jones was one of many members with combat experience: for example, 13 of the 18 officers with the rank of squadron leader or above in 1927 had earned awards for bravery. One senior World War II veteran recalled that these commanding officers were 'a fairly wild lot' who counted the ability to hold drink as a key quality in any recently arrived cadet.[9]

The pilots tended to view themselves as dashing and skilful men—a perception that did not discourage reckless flying behaviour. In the Citizen Air Force, members tended to be preoccupied with the social rather than the technical side of their part-time jobs. There were 24 crashes in the first Citizen Air Force course, but at the graduation ceremony for those newly qualified pilots, the flight training school commander chose to joke about it. Permanent fliers sometimes also made a poor impression on the viewing public. At Melbourne's Flemington racecourse in 1924, four aircraft in succession crashed on landing. The crowd found the spectacle farcical and comical, and an infuriated pilot offered to take them on in a fist fight. In 1927, four pilots died in a crash during a flypast for the Duke of York in Melbourne, and yet another one at a flypast for the opening of Parliament House in Canberra. Although aircraft reliability improved through the 1930s, the accident rate did not. That it owed much to attitudes is suggested by the behaviour of two pilots destined for distinguished Pacific War careers: Fred Scherger, who loved flying low and inverted, and often did so over crowds in the 1930s; and Richard Cohen, who as a cadet made a risky landing in his Cirrus Moth near a country school to take an attractive schoolteacher joyriding. Pilots of the RAF had a similar attitude, as famously exemplified by Douglas Bader, who lost his legs in an accident while performing dangerous aerobatics in 1931.

In 1932 the new Lyons government raised again the question of the RAAF's separate existence. Williams defended his service by pointing to its cost-effective potential for defending the country, and also the continuing independence of the RAF. George Pearce, Minister for Defence, came to the rescue again, declaring that no merging would occur. Japan's conflict with Chinese forces in Manchuria and Shanghai in 1932 fostered growing Australian concern about the need for stronger defence forces.

The RAAF was now on the rise. Even though the Navy was still the number one priority—for as Prime Minister Lyons said, Australian defence was related to British Empire defence, of which the 'fundamental basis' was 'Empire sea-power and the Singapore naval base'[10]—the air force became the second spending priority. In 1934 the Salmond report was revisited and approved in a modified form. The government ordered modern aircraft: 24 Seagull seaplanes and 18 Hawker Demons, to be followed in 1936 by Avro Anson reconnaissance bomber aircraft. Political will fully emerged in 1938, when the government pledged to raise the number of squadrons from the existing eight to 18. The source of that will was fear: the British High Commissioner reported in November that Prime Minister Lyons exhibited 'a kind of desperate anxiety about the defence of Australia against Japan'.[11]

Yet a problem that would torment the wartime RAAF now emerged: it became increasingly difficult for the RAAF to procure modern aircraft. Great Britain, Australia's supplier and mentor in military aviation, was itself rearming after years of neglect. War appeared more likely every year after Hitler became Chancellor in 1933, and particularly after he announced in 1935 that Germany had achieved air parity with Britain. In addition, Britain's—and therefore Australia's—potential enemies were exhibiting a willingness to use air power to achieve their aggressive political goals: Italy in Abyssinia in 1935, Germany in Spain in 1936, and Japan in China in 1937. Britain was developing some formidable aircraft of its own. In 1936 she began producing the heavily armed Hurricane fighter, and in the same year the Spitfire achieved world attention by achieving a speed of nearly 550 kilometres per hour. Nevertheless, it soon became clear that Australia would not be a high priority for such aircraft, and also that if Britain became involved in a European war, exporting aircraft all the way to Australia would be physically difficult. America was an alternative supplier, but its then limited capacity to produce military aircraft was being tested by the pressing demands of Britain and France. Besides, if a European war began, America's determination to remain neutral might legally prevent her from selling weapons—including aircraft—to any of the belligerents.

A partial solution to this predicament was to revive hopes of making Australia militarily self-sufficient, or at least able to provide much of its own equipment. In 1936, the managing director of BHP, Essington Lewis, convened a conference, backed by Richard Williams and the government, which resulted in a syndicate to establish factories for producing aircraft and engines. This would prove momentous in Australia's coming air war.

Lawrence Wackett was appointed chief engineer and manager of the Commonwealth Aircraft Corporation (CAC) that was established in October 1936. He led an overseas mission to find an aircraft suitable for manufacture in Australia. The local industry was not yet capable of producing an advanced fighter, so a general-purpose military monoplane was needed. In particular, it had to be a two-seater, so it could be used as an advanced trainer for an expanding air force. After visiting Germany, England, the US and four other countries, the mission unanimously recommended the North American NA-33 as best fitting their brief. There was considerable criticism of the decision not to take a British design, though none then available met the requirements of the mission's brief.

In 1938 the RAAF named the new aircraft 'Wirraway', from an Aboriginal word for 'challenge'. It was appropriate, given the roles that this modest aircraft would unexpectedly be required to perform once war with Japan commenced: reconnaissance, supply dropping, army cooperation, dive-bombing and flying as a fighter interceptor. The Wirraway was modified, carrying twin Vickers machine guns in nose troughs rather than a single gun, and a third aft (rear-facing) gun on a flexible mount in the rear cockpit. There was provision for underwing bomb racks, a radio and camera, and the tail and wings were strengthened for dive-bombing. However, with a top speed of 354 kilometres per hour, it was not well suited to combat roles. The first 'Wirras' were not produced quickly: the contract to build them was only signed in April 1938, with an agreement to make a modest 40. The first Wirraway produced by the Commonwealth Aircraft Corporation factory, at Fisherman's Bend, Port Melbourne, did not fly until March 1939, when Flight Lieutenant Fred

Scherger took it for a test flight. This aircraft, A20-3, was the first of 755 Wirraways to be produced.

The attempt to turn a trainer into an all-purpose aircraft reflected the quandary of the RAAF and the Australian government in the late 1930s. By 1939, Australia had no modern fighter. Its Bristol Bulldogs and Hawker Demons were open-cockpit biplanes, with a range, speed and ceiling inferior to contemporary civil aviation transports such as the Douglas DC-2. In the 1930s, new monoplane bombers were appearing and, being faster than the Bulldog and Demon, gave the impression that 'the bomber will always get through', as British politician Stanley Baldwin put it. Hence bombers seemed an attractively cheap purchase, especially as they could defend against enemy ships at longer range than any coastal defence guns.

The Avro Anson was a reconnaissance-bomber, and more Ansons would fly in RAAF service than any other type, but even before World War II began the 'Faithful Annie' was suitable only for training. The gun turret's movement was leg-powered, retracting or extending the undercarriage required about 150 turns of manual winding, and a foot pump was used to prepare the brakes for landing. It could barely reach 300 kilometres per hour.

Militarily and politically there were good reasons to provide service aircraft of speeds comparable to the 390 kilometres per hour of civil aircraft. One possibility was the Bristol Beaufort reconnaissance-bomber, with a maximum speed of 435 kilometres per hour; however, the RAAF waited in vain for the 90 Bristol Beaufort reconnaissance-bombers ordered from Britain. So in December 1938 the government sought, and quickly obtained an order for, 50 Lockheed Hudson bombers—top speed nearly 400 kilometres per hour—from the US. This was a momentous coup, for the versatile Hudson would prove invaluable. Yet Alan Stephens points out that an attempt to obtain modern American *fighters* from the same source might also have succeeded, except Australia was too willing to wait for aircraft from hard-pressed Britain.[12] The emphasis on 'general purpose' aircraft, such as the Wirraway and the Hudson, was based on the belief that Australian airspace was best defended not by fighters, but by aircraft capable of destroying enemy airfields and aircraft carriers before they could launch aircraft against the mainland. Australia felt that the great distance of its vital assets from any potential enemy meant that it did not need fighter aircraft. However, in February 1942, Hudsons would be unable to prevent the attack on Darwin, and the failure to obtain fighters would prove a disaster. An aggressive, long-range fighter was, on the other hand, pivotal to Japanese planning, as it could escort bombers and contribute substantially to ground attack.

Australia and Britain did reach an agreement about Beauforts in 1939. In its factory almost next door to the Commonwealth Aircraft Corporation, the Department of Aircraft Production (DAP) would produce Beauforts for the RAF and RAAF. None would emerge until 1941, but when one considers too the Tiger Moth trainers that de Havilland Aircraft began mass-producing in Bankstown at the end of 1939, portents for a home-grown aircraft industry were encouraging. By 1939 some 4000 workers were employed in Australian aircraft factories.

Nevertheless, in mid-1938, Australia's dependence on Britain in air matters became strikingly clear. Following criticism of the RAAF's accident rate in the press and in Parliament, the Lyons government initiated a review of the RAAF by RAF Marshal Sir Edward Ellington. Williams allegedly first learned about this decision through the press. Ellington, whom Stephens calls 'boorish and patronising', pointed out 'deficiencies' in the RAAF.[13] He criticised the adoption of the Wirraway, suggesting that it be seen as only temporary until a suitable British alternative could be found, and allegedly refused to attend a specially organised demonstration of the Wirraway.

Ellington did not deign either to talk to Williams, and was highly critical of him and the Air Board. To them he sheeted home a supposed lack of discipline and excessive accident rates. These rates he based on the fact that of 12 accidents that had occurred in the previous three years, three or four had been caused by bad flying discipline or disobedience. Indignant, the Air Board defended its accident record and discipline in comparison to the RAF. It also defended the Wirraway as the best available aircraft in its class. However, the press added to the criticism of the RAAF and its CAS. So too did the government, which said that the 'main responsibility rests on the Chief of the Air Staff', despite his previous good work.[14] Williams, suspicious that the government had been conspiring for his head from the outset, only saw confirmation of this in the government decision, again announced to him via newspapers, to second him to the RAF for two years. Air Vice-Marshal Goble became Acting CAS in February 1939.

Ellington may have been haughty, but he was entitled to question the RAAF's professionalism. Williams had suffered the consequences of longstanding nonchalance about safety in Australian military aviation. His departure was part of a slow transition of the RAAF from a flying club to a professional service. Yet it was also badly timed, for with war looming, no one with Williams' intellect or charisma took his place. There were Australians with ability and promise, but rather than appoint one of them, the government decided to ask Britain to send an RAF officer to replace Williams. In this they were supported by the press, but not by senior RAAF officers, who preferred Williams. The man Britain sent, in 1940, was naturally not one of their best, given that Britain was fighting a war for survival. Instead they dispatched a retired officer, Air Marshal Sir Charles Burnett, eight years older than Williams and with a less distinguished record. His appointment was a serious blow to the RAAF's independence, and the prelude to what the RAAF Historian calls 'the plundering of Australia's air defence resources for the benefit of Britain's war effort in Europe'.[15] Burnett would also weaken Australia's effort in the Pacific War by fostering divided leadership within the RAAF, and doing too little to obtain aircraft—especially fighters—to defend Australia.

On the eve of World War II, the single most important achievement of the RAAF since 1921 was its survival as an independent service. Its leaders and subordinate personnel had been forced to spend too much time justifying the RAAF's existence and worrying whether it would continue. There were no long-established models in other countries to follow. Much emphasis had necessarily been put on training, albeit with room for more professionalism. At the end of August 1939, days before the war began, the RAAF's strength stood at 3489 personnel, including 310 officers. While there was some superb material there, without modern aircraft no air force can thrive, and because the dangers of having a weak air force were recognised too late, Australia possessed only a small and obsolete fleet of planes. On the eve of war this comprised just 246 aircraft, all obsolescent: 82 Ansons, 54 Demons, 7 Wirraways, 21 Seagull seaplanes and 82 trainer aircraft. There were just 12 squadrons, of which two existed only as a nucleus and four were citizen force, not fully professional. RAAF official historian George Odgers likened this force to a blunt sword waiting to be sharpened by Australia's willing youth.[16] Many hundreds of young Australians would die because that 'sword' was so fragile when struck by a well-tempered samurai blade.

A growing bully—Japanese air power

What of the Japanese air forces that were destined to meet the RAAF during the coming war? In 1910, two Japanese army officers had flown the first aeroplanes seen in Japan. Within a year one of them, Captain Tokugawa, had produced the first aircraft built in Japan. By 1920, the 'Big Three' of the Japanese aviation industry—Mitsubishi, Nakajima and Kawasaki—were operating. Until the mid-1930s the Japanese depended on foreign technology and expertise, but at the same time were sending young technicians overseas to factories and technical schools. As early as 1921, Mitsubishi invited Herbert Smith of the British Sopwith company to Japan to design an original fighter capable of being launched from an aircraft carrier, which was at that time a type of vessel still in its infancy, but destined to be central to Japan's Pacific War. In 1923, an Australian MP, Walter Marks, visited Japan and saw the *Hosho* and *Akagi*, two of five aircraft carriers Japan was planning to build. He presciently asked in Parliament what Australia had to prevent these vessels coming south and launching their aircraft over Sydney to force a surrender. In 1942, the *Akagi* would indeed launch aircraft to attack Darwin. Marks reported that Japan was planning to spend £5 million on its air force between 1923 and 1927—twice what Australia would spend.

Japanese army and navy leaders were determined to make their aircraft industry self-sufficient and by 1936 were producing several aircraft equal or superior to foreign equivalents. Other firms emerged, including Kawanishi, which produced superb seaplanes, and Aichi, which made seaplanes and Japan's first dive-bomber. From 1937, when Japan invaded China, its aircraft production soared. The following year the government took over the production plans and techniques in sizeable aircraft factories, which were encouraged by tax exemptions. The aircraft industry it had developed before the war would enable Japan to produce well over 100 new types of military aircraft between 1940 and 1945. Such development was hidden as much as possible from the world, especially from 1937, and the few warnings American and British observers gave as to the high quality of Japanese aircraft continued to be ignored by their superiors until December 1941. In the West the Japanese aircraft were complacently regarded as second-rate derivatives of Western designs. In fact, the 'Nell' bomber produced in 1936 was the equal of contemporary bombers, and would prove destructive in Malaya. The 'Sally' bomber, the 'Mavis' seaplane and the 'Kate' carrier-bomber that all emerged that year would also contribute substantially to the Pacific War. The Kate in particular was outstanding: it could carry a torpedo or bombs, and would wreak devastation at Pearl Harbor and beyond. In 1939, the 'Val' dive-bomber joined the Japanese arsenal. With the famed Mitsubishi Zero fighter that appeared in 1940, the Kate and Val would form a trio of Japanese naval aircraft that would surprise and terrorise Western powers from 1941. The fast and long-range 'Betty' bomber of 1940 would also work in tandem with the Zero, for example over Darwin. Japan's fighter aircraft in 1939 were the 'Nate' and 'Claude', which looked unimpressive and by 1941 would be obsolete, but they were sophisticated aircraft that dominated the skies against Russian fighters over China and the Mongolian border.

In 1923, Marks rebuffed claims that the Japanese had no 'air' sense. He declared 'the Japanese are not inferior to the Australians or British—they can fly all right'.[17] Japanese aircrew were indeed well trained and experienced. An Army Air Division was established in 1919, and an Army Air Corps in 1925. Their pilots saw small-scale action in Vladivostok in 1920 and the Tsinan Incident in 1928, then larger-scale involvement in the Manchurian Incident (1931), Shanghai Incident (1932) and the Sino–Japanese War from 1937. These 'incidents', most of which were acts of Japanese aggression, gave experience to individual members of the Japanese Army Air Force (JAAF). They also allowed the JAAF's commanders to refine the force's organisation and, especially from 1937, introduce and test improved aircraft types.

The Japanese Navy Air Force (JNAF) would be more important quantitatively and qualitatively than the JAAF in the Pacific War. By the end of 1921 Japan had the world's first purpose-built aircraft carrier, the *Hosho*. In the Sino–Japanese War from 1937, Japanese naval aircraft operated over long distances from aircraft carriers and land bases. 'Nell' navy bombers that flew from Japan and Formosa to bomb Hankow and Nanking made the first trans-oceanic bombing raids in history. Such destructive experiences allowed them, like the JAAF, to fine-tune their organisation and tactics. Their experience of long overwater flights, using not only bombers but also escorting fighters, made them the key force when Japan spread its aggressive attentions beyond China to the rest of Asia and the Pacific. If Japan was to extend its empire over that vast area, air power would be an essential means of attack, especially against strong enemy navies. Once it had acquired the land it wanted, air power would also be the key to defending that ground flexibly. Should Australia and the other Western powers in the region be attacked, Allied aircraft, flying well forward of their bases, would be the first Allied forces to fight.

In 1939, the nightmare Pacific scenario still lay two years away. There was the consolation for worried Australians that if and when war with Japan came, Australian aircraft would not have to face Japanese aircraft alone. In June 1938, soon after arriving in Australia, Sir Edward Ellington was quoted as saying reassuringly that Japan could only attack Australia if it first overcame British power, so that local defence was of secondary importance. Moreover, he reportedly stated that the only air attack that could reach Australia was by seaborne aircraft, which at present would be ineffective.[18] In fact a year before, Japan had launched two great carriers, the *Soryu* and *Hiryu*, two of the four carriers that would one day send aircraft to bomb Darwin.

Ellington's complacency, typical of Western senior air commanders, was soon to cost the lives of many Australian fliers. Airmen from many nations were about to die in a war in which air power—as politicians and military men had foreseen since the last world war—would be important in every campaign.

2 'They will follow you through hell': The RAAF and war in Europe

On 3 September 1939 the Australian government dutifully and willingly followed Great Britain in its declaration of war on Germany. Immediately all RAAF squadrons were fully mobilised at their Australian war stations. For the next two years the RAAF would become so deeply involved in the European war that when a real threat to Australia materialised, its home forces were terribly weak.

Within days of the declaration of war, Australia's noble but risky willingness to help Britain's air campaign became manifest. On 3 September the nucleus of No. 10 Squadron RAAF was in Britain to collect Short Sunderland flying-boats from an English factory. When the British government requested that this squadron remain in England, build up its full strength there and come under British control, the Australian government consented.

On 20 September, the Australian War Cabinet offered Britain six more squadrons, as an air expeditionary force. The Menzies government believed, as the Prime Minister said at the end of September, that in the difficult times ahead it might well be that 'the Mother Country' would ask 'more insistently for help in the air than for help on the land or sea'.[1] This supposition was perceptive and reasonable, but when the Australian government offered six squadrons, the entire RAAF comprised just 12.

There were only 3000 regular airmen, another 500 in the Citizen Air Force, as well as about 150 officers in the reserve and a further 1400 civilian pilots. If the Cabinet's offer were accepted, most of Australia's trained airmen would be sent overseas. Another substantial number of Australian airmen—about 450—were already in Britain's Royal Air Force when the war began. Nearly all were pilots, so the RAF contained more Australian aircrew than did the regular RAAF.

The six-squadron offer was soon withdrawn on British advice, for within days of it being made, Great Britain proposed a scheme that would profoundly influence all wartime British Commonwealth air power. Acutely conscious of its inability to provide sufficient aircrew for the 2250 aircraft it would soon be producing monthly, Britain sought assistance from the Dominions. Pre-war British plans had identified the required annual increase of aircrew as being 50,000, but Britain itself could supply and train only 22,000 of these. She proposed that the remaining 28,000 per annum should come from Canada, Australia and New Zealand.

In November 1939 Australia duly sent Minister for Air James Fairbairn to Canada, where an agreement was reached. Prime Minister Menzies said Australia would concentrate its efforts on this 'Empire Air Training Scheme' (EATS), while giving assurances that Australia's air defences would be completed. Fairbairn insisted that about half the Australians be trained not overseas as originally planned, but at home, and so Australia agreed to establish four schools for initial training, nine for elementary flying training, seven for service flying and 13 other schools. Two-ninths of Australian students would go to Canada for training, but only after completing elementary training in Australia. The Australian government would not only recruit and train its portion, but also provide all necessary facilities such as airfields, buildings, instructors and aircraft. Complex cost-sharing arrangements made with Britain included British payments to Australia in kind (including aircraft and engines), cash, and subsidised pay for RAAF aircrew in the RAF. The Dominions would have first call on their graduates from the EATS, but it was expected that the vast majority would fight for the RAF in Europe.

Fairbairn's insistence on substantial Australian training at home proved judicious, for it ensured that some advanced training machines with potential military value were sent to Australia. Wise too was the approval of the CAS's recommendation to establish 38 advanced operational airbases on Australia's coast.

Not so astute was Australia's acceptance of Britain's concept of a united Empire air force, in which all senior ranks were held by British officers. This ensured that few leading Australian airmen reached positions of senior command in Europe. Although Australian airmen continued to wear their distinctive dark blue uniforms and to receive Australian rates of pay, acceptance of the British plan also meant there was no distinct, unified Australian aerial force in Europe. In the Middle East, soldiers of the AIF fought together in brigades and divisions, but most Australian airmen in the war against Germany and Italy were unable to operate like this. (No. 10 Squadron was joined by No. 3 Squadron and No. 1 Air Ambulance Unit, but these were the only RAAF units sent from Australia's home defence force.)

Menzies assured Australians that his government would 'preserve the Australian character and identity of any air force that went abroad', and Article XV of the Ottawa agreement which codified the Empire Air Training Scheme decreed that graduates of each contributing country would be 'identified with their respective dominions'.[2] The British Air Ministry determined that Australia was entitled to raise eighteen Article XV squadrons, numbered 450 to 467. Together these would include some 2500 aircrew, which looked very impressive on paper, yet that Air Ministry also decreed that an 'Australian' or 'Canadian' or 'New Zealand' squadron would qualify as such as long as a majority of its members were from the Dominion concerned.

Furthermore, the Dominion governments allowed the British Air Ministry the power to determine what postings their reinforcements would receive, which meant that reinforcements from Britain and all her Dominions were sent to whichever squadron needed them, regardless of nationality. Most so-called 'Australian' squadrons were thus quite cosmopolitan. Insultingly, command positions in 'RAAF' squadrons were often given to British officers, not always better qualified than available Australian officers. The Australian government's willingness to give up the independence of its air force in a way that would never have happened with the Army, Navy or even the AFC was probably due to the urgency of Britain's need, especially for airmen to man its aircraft, and the relative youth of the RAAF, the independence of which apparently mattered relatively little to the Australian government.

The EATS took over 1000 Australians per month from their homeland from 29 April 1940, when the first course was inducted. Australian politicians did not ignore the imperative for home defence, and at this time Menzies declared that Australia's local air strength would now grow enormously. He described the 591 Avro Ansons and 336 Fairey Battles that Britain was to send for training purposes as 'capable of holding their own against any seaborne aircraft likely to be brought against them in Australian waters'. In fact, most Japanese carrier-borne aircraft outclassed the Anson and Fairey Battle. Similarly hollow was the prime minister's further claim that this increase in air strength, with that of the Navy and Army, should render Australia 'secure against any serious attack'.[3]

Australia's commitment to the EATS did bring some advantages for the coming Pacific War. Firstly, because no more squadrons based in Australia were sent away to England, they remained as unified units for the challenge ahead. Secondly, by the time the war with Japan began, many Australian airmen had up to two years' experience in combat against the Luftwaffe. Some would return to give their homeland the benefit of that experience.

There was no shortage of Australians keen to join the air force. Of the 100,000 Australians who had volunteered for the armed services by the end of March 1940, about 68,000 had applied to join the RAAF. Free from conscription, the air force's all-volunteer status gave it the elan of the First and Second AIF, and like air forces everywhere it would contain many of the nation's brightest eligible personnel. The exploits of Australian airmen during the Great War, their pioneer successors in the 1920s and 1930s, as well as the fictional exploits of heroes such as 'Biggles' all made for an appealing contrast to the horrifying loss and hardships of footsloggers on the Western Front. Menzies' comment that Britain would need airmen more than troops probably also contributed to this rush.

Nearly 57,000 of the 68,000 volunteers applied as ground staff rather than aircrew. Ground staff were indispensable, and given that there were more than 60 separate 'musterings' or trades within the RAAF, a great variety of skills was required. Technical ground staff musterings were hard to fill, and from the outset politicians and industry worried about the domestic effects of the government's plan to call up thousands of air force mechanics.

Early in the war there were more volunteers than the RAAF could process, let alone induct. Fewer than one-tenth of the ground staff applicants had been enlisted by March 1940. At that time fewer than 40 per cent of aircrew applicants had been interviewed, and fewer than 2000 recruited. This embittered eager young men who had been told by their government that providing trained airmen to Britain was vital. Yet delays were inevitable, given that the pre-war regular air force had trained fewer than 100 pilots annually, and that there were, early in 1940, only 16 of the 1000 flying instructors needed to meet the task of graduating some 3700 pilots annually. Courses for instructors had quickly been instituted, through a reconstituted Central Flying School, and the air force doubled in size—to 6000 men—between September 1939 and April 1940. By then its waiting list contained all the men it could cope with for six months.

The other services wanted men too, so the RAAF maintained a recruiting campaign while still unable to place many who had already applied. A 'reservist' scheme was established to mollify these men and to attract more. Under this scheme, men waiting to be called up could begin learning the necessary physics, mathematics and morse code. Thus, for example, John Grey Gorton would regularly leave his orange orchard to visit the post office at Kerang to learn morse code while waiting for the call. When Gorton had first registered, the recruiting officer had his doubts as to whether the air force would want the 29-year-old farmer, although he did have a pilot's licence and an MA from Oxford. By the end of 1940, more than 7000 reservists were being instructed by more than 1500 instructors at 400 centres.

Once an applicant had been provisionally accepted, he had to undergo medical and other tests. General fitness was assessed, but special emphasis was laid on eyesight: colour blindness, poor hand–eye coordination and ocular muscle imbalance (that is, an inability to judge distances when, for example, landing an aircraft or firing its weapons) could cost lives. Trainee pilots needed a minimum IQ of 110. At Initial Training Schools men were evaluated on the Wright Coordination Machine, which tested the ability to keep two lights together with hand and foot controls.

Training for war

The first new training schools designed to send an increasing flow of aircrew to Europe opened in March 1940, often in aero clubs or hastily formed establishments with inadequate or non-existent facilities. Meeting the demands of the EATS would be possible only if training were made much more specialised than the pre-war system, which prepared pilots to fly or navigate any aircraft or work in an administrative position. Under the EATS, the new pupil (with rank of Aircraftman Second Class or AC2) first attended one of six Initial Training Schools, where for three months he studied mathematics, physics, navigation and morse code, among other subjects. John O'Keeffe, who left teaching at a country school to become an airman, described the process as 'lectures, needles by the dozen, hours and hours of drill, parades and route marches', all the while being 'made to feel like human excreta by NCO disciplinary staff and commissioned lecturing staff'.[4]

On crossing that hurdle successfully, if the recruit was chosen to become a pilot—the goal of the vast majority of aircrew recruits—he would spend two months at an Elementary Flying Training School (EFTS), learning to fly a light aircraft, generally the Tiger Moth or Gipsy Moth. For about 10 hours he flew with an instructor, who sat in front of him and shouted advice down a tube. Here many—perhaps most—pilots experienced their first flight. Then came the even more momentous first solo flight. The Tiger Moth brought pilots into close contact with the elements and, for many, epitomised the beauty of flying. Yet there were many accidents and hard or forced landings. The histories of 2, 3 and 4 Elementary Flying Training Schools, for example, note that there were 'constant aircraft incidents', 'many aircraft incidents' and that 'accidents were common', respectively.[5] At this level, however, few crashes were serious, and of these three schools, only 4 EFTS had a fatal accident, when a pilot officer fell from his aircraft while performing a slow roll. Some of the incidents were not without humour, as in the story of Leading Aircraftman Joseph Gribble of 3 EFTS, who became lost flying from Melbourne to Ballarat. He landed to seek directions, then took off and again became lost. With darkness approaching, Gribble parachuted from his aircraft, which crashed. He was fined.

There was nothing humorous in incidents such as the death in a crash of a 1 EFTS instructor and air cadet at Parafield, South Australia, in 1940, or the deaths of four members of 8 EFTS killed in one accident at Narrandera, New South Wales in 1943. At this level the trainee received a 'flying log', an official but also intensely personal document in which all the flights he would undertake in his RAAF career were briefly recorded. One recruit, Wilfred 'Woof' Arthur, discovered at this level that he was prone to airsickness, becoming violently ill and suffering bad headaches. He overcame it to become one of Australia's best fighter pilots.

If, like Arthur, the trainee pilot passed successfully through the EFTS, he would be sent to a Service Flying Training School (SFTS); 37 per cent of RAAF pilots completed this training in Canada. Another 700 trainees attended an EFTS and SFTS in Rhodesia, while the rest completed their SFTS in Australia. Irrespective of location, for four months the trainee learned more advanced skills such as instrument and formation flying, gunnery and complex aerobatics in an advanced trainer, which was twice as fast as the Tiger Moth and, unlike the yellow 'Tiggy', had the enclosed cockpit and retractable landing gear of operational aircraft. If the trainee was considered suitable to pilot a single-engine aircraft, this trainer would be a Wirraway. Arthur Tucker said he and others were sent to single-engine rather than twin or four-engine aircraft purely because they were tall enough to push the rudder bars on a Wirraway. The 'Wirra' could be a daunting prospect. One pilot called it a 'huge, noisy, clumsy brute', though he and others came to admire it.[6] 'Black Jack' Walker, one of the RAAF's best and most experienced pilots, dubbed it 'a jolly good trainer' that would prepare a pilot for almost any single-engined fighter, especially if he could cope with its 'vicious stall'.[7] If the trainee was to fly multi-engined aircraft, such as bombers, he would learn on the Anson or, from late 1941, the Oxford.

There were many more accidents at the secondary than the elementary training level. One that made worldwide news occurred at 2 SFTS in September 1940, when two Ansons collided and became interlocked in mid-air. The trainee pilot in the top aircraft, LAC Leonard Fuller, managed to direct the combined planes away from the nearby township of Brocklesby and, once the lower pilot had parachuted clear, to use the flaps and ailerons of the top aircraft to make a gliding landing on the lower aircraft. Another accident claimed Fuller's life later in the war.

Some schools had excellent accident-free runs: though 4 SFTS at

Geraldton, Western Australia, received second-hand Ansons, it had no fatalities for the first 22 months of its existence, and averaged an impressive 1469 hours flying between accidents. On the other hand, more than 30 of the 2200 pilots who entered 7 SFTS at Deniliquin, New South Wales, were killed in air accidents there. The first air accident at 5 SFTS, in Uranquinty, New South Wales, occurred in April 1942, following 'unauthorised diving at ground targets'.[8] Drought conditions there engendered dust storms, adding to the dangers typical in the hot months in the many schools north of the Great Dividing Range and in South Australia and Western Australia. Flying conditions there were often ideal in the morning, but later in the day turbulent air, massive cloud formations and occasional thunderstorms made for flying that was frequently uncomfortable and sometimes dangerous. In fact, while 485 Australian aircraft were lost to enemy action in the South-West Pacific Area throughout the war, a staggering 740 were lost in accidents at flying training schools.

Those who graduated through the SFTS moved on to real warplanes, early on in service units, and from the fateful date of 7 December 1941 in Operational Training Units (OTUs). Common in the latter were Beauforts, but also Hudsons, Vengeances, Beaufighters, Catalinas, Spitfires, Mosquitos and Liberators. These were significantly more powerful than training aircraft, so losses at this level occurred at an even higher rate than at the flying training schools. There were so many accidents among 1 OTU Beauforts at Bairnsdale, Victoria, that it became known as 'Death Valley'. Bill Deane-Butcher was medical officer to 75 Squadron during its intense fighting at Port Moresby early in 1942, but said he did more of the awful task of identifying and burying remains with 1 OTU than with the Kittyhawk squadron, which lost many of its men far from base. Instructors reportedly went pale on being told that they were posted to 1 OTU, which by war's end had lost 131 aircrew dead or missing. The official medical history tells in sober terms of the fate of pilots who crashed while at Mildura's No. 2 OTU:

> The terrain over which exercises were carried out was desolate and uneven, and it would have been possible for a searching ambulance to pass by without noticing a crashed aircraft lying in a depression only a few yards away. The operational aircraft sometimes crashed many miles

> from base, and, if the search was not well organised, the pilot, if not already dead, might die before help reached him.[9]

The traditional cavalier RAAF attitude no doubt contributed to the accident rate, and as they had in the 1930s, newspapers and politicians occasionally brought accidents to public attention. However, the training accidents were due mainly to attitudes and needs peculiar to this extraordinary time. Factors such as the inexperience of fliers and instructors that was unavoidable in a mass air force, the inherent difficulty of landing many of the aircraft in use, the need to train hard for imminent action, and the necessarily truncated flying courses all made for high accident rates. Alec Boxall, who became a navigator, wrote that training accidents often occurred when aircraft became lost in cloud.

> You have a navigator who is half-way through his course, thinks that he knows it all, sets the wind drift to port instead of starboard and, instead of flying to the side of the Grampians they fly straight into them. That sort of thing happened every week.[10]

Boxall was nearly killed himself on one training flight when a recently commissioned pilot tried to show off in an Anson by doing acrobatics over Port Lincoln. Instead he stalled the aircraft, throwing three of his passengers violently around the plane and only just avoiding disaster. Dying in training seemed pointless and inglorious, but the man killed this way sacrificed his life for his country every bit as much as the veteran who died in his umpteenth dogfight.

Those emerging successfully back at the Initial Training School who were not chosen as pilots, or did not want to be, were categorised as potential observers (later called navigators), bomb-aimers, wireless operators or air-gunners and sent to the relevant specialist school for a six-month course. Similarly, those who in 'flight grading' at EFTS were not selected as pilots, would, if not discharged or transferred to ground crew, be streamed to these specialist positions. The specialists completed their training on Ansons, Oxfords and Fairey Battles. The upper age limit for these specialists was 32, for pilots 31. Navigators tended to be men of what the official medical history calls 'a high intellectual standard', and were regarded as the brains of the multicrew aircraft.[11] About 80 per cent of pupils graduated, and of the remainder about half were sent into ground staff 'musterings'. Each group entering initial training was called a course, and numbered '1 course', '2 course' and so on. Leave between schools was irreverently known as 'intercourse leave'.[12] Men measured their own success and luck against those in their course.

Luck had already often played a part in determining ranks. Some aircrew graduates became officers, the rest sergeants. By the beginning of the war against Japan, fixed proportions of graduates were commissioned as officers: one-third of pilots and navigators, one-tenth of wireless operators, and just one-twentieth of air-gunners. The proportions were made less rigid from mid-1942, though methods of selection remained the same. Although proven ability was essential, so too was performance in an interview, often of three candidates at once. Age and educational background made a difference here.

The men who qualified as aircrew tended to be middle or upper class. Ninety-two per cent of aircrew recruited in the first year of the EATS had at least four years of secondary education; 96 per cent of pilots and 99 per cent of navigators were thus qualified. This was at a time when of more than 80,000 Victorians aged 15–19 years, just 2866 students had qualified for the fourth-year Intermediate Certificate in 1935. Those with a mechanical inclination, especially towards motorbikes and cars, had a better chance of being accepted as aircrew. Australians, like Americans, supposedly had an advantage over the Japanese in that they tended to be more familiar with complex machinery. John Piper said what secured his selection was his membership of the Light Horse, where a light touch was necessary, and his sailing experience. Bill Deane-Butcher, who worked on an aircrew selection board, said they looked for highly motivated, practical, confident and healthy men, but admitted that it was difficult to predict features like 'temperament, fear of heights, allergies, tendency to motion sickness, [and] inability to cope with subjects like navigation and aerodynamics'.[13] Applicants were required to give their parents' nationality and state whether they were 'of pure European descent', although unlike the Royal Australian Navy (RAN) and AIF, the air force was permitted to enlist aliens and non-Europeans. Only one of the 10,000-plus pilots trained under the EATS was Aboriginal, and we shall hear his story later. The typical RAAF aircrew trainee was single and aged 25 or under. Nearly two-thirds of recruits were from New South Wales and Victoria, and the city/country divide was extremely close: 51 to 49 per cent in favour of urban-dwellers.

The expansion of the RAAF was well underway before the first EATS trainees graduated, in November 1940: by then, for example, 400 new pilots had already been commissioned. When Air Marshal Sir Charles Burnett was appointed CAS in February 1940, he was eager to send Australian airmen to Europe, and he concentrated on a training organisation suited to that purpose. He did not press for a distinctively Australian identity within the unified air force, or concentrate on developing an operational force for defending Australia. Soon after arriving, he and the Air Board did reorganise Australia into four 'Areas': Southern, Central, and from early 1941, Northern and Western—yet when decisions needed to be made about the use of existing forces (for example to protect shipping), they were not taken at these headquarters, but by Burnett, at Air Force Headquarters in Melbourne. This, together with Burnett's failure to allow senior RAAF officers to obtain experience in European operations, meant that the RAAF lacked the leadership and organisation necessary when a war for national survival began.

In September 1939, an RAAF squadron had for the first time been sent to New Guinea: No. 11 Squadron, based at Port Moresby, and initially equipped with just two Short Empire flying-boats impressed from Qantas. To help expand and modernise the air force, Richard Williams, now Australia's first Air Marshal, returned from Britain to occupy the new post of Air Member for Organisation and Equipment on the Air Board. Group Captain Bill Bostock had been appointed Deputy CAS in 1939, and Burnett retained him in that post. In April 1940 the significant post of Director of Training went to Wing Commander George Jones, who deserves much of the credit for the success of the production line that training became in Australia. The expanding air force required a large bureaucracy; recruits with professional and executive ability were needed for the 'Administrative and Special Duties' (A. and S.D.) branch, which complemented the 'General Duties' branch, comprising all officers qualified for flying duties. Integrating these many former civilians into the RAAF was a huge undertaking.

By December 1941, on the eve of the war with Japan, there were 34 EATS schools for aircrew in Australia. Many had staff of 500 or more and at least 50 aircraft. While some were at established airbases such as Point Cook and Laverton in Victoria and Mascot in Sydney, the creation of others at places such as Uranquinty in New South Wales necessitated land clearance and grading, as well as significant building of accommodation for personnel, aircraft and other stores. In July 1942, of 1630 servicemen and women at No. 1 OTU, Bairnsdale, 320 were still without a bed seven months after the unit was created. During the course of the war, most of these schools trained 2000–3000 men each. For all the disappointments and dangers in the EATS training program, most of those who passed through it loved it: there was the sheer physical enjoyment of using a powerful machine with, but also against, the forces of nature, as well as the comradeship, the new status, the places visited, and the sense of combined purpose. All these elements were inherent to a degree in the other services, but there was something special in being in aircrew, as was brilliantly evoked in this letter from a 19-year-old trainee pilot:

> . . . you arise and don your flying suit, then making your way to the tarmac, you see your crate waiting for your familiar hands to bring it to life.
>
> As you look at it, you ponder over the wonder that here before you is a multitude of pieces of metal constructed in the shape of a bird, which has in it an engine driven by explosion, which, in turn, causes another piece of metal to revolve at such a great speed as to cause the whole construction, plus man, to be lifted into the air and transported from place to place at almost incredible speeds ...
>
> So one climbs aboard and feels the bouncing heart-throbs as the engine comes to life at his touch on the controls. Then the surge of power which flows through the machine as the throttle opens and one feels oneself move forward with ever-increasing rapidity until soon one feels the smoothness of the flight of the aircraft as it has dissolved from earth.
>
> Upwards one sails, and looking down on the world beneath, the feeling of lightness seems to enter one's heart, causing a wave of happiness to surge from the toes, which tingle, to the head, where it breaks out in a wide grin.
>
> Then to fly through the mist of clouds, reappearing above them in time to see the first rays of sunlight strike their fleecy surfaces and reflect with a golden glow.

> Then the thrills in the pit of one's stomach as the plane alters its altitude in relation to the earth while the pilot performs what he fondly refers to as 'aerobatics', as he loops and spins, rolls and dives. One of his biggest thrills is flying upside down. It's great.
>
> Then down he goes to skim the surface of Mother Earth at a height of anything from three feet to 15,000 feet. This, too, is his big thrill.
>
> Finally he realises he must return, and slowly and reluctantly the obedient thing he is flying descends and settles once more on the ground, both pilot and itself giving one last sigh as their journey ends.[14]

The necessity of confronting the possibility of death every time they climbed aboard was present, but would become more pressing in operations. John Piper and Raynor Barber, who in New Guinea would fly Kittyhawks and Beaufighters respectively, stated that from the outset they and many other pilots considered it unlikely that they would survive the war, and it is hard to imagine many Australian airmen disagreeing with an American pilot's claim that every pilot or crewman in World War II came within an ace of death at least once.[15] Whatever their attitude to death, there was a general conviction that they were fighting for a just cause and, especially after the involvement of Japan, for the survival of all they held dear.

After a while, the experience of flying was not so novel and exhilarating for the flying instructors, whose role was indispensable. Their work, training for example four or five pupils at a time at the Elementary Flight Training Schools, was fatiguing in itself, but as the war went on, was often done by men returning exhausted from demanding operational duties. Most instructors were themselves trained at the Central Flying School at Point Cook, which provided 3601 instructors during the war. On returning from the Middle East in 1941, fighter ace John Jackson was briefly appointed as an instructor at Point Cook. He told his wife:

> I just loathe this joint. This training is a tough job and I take my hat off to the boys who have been doing it since war broke out. They have done a fine job, and are turning the pilots out solidly trained and ahead of schedule. They fly night and day, long hours; every one of these instructors is longing to be sent overseas, but I doubt if they have any chance of ever getting there—they are so valuable here.[16]

Jackson would go on to lion-hearted exploits in New Guinea, but those instructors who did not make it overseas were unsung heroes of Australia's air war.

Europe and the Middle East

Those accepted into the air force from 1939 to 1941 were keen to go where there was action: Europe. This would change in December 1941, though for some Europe would always be more appealing than the Pacific.

Most RAF squadrons contained at least one Australian, so Aussies participated in virtually all major air operations in the first years of the war. On the first day of the war, Tamworth-born Ellis Ross flew a sortie, or operational flight, in a Hampden bomber of 83 Squadron RAF. Ross would earn a DFC before being killed by flak over Germany in August 1940. The first Australian airman—and indeed the first Australian—killed in action in World War II was Wing Commander Ivan Cameron who, on 28 September 1939, was shot down over Germany on a reconnaissance mission. In 1940, even before the EATS brought Australians to British skies, Australian aircrew fought and died in relatively large numbers. Between 11 and 14 May, Hurricane pilot Leslie Clisby became the first Australian ace of the war, downing eight aircraft. On one occasion his rudder had been blown away and he was manoeuvring to crash-land when an enemy bomber flew across his nose. The quick-thinking Clisby fired a burst, which disabled the Heinkel. Both planes landed in the same paddock, and within minutes Clisby was chasing the German crew across a field. After he brought one down with a rugby tackle, all five surrendered to the determined Australian. On 14 May Clisby's luck ran out and, after shooting down two of a large group of enemy fighters, he was killed by Messerschmitt Bf 110 fighters near Rheims. Thirteen of the 37 Australian pilots who flew for Fighter Command in the Battle of Britain were also killed.

Following Italy's entry into the war in 1940, the conflict spread to the Mediterranean, where Australians in RAF squadrons fought Italian and German pilots. No. 3 Squadron RAAF arrived there in October 1940. By the time the desert campaign ended in Tunisia in early 1943, the squadron had destroyed around 200 aircraft in air combat alone and produced 17 aces. From mid-1943 it fought in Sicily and Italy, where amidst Allied air superiority it concentrated on ground-attack operations.

The first Article XV RAAF squadron formed in England was No. 452, which flew Spitfires. Its Commanding Officer (CO) was RAF ace Roy Dutton. Though its Australian pilots were inexperienced when it began combat flying in June 1941, it soon established an outstanding reputation. In August it destroyed 22 enemy aircraft, more than any other Fighter Command squadron that month. Irish ace 'Paddy' Finucane claimed ten enemy planes, but seven Australians contributed. Finucane commented: 'These Australians are tough. Waggle your wings, and they will follow you through hell and high water.'[17] Among those he had in mind was Pilot Officer Keith 'Bluey' Truscott, who in August achieved his first two kills. He was fortunate to have become a fighter pilot at all, for despite considerable physical and mental gifts he had struggled in flying lessons, taking an unusually long time to go solo. He almost certainly would not have made it had he not been a household name in Victoria, where in 1939 he had been a member of the Melbourne football team that won the VFL Grand Final. He had been granted leave from the air force in 1940 to play in that year's premiership-winning team too. By October 1941 Truscott's kills had risen to six, and he was awarded the DFC. By January 1942 he was commanding the squadron, now firmly established as one of Fighter Command's best. 'Bluey' was a celebrity in Britain, popular not only for his flying skill but also for his personal qualities of openness, intelligence, good humour and determination. In a publicity exercise, the Marquess of Donegall was able to persuade red-headed Britons to donate £5000 to 'buy' Bluey a Spitfire. In March 1942, when Truscott destroyed a Focke-Wulf 190, he brought the squadron's total kills to 62, with a further seven probables, for the loss of 22 of its own pilots. Truscott's was the squadron's last European victory, for it was earmarked for Australia and war with Japan.

No. 457 Squadron, the second Article XV RAAF fighter squadron formed, was not given the same early opportunities as 452 to show its ability. Not until March 1942, some eight months after becoming operational, did it contact the enemy, and then the Australians found their Spitfire Vs inferior to the Focke-Wulfs they encountered. The unit had destroyed five enemy aircraft, with four probables, by June, when it too was withdrawn for a move to Australia.

A number of Australian airmen who achieved success in Europe would eventually fight the Japanese. No. 10 Squadron's Dick Cohen (who later changed his name to Richard Kingsland) showed his mettle in June 1940, when ordered to fly British officials Lord Gort and Alfred Duff Cooper to Rabat, Morocco. After landing his Sunderland in a narrow estuary, Cohen waited for his two passengers as they went ashore to make delicate negotiations concerning that French colony's future. French guards picketed Cohen's aircraft in small boats. After nightfall Cohen received an urgent radio message from British Prime Minister Winston Churchill warning Gort and Cooper that their reception would probably be hostile. Cohen went ashore to investigate. The guards refused to take him to the jetty, so he seized a boat at gunpoint and, on getting ashore, stole a car. At the hotel where Gort was speaking, hostile guards again confronted Cohen. Undaunted, he drew his revolver and engaged in a gunfight. He entered the hotel, found Gort and explained the danger. Before they could leave, they were arrested and locked up. The negligent guards did not disarm Cohen, who again shot his way out of danger: destroying the lock, escaping the building and stealing a car that took all three men to the jetty. They reached the Sunderland and, dodging hostile boats and other obstacles, taxied out to sea before escaping. Cohen received the DFC for this exploit, the first of many that would see him lead No. 11 Squadron's flying-boats against Japan.

Clive Caldwell, who following a private-school education had worked in jobs as varied as jackeroo and insurance salesman, joined the RAAF aged 29 in 1940. Previous experience in Tiger Moths helped him gain a commission in January 1941. He was soon on his way to the Middle East, where he joined No. 250 Squadron RAF, flying P-40 Tomahawks. After some 40 sorties, Caldwell had just one confirmed kill to his name, but then followed a momentous revelation. One day while flying low over the desert in formation and wondering why he was not achieving more hits, he whimsically released a burst of machine-gun fire. He could now see how the bullets fell in relation to his aircraft's shadow and realised that this was a way he could practise firing for deflection: that is, firing while taking into account the lead of the enemy aircraft. Only in firing from head-on or behind (astern) could one avoid the need to calculate deflection. This was very complex in one moving aircraft shooting at another aircraft, especially in the usual case where one aircraft was higher than another, for then it was easy to miss to left, right, above or below the enemy plane; it was three-dimensional shooting. After further experiments with this technique, Caldwell quickly formed mental images of the amount of deflection needed at different speeds. Within two weeks, he had gained 'ace' status. His 'shadow-shooting' method became standard gunnery practice in the Middle East, though few could apply it in combat as effectively as Caldwell. While leading 250 Squadron in December 1941, Caldwell destroyed five aircraft in one sortie. He achieved further success with 112 Squadron. This included not only kills in the air, but strafing ground targets: one estimate says he killed 600 enemy soldiers. Understandably, he was nicknamed 'Killer'. Following the Japanese onslaught, the Australian government sought the return of such experienced pilots, asking for Caldwell specifically. When he left the Middle East, the British air commander there, Air Marshal Arthur Tedder, wrote in Caldwell's flying log: 'A fine commander, an excellent leader and a first class shot.'[18] Caldwell had achieved 19 individual and three shared confirmed kills, as well as six probables and 15 damaged. More were to come.

Caldwell would be joined in Australia by Tim Goldsmith, another RAAF fighter pilot who distinguished himself in the Middle East. A year after enlisting at the age of 19, he was flying RAF Spitfires. Posted to the beleaguered and strategically vital island of Malta, he achieved 12 victories in four months. In that time he was commissioned, won the DFM and DFC, and on leaving the island in July 1942 received the Malta Cross from the Maltese government. By the end of 1942 he was in Darwin.

Like Goldsmith, Queenslander Charles ('Chas') Crombie flew in Malta. He piloted Blenheims and Beaufighters before converting to Hurricanes. He shot down three German bombers in Egypt and was sent to Malta in 1942. He had destroyed another seven aircraft by year's end, when he was sent to fight the Japanese in Burma. Also sent to Burma was Spitfire pilot 'Larry' Cronin, victor over three German fighters. Many other Australians, including bomber crews, would also fight there.

Among Australians of 3 Squadron who would return to fight Japan was Peter Jeffrey, a permanent air force officer. By December 1941, when he was called home, he commanded the squadron, was an ace, and had won a DSO and DFC. He was joined in Australia by John Jackson, who in a 3 Squadron Hurricane in February 1941 shot down three Stukas in one action. By January 1942, Jackson had destroyed at least six aircraft serving three of the king's enemies: Germany, Italy and Vichy France.

By the time his DFC was gazetted in April 1942, Jackson was fighting the fourth enemy, Japan, in the most important struggle of his and his country's life. He had three airmen brothers: Ed, Les and Arthur. While trying to accumulate enough flying hours to be called up as an RAAF pilot, Arthur was killed in an aircraft accident in October 1939.

In all, 27,899 RAAF aircrew graduated from the EATS and contributed to the war against Germany. It was a remarkable achievement for an organisation that since 1921 had graduated only about 50 pilots annually. In addition, Australia trained another 9138 aircrew who served only in the South-West Pacific Area. RAAF deaths in Europe and the Middle East totalled more than 6600, with a further 1382 wounded. Those numbers reflect the risks Australians took and the courage they showed in the war against Germany and Italy.

While so many Australian airmen risked all for victory in Europe, the way in which their effort was organised hampered the RAAF at home. At war's end, although there were far fewer men in the RAAF in Europe than in Australia—about 15,500 to 138,000—the comparative totals of aircrew were very close: 12,300 to 14,500. Australia's commitment to the EATS denied the country many talented airmen, and the failure of Australian and British leaders to give opportunities for Australians in Europe to rise to high ranks contributed to the RAAF leadership crisis in its campaign against Japan. On the other hand, those Australian airmen who returned to the South-West Pacific Area from the European war brought the benefits of experience, and the Australian contribution to victory over Germany also helped ensure victory over Japan.

The other half of the sky: women join the air force

Several months before war was declared, Mary Bell established in Brisbane a voluntary organisation called the Women's Air Training Corps (WATC). Its members were women keen to train for aircraft work should Australia go to war. Mary was a pilot, and the wife of John Bell, a former AFC pilot and then Queensland manager of Airlines of Australia Ltd. When war broke out, Mary's husband was posted to Melbourne. She followed and formed a division of the WATC there. This group soon had ten 'squadrons' and about 1000 members. They trained on motor transport and aero engines, wireless telegraphy, stores, cooking, photography, draughting, clerical work, and as aircraft hands. Divisions were also formed in the other states. Each division had a commandant, with Mary the Australian Commandant. They did much voluntary work for the RAAF, for example as drivers and clerks. Early in the war Mary proposed to the Air Board that it consider enlisting women in the air force. The Air Board showed little interest, but the Minister for Air, James Fairbairn, sought information about the British Women's Auxiliary Air Force. He would not live to see the new women's force, for near Canberra on 13 August 1940 he was killed in an air accident that cost the lives of some of Australia's most distinguished military leaders.

The air force was seriously short of telegraphists, so despite reservations and opposition from some men on both sides of politics, on 9 January 1941 the Advisory War Council agreed that women should be enlisted 'to the minimum number for the minimum period'.[19] Mary Bell became acting director of the new service. Despite a lack of facilities and the unhelpful attitudes of some male officers, recruiting of airwomen began on 15 March 1941. Ten days later the new Minister for Air, Mr McEwen, announced the formation of the Women's Australian Auxiliary Air Force (WAAAF). Some 320 women aged 18 to 40 (or 50 in special circumstances) would be enlisted as wireless and teleprinter operators and for administrative and domestic duties. They would be paid at two-thirds the rates for corresponding ranks of airmen. Speaking for the Opposition, Mr Makin raised various objections, concluding with the rather desperate line that 'the air force was a man's job, anyway'.[20] Nevertheless, women were not dissuaded by such attitudes and discriminatory regulations. The need for women's auxiliaries would grow, rather than decline, and there was no shortage of applicants.

Mary Bell resigned in May, having learned that a new director would be appointed. Her replacement was Clare Stevenson, a former General Secretary of the Young Women's Christian Association and executive of Berlei Ltd. By November 1941 there were nearly 750 airwomen and officers, and the WAAAF was on its way to becoming the largest of the three women's services. In 1944 its strength would surpass 18,600. Once war with Japan began, the WAAAF's roles would increase, including for example aircraft maintenance and repair. By 1945, 77 per cent of RAAF positions were open to women.

The creation of an RAAF Nursing Service in July 1940 was not a contentious employment for women in the air force. The original strength was 38, soon rising to 61. Recruits were required to be unmarried females who were registered nurses aged between 21 and 40, though specially qualified older nurses could in some cases be appointed. More than 50 RAAF nurses travelled overseas with the first EATS group.

Four RAAF nurses were posted to Darwin in October 1941. Their facilities were pleasant, but initially they found life there rather monotonous. That would soon change.

3 'We may not have much time to spare'

Deliveries of aircraft to Australia were slow in 1940, thanks mainly to the disastrous turn of events in Europe. By June 1941 Australian factories had produced 461 Tiger Moths and 313 Wirraways and trainers. The first of 700 Australian-built Beaufort bombers was delivered in August 1941. This was an impressive achievement for a country that was still not building entire motor cars. The fledgling industry's production figures were notable, too, although the press criticised the Commonwealth Aircraft Corporation and the Department of Aircraft Production for being too slow. Moreover, by December 1941, on the eve of war with Japan, most of Australia's 19 home defence squadrons were only at two-thirds of their proper establishment and thus pitifully equipped for combat.

By mid-1941, the only genuine front-line aircraft delivered to Australia were 100 Hudsons and four Catalina flying-boats, though the hundreds of Anson and Fairey Battle light bombers being used for training might serve a limited purpose in an emergency. The Wirraways became ersatz 'fighters'. In January 1941 the Minister for Air reported to the War Cabinet on the Japanese aircraft types that aircraft carriers might bring into Australia's operational zone. The politicians were interested in references to a new naval fighter plane put into production in 1940 and which seemed to be a development of their Type 96 'Claude' fighter.

'Type 96' referred to a Japanese dating system, as did the name of this new fighter, the Type 0, or as the Allies would come to write it, the 'Zero'. It was said to have two cannons, two machine guns and a top speed of 300 miles per hour; in fact its maximum speed was 332 miles per hour (534 kilometres per hour). When using drop tanks for extra fuel it also had a phenomenal range of over 3000 kilometres. However, when the Minister of the Army, Mr Spender, said shortly afterwards that this recent information suggested Japanese seaborne aircraft would outclass the Wirraway, the CAS Sir Charles Burnett replied that there would not be many of these high-performance Japanese aircraft, and that against the Japanese types that might be used to attack Australia, the Wirraway would put up 'quite a good show'.[1]

That month, January 1941, Catalina aircraft made a momentous ferry-flight from Hawaii to Australia. It was only the third recorded direct trans-Pacific flight to Australia. So that American neutrality laws were not broken, civilians had to transport the 18 Catalinas ordered for the RAAF from the Consolidated Aircraft Corporation in San Diego. Nearly every Qantas captain and first officer contributed to the operation. The Catalinas would be a mainstay of the RAAF in the Pacific, and eventually 168 would be delivered. They were by no means fast: it was joked that to make a rendezvous the Cat's navigator needed a calendar rather than a stopwatch, and that Catalinas had endured bird strikes *from the rear.* Athol 'Attie' Wearne, a veteran of the Atlantic war, initially found the interior of a Catalina gloomy and restricted compared to the twin-decked Sunderland. However, he grew to love the Cat, especially for its efficiency. To those not accustomed to the Sunderland, the Catalina with its bunks and galley was luxurious. Its two Pratt and Whitney engines were noisy but wonderfully reliable. The Cat sat low on the water, so in heavy seas waves washed over the cockpit. In slightly bumpy seas and once airborne it was a fine aircraft to pilot. Its load was critical to its handling: the heavier the load, the harder it was to climb and manoeuvre. Another veteran of both the Sunderland and Catalina, Sir Richard Kingsland, considered the Catalina 'delightful to handle', and its engines superior to those of the Sunderland.[2] Yet he also emphasised its vulnerability, for its lack of speed (170–220 kilometres per hour, depending on load) and manoeuvrability made it a sitting duck for any other aircraft it was likely to face in the Pacific. Its antiquated Lewis waist guns were symptomatic of the state of Australia's defences. Within six months of their arrival, eight of the 18 Catalinas would be lost to enemy action. Moreover, although its independence from established airfields was an advantage to senior RAAF officers planning operations, the Catalina's light hull was designed to operate from the calm waters of harbours, lakes and rivers rather than the open sea. Yet the Catalina would become the go-to aircraft when airmen had to be rescued after ditching in the sea. Every such rescue was dangerous. One pilot put a brave face on it when he said that even if it was not the RAAF's best aircraft in terms of handling, it was arguably the best in terms of interesting missions. The Catalina was possibly Australia's greatest aircraft of the war, for it flew from the first operations to the last, in areas stretching from New Guinea to China, Sumatra to the Caroline Islands, and in an extraordinary range of roles.

If Australia's aircraft were vulnerable, so was its main northern base, Darwin. In November 1940 the War Cabinet approved plans for evacuating Darwin's civilians if circumstances demanded. Air-raid and anti-gas drills were performed and slit trenches dug, but lack of equipment limited the degree of aerodrome defence. No. 12 Squadron's Wirraways and 13 Squadron's Hudsons toiled on coastal patrols and shipping escort. The crews of some Japanese luggers that came illegally close to the north coast shook their fists at Wing Commander John 'Sam' Balmer of 13 Squadron, who flew so low over them that his Hudson's slipstream rocked the boats violently. The modern Hudson made a wonderful initial impression on its crews. As might be expected in an aircraft that was a modified version of a commercial airliner, the Hudson had a beautiful instrument layout and nice controls, its gauges could be illuminated at night and it had an autopilot. However, compared to purpose-built bombers it could not carry a heavy bomb load. More worrying to the crews was its tendency to stall and flick-roll with no warning if flown too slowly while heavily loaded. At low altitudes, this left no time for recovery.

By April 1941, Nos 12 and 13 Squadrons were operating from the RAAF aerodrome at Darwin (just eight kilometres east of the town), where there were nearly 700 RAAF officers and airmen. Some 90 kilometres south was the Northern Territory's main subsidiary base, Batchelor. For servicing, aircraft based in Darwin had to go to Richmond in New South Wales. Numerous bases were established in northern Australia in 1941, though most were undeveloped. Pacific island airbases that would soon be battlefields were also created or developed from 1939 to 1941. Australia and New Zealand agreed in 1939 to form a line of such bases as an outer defensive ring. The line comprised New Guinea, the Admiralty Islands, the Bismarck Archipelago, the Solomon and Santa Cruz Islands, the New Hebrides and New Caledonia. Port Moresby would be the main operational base in this chain. Its main new aerodrome was the 'Seven Mile', which was broad and flat, but not yet long enough for heavy bombers. Bases suitable for seaplanes were established off various islands, but there were few aerodromes from which land-based aircraft could operate. Port Moresby and Rabaul were the most developed, while there were also airfields at Lae, Kavieng, Salamaua, Wau and Wewak.

The Darwin squadrons were not the only ones expending time and energy on reconnaissance and escort duties. For example, after a series of attacks on Allied shipping by German surface vessels and losses to enemy sea-mines, aircraft from four states and Darwin searched 2,641,800 square kilometres with no sightings. In July 1941 a Hudson crew believed they had at last detected and destroyed a submarine, but the submerged dark object that gave off various dark substances when hit proved to be a whale. Valuable lessons in reconnaissance were learned in the sad task that fell to airmen searching for HMAS *Sydney* in November 1941. When the ship failed to arrive at Fremantle, Hudsons from Pearce (Western Australia) and Darwin, Catalinas from Port Moresby and Ansons from Geraldton were sent to locate her. In many hours of searching, the airmen found only boats containing surviving German crewmen of the *Kormoran*, which, like the *Sydney*, had been sunk in their deadly naval engagement. From his Hudson, Charles Learmonth misidentified one boatload of Germans as Australians, and dropped his favourite pipe to them. By 1 December, when the search came to an end, Learmonth had managed just 31 hours of sleep in eight days. Among the 645 Australians who perished in the *Sydney* were the RAAF pilot of its Walrus amphibian, and five support airmen.

In October 1941, John Curtin became Prime Minister. As Leader of the Opposition he had urged the Menzies government to concentrate on strengthening the RAAF and promoting Australia's ability to make its own aircraft, warning 'we may not have much time to spare'.[3] His government faced extraordinarily tough times, for there was little hope of restraining Japan from aggression against the Western powers in the months ahead.

Malaya—preparing to fight

While meeting its obligations under the EATS and providing home defence for a continent, in 1940–41 the RAAF also had to help Britain develop its defences in the Far East. Britain and Australia were determined to hold Singapore. Successive Australian governments believed that a British or American fleet based at Singapore could prevent a Japanese invasion of Australia, even though Japanese island bases in the Pacific were thousands of kilometres from Singapore. In May 1940, responding to a British request, the Australian government offered its first operational Hudson squadron, No. 1 Squadron, for service at Singapore. The offer was accepted, and No. 1 was soon joined by another RAAF Hudson squadron, No. 8, at a new airfield at Sembawang, in Singapore. They were followed in September by No. 21 Wirraway Squadron, as well as an RAAF station headquarters staff. Each squadron comprised 12 aircraft plus six reserves.

By September 1940 the threat in the Far East had increased greatly. Germany's conquest of the Netherlands weakened the administration of the Netherlands East Indies (modern Indonesia). Following the fall of France, Japanese troops marched into French Indochina in September. A conference of British, Australian and New Zealand representatives at Singapore in October 1940 agreed that Malaya's garrison was inadequate and estimated that 582 aircraft, rather than the 88 largely obsolete ones available, would be needed to defend the peninsula.

In the year following the conference, Australia and Britain tried to provide the forces needed. They surpassed an identified target of 26 army battalions in Malaya, including six from Australia's 8th Division. However, there were only 161 aircraft, one-quarter of them Australian. These included the 16 Brewster Buffaloes of a fourth RAAF squadron, No. 453, which arrived in August 1941.

RAF Far East Command was led by the Commander-in-Chief Far East, Air Chief Marshal Sir Robert Brooke-Popham, a 62-year-old retired RAF officer. It was said that he tended to fall asleep in conferences, but he was alert enough to tell the Australian War Cabinet in February 1941 that the Japanese were not really air-minded and their aircraft not highly efficient. He reported to England that he 'had some difficulty in explaining to Ministers and others in Australia why [the] Wirraway was able to give effective war service in the Far East'.[4]

Australia was also misinformed about Japanese numbers. In February 1941 the information available to the government suggested that Japan had 990 front-line aircraft: 340 carrier-borne, the rest land-based. In fact, the total was 2625, of which 1250 were carrier-borne; carrier-borne aircraft could most readily be brought within range of Australia. British Commonwealth and Dutch forces in the region were calculated at 503, some of them obsolete.

Intelligence about Japanese air forces was still scandalously inadequate by December 1941, so training in Malaya was hampered by lack of knowledge of Japanese organisation and aircraft. Zeros had been in use in China since July 1940, where they had virtually destroyed the remnants of Chinese air strength. Claire Chennault, an American adviser to the Chinese, and who later in 1941 would establish the famous 'Flying Tigers', had warned in vain of the Zero's capacity. In May 1941 Chinese anti-aircraft guns shot down the first Zero lost in action. After it was inspected, the British Air Ministry forwarded details of its performance to the Far Eastern Combined Bureau in September 1941, but because of staff shortages these had not been distributed by the time war broke out.

British sources offered more respect to the Japanese Naval Air Force (JNAF) than to the Japanese Army Air Force (JAAF). Although they assessed the latter as numerous, fanatically brave and possessing long-range fighters, the force was considered inefficient and unable to beat 'reasonable opposition'.[5] Analysts seem to have ignored the 'Oscar', the JAAF's best fighter. It was even lighter and more manoeuvrable than the Zero, but was slower and armed with just two machine guns. The outmoded fixed undercarriages on the more numerous A5M Claude and Ki-27 Nate fighters probably encouraged Allied commanders to be complacent about the Zero and Oscar.

Despite the underestimates of Japanese air power, much of the high-level policy emerging from Britain and the US in 1941 was deeply worrying to Australian politicians. Australia's national defence strategy depended on those two great powers, and more particularly on the Singapore strategy. It became apparent that should Japan and the US enter the war, both Churchill and Roosevelt had decided to beat Germany first. The Australian government realised too that Britain would not be able to send a fleet to Singapore, although there were assurances that if Singapore could hold out for six months the fleet would arrive. Britain hoped that America might make a commitment to send part of its Pacific Fleet from its base at Pearl Harbor, Hawaii, but in line with its 'Beat Germany first' attitude, the US would probably go on the defensive in the Pacific, so Australia might well be fighting alone. Country Party leader 'Artie' Fadden, Curtin's predecessor as Prime Minister, feared that if these great powers ignored Australia until the European war was over, 'we and our countrymen might well be pulling rickshaws before long'.[6]

As Prime Minister, Sir Robert Menzies had visited London in February 1941, determined to obtain more reinforcements for the Far East. He received brusque treatment from the UK Chiefs of Staff, who told him that although the desired total of British aircraft was unlikely to be reached in Malaya before the end of 1941, the 'majority of the 450 shore-based aircraft which the Japanese can muster against us [the actual number was much higher] are of obsolete types and . . . we have no reason to believe that Japanese standards are even comparable with those of the Italians'. The Brewster Buffalo fighter then being made available in Malaya was described as an 'eminently satisfactory' type that 'would probably prove more than a match for any Japanese aircraft'.[7] Menzies was not told that the Buffalo was known to lack the performance necessary to match enemy aircraft in Europe and the Middle East, and was thus being sent to the area perceived as third priority.

Britain sent 600 modern aircraft to Russia in the second half of 1941; some of these surely could have been sent to Malaya, where the available front-line aircraft on 7 December numbered barely a quarter of this total. Moreover, no long-range bombers were sent to Malaya.

To defend Australia from as far forward as possible, the Australian Chiefs of Staff wanted to establish RAAF squadrons in the islands of the Netherlands East Indies and New Guinea. To protect these forces, the 2/22nd Battalion was sent to Rabaul, and Australia entered an agreement with the Dutch to send two more battalion groups to Ambon and Timor should hostilities break out. Well-prepared advance bases on those two islands would then each receive an RAAF bomber squadron from Darwin.

Japan's relations with the US soured in 1941 over her refusal to end its invasion of China and occupation of French Indochina. In July the US, Britain and the Netherlands froze Japanese assets. At a conference in Singapore in April, the Allied members had agreed that the Japanese would not attack simultaneously at several places in the Far East, and would not challenge 'the combined British, American and Dutch might'.[8] In fact they proposed to do just that. On 1 December 1941 Japan decided to put long-formed plans into operation and attack across a vast area stretching from Burma to the north Pacific. As British and Australian experts had feared as early as 1919, Japan did not attack in the Far East until Britain had become embroiled in a European war. Malaya and Singapore, so fundamental to Australian defensive planning, were among the main objectives of Japan's combined operations assaults, timed to begin on 7–8 December 1941.

Malaya—from siesta to battle

On arriving in Singapore, the eager airmen of Nos 1 and 8 Squadrons were surprised and disappointed by the routines that awaited them. They were untried in battle, but were experienced in patrolling, well trained and equipped. They wanted and expected to learn from the RAF organisation in Malaya, but found equipment and methods underlying fundamental tasks such as patrolling, signalling and direction-finding to be inadequate. Flight Lieutenant Roy Bulcock, an experienced Australian businessman who had come to serve with the RAF in Singapore, was staggered by the palatial conditions at Seletar aerodrome, where facilities within the 11 kilometre enclosing fence included tennis and squash courts, football fields, a swimming pool, golf course, movie theatre and yacht club.[9] He was concerned at the slow pace and pedantic form-filling approach that accompanied these marvels. Furthermore, the working hours at Sembawang and Seletar were short: from only 7.30 a.m. to 12.30 p.m. The three Australian squadrons—1, 8 and 21—soon added a further two hours per day, but flying hours were nevertheless very limited. Many exercises were 'tarmac patrols', with the aircraft moving only on the ground, or courses identifying ships from silhouettes or models.

To protect Singapore, once hostilities began enemy aircraft would have to be kept as far as possible from it. This required bases for Commonwealth aircraft in northern Malaya. These airfields were crucial too in that the defenders' best hope of defeating an invasion was to cripple the assaulting fleet by air attack. If the Japanese attacked, Allied air and ground forces would need to deny them airfields. Indeed, throughout the war with Japan, control of airfields would be central to most operations. The key airstrips were on Malaya's east coast, including Kuantan, halfway between Singapore and the Malaya–Thailand border, and Kota Bharu, close to that border. The east coast had long been purposely neglected in a defence strategy that prioritised the west coast in allocating the scarce available troops. However, it was not practical to base aircraft on the west coast airfields, for heavy cloud and rainfall over the central mountain spine presented a constant threat to aircraft flying over it. Relatively isolated and difficult to reach on the ground, both eastern bases were now obvious military targets. Pilot Officer George Burlinson saw Kota Bharu up close in July 1941 during a tour of inspection of Malayan airfields. Burlinson, like Bulcock, was one of more than 100 Australian officers recruited for administrative duties with the RAF in Malaya. As Command Defence Officer in Singapore, Burlinson met Brigadier Key, the British officer commanding the defence of Kota Bharu. Key had barely 3500 men to guard more than 70 kilometres of frontier and 60 kilometres of coastline. He had just one field gun for the defence of Kota Bharu. On returning to Singapore, Burlinson wrote a report on this vital base's perilous condition. The report reached the British army commander in Malaya, General Percival, but he said he was satisfied with the dispositions, and questioned the need to receive a critical report signed only by someone of Burlinson's low rank. A mendacious contemporary newspaper report described Kota Bharu as 'magnificently defended' from ground and air, but another journalist was more honest when, after visiting the base, he described life there as bleak: devoid of amenities, so wet that ground crews worked in bathers, and with food and drinking water scarce, poor and responsible for universal stomach complaints.[10]

Bulcock was later posted to RAF Station Kuantan. The feverish pace of work there contrasted with the torpor of Singapore, but some of it was misdirected. Enormous effort was put into clearing the rubber trees around the base, but these offered natural cover. No attempt would be made to camouflage buildings on Malayan aerodromes until the campaign had begun.

Authorities had foreseen the need for radar stations, but by December 1941 only six of 20 planned stations were completed, all of them around Singapore. Similarly, plans to provide 16 anti-aircraft guns per aerodrome had nowhere been met by December, when some airfields had just one. Buffalo fighters began arriving from the US in February 1941, and by December armed four squadrons. As mentioned, 453 Squadron was one of these. Formed at Bankstown, New South Wales, in May, it was the only Article XV RAAF squadron in Malaya, and this status caused confusion as to whom its personnel belonged. The original aircrew and ground staff were Australians, and wore Australian uniform. The RAF's ultimate authority over the unit was apparent in its command arrangements. Squadron Leader Bill Allshorn, a permanent RAAF officer, was initially given command, with the assistance of Flight Lieutenant Les Jackson. However, their role with 453 was temporary, as the British Air Ministry advised that there was no suitable Australian available to lead this squadron and that it had appointed an RAF officer. Their choice, 25-year-old Englishman W.J. Harper, arrived in October. He was an experienced Spitfire pilot, but his relationship with the unit would be unhappy. He later claimed that from the outset some of the Australians were contemptuous of all 'Pommies', an accusation that his Australian adjutant disputed. Harper believed that in turn some RAF personnel in Malaya ostracised Australians, partly because the RAF Fighter Group Controller harboured an unwarranted dislike for the Australian fighter squadrons. Most of Harper's pilots were recent EATS graduates, with no experience flying single-seat fighters. Fortunately they were able to get that experience in Malaya at an improvised OTU at Kluang, equipped with the Wirraways allotted to 21 Squadron before it too received Buffaloes. Within three months of arriving, 453 Squadron was approved as 'operational'. Harper was so unhappy with the quality of his pilots, however, that at the beginning of December, with Malaya on alert, he flew to Australia on a vain and ill-advised quest to obtain better ones. This generated much ill-feeling within the squadron, which would go into action under the temporary command of a popular Irishman, Flight Lieutenant Tim Vigors DFC.

Inexperienced pilots were by no means confined to 453 Squadron. Between January and September 1941 there were 67 air accidents in Far East Command, and 48 aircrew killed.

On 19 November, the day 453 Squadron was pronounced operational, so too was No. 21. This was quite an achievement, since as recently as September, it had converted from a general reconnaissance squadron to a fighter and army cooperation squadron, even though some of its pilots proved unable to make that transition. Moreover, it lost five of its best pilots to the Kluang OTU and other valuable aircrew when their 18-month operational tour ended. Bill Allshorn, appointed to command in October, faced many challenges. One, which confronted all fighter pilots in Malaya, was to get the best out of the Buffaloes. Allshorn reported that the undercarriage, or wheels, once retracted was hard to lower. Other complaints about the 'flying beer barrels', as some called the Buffaloes, included their poor condition on arrival, their inadequate radios, malfunctioning machine guns and their slow rate of climb, which necessitated the use of a manual fuel pump above 18,000 feet. These Buffaloes were modified, notably with armour, radio and more armament, but this reduced the aircraft's speed, climb, manoeuvrability and service ceiling. They were faster than the common Nate fighters, but the Japanese aircraft were lighter and more manoeuvrable, and could climb and accelerate faster. Nevertheless, Air Chief Marshal Brooke-Popham told the Australian Advisory War Council on 16 October that the Buffalo was superior to Japanese fighters and well suited to Malaya. At the same time he reportedly told Charles Burnett, 'we've just got to tell the jolly old Japs to go back', to which the Englishman replied in a lowered voice, 'You never know what these Australians will do.'[11]

How the Buffaloes would perform in battle remained to be seen, as did the performance of the inexperienced pilots of all four fighter squadrons in Malaya. The two RAAF Hudson squadrons were considered 'seasoned' by the eve of battle. Their skills in bombing-up, navigation and bombing were well honed, though as with No. 21, some of their best-trained aircrews returned home when their operational tours expired. The Australians' Hudson II had self-sealing fuel tanks and protective armour. It was equipped with five machine guns, could carry about 1500 pounds (680 kilograms) of bombs and had a top speed of 410 kilometres per hour. Christopher Shores' authoritative history of Malayan operations calls it 'a reasonably useful aircraft'.[12]

In October 1941, Brooke-Popham announced that a campaign in the south was 'the last thing Japan wants at the moment'.[13] In November he stated that such an attack was now unlikely until February, as landings in north-eastern Malaya would be difficult in the monsoon. He was wrong about Japanese intentions, but the monsoon was an obstacle—to Allied reconnaissance aircraft trying to detect any Japanese approach through the South China Sea. Reconnaissance duties over Malaya and as far east as Borneo were divided among three groups: Catalinas of the Dutch Naval Air Service, Catalinas of No. 205 Squadron RAF and Hudsons of Nos 1 and 8 Squadrons. It was hoped these aircraft would detect any invasion fleet before it came within about 330 kilometres of the coast; Allied strike forces would then be able to hit the seaborne invaders in daylight.

However, there was uncertainty about how best to react once a potential enemy convoy was spotted. What if it was headed for neutral Thailand, not Malaya? What if the Japanese sent out ships as bait to draw a British attack and thus discredit Britain in the eyes of still neutral America? Because of these concerns, orders were issued that any aircraft that found a convoy must not attack until directed to do so. In the event of a Japanese attack on Thailand, there was a plan, Operation Matador, to send Indian troops across the Thai border, with strong air support. No. 21 Squadron was transferred to Sungei Patani, in north-western Malaya near that border, to support Matador should it be ordered. Conditions here were poor. Lacking transport, officers and airmen had to walk four kilometres each way across boggy ground to and from their mess huts. More importantly, maintenance of their aircraft had to be done in the open, in the rainy season. Like all aerodromes across northern Malaya, its negligible air-raid warning system and anti-aircraft defence left it open to surprise attack.

When on 2 December the fast and powerful British warships *Prince of Wales* and *Repulse* arrived in Singapore, it appeared at last that the Singapore strategy was not merely a dream. Churchill had insisted that three capital ships be sent, including one carrier. That carrier, *Indomitable*, had been damaged in an accident, which prevented it accompanying the *Prince of Wales* and *Repulse.*

Churchill hoped that the presence of these two ships would deter Japanese bellicosity. Yet, modern and majestic though they were, their anti-aircraft defences were weak, and they would now depend for air support on the local land-based aircraft, which were dangerously few and limited in range. No. 453 Squadron was chosen to provide fighter protection for the 'Eastern Fleet'.

On 1 December, as the second degree of readiness (the second-highest on a three-level scale) was ordered, No. 8 Squadron was transferred from Sembawang to Kuantan—but due to lack of air transport, they only reached there on the eve of the Japanese attack. At Kuantan, all but the landing strip was a quagmire in which vehicles sank axle-deep. Scandalously few preparations had been made for receiving this unit, which would play a critical role if enemy landings were to be detected and opposed.

In the first week of December, six Australian-made Beauforts arrived in Singapore. Many hopes rested on these aircraft, but they proved toothless. Incredibly, they were unarmed, and their crews had not received operational training. Five of these Beauforts were returned to Australia, with only one being retained for photo reconnaissance, a pressing need for the RAF.

Americans on the horizon

While conflict with Japan loomed ever closer in late 1941, the possibility of a close friendship with another great power emerged. Contacts with leading American servicemen led Australian politicians to hope that the US would protect Australia from invasion. Since 1933 America had put faith in long-range aircraft, especially bombers. The destinations they had in mind when ordering such aircraft were their bases in Alaska, Panama and Hawaii. From 1939, America's preoccupation with the war in Europe meant that the US government did not greatly reinforce its strength in the Pacific. However, that region was bound eventually to benefit from expansion in aircraft production. By 1940, for example, the industry was doubling its production from 2000 to 4000 aircraft per month. The ten types then accepted for production were:

- **Heavy bombers ('B' designating 'bomber'):** B-17 Flying Fortress and B-24 Liberator
- **Medium bombers:** B-25 Mitchell and B-26 Marauder
- **Light bombers or 'attack' aircraft:** A-20 and A-24 Dauntless
- **Fighters ('pursuit', as designated by the 'P'):** P-38 Lightning, P-39 Airacobra, P-40 Warhawk (known in Commonwealth service as Tomahawk and Kittyhawk), and P-47 Thunderbolt.

In August 1941, the American government decided to send substantial reinforcements to the limited air forces commanded by General

Douglas MacArthur in the Philippines. This was wonderful news for British, Dutch and Australian commanders. First among the additional forces were nine of the awe-inspiring B-17 Flying Fortresses, which reached Port Moresby in September. During a two-day rest there, the crews were made very welcome by the RAAF and other Australians, all of whom were intensely interested in the flight. The Flying Fortresses flew on to Darwin and then Manila. The American government was keen to continue using this South Pacific run to Manila, and in mid-October submitted to a delighted Australian War Cabinet its desire to establish an air route from Hawaii to the Philippines via Rabaul, Port Moresby, Townsville and Darwin. The US War Department would leave the construction of the bases to the Australian government, but would give financial and technical assistance. The Americans wanted American heavy bomber crews to train and undertake maintenance and other duties at these bases. The Australian government, conscious that these steps brought Australia into American strategic planning, readily agreed. MacArthur's chief air commander, Major-General Brereton, visited Australia and New Guinea in November to look at the bases. Brereton would prove the most congenial of the senior US air force leaders who negotiated with the Australians over the next few years, and though disappointed by the condition of the strips at Batchelor, Port Moresby and Rabaul, he was impressed by the RAAF officers he met: Group Captain Scherger at Darwin, Air Commodore Lukis at Townsville, Squadron Leader Pearce at Port Moresby and the CAS, Burnett, in Melbourne. A plan emerged, which included the development of sufficient aerodromes and other major facilities to allow training, aircraft assembly, repair and general operation of 50 per cent of the United States Far East Air Force from Australia. From there, American forces would be able to operate over the Netherlands East Indies, New Guinea, the Solomons and New Hebrides. The US would meet the cost, totalling more than £5 million. The Australian War Cabinet approved this plan on 4 December 1941.

While these cordial negotiations were proceeding, relations between the US and Japan were at an all-time low. On the night of 7 December (6 December in Hawaii), American airmen in Manila held a dinner for General Brereton. At one point during that night he slipped out, to be told that in Washington the War and Navy Departments believed war was imminent. He put his force on 'combat alert'.

Enemy sighted

When Japan decided to go to war with the US and Britain, a primary goal was to secure oil supplies that the Allied embargo was denying them, in Borneo, Sumatra and Java. To this end the Philippines and Malaya would be attacked, to be followed by an advance into the Netherlands East Indies. The Japanese Army's commitment would be a modest ten divisions. However, Japan's navy was stronger than America's Pacific Fleet, and its air forces were superior in numbers and equipment to its American, British, Australian and Dutch opponents in the Far East. The Japanese air strength of about 4600 first-line aircraft probably outnumbered all the Allied air forces by about three to two. Moreover, whereas the Allies were holding a vast area, the Japanese attackers could concentrate their forces on particular objectives. Though the Allies planned to initiate a combined American, British, Dutch and Australian (ABDA) command if hostilities commenced, coordination would inevitably be more difficult than it would be for Japan, with its unified command and single acquisitive purpose. The Japanese airmen who were to play key roles in these assaults were amongst the world's best trained and most experienced. Their equipment and tactics had been proven in action. The Australian pilots who faced them were less experienced and were flying, in the case of the Brewster Buffaloes, aircraft that were second-rate even under optimum conditions.

RAAF reconnaissance aircraft were part of a long line of pickets designed to warn of Japanese air or naval approaches towards islands from New Caledonia in the east to the Netherlands East Indies in the west. If the US came into the war, it could be linked into the chain. Australians were at many places in the chain—including Noumea, Vila, Tulagi, Rabaul, Lae, Salamaua, Port Moresby, Morobe, Madang, Wewak, Lorengau, Kavieng and Malaya—yet their presence was small. The RAAF's first-line aircraft outside Malaya in December numbered 180. About 100 were Wirraways, and 45 Hudsons. Just 11 Catalina flying-boats of Nos 11 and 20 Squadrons, based in New Guinea, were responsible for the outer defence line there. The main bases in Papua and New Guinea—Port Moresby, Rabaul, Lae and Salamaua—had an average strength of just 18 men. In the first week of December, four Hudsons of No. 24 Squadron were sent to Rabaul, followed from 10 December by the squadron's Wirraways. As planned, advance parties of the RAAF moved to various Dutch bases in that first week. On 7 December, Hudsons of Nos 2 and 13 Squadrons flew to Koepang in Dutch Timor and Laha at Ambon, respectively. These squadrons were at a superb state of readiness. Their advance parties had spent much time looking over the area where they would soon be operating, but their means were still very limited.

By the first week of December, Brooke-Popham was worried at news of Japanese naval and air movement into Indochina and the South China Sea. He was anxious to hear whether Zero fighters with detachable fuel tanks were among the aircraft, which they were. The monsoonal low cloud cover was perfect for the enemy to assemble and move invasion convoys. The rains were rendering Malayan airfields all but impassable for aircraft and vehicles, except where roads and runways had been soundly constructed. At Kota Bharu on 4 and 5 December, for example, the airfield was unusable. No. 8 Squadron and the Dutch Catalinas were still operating, but found no suspicious activity.

On 6 December, three No. 1 Squadron Hudsons were able to take off and search their three allotted sectors. The weather was still difficult, but at about 12.15 p.m. came a staggering discovery in Sector 1. From his Hudson, Johnny Ramshaw sighted three small Japanese warships 300 kilometres from Kota Bharu. At 12.30 p.m., he made a second sighting, this time much bigger. After flying the length and breadth of the convoy at an altitude of just 900 feet, the crew counted one battleship, five cruisers, seven destroyers and, most ominously, 22 transports. The convoy looked to one of the aircrew like a swimming scorpion with a broad head and segmented vertebrae. It was headed due west, perhaps towards Kota Bharu, some 425 kilometres away. While scrutinising this armada, the crew saw one warship launch a float-plane. Ramshaw flew into cloud cover and signalled his momentous news to base.

At around the same time as Ramshaw's second sighting, another Hudson, under Jim Emerton, found a large force in Sector 3, also apparently bound for Kota Bharu. Japanese aircraft were flying above the convoy. When Emerton prepared to send a signal of his sighting, his wireless air-gunner recommended waiting half an hour, as their 'key clicks' would be intercepted by the fleet below. When it came time to send the sighting signal, Ramshaw's wireless air-gunner came on the air with news of his sighting. Ramshaw had requested permission to shadow the force but, amazingly, was refused and told to continue his patrol. Brooke-Popham later claimed that the two Hudsons were at the limit of their range and could not shadow the force. The crews themselves believed that they could have stayed with the convoy for two to three hours until relieved.

Once back at Kota Bharu, the crews were questioned closely. Intelligence staff concluded that both Hudsons had reported the same force. In Singapore, the Combined Operations Staff and Brooke-Popham believed, correctly, that there were two forces, destination as yet unknown. The smaller force first seen by Ramshaw appeared to be heading for Thailand. Brooke-Popham was acutely aware of the need to avoid being seen to provoke the Japanese, so did not yet order Operation Matador. Instead he put forces in the first—highest—degree of readiness. Not until 4.20 p.m., however, did orders reach Kota Bharu to send out another Hudson to locate the Japanese force. It had no luck in the dark, so 6 December finished with many vital questions pending.

That night, Catalinas of No. 205 Squadron RAF were searching for a reported Japanese convoy south of Cambodia Point. One Catalina sent a signal at 8 a.m. in the approximate area of the supposed convoy. She and her crew of eight were never heard from again. Japanese records show that the flying-boat encountered a 'Jake' float-plane. The Japanese pilot fired at the Catalina from behind and below, and then maintained observation as the British plane managed to escape. However, a patrol of five Nate fighters had spotted her too. The British crew fought back but their Cat was soon on fire. Eventually, after attacks from all five aircraft, the Catalina exploded and fell into the sea.

This attack, which occurred 14 hours before the assault on Pearl Harbor, was significant. The dead were apparently the first Allied servicemen killed by the Japanese, and this was probably the first Japanese act of war against the British Commonwealth. The Catalina's second navigator was an Australian, 21-year-old Sergeant Colin Treloar of Adelaide, who became the first RAAF member to die in the war with Japan, and the first Australian killed in action against Japanese forces. Known as 'Ike', after a popular racing broadcaster, Treloar had in 1937 been a prefect, first XVIII footballer and bow of the first rowing VIII at Scotch College, Adelaide. The RAAF had been his first job. Within days of his death, his parents knew that he was missing, and for years thereafter his father—who as a Light Horseman had won a Military Cross in 1918—made enquiries based on possible sightings of the wreckage of his aircraft or of Colin in a Japanese prison. The National Archives of Australia contain a file with more than 50 pages of documents produced between 1941 and 1946 in that fruitless search. Treloar's body was never found.

The captain of Treloar's aircraft, Pat Bedell, apparently had an Australian connection too. A letter in the Treloar file from 205 Squadron's Operations Officer refers to Bedell as being from Adelaide. It seems that he too should be commemorated as among the first Australians killed.

The Japanese invasion force included 28 troop transports, 25 of which were headed for Thailand. The remaining three were directed at Kota Bharu, with an escort of eight warships. Weather conditions on 7 December made it perilous to search for these vessels. Colonel Tsuji, chief of operations and planning for the invading 25th Japanese Army, wrote that the odds were 10,000 to one against the enemy locating the convoys by 7 December. However, Australian Hudsons and Dutch Catalinas tried. Two of three No. 1 Squadron Hudsons were forced back by rain and low cloud, and the third found nothing over the Gulf of Siam. Only late in the day did a Hudson of No. 8 Squadron spot a Japanese merchant ship carrying a large number of khaki-clad men, but well north of Kota Bharu. So too were four Japanese vessels sighted after nightfall by a 1 Squadron Hudson piloted by James Douglas, and two spotted by John Lockwood and his crew. One of the warships fired about ten broadsides at Lockwood's aircraft, only missing due to the pilot's skilful manoeuvring. As Lockwood and Douglas returned to base, the weather was so bad that over the last 80 kilometres they flew at just 200 feet. The cloud cover then dropped still further; it was a black night.

The ships the two Australians had sighted were headed for the Australians' base; Japan had mustered nearly 600 aircraft to support its invasion of Malaya. The British forces' operational aircraft numbered just 155.

4 'We were actually going into action!!': Malaya

Shortly before midnight on 7 December, Flying Officer Peter Gibbes arrived at Kota Bharu to join No. 1 Squadron. A pre-war commercial pilot, he had recently been with No. 6 Squadron at Richmond. He was looking forward to flying the sophisticated Hudsons on reconnaissance missions and perhaps even getting to grips with the Japanese should they attack. He had flown to Singapore in the unarmed Beaufort that the RAAF had kept for photo reconnaissance, and had then made the slow journey north. Though dark, it was still terribly hot at Kota Bharu, where a truck took him from the railway station to the base. Everyone seemed to be asleep. But as the Indian driver showed him to his quarters, deafening explosions rent the thick air. The driver reassured him that it was just an exercise, so Gibbes went to his room and lay down under a mosquito net. Yet rather than subsiding, the noise grew louder. People were running down the corridor and shouting, while outside aircraft engines were roaring into life. Gibbes went to his door and, not knowing anyone, grabbed a passer-by and asked what was happening. The astonishing reply was 'The Japs have landed!'

In shock, Gibbes got dressed and followed someone to an operations room where an officer was telling the assembled crowd that Japanese troopships and warships were some eight kilometres out, shelling Kota

Bharu and landing troops. He finished with the dramatic exhortation: 'Move fellows! Get into the air!'[1] To a question of what they were to do, he answered, 'Sink everything you can see.'

Eventually the officer spotted Gibbes and asked him who the hell he was. After quickly ascertaining that the new man could fly a Hudson, he ordered Gibbes to 'grab A16-43' (RAAF Hudsons were designated A16) and 'go drop some bombs'. Gibbes took a parachute and Mae West life-jacket and ran outside. He found the runway, as a flare path of lights was being laid, but he was unsure of its orientation. When he found his A16-43, three crewmen were standing by. With no rank badges or wings, he introduced himself simply as 'Peter Gibbes', who would be flying them. There were mumbled replies and all went to their stations. Despite the somnolent air that Gibbes had sensed on arriving that night, six of No. 1 Squadron's Hudsons had been fully armed and ready to attack any approaching force, and the remaining four had since been readied. His engines fired immediately he pressed the starters, and he followed the exhaust flames of the nearest Hudson on to the sodden strip. After take-off and once the flare path was behind them, the darkness forced him to fly on instruments.

Gibbes' Hudson and six others headed for the light-show created by gun flashes, bursts and tracers. When 500 metres from the source of these lights, he dropped close to sea level, opened his bomb doors and sped towards a shadowy vessel. Just 20 metres away he jettisoned his bombs, then swept over the target. Anti-aircraft guns chased them as they flew on, then he turned back towards his new home as quickly as possible. It was the first of numerous 15–20 minute shuttles the Hudsons would make as they bombed, strafed, replenished their weapons (a five-minute job) and returned to the action. Refuelling was not necessary after each sortie, as the enemy was just a few kilometres away. On returning to base from one flight, a crewman was smoking the same cigarette he had lit on take-off.

The first Hudson to drop its bombs was that of John Lockwood, who had arrived in Malaya with No. 1 Squadron in July 1940 and whose plane, as we have seen, had already been fired on as he searched for the invaders the previous day. Lockwood was interested in history: in 1940 he had ordered the complete set of the official history of Australia in the Great War. Now he and his crew were themselves making history, being the first

Australians—and quite possibly the first *Allied* servicemen—to attack the Japanese in World War II, for the Pearl Harbor attack, on the other side of the International Date Line, occurred more than an hour later.

At Geelong Grammar, Lockwood had been a member of the cadet unit and of the prestigious rowing VIII in 1938. The following year, when war broke out, he enlisted on the first possible day, 4 September, receiving the low RAAF enlistment number 554. In Malaya, at age 20, he met and married an English typist working at headquarters.

At 2.08 a.m. on 8 December he took off with his crew, Flying Officer Tony Jay, and Sergeants Adrian Munday and Bob Thomson. Wing Commander 'Curly' Davis, commanding No. 1 Squadron, had, after consultation with Singapore and Brigadier Key, ordered his aircraft into action. Orders were simultaneously given to the other squadrons in Malaya, including No. 8 RAAF, to attack at first light.

The sight of tracers flashing from anti-aircraft guns at night, such as No. 1 Squadron observed now, could be very unnerving to aircrew, as they seemed to be aimed at the individual. Yet these ones reminded Thomson of Guy Fawkes night. They were deadly skyrockets, but Lockwood dived to 50 feet and dropped two bombs towards the northernmost transport. They missed but, evading the flak as he turned, he came in again and released his remaining two bombs. These were semi-armour piercing bombs, designed to penetrate armoured decks. They succeeded, for John Ramshaw saw them hit the transport amidships. Ramshaw was piloting the second sortie behind Lockwood, but on 4 September 1939 had been two ahead of Lockwood, receiving at Point Cook the RAAF enlistment number 552. A third recruit that place and day was John 'Spider' Jones, 'a gutsy little fellow' who flew the fourth sortie. However, 21-year-old Jones and his crew never returned. Theirs may have been the aircraft that the Japanese later reported having seen hit by flak and then, presumably because it was damaged beyond repair, being flown by its pilot directly at a Japanese landing barge. The Japanese report said this suicidal attack killed 60 soldiers.

Ack-ack (anti-aircraft fire) also holed several of the six aircraft that did return. The crews reported seeing six warships, three transports and a large flat vessel that was probably a seaplane tender. Joined by three more Hudsons, the Australians made another ten sorties, bombing and strafing the transports and the barges carrying troops from them to shore. Ken Smith saw two of his bombs land amidst ten barges near the beach. The explosions overturned some completely. The crew fired the Hudson's machine guns too, including two Browning .303 machine guns mounted unorthodoxly in a side window. As Smith fired the two forward guns at a landing craft, he saw one Japanese soldier run for cover behind an upright boiler mounted precariously in the vessel.

Unfortunately for the Australians, most of the heavy fire would now be directed at—rather than from—them. The crews of the ships' anti-aircraft guns were now fully alert. The cruiser *Sendai* carried up to 50 anti-aircraft guns, the five destroyers about 30 each. Little wonder that when, on his second sortie, Ramshaw flew at mast-height towards a warship (probably the *Sendai*) he was shot out of the sky. Ramshaw and Don Dowie were thrown out through the Hudson's perspex roof. Trapped in the body of the aircraft, the two gunners, Jeffery Coldrey—who the previous day had flown with Lockwood—and Garry White had no chance. Dowie and Ramshaw were alive, but barely. On regaining consciousness, Dowie found that he was floating in his life-jacket, which he had half-inflated before the crash. When Dowie called out, Ramshaw replied, but after a few minutes' conversation told Dowie that he felt he could not survive. That was the last Dowie heard from his courageous captain. Dowie himself expected to die any minute, for he saw the loaded Japanese landing barges coming towards him as they made for the shore. Though in great pain from a fractured spine, he managed to blow more air into his life-jacket. After several hours he had floated north and regained enough feeling in his limbs to grab on to an empty prahu, or sailboat. Within days he was captured and began nearly four years of imprisonment.

On his second sortie, 'Ossie' Diamond's Hudson machine-gunned the bridge and decks of the leading and already burning transport, then flew in slowly and deliberately in the hope of ensuring accurate bombing and confusing the enemy gunners. It was a sound plan, for he scored a direct hit. A fireball rose under the aircraft, and the force of the explosion pushed him down towards the sea. He pulled the Hudson up, but on the way home realised his plane had been severely damaged, with holes in the tailplane, wings and fuselage, one engine out of action and a piece of shrapnel in the oil tank.

During No. 1 Squadron's sorties at Kota Bharu, the BBC broadcast news in London of the Japanese assault on Pearl Harbor. Churchill was ecstatic, for he was convinced that American involvement in the war guaranteed an Allied victory. However, a breakdown in communications between Singapore and London prevented Churchill hearing of the Japanese attack at Kota Bharu. Communications were absurdly poor at Kota Bharu. Wing Commander Noble, the RAF commander there, was having a crucial telephone conversation with Air Vice-Marshal Pulford, Air Officer Commanding the RAF in Singapore, when after the standard six minutes an operator asked whether he wanted an extension. After nine minutes he was told he had to be cut off and, when Pulford complained, was informed that three other more senior commanders were waiting to talk on this one and only line to Kota Bharu. Once operations commenced, neither Air Headquarters in Singapore nor Noble spoke to Wing Commander 'Curly' Davis. The Australian had to make his own decisions.

Davis decided at 5 a.m. to pause for an hour, so he could take stock of the serviceability of his aircraft and rearm, refuel and make temporary repairs to those still airworthy. He could also interrogate his aircrew, who told him they had sunk one enemy ship and at least 24 barges. Two transports were on fire: the *Awazisan Maru* had suffered ten hits, the *Ayatosan Maru* about six. The smaller *Sakura Maru* had also been damaged, suffering 19 casualties. So serious was the damage to the convoy that the Japanese naval escort commander withdrew. The *Awazisan Maru* was left behind with its 40 dead, but the other two transports escaped. Flight Lieutenant Jack O'Brien, making a reconnaissance sortie, saw them and their escort some 50 kilometres north retiring at speed. Ominously, he also saw the first enemy aircraft spotted since combat began: nine Japanese bombers that flew over the ships and on towards targets inland from Kota Bharu. Early that morning RAF Vildebeest biplanes—cruising speed 137 kilometres per hour, and several with RAAF observers—made unsuccessful torpedo attacks on these ships.

The Hudsons responded to calls from the hard-pressed Indian brigade to help them fight the Japanese troops who had established themselves ashore. Lockwood and Smith bombed and strafed Japanese personnel near a river mouth, killing many. Return fire penetrated the fuselage near Sergeant Adrian Munday's machine gun, but he stuck to it. The courage, skill and doggedness of the No. 1 Squadron crews could not prevent the Japanese penetrating further inland towards their main objective: Kota Bharu airfield.

The ultimate goal of the Japanese operations, Singapore, had by now tasted air attack. The Japanese boldly sent a bomber force more than 1100 kilometres from north of Saigon to bomb the island's naval facilities and airfields. At 4.15 a.m. bombs hit those targets and Chinatown, where nearly 200 people were killed or wounded. Radar detected the approach of the 17 Nell bombers 120 kilometres north-west of Singapore, but there was no black-out of the brilliantly lit island. Warning sirens did not sound until the raid was in progress, and, worst of all, the inexperienced anti-aircraft gunners barely troubled the attackers.

Australians were ready to use a more potent weapon against the bombers: three Buffaloes of 453 Squadron were fully armed and their pilots were prepared and eager to take on the intruders. The acting squadron leader was Tim Vigors, a young Irish ace who had flown as a night-fighter in Europe. RAAF pilots Doug Vanderfield and Mick Grace, both with European experience, were keen to join him. Amazingly, though, they were refused permission to take off. Vigors declared they would take off anyway, but was told that if they did so they would be placed on a charge. The reason given for this astonishing order was that the anti-aircraft commander wanted to ensure that his green gunners did not shoot down their own aircraft.

Nos 8 and 21 Squadrons did become involved early on 8 December. No. 8's Hudsons, as well as four RAF squadrons of Blenheims, left at dawn to attack enemy shipping at Kota Bharu. No. 27 Squadron RAF's Blenheims took off from Sungei Patani, in north-western Malaya. Rainstorms would force them back, but soon after they left came a report that five Sally bombers were approaching Sungei Patani. The only protection for the airstrip was four Bofors guns and the fighters of 21 Squadron. Two of its pilots sat in their Buffaloes, awaiting orders, while two more were ready to jump in. Bill Allshorn wanted to scramble his squadron, but the British station commander, Squadron Leader Fowle, refused. A noisy debate in the crew room suddenly ceased when a telephone call reported the imminent arrival of the enemy aircraft. As Allshorn and his pilots ran towards their aircraft, the bombs began falling. Fred Williams, a flight leader sitting in one of the Buffaloes, called on everyone to leave their aircraft and take cover. He was concussed by a bomb fragment that struck off his helmet. Ignoring his orders, two pilots, Bob Kirkman and John Hooper, took off through the bombardment and chased the enemy. Each caught bombers in their sights, but their temperamental machine guns failed to fire. When they returned to base, they discovered that the bombing had knocked out seven of their squadron's aircraft and inflicted 18 casualties. The airstrip was now unserviceable, so an emergency one had to be hurriedly marked out for the returning Blenheims. Life would become rougher still at Sungei Patani before the day ended.

No. 8 Squadron's Hudsons were luckier. Initially they encountered fine weather. Air-gunner Doug Scott was in Jim Marshall's Hudson. When they took off that morning he reflected:

> *We were actually going into action!!* There was no thought of danger. I was too busy checking the movement of the turret and making sure the guns were in good firing order. What time I had to think, I thought of home and loved ones.[2]

Squadron Leader Pete Henderson and his flight found the still-burning *Awazisan Maru* and some 50–60 small power-driven boats, landing barges and armoured patrol boats. The Hudsons made independent attacks at 'mast head' height. On their second run over the frantically circling patrol boats, Scott could see the flash from the barges' mounted machine guns while he strafed with his own guns. He saw aircraft 'flying in all directions. One of them turned out to be enemy and had a go at us.' Scott fired at it until his gun jammed. Marshall fired his front guns, dived to sea level and, despite a damaged engine, returned to Kuantan. There, Scott remembers, 'A nasty shock awaited me when I backed out of the turret. There were bandages strewn around, a first aid kit and whatever else goes with a casualty.' Only now did he discern that Pilot Officer David Hersey had been wounded. 'Suddenly I realised,' says Scott, 'how close we had been to not coming back from that flight. There were bullet holes in A16-82 to substantiate the feeling. That night I didn't sleep too well.'[3]

Geoff Hitchcock's crew had probably been the first to encounter enemy fighters, for they were set upon as they strafed the barges. Scotty Jansen fired a 15-second burst into an attacking Zero, which fell into the sea, thereby almost certainly becoming the first Japanese aircraft shot down by the RAAF. (A comprehensive list of Australian aerial victories in the Pacific War appears in Appendix C.) Once the fallacy of underestimating the Japanese aircraft had been exposed, there was a tendency to misidentify enemy aircraft as German. Moreover, nearly every Japanese single-seat aircraft seems to have been identified as a 'Zero'. This tendency persists even in post-war Australian publications, such as the official history. Japanese sources reveal that there were no German aircraft and that the 'Zeros' were often other types, inferior to the Zero but still redoubtable opponents.

Rain prevented a second flight of No. 8 Squadron from catching the enemy fleet as it headed away, so instead they attacked the enemy boats near Kota Bharu. 'Spud' Spurgeon bombed the stricken *Awazisan Maru* yet again. In his 'haste and anxiety' he had forgotten to make allowances for the time fuses on the bombs, and after dropping them 'got the bloody lot back'.[4] Shrapnel penetrated his aircraft. Clocks unwound on his instrument panel, the windshield cracked and a machine-gun barrel bent back. Spurgeon had enlisted at 19 at the same time and place as Lockwood and Ramshaw. He later recalled that on his entry to war his knees were knocking, but thoughts of death or defeat never entered his or his mates' heads, for theirs was the gung-ho outlook of 'young cowboys'.[5] Death was at his shoulder now, but he was able to keep airborne long enough to crash-land at Kota Bharu.

Don Stumm strafed the barges at a height of just 400 feet—close enough for his machine-gunner, 'Dusty' Hensel, to be able to see Japanese troops fall when hit. Hensel initially had misgivings about killing people, but the reflection that it was them or him was decisive. This view was confirmed when they returned to Kuantan and counted 48 bullet holes in their Hudson. No. 1 Squadron's Hudsons were still flying from Kota Bharu and were also strafing the beaches. For example, Peter Fowler attacked a launch towing three barges. Return fire blew a hole in Fowler's instrument panel, and he had to land without an airspeed indicator. He was nearly without something even more delicate, for ground staff pointed out that the bullet that hit the instrument panel had first penetrated underneath Fowler's seat and passed between his legs.

The Blenheims' vulnerability was exposed, with two shot down at Kota Bharu. Oscars chased several more on the way back to Butterworth, on the west coast. During one frightening treetop-level pursuit, a bullet hit Keith Burrill, Australian WAG of a Blenheim, in the mouth and jaw. The impact threw him to the floor of his gun turret, but he got up and returned to his weapon. The Oscar closed in for the kill, but Burrill had the satisfaction of shooting it into the jungle. For the courage and skill that had saved his crew and aircraft, Burrill received the DFM.

Flying the Australian reconnaissance Beaufort, an RAF crew discovered the main enemy convoy at Singora, in Thailand, where some 60 Japanese aircraft were also seen to be based. The Beaufort was irretrievably damaged in combat, but the valuable photographs, once developed by an Australian photographer of No. 1 Squadron, were sent to Singapore. That morning, the enemy aircraft revealed in the photos hit the British airfields, or more precisely their grounded aircraft and personnel. They dropped light fragmentation bombs, so as to spare the runways for their own future use, while still destroying their present occupants.

Japanese aircraft raided Kota Bharu five times that day, 8 December. Groups of up to nine Nates and Oscars dived from 6000 feet, strafing any movement. These attacks were frightening, but the Australians were also intrigued by the unexpected skill and daring of the pilots, who showed off their aerobatic ability. 'Curly' Davis was so absorbed in their manoeuvres that a bullet shot the heel off his boot as he stood and watched.

Meanwhile Johnny Lockwood, who had made No. 1 Squadron's first sortie of the day, made his fourth, bombing and strafing enemy vessels. It was the squadron's 27th and second-last sortie of 8 December. For 'distinguished service' in this campaign, notably on that day, Lockwood would be Mentioned in Despatches. 'Ossie' Diamond flew the last sortie, bombing a bridge near the Thai border. He would receive a DFC in this campaign. The Jewish dry-cleaner from Brisbane had shown that in the RAAF any Australian could prove his worth. Yet even heroics such as Lockwood's and Diamond's could not affect the outcome of the enemy landings, for by midday, Japanese ground troops were firing sporadically on the airfield. By late afternoon the small-arms fire was heavy, and Japanese troops were approaching the radio transmitting station. Ground and aircrews had been working and fighting continuously for more than 14 hours. The ground crew had ensured all Hudsons were quickly rearmed, loading each aircraft's four 250-pound (115 kilogram) bombs in minutes, but had also ingeniously kept aircraft running by stripping the seriously damaged to keep the others aloft. Yet by late afternoon only five Hudsons were still serviceable. Two other aircraft required only a single wheel replacement to become serviceable, but the enemy fighters and ground fire halted every brave attempt.

Air Headquarters in Singapore, aware of the enemy's proximity to the airfield, ordered that all aircraft at Kota Bharu be flown to Kuantan, and that the airfield installations be demolished. This led to some recriminations later among the air and army commanders in the area, who argued that the order was hasty. 'Curly' Davis supervised the destruction of aircraft unable to make the journey, and then ordered his crews to take off in the overloaded Hudsons. James Douglas' aircraft was damaged to the point where he had to wire the wing flaps into position and fly with wheels down all the way to Kuantan, carrying nine outwardly nonchalant airmen. Jack O'Brien carried 17 passengers in his damaged Hudson, which came under Japanese machine-gun and rifle fire as he cleared the treetops. To evade six Zeros he flew just 10 feet above a beach fringed by protective coconut palms. The rest of the station's airmen left by truck. In the hasty withdrawal, the airfield was not demolished and petrol and weapons were left behind. Brigadier Key ordered the destruction of other nearby airfields and withdrew his brigade.

The RAAF's departure from Kota Bharu was not their finest hour—it earned participants the derisive nickname 'Kuantan Harriers'. Nevertheless, the 14 hours in which air and ground crew had done everything they could to harass and smash the Japanese amphibious assault had been far more indicative of the spirit and skill with which the RAAF would fight in future. One estimate says that the two RAAF squadrons and Blenheims killed 2000 Japanese on the beach and at sea that day, although a Japanese estimate, probably much too low, was just 320 dead at Kota Bharu.[6]

We left No. 21 Squadron frustrated after a Japanese attack had hit them at Sungei Patani. John Hooper, whose temperamental guns had prevented him downing a bomber then, was patrolling two hours later when he spotted Sally bombers in formation. After trying unsuccessfully to radio his base he climbed towards the enemy. As he did so, six Zeros attacked him. Perhaps instinctively, Hooper turned his Buffalo on its back and dived away, thus employing one of the few tactics that would prove effective against this formidable opponent. He landed safely, and the bombers flew past Sungei Patani.

After Hooper's return, Flight Lieutenant Jack 'Congo' Kinninmont and Sergeant Norm Chapman took off on a reconnaissance of Singora, the main Japanese landing zone in Thailand. Inevitably, they encountered enemy fighters. Kinninmont's description of the subsequent battle with 12 Nates is wonderful:

> Then the sky seemed full of red [roundels] and the Japs all tried to shoot us down at once. I pulled up to meet one as he dived down . . . I was in such a hurry to shoot something that I didn't use my gun sight. I simply sprayed bullets in his general direction. Somebody was on my tail and tracers were whipping past my wings . . . Chapman was turning and shooting with four Japs. I decided to get out. I yelled to Chapman (over the radio telephone) 'Return to base. Return to base' and went into a vertical dive. As I went down I glimpsed the sergeant diving straight for the ground with three Japs on his tail, shooting . . . I had a quick shot at a four-engined Kawanisi Jap flying-boat and missed . . . Of the three Japs that followed me down in that dive one . . . stuck like a leech . . . As I watched him, my neck screwed around, I saw his guns smoke and whipped into a tight turn to the left. It was too late and a burst of bullets splattered into the Buffalo . . . I opened the throttle and the motor took it without a murmur. It was then that I felt the first real fear in my life . . . It struck me in a flash. This Jap was out to kill me. I broke into a cold sweat and it ran down into my eyes. A noise throbbed in my head and I suddenly felt loose and weak. My feet kept jumping on the pedals. My mouth was stone dry and I couldn't swallow. My mouth was open and I was panting as though I'd just finished a hundred yard dash and I felt cold. Then I was jibbering . . . 'Watch those trees—that was close. He'll get you next burst. You'll flame into the trees. No, he can't get you—he mustn't get you. You're too smart. He'll get you next time. Watch him, watch his guns. Watch those trees—it's cold.' My feet were still jumping on the pedals. I couldn't control them. Then I saw his attacks were missing me. I was watching his guns. Each time they smoked I slammed into a tight turn. And then my whole body tightened and I could think. I flew low and straight, only turning in when he attacked . . . We raced down a valley to the Thai border and the Jap quit . . .[7]

Kinninmont and Chapman got back to Sungei Patani, which was the target of 24 Sallys mid-morning. Again Squadron Leader Fowle refused to let the waiting Buffaloes take off. The Japanese bombers destroyed a 200,000 gallon petrol dump and barracks buildings. Fowle ordered the Buffaloes to be flown to Butterworth. Before this movement began, the Army sent an urgent request for another reconnaissance of Singora. Kinninmont volunteered to fly the perilous journey again. He made it there, observed much movement, and left. The five Zeros that pursued him scored hits, but once more the intrepid 'Congo' got home.

Butterworth proved an unhappy location. It had been strafed during the morning. The aircrews, who had managed on just bully beef and biscuits through this demanding day, were not fed and had to find accommodation either on the beach or three kilometres from the airstrip. It was symptomatic of a day where much had gone wrong. The RAF's bases in northern Malaya were virtually out of action, Operation Matador had been rendered irrelevant, and Japan was poised to build on its impressive gains. Japanese air forces had attacked with devastating effect at Pearl Harbor and the Philippines. Raids on Wake Island, Guam Island and Hong Kong gave grim warnings that these places were doomed. Allied forces everywhere had been amazed and horrified to learn how much they had underestimated their enemy's strength and overestimated their own. For Australia, the attack on Pearl Harbor brought about a long-feared scenario: Japan had entered a war at a time when neither Britain nor the US could send their navies to defend Australia.

Australia's declaration of war on Japan, to which the King assented on 9 December, was dated 8 December. In a broadcast to the nation on 8 December, Prime Minister Curtin called it 'the gravest hour of our history'. Nevertheless most Australians felt, like Churchill, that Singapore was impregnable. That belief was to be put to the test sooner than they imagined.

9 December

Butterworth and Kuantan airfields were Japanese targets on 9 December. At Butterworth, 21 Squadron prepared its four Buffaloes for action. On a mid-morning reconnaissance Geoff Sheppard and Daryl Sproule spotted a dozen Japanese tanks heading from Thailand towards the Malayan border. As the Australians dived to attack, neither anti-aircraft fire nor aircraft attempted to halt them, and one confused Japanese soldier waved a flag to them. The Buffaloes did not halt the tanks, but set four trucks alight.

Lunch for the airmen, who had spent the night on the beach, was their first food since the previous night, but was less than appetising: a biscuit and a sardine.

The four Buffaloes were due to escort an attack by Blenheims from Butterworth that afternoon. The Australians had not previously flown Buffaloes with full ammunition and fuel loads, and now found it disconcerting that whenever they wanted to turn steeply, the aircraft threatened to stall.

The Buffaloes were airborne first, but after waiting about an hour for the Blenheims, Fred Williams and Dick McKenny headed back to land. On the way, they encountered numerous Japanese fighters. Williams' windscreen became smeared with grease, but he saw an aircraft and got off a short burst before realising he was shooting at McKenny. The two landed at Butterworth, but were almost out of petrol and found themselves in the middle of an air raid by 54 aircraft, which had prevented the Blenheims taking off. The Australians taxied to a fuel tanker, only to find that conscientious aerodrome staff had padlocked it before taking cover.

The Japanese bombers were returning, so the Australians took to the air again to join their still-airborne colleagues. They hit two bombers, but were soon under intense assault by Japanese fighters. McKenny's Buffalo was set alight and plummeted. His face was severely burnt, but he managed to bale out into the sea, where an elderly English naval officer in a boat rescued him. Three Nates attacked Williams, who on finding his guns inoperable headed for the airfield. As he approached the runway, his engine cut out completely and he had to make a 'dead-stick' landing, gliding to the ground with enemy fighters on his tail. As he leapt clear, he saw his Buffalo explode under Japanese gunfire. The other two Buffalo pilots, 'Monty' Montefiore and Max White, were shot down too. Montefiore parachuted clear and, after landing, rode back to Butterworth on a bicycle borrowed from a passing Malay. White's aircraft was hit many times but he managed a forced landing.

Two Blenheims had taken off at Butterworth when the raid commenced. One, under British Squadron Leader Scarf of 62 Squadron, flew to Singora in a lone attack. Enemy fighters attacked him on the way home, but though mortally wounded, Scarf brought his craft down and saved his crew. He was awarded the Victoria Cross. The other Blenheim was soon forced back to Butterworth by a Zero. The aircraft's Australian

WAG, Harold Burn, called the squadron's first two days of war 'a shattering experience', revealing as it did the inadequacies of their aircraft and of Malaya's defences.[8] By day's end, just two of the 50 Blenheims with which the RAF had begun the campaign were still operable.

Butterworth's buildings were incinerated in the raid, so in the evening the station commander ordered 21 Squadron and its two serviceable Buffaloes south to Ipoh, an advanced landing ground rather than a station. Finding Ipoh virtually deserted, the squadron camped by the roadside. Food and drinking water were again inadequate. Later there was much criticism of the ill-discipline of 21 Squadron ground crew. Jack Woodward, an Australian Sergeant with No. 27 RAF Squadron, wrote a month later on the basis of rumour that:

> our own Australian squadron (21) put on an awful show, not only clearing out from S.P. [sheer panic], but also abandoning all their equipment . . . it will take quite a lot of living down. [An Australian colleague] and myself have even copped some abuse from our own squadron lads over 21's effort, but I'm afraid the RAF were really not much better.[9]

Indeed his own squadron had faced similar accusations. This harsh criticism of the inexperienced Australian squadron was passing the buck, which stopped with the disorganised senior British RAF command.

Kuantan also suffered that day. Squadron Leader Pete Henderson requested Air Headquarters to return 8 Squadron to Sembawang that morning, to avoid air attack. The supercilious reply from Air Headquarters that he must stay put and that the bombing of Kuantan 'was not in the scheme of things' reflected its ignorance. Even before the message arrived, Japanese aircraft attacked the base. Doug Scott was in the armoury loading machine-gun belts, and in the clatter did not hear the warning siren. When someone rushed in to warn of approaching aircraft, Scott and those around him grabbed helmets and gas masks and tried to put as much space as possible between themselves and the ammunition hut. He detected nine enemy bombers approaching, line abreast, about 500 feet up.

'We dived into a deep concrete drain', he wrote later, 'and squatted there with our fingers in our ears. I reckoned; "This was it". Next thing we heard, "Crumf, Crumf".' He risked looking over the rim of the drain and saw bombs exploding on the far side of the drome. After briefly hiding in chest-deep water in a stormwater drain, he got out into the open. It was quiet, and the attack seemed to be over. But then:

> . . . suddenly I heard them, I looked up and there they were, line abreast and coming our way; but this time much lower. As they positioned themselves and approached, they opened fire with all their machine guns, strafing the whole area. I threw myself to the ground and tried to make myself as small a target as possible. There were no shelters.

To Scott's relief and amazement, suddenly the shooting stopped coming towards him. He looked up to see 'a lone Hudson swooping across the bombers with all guns blazing'.[10] The bombers scattered, one apparently on fire and with two figures parachuting clear. Scott's saviour was Ron Widmer, who was returning from a reconnaissance flight in his Lockheed Hudson. Having seen smoke rising from Kuantan, Widmer had jettisoned his bombs and made a frontal attack on the bombers before swinging around so that his rear turret could have a spray. Scott recalled that as Widmer sought to land, an anti-aircraft gun opened fire on him. Scott ran over to the Indian crew and told them to stop. They ignored him until he drew his revolver, after which they realised their mistake. Widmer landed safely, but more Japanese bombers arrived and attacked the airfield virtually unopposed. Three Hudsons were destroyed, numerous other aircraft damaged and four buildings—including the armoury—wrecked.

When news of this raid reached Air Headquarters, it revised its views, ordering all serviceable aircraft at Kuantan to Singapore. Scott's pilot, Jimmy Marshall, ordered that everything inessential be discarded from his Hudson and flew it and 17 passengers to Singapore. A rumour that Kuantan station would be entirely evacuated led to a stampede for transport to a nearby railway station. Roy Bulcock, the RAAF ground officer mentioned earlier, was horrified by the behaviour of Australians who left behind bombs and equipment, drove away in mass panic, and in one case stole a car and, after crashing it, commandeered a bus at gunpoint. 'For the first and last time', he wrote, 'I felt ashamed of being an Australian.'[11] A later court inquiry into this mass panic cleared Henderson of blame and criticised RAF authorities, especially the Station Commander.

No. 1 Squadron travelled to Singapore too.

10 December—lost at sea

On 8 December the Commander-in-Chief of the Eastern Fleet, Admiral Tom Phillips, sailed out from Singapore in command of the powerful 'Force Z', based on the great capital ships *Prince of Wales* and *Repulse*, with four destroyers. From the *Prince of Wales*, he requested that fighter protection be provided when he reached Singora in Thailand. A reply signal declared such protection impossible, without specifying that this applied only to Singora. Further south it would be feasible, and the RAAF's 453 Squadron was allotted to fleet protection. By the evening of 9 December Japanese aircraft were shadowing Force Z, and Phillips decided to return to Singapore. However, when a signal that night informed him of an enemy landing at Kuantan, he decided to intervene. Early on 10 December Kuantan was in sight, but no Japanese ships were visible. Phillips turned again for Singapore. He was now within range of 453 Squadron's Buffaloes, but did not alert Singapore as to his movements. Meanwhile, more than 80 Japanese bombers and torpedo-bombers were searching for Z Force. It was spotted at 10 a.m. and subjected to a succession of attacks. Herb Plenty of 8 Squadron passed through the area while returning from a reconnaissance. Confident that his Hudson would not be attacked, but helpless to intervene, he and his crew watched the destruction of the two great warships. First news of the attack arrived in Singapore nearly an hour into the action, when *Repulse* sent an emergency signal. Within six minutes, ten Buffaloes of 453 Squadron were airborne and heading off on the 265 kilometre journey. By the time they arrived, *Prince of Wales* was sinking on the horizon, and the unescorted enemy bombers had left the scene.

Hundreds of seamen were rescued, but 840, including Phillips, were lost. Had the Buffaloes been dispatched earlier, or based in Kuantan, they might have changed the course of events. Instead, when the pilots returned, the Commander-in-Chief was in the Operations Room to hear their dreadful news. It was a great blow to the morale of the forces in Malaya, signalling as it did the loss of naval supremacy in the region and the failure of the Singapore strategy, with its dependence on capital ships and air power.

11–21 December

For a few days after the destruction of British air power in northern Malaya and of Force Z there was a lull in RAAF activity. The Japanese air forces concentrated on supporting their troops, establishing themselves on airfields in Thailand and northern Malaya and bombing Penang Island off the west coast.

In response to these raids, Brooke-Popham ordered more fighters north. No. 453 Squadron, frustrated in its desire to show what it could do in Singapore and with Force Z, would now get its chance. On 13 December its 16 Buffaloes took off. The first three aircraft were headed for Butterworth, where they would refuel before reconnoitring southern Thailand.

No sooner had they landed, however, than they were directed to intercept bombers headed for Penang Island, just across the straits from Butterworth. The flight leader, Doug Vanderfield, found that his undercarriage would not retract, but still flew towards the raiders. Using cloud cover, his flight attacked the 'Lily' light bombers. Jack Woodward saw what followed: 'One Buff got underneath and behind a bomber . . . and gave it one burst. It just rolled and then burst into flames and fell into the sea.'[12] Vanderfield's troubled aircraft had achieved this kill. Although six 'Sonia' dive-bombers were seeking to intervene, Vanderfield then sent a second bomber plummeting. His wingmen, Mac Read and Bill Collyer, probably shot down two Sonias. Vanderfield flew to Ipoh for repairs, while Read and Collyer, whose plane had been damaged, rearmed and refuelled at Butterworth before flying on to strafe enemy transport further north. They left six trucks burning, yet this was a mere pinprick to the advancing army.

Another flight of 453's Buffaloes comprised an Englishman, a New Zealander and an Australian. The Englishman, Wing Commander Neale, was to take command at Ipoh Station after recently arriving from England. The Australian, Pilot Officer Tom Livesey, gave him a cockpit drill on the Buffalo, before Neale flew a practice circuit. He insisted that Livesey lead the way to Ipoh, even though the Australian did not know the area. They lost their way in a storm. Running out of fuel, Livesey flew low to find a suitable landing ground. He landed in what looked like a wheatfield, but was in fact a paddy field. On touching down, his aircraft flipped over. Realising the danger this ground represented to his fellow-flyers and despite painful cracked ribs, Livesey scrambled out and signalled frantically to Neale and the New Zealander, Brown, to bale out. Instead both sought to land and were killed in fiery crashes. On being arrested by a local Dutch policeman, Livesey realised he had landed on the island of Sumatra.

A third flight was confronted by 30 Nates at Butterworth. Tim Vigors and two other pilots fought well before being shot down or forced to land. Vigors was badly wounded. Two Australians then took off against the same swarm. Geoff Angus' aircraft was soon emitting smoke and he was hit in the ankle by a metal fragment. In landing wheels-up in a field he struck his face, but could not pause to take stock, as the victorious enemy pilot strafed him and his Buff. Nevertheless, he made cover. Ron 'Doc' Oelrich was under fire as soon as he took to the air; Woodward counted eight attackers. Oelrich led them through the fire of Bofors guns on the airfield—eyewitnesses said deliberately—but crashed when a bullet penetrated the back of his head. Oelrich was later Mentioned in Despatches for this day's efforts. Over six feet tall with fair hair and blue eyes, he had achieved first-class passes in most of his Intermediate Certificate subjects at Sydney's prestigious Fort Street High School. Now he had become the first RAAF Buffalo pilot killed in action. His body was recovered from the wreckage and buried, wrapped in a blanket and strapped to part of a door, at Butterworth, but could not be located again after the war. Woodward, in light of what he had seen, mused that 'Man for man, I'm certain that our chap is far superior to the Jap.'[13]

Nevertheless, in its first day of action, 453 Squadron had lost seven Buffaloes.

On 14 December, five RAAF Buffaloes, led by Max White, were sent to attack Japanese ground forces in northern Malaya. Two became separated and returned to base, but the remaining three carried out their mission and then ran into three Sonias, and possibly some Oscars. The Buffaloes attacked, but White was shot down and killed, apparently by the rear-gunner of a Sonia. Greg Board got on to the tail of one aircraft, fired and saw it explode in a red ball. Geoff Seagoe shot bits off the tail of another before it escaped. He turned to strafe the enemy column again, but an explosive bullet, apparently fired from the ground, penetrated his aircraft and wounded him severely in the shoulder. He made it back to Ipoh.

Reinforcements arrived at Ipoh next day from Singapore: ten Buffaloes, led by Squadron Leader W.J. Harper, who had just returned from Australia. No. 21 Squadron was at this stage providing the ground crew for both squadrons at Ipoh, and was overstretched. They were unable to fix the Buffaloes' problematic guns, so that when Vanderfield, Board and

Matt O'Mara intercepted a raid by 19 Lilys that day, only four of their combined total of 12 guns operated. Board was nevertheless able to shoot one Lily until it fell, burning and disintegrating. After Harper brought 453 Squadron armourers under Sergeant Eric Haines to Ipoh, the machine guns' reliability improved greatly. Haines' extraordinary efforts in the early campaigns—working tirelessly on poor machines with inadequate spares and risking his life to put out a burning aircraft—would bring him a British Empire Medal.

To reduce Buffalo losses, Air Headquarters now ordered the fighter squadrons at Ipoh to concentrate on airfield defence and reconnaissance rather than aggressive sorties. Some pilots were put on airborne standing patrol, while others sat sweating in their oven-like cockpits waiting to be called. Thus when on 17 December three Oscars appeared at Ipoh, an identical number of Buffaloes confronted them. However, their flight characteristics were not identical: one Buffalo escaped its pursuers, the other two barely survived. Buffaloes did chase away approaching fighters later that day, but thereby left the field open for an incursion by ten bombers. Next day the enemy raided again, destroying two Buffaloes on the ground and killing the equipment officer, Frank Hordern, as he drove onto the airfield to help. They also destroyed a DH Dragon aircraft and the urgently needed spares it had brought for the Buffaloes, as well as killing the pilot and two unloaders. Conditions at Ipoh were so primitive that ground staff were refuelling aircraft with buckets and funnels.

On 19 December the weary squadrons were ordered to Kuala Lumpur. Though safer, it was still raided. There 453 Squadron's ground staff 'had their first real taste of the Jap'. Two 'Buffs' were airborne when the Sonias, Lilys and Oscars attacked. They saw the Sonias first, which they identified as Stukas, and which to one of the pilots, Ross Leys, looked like frightening red spiders. Eric Peterson downed one, while the escorting Oscars chased Leys. Jack Shanahan, of the ground staff, saw Leys run into 'all the strife in the world and the last we saw of him was when he bailed out and the Japs began shooting him up as he hung helpless in the "chute".'[14] As the aircraft approached, Leys thought the pilot was merely having a look, but then puffs emerged from the Oscar's nose. The aircraft passed so close that Leys' parachute rocked violently. He pulled hard on the parachute cords as two more aircraft attacked him, but although they holed his parachute his only injury was rope burns to his hands.

22 December: climax

On 22 December Kuala Lumpur saw the biggest air battle of the Malayan campaign. For more than half an hour 18 Oscars, flying from Kota Bharu, took on 12 Buffaloes of 453 Squadron under Vanderfield. Shanahan, spectating with other ground crew, later wrote: 'It was a wild and woolly show ... the whole mix-up lasting half an hour ... and from zero feet to up to 7000 feet.'[15] The superior Japanese aircraft took a heavy toll on the Australians. Tom Livesey, his ribs heavily strapped, accidentally knocked off his own undercarriage on a sandbank on take-off, then found himself taking on six Oscars. Shrapnel struck his calves and an ankle, while bullets ripped into his engine and cockpit. 'Friendly' Bofors guns tried to shoot him down too, but he survived this and a belly-landing. Harry Griffiths downed one, and possibly two, aircraft before a cannon shell shattered his windscreen. Griffiths tried to wipe the smile off one enemy pilot's face by shooting at him with his revolver. The cheeky pilot did a barrel roll right around Griffiths' stricken aircraft. Despite hand and head wounds, Griffiths landed safely. His ground crew counted 70 bullet holes before they were ordered to do something more urgent.

Bob Drury also made a belly-landing, in which the engine of his badly damaged Buffalo broke loose from the front. He was lifted gently from the wreckage, but his injuries proved fatal. Drury had been one of the pilots Squadron Leader Harper had criticised as inadequate, but in previous days had shown his mettle in solo reconnaissance missions and effective ground strafing. An RAAF clerk at the outbreak of war, he had transferred to aircrew. He left a wife and a one-year-old daughter.

Mac Read also died, apparently ramming or crashing into an enemy aircraft as he dropped. Bill Collyer was attacking one Oscar when another stalked him and, in firing on the Buffalo, also hit Collyer's target. He thought this first Oscar was going down, but then had to concentrate on his own predicament. One bullet passed his ear, but hit the instrument panel and his foot. By the time he had evaded his opponent and reached Sembawang, his aircraft had taken about 70 hits.

George Scrimgeour took on an Oscar head-on. His plane caught fire and when he opened the hood his face and hands were burnt. While Scrimgeour floated down in his parachute, the Japanese pilot tried three times to shoot him. He missed the 21-year-old Australian, but put

25 holes in his parachute. Twenty-three days later, Scrimgeour would be flying again.

Greg Board had an Oscar in his sights when his Buffalo was struck from behind, destroying his instrument panel and setting his fuel tanks brilliantly aflame. He baled out into jungle.

Japanese casualties in this battle are uncertain, but numbered between three and eleven, with one chutai (squadron) commander shot down.

Soon after this battle, another raid was reported coming in, and four Oscars reached the strip before the Buffaloes could take off. Following established doctrine, the pilots leapt out of their planes to take cover—all that is, except Eric Peterson, who apparently had not seen the attackers and took off. Over six feet tall, and passionate about engines, Peterson had at Canberra Grammar been a champion mile-runner and swimmer and was a first-grade cricketer. Now Eric's considerable physical skills availed him nothing. An Oscar 'jumped' him at just 700 feet, and Peterson crashed to his death.

Down to just three serviceable aircraft, 453 Squadron was ordered to Singapore. There the last scenes of the frantic drama that began in Malaya would be played out.

5 The Fight for Singapore

On Christmas Eve at Sembawang, 453 and 21 Squadrons temporarily amalgamated as 'No. 21/453 Squadron', under Squadron Leader W.J. Harper. The inadequacy of the Buffalo was now more apparent than ever. Radical changes were made to improve performance, including removing radio masts, rear-vision mirrors and cockpit heaters, reducing gun cowlings and gunports, and replacing .50 calibre machine guns with .303 calibre guns. The resulting 'Super Special' Buffalo was 1000 pounds (455 kilograms) lighter and a much better performer. Nevertheless, the engine remained inadequate, as did the aircraft's performance above 18,000 feet. The Zero and Oscar could operate well above that altitude, thus staying out of reach. The Buffaloes remained, as one 453 Squadron member said, 'apologies for an aircraft'.[1] At about this time, Jack Woodward acknowledged that 'The Jap has done really remarkably well, and I have come to the conclusion that we very much underestimated his strength.'[2] It was a common feeling, though few would have put it so sportingly.

At Sembawang, the busiest airfield on Singapore, Australian Group Captain McCauley now commanded the amalgamated RAAF squadrons, two Dutch bomber squadrons and the two RAAF Hudson squadrons. The Hudsons undertook, with No. 205 Squadron's Catalinas, extensive reconnaissance searches, which overtaxed their aircraft. To reinforce these, Australia had to spare six precious Hudsons from home defence.

January 1942: reinforcements arrive

In late December, the British authorities at last responded to the urgent need for reinforcements, promising to send Hurricanes. None were aboard the first convoy, which under RAAF escort brought much-needed infantry on 3 January 1942. Three days later the Buffaloes had a rare chance to turn the tables on the Japanese, when Bob Kirkman and Geoff Sheppard found nine unprotected barges laden with Japanese troops on the Bernam River. The Australians expended all their ammunition strafing the barges. Kirkman later succinctly explained the grim outcome to fellow pilots: 'We saw a lot of Japs in the water—dead ones.'[3]

Generally, however, the Allied air force concentrated on surviving, defending Singapore from growing air attacks, and protecting convoys as they arrived. It could do virtually nothing to protect the army, which was concentrating on denying Malayan airfields to the Japanese: if these airstrips fell, Japanese aircraft could wreak havoc on the Allied airfields in Singapore, and on the convoys in which lay the Allies' only hope.

Allied aircraft did try to disrupt the Japanese occupation of Kuantan airfield, but torrential rain and accidents stymied every attempt. The disparity in numbers and aircraft quality at the heart of the Allied aerial nightmare was apparent on 12 January, when more than 100 enemy aircraft attacked Singapore. Eight Buffaloes of 21/453 Squadron, as well as 14 New Zealand and two Dutch Buffaloes, took off to intercept. The Australians were directed to three sectors in succession and finally pursued a formation of 27 bombers as they left the island. The Australians threw their throttles wide open and gave chase. When the Japanese aircrews saw the Buffaloes approaching, they too accelerated and, going into a shallow dive, were able to leave the Australians behind. 'Bombers outpacing fighters,' said one Australian pilot afterwards. 'You've got to **** well laugh!'[4] The Buffaloes could not obtain sufficient altitude to meet the bombers at 25,000 feet, or their fighter escort at 28,000 feet. The Buffaloes on Singapore needed 30 minutes' warning of the enemy's approach if they were to reach 20,000 feet in time to meet them. Such warnings were virtually impossible with the successive evacuation of Observer Corps posts on the peninsula, and inadequate radar cover. Even if they made it to that altitude, the Buffaloes were outnumbered in ratios of between six and fifteen to one. Only 40 anti-aircraft guns on the island could reach enemy aircraft at those altitudes.

The Hudsons were still undertaking reconnaissance, twice daily in pairs. After they lost two aircraft, their flights along the east coast became known as the 'Clay Pigeon Run'. Peter Gibbes' Hudson was holed on four successive sorties. Convoy escort was also critical, although almost all the troops who arrived in the six convoys to Singapore lacked training, equipment and experience. The convoy that arrived on 13 January brought the greatest joy: as well as troops, it carried 51 Hurricane fighters and 24 pilots, including three Australians. Bad weather protected them from 100 approaching enemy aircraft.

The Australian Army's entry into the fighting on 14 January gave the Allies in Malaya a fillip, for the 2/30th Battalion carried out a brilliantly successful ambush at Gemas. For two days afterwards Australian Buffaloes attacked enemy convoys on the Gemas road, though ground fire damaged five 'Buffs'. Allied aircraft hit enemy barges and vessels on the west coast, where the Japanese were exploiting their control of the seas to make amphibious landings. In the meantime, three Buffalo pilots—Doug Vanderfield, 'Congo' Kinninmont and Leigh Bowes—claimed bombers over Singapore, even though their fighters had been too slow to permit more than one pass against these enemies. On 16 January, Harper destroyed a tank, one of many vehicles set alight as the Buffalo pilots sent Japanese vehicles scattering desperately under their guns.

Early on 17 January, Vanderfield, Mick Grace and Sergeant Alf Clare intercepted three enemy fighters and claimed them all. Half an hour later came the first heavy raid on the RAAF Station at Sembawang, which had previously led a charmed life. Japanese radio had asserted that this was intentional and joked that when Japanese paratroops landed on the island, geisha girls would land among the Australians on Sembawang. However, in the 17 January raid, the 27 Japanese bombers dropped nothing so enticing. Instead they pattern-bombed the airfield, putting the station's water supply out of action. Flight Lieutenant John Wright, who had arrived just two days earlier from Darwin, was sitting on the edge of a trench engrossed in conversation about pay when he suddenly saw earth spurting up and coming straight towards his group from the end of the runway. They dropped into the trench, but in the bombing that followed he was knocked out and concussed. After the raid he emerged to nightmare scenes: men digging themselves and others out, aircraft burning, ammunition exploding everywhere, dead Indian labourers heaped in sheds, men killed by blasts and squashed into a drain like sardines. The station's main buildings were hit, and six aircraft destroyed. Few who made it to the slit trenches were hurt, even though some took risks to salvage aircraft and extinguish fires. For weeks afterwards Wright could not settle to his work until after the usual late-morning air-raid time had passed.

Even here, men found a release in humour. Jack Shanahan told his diary, 'the funniest sidelight was the "death of Albert"'. A member of the ground staff, Albert had been working only in shorts inside an aircraft until the last moment, when he had gone to a slit trench. After the raid, men had found his torn and singed shirt and burnt identity disc. In Shanahan's words:

> The cry immediately went up . . . Alberts gone . . . he's had it . . . and the boys began to look for some earthly sign of the late lamented Albert. All this time the late lamented was strolling, leisurely back to what had been his post of duty, and to find everyone at the stage of saying . . . well, he wasent such a bad b.....d.[5]

More laughs concerned an Australian who, during another unexpected raid, tried to reach shelter on a bicycle. Man after man passed him, and with the enemy aircraft coming ever closer, he threw the bike away. He was said to have made up 40 metres to dead-heat with the first man into the shelter.

The already hard-pressed RAAF ground staff came under more pressure after that raid, as many of the local labourers fled. Nevertheless, later raids caused little damage.

By 18 January the three fighter squadrons mustered just 28 Buffaloes to oppose an estimated 150 Japanese fighters and 250 bombers. The previous night, Norm Chapman had confided in a mate that the squadron had 'no show at all', illustrating the point by describing how a Zero had looped around his Buffalo while Chapman flew along straight.[6] His analysis would be grimly vindicated the next day. During the morning at Gemas, Daryl Sproule probably downed a Nate, but later that day positions were reversed when Chapman and Henry Parsons escorted Hudsons on a mission. They ran into four Oscars, which quickly sent Chapman's Buffalo down in flames. Chapman had been a clerk, mechanic and salesman at a Melbourne motor engineering works. One of his officers remembered him as 'a very well liked and extremely game man'.[7]

From his Hudson, Herb Plenty saw Chapman go down, and on flying over his burning wreck wondered how long before the same happened to him. By then he had become separated from two other Hudson pilots, Russ Bell and Bob Arnold, but by flying full speed at treetop height he evaded enemy fighters and got home. Chapman's wingman, Henry Parsons, sought to keep the Oscars off Plenty's tail, and claimed one possibly destroyed. He too returned to Sembawang, where he told his mates he wanted to get a Japanese aircraft to 'make up for Norm'.[8]

Bell and Arnold were flying at wave-top height towards home, when Bell's turret-gunner, Doug Scott, saw a black spot approaching from the rear. It soon grew into a Japanese fighter, which so positioned itself behind Arnold's aircraft that neither Scott nor Arnold's turret-gunner, John McNeill, could hit it. Scott watched helplessly as the Japanese pilot skilfully put McNeill out of action and set one engine alight. The fighter then dropped in behind Bell and started spitting fire. For a split second he showed his underside to Scott, who 'gave him everything those guns could fire'. The Japanese pilot flew off. Though hugely relieved, Bell now had to shepherd Arnold home. Scott recalled:

> We reformed on them and signalled to follow. I looked over at the Hudson, she looked badly shot up ... When we reached Sembawang, F/Lt Bell signalled that we would follow them in to land. They acknowledged and were making their run in [but] the hydraulics must have been damaged because only one flap operated. The aircraft keeled over and exploded on impact. The feeling of absolute frustration and sadness that swept over me at that moment as we passed over what was left of the Hudson cannot be expressed.[9]

Like Scott, the Australians on the ground who sought to help the crash victims knew the men who had just died horribly. 'Dusty' Hensel was haunted forever after by the sight of burnt hands rising from the wreckage. His wing commander gently admonished him and others who went to look at the wreckage, when they themselves had to fly a Hudson that night.

The day of 19 January saw the Anzac spirit rekindled in the unexpected form of the Wirraway. The RAF OTU at Kluang had been renamed 'Y Squadron', a combat unit. It had all RAF ground staff, but mainly New Zealand pilots and RAAF observers. Now, with eight RAAF Buffaloes as escort, five Y Squadron Wirraways attacked enemy launches and barges at Muar. The Wirraways were unusually loud, for the crews had fitted a metre-wide 'soup-plate' siren, which made a fearful scream when turned into the wind. Each carried twenty 40-pound anti-personnel bombs and was armed with the standard two forward-firing guns, but also two locally fitted rear Vickers guns.

As the Wirraways approached their target, the escorting Buffaloes spotted and engaged three Sonias. The Australians destroyed two, but when five Oscars arrived on the scene, Henry Parsons, so keen to avenge his mate Norm, was killed. The Wirraways attacked the enemy barges with all their guns and bombs. They reportedly sank no barges, but return fire hit every one of them. As RNZAF pilot Ray Hemus banked his Wirraway so that his RAAF gunner, Abe Moritz, could spray the enemy from just 400 feet up, ground fire hit the port side, spraying metal parts into Moritz's forehead and cheek. Hemus tried to climb away and save his crewmate, but the joystick would not move forward or back. Somehow he got home, but Moritz's damaged eye subsequently had to be removed. Four Wirraways returned to base, and the crew of the fifth parachuted to safety. It was a brave performance at a time when Wirraway crews were also fighting courageously, as we shall see, at the eastern end of the arc of Australian defences, in Rabaul. That afternoon nine Buffaloes confronted 40 Oscars near Muar, where 'Congo' Kinninmont achieved the only success, his second kill that day.

On 20 January, the Vildebeests continued their daring attacks on enemy columns. RAAF observer 'Skip' Glowery thought his luck had run out during an attack at Kuala Lumpur. After the crew released their bombs in a dive, there was a huge bang, and Glowery felt hot blood spurting over his neck and head. He told his British pilot 'Al' Allanson that he had been hit but could not locate the hole. Allanson took a torch and inspected him, but after smelling his fingers concluded that Glowery was all right: the culprit was Allanson's 'pee tin'!

Most ground staff of Nos 1 and 8 Squadrons left by ship that day for Sumatra, where they were established at an aerodrome known as P.2. While this was an early admission of defeat in Malaya, that day brought the first Hurricanes into battle. In the biggest raid yet on Singapore, 80 Japanese aircraft approached that morning. The Hurricanes shot down at least eight Sallys and two fighters, but themselves lost three, including their squadron leader. After the bombers had hit Sembawang, the 453 Squadron diarist wrote that when the smoke had cleared it was apparent that:

> ... once more Tojo had dropped million dollar bills, champagne and geisha girls on his beloved Aussies—blast him! Not much damage was done and once more, after the boys had had the usual 'nervous one', they soon recovered their good spirits.[10]

The Hurricanes raised morale throughout Singapore, but the Zero outclassed them in manoeuvrability and speed below 20,000 feet. These Hurricane IIs had been fitted with desert air intake filters, which deprived them of nearly 50 kilometres per hour in speed. Moreover, they had 12 machine guns rather than the usual eight, and the extra four added much weight. Most importantly, the Hurricanes were vastly outnumbered, with the daily number available averaging only 16. As Shanahan noted, 'When the sirens go now, the only time we see an Allied kite is when we see one poor little fellow being chased by half the Jap Air Force.'[11] He likened Sembawang airstrip, covered in bomb craters, to Swiss cheese.

There were now five RAAF Hurricane pilots in Singapore. On 21 January, one of them, Pilot Officer John Gorton, was in a flight trying to intercept enemy bombers when he emerged from cloud and found himself confronted by Oscars. Eventually he had to crash-land his damaged aircraft on Bintan, an island south of Singapore. Indigenous soldiers fired on him before recognising him as friendly. Identifying him as John Gorton may have been difficult even for acquaintances, because in crashing he had sustained terrible injuries to his nose, cheekbones and forehead. His arms were badly lacerated too, and on freeing himself from the wreck, he collapsed. Locals carried him to a planter's house. When an RAF launch arrived for Gorton, the sergeant aboard considered that the unconscious Australian was too seriously injured to survive the voyage and so declined to take him. Within days, however, Gorton was improving.

Three other RAAF Hurricane pilots experienced intense dogfights on 23 January. Geoff Schaffer shot down an Oscar, but had to bale out after another set his aircraft alight. Suffering burns and shock, he was hospitalised. Bill McCulloch and Ian Fairbairn also claimed one fighter each. McCulloch survived being shot into the sea, while Fairbairn had to crash-land.

On 24 January, 8 Squadron's Herb Plenty and 'Spud' Spurgeon were returning from a reconnaissance of Malaya's east coast, when two Zeros attacked. In Spurgeon's words:

> The first [Hudson] escaped into cloud and I was the bunny left. Almost immediately the aeroplane was set on fire. It was a fiery sort of aeroplane, the Hudson. The only alternative I had was to land on the water. That effectively dowsed the fire and of course wrecked the aeroplane, which then sank. Two of the crew of four were killed. The other one [Syd Chesterman] I'm sure was wounded. Together we got out. We had no possibility of getting to the dinghy so we relied entirely on the Mae Wests [life-jackets] . . . That was at ten o'clock in the morning. We remained together until about nine o'clock that night. He was getting weaker all the time and I suspect . . . [he] had a pretty severe injury . . . During the night, the wind got up and the sea got so strong that we had to separate and that was the last I saw of him. In the morning at about seven o'clock I saw the outline of an island and I swam as hard as I could to get to it and I was flung up on a coral reef . . .[12]

On 30 January a Japanese patrol captured Spurgeon. He was tied to the outside of a car, his feet on the running board and arms through the window, and driven into a long captivity.

Immediately after Spurgeon's Hudson was set alight, the Zeros played a deadly version of hide-and-seek with Plenty's 'kite', which they eventually spotted. He flew just above the water, but they quickly hit both engines. Although the Hudson crashed and sank, all four crew members escaped. Before leaving, the Zero pilots waved to them from their opened canopies. Plenty's crew inflated a dinghy and reached the same island as Spurgeon. With the help of locals they eventually returned to the mainland and paddled a prahu to Singapore.

On 24 January, another reinforcement convoy reached Singapore. Their passengers included RAAF pilots, all inexperienced and some requiring more training. More than 20 went to 21/453 Squadron, which now had only four serviceable aircraft.

RAAF Hurricane pilot Alan Coutie was lost, permanently, when his aircraft disappeared in bad weather over Singapore. Early that day, 25 January, two Hudsons, under 'Ossie' Diamond and Dave Colquhoun, sighted a Japanese invasion fleet heading for Endau. Their radios were jammed, but they escaped three chasing Nates and reached Sembawang. Fewer than 40 aircraft—Hudsons, Albacores and Vildebeests—could be mustered to oppose the invasion fleet. They had to fly within range of enemy airfields at Kuantan, which had about 100 fighters, and Kota Bharu, while the invasion force was also accompanied by an aircraft carrier! 'Curly' Davis rightly called the attack on the invasion fleet 'heroic'.[13] One of the Vildebeest crewmen likened the battle to something from a movie, with 'kites everywhere in the sky and here and there some coming down in flames'.[14] When the Vildebeests and their Hurricane escort approached the landing beaches at Endau, many enemy fighters attacked. RAF Vildebeest pilot Tim Lamb, who had RAAF Sergeant Gil Sharp as his gunner, recounted what happened:

> We put our noses down and headed flat out for the beaches ... It's a wonder the old crates didn't fall apart. Within seconds the sky was full of aircraft and our Squadron Commander gave orders to attack individually ... by a lot of crabbing, jinking and a hell of a lot of luck [we] had no vital hits, although it was disconcerting to see rows of holes appearing all over the place in fabric and hear the twang of parting wires. I could hear Sharp blazing away and I heard him shout that he had got a Zero ... Immediately I was over the beaches, which were seething with troops, I turned north and dropped my bombs ... With the last one away I banked into the jungle ... Suddenly Gil Sharp gave a shout, and a Zero shot over my head. I didn't know at the time but a shell had got him right through the knee and the lower half of his leg was hanging off.[15]

After a hair-raising trip home, Sharp was taken from the tattered plane to hospital, where his leg was amputated.

Behind the Vildebeests came RAAF Hudsons which, on approaching the fleet, found some 50 Zeros attacking them from above. The first burst at Jack O'Brien's aircraft killed his wireless operator. Another burst struck his second pilot in the head, killing him and then striking O'Brien on the shoulder. O'Brien was thrown forward over the controls, but recovered, although the dead pilot's legs were so entangled in various levers that O'Brien had to leave Endau without dropping his bombs.

The other Hudsons attacked ships and troops, and all made it home. Peter Gibbes dropped bombs from just 500 feet and scored direct hits on a motor vessel. He later recalled seeing bodies and soldiers' equipment hurtling skyward and then rotating grotesquely before falling back into the sea. Buffalo pilots Mick Grace, Geoff Sheppard and Ross Leys each claimed enemy aircraft destroyed. Eighteen Allied aircraft, including 11 Vildebeests, were lost in the brave but futile Endau operation, which was the last major RAF effort in the Far East. It could not prevent the Japanese from bringing ashore valuable troops and equipment.

On 27 January General Wavell, Supreme Commander of ABDA, ordered the army to withdraw to Singapore Island. This made Singapore's airfields more vulnerable to air attack and, all being in the island's north, they were now within Japanese artillery range. When the first rounds fell around 21/453 Squadron, the men raced for slit trenches, and someone was able to see some humour in their situation, quipping that the next thing they saw would be 'the whites of the Jap's eyes'. Another airman was caught sitting on the latrine, and in the words of an eyewitness 'took off... unfortunately for him without his overalls and down he went with a "dicky" knee. The poor blighter had to crawl and drag himself to the nearest trench where his predicament was the cause of much ribald mirth.'[16] Air Headquarters now decided to withdraw its forces gradually to the Netherlands East Indies. That day No. 8 Squadron's aircrews were flown to Sumatra, while No. 1 Squadron continued the reconnaissance flights.

Also that day, Nos 21 and 453 Squadrons resumed their separate identities. All No. 21 Squadron Buffaloes and some pilots went to 453 Squadron, as did personnel and aircraft from another Buffalo squadron. No. 453 was now the sole remaining Buffalo squadron, and was left to defend the island alongside the Hurricanes. While they faced terrible odds, an investigation into accusations of desertion and a pep-talk by senior British commanders, who accused Australians of cowardice, angered and hurt members.

On 30 January, Sergeant O'Mara of 453 Squadron became separated from two other Buffaloes while patrolling. He belly-landed on Bintan

Island, close to where John Gorton had landed nine days earlier. Like Gorton he was cared for by locals. Both were rescued by an air–sea rescue launch and returned to Singapore. By then, 11 February, their squadrons had left Singapore for the Netherlands East Indies.

Ground troops on Singapore were bitter that the island's remaining aircraft were withdrawn, but doing otherwise would have invited the complete destruction of this air force. In February Doug Scott was taken with a group of airmen to help unload stores on the island and found himself among British soldiers. On discovering that they were air force, one Scottish soldier went berserk and had to be restrained by his mates. 'Why didn't ya come and help oos?' was his plaintive cry.[17] It was a common attitude among the ground troops, but not a fair criticism of the airmen, as opposed to the leaders responsible for equipping them.

O'Mara and Gorton boarded SS *Derrymore* with hundreds of other airmen and troops bound for Java, but when it was torpedoed on 13 February, they took to rafts. Eventually by pure chance the pair were spotted and rescued by HMAS *Ballarat*. They reached Batavia on 15 February. That day saw the fall of Singapore, the greatest military disaster in their country's history, in which Australia lost more than 15,000 troops. The long-feared danger to Australia was now greater than ever.

At Batavia, on 17 February, Jack Woodward pondered the fall of Singapore, blaming it on the lack of fighter planes. With sufficient of them, he believed, the story would have been different. 'Of course, in addition,' he noted, 'we would have required more competent men in charge of the Air Force, for a more incompetent blithering lot of idiots it would be difficult to come across.'[18]

What had gone wrong would long preoccupy the relatives of those airmen who died in the campaign. In 1949, for example, the widowed mother of Norm Chapman wrote to the Department of Air, which had recently informed her that her only son's body had still not been found, but would be commemorated on a memorial yet to be built in Singapore. 'To me' she said, 'it will be a constant grief at the loss of our gallant and worthy son, but also that he, with others, were so poorly equipped, directed and eventually abandoned. Australia, the land of his birth sent these lads to their death.' She also hoped that the memorial would 'prove more worthy than the treatment they received whilst trying against superhuman odds, to preserve the freedom of their loved ones'.[19]

6 'We who are about to die, salute you!'

After Japan entered the war, Australia's primary goal changed from protecting the Empire to national survival. The best way to survive was to keep Japanese forces out of range of the mainland. Malaya and Singapore were central to this strategy, as was the archipelago of islands running from New Britain in the east to the Netherlands East Indies in the west. Australia greatly valued the airfields on these islands. The government hoped that they could hold them, with Allied help, although in some cases they only expected to delay a Japanese advance. Those same islands were also major Japanese strategic objectives, so a clash was inevitable.

Immediately after the bombing of Pearl Harbor on 7 December 1941, the Australian War Cabinet asked the Chiefs of Staff for their estimate of Japan's intentions. The reply was that Japan might try a similar strike directly against Australia, launched from aircraft carriers. Alternatively, they could move step by step and, if they took Singapore and the Netherlands East Indies, could invade Australia. They might well seek to take advanced bases in Rabaul, Port Moresby and Noumea, and might even attempt to take Darwin. Given the scant resources at Australia's disposal, these were disturbing scenarios.

The Australian War Cabinet decided in December that the flow overseas of EATS trainees, then running at 620 per month, should halt 'for the present'. Australia needed aircrew urgently for local duties, and sending them overseas past the Japanese Navy was now hazardous. Searching for Japanese vessels became a priority for Australian aircraft, especially the Hudsons at Rabaul and Catalinas at Port Moresby. The Catalinas of 11 and 20 Squadrons undertook more than 100 reconnaissance and search flights in December 1941, to places as far afield as New Caledonia, the New Hebrides, the Solomons and New Ireland. On 8 December Lincoln Sloan, a Catalina pilot, spotted three Japanese pearling luggers in Australian waters and ordered them to Thursday Island. After completing the ten-hour patrol, Sloan landed at Port Moresby. Just two hours later Bill Dawson, a young seaman on lookout on HMAS *Adelaide*, photographed Sloan's crew taking off for another long patrol. Dawson and the rest of the ship's crew were excited and alert, as the ship's captain had announced that Australia was at war with Japan. But soon a dose of horror was added to Dawson's mixed emotions as he watched the aircraft crash into a hillside near the town and burst into flames. Sloan and his crew were killed.[1]

Catalina crews in the early months of the war were, apart from first and second pilots, generally culled from ground staff, who were not officially classed as aircrew. Only after many months, when some of these converts had flown over 1000 operational hours and others been killed, were the survivors given full crew pay and acting rank. Comradeship in Catalina crews was generally strong, engendered partly by the ad hoc way in which they were assembled, with mates teaming up with mates and 'friends of friends'. This encouraged unit pride, as did the fact that being sent to a Catalina squadron was considered an honour, reserved for above-average crew.

General Brereton's visit to Australia on the eve of Pearl Harbor and the subsequent agreement about American bases there ensured Australia would have allies in its defence. The Japanese whirlwind that struck American forces in the Philippines at the same time as Pearl Harbor and Kota Bharu blew American aircraft Australia's way unexpectedly quickly. Fourteen Flying Fortresses landed at Batchelor on 20 December before moving on to Java, and three days later an American convoy reached Brisbane, having been diverted from a voyage to the Philippines. Together with 20,000 US troops, it brought eighteen P-40 fighters and 52 dive-bombers.

Lieutenant-General George Brett, Wavell's American deputy in ABDA command, arrived in Darwin on 31 December to look after US forces in Australia.

Rabaul—Japanese target

In early December, No. 24 Squadron's few Hudsons and Wirraways had been sent to Rabaul. Just arriving was an achievement for the Wirraways, which had to make an unprecedentedly long 450-kilometre ocean crossing. They made it by staging at a precarious little grass and coral strip at Gasmata, on the south coast of New Britain.

Rabaul, located on the huge Simpson Harbour in north-eastern New Britain, and with volcanic craters surrounding it on three sides, was an isolated posting. There were good local roads, but none suitable for motor traffic connecting Rabaul with the rest of the mountainous, jungle-clad island. Moreover, the airfields were primitive. The main airstrip, Vunakanau, lay some 16 kilometres south of Rabaul and offered one runway hacked out of the long kunai grass. There were no dispersal bays in which to hide the aircraft, let alone protective revetments, so when enemy reconnaissance aircraft came over to spy on RAAF strength, the Australian planes were conveniently lined up on the strip. A corrugated iron shelter acted as workshop and hangar, but there was no storage or accommodation of any other kind, and refuelling was by hand. Tools were pathetically inadequate: all that was available to repair a Wirraway undercarriage at Horn Island, on the way up, was an axe and a chisel, while corrugated iron was used to repair another at Rabaul. The squadron also had a skeleton staff, just 115 of the 650 men it had at Townsville. Progress was slow, even with local help. A lesser airstrip was at Lakunai, adjacent to Rabaul township.

The 1400-strong Australian garrison stood in the way of Japanese determination to make Rabaul a major base. Ominously, Japanese reconnaissance planes flew over Rabaul on 8 December.

The Australian Hudsons also undertook reconnaissance. While looking over Kapingamarangi Island, nearly 500 kilometres north of Rabaul in the Caroline Islands, a Hudson crew spotted slipways, barges and other small vessels, but also a merchant ship speeding north and firing at these spies. Three Hudsons were sent to sink the ship, but their inexperienced crews attacked without coordination and from too high to achieve a hit. Squadron Leader John Lerew arrived with his Wirraways at Rabaul just in time to receive a signal from CAS Burnett threatening to replace the squadron unless they improved their efforts. Even more stinging was a signal from Wing Commander Bill Garing, the tough and aggressive Senior

Air Staff Officer at Northern Area Headquarters in Townsville. Garing's criticisms hit like a torpedo. He described the bombing effort as 'lamentable' and pilloried the crew that failed to take worthwhile photographs on the sortie that spotted the ship. Lerew was much more sympathetic to his men. He understood the unwillingness of the flight commander, who had flown the reconnaissance and bombing missions for a total of 13 hours in 24, to risk his aircraft in masthead attacks so far from base.[2]

Garing finished his signal with a phrase reminiscent of Horatio Nelson and Winston Churchill: 'The Empire expects much of a few.' Lerew, whom a smitten interviewer once described as a cross between Errol Flynn and David Niven, was not afraid to respond in kind. 'The Empire expects much, repeat much, of a few,' he retorted. To another criticism, of his failure to keep Headquarters fully briefed as to his situation, he impishly expressed 'Disappointment in lack of assistance rendered by Almighty.'[3] On another occasion he complained that more worry was coming from the south than from the enemy in the north.

On 18 December two Japanese 'float-planes' flew over Rabaul, easily evading two Wirraways that tried to intercept. They were probably Nell bombers, flying from the great Japanese base at Truk. Townsville ordered a single Hudson reconnaissance to Kapingamarangi and warned that a Japanese aircraft carrier might be in the area. Knowing the Hudson was likely to meet opposition and that this message was a challenge to his squadron to prove its guts and value, Lerew decided to fly the sortie, which would be his first operational one.

Three hours in, after flying for a long time with only sea in all directions, the crew saw the island 10,000 feet below. All became tense as they looked also for an aircraft carrier. There was none, and Lerew gently flew over the circle of islands so they could take effective photographs. They soon heard an intermittent thudding sound, which they eventually identified as flak. Stuart Hermes, the second pilot (or 'second dick', in air force slang), also spotted two float-planes taking off to intercept. Lerew decided to attack them before they became airborne. He dived, all instruments going 'off the clock'. The squeal of the engine on full power was exhilarating, but a sudden explosion next to the Hudson deafened everyone and, amidst a flash, seemed to flip the aircraft over. Lerew righted his 'kite' and, detecting the float-plane travelling fast across the glassy lagoon, opened fire with his front guns. 'Bullets seemed to be ripping through him', he wrote later, 'and splashes in the water around him assisted in keeping my sights on him.'[4] The Japanese rear-gunner appeared to collapse, but the float-plane kept going. Lerew evaded the Jake when it gave chase, but his bombs did no damage to the slipways. Three hours later, on reaching home, he rued his missed opportunities.

By Christmas there had been two similar reconnaissance flights. They did no damage, but from their photographs the first RAAF target map was made.

On the day of Lerew's flight, the War Cabinet approved the Chiefs of Staff recommendation to leave the Rabaul garrison where it was. The Chiefs knew Japan could send forces that this small garrison could not possibly defeat, but decided the base should not simply be surrendered. They argued that American naval forces might arrive to resupply and reinforce the garrison. Three more Hudsons were sent.

Five Wirraways were based at Lakunai. Lerew gave all Wirraway aircrew a demanding schedule to ensure that they spent seven hours a day at their aircraft, with another seven 'available' should they be needed. All had their engines running before dawn in case of enemy attack.

On New Year's Day, Lerew led four Hudsons in a raid on Kapinga-marangi, and this time returned with the satisfaction of leaving a huge column of smoke there. The Australians had hit oil and bomb storage facilities, barracks, a lookout tower and several aircraft. The fire was still burning when three Hudsons, including Lerew's, returned to destroy a 'Dave' float-plane and inflict more casualties.

On 4 January 1942, the first air attack hit Rabaul. Sixteen Nells approached Lakunai, looking to the Australians below like a beautiful arrowhead. Two obsolete Australian anti-aircraft guns tried vainly to reach them. Their height protected the bombers, but also affected their accuracy. Of more than 60 bombs, just three hit the airstrip, though 15 labourers were killed and as many wounded, with the result that the RAAF lost its local workforce. The Wirraway crews' long-awaited chance to defend the base proved disappointing. Two had to abort their take-offs amidst a huge cloud of dust and ash thrown up by the bombing. Two did become airborne; owing to a shortage of personnel, the Medical Officer was directing them, by radio telephone, and provided material for some good humour afterwards when he called, 'There they are[,] going for the clouds.'[5] Given that there was at the time 8/10ths cloud cover, it was not a very precise direction! In any case, the two Wirraways could not climb fast enough to reach the Nells. One of them was piloted by Squadron Leader Arch Tindal, the cheerful and handsome armaments officer of Northern Area Headquarters who was visiting Rabaul on inspection. Eight huge Mavis flying-boats attacked later that day, but their 90 bombs all missed the Vunakanau airfield.

RAAF Headquarters was now putting into motion a daring reconnaissance. This would not help Rabaul's garrison, but would expand Allied information about Truk, the little-known but vital Japanese base some 1000 kilometres north of New Britain. No. 6 Squadron, based at Richmond, New South Wales, was given the mission, using two new, specially modified Mark IV Hudsons, named 'Tit-Willow' and 'Yum-Yum'. These had extra fuel tanks and two 20-inch cameras, considerably more powerful than the standard eight-inch camera. The pilots chosen for the task were Bob Yeowart and Bob Green, who were briefed for four days and told that they would probably have to fight their way through enemy Zeros at Truk. They could have had few illusions about their prospects of survival. On 4 January the two Hudsons left Townsville for Rabaul, avoiding Port Moresby and possible intelligence leaks. For two days the fates kept them from Rabaul, first through a Japanese air raid and then a rain squall. When they reached Rabaul, on 6 January, Green's aircraft had developed engine problems that could not be fixed there, so Yeowart was left to carry out a suicide mission that had, if possible, just become more suicidal. Lerew was upbeat about the reconnaissance mission, and did all he could to help Yeowart, including flying alongside in his Wirraway as Yeowart took his Hudson to New Ireland for greater safety from Japanese air raids. There, at Kavieng airstrip, the Hudson was camouflaged with pawpaw branches, complete with hanging fruit.

Lerew followed up his flight to Kavieng with another attack on Kapingamarangi. In return, nine Mavis flying-boats attacked Vunakanau. Unusually, the indefatigable coastwatchers gave no warning of their approach. Japanese bombs wrecked a nearly complete direction-finding station and a control hut, damaged the runway and wrecked a grounded Wirraway. Col Butterworth was observer in another Wirraway on the strip. As the enemy formation approached, he started the engine and saw his pilot, Bruce Anderson, run the 50 metres from the mess and climb swiftly aboard. Looking back from his observer's seat, Butterworth saw bombs hit the far end of the strip and then seemingly follow the Wirraway as it sped up before taking off. Dust, smoke and flying debris reduced their vision, but the two Australians saw the enemy formation heading across the harbour for home. Climbing with all the power his strained engine could muster, Anderson sought to intercept the big Japanese 'V' formation. When their courses met, the flying-boats were still 1000 feet above the Australians, who on levelling out and flying at their maximum airspeed saw the flying-boats drawing away. Over New Ireland, Anderson tried diving almost vertically so as to build up speed and then climb again towards the intruders. As they got closer again, Anderson fired his two fixed Browning machine guns. Then, after the shuddering Wirraway had stopped climbing and begun diving again, Butterworth tried a burst of his Vickers machine gun from the rear cockpit. Japanese gunners fired back from the Mavis bringing up the rear. It was a routine repeated a few times, but to no effect. Now 100 kilometres from home, with smoke streaming ominously from the engine, and fuel and ammunition low, Anderson had to turn back. He and Butterworth made history, as theirs was the first RAAF aircraft to fire on the Japanese in the South-West Pacific. Yet while they may have damaged one or two aircraft, this had not affected Japanese strength. On landing, Anderson and Butterworth received a dressing-down from Lerew for damaging their engine. However, this was nothing compared to what Anderson was destined to face in the few hectic months of life that remained to him.

At about this time, Tindal returned to Townsville, where he spoke plainly about the lack of signals equipment, ammunition and adequate aircraft in Rabaul. This seems to have placated Headquarters somewhat.

A fourth Japanese raid hit Rabaul on 7 January, when about 20 Nells destroyed three aircraft and damaged buildings and other aircraft. Anderson, Lerew and Flight Lieutenant Peter Turnbull, a veteran pilot attached to the unit but temporarily grounded by injuries sustained in a car accident, bravely tried to save a burning Wirraway. As they did so, a blazing Hudson just 50 metres away exploded and detonated nearby bombs and petrol drums. The airmen dived under the squadron doctor's car, which had just driven up. Despite the tiny clearance, they survived the shower of aircraft and bomb fragments that hit the car above them.

That day, Japanese aircraft flew over Yeowart's Hudson at Kavieng, on their way to and from Rabaul. One even came down to 5000 feet to inspect the strip, but did not detect 'Tit-Willow'. Early on 9 January, after receiving the code words 'North Wind', meaning 'Proceed on reconnaissance to Truk', Yeowart and his crew took off. 'Staggered off' was how he described it, for the heavily laden Hudson barely made it through thick kunai grass on a bank at the end of the short strip.[6] Unknown to him, watching Diggers held their breath, for they had not told Yeowart of coconut palm stumps hidden in that grass. Their estimated time of arrival over Truk was 10.13 a.m., and although there were intermittent rainstorms on the way, after more than four hours flying they broke through a severe squall to see Truk below them, right on time. Maintaining their height of 13,000 feet and with their engines de-synchronised to sound like a Japanese bomber, they proceeded to photograph and take notes on all that appeared below them at the secret base: flying-boats on the water, 12 warships in harbour, recently constructed buildings, and float-planes flying around and landing. An ingeniously constructed airstrip that was cut through a hill was packed, 'wing to wing', with Japanese bombers. Halfway through their first run, anti-aircraft guns began firing at the Hudson and the rear-gunner, Frank Marriner, reported enemy aircraft climbing towards them. Yeowart pressed on with a second run, so as to complete all the tasks originally allotted to both Hudsons. As the 25-minute run came to an end, the ack-ack was getting the range and Marriner was firing on a chasing fighter. 'For God's sake keep her going,' he called to Yeowart, who dived into an electrical storm, evading three approaching float-planes but also creating even more scares.[7] Eventually he took the Hudson down to 500 feet and lost his pursuers before flying back to Kavieng. Yeowart landed long after expected and with barely enough fuel. The only damage was a wingtip that had been shot off. Most importantly, they had 280 films of photographs. After refuelling they flew on to Rabaul and landed between the bomb craters. Following Lerew's hunch that 'Tit-Willow' and its crew should move on quickly, Yeowart took off again at 2 a.m. The Rabaul strip looked to him like Luna Park, with green and white lights marking the safe passage between the red lights that signified bomb craters. While flying over Milne Bay, they heard that Rabaul was experiencing an air raid. A passenger on this flight was Peter Turnbull, whose name was destined to be forever linked with Milne Bay.

Once Yeowart landed at Townsville, the films were rushed to a darkroom for developing. To everyone's relief the cameras had worked and the films had survived to make excellent pictures. Strangely, neither Yeowart nor his crew were rewarded for the courage and skill with which they carried out their mission. This was especially sad for Yeowart's crewmen, for by July all three would be dead: Patrick McDonnell, a 23-year-old commercial pilot from Manly, Sydney, who wrote invaluable notes at Truk; Murray Ellis, a 24-year-old shop assistant from South Australia, who would die with McDonnell when their Hudson exploded in mid-air; and Frank Marriner, a Victorian salesman, killed the following month. Later, in 1944, when the US media published some of the Truk photographs, they were not credited to the Australians until Lerew and others complained.

RAAF Catalinas were ordered to launch a night raid against targets revealed in the photographs. Six Cats from Nos 11 and 20 Squadrons, but flown largely by No. 10 Squadron veterans, set out for Truk on 11 January. However, appalling weather forced them back. There were further hazardous reconnaissances on 14 January, by Yeowart, whose Hudson was hit by ice chunks from its propellers as it flew high over Nomoi in the Carolines, and Squadron Leader Dick Cohen, covering islands in the Gilberts. Both missions were fruitless. Had Yeowart been sent to Truk instead he would, assuming he survived, have reported two aircraft carriers among an invasion fleet gathering to hit Rabaul within a week.

The following day, Catalinas tried again to hit Truk. Three went from Lorengau, in the Admiralty Islands, and another three from Kavieng. In heavily overcast skies the Lorengau Catalinas failed to find the base. Of the three at Kavieng, one crashed on take-off, killing the entire crew. The second landed again to try to help the doomed crew. Only the third aircraft, under 23-year-old regular air force officer Ernest Beaumont, managed to reach Truk, where a temporary break in the cloud cover allowed him to make two runs and drop 16 bombs. Then the murk closed in and they flew home, unable to observe the results of their handiwork, which apparently included killing five and wounding more Japanese in three ships.

The Australian efforts were mere pinpricks in the side of a dragon, but they did not go unnoticed. When on 9 January Japanese float-planes approached the Japanese base at Kapingamarangi, an air-raid alert went up, and the Japanese airman in charge noted in his diary that recent bombings by Hudsons had stretched nerves on the island.

On 11 January, Lerew signalled Townsville and Melbourne, asking in vain for more labour, equipment, anti-aircraft guns, bombers and six 'modern' fighters, which unlike his 12 Wirraways could halt the unescorted Japanese bombers. Sixteen USAAF P-40 fighters passed through on 16 January on the way to the Netherlands East Indies: how useful they would have been had they stayed! Yet even they could not for long have delayed the inevitable.

Despite their parlous situation, the men's spirits were incredibly high. When enemy bombers approached, airmen of all ranks stayed above ground dangerously long, laughing and barracking them. Others stayed by the radio in the operations room, repeatedly ignoring Lerew's warnings to go to the slit trenches. Wing Commander Garing sent a signal from Townsville, reminding Lerew to do his best with what he had. More practically it told him to extract his force if the enemy invaded.

The day of 17 January brought an extraordinary confrontation. While Lerew was inspecting a new dispersal bay at Kavieng, a lone Mavis bombed the strip. Lerew quickly drove to his Wirraway and took off, without shirt, helmet, goggles, or the harness that normally pinned the pilot to the seat and his parachute to him. Once at 16,000 feet, Lerew's teeth were chattering with cold, but then his dreams came true as he looked down and saw the flying-boat *below* him at 8000 feet. He stalked the Mavis and about 100 kilometres from Kavieng made a head-on attack. He fired at close range and saw his bullets hit, but the enemy flew on. When he turned for another go, the Mavis was climbing away at a speed Lerew could not match. Long after the war he met the Japanese pilot, who praised Lerew's courage and acknowledged that his puny machine guns had damaged the Mavis and killed two crewmen.

During the afternoon of 20 January, Lieutenant Selby's men in the Rabaul anti-aircraft battery heard roaring engines, then spotted the fastest aircraft they had ever seen. They were fighter planes, the 'O' type they had only previously heard about. Their arrival heralded doom for 24 Squadron.

By 12.48 p.m., three groups of aircraft had been identified approaching Rabaul. Max Bridgman, an RAAF signals operator, was off duty cruising in a launch in the harbour when they came over. He lost count of the number somewhere around 100. In fact there were 109, carrier planes launched from the *Shokaku* and *Zuikaku.* Not only would these vastly outnumber the ten Wirraways spread equally between Lakunai and Vunakanau, but their crews, veterans of Pearl Harbor and China, were the best in the Pacific region. The 'fantastically uneven combat' that now unfolded was reminiscent of Polish cavalry trying to defend their country against German tanks.[8]

An airborne standing patrol of two Wirraways met the intruders. John Lowe and Clive Ashford took on six Zeros, until three got behind their Wirraway and tailed it, before sending it flaming into the sea. Lowe and Ashford died. George Herring and Bert Claire, in the other Wirraway, soon had three Zeros on their tail. The nimble fighters' manoeuvres astonished Claire, who sought vainly to nail them with his machine guns. He missed, whereas they riddled the Wirraway with holes. Shrapnel tore Claire's clothes and skin, and blood temporarily blinded him. Pilot and gunner both sustained leg wounds, and the Wirra's tail was shredded, but Herring somehow pulled it out of a spin and crash-landed at Lakunai. They leapt clear and watched strafing Zeros quickly destroy their kite. Flight Lieutenant Wilfred Brookes, commanding the Wirraways, drove up in his car to see if he could help. After inspecting the wreck, he turned round and 'two bedraggled forms covered in blood rose from the ground and proved to be Herring and Claire'.[9] Herring would later serve in Kittyhawks, while Claire returned to Rabaul the following year, in a Beaufighter.

For the moment, fighting impossible odds, the aircrew seemed to have no hope of escape. Yet they had no intention of fleeing. Their long-awaited chance to engage the enemy had finally come. Indeed, as soon as the Japanese aircraft had arrived, the Wirraway crews on the ground had climbed towards them. Bill Hewett used cloud as cover and looked to attack the rear of a flying-boat formation. Suddenly he and his observer, Jack Tyrell, looked up to see a Zero roaring towards them from just 500 feet overhead. Tyrell described what followed:

> [Hewett] pulled our nose up hard, firing at the same time. Our aircraft stalled out of the turn. The Zero was sitting waiting as we almost stopped in the stall. With a magnificent piece of shooting he raked our bus from end to end. Cannon fire whizzed pieces out of the wing. Chunks flew

> off the fuselage. A small calibre bullet struck the left hand gun through the cowling. It entered one of Hewett's knees and burst out his shin. Hewett blacked out temporarily. The aircraft went into a spin.

Tyrell was standing at the rear gun. He should have been strapped in, but this Wirraway lacked the equipment. His own rotating machine gun struck him in the face and he was hurled from the cockpit. Usually they flew without parachutes too, but today Tyrell had worn one. Another miracle occurred when his parachute mysteriously opened, the ripcord having apparently caught on the cockpit as Tyrell was thrown out. He could see the Zero chasing Hewett's spinning aircraft. Hewett regained control, found a cloud and eventually landed the severely damaged Wirraway. After Tyrell had made a long bushwalk, in which he had to convince Australian troops that he was not a 'Japanese paratrooper', the two crewmen were joyously reunited.[10]

A Japanese bullet killed Charles Bromley, piloting another Wirraway, and when he crashed into the sea his observer, Richard Walsh, died too. Bob Blackman and Stanley Woodcroft also 'went in' when their Wirraway was destroyed. Selby wrote poetically of the death of one unidentified Wirraway:

> There was a puff of white smoke from the cannon of a Zero, a red flash as the shell found its mark on one of our planes, and before the boom of the explosion floated down to us a Wirraway was screeching earthwards, angry red flames and black smoke pouring from it.

To this vivid but grim description he added the epitaph: 'Within a few minutes there was not an Australian plane in the sky.'[11] The battle had lasted just seven minutes. Bruce Anderson and Col Butterworth had crashed on take-off and been injured. Ron Little, who initially tried vainly to fly in formation with other Wirraways, had cloud-hopped, evading up to 13 Zeros and landing his heavily damaged plane after the attackers left. Lerew counted five Wirraways destroyed: three shot down, one destroyed on take-off and another destroyed by strafing. Two others that had crash-landed were seriously damaged. More worryingly, six aircrew had been killed and five wounded. They had obtained no confirmed kills, though Japanese records suggest that Selby's anti-aircraft gunners scored a few successes. The anti-aircraft boys had been, Selby thought, inspired by the Wirraway pilots' 'cold-blooded heroism' in the face of certain death. In their report on the day's action, the Japanese meanly reported a supposed lack of spirit in their enemies.[12]

In the words of an official Australian report, on 20 January No. 24 Squadron was 'wiped out for all practical purposes'.[13] Lerew now commanded just two Wirraways and one Hudson. He signalled to headquarters his intention to send the Hudson with casualties to Port Moresby. He told them too that the Wirraways were useless for defence and asked again, 'Will you now please send some fighters?' The answer, which at last showed a spark of sympathy, was: 'Regret inability to supply fighters. If we had them you would get them.'[14] By late afternoon the next day, the invasion fleet was approaching. Lerew was ordered to send 'all available aircraft' against the fleet, but he had just one Hudson suitable for the job. One hundred locals helped pull it out of the trees and through a quagmire, but though it became airborne, night fell before the crew could find their target.

RAAF Headquarters sent a message that all aircrew should be evacuated from Rabaul, though it may never have arrived. Lerew said he never received the signal, but the two Wirraways left that night for Lae. Lerew sent a message to headquarters implying that it was time for the RAAF men to get out, but oddly, given the earlier message to do just that, he received a reply reminding him that Rabaul had not yet fallen and ordering him to keep the aerodrome open.

On the morning of 21 January, Lerew attended the burial of two of his aircrew at the Rabaul cemetery. Chaplain John May, of 2/22nd Battalion, officiated. When he, Lerew and the 24 Squadron Intelligence Officer, Geoff Lempriere, gathered afterwards in Lerew's headquarters, all felt bitter about the failure of Australian authorities to provide better support. May was struck by Lerew's 'calm and yet forceful manner', his concern for the men under his command and his determination to get them out safely. He later recalled someone mentioning gladiators in the Roman arena. Lerew, using his rusty schoolboy Latin, and with assistance from May, decided to send as a signal to Northern Area Headquarters the simple phrase *Morituri vos salutamus*: 'We who are about to die salute you.' Initially they sent a misspelling, 'Moriturb', but then quickly corrected it in a second signal.[15] The comment has entered RAAF folklore. Lerew and most of his men would not die in Rabaul, but the soldiers there would be far less fortunate. Still, Lerew's comment epitomised a justifiable spirit—of cynicism, self-pity and resigned duty—among all Australians on New Britain at the time.

In its response Headquarters ordered Lerew to Port Moresby to take over a new Hudson squadron. He had no intention of leaving his current squadron behind. He had designated the one available Hudson to take out the wounded first and that night it took off, fully loaded, from Vunakanau, guided by a few barely adequate lights. Last aboard was Corporal Allan Brasch, a fitter told to leave the hospital at the last minute; had he stayed, he would not have survived, as all males in the hospital were butchered after the Japanese arrived.

On 22 January, as the Japanese armada approached Rabaul, Lerew assembled his men and, with the garrison commander's agreement, announced that they were to evacuate Rabaul while the Army fought it out as best they could. In a convoy of trucks and cars, the airmen headed along the south coast. Tyrell described Lerew as 'tireless', and 'an inspiration to all of us'.[16] They were joined by another Australian, Leigh Vial, Assistant District Officer at Rabaul, whose local knowledge proved valuable and who would later render further great service to the RAAF. The party had to abandon their trucks at the Warangoi River. Over a few nights, RAAF flying-boats rescued some 120 airmen. Signals operator Sergeant Fred Higgs contributed vitally to these rescues by going alone to Wide Bay, where he was able to use a teleradio set in an abandoned homestead to call Moresby. On being ordered to escape, he and two other airmen appropriated a five-metre boat and, using just a school atlas and a compass taken from a Wirraway, sailed through enemy air attacks and other dangers to reach Cairns 21 days later. Lempriere tried to escape in a launch, but was captured. Two other squadron members died as prisoners: Warrant Officer James Kelly perished in July 1942 when an American submarine sank the *Montevideo Maru*, in which he was being transported, while Corporal Reginald Smalpage died in captivity after volunteering at the Warangoi River to return to Rabaul to retrieve a box of secret documents left behind.

On 23 January the Japanese invasion force landed and, after a short fight, took Rabaul. They then began to turn it and the rest of New

Britain into a formidable, unsinkable aircraft carrier. It was a fine base for protecting Truk and for snooping on Allied activities north-east of Australia. Recapturing Rabaul would be the primary Allied objective in the South-West Pacific for the next two years.

The burden of the Catalinas

Rescuing most of 24 Squadron was one of many tasks that 11 Squadron's Catalinas fulfilled in early 1942. Their heavy reconnaissance burden included a patrol between Samarai Island and Lae on 21 January. Eight Australians crewed the aircraft under the command of American Lieutenant Hutchinson. Port Moresby was about to send him a message that enemy fighters were over Salamaua, when he sent them one: 'Being attacked by five fighters.' Flying at about 1000 feet, they saw 12 Japanese Zeros approaching from the opposite direction. Hutchinson climbed towards cloud, 6000 feet higher, and had made it to 5000 feet when the fighters came behind in formation. Tom Rowe, a 22-year-old engineering student who seemed 'no more than a boy', came down to the waist gun blister to direct the gunners, Tom Keen and John Craigie.[17] Keen described what followed:

> . . . while the fighters were still some distance astern I saw white smoke come out the front of one of them. The blister glass alongside me flew to pieces. As he was out of range I held my fire. Another white flash followed by a crash on the hull. He came into my range and I gave him a burst. He fired at the same time and a row of holes appeared alongside me. He faltered in his flight so I gave him a prolonged burst. He faltered again and then dived. Pilot Officer Rowe said 'You've got him.' While I was watching him dive I heard a crash beside my head and there was another one attacking.

Craigie's gun was firing too. Keen's senses were assaulted by alarming signs: he smelt fire, saw smoke in the cabin, heard Craigie screaming and saw him clutching his shoulders. Then enemy aircraft seemed to be coming from all directions. The fabric above Rowe disappeared in flames. Hutchinson now sent Moresby the laconic message, 'On fire'. Flames were licking at Keen's back and his gunsights were shot away. The Cat was trying to climb, but losing altitude. Keen, aware that the bomb-load was still on board and could blow up, decided to get out. As he turned to leave, he saw Craigie 'just sitting in his seat holding his gun. He was staring out astern. He was dead.'[18]

Hampered by smoke and flame, Keen put on his harness and parachute and jumped. In the slipstream his damaged harness split his mouth. His parachute pack threatened to fly off, but he managed after a struggle to pull the ripcord. He looked up to see a fighter diving towards him. With bullets whipping past his leg, Keen shammed dead. The rest of his crew could no longer sham. He heard a long crash, followed by an explosion, which threw him higher. The aircraft was blazing on a ridge in the distance, a funeral pyre of his mates. He landed in trees, and after freeing himself, found some locals who guided him to safety. Keen had shot down a Zero, from the aircraft carrier *Kaga,* which had sent out its aircraft to help crush potential opposition to the landings at Rabaul. His was the first Catalina shot down in the Pacific area.

A 20 Squadron Catalina spotted the invasion fleet west of Kavieng and sent a warning to Rabaul. Second pilot Paul Metzler glimpsed enemy aircraft taking off from a carrier in the fleet. Soon afterwards four Zeros burst from cloud and onto their tail. The captain, Bob Thompson, sought cover in the clouds while Metzler coordinated the guns firing at the circling vultures. All four gunners were hit in the uneven exchanges, one fatally. To Metzler, cannon shells rushing past the cockpit looked like 'blurred oranges', while bullets striking the armour plate behind him sounded like gravel hitting a window pane.[19] They also hit the non-self-sealing fuel tanks, and the Catalina became a ball of red and black flame. It hit the water at high speed and bounced along. All who could got out, and watched it sink, hissing as the burning metal met its watery end. Three crewmen died; the rest were captured by one of the cruisers they had spotted.

A Catalina squadron member told his diary that the fall of Rabaul 'has left us all with a horrible feeling of the inadequacy of our fighting strength'.[20] The Catalinas were now Australia's only 'strike force' capable of reaching that base. Bad weather and darkness had thwarted five Catalinas sent to intercept the invasion fleet, but five did bomb the ships in Simpson Harbour on 24 January. It was the first of many such missions. By 30 January they had made four 'bashes' on Rabaul, where the flak was already becoming heavier and more accurate. The 'Cat-boat' was not difficult for enemy searchlights to detect. Little wonder that Dick Cohen, CO of 11 Squadron, considered this period the 'most uncomfortable' of his life.[21] It did not help the Cat pilots' sense of security that the armour plating behind their seats was removed in the quest to reduce weight so that bomb-loads could be maximised.

On returning to Port Moresby from Rabaul, Lerew took temporary command of a new Hudson squadron, soon to be No. 32, formed from flights transferred from three existing squadrons. Its first four pilots were all fine aviators: Bob Yeowart and Bob Green, and two pre-war regular officers, Bill Pedrina and John Hampshire. Yeowart took his Hudson on one of the new squadron's first sorties, a reconnaissance to Rabaul on 23 January. They counted the ships before six Zeros attacked; using clouds for cover, he returned safely to Salamaua. Yeowart's last job, before he was evacuated with malaria, came on 2 February. For more than six daylight hours he provided 'fighter escort' to an Empire flying-boat in which Dick Cohen evacuated government officials and planters on many stops between Buna and Samarai. Brave as he was, Yeowart was later horrified to contemplate what might have happened had he encountered Zeros.

In February 1942, there were still many more occasions on which Hudsons would have to take on Japan's great fighter.

7 'Thrilling but terrifying': The Netherlands East Indies

No. 2 Squadron Hudsons based at Penfui, Timor, were already airborne on 8 December when their crews were informed that Australia was at war with Japan. They soon achieved a coup, finding and attacking a Japanese radio ship headed for Dili. The Hudsons set the vessel alight and watched its crew abandon ship.

This first Australian attack on enemy shipping in the Netherlands East Indies was followed on 10 December by a raid on an enemy land target. No. 13 Squadron Hudsons based at Laha, Ambon, were sent to attack Tobi Island in the Halmaheras. Wing Commander Joshua McDonald, a regular air force officer who had recently taken over the squadron, briefed the six crews beforehand. When he said he would lead off and then slow down to 110 knots (204 kilometres per hour) to let the others catch him, Flight Lieutenant Archie Dunne spoke up. As a former instructor who knew how touchy Hudsons could be, Dunne urged McDonald to flash his lights and maintain a higher speed instead.

When the aircraft left, Dunne took off second. Though flying as slowly as he dared with a heavy load, Dunne was soon passing his squadron leader's painfully slow Hudson. Suddenly McDonald's aircraft stalled and spun down towards certain destruction. Led by Dunne, the Hudsons flew on. When one pilot broke radio silence to ask what was happening,

Dunne replied laconically, 'C.O.'s gone in. I'm taking over.' Shaken but determined, the crews reached their distant target, where, unopposed, they attacked enemy buildings. One pilot's exclamation, 'That will fix them!', was heard by radio operators at the Area Combined Headquarters at Halong, Ambon.[1]

Squadron Leader John Ryland succeeded McDonald as 13 Squadron's commander. When war broke out, Ryland had been a captain at the recently formed Ansett Airways. Soon his courage and leadership would earn him the DFC.

Laha and Namlea

On Ambon, as at Rabaul, Australian commanders worried about the inadequacy of their forces. The two main airstrips were Laha, which even with just ten Hudsons was crowded, and Namlea, on Buru Island west of Ambon. The RAAF at Laha asked for fighter aircraft, as the two Dutch Buffalos available offered 'utterly inadequate' defence. Even Wirraways would do, but the reply was 'No fighters available'.[2] Sergeant Albert Fletcher wrote that the Hudsons were being used as 'stand by fighters, reco. planes, fighter escorts for Catalinas, bombers in fact for everything bar their original purpose—Passenger planes.'[3]

After a Mavis flying-boat raided Babo in Dutch New Guinea on 30 December, Laha dispatched three Hudsons there as 'fighters' to intercept it. During the fruitless search, Bernnie Hack, a WAG in John Turnbull's Hudson, noticed an unusual sound in the motors. On leaving his turret and going forward he discovered that the starboard motor had cut out and the pilot was about to release their bomb-load. Back at his turret, Hack heard a 'terrific explosion'. He thought it was the bombs detonating, but then saw 'a huge sheet of flame', which came down the Hudson's side and extended three plane lengths behind it, setting the tail alight. All the windows and the emergency exit door were blown out. More frighteningly still, the port motor had blown up under the strain. Hack started moving towards a parachute, but then realised they were only 300 feet up. He ducked to avoid the intense heat, but then the aircraft nosed up and threw him on his back. The next thing he remembered was regaining consciousness, underwater. He was wearing a Mae West, and on surfacing was surrounded by blazing petrol. He soon realised something was wrong with one of his legs—it was badly broken—and he used his good leg to support it. A Catalina appeared overhead and rescued him, still conscious but terribly burnt.[4] His three crewmates were dead. Hack would spend much time in Ambon and Darwin hospitals, both during Japanese bombing raids.

On 7 January, in bright moonlight, seven Mavis flying-boats unexpectedly bombed and strafed Laha and Namlea. Fletcher was at Laha when, soon after 3 a.m., his unit experienced this first raid:

> I was awakened by the 'crumping' of bombs and the crackle of machine gun and cannon fire. It was a curious feeling, I could see flashes of red through an open door and realised at once the full significance of it all, it was on, the game had really started. I got hurriedly dressed, expecting at any moment that blinding flash that I somehow had always associated with death from a bomb-burst.[5]

Three locals were killed and two Hudsons damaged, but the Australians suffered no fatalities. Nevertheless, the 13 Squadron Operations Record Book acknowledges that this raid had 'an adverse effect on morale of the R.A.A.F. personnel', who from then on virtually evacuated their camp every night. Without the protection of their malaria nets, many fell sick.[6]

Wireless operator Jim Cunneen, a cobber of fellow operator Fletcher, wrote to his father from Laha on 10 January. He gloomily predicted that the Japanese would take the island soon and easily. He believed that while the aircrew would have a sporting chance of being evacuated, the ground staff and Army had 'not even a fighting chance'. He feared the fall of Ambon would represent a menace to Australia, which the Japanese might come to dominate. 'We can only hope', he felt, 'for some sort of comeback on the part of America and perhaps aid from Britain who seem to have deserted us.'[7]

That same day, an enemy convoy was discovered heading for the northern Celebes, so before dawn on 11 January all available Hudsons were sent to oppose it. Dutch and American Catalinas were unable to penetrate the enemy fighter cover, but the Hudsons were fast enough to get through and attack. When they arrived at daybreak, 'great columns of smoke from fires on Dutch ships and from the town made a thrilling but terrifying sight'.[8] It was cloudy and dark, but gunflashes from the warships marked them out among the 30 vessels. Ron Cornfoot headed his Hudson for a large transport, soon surrounded by warships and their spitting anti-aircraft guns. Arch Dunne, piloting another Hudson, considered the flak so thick that a man could almost walk across it. Despite the flak and the attentions of four float-planes, the Hudsons loosed their bombs before heading home. Their three hits included one on the cruiser. Subsequent assaults hit the cruiser again and strafed enemy troops.

Fletcher was in one of five 13 Squadron Hudsons on this mission. His aircraft, piloted by Flight Lieutenant Geoff Newstead, had just dropped its bombs when their Hudson 'suddenly shook as a fighter shot past leaving us with 3 holes in the wing and one in the tail to tell of its passage'.[9] All five Hudsons returned safely.

Bombing-up the Hudsons in the Netherlands East Indies was difficult. With no bomb hoists, four men had to manhandle 500 pounds (227 kilograms) of bombs into place. Sometimes after landing, the crews requested a quick change of bomb type. The already loaded bombs could not be simply dropped onto the ground, so someone in the bomb-aimer's compartment had to release the bomb onto the neck of someone underneath, and other ground crew would then lower it to earth.

Later on 11 January, float-planes attacked four Hudsons that were bombing a transport. No. 2 Squadron pilots Parker Hodge and Peter Gorrie sent two down in flames, and put a third into a spin. These sorties each comprised more than six hours flying time, and many crews flew twice that day.

Fletcher called the next day, 12 January, 'black and fateful'. The Hudson's limitations against fighters were painfully exposed when the Australians resumed operations at Menado, in the Celebes. Five Hudsons met eight opponents. Three were float-planes, but the remainder were a type not yet encountered in the area: Zeros. Gorrie's Hudson was seen to catch fire and spin into the sea. Hodge, the previous day's other hero, was also shot down, as were the Hudsons of Geoff Sattler and Arthur Barton. Fletcher wrote in his diary of the day's losses: 'All gone. It really does seem fantastic and unbelievable.'[10] Among the dead was Reg Hunter, Fletcher's cobber with whom he had worked, drunk and played for two years. Only Rob Cuming's Hudson returned. Among the four lost crews, just one man, Ted Howard, survived. He was captured.

The Celebes and Tarakan fell to the Japanese, and Area Combined

Headquarters decided on 12 January to cease air attacks on strongly held targets and preserve their strength for the enemy assaults expected on their own bases. It calculated that if enemy carrier-borne aircraft attacked, its forces would be destroyed in one day. It requested P-40s and Wirraways in as large a number as possible. Predictably, the reply was negative.

Sir Charles Burnett, the CAS, sent a personal message to Wing Commander Dallas Scott, the senior RAAF officer at Area Combined Headquarters, congratulating his men on the good work done, but reinforcing the need to stand by the Dutch and hold Ambon. Scott replied that the Australians would follow General Wavell's orders in a way that would 'not derogate from their reputation'.[11] Scott's men sympathised with his predicament of having to send them on suicide missions without being able to lead them himself. A former Melbourne Grammar school captain, junior Victorian boxing champion and a commercial pilot who had flown Lockheed 14s, the predecessor of the Hudson, 28-year-old Scott was undoubtedly keen to fly.

There was in Australia some sympathy for his position. So intense was the pressure on Northern Area Headquarters in Australia, concerned primarily at the time with Rabaul and Ambon, that from 15 January its responsibilities were divided between new commands: North-Eastern Area, based at Townsville, and North-Western Area, with headquarters at Darwin. On 15 January, North-Eastern Area asked RAAF Headquarters to consider withdrawing the Ambon Hudsons, because their retention was crucial, only to be told that the forces at Ambon were under Wavell's operational control. Their plea seemed all the more justified when that same day a heavy air raid struck Laha, now well within Japanese range and lacking camouflage. A two-hour raid rendered the runway unserviceable for 24 hours and destroyed three aircraft. In one raid on Laha, bomb splinters caught Pilot Officer Alan Morley in the backside. After this he was physically discomforted whenever he sat down, but also received ribbing along the lines of 'Did it have BHP on it?'—a reference to the pre-war export of pig-iron to Japan.

Two crews were selected to secure photographs of Japanese aerodromes at Menado on 19 January. Fletcher flew with Flying Officer Henry Birley, alongside an aircraft piloted by 23-year-old regular air force officer Maurice Willing. Willing's crew included Jim Cunneen, replacing another member of the crew who had just come down with malaria. After reaching Menado and taking photos, Fletcher's crew spotted a Zero 'weaving and climbing about 1000 ft below us'. They warned Willing over the radio and, while darting for a nearby cloud, saw him do the same. Eventually Birley's aircraft got home, and the crew sat down and waited for their companion 'ship'. Fletcher later wrote in his diary:

> We waited long and with slowly sinking feelings. There is something undiscribeable [sic] in watching hour after hour in the direction which a plane must come if come it does and then to realise that that particular plane will never fly that way again.[12]

After barely surviving a patrol the previous day, Willing had told armourer Les Dalkin 'We have to go tomorrow, too.' Dalkin felt that Willing believed he would not survive the mission.[13] Sadly, his premonition proved correct.

When Cuming and his crew arrived on Timor after a flight from Namlea for supplies and reinforcements on 20 January, their exhausted and emaciated condition shocked their compatriots. Sympathy turned to apprehension as they watched Cuming's overloaded Hudson struggle to take off on the return trip. It accelerated rapidly and its tail lifted from the ground, only to fall back suddenly. With engines screaming, the Hudson then lifted off, pitched up steeply almost to the vertical—and stalled. It landed nose-first, exploding in a ball of flame and ammunition. Eleven airmen, including Cuming, were killed.

On 22 January, Fletcher had just moved into a Hudson gun turret during convoy duty when a Mavis flew overhead. The Hudson gave chase, jettisoning its bombs to speed it along. The captain, Les Ingram, manoeuvred into position to dive on the Mavis, firing his forward guns, and when he broke away Fletcher had a chance to fire. Fletcher wrote: 'It really was great fun with the knowledge that our fire was being returned giving us that extra thrill that made it all worthwhile.' Eventually Ingram had to leave, for his ammunition ran out. On landing, Fletcher saw the 'fun' differently. A bullet had pierced the wing just 20 centimetres from the engine: 'knowing our Hudson we knew what a bullet in the engine meant'. They had, he felt, been 'within eight inches of death'.[14]

Dallas Scott and John Ryland were permitted to visit General George Brett, Deputy Commander of ABDA, at Bandung. They stated that if fighters and anti-aircraft guns could not be sent to Laha and Namlea, all but small parties able to refuel and rearm aircraft should be withdrawn to Darwin. Brett, a compassionate, gentlemanly and dynamic leader, agreed to a withdrawal, and on 24 January ABDA ordered that only enough aircraft to maintain the necessary reconnaissance patrols need remain. Scott was told that if Laha and Namlea became untenable, he could use his discretion to order reconnaissance to operate instead from Timor or Darwin.

By 25 January the two squadrons had lost 13 Hudsons. That day Arch Dunne arrived at Babo to evacuate an RAAF detachment. With Dutch permission, they destroyed what they estimated as millions of pounds' worth of equipment. Dunne, knowing that carrying 15 people and special tools to Darwin would push his Hudson to its limits, demanded five hours' fuel for the four-hour trip. He just cleared the trees at the edge of the short strip, but then found that he could not climb. For 20 minutes he fought to keep the sagging plane aloft, and then began slowly to raise it. Suspecting that a fuel tank was leaking, he switched to it to drain it, which took just five minutes. He now had four hours' fuel for the four-hour trip, with nothing for emergencies such as the forecast bad weather front. Now at altitude, the passengers were very cold, as they had climbed aboard in their flimsy tropical clothing. Dunne nursed the aircraft to Darwin, then landed as quickly as possible. One engine stopped as he was taxiing. Ground staff found just three gallons of fuel remaining: enough for five minutes' more flying. Had the crew at Babo put in the extra 70 gallons the aircraft was capable of taking, they may never have cleared the trees. It was a brilliant achievement by a superb pilot.

On 26 January, damaging air raids struck Laha and Namlea. The attackers were Zeros, and as they approached, Dunne—now back at Namlea—and fellow pilot Bob Law-Smith broke off a game of chess. When one of Dunne's crewmen called, 'Are you going to take off?', he replied, 'Yes, into the scrub.'[15] The exuberant Japanese fighters flew over virtually unopposed. One pilot had the temerity to lower his wheels and briefly touch down on the runway to show his contempt.

That day ABDA command asked Darwin to send Empire flying-boats to evacuate personnel from the two bases. One was sent. It was so full that the pilot, John Hampshire, was initially unable to take off. Four unknown 'A and SD' RAAF officers manfully volunteered to stay behind and try to take a later flight.

The same day, a Hudson crew spotted 22 Japanese ships headed towards Ambon. The Hudsons not shadowing the armada were stripped down to evacuate as many personnel as possible. In one aircraft, 23 men stood for the four and a half hour journey in conditions so cramped that on reaching Darwin some could not lift their arms. Law-Smith's Hudson was bullet-riddled from the 26 January raid and its instrument panel and compass were useless. Nevertheless, he and his crew were determined to get it to Darwin. They succeeded, partly by using a file tang as a fuel transfer valve, and won for their aircraft the nickname 'The Flying Colander'. John Trim, who had been Mentioned in Despatches after courageously manning a Lewis gun on Laha airstrip, arrived 'complete with one pair of shorts'.[16] Fletcher had also left behind all his possessions when he landed at Darwin at 1 a.m. on 30 January. But as he highlighted in his diary, he was 'Once more on Aussie soil.'[17]

By 30 January, Scott's last two Hudsons were due to leave for Darwin. Twenty-eight officers and men were waiting to board when it was discovered that a bullet had damaged one aircraft's main fuel line. Scott ordered 17 airmen aboard the undamaged plane and, after it took off, went to work with the remainder on fixing the other aircraft. Their equipment proved inadequate, so Scott sent a radio message asking Hampshire to evacuate them in the Empire flying-boat. However, Hampshire was halfway to Darwin with the last staff from Halong and had insufficient fuel to turn round and then back. It had been arranged that any parties left behind should head for northern Ambon, then travel by boat to Geser Island, to the east. Hampshire flew there on 12 and 15 February, but to no avail: a patrol boat had captured Scott's party. He and his brave group were executed between 6 and 20 February, amidst frenzied Japanese activity that entailed the killing of more than 300 defenceless prisoners. Among them was Corporal Eric Gaskin, an armourer said to have given up a place in the last Hudson to a younger man, declaring his own life 'a bit of a mess anyway'.[18] The dead were buried in unmarked graves.

★ ★ ★

The group at Namlea, under Squadron Leader 'Tich' McFarlane, fared better. When he asked for volunteers to remain behind to complete demolitions, there was an instant unanimous raising of hands. He selected 60 to travel on the three available Hudsons. The eight men who remained behind followed McFarlane on a dangerous, confidence-sapping 250-kilometre trek across Buru island, where Hampshire's flying-boat rescued them on a lucky Friday 13 February.

Douglas Gillison, the official RAAF historian, asserted that the squadrons at Ambon and Namlea had provided 'much valuable information' through reconnaissance, and damaged the enemy considerably in relation to the size of their force. However, as he also acknowledged, they had no chance of fulfilling their main role of blocking the enemy advance. As Ron Cornfoot reflected, the great efforts of the two squadrons had probably not delayed the Japanese advance for more than 'moments', while costing a substantial number of aircraft (he says 70 per cent) and, even more importantly, their irreplaceable captains and crews.[19]

How did the men cope with the knowledge that death was so close to them every time they flew a mission and as Japanese land and naval forces approached? We have read of Cunneen's despair. Yet as Fletcher also stated, in the weeks after that fateful 12 January, work and continuous flying gave them little time to reflect. Telling also are Fletcher's comments on the mission that cost the lives of Maurice Willing and his crew. He says that in preparing for this mission, 'we looked upon this as a sort of suicide job, *but also looked forward to it with some sort of a thrill*'.[20] That youthful, adventurous spirit, as well as the general air of unreality and the frantic pace of events, all combined to prevent the RAAF men going mad.

Timor under attack

On Australia Day 1942, Japanese aircraft first raided the airfield at Penfui. The Hudsons had already been moved to an emergency landing ground near Mina River, but the raiders destroyed several other aircraft, and intercepted and shot down an RAAF Dakota (C-47) heading for Penfui. The Dakota's four crewmen spent 30 hours in the water, at times fighting off sharks, before reaching land and local assistance.

USS *Peary*, which had narrowly survived an accidental Australian bombing in December, brought fuel supplies to the Australians at Mina River, where through tremendous effort over two weeks, the fuel was carried to the airstrip. Before that, six Zeros had found the strip and destroyed a Hudson. Zeros also shot down a Qantas Empire flying-boat, *Corio*, which had been taking mail, supplies, servicemen and evacuees to and from Singapore. Only five of 18 on board survived, by swimming eight kilometres to shore.

By mid-February, both 2 and 13 Squadrons were operating from Darwin, with some personnel remaining at Penfui to enable the squadrons' reconnaissance aircraft to land there at dusk or depart at dawn. The free-ranging Japanese repeatedly bombed Penfui, and especially nearby Koepang. The crew of Geoffrey Mitchell's Hudson were unlucky when lightning struck them during a storm at Penfui, killing all aboard.

With invasion imminent, on 18 February Wing Commander Frank Headlam was ordered to evacuate all RAAF personnel at Penfui, except small parties necessary for maintenance and signals. All personnel volunteered to remain behind, but 23 were chosen. At dusk, Squadron Leader John Ryland arrived with six Hudsons to evacuate the remainder to Darwin, which they reached on the fateful morning of 19 February. The men who stayed behind undertook demolitions and mining and, after the Japanese landed and dropped paratroops on 20 February, headed into the hills. Various attempts to supply and rescue them failed until, after great hardships in which four men died, an American submarine rescued them in mid-April.

Sumatra—P.1 and P.2

We saw that the RAAF Hudsons and Buffalos that had fought in Malaya and Singapore moved to Sumatra late in January 1942. They were part of a force of ten squadrons based at airfields called P.1, 13 kilometres north of Palembang, and P.2, a huge natural clearing 65 kilometres south-west of that town. On both bases communications, living quarters, transport and anti-aircraft defence were inadequate, yet as airstrips they were significant enemy targets. Moreover, they were located near one of Japan's main strategic goals, for Palembang held over half the Netherlands East Indies' oil reserves. In the first week of February, as air force units withdrew from Singapore, accommodation intended for 250 men at P.2 had to house 1500, with 2500 more in Palembang town. Among these new arrivals was No. 21 Squadron. Initial plans to disband the unit sparked great resentment and were thwarted only by the intercession of Australian Group

Captain McCauley, Station Commander at P.2. The squadron performed various aerodrome duties in the Indies before embarking for Fremantle in mid-February.

McCauley had eight bomber squadrons at P.2, some only nominal. There were some new British Hudsons for the two RAAF squadrons (Nos 1 and 8) and No. 62 Squadron RAF. Two RAF Blenheim squadrons, Nos 84 and 211, arrived from the Middle East, with numerous Australian aircrew. Many of the latter were inexperienced, but there were also veterans, like Sergeant George Sayer, who had served in Hurricanes and Blenheims in the Western Desert, Abyssinia, the UK and Russia. Forty-eight Hurricanes flew off the British aircraft carrier *Indomitable* to join the two fighter squadrons based at P.2. That base's natural cover prevented the Japanese locating it during the forthcoming operations, whereas P.1 came under enemy air attack from 23 January.

No. 1 Squadron sent five Hudsons against a Japanese base in northern Malaya on 31 January. A round flight of more than 2000 kilometres, including violent storms and stops for refuelling, brought the satisfaction of hitting the target, but flying such missions was stressful. Peter Gibbes recalled of Sumatra that before every mission he and his fellow pilots were anxious, pallid, at times even shaking, liable to vomit and completely free of bravado. On the other hand, 'Curly' Davis was struck by the continued good humour and banter among his squadron, especially the ground crew. On this mission Adam 'Curly' Brydon's crew got some laughs out of throwing beer bottles at the enemy. These bottles screamed through the air thanks to razor blades fitted in their necks.

Gibbes flew one extraordinary reconnaissance mission. Following reports that an invasion fleet had departed Saigon for Sumatra and was sheltering in the Anambas Islands, on 6 February Gibbes flew from P.2 through clear skies towards the enemy. Seven hundred kilometres into the flight, the crew spotted thick cloud around their island destination. Ten enemy fighters climbed menacingly towards them, but Gibbes was cool enough to ensure that before he headed for the clouds his second pilot, Tony Jay, sketched the harbour and nine ships now visible below. Gibbes evaded the Zeros, but had used up so much fuel that he could not reach Palembang. He headed instead for Singapore, where he reported personally to Air Vice-Marshal Pulford, who invited his crew to lunch.

Two other No. 1 Squadron pilots, Jim Emerton and John Lockwood, had made the hazardous trip to Singapore the day before, with orders to bring Pulford and his senior staff officers back to Sumatra. Pulford declined to go then, as he did when Colin Verco and Ken Smith made a similar mercy mission on 10 February. Pulford would reluctantly leave Singapore, by boat on 13 February, only to die of starvation and illness on an uninhabited island.

By early February there were on Sumatra just 55 serviceable combat aircraft, all doing their utmost to fly reconnaissance missions or to attack enemy bases, even in monsoonal storms. After Gibbes' long reconnaissance, the Blenheims' attention switched to the Sumatra-bound armada. They flew out on the night of 11/12 February, while the Hudsons were to bombard the Japanese airfield at Kluang. Bad weather hampered the Blenheims, as did several crashes on take-off. After one had burst into flames on hitting trees, a second, captained by Australian pilot Bevan West, also crash-landed. Sergeant Ray Wheatley of No. 8 Squadron had been preparing a Hudson for take-off and saw West's crash. A man whose courage had been apparent in Singapore, Wheatley now rushed to the wrecked Blenheim and, forcing his way into the cockpit, unstrapped the injured West before helping the gunner and observer to safety. Within minutes the bombs in the first crashed Blenheim exploded and destroyed both aircraft. Wheatley received the George Medal for his 'courage and leadership without thought of self'. The Hudsons sent out that night all reached and hit the target area in Malaya. Johnny Lockwood was well on the way home when the crew discovered that three bombs were still 'hung up' in the bomb bay. Lockwood turned back and, with dawn breaking, dropped the three bombs onto an enemy hangar.

After General Wavell ordered an aerial and naval assault on the enemy fleet on 13 February, Commonwealth aircraft found more than 30 ships. During the search, two Blenheims crashed in a storm, one losing an Australian crewman and the other its all-Australian crew. Other Blenheims and RAAF Hudsons attacked early on 14 February. The Hudson squadrons were sent to sink enemy vessels approaching the mouth of Sumatra's Musi River. Nos 8 and then 1 Squadrons used cloud cover to evade enemy fighters and reach the target. No. 8 got through, but their bombs missed. As No. 1 attacked the convoy, Zeros arrived and interfered violently. The ships threw up heavy flak too. Jim Douglas, one of the first pilots to spot the invaders in December, was making a second attack on a transport when his Hudson caught fire and crashed in the sea. One man baled out, only to land in the burning wreckage that signalled the deaths of the entire crew. 'Curly' Davis, who admired Douglas' courage, clear-thinking and inspiring leadership, recommended the 25-year-old for a Victoria Cross, but the recommendation was rejected. Jack O'Brien believed his Hudson scored three hits on a Japanese transport, which was seen to be burning and listing. Three other Hudson pilots claimed hits, including Brydon, whose kite was so severely damaged by flak that he had to crash-land at P.2, where it was likened to a sieve and declared unserviceable.

Even the veteran 'Ossie' Diamond was shaken, first by heavy anti-aircraft shells whizzing past as he flew at low level, and then by bullets two chasing Zeros shot through his aircraft. At one point, after standing out of the seat to manoeuvre near the water, he sat back to find the seat hot from bullets passing through it. With smoke trailing from one engine, the situation looked hopeless until the Zeros pulled away. Part of the tailplane had also been shot off, but Diamond managed to fly low all the way to P.1 (P.2. was too distant) and make a superb landing. His crew's adventure was not over, though, for they had not realised that Japanese paratroops had that morning descended around P.1. Diamond and his crew were told this as they rushed across the strip to another Hudson. Diamond mustered all the power he could in the aircraft but, on nearing the end of the runway, realised it would not take off: its propellers were damaged. He pulled up, got out and set the aircraft alight with a shot from a flare pistol. Then he realised that shots were coming at him. Taking weapons from the aircraft, the crew sought to fight back, but were soon pinned down by enemy machine guns. They took to the long grass and after a ten-hour trek featuring nearby explosions, found their way to Palembang and P.2.

Two Australians, Jack Woodward and 'Clicker' Clark, were in one of three Blenheims sent to strike the invasion force. Woodward believed that their bombs inflicted 'a hell of a lot of damage', while they in turn were flying too low to be hit by the heavy flak. When two fighters got on their tail, Clark fired from close range into a float-plane. They saw it spinning out of control towards the waves, but before it crashed another fighter was firing hard at them. Clark fired a long burst in return, and saw the smoking plane go into a shallow dive. To his disgust, these two aircraft were acknowledged only as a 'probable' and a 'possible'—but at least these Australians survived. They experienced great anguish wondering what happened to a fellow crew, which they last saw under fighter attack. Their worst fears were confirmed.[21]

Other Australians, including George Sayer and Allan Ross, in Sayer's 84 Squadron Blenheim, and Bill McCulloch of 232 Squadron, had seen the paratroops descending. On a flight from Tjililitan, on Java, McCulloch's Hurricane flight noticed twin-engine aircraft below them. They mistook them for Hudsons until they saw the paratroops and their escorting Oscar fighters. Two Oscars quickly shot at McCulloch, wounding him in both legs and the arm. His aircraft was hit in the tail and, given its position just above the treetops, McCulloch could not bale out before it crashed into a swamp. After struggling through jungle and using his dinghy to cross a river, he reached Palembang.

While Diamond's and McCulloch's dramas were unfolding, two more No. 1 Squadron aircraft had attacked the convoy. Lockwood and Gibbes dived towards separate ships. Lockwood's Hudson was later seen with smoke issuing from an engine and two Zeros chasing it. He and his fine crew—George Christensen, Adrian Munday and Eddie Edmondson—all perished when their aircraft crashed into the sea. In a letter to his parents, Lockwood had tried to prepare them for the worst, saying that if he did not survive, 'it is not me who is giving the life but you, because you gave me life, and please don't regard it as my loss'.[22]

P.2 was now being prepared for evacuation. Twenty-one Hudsons flew to Java, all loaded with men and equipment and made ready because of excellent routines and brilliant improvisation from Flight Sergeant Harold Musicka and other ground crew. The day of 14 February had been a sad one for the RAAF Hudsons, with Davis calling his squadron's attacks on the invasion fleet 'little less than a suicidal mission'. Although only three Hudsons had been lost, with Diamond and his crew recovered, 'the loss of two experienced flight commanders and crews was a significant blow to the squadron and deeply felt by all members'.[23]

On 15 February, the day Singapore fell, Hudsons (three of them RAAF), Blenheims and Hurricanes that were still based at P.2 resumed the fight. Late in the day enemy fighters ceased interfering and the Allied aircraft seized a rare opportunity to take revenge on enemy troops coming down the rivers in barges. Afterwards, one airman likened the river to 'a bowl of water into which a box of matches had been emptied'.[24] Hurricanes decimated some enemy aircraft lined up on a beach.

Piloting one Blenheim was Australian Sergeant Bill Cosgrove. Return fire hit his RAF gunner, Sergeant Hayes Harding. Cosgrove wrote home:

> He's a damned good boy. I said as we were pulling out from the dive 'Are you hit, Ticker?' 'No', he shouted 'Go down on the bastards again!' And he's only a little fellow too. The second time we went down there was blood all over the turret and this time we got hit in the engine, elevator and hydraulic pipe.[25]

Harding later praised Cosgrove's skill as a pilot—'a bit wild but a good formation flyer'—in all respects but landing. So when Cosgrove told him they were belly-landing, Hayes said he would bale out rather than risk it. 'Keep quiet you little bugger and cross your fingers' came the reply. Hayes described the subsequent landing as Cosgrove's best ever.[26] In his letter home, Cosgrove acknowledged that in the Netherlands East Indies, 'in four flights, I had four crashes,' but explained, accurately, that the cause was 'being shot up by the Japs each time'.[27] This day's aerial activity threatened Japanese operations around Palembang, but the Allied high command had no reserves of troops and ships with which to exploit it.

Nos 1 and 8 RAAF Squadrons, with No. 62 Squadron RAF, were now based at Semplak in north-western Java. Their combined strength was just 25 worn-out Hudsons. Soon all 25 were transferred to No. 1 Squadron, while most of their personnel and those of RAAF Headquarters sailed or flew to Australia. So too did 453 Squadron, but only after Air Vice-Marshal Maltby, now commanding the RAF in Java, summoned its officers and again raised the slur of their supposed misbehaviour at Sembawang in January. There was also a clash between the 453 Squadron adjutant, Flight Lieutenant Wells, and Squadron Leader Harper, who did not want the unit to return to Australia. Australian Group Captain McCauley ensured that it did return, but on reaching Australia it was disbanded.

The treatment of 453 Squadron was just one element of ill-feeling between the RAAF and RAF during this period. Davis fumed when RAF Headquarters proposed to put RAF personnel in charge of No. 1 Squadron's flights, and then to renumber the squadron with an RAF number. Davis stalled for long enough to see the RAF station commander replaced, and the plan dropped. There was a depressing atmosphere, with rumours rife and great uncertainty. Davis wrote afterwards that 'If asked to state the role of No 1 Squadron in Java, it would be difficult to nominate anything specific.'[28] They carried out reconnaissance and attack missions, but were generally outnumbered by as much as 10 to 1 by enemy aircraft, which raided every Allied base in Java almost daily. Japan provided 409 naval and army aircraft for the Java operation. The Allies occasionally hit back, raiding their former airfields on Sumatra. Sayer's Blenheim was one of seven sent to attack P.1 airfield on 19 February. On the return flight, two Japanese fighters with fixed undercarriages suddenly dived towards them. One of them approached close and slow enough for Sayer's gunner, Allan Ross, to shoot bits off before seeing the pilot slumped forward and the plane dropping earthwards. Sayer avoided the other fighter in cloud.

Tom Young, an Australian Hurricane pilot with 232 Squadron, recognised a Dave float-plane over Bantam Bay on 20 February. Eventually he gave up trying to outmanoeuvre it and stood off to fire into it at long range. Smoke poured from the Japanese plane, but its pilot turned towards Young and tried vainly to ram him before going down. This was a rare triumph. On 22 February, twenty Zeros strafed the virtually defenceless airmen at Semplak for 30 gut-wrenching minutes. There were no casualties, but six Hudsons were destroyed and more damaged.

On 1 March the Japanese landed on Java. Earlier that day, RAAF personnel had died when HMAS *Perth* was sunk in the Java Sea. RAN cruisers operated Walrus aircraft, flown and maintained by RAAF members of No. 9 Squadron. Now three were dead, and the remaining ground crew and pilot, Allen McDonough, went into captivity. One, LAC Ernest Toe, would die as a prisoner of war (POW). Meanwhile, despite the remarkable efforts of ground crew to keep the Hudsons aloft in preceding weeks, just two could join the Blenheims and Hurricanes that made exhausting but vain attempts, like HMAS *Perth*, to hamper yet another invasion. Allan Ross fractured a bone in his back and was knocked unconscious when Sayer's aircraft was forced down in a paddy field. Eventually the crew rode to Kalidjati, the Hudsons' new home, on pushbikes.

The Japanese forces landing at Eretanwetan were soon marching hard towards the same objective. Two of four now airworthy Hudsons were ordered to fly out. More ignominious was the flight of the British station commander, who had previously expressed his dislike of all

Australians and meanly denied them transport from their quarters to the airstrip. Now Japanese fire killed him as he sought to drive away. This was in stark contrast to the courage of the British and Dutch aerodrome defence force, which held up the Japanese until overwhelmed by tanks. Gibbes was among airmen pinned down by enemy fire. He and two others decided to make a run for a Hudson; his companions were shot dead. He crept on his belly towards the aircraft and when the enemy fire briefly subsided, leapt up, flung open the door and jumped aboard. He had to lie on the floor, as bullets were cutting holes just above his head. From a prone position, he reached the controls and managed to start both engines. Taking no time to warm up the motors, he opened the throttles and moved forward. Every Japanese gun within range opened fire on the lone pilot and his Hudson, but he managed to clear a hedge and become airborne. Too angry to fly from the scene, he turned the aircraft towards a motorcycle–sidecar combination that had shot his companions and was now firing at him. He was surprised and satisfied to see his machine-gun bullets send the driver and his bike cartwheeling wildly. Several other Hudsons got away under fire.

On 2 March, No. 1 Squadron was ordered home. Demonstrating characteristic ingenuity and initiative, the crews used four-gallon tins carried in the aircraft to allow in-flight refuelling. A side window was knocked out and petrol poured through a length of rubber tubing into a wing tank. The last of the Hudsons left for Port Hedland, Western Australia, on 7 March. When Gibbes landed at Roeborne, Western Australia, a suspicious old farmer carrying a shotgun gruffly asked, 'Who are you bastards?' Broome had been raided by the Japanese just days earlier. Doug Scott recalled, 'When we set foot on Australian soil again, there weren't many of us who didn't squat down and scrape up a handful of good old Aussie soil.'[29]

While 120 members of No. 1 Squadron had reached Australia, 160 were left behind. Flying-boats were supposed to rescue them but, thanks to the raid on Broome, these never came. Wing Commander Davis, their brave leader, went into captivity rather than leave his men. The lack of reward for his squadron's three months of solid effort left him 'despondent'.[30]

Wing Commander Jeudwine of 84 Squadron RAF led 12 airmen in an escape from Java. Originally there were 13, but as rations had only been apportioned for 12, one had to go back: RAAF Warrant Officer Neville Jeanes, who had to endure three years of captivity. There were eight Australians in the open boat that left under Jeudwine's command on 7 March, including George Sayer and Bill Cosgrove. For 44 days they sailed. When spotted by a surfacing Japanese submarine, its chivalrous captain, Katsuo Ohashi, chose not to harm them. Another day, a large whale surfaced and examined them, but it also chose to leave them alone. A huge shark threatened to interfere when men were fixing the rudder, and had to be driven off by rifle fire. By the time they reached Fraser Island on 18 April, Jeudwine's party had covered some 2400 kilometres.

With the surrender of Java on 8 March, Japan had completed its conquest of the Netherlands East Indies, part of the largest amphibious campaign in history. In every conquest, from Malaya to Rabaul, their air power had been critical.

8 Crisis of leadership: Darwin and the RAAF

A Japanese attack on Darwin was likely as soon as it became practical. Darwin was a key port and airbase in the chain linking Australia to Malaya, the Netherlands East Indies and the Philippines. The Australian government's concern about Darwin was reflected in its evacuation of more than 2000 civilians to the southern states from 7 December. On 18 February 1942, barely 2000 civilians remained in the town.

By then the danger of air raids on Darwin was acute. The Japanese had conquered Ambon, which was within flying distance of Darwin, and were about to invade Timor. Four Japanese aircraft carriers—*Akagi*, *Kaga*, *Hiryu* and *Soryu*—were in the area to support the Timor invasion. They could launch air raids, or could support a Japanese landing at Darwin. Given the impeccable record of such landings in the last two months, this was a frightening prospect.

The Japanese were not actually planning such a landing, but knew that ships and aircraft based at Darwin were supporting the defenders of Timor and Java. Consequently, Admiral Yamamoto, Commander-in-Chief of the Combined Fleet, ordered the Carrier Task Force, based on the four carriers, to bomb the port on 19 February. First their 188 carrier-borne aircraft would attack, followed by 54 land-based bombers. The Japanese air commander in the operation, Commander Mitsuo Fuchida, had led the attack on Pearl Harbor. He likened using his force on Darwin to employing a sledgehammer to crack an egg.

The egg already contained cracks when Group Captain Fred Scherger arrived as Darwin Station Commander in October 1941. Relations between the RAAF and other services were not cordial, discipline within the RAAF was weak, and facilities were poor. Scherger, probably the RAAF's foremost inter-war pilot, was slightly built, but a determined and jovial extrovert. He worked energetically to overcome the station's weaknesses, for example by instituting daily bayonet practice for all ground crews, and in an effort to facilitate American use of the base, had the Batchelor runway strengthened and extended. Yet administrative problems mounted in the New Year. The creation of North-Western Area Headquarters at Darwin in mid-January eased pressure elsewhere, but its coexistence at Darwin with the station headquarters and Area Combined Headquarters (part of ABDA command) made facilities even more crowded for the 2000 RAAF personnel in the area. Some airmen had already been living in garages or under buildings. One officer reported that senior American officers, on arriving from the Philippines, 'slept in the "Ladies Room"'. He added, cryptically, 'and liked it'.[1]

While the bureaucracy expanded, the threatened area's aircraft strength remained pitiful. American aircraft were regularly passing through to the Indies and the Philippines, thereby raising hopes that a fighter force may develop there, but on the eve of the Japanese raid, the only USAAF fighters present were ten P-40s preparing to fly to Java via Koepang. The serviceable Australian aircraft at Darwin comprised only nine Hudsons, six just arrived from Timor that morning. The lack of Australian aircraft there was partly due to the sensible policy of dispersal, which, for the protection of the few available aircraft, saw eight Hudsons stationed some 500 kilometres south-east at Daly Waters airstrip; nine Wirraways were at Batchelor, and another five unserviceable Wirraways at Darwin's civil aerodrome. Anti-aircraft defences were thin: just ten twin-Vickers machine guns and twelve borrowed American .50 calibre anti-aircraft guns at the RAAF Station, and no anti-aircraft guns at any other advanced operational base. A lightweight radar set had arrived at Dripstone Caves north of Darwin in early February, and by March would be picking up aircraft 120 kilometres away. On 19 February, though, it was still under construction. Enemy reconnaissance aircraft had flown over the area at least four times, most recently on 18 February, but when the attack on Darwin finally came, it surprised the ill-equipped defenders.

At 9.15 a.m. on 19 February, the USAAF P-40s took off from Darwin for Koepang, but when the Darwin operations room warned their commander, Major Floyd 'Slugger' Pell, that the weather ahead was poor, he turned back with his inexperienced fliers. They reached Darwin at about 9.40 a.m., when Pell ordered his one experienced pilot, Robert Oestreicher, and four others to maintain a patrol while the remaining five landed to refuel. During the patrol Oestreicher looked over his left shoulder and suddenly saw fighters diving towards them. On seeing the tell-tale red circle he called 'Zeros, Zeros, Zeros' into his radio-telephone and dived away.[2] Bullet holes appeared in his plane, which he likened to those made by a sewing machine. He shot down two Vals—the first enemy aircraft shot down over Australia—and survived the action, but two of his fellow pilots were killed and the other two were forced down.

During the American pilots' fight, Australians made a series of errors on the ground. Observers on Bathurst and Melville Islands saw the Japanese aircraft approaching Darwin from the north, and sent a warning that reached the RAAF operations room in Darwin at 9.37 a.m. The reasons why this and other warning messages to the services in Darwin—including one from a group of RAAF codebreakers—did not precipitate an immediate alarm are somewhat mysterious. The recently appointed station master, Wing Commander Sturt Griffith, apparently thought the aircraft might be American and was keen to avoid a third false alarm after two demoralising ones in recent weeks. The siren only sounded at about 10 a.m., just as the attack was beginning.

The raid on Darwin lasted about half an hour and was delivered initially by glinting high-level bombers, whose pattern-bombing then gave way to strafing and bombing from dull-green dive-bombers and fighters. They concentrated first on the harbour, where 47 merchant and naval vessels presented inviting targets, and then on the town. Fighter-bombers with escorts hit the RAAF Station, where Pell and his novice pilots, having flown back to refuel, took off in a hopeless attempt to fight back. Pell was just 25 metres up when three Zeros attacked and sent him crashing in flames. He survived baling out and was crawling towards help when a strafer's shells killed him. Another pilot was killed taking off, while the remaining three were shot down, but survived.

Although no Australian aircraft defended Darwin that day, some RAAF airmen on the ground fought back. More than 50 Australian airmen manned machine guns during the attack. One was Squadron Leader Andrew Swan, a tough Scottish-born regular. He had twice been Mentioned in Despatches while serving with the Black Watch in 1914–18, and as Administrative Officer at Darwin had recently done much to improve discipline. Now he manned a Lewis gun with Warrant Officer Harry Chapman. The two also pulled ammunition from a burning hangar. Wing Commander Arch Tindal, who had risked his life flying Wirraways in Rabaul and his career by standing up for Lerew and his men on returning to Australia, now put all on the line again. He went to his quarters and grabbed a Vickers 'GO' (gas-operated aircraft machine gun) that he had mounted on a mobile stand. He set it up on a trench and fired at enemy aircraft until one of their shells killed him. He was the first RAAF fatality sustained in combat on the Australian mainland. His bravery would be commemorated in the naming at Katherine of Tindal RAAF base, destined to be the largest in post-war Australia.

Before noon, the second raid arrived, delivered from the south-west and north-east by 27 Nell and 27 Betty land-based bombers. For 20 minutes they concentrated on the RAAF Station buildings and aerodrome. Their pattern-bombing was, to Squadron Leader Francis McMahon, the day's 'most terrifying experience', as 'the ground rocked to the explosions of salvos of bombs'.[3] Even to relatively experienced men, like LAC Richard Taylor, of No. 2 Squadron, waiting between the bomb release and the explosion of those swishing weapons was nightmarish. From his trench, LAC Aubrey McEgan saw low-flying Japanese fighter pilots leaning from their cockpits and choosing their targets, then ducked as a bomb landed some two metres from his slit trench. The tremendous vibration blew off his helmet.

The raids, delivered with frightening efficiency by some of the world's best military airmen, were very destructive. Dazed and shaken RAAF personnel emerged from their trenches to see the station's two hangars burnt out, and most other buildings destroyed or severely damaged. Ten ships had been sunk (including USS *Peary*), and 23 aircraft destroyed, together with the wharf and many buildings. At least 243 people were killed, though at the time the government admitted to only 17. Seven

RAAF personnel died. In return, between five and ten Japanese aircraft had been brought down.

Rumours that the raids were a prelude to a Japanese invasion spread in the town and among the RAAF on 19 February: McMahon heard junior non-commissioned officers (NCOs) insisting that 25,000 Japanese had landed and were about to cut them off. The subsequent flight of some airmen tarnished the RAAF's reputation. After the second raid Wing Commander Griffith, visibly rattled by the attacks, gave Squadron Leader Swan a vague verbal order for all airmen to assemble 'half a mile down the road and half a mile into the bush'.[4] This instruction seems to have turned into a rumour, which 'spread with incredible rapidity', of an order to evacuate the station immediately, to a distance well beyond half a mile.[5] The instruction was later used to excuse a large-scale rush for the rear. McMahon, an administrative officer, stated that 95 per cent of those who ran honestly thought they were following orders and that they returned when ordered. RAAF historian Alan Stephens suggests that it was simply desertion: as late as 23 February, 278 were still absent without leave, having scattered to places as distant as Batchelor, Adelaide River, Daly Waters, and in one case Melbourne! However, other units, such as the RAAF Transport Section and the experienced RAAF Hudson squadrons, had remained calm. Squadron Leader Brian Walker reportedly fired warning bullets close to the ears of two senior NCOs trying to desert 12 Squadron at Batchelor, but otherwise that unit remained unruffled.

Two weeks after the Darwin raids the government instituted a commission of inquiry, headed by Mr Justice Lowe. He criticised all three services. The RAAF was faulted for its inadequate preparation for war and tardy response to reports of approaching aircraft. Most of the senior RAAF officers in the North-Western Area were replaced, but Scherger, who had been acting Air Officer Commanding North-Western Area on 19 February, was praised for demonstrating 'great courage and energy'.[6] McMahon, whose bravery in the raid Scherger himself praised, wrote later that many of the stories of disgraceful behaviour were invented by airmen who were not present and thus did not experience 'conditions not previously encountered on the Australian mainland'.[7] He acknowledged that some individuals did run away, and that many were so scared that their teeth chattered, but the key determinant of behaviour, he felt, was training. The well-disciplined did a good job, others did not:

> The big majority suffered badly from lack of leadership; lack of personal intimate leadership from officers they had grown to know and trust—commissioned and non-commissioned . . . the air force was paying more attention to technical ability in N.C.O.'s and officers than to qualities of leadership . . . Cypher books, machine tools, aircraft, were more important than men.[8]

Alan Powell, the leading authority on the war in northern Australia, reinforces this point in arguing that the wartime RAAF's rapid expansion ensured that no tight bond had developed in Darwin between officers and most technicians. He says too that the growth entailed 'a drastic dilution of professionalism', with the core of pre-war airmen in the squadrons more professional than the droves of administrators and technicians who had joined since 1939.[9] Yet the way inter-war governments treated the RAAF as a poor relation of the other two services was also fundamental to the poor performance of men and the absence of proper equipment at Darwin. While 19 February 1942 represented a low point in RAAF history, the story thereafter was of a climb towards victory.

This ascent would not be smooth. Immediately after 19 February, it was difficult to be optimistic, and indeed, Darwin endured 62 more raids. Reflecting the hopelessness they felt, servicemen in Darwin told the Lowe Commission, off the record, that should Japanese forces attack, the port was doomed. It was unusual that a civil judge should be commissioned to examine a military disaster, but Lowe's conclusion that Darwin desperately needed fighter squadrons and anti-aircraft guns was commonsense, given that the North-Western Area was virtually unprotected. A senior officer later recalled that the sight of formations of Japanese aircraft:

> arrogantly holding their course, unmolested (except for the Army A.A.) and flying with air pageant precision, induced a sense of inferiority and frustration. The enemy was endowed with an aura of invincibility and we suffered a sense of the inevitable so long as we had no fighters to oppose him.[10]

Enemy superiority was brutally obvious on 3 March, at Broome. With its three hospitable pubs, that tiny port had long been a favourite overnight stop for aircrews on coastal patrols. During the operations in the

Netherlands East Indies, it became a staging point for those travelling between Perth and Java, and its runway had been extended and strengthened to take four-engine aircraft such as Flying Fortresses. Many aircraft, mainly USAAF, passed through during the retreat in late February, with 57 aircraft landing there in one day. However, there were no fighters or anti-aircraft guns there when a Japanese reconnaissance plane came to have a look on 2 March.

At about 9.30 the following morning, Sergeant Frank Russell and five other crew members were sitting in the RAAF Empire flying-boat *Centaurus*, one of the Australian and Dutch aircraft that had brought thousands of passengers through Broome in the previous fortnight. Theirs was one of four Qantas flying-boats impressed into the RAAF. Russell described what followed:

> We were all on our ship, 3 miles from the shore, drinking our morning cocoa, when the first kite appeared and dropped a bomb within 30 feet of us. Then it dived, and next minute, a prolonged burst of machine gun incendiaries entered some of our tanks and set them on fire. I shall leave the panic to your imagination. I personally ran around in circles, trying to work out what one should do on a burning flying boat with 2000 gals of gas on board and incendiaries whining into her obviously in search of further containers of fuel. All that in 5 seconds!!! Then came a second burst of, I suppose 70 or 80 rounds. Some of them came so close to me and a 44 gallon tin of gas I quickly decided to place my fate in the jaws of the excellent specimens of grey nurse sharks we had seen rather than collect a gutful of lead and suffer a consequent roasting. The third burst found me disappearing through the aft hatch . . .

Around him he saw:

> . . . a scene of ghastly devastation! . . . Our flying boats all over the place were sending up huge clouds of smoke. Burning petrol, and sinister patches, floated all over the sea. From the diving Zero fighters, came a very hell of clamour that seemed to fill the earth, the sky, the sea, yet, through the ghastly noise, we somehow heard the chatter of our and the enemy's machine guns and the clatter of our ack-acks. All around us there fell a ceaseless stream of tracer bullets.

Russell likened the ordeal to a nightmare or a horror movie.

Though under fire, Corporal Andrew Ireland released a rubber dinghy from the flight deck and, after diving into the sea, inflated it and saved his fellow crewmen from their now-burning aircraft. This feat earned him a British Empire Medal. When at last the Zeros left, Russell and his mates searched for survivors. They saw 'pitiful sights' among the civilians who had been in the Dutch flying-boats.

Within 20 minutes, the Zeros had methodically destroyed all 16 flying-boats at Broome, as well as the six aircraft on the airfield and a US bomber that took off: only one of the 33 men on board survived. Russell and his bedraggled crewmates were flown to Melbourne, treated like 'ruddy 'eroes' and interviewed about the disaster.[11] Russell had eluded death, but just two years later he and his damaged Catalina were lost while returning from a mission to Java.

On the same day as the Broome raid, which cost about 70 lives, other unopposed Japanese aircraft struck Wyndham, in Western Australia. In Broome, there was an understandable conviction that invasion was imminent; when Wing Commander Snook visited on 20 March, he found the 65 white inhabitants panicky. That day, the Japanese raided Broome again, though the seven bombers and two Zeros found slim pickings: they had to settle for destroying Snook's transport plane on the ground. On the same day, Zeros strafed Derby, Western Australia.

In early March, American staff in Australia calculated that an amphibious attack might occur in north-western Australia on or before 25 March, while the Australian Chiefs of Staff determined that in early April the Japanese could attack with vastly superior air and land forces. The forecasters were not of course aware that the Japanese decided in March, at an Imperial General Staff conference, not to invade Australia. They had already achieved their initial goals and would concentrate on cutting Australia off from the United States. For north-western Australia, this decision ensured that the struggle in that area would primarily be an air war.

The defensive work in that air war would for now fall mainly to the American air force. On 17 March General Douglas MacArthur, following orders to leave his doomed command in the Philippines and travel to Australia, landed at Batchelor airfield en route to Melbourne. By mid-April a new command structure had been established in Australia, with MacArthur the Supreme Commander of the newly created and vast

South-West Pacific Area, including the Philippines, Borneo, the Netherlands East Indies (except Sumatra), Australia and New Guinea. General George Brett had already done much to turn Australia into 'a second England'—a great airbase from which to take the fight to the enemy—and now took command of the 'Allied Air Forces'. His headquarters, established on 20 April, were initially based in Melbourne. Australia had replaced the Philippines in American planning as a destination for resources. This virtually ensured that Japan would not conquer Australia.

MacArthur's initial orders from the Allied Joint Chiefs of Staff in Washington were to 'hold the key military regions of Australia as bases for future action against Japan and strive to check Japanese aggression in the South-West Pacific Area'.[12] He and other American commanders were very concerned about security in northern Australia, which initially took priority over the strategically vital Port Moresby. Even so, Darwin had no fighter garrison for more than three weeks after the initial raid. On 16 March—the day that the fourth Darwin raid killed two and wounded eight RAAF personnel—an advanced echelon of 49th Pursuit Group USAAF flew there with P-40s. By the end of April, Darwin had received all three squadrons of this pursuit group, which from May was called 49th Fighter Group. Thanks primarily to the high quality of 49th Group's pilots and leaders, especially their commander, Lieutenant-Colonel Paul B. Wurtsmith, this Group outfought the Japanese aircraft that frequently returned to fight them.

The radar station and early warning stations helped substantially. On its first day of operation, 22 March, the radar station at Dripstone Caves, initially called No. 31 Radio Station, gave warning of an enemy attack, which resulted in one enemy fighter destroyed for no loss to the Americans. More stations would be established from June, but in the meantime RAAF coastwatching units on Bathurst Island and Point Charles helped provide early warning. Wurtsmith commended the efficient RAAF wireless crew operating at their lonely post on Bathurst Island.

On Anzac Day, 24 Japanese bombers and 9–12 Zeros launched the fourteenth attack on Darwin, but faced all 50 P-40s of the Group for the first time. The Japanese lost 11 or 12 aircraft, while bringing down none—but they did drop anti-personnel bombs on the RAAF living quarters. When two days later Sergeant Tom Calder returned from a job and called out to two mates in his hut, the reply came: 'They're dead.

Bloody air raid. Got them in the trench.' Incredulous, Calder demanded that the respondents show him the trench, for he felt the one he and his mates had used was invulnerable. He discovered that his two mates and a third man had that day gone to a different trench and been killed. 'No way would I have changed our trench,' Calder reflected dolefully.[13] After another costly attack on 27 April, the Japanese launched no more raids for nearly seven weeks.

By the end of April, Wurtsmith's Group had destroyed 38 Japanese aircraft and lost just seven P-40s. They flew from Darwin RAAF base, Batchelor, and two new airstrips, named Strauss and Livingstone after two of their dead pilots. Australians should not forget that the first direct air defence of their country was provided by these American fighter pilots. They raised the morale of all in Darwin, for as a senior RAAF officer observed, once the P-40s began shooting down Japanese aircraft, 'excitement and anticipation began to replace frustration'.[14]

American engineer units were also sent to 'Northern Territory Force', under Australian General Ned Herring. These units, with growing Australian help, worked rapidly and efficiently, building and extending airstrips on the north–south road, including Strauss, Hughes, Livingstone, McDonald, Fenton, Pine Creek and Katherine. Others were built around Alice Springs, at Gorrie (named for the Hudson pilot), and near Katherine. The great logistical brake on growth was the need to bring the materials for construction vast distances from eastern Australia by rail and/or road.

From 25 March, operational command over the American Fighter Group fell to RAAF Air Commodore Frank Bladin, who that month became the new commander of North-Western Area. He was an excellent choice. He had the leadership skills and commonsense required for supervising tasks as diverse as constructing airfields, improving the training of ground crews and conducting air operations in the huge area between Torres Strait and Western Australia. He worked superbly with allies and the other services, for example showing his readiness to accept orders from General Herring when an invasion alert was issued late in March. Known in the inter-war RAAF as 'Dad' or 'Pop' because of his concern for his men, he was also ideally suited for the role of restoring the morale of the Australians in the command after 19 February. He was shocked to see the results of the destruction: 'The men were forced to eat, sleep and work in vastly downgraded conditions, and cohesion was affected.'[15] Ground crew in particular were sleeping in shattered barracks, then scattering by day to service their aircraft, all the while avoiding the station buildings, which they dubbed 'the million pound bombing target'. They had virtually no recreational facilities, and the main topic of conversation was how long it would be before they were posted 'down South'.

In the two weeks after the first raid, at least half the civilians in Darwin fled in the so-called 'Adelaide River Stakes'. A month after the raid, Bladin saw plates of food still on dinner tables in civilian homes abandoned on 19 February. Ever since 19 February 1942, the thought of Australian civilians rushing away from the scene of action has seemed embarrassing. Yet it was entirely understandable, and during the war civilians all over the world headed for refuge whenever enemy aircraft were likely to attack them with impunity. A more organised departure of RAAF personnel also occurred. The policy of dispersal, which had saved aircraft and lives on 19 February, was further extended now to the few Australian air assets in the Northern Territory. Bladin sometimes found it challenging to maintain the line between 'dispersal' and 'disintegration', though he recognised that should there be an invasion, Darwin was the worst place for his aircraft to be based. Instead of his forces being in the target area of an amphibious assault, they needed to be based away from the battle zone so as to help smash the invaders. Most of the aircraft and ground staff of Nos 2 and 13 Squadrons were sent to Daly Waters. Though Darwin remained a fearful place, as the lack of an efficient warning system kept everyone on tenterhooks, Daly Waters was dusty, smelly, dry, exceptionally hot and insect-ridden. One 13 Squadron officer recalled that on waking in the morning it was difficult to see through his mosquito net, so thick were the flies waiting to start work on him. Morale was low, facilities and transport poor, and dispersal for fear of air raids taken to extremes: the base was nearly 10 kilometres wide! As McMahon wryly noted, a thousand-bomber raid could barely have harmed it, but its half a thousand men could not run it efficiently.[16] In time, however, a far more efficient base would develop.

'All available Hudson aircraft' to attack

The two Hudson squadrons still bravely flew missions to the Netherlands East Indies and would bear the main burden of attacking from the North-Western Area until October. No. 12 Squadron's Wirraways could not reach the Hudson targets, so could not fly escort; instead, they patrolled the Northern Territory, a task that rapidly 'browned off' the pilots.

The Hudsons flew unescorted, meaning that throughout the seven or so hours in the air their crews had to scan the sky continuously for enemy fighters. They flew via an advanced operational base at Drysdale Mission in Western Australia. From that fly-infested outpost they could ensure that they attacked at first light, last light or in moonlight to reduce the risk of encountering enemy fighters. It was still a wearying, worrying task. Like the Japanese bombers attacking Darwin, they sought to reconnoitre for signs of enemy intentions and movements, to reduce the enemy's offensive ability and to damage their supply lines. As a wartime publication stated, every flight they undertook involved a 'quadruple risk': from water, weather, and the enemy's anti-aircraft fire and fighters.[17] The squadrons' main targets were Timor and Ambon. On Timor, they hit the Japanese bases at Koepang and Dili, and dropped supplies for the RAAF rear party and Australian soldiers fighting a guerrilla war. Whereas individual Japanese bombers could carry 2000-pound (910 kilogram) bomb-loads to Darwin, the Hudsons could carry just 1000-pound and 500-pound loads to Koepang and Ambon, respectively.

After a reconnaissance flight reported 36 Japanese aircraft at Penfui in March, the Australians were rather grandiosely ordered to send 'all available Hudson aircraft less one' to strike them.[18] This meant just three aircraft! Bad weather scotched this mission, but on 18 March six Hudsons attacked, leaving fires visible 80 kilometres away.

Jack MacAlister's Hudson bombed an enemy flying-boat at Koepang in March, but then 15 enemy aircraft took off to intercept. Ten kilometres from the coast, they caught him. His crew downed one fighter—said to be the first Zero shot down over Timor—yet with their starboard engine on fire, and the turret-gunner dead, MacAlister's crew had to bale out. Only MacAlister survived. He landed in a tree, where the fighters tried to shoot him; eventually he was captured. MacAlister and seven other prisoners later escaped their compound and rushed to a nearby airfield. He broke the window of a Japanese DC-3 and got inside, only to discover that the battery had been removed. He and his companions made it back to camp before daybreak and roll-call. MacAlister was moved to Changi, where after another foiled escape attempt, he was tortured and treated appallingly during nine months' solitary confinement. He survived the war, receiving a DFC for his flying and an MBE for 'exemplary behaviour' in captivity.

Bob Dalkin led four Hudsons on a raid on 31 March. The laconic Dalkin dropped bombs on the Penfui airfield from too low and then felt an 'awful thump' from the explosions. Hoping the plane was still in one piece, he made a quick turn to give the gunners a chance to do more damage, then flew low to the Koepang flying-boat base. The turret-gunner saw anti-aircraft fire passing between the aerial and the fins. The attackers claimed six grounded aircraft destroyed, and four flying-boats damaged. It was, in Dalkin's words, 'quite a night'.[19]

Harold Cook led a dramatic three-Hudson attack on Japanese shipping at Koepang in mid-April. As he was approaching a ship, his bomb doors open, Cook saw Zeros. Instinctively he closed the doors and headed for cloud, but then realised he wouldn't make it before the fighters reached him. He turned again towards the ship and, though three Zeros tried to head him off, scored hits with two bombs. His bombing done, survival became the priority and he flew as close as possible to the water. He caught sight of a Zero attacking his wingman, Roger Blanchard, but three Zeros were soon attacking him viciously too. A cannon shell penetrated the cockpit, temporarily crippling Cook's right arm. His second pilot, Viv Leithhead, saw his tracers enter the belly of a Zero, which went down in flames. Another Zero took the downed fighter's place on the Hudson's tail, and severely wounded the turret-gunner, Herbert Hearle, in the hand and leg. William Witham was knocked unconscious when a bullet entered his cheek and lodged in his chin. After 30 minutes of this deadly chasing game, Cook's controls were damaged, one engine losing power and the other on fire. He brought the plane down in shallow water. With their two WAGs badly wounded, Cook and Leithhead had to choose whether to stay and be captured with their crewmates, or to head north, where they knew others of 2 Squadron were awaiting rescue. Hearle and Witham were left in the care of locals, but the Japanese captured and executed the stricken airmen. Cook and Leithhead rejoined their other stranded colleagues and were rescued by a US submarine. Blanchard, whom Cook had seen struggling against a Zero, flew home safely, thanks largely to Don Gitsham, who despite wounds to the foot and buttock, fought on and brought down the Zero. Blanchard and his crew never returned from another mission to Koepang, flying unaccompanied.

By May, 49th Group's efforts had made it safe enough for the Hudsons to move to more forward bases, Darwin and Hughes. For 13 Squadron, moving to the new field at Hughes ended a frustrating period of shortages, illness and poor conditions, though initially rice was so prevalent in the diet that men quipped it was preparing them for Japanese invasion.

A scandal begins

The Allied Air Forces were created as Charles Burnett's term of service as CAS was ending. There were three obvious candidates to succeed him. One was Air Vice-Marshal Bostock, whose impressive CV included his record as a World War I pilot, a graduate of the RAF Staff College, experience with an RAF bomber group in England, and one of the best intellects in the RAAF, to which he had given excellent service in varied posts. He was a protégé of Burnett, who told him that Bostock would succeed him in May 1942. Unfortunately for Bostock, Burnett's open disdain for Labor politicians and his friendship with United Australia Party leaders made a poor impression on the Labor government: the Minister for Air, Arthur Drakeford, would not appoint Bostock CAS.

Drakeford's own choice, Richard Williams, was an obvious alternative, but Prime Minister Curtin was wary of Williams' reputation as a political animal. A third capable possibility, Australian-born Air Marshal Peter Drummond, now a distinguished RAF officer, declined the offer, reportedly because of concern as to the place of the CAS within the new Allied Air Forces arrangements. The best three Australian candidates having been disqualified, the government faced limited choice. Australia's failure to insist early in the war that its senior officers go to Europe for operational experience now came home to roost. On 28 April, the War Cabinet decided that while operational control of RAAF service squadrons—that is, control of their activities on campaign—would rest with the Commander of the Allied Air Forces, the Australian CAS would be responsible for 'all matters associated with RAAF personnel, provision and maintenance of aircraft, supply and equipment, works and buildings, and training'.[20]

On 2 May, Bostock officially became General Brett's Chief of Staff, and thus directly involved in the operational employment of the RAAF. Under great pressure to appoint a CAS, the government fixed on George Jones. He was a surprise choice within the RAAF, and he admitted that he himself was stunned. He has received short shrift in official RAAF publications, where he is described as 'mournful looking', 'diligent but uninspiring', and a 'mediocre' leader and thinker.[21] They and senior air force officers of the time suggest too that Jones was selected by mistake. His rank on appointment was Wing Commander (equivalent of an army Lieutenant-Colonel), though he was an acting Air Commodore (equivalent to Brigadier). To become CAS he was promoted above Bostock and seven other colleagues more senior than him on the *Air Force List*, an annual booklet listing every RAAF officer in order of seniority. This list was reportedly part of the mistake, for when Drakeford asked Assistant CAS Joe Hewitt for advice, the latter advised him to consult 'the list'. Drakeford allegedly thought 'the list' referred to a diagram drawn up by Brett and Burnett which showed Jones, then in charge of training, as fourth in an organisation chart of the Allied Air Forces. Drakeford mistakenly suggested Jones, who not only jumped over eight other officers, but also won a promotion of three ranks at once! Peter Helson's recent research suggests that Drakeford quite consciously chose Jones, whose administrative ability he admired and whose working-class origins may have appealed to the Labor government. Nevertheless, even if the government did not demonstrate incompetence in choosing the wrong man, it exhibited disdain for its own air force by snubbing the RAAF's established hierarchy and overlooking the eight men most qualified for the top job. The government's uncertainty about what it was doing was also reflected in its decision to promote Jones to Air Vice-Marshal rather than Air Marshal. His rank was not unambiguously that of the head of the service, but instead was equal to Bostock's. Jones himself declared after the war that Curtin had little knowledge of the armed forces and little inclination to expand his knowledge, and that most politicians on the Advisory War Council exhibited 'abysmal ignorance'.[22]

Jones had some impressive credentials. In the Great War, he had served as a Light Horseman at Gallipoli, then as an airman had become an ace. In World War II, he had been a very effective RAAF Director of Training, one of the most important service jobs. He had now risen from the lowest rank in the services to become chief of one of them. This shy and slightly awkward man had actually recommended Bostock for the post of CAS, and had previously looked to him as a mentor.

Their friendship now evaporated, for Bostock had expected to be named CAS, and was never able to accept this strange turn of events.

Moreover, Jones, once appointed, was determined to receive his due. The lack of cooperation between these two senior officers would damage the RAAF's efficiency. So began a period which subsequent historians have described as 'The RAAF Command Scandal' and 'How Not to Run an Air Force!'[23] There were to be various twists in this tale, not least because Bostock would find opportunities to increase his power via American attitudes towards the organisation of air operations in the South-West Pacific Area. For the moment there was a diplomatic arrangement between American and Australian senior air force officers, whereby staff officers of the two nations alternated almost automatically down the chain of command. There was goodwill between both nationalities. From mid-May both operated in five areas: North-Eastern, Eastern, Southern, Western and North-Western. Australians commanded each area, and RAAF officers actually held a majority of command posts.

Given the expansion of American power in the area, it was impossible for this arrangement to last.

9 The fight over Port Moresby

Japan wanted New Guinea. That green-clad island would be a strong shield protecting its other conquests. In particular, if Japan captured Port Moresby, the main settlement in Papua, it could launch attacks against the Australian mainland, could close Torres Strait as an Allied route for supplying Darwin, and could ensure that for the Allies, assaults on Japanese bases north of New Guinea would be logistically difficult or even impossible. Moreover, unless Japan took Port Moresby, Rabaul would not be entirely safe. These considerations profoundly affected the RAAF's Pacific War.

By late February 1942, Australia's prospects of avoiding invasion of its home soil—let alone holding New Guinea—looked grim. Although the US was building up its forces in Australia, its government and Britain's had, as expected, decided to concentrate on beating Germany first. This meant that no Allied offensive could be mounted against Japan in the foreseeable future. Instead, the priority was to stop the advance of the Japanese, who for the past three months had proved unstoppable. The only means of taking the fight to Japan was by air. For that purpose New Guinea, and especially Port Moresby, was theoretically ideal, as from it Allied raiders could hit much Japanese territory.

Yet theory and reality were at odds in early 1942. The RAAF had just three understrength squadrons in Port Moresby: Nos 11 and 20 with their

Catalinas, and the composite squadron with its Hudsons. There were no dispersal bays or taxiways for the Hudsons and any new aircraft that might arrive at Port Moresby, where personnel sensed that the government had abandoned them to the same fate as Rabaul.

Moreover, while Australian aircraft from Port Moresby could attack the Japanese, for example in Rabaul, the reverse was the case too. And in early 1942 Japanese aerial resources were of course more plentiful than Australia's. The mutual destructiveness of this scenario was exemplified on 3 February. At 3 a.m. that morning the Port Moresby garrison was woken by a low, distant, but ominous sound. It was unfamiliar to most, but they recognised that it presaged the first air raid on the port. The 21 bombs dropped by the half-dozen bombers that launched this first of many raids on Moresby killed an Army sergeant, and prompted many local workers to flee. Otherwise the raid was ineffectual, if nerve-racking. That night five Catalinas launched a return raid on Rabaul. Unlike the Japanese raiders, however, the Australians were greeted by enemy night-fighters, operating for the first time. (The Japanese rarely used them thereafter, even though if used in conjunction with searchlights they probably could have wrought havoc.) One of the Cats intercepted on 3 February took cover in the convenient smoke of a live volcano overlooking the harbour, but the crew of another, piloted by Godfrey Hemsworth, had to fight for their lives against a Claude fighter, probably flown by Hiroyoshi Nishizawa, who would become Japan's top ace.

Hemsworth, a pre-war civil airline pilot, had in 1941 been characterised by his squadron leader, Charles Pearce, as a competent pilot, but marked by the '"Quantas"[sic] outlook in that he will not take the slightest risk in flying in case it will jeopardise his position with "Quantas Airways" after the war'.[1] This was a slur on Hemsworth and other Qantas pilots. In their civil aviation jobs these pilots would indeed 'not take the slightest risk', but less for personal gain than because minimising danger was the essence of their training and their work. However, when flying in defence of the country, their self-sacrifice was exemplary: three of the first four Qantas pilots who signed up for active duty with flying-boats in 1939 would be dead within six months of Pearl Harbor. Keith Bolitho, a famous Catalina pilot, believed that 'Old Qantas pilots contributed very largely to the success of the Cats . . . All [were] steady, experienced captains.'[2] Pearce acknowledged that Hemsworth, who would prove himself risk-taker enough to win promotion to squadron leader within months, commanded the respect of his crew.

One of his crew, Sergeant Douglas Dick, flying his first operation, fired accurately at the Claude with the twin Lewis guns in the port blister. The Cat was already damaged, but as a second fighter climbed and then dived, it went right through the stream of bullets from Dick's guns. Its belly full, the enemy eventually spiralled uncontrollably towards the water, into which other crews saw it crash. Its demise was counted officially as a 'probable'. Hemsworth now had to control an aircraft with gunfire damage to its tail, both wings, its fuel tanks, oil feed line and, most threatening of all, to a propeller. While putting the heavy Catalina into an evasive dive, he had to shut down the associated engine and 'feather' the damaged propeller: that is, press a button to rotate the blade side-on into the airflow. An unfeathered propeller would continue to rotate and cause high drag, badly affecting the aircraft's performance. The crew also jettisoned their bombs and all dispensable gear. Flying on one engine and with petrol pouring into the aircraft from a damaged fuel tank, Hemsworth kept the Cat aloft for five hours before making a perfect 'let down' in darkness near Salamaua. Knowing that Salamaua had recently been an enemy target, he waited only until temporary repairs allowed him to take off again on two engines. Still feathering the propeller, he could not fly over the mountains to Moresby, so flew around the coast at a height of just 50 feet. On alighting at Moresby Harbour, Hemsworth had spent over 25 hours on this operation, 14 of them on one engine and in an aircraft containing more than 100 bullet holes. Nishizawa claimed this Catalina as the first of more than 80 victories.

War correspondent Osmar White often went to the wharf to watch the Catalinas return from missions, where the crews regularly arrived 'so exhausted they could hardly stand, eyes like raw beef from glare, and bodies palsied by snapping nerves'.[3] Apart from the fatigue, the tension inherent in their long flights, ironically called 'milk runs', was awful. All their flying time except the small percentage within about 100 kilometres around Moresby was over hostile territory, in a slow-moving aircraft with little hope of returning to base if seriously hit. The Catalinas were not just reconnaissance planes or ersatz bombers. They escorted convoys, searched for lost aircraft and followed up reported submarine sightings, dropped supplies to coastwatchers, and acted as 'Scarlet Pimpernels', rescuing fellow airmen and civilians from dangerous locations. The squadrons were supposed to have nine aircraft each, but for much of the year they struggled to have four operational Cats between them.

The heavy operational demands on Lerew's composite Hudson squadron were fatiguing its aircrew too. David Campbell, 26-year-old navigation officer attached to Port Moresby station headquarters, eased the load by piloting a Hudson on a daylight photographic reconnaissance mission on 6 February. Campbell epitomised the RAAF pilot. His old school tie was that of King's School in Parramatta, New South Wales, where he had been Captain of the School, captain of the Rugby XV and of rowing, and a champion boxer. Yet he was also a man of intellectual gifts above the high average even of RAAF pilots. He attended Cambridge University where, as well as obtaining a Blue in rugby, he developed a passion for writing and for flying. Campbell combined both enthusiasms in a marvellous short story about this reconnaissance flight. The goal was to photograph, in daylight, both Rabaul and Kavieng, where enemy fighters were present. He was full of disquiet as he flew the Hudson, heavily loaded with extra fuel, over the Owen Stanley Range. Though ordered to return if he found no cloud cover, he knew that even if there were cloud over the target, there would be none in stretches of the vast sea between them, and he felt obliged to gather information for the Catalina crews. The night before the flight, while enemy bombers circled unmolested over Moresby, he pushed his apprehension to the back of his mind and devised a plan to minimise the chance of an encounter with the fighters. He would fly initially to Rabaul, then head due west as if going home, before turning north-east to Kavieng—then head home.

Mercifully, heavy cloud hung over New Britain when they reached it. They landed at the still friendly but bomb-cratered airstrip at Gasmata. In December, Lerew's Wirraways had landed there before being shot down over Rabaul. In planning the Wirraways' flight at the time, Campbell had warned them away from cloud, which could harbour dangerous storms, ice and down-draughts. Now these dangers were forgotten: 'We wrapped its greyness around us and felt secure.'[4]

Eventually the cloud broke sufficiently for Campbell's crew to see 'patches of rain-soaked jungle' and then, through a crescent of cloud, Rabaul. They photographed the town and the 30 or so ships in the harbour, as well as the aircraft lined up on the runway at Lakunai airfield, where construction was continuing. There was no anti-aircraft fire and indeed no movement except a circling tugboat. While making notes for military intelligence, Campbell's mind was working at another level, enjoying the beauty of the sunlit harbour. But:

> Then I saw the Zero. It was taking off from Lakunai, a small silver T pulling up over the tops of the coconut palms. I thought quickly. I had not quite finished the recco and I had at the most four minutes before the Zero gained our height.

He warned the crew, finished his notes and put the Hudson into a steep turn. After three—not four—minutes, as he straightened and made for clouds, Campbell:

> felt a sudden hammer blow on my left wrist and pins and needles in my hand. At the same moment the instrument panel began to fall to pieces. I looked at my wrist in surprise. Where my watch had been there was a round blue hole.

A bullet fired from the rear had ripped through his wrist, torn open his palm, penetrated the control wheel and removed his little finger before lodging in the control panel. Campbell's next lines give rare insight into the thought processes of airmen facing imminent death:

> And I was surprised; completely surprised. I am convinced that a man, until he sees bullets flying around him, does not basically realize that war is serious, that the enemy is out to kill him.

Flying at altitude, Campbell asserted, detached the pilot from his violent deeds. A plume of smoke from his exploding bombs gave him cause to congratulate himself. He knew little of the 'panic and distraction' he inflicted. The bomber pilot, thought Campbell, 'is immune from this until his instrument panel begins to fall apart and he sees his hand flapping suddenly like a dying fish'. It was a sudden shock, too, that he, 'having done and thought the things that make up my particular existence, should end my life here in a burning aircraft ten thousand feet above a town I had lived in not a month back'.[5]

Yet at the same time as these existential thoughts flashed through Campbell's mind, so did the practical demands of being a pilot. He had instinctively dived for the clouds. Hearing the turret guns recommence firing, he realised that the Zero—he later calculated there may have been two—was attacking again. Banishing a quick fear of hitting a mountain, he turned one way and another before heading west on the few instruments still functioning. They eluded the interceptor, but the two attacks had done tremendous damage. Geoff O'Hea had been hit in the leg while firing the turret guns, and Harry Lauder's right bicep and calf had been smashed, with his right index finger shot off and his second finger hanging from a thin cord. Lauder's first comment was to thank God that the camera he had been holding was undamaged. On seeing this 'butcher's shop', Jock Thomson had vomited. Then his training kicked in and he went to work, first by stopping the spray of aluminium powder that was filling the cabin from damaged sea markers, and then by administering first aid. The blood-soaked Lauder asked if they were going on to Kavieng. Campbell decided it was time to go home—if they could make it the remaining 800 kilometres to Moresby. Losing blood and, even more worryingly, fuel from holed tanks, Campbell had to fight a great mental battle to reach safety. At one point he slapped himself in the face hard several times to stay alert. As they approached home, their fuel had almost run out. Ditching into the sea would be fatal for the wounded men, but with crucial help from Thomson, Campbell landed on one engine, with no fuel and an unserviceable wheel. He then proceeded to give what the recommendation for his DFC called 'a clear, full and concise reconnaissance report'.[6] Thomson received a DFM. Their aircraft had received 268 holes.

Gasmata, Campbell's stopover, fell to a Japanese amphibious landing on 9 February. After several unsuccessful attempts to bomb Japanese ships there, on 11 February three Hudsons, piloted by Lerew, Bill Pedrina and Ian Gibson, made a mast-height attack. Four bombs from the first aircraft struck a transport amidships, while the second scored a direct hit on another vessel. Pedrina's incendiary rounds set one of the two ships alight. The enemy ships' anti-aircraft guns and four Claudes fought back ferociously. Even before Lerew's aircraft finished its dive it was alight. Pedrina's crew saw Gibson's aircraft plummeting, one engine blazing and fighters on its tail, into a jungle-clad hillside. Gibson and his crew—Frank Thorn, Arthur Quail and Bill Coutie—died instantly. The wreckage of their aircraft was not discovered until 2008. As Lerew told Gibson's father, the young pilot had done 'a grand job of work . . . on his first real trial as captain of his aircraft'.[7] Satoshi Yoshino, the pilot who had consigned them to their deaths, had also set Lerew's aircraft alight. Unable to extinguish the flame, and after toying with the thought of smashing his Hudson into one of the ships, Lerew ordered his crew to bale out. While the other three crewmen headed for the rear door, Lerew jumped out of the cockpit window. Nevertheless, as he later wrote, his jump 'was at such low altitude that I struck the trees almost immediately the parachute had opened'.[8] The tree from which he hung almost became a gallows, for his Mae West threatened to choke him. He pulled himself up into the tree.

Among those watching the aerial action was Geoff Lempriere, who had been Lerew's Intelligence Officer in the fight for Rabaul. Now, a prisoner at Gasmata, he looked on helplessly as only one parachute—Lerew's—emerged from the aircraft. Lerew, by what he later acknowledged as great luck, again evaded death on New Britain, as Japanese troops sought him amidst the jungle, wide rivers and swamps. Aided by locals and a coastwatcher, he returned to Port Moresby in a schooner. Neither of the damaged ships had been sunk, and no Japanese aircraft shot down, though some 18 Japanese seem to have been killed. The seven airmen who died over New Britain that day were among 275 Australians killed on 11 February—the vast majority in Singapore, as the fall of that 'fortress' approached.

While Gasmata became a Japanese base, William Milne's intrepid Hudson crew survived a reconnaissance of Rabaul that revealed a formidable Japanese build-up there: an aircraft carrier and five other warships, 11 transports and 26 aircraft. Interception of such reconnaissance flights became virtually routine, and it was Pedrina's turn on 19 February. While Japanese bombers hit Darwin, two of their fighters intercepted Pedrina over Arawe, in south-west New Britain. Wireless operator Frank Marriner, who had been with Yeowart over Truk, received multiple leg wounds which severed his femoral artery: he died on the return trip. The turret-gunner, Edwin Hockings, received powder burns to the legs, and a spent bullet lodged in his boot. He had fired 2000 bullets at the attackers, one of which he saw diving out of control. Pedrina managed to land his heavily damaged Hudson. White wrote of the handful of Hudson and Catalina crews in this period that their 'endurance and heroism were prodigious'.[9] No senior officers from North-Eastern Area visited to observe, praise and encourage these prodigies.

In mid-February twelve Flying Fortresses allocated to the South-West Pacific arrived at Townsville. On 23 February they flew to attack Rabaul. Squadron Leader Dick Cohen accompanied the American commander of the Fortresses, while two RAAF Catalinas joined the mission. The results were not spectacular, but it was the first of many examples of operational cooperation between the two air forces.

Catalina pilots would fly with the American formations for some time, helping them with target selection and defensive tactics. Later that year, Ron Munro, of a Beaufort squadron, flew in a B-17 mission to Rabaul and was shocked by the laxity of the American crew. When Munro spotted a Zero some eight kilometres away and told the captain, the American was unable to raise his gunners on the intercom, so Munro had to go and call them away from a card game. By contrast, Munro said, the crews of Australian bombers 'never left our stations, never used the intercom unless it was absolutely essential and never took our eyes off the surrounding air space or sea'.[10]

In February the composite Hudson squadron became 32 Squadron. Its commander was Squadron Leader Deryck Kingwell, who had graduated in the 1937 class with awards as best pilot and top cadet at Point Cook. He would prove a fine leader, but six of his ten original crews would die on operations.

Some Hudsons were dispersed to the greater safety of Horn Island in Torres Strait, but Kingwell's new squadron suffered on 24 February, when the Japanese launched their third air raid on Port Moresby, and their first daylight one. Ten bombers in what one observer called 'silver make-up' hit the squadron's camp and the Seven Mile airfield.[11] All the aerodrome's buildings were wrecked, as was a Hudson, and one airman died. That night Ernest Beaumont, who had heroically pressed on to attack Truk on 15 January, was sent to raid Rabaul, but he and his Catalina crew were lost forever. Bert Bates recorded the news sadly, for his crew and Beaumont's had been sharing a house in Moresby. The survivors were 'beginning to wonder', he reflected, 'how much longer the "Cats" can continue to do an impossible job'.[12] The following night, Cohen dived his Catalina like a Stuka at enemy shipping in Simpson Harbour, straddling one vessel with eight bombs, while on 26 February Squadron Leader Frank Chapman bombed a wharf at Rabaul, creating a fire visible nearly 50 kilometres away.

Then came 28 February. The Catalinas had as usual been berthed on the far side of the harbour, away from the town, and Bates was undertaking maintenance on one of them when an old launch pulled alongside. The coxswain shouted that an air raid was imminent, so the airmen donned their helmets and piled aboard. They:

> ... chugged steadily out to mid-stream, possibly a little sceptical that any air raid would eventuate ... Just as we neared mid-stream, four incredibly fast machines hove into view seemingly from nowhere and flying at a height of about 100 ft. 'Lockheeds' ejaculated one of my companions, 'struth, look at 'em go'. Suddenly the leading plane did a swift right turn revealing a single radial engine. 'No, Wirraways,' I corrected, when realization suddenly dawned on me. 'Wirraways be buggered they're Jap. fighters', and Jap. fighters they were. Manoeuvring swiftly into position the dreaded fighters banked sharply to the right and in follow the leader order dived straight for the helpless 'Cats' ... Immediately columns of spray shot into the air from the nearest 'Cat' as the incendiary cannon bullets tore thro' and around its helpless frame. Almost as soon as the first of the fighters had dived onto its prey, the foremost Catalina was enveloped in flames across its entire wing. In a few seconds the whole blazing structure was sending up towering billows of black smoke high into the sky. Another 'Cat' also blazing furiously added mute testimony to the success of the raid.[13]

A third Catalina was destroyed, another damaged. The enemy did not finish there, but also struck the town, where they scored a direct hit on the Catalina squadrons' headquarters. The raid left just three serviceable aircraft in Moresby. A slight consolation was the downing of a Zero by anti-aircraft fire and the capture of its pilot, the first Japanese captured in New Guinea. Bates encountered him soon afterwards, when both were passengers on a Catalina returning for an overhaul to the flying-boat base at Rathmines, New South Wales. During the flight, Bates wrote:

> ... I am in my W/T's chair, Bol's [Bolitho, the pilot] at the controls, that's Reg's leg there dangling from his Engineer's position, that singed

and bandaged propped up figure on the bunk is the Jap, the boys are smoking and chatting happily—'heigho Rathmines'.[14]

Taken to Melbourne, the prisoner provided beneficial information about Japanese forces at Rabaul.

Rathmines was known to those based there in 1942–43 as 'Cohen's Country Club', after its 26-year-old CO, Wing Commander Dick Cohen. With its facilities for fishing and sailing, it was probably the only RAAF base where airmen often chose to spend their leave.

By early March, the three squadrons at Port Moresby comprised just six Catalinas and seven Hudsons. The Chiefs of Staff calculated that to defend New Guinea and attack Rabaul effectively, they needed 13 squadrons, which would total at least ten times this number of aircraft and include four fighter squadrons. Darwin was considered a priority for fighter support at this stage, but one squadron of P-40s was expected at Moresby in mid-March.

On 7 March, Stuart Hermes, formerly Lerew's second pilot and now captaining a Hudson on reconnaissance, spotted transports and warships headed for Lae. This first assault on the main island of New Guinea was momentous, but by the time the first Hudsons reached the amphibious attackers at 11.35 a.m. on 8 March, the invaders were ashore unopposed at Lae and Salamaua. Kingwell scored a direct hit on a transport, which was left burning and listing, but this and other Allied raids did not delay the Japanese consolidation of their two new bases. Lae would soon be a major airbase and a thorn in the side of all at Port Moresby.

An unexpected fillip to Australian hopes, and for Allied morale generally, came on 10 March. Aware of the landings, a naval task force including the American aircraft carriers *Lexington* and *Yorktown* sortied to within 75 kilometres of Papua's south coast. They launched 104 aircraft to fly over the Owen Stanleys and make a surprise attack on the enemy fleet. Together with Flying Fortresses that launched a second raid, they sank three warships and damaged other vessels.

During the landings and for the six months thereafter, Pilot Officer Leigh Vial, who had helped Lerew's party escape from New Britain, provided unique intelligence about Japanese movements around Lae and Salamaua. A pre-war assistant district officer in New Guinea, Vial had unusual insight into the geography and ethnography of the area. He was the first white man to climb New Guinea's highest mountain, Mount Wilhelm. Using a radio, maps and binoculars, and alone but for the occasional assistance of two locals, the unassuming Vial fought a solitary war. The enemy became aware of his radio transmissions and were keen to destroy him. He saved many lives and much equipment by warning of enemy attacks and providing intelligence useful for planning Allied air raids. When he first emerged from the jungle after six months of lonely work, the Americans awarded him the prestigious Distinguished Service Cross—only the second awarded in the South-West Pacific Area. 'Golden Voice Vial' would die in an aircraft accident in 1943 after being recalled to Moresby to help with psychological warfare.

On 14 March 1942, eight Japanese bombers and nine fighters attacked Horn Island, only to receive a bloody rebuff from nine American P-40s temporarily stationed there. Yet the presence of Japanese fighters so far south was worrying, reflecting as it did the fact that there were now Japanese bases within 320 kilometres and an hour's flying of Port Moresby. This new reality made life still more perilous for the Allied aircrews in New Guinea. For example, Kingwell returned from raiding Gasmata on 13 March to find five Zeros waiting for him over Moresby. White observed Kingwell exploiting the low cloud cover:

> He skipped so agilely in and out of it, blasted away so valiantly with his pathetic turret guns, defied every rule of aerodynamics and ignored the limitations of his aircraft so successfully that after 20 minutes the Zeros gave up and buzzed angrily home.[15]

Australians on the ground yelled and cheered at this impressive display, for it was an exception to the rule now exercised by the Japanese over Moresby's skies.

Tomorrowhawks and Neverhawks

Fighter support at Port Moresby was needed more than ever, and its absence drained the garrison's ebbing morale. However, by February 1942 there was still not a single RAAF fighter squadron in Australia. With Darwin the defence priority, hopes that American pilots and planes would arrive in Moresby proved fruitless. Australian plans for three fighter squadrons—one each based in Sydney, Townsville and

Port Moresby—depended on supplies. When at the end of February 25 P-40Es ('Kittyhawks', as the Australians knew them) became available, they were immediately allotted to a squadron to be sent to Port Moresby. This squadron, No. 75, was formed at Townsville on 4 March, while sufficient Kittyhawks were also made available for two further fighter squadrons to be raised a fortnight later: No. 76, at Archerfield, Queensland, and No. 77 at Pearce, Western Australia. For the moment, 76 and 77 Squadrons would remain in Australia.

Squadron Leader Peter Jeffrey, DSO, DFC, 'blunt' and 'rugged' but also a superb pilot and leader in the Middle East, was given temporary command to prepare 75 Squadron for operations.[16] Bill Deane-Butcher, a young doctor in a Brisbane hospital, was a close friend of Peter Jeffrey's brother, Rod. Bill and Rod enlisted together as doctors in 1939. Rod, who joined the Army, would die on the infamous Sandakan Death March in 1945. Bill was at the EFTS at Archerfield when he heard about the new fighter squadron. He rang Peter Jeffrey in Adelaide and got the job as squadron doctor. Jeffrey knew the value of squadron doctors, not least as confidants to the CO and to the pilots, and by assisting Deane-Butcher into that position Jeffrey had made an astute choice. Most of the ground crew and some of the pilots of 75 Squadron were to come from 24 Squadron in Townsville, but others came from RAAF units throughout Australia.

Jeffrey's pilots had first to ferry ten Kittyhawks from Bankstown, New South Wales, to Townsville. When they encountered bad weather in northern New South Wales, three pilots crashed, and two were killed. The seven that made it safely were joined at Townsville by five flown from Amberley airbase near Brisbane under Peter Turnbull, DFC. Turnbull and Jeffrey were not the only pilots with combat experience. John Jackson and David Ellerton had also flown with No. 3 Squadron in the Middle East. There Turnbull had achieved nine aerial victories, Jeffrey five, Jackson six and Ellerton two. 'Pop' Woods had flown second pilot in a 32 Squadron Hudson from Port Moresby, while Bruce Anderson had combat experience from Rabaul. As Commanding Officer of No. 3 Squadron, Jeffrey had recommended in late 1941 that Turnbull and Jackson be returned to Australia, having 'done their bit' for the war effort. Consequently he was surprised to see Jackson, a family man in his thirties, eager for more. When he told Jackson he may have done enough, the reply came: 'What are you fighting for? King and country? Well, I'm fighting for my wife and kids and no Jap bastard's going to get them!'[17]

The desert veterans had flown Tomahawks, a slower and more lightly armed version of the P-40, but the remaining pilots had little or no experience of the new fighters. One pilot new to them described the P-40E as 'awe-inspiring', with its huge engine, its long nose blocking the view when you first sat in the cockpit, innumerable levers and dial switches, and the unfamiliar smell of the glycol used as antifreeze.[18] Another pilot who was not so impressed said of its 'rows and rows and rows of electrical switches—I never ever did find out what half of them were for'.[19] Before a standard 'T-shape' arrangement of controls was introduced in 1953, aircraft designers could choose where to place their instruments, so that learning each configuration was sometimes difficult.

The familiarisation experience of Sergeant Jack Pettett in March was reportedly typical. By the time he went into action, he had flown 12 hours 50 minutes in a Kittyhawk, including the ferry flight to Moresby and just one hour of shooting practice. About ten pilots of the squadron had flown Kittyhawks for fewer than 10 hours before entering operations. There was no teaching or development of tactics, perhaps because of lack of time, though this would become an issue in the months ahead. In the nine days of 'crash course' training, there were indeed actual crashes, especially on take-off and landing. The P-40's narrow landing gear made it notoriously liable to 'ground loop'—that is, to rotate dangerously on landing or take-off. Many factors made take-off 'hairy', including the difficulty of seeing from the cockpit of this and all other aircraft types that sat back on a tail wheel, the absence of steering gear other than rudder and brakes, the mud and dust that typified many operational strips, the leftward pull that propellers exerted on aircraft, and the weight and power of World War II planes.

The Kittyhawk, which was destined to be the main RAAF fighter in the Pacific, had other strengths and weaknesses. It was superior in every way to the makeshift fighter it replaced, the Wirraway, but the comparison that would really matter was with the Zero. The 'Kitty' was neither highly manoeuvrable nor very fast. In many ways it was reminiscent of a big American automobile: heavy but strong, comfortable and enjoyable to drive with a good all-round view, and able to survive rough handling from the driver and a battering from other vehicles. Of course, unlike a car, it was designed to kill, and in this it could be highly effective. Bruce 'Buster' Brown, who flew Kittyhawks in 75 Squadron, criticised the aircraft's power–weight ratio as leaving it underpowered, but praised its 'beautiful firepower'.[20] It had six .50 calibre machine guns, whereas the Zero had two 7.7 mm machine guns and two 20 mm cannons.

Which armament was better? The Kittyhawk could put more rounds in the air, and the .50 calibre rounds were very destructive, penetrating engines and even pilot armour, which Zeros rarely carried. The P-40E could fire off its 1400-plus rounds in just over 10 seconds, though a standard burst in a Pacific War dogfight was considerably briefer, and the guns were a bit prone to jam. The Zero's machine guns were faster-firing, but not as destructive, and had a shorter effective range. Its cannons were more powerful, but it carried just 60 cannon rounds, which exited the short cannon barrels with a low muzzle velocity. It was hard to bring down opponents with a Zero cannon. Moreover, the Kittyhawk was sturdy enough to survive many hits from any aircraft, and the armour plating behind the pilot's seat saved lives. Yet it was not a first-rate dogfighting aircraft: its weight, lack of manoeuvrability and poor performance at high altitudes meant it was not comparable to the Spitfire or Messerschmitt Bf 109. The lacklustre performance at high altitude, attributable primarily to the Allison engine's inadequate supercharger, was especially worrying: in the rarefied air above 20,000 feet, Kittyhawks tended to become unstable and, in fighter pilot parlance, to 'fall out of the sky'.[21] And 20,000 feet would prove to be the height at which Japanese aircraft sought to meet them.

Kittyhawk pilots were warned to avoid head-on confrontations with the nimble Zero. Nevertheless it was by no means doomed in dogfights with Japanese fighters. Though its climbing rate was poor—inferior to the Tomahawk, let alone the Zero—it was faster than the Zero in a dive. Japanese fighters, with their light construction and design features intended to maximise manoeuvrability, were generally not as well suited to diving as their heavier Allied opponents. The Kittyhawk's speed (582 kilometres per hour at 15,000 feet) was respectable and slightly superior to the Zero's, meaning that the P-40 should be able to escape a fight, and to prevent a Zero from doing so. If both aircraft were around their top speed, the Kitty could out-turn and out-roll the Zero, as well as the Oscar. However, every manoeuvre costs speed, and thus the Kittyhawk could soon be reduced to the low speeds that favoured its agile opponent. Its liquid-cooled Allison engine was reliable; unlike the Zero, it had self-sealing fuel tanks. John Jackson's brother Ed, flying with 3 Squadron in Libya, wrote to John on Christmas Eve 1941 that Kittyhawks 'were nice kites and an improvement in all ways' over the Tomahawk.[22] John agreed. If the Kitty pilot could take on a Zero from higher or equal altitude in a head-to-head pass and then dive away, his superior firepower might give him victory; then perhaps he could climb and try again.

The Spitfire was every Australian fighter pilot's dream early in the war, but those who flew the P-40 in this period seem universally to have liked it. Spitfires may well have done a better job in the defensive battle ahead, but in other roles their inferior range and tendency to overheat in the tropics were problematic. John Piper, who would score kills in P-40s, felt that moving from the Wirraway to the Kittyhawk was like having a Rolls-Royce after driving a Model T Ford. Another admiring 75 Squadron veteran called the Kittyhawk 'a wonderful warhorse'.[23] Like knights of old, the pilots of 'Seventy-five' would depend on their warhorses for survival.

'Samurai', the Japanese equivalent of medieval European knights, was the title of the memoir of Japan's most famous air ace, Saburo Sakai, who would clash with 75 Squadron over New Guinea. He wrote that the Allied fighter planes in that clash 'were clearly inferior in performance to our own Zeros'.[24]

On 19 March, John F. Jackson was appointed to command 75 Squadron. Though tall and blue-eyed, Jackson did not have the air of a 'boy's own' or movie star pilot. White described him as a 'clumsy looking man with a brown drooping mustache, a florid face and prominent eyes'.[25] He was balding, ambling and no extrovert. Educated at Brisbane Grammar and Scots College in Warwick, Queensland, he had become a grazier and businessman before the war. He had learned to fly and was able to purchase his own aircraft, competing in a Brisbane–Adelaide air race in 1936. That year he had joined the RAAF Reserve. By the time he took off for Port Moresby with the main body of the squadron on 19 March, he had flown 129 wartime sorties. His letters reveal that he thought a Japanese invasion of Australia quite likely. In February he enquired about moving his family from Queensland to the US rather than face 'a fate worse than death at the hands of the rotten yellow Japanese swine'. At other times he urged his wife to move south. On 20 March he toned down his anxiety about his family's predicament, saying: 'I agree there is no immediate danger, and there's always the chance that the tide will be stemmed outside Aussie—here's hoping.' He personally looked forward to going back into action, and said they would beat the Japanese. 'I reckon', he said, 'I can fight ten times as hard now that our shores are threatened.'[26]

In the days ahead, 'John F' would inspire his heterogeneous and inexperienced squadron with his infectious confidence, his quiet but deep-voiced paternal manner, his willingness to lead from the front, and his rugged determination. Jeffrey admired Jackson's courage, but considered him too aggressive, hard to fly in formation with, hindered by less than perfect eyesight and hearing, and generally too old to be a fighter pilot. On the other hand, Arthur Tucker recalled later that 'for those of us who were such raw "sprogs" [new recruits], his presence and mature strength were an immense source of reassurance'.[27] Jackson was, he said, the sort of solid countryman that most Australians would like to think they are, but rarely match.

Tucker was not so reassured by other leaders within the squadron. He had been a Queensland country schoolteacher since the age of 16, was a keen shooter and rugby player, and although only 20 when he joined the RAAF in 1940, these experiences and a tough physique made him confident beyond his years. Tucker's informed commentary on the battles that followed challenges some of the myths that surround them. Concerning this training period he criticised the experienced pilots who, with the exception of John Jackson, on returning from the Middle East did not help the novices in the unit. He felt they did not bring the squadron any marked confidence, but did import cliquish loyalties and their own prejudices. They were, Tucker argued, as ignorant and nervous about the Japanese as everyone else in the RAAF, and their experiences in the mobile desert operations had not prepared them well for the coming struggle—a fight in the style of the Battle of Britain for control of a base. He saw the veterans' attitudes to landing the P-40 as revealing. The new pilots had learned from the Americans to land in the three-point position, like a modern Jumbo jet, with all three wheels touching down at once, whereas the Middle East veterans insisted on 'wheeling her in' on the main undercarriage, front wheels only, probably to avoid landing gear collapses. Tucker later called this approach unnecessary and wrong, for it made pilots use more runway, land faster and end up bouncing on the strip.

Tucker's criticisms may be harsh, but Bill Deane-Butcher also notes that soon after the squadron formed, so did a rift between some inexperienced pilots and some more senior fliers, not including John Jackson. There was, he says, some rough handling of younger men who probably would have responded better to encouragement. The upshot was some 'bitterness and resentment'.[28]

No. 75 Squadron's 17 aircraft flew to Papua via Cooktown and Horn Island. At last Port Moresby's long-suffering garrison would receive the fighter support that had been so conspicuously lacking during 16 air raids. Repeatedly dashed hopes that Kittyhawks would arrive had spawned for them derisive epithets such as 'Tomorrowhawks' and 'Neverhawks', and also fostered anxiety that Japanese invaders would appear before Allied fighters. On 17 March, 33 ground crew of 75 Squadron arrived by Empire flying-boat in Moresby, thus giving substance to rumours of imminent arrival. When four fighters approached on 20 March they were greeted by waving and cheering, until the aircraft's gunfire identified them as Japanese raiders. Thus when, on 21 March, the first flight of four Kittyhawks approached the Seven Mile Aerodrome, led by Peter Jeffrey, machine-gunners defending the airstrip ignored official notification, as well as the sight of extended wheels and flaps—a sure sign that aircraft were landing. First one, then several, machine-gunners opened fire. No pilots were injured, but one bullet missed Jeffrey's head by half an inch. All four aircraft were damaged, one so badly that it would never fly again. However, within two hours, two were serviceable enough to permit the first squadron scramble.

That scramble occurred at 3.53 p.m., when Wilbur Wackett, son of Lawrence, and Barry Cox took off to intercept the daily Japanese reconnaissance flight. Gunner Raymond Neal was part of the Paga Coastal Defence Battery at Port Moresby and remembered it as:

> . . . a typical tropical afternoon with about 60 to 70 percent cloud cover. We observers were watching for the appearance of the Jap bomber between cloud breaks and trying to track his location by the

> sound of his engines. Imagine our delight to hear our fighters come on to the scene. Troops came out from cover on every hill and ridge and were screaming directions to our fighter pilots whenever the enemy aircraft appeared in a clear patch of sky. Unheard, of course, but a reflection of the long months of not being able to deal with an enemy aircraft outside the range of [the anti-aircraft guns] . . . I stood on Paga Hill outside the Battery observation post and watched the battle between our new fighters and the frantically manoeuvring Jap bomber. A break came in the cloud and there the bomber was—my binoculars up and in time to see the final attack by our fighters. A bright burst of fire inside the aircraft then a rapidly developing conflagration and one Jap bomber falling in a screaming uncontrolled dive to make a large splash in the sea beyond the reef outside Moresby Harbour. On every hill and ridge around the shores of Moresby assembled spectator troops cheered this first victory over one of those who had been harassing us for months.[29]

Wackett and Cox had surprised the enemy bomber at 10,000 feet. Pressing the gun trigger on his control stick, each Kittyhawk pilot set an enemy engine alight and saw their target lose height rapidly before exploding 500 feet above the sea. White said, 'We onlookers fell on one another's necks, howling hysterically with joy', while according to Neal's diary, 'Morale rose 1000%'.[30] Truckloads of servicemen drove up, cheering and laughing, staring at the new aircraft in awe. When the main body of the squadron arrived, later in the day, they too were cheered by truckloads of troops.

Some of the garrison naively thought 75 Squadron's presence meant that every enemy bomber would now be shot down. That was impossible, but the Kitties' arrival did ensure that Japanese raiders would now be opposed. It signalled too that there would now be a true fight for Port Moresby, rather than a bloody walkover.

10 The 44 days

While Barry Cox and Wilbur Wackett intercepted the troublesome bomber, LAC Ron Petrich in the squadron signals office was ordered to hold down his morse key in the hope of jamming the intruder's operational frequency. He seemed to have succeeded, for the Japanese base was heard calling the bomber for hours afterwards. Banking on this success, John Jackson decided to take the battle to the Japanese rather than wait for their next raid. Two 32 Squadron Hudsons had been over Lae early on 21 March and, although Zeros wounded two crewmen, they returned with excellent photos of the base and its aircraft lined up wingtip to wingtip.

At 6.30 next morning, ten P-40s took off to make an audacious raid on Lae. Most flying in the months and years of aerial fighting that lay ahead in the South-West Pacific would occur in the morning, before clouds over the mountains made it too dangerous. John 'Cocky' Brereton swerved to avoid a Hudson parked on the side of the airstrip and, after his wingtip touched a mound of earth, felt the undercarriage tear off. His injuries were only superficial, thanks largely to the bravery of medico Deane-Butcher and Ted Church, the equipment officer, who pulled him out unconscious before the aircraft caught fire.

The remaining aircraft approached Lae from the seaward side and, diving through cloud, achieved complete surprise. Five Kittyhawks, piloted by John Jackson, Anderson, Cox, John Piper and Jeffrey Woods, were to strafe the airfield, while the remaining four, flown by Peter Turnbull, Wackett, Pettett and Les Jackson, provided top cover. Facilities at Lae were poor, with no hangars or control tower. Japanese fighter ace Saburo Sakai considered it the worst airfield he had seen. On 22 March, though, it presented a beautiful target to the Australian airmen flying low overhead. After the five strafers had finished their run unopposed, John Jackson turned left and brought his formation back for a second pass over the strip and then a seaward escape. Piper flew so low through the smoke of burning aircraft that his Kittyhawk nearly became a wreck too. He heard a loud clang as the propeller of a grounded Zero ripped out one of his guns and nearly severed the wing's main spar.

Japanese fighters were over the base, supposedly providing top cover, but they had done nothing to impede the attackers. Eventually they reacted, and began dogfighting with the Australians' top cover. Pettett, who had had just one hour's shooting practice in a Kittyhawk, now sought to employ it against a skilled Zero pilot. He twice fired and missed as the Japanese executed a stall turn, then again after the enemy pilot had come head-on and passed him to starboard. The speed and confusion of the action left uncertainty afterwards as to who did what. Piper, whose aircraft was tough enough to survive its brush with a stationary aircraft, found a live one on his tail, and had the uncomfortably vivid experience of watching a Zero fire its cannon at him. He recalled that the shells looked like burning 'cricket balls dipped in petrol' when fired from behind; they then zipped past his cockpit at a disconcerting speed.[1]

Bruce Anderson did not return to base. Flak had reportedly crippled his Kitty during the second strafing run. However, the crash of his Kittyhawk was not the end of the tale of the first man to fire at the Japanese in New Britain. He survived, was captured and, in a bitter twist, was taken back to ill-fated Rabaul. Japanese records indicate that he was murdered there later in 1942. Lerew considered Anderson 'one of the most charming young blokes I've ever known; so full of enthusiasm and so keen to have a go at the Japs'.[2] He must have enjoyed extracting revenge at Lae for the suffering his squadron endured at Rabaul.

The Australians claimed 12 destroyed on the ground and two in combat. Japanese records suggest no air combat losses, but six destroyed and eight damaged on the ground. Of those eight, seven were irreparable with the facilities at Lae.

Another Australian who did not return to share the elation of that success was Wilbur Wackett, victor of the previous day. His reflector gunsight was not working and only one of his guns was firing, but he scored some hits on one Zero before another achieved many hits: on the armour plating behind Wackett's seat, on the seat headrest, which disgorged its horsehair padding all over him, on his wristwatch, and most worryingly, on the engine, which was soon smoking and failing. Wackett dived into cloud. On emerging, he believed he saw two burning Zeros crash into the water, and prepared for a similar watery fate. Protecting himself as best he could, he hit the water at 170 kilometres an hour. He was halfway between the Japanese bases at Lae and Salamaua, some 13 kilometres offshore. He escaped the fast-sinking aircraft and evaded curious sharks as he swam, helped by his Mae West, for up to nine hours towards the shore. Two Rabaul 'natives' saved his life, first by protecting him from other locals inclined to hand him over to the Japanese, and then by guiding the fatigued and sore Australian through exceptionally rough country. When he rejoined the squadron at Moresby, on 22 April, Wackett had crossed Papua from north to south, mainly on foot. By then much had transpired at Moresby.

On 23 March, the day after the Lae raid, the Japanese retaliated. The Kittyhawks were unable to reach the bombers in time to prevent them dropping their bombs. After the bombs had hit, the Kittyhawks were at 7000 feet, the raiders at 20,000, and the P-40s could not catch them. Meanwhile, strafing Zeros destroyed two bogged Kittyhawks, and lost one of their own to anti-aircraft fire.

That day North-Eastern Area Headquarters gave authority for 75 Squadron to withdraw to the greater safety of Horn Island, but left it to Jackson whether to act on this permission. 'Old John', as Jackson was now affectionately known, was well aware how valuable his squadron was to all at Moresby, and decided to stay. Pilots and ground crew were steadily arriving to make his job easier, but the obstacles were still formidable. The squadron's inability to intercept the attackers that afternoon demonstrated the Kittyhawk's technical deficiencies, but also the inadequacy of the air-raid warning system. From 18 March the first RAAF radar station outside mainland Australia, 29 Radar Station, was operating at Moresby, but the surrounding mountains blocked reception to the north. It would only really become effective in 1943. An extensive system of observation posts placed at intervals of 30, 60 and 100 miles from Moresby was planned, but at this time operated only at the 100-mile radius. At that distance there were 20 posts in the Owen Stanleys, but they could not always provide sufficient warning. Fighter sector control, which gave the Kittyhawks information and directions to enable them to scramble and intercept, was primitive, for it depended on unreliable radios. Initially the controller operated from a tent at the top of the airstrip, later from a hillside tunnel overlooking the strip.

No. 75 Squadron faced other difficulties. As the two destroyed Kittyhawks testified, there was virtually no 'hard standing' for aircraft, which frequently became bogged. The incomplete end of the airstrip was especially treacherous for inexperienced pilots. Within the first three days of operations, seven of the 17 P-40s were destroyed, several in accidents. Facilities for servicing the aircraft were poor, and the dust and heat hampered the ground crew. The aircraft were painfully hot to touch. Moreover, there were no instruction manuals. Deane-Butcher said of this oft-forgotten group:

> Some of the ragged looking men servicing the aircraft and guns were a lot older than their young pilots and developed a close personal bond. When their aircraft were damaged or their pilots were hurt their anger was real. When one was lost there was genuine grief.[3]

In an admiring pilot's words, the ground crew 'went about their business working miracles every day'.[4] They were essentially working from dawn to dusk, their only shelter and camouflage bits of tarpaulin strung from trees, unable to hit back personally at those attacking them and their charges.

The squadron's living conditions at Port Moresby, like the Japanese ones at Lae and Rabaul, were not conducive to efficient dogfighting. The original campsite was in a mosquito-infested spot, where toilet facilities comprised a shovel, the nearest long kunai grass and possibly some newspaper. With no labour available to improve these amenities, there was an outbreak of gastroenteritis. When Arthur Tucker mentioned the 'shits' in the logbook entry for his first dogfight, the source was not fear but gastroenteritis, which sent the liquid running down his leg as he flew.[5] 'Leakage' was widespread, and the universal suffering from gastro became an outstanding memory of the battle for Moresby. The intestinal gas associated with 'the trots' and promoted by the baked beans that were often on the menu became much worse at higher altitude. Throughout the war, 'farting like fury' was common among Australian pilots at an altitude above 12,000 feet.[6] Those afflicted with gastro or tropical diseases sometimes had to vomit, first taking off their oxygen mask and trying not to deliver their load onto the windscreen. Eventually the tent camp became so unhygienic that a new one was constructed about 1200 metres from the runway. The camp was also 25 kilometres from the Army hospital, to which the squadron's serious casualties had to endure a rough ride.

The daily routine for those able to fly began at about 4.45 a.m., when they were woken. They dressed, washed and shaved, and shook any creepy-crawlies out of their fleece-lined flying boots before assembling their gear: flying helmet, goggles, oxygen mask, throat microphone (which fitted round the throat like a garter, fastening at the back; though for security reasons, most communication was in radio silence and by hand signals), parachute, Mae West life-jacket, revolver and maps. Most flew in khaki short-sleeved shirt and shorts. If a mission was planned, they would be driven to their aircraft. Otherwise, several would fly on the daily security patrols over Moresby, and the remainder would go to the stand-by tent to await developments over the next 12 hours. They lay on wooden stretchers, or sat in wooden chairs or armchairs taken from deserted homes in Moresby. There were pin-up girls on the tent poles, and an old gramophone player repeatedly played 'Daddy' and 'Frenisi', while, like other RAAF airmen throughout the war, they talked, read, played cards or wrote letters. On the firing of three shots—a red alert—or if the telephone rang, the Intelligence Officer, Stu Collie, would call out 'It's on!' or 'Pilots!' With their adrenaline rushing, men would run to their planes and climb in. Ground crew leaned over to position the safety harness and parachute and to help ensure that microphones and oxygen were working. Some pilots were very anxious at this point. Tucker remembered that once when one of these scrambles proved a false alarm, he quickly got out onto the wing and, with the tension suddenly lifted, his legs lost all feeling and he fell embarrassingly to the ground.

Once airborne, though, the pilots became too busy to reflect on the horrible death that could be their fate at any minute. From the outset they had to be vigilant, scanning the sky for any sign of the enemy. Once aloft, the Kitties assembled in formation and climbed together as fast and steeply as possible. Ideally they would attack from above, with the sun behind them, but only rarely did they get above the Zeros. Though tactical coordination was minimal, it was generally agreed that once you had attacked a Zero, you dived away, using the Kitty's superior speed in the dive, and climbed again to have another go if possible. If attacked from behind, you 'bunted', that is, went into a steep and physically uncomfortable dive from level flight. An alternative description was to 'push everything'—meaning control column and rudder—'on to one corner', and then go straight for 'the deck'.[7] Tucker later recalled that the most important lesson John Jackson taught him was the need to push his stick hard forward in this way to disengage from a Zero in close pursuit.

On 24 March, the squadron's fourth day at Moresby, the Australians had the better of operations. Johnny Piper took off early to intercept a lone bomber, which avoided the P-40's first burst. Piper himself was fired upon, but his second burst started a fire in the enemy's port wing tank, and his third sent the bomber diving out of control. It dropped two bombs before flipping onto its back and falling into the sea.

A Japanese raid on Moresby on 27 March did no damage. Four Kittyhawks intercepted, and seemed to wound one bomber fatally. Flight leader Jeffrey Woods emerged safely from a confrontation with two Zeros, but then noticed a parachute drifting below him and a fire on the ground. He deduced later that the parachute and burning aircraft belonged to Ron O'Connor. Despite the efforts of 39th Battalion patrols, O'Connor's body was never found. The former bank clerk had been the sole survivor of the crashes on the original flight to Townsville.

On 28 March, John Jackson became bogged on the runway, but four other Australians intercepted a formation north-west of Moresby. Five escorting Zeros, flying at 24,000 feet, confronted the Australians. They hit 'Ozzie' Channon's elevator and rudder, and his wrist, but he managed to land perfectly. Sergeant Ron Bailey was last seen diving steeply with a Zero giving chase. After the war his aircraft was found, sunk deep in a swamp, but his body could not be recovered.

Before his death, as an NCO pilot Bailey had not been excluded, as was standard British protocol, from the officers' mess. Instead, in accordance with a practice Peter Jeffrey had instituted for No. 3 Squadron in the desert, a humble marquee acted as mess for all the pilots. This was a common, but not universal, practice among RAAF aircrew in the Pacific. Peter Masters, who joined the squadron on 23 March, described the pilots as 'always good company for each other'.[8] They would share a modicum of beer, then return to their tents.

John Jackson was quite happy when, on 29 March, he wrote home with evident pride: 'The boys already have about 5 scalps and about 12 aircraft destroyed on the ground and some damaged. I think we will hold the yellow B's here, and we have already given them a few decent cracks.'[9]

A few reinforcement aircraft were arriving, but by 31 March, the squadron had just ten serviceable P-40s. Eleven had been lost: four each in dogfights and to Japanese ground attack, three in accidents. As Osmar White observed, 'When a fighter came spinning out of the brazen morning sky above Moresby, writing its own brief epitaph in a thin line of flame and smoke, the chances were even on it being a Zero or one of ours.'[10] The Japanese could better afford this war of attrition. Their 25th Air Flotilla, formed at Rabaul, included 45 Zeros and 36 bombers based at Vunakanau and Lae, as well as 12 flying-boats at Rabaul. Among the forces gathering at Rabaul was the Tainan Air Corps, an elite unit destined to fight over Moresby.

However, the arrival of USAAF aircraft at Moresby on 31 March was a portent. These were Douglas Dauntless dive-bombers, which on 1 April, with 75 Squadron escort, successfully raided Salamaua airfield. That day, Bert Bates and his Catalina crew returned to Moresby after two weeks' leave in Australia. Bates perceived that although the town looked much the same:

> ... a more confident outlook had replaced the old feeling of hopelessness which had become a noticeable characteristic just before we left. Apparently the moral effect of even a comparatively few Kitty hawkes [sic] was enough to give the men a new confidence and the hope of better things to come. No doubt this new feeling was encouraged by the evidence of portions of Japanese planes scattered about ... these signs indicated that the Jap. was no longer going to have it all his own way.[11]

Leading by example, John Jackson made a lone reconnaissance of Lae early on 4 April. He strafed aircraft and personnel from 500 feet up and, on returning, planned another strike on Lae that day. Coming in from the landward side, five Australians made one pass over Lae's neatly parked bombers and fighters, leaving an estimated seven aircraft burning. The smoke from these pyres was still visible as the Kitties strafed enemy huts at Salamaua.

The Japanese reciprocated on 5 April, when seven bombers with fighter escorts approached Moresby at 21,000 feet. Seven Kittyhawks went to meet them. Les Jackson brought down a Zero, while others damaged bombers. Nevertheless, the bombers got through, hitting ammunition and petrol dumps. Two welcome groups of friendly aircraft also arrived that day. One comprised seven replacement Kittyhawks, the other two USAAF P-39 Airacobra fighters. The Americans stayed for about two weeks, gleaning experience and advice from the Australians.

When on 6 April another seven escorted bombers attacked Moresby, nine Kittyhawks and the Airacobras intercepted. The Allies claimed some hits, but no kills. Les Jackson had to crash-land on a reef, but was uninjured. Overhead in his Kittyhawk, his brother saw but did not recognise the man waving and doing a jig on the still dry wing.

On 7 April, Kittyhawks escorted the Dauntless dive-bombers again. The Americans bombed Lae airstrip, claiming 12 aircraft destroyed on the ground and shooting down one Zero. One of their aircraft was downed; its crew appear to have been executed.

John Jackson was also about to experience life behind enemy lines. When the squadron received orders for a lone reconnaissance over the Lae–Salamaua–Nadzab area, he chose to go. He took off at 6 a.m. on 10 April; by 9.30 a.m. he had not returned, and was posted missing. It was a shocking blow to morale. Dauntlesses and Kittyhawks searched for Jackson in subsequent hours and days, with no luck. By 10 a.m. on 10 April the squadron was fighting off enemy aircraft over Moresby, shooting down at least one and possibly three. Pilot Officer Geoff Atherton took credit for a bomber, the first of five Japanese aircraft this quiet, self-assured and inspiringly courageous Tasmanian would count as shared, probable, damaged or destroyed in his time at Moresby.

The next day, the squadron launched a dramatic raid on Lae. Seven Kittyhawks escorted the Dauntlesses, following them as they dived towards their targets, with three Zeros in pursuit. Masters went to assist a Kitty being tailed by a Zero. As Masters hunted the hunter, the Japanese unaccountably executed a high turn into his line of sight. 'With a lot of rudder and all my strength on the stick', Masters later recalled, 'I got about one aeroplane's length lead on the Zero and kept pulling the trigger. I was then very close as I saw part of the wing fall off and pieces from the canopy and cowling.'[12] He watched the Zero fall, out of control. Masters felt no remorse, just elation at performing the job he had been sent to achieve.

Piper got two Zeros, one of which plunged into the sea. He felt satisfaction in shooting the pilot of one of them as he got out on the wing. Other Zeros chased him until he escaped, flying fast and low over the water. One Dauntless went down, and Sergeant David Brown made a forced landing after flak hit his Kittyhawk. With a pistol in one hand and a knife in the other he tried to escape over a hill, until Japanese troops confronted him. Menaced by their machine gun, he surrendered. He was visibly upset when they confiscated a photograph of his fiancée, which was reportedly later returned to him. His captors flew him to Rabaul. The National Archives holds a copy of an RAAF Casualty Section letter written to Brown's father in 1950 informing him that his son's body had been found in a mass grave with ten other RAAF members executed by the Japanese Navy at Rabaul. It reported that:

> After the execution a Japanese officer addressed his men and spoke of the fearless manner in which all the prisoners met their deaths and said that he hoped the Japanese would be prepared to die for their country as bravely as their enemy had done.[13]

When Dauntlesses and Kittyhawks again raided Lae two days later, 'Bink' Davies was shot down, last seen spinning uncontrollably earthwards. Ten years after the war, Davies' elderly father approached Deane-Butcher, clinging to the futile hope that his son had somehow survived, disabled in a remote village, waiting for his father to save him.

Squadron Leader 'Barney' Cresswell, 76 Squadron's CO, was attached to 75 Squadron to gain experience, and flew on a reconnaissance flight in the Lae area with Woods on 17 April. Over the Wau–Bulolo area, a

Zero fired at Woods. Though unable to return fire he waggled his wings to warn Cresswell, 150 metres behind him, and then dived into cloud. Zeros chased Woods for 15 minutes, but he made it home. Cresswell did not. His crashed aircraft was found and he was buried with full military honours. Cresswell was a regular air force pilot and instructor with eight years' experience, but this was his first combat flight.

Later that day came a wild dogfight. Les Jackson led nine Kittyhawks in a clash with an incoming formation about 100 kilometres from Moresby. As usual, the Zeros had a height advantage as the Kitties climbed towards them. One Zero pulled up in front of Tucker, who drilled a devastating long burst into its belly. It was poised to drop when Tucker felt bullets hit his own starboard wing and elevator, and his kite stalled out of the fight. Bill Cowe was heading for the bombers but soon found himself tackling Zeros. His aircraft was hit 12 times, but he reached the sanctuary of clouds. Les Jackson fired tracers into one enemy's cockpit and saw smoke trailing from the damaged engine. Japanese records confirm the loss of two aircraft that day, but mendaciously claimed 18 Allies destroyed.

Flight Sergeant Herbert Brumby and two mates rushed to help men wounded by 'daisy-cutter' bombs dropped by the raiders. The sight of two men with their legs cut off and bodies torn by these anti-personnel bombs moved Brumby to tears. In a post-war interview, Piper reflected that the raids on Moresby were made with 'small aeroplanes and small bomb loads', and that no one should have been as frightened as they were, but sights such as this made it impossible to think so clearly.[14]

On 18 April, eight Kittyhawks confronted twelve Zeros approaching Moresby. The Australians damaged two, but lost Sergeant Richard Granville, whose burning kite was last seen diving steeply. His body was located and Deane-Butcher and his staff had the grim task of carrying his remains on a long, hot trek back to the ambulance. Granville was buried in a coffin draped with an Australian flag made by the women of the Itikinumu plantation. Les Jackson suggested that the flag be forwarded to Granville's parents. Granville was the only son of Lieutenant-Colonel 'Granny' Granville, DSO, a prominent Light Horse commander in the Great War.

However, welcome news also arrived on 18 April: John Jackson was alive! On leaving Lae after his reconnaissance, he had been chased by three Zeros. Unable to outrun them, he turned to take them on, only to find that his guns would not work. With his aircraft 'a mass of holes, windscreens etc all shot away, and on fire', he crashed into the sea. His Kitty sank within seconds. Menaced first by the circling Zeros and then by a crocodile—which initially he took for a log and clung to—he swam for shore. Most locals were too frightened to help, but two 'good lads', mission-educated Edmund and Arthur, offered to guide him to safety. On sighting Japanese search boats all three went bush, 'swimming creeks in my clothes and struggling through swamps and jungle, going down to my waist in slime and mud'. Japanese troops, guided by villagers, landed and chased Jackson's party. He had shed his shoes and socks in escaping the aircraft, but Edmund and Arthur carried him through darkness along the narrow track, sheltered him from rain and fed him. Their quinine also helped him endure. Next morning the sound of a gunshot showed they were still in peril. Jackson's helpers made crutches and cut up a bag to protect his pulpy feet. The sound of American bombers hitting Lae comforted him, but pain haunted his every step while negotiating mountainous terrain in an 'endless climb up and up'. Once when he woke to strange voices, he was grateful they turned out not to be Japanese, for he 'couldn't have run a yard'. Eventually meeting up with a patrol of the New Guinea Volunteer Rifles, Jackson went to Wau. At one point he saw a Kittyhawk 'surprised and shot down in full view of our army'. He later discovered that the victim was 'poor old Barney Cresswell'.

Jackson was flown back to Moresby in a Dauntless on 23 April, with Piper flying escort. As the Dauntless flew low over the Seven Mile airstrip, Jackson waved to the large crowd that had assembled. Suddenly two Zeros that happened to be overhead fired at the Dauntless, until Piper came in and drove them off from Old John's parade. Jackson, manning the rear gun, had a fingertip shot off, but all in all it was, as Deane-Butcher remarked, a brilliant piece of theatre and there were smiles all round.[15]

When Piper damaged a Zero that day, it was the seventh sortie in which he had destroyed or damaged an enemy aircraft; all seven were flown in different P-40s, which was typical in this squadron with its fluctuating numbers of available aircraft. It was also a fine effort from a pilot who considered himself 'a hopeless shot'.[16]

The day of 24 April saw intense action, after four Kitties took off to intercept Zeros. Les Jackson and Bob Crawford tackled Zeros harassing an American Marauder bomber. They forced two away from their prey, but Crawford soon found two Japanese tailing him. One of many hits on his aircraft struck the oil tank, another rendered the rudder bar useless, his throat microphone was shot away, and his arms and legs were lacerated. He was too low to jump, so he made a water landing. After three bounces, the Kitty settled in shallow water. He was rescued.

Seven and a half kilometres (25,000 feet) higher, other Kittyhawks were still fighting. While diving from this great height to intercept, Tucker's windscreen fogged up due to the rapid change in air temperature. He wiped it, then opened the canopy to de-fog it, all the time concentrating on three Zeros, each of which he hit. Channon, who had been leading Tucker's flight, was last seen under attack from a Zero. Tucker believed that Channon, 'a gentleman and extremely game fighter', had probably also been troubled by a fogged-up windscreen.[17] Mick Butler took on two Zeros but, when two more joined in, had to seek cloud cover. He crash-landed his damaged Kitty, careering through high grass at 320 kilometres an hour. An ant hill sheared off the tail and the wings were badly damaged, but he walked away, living testimony to the Kittyhawk's toughness. The 15 Zeros destroyed a moored Catalina before departing.

On Anzac Day 75 Squadron moved to 11 Mile Strip at Bomana. Seven Zeros strafed them during the move. Alan Whetters, flying one of four Kitties airborne at the time, was surprised by a Zero on his tail. The bullets thumping into his armour plate sounded like 'piano notes without the music'.[18] Whetters landed safely, but Japanese strafing destroyed two US bombers on Seven Mile airstrip. Despite these losses, John Jackson declared, in a letter to his wife that day, that he was more optimistic about the war.

Airborne Kittyhawks were again outnumbered by Zeros on 26 April. For one scary moment, Butler was under long-range fire from all five Zeros. By skilfully exploiting the P-40's superior diving speed, he managed to evade his attackers, but only after a 200-kilometre chase. Masters and Cox emerged from six days' hospitalisation for dysentery, though Cox still looked ill. Within two days they would be flying, and fighting for their lives.

David Ellerton was flying a Kittyhawk to Townsville on 27 April when he noticed a P-39 stranded on a Queensland beach. He landed to check on the pilot's well-being, only for his Kittyhawk to flip over on its back while landing on the soft sand. Trapped, Ellerton drowned. He was the fifth tentmate Masters had lost in five weeks. Ironically, 23-year-old Ellerton had been born in Japan.

What came to be known by 75 Squadron as 'the last attack' over Port Moresby occurred the following day, 28 April. John Jackson, Masters, Cox, Cowe and 'Cocky' Brereton were on morning standby when the phone rang, followed by the call 'It's on!' Jackson was first to his aircraft, calling out that Masters would be his No. 2 in their 'V' formation. At 11.15 they became airborne against the approaching eight bombers and 14 Zeros. After 15 minutes, Jackson pointed ahead to aircraft that Masters estimated were 8000 feet above them. Though climbing as high and fast as they could, by the time they intercepted they would still be below the attackers. Jackson motioned for Masters and Cox to move right. They would gain height and attack the Bettys from side-on and below before the Zeros came down on them from above the bombers. With his aircraft straining at its limits at 20,000 feet, Masters fired at a Betty and saw the grimacing side-gunner and the Kitty's bullets puncturing its underbelly and rear fuselage. However, his aircraft stalled, flipped over and went into a dangerous flat spin. After he regained control, through a break in the clouds he could see four specks dogfighting far above. Brereton, who had positioned himself behind the last Betty bomber and inflicted some hits, possibly saw the same fight. Brereton did observe two Zeros harassing another Kittyhawk, which was trailing smoke, but before he could grasp more, two fighters attacked him, damaged his P-40 and forced him to head home. Jackson eventually broke radio silence, and Masters heard him swearing loudly about his inability to get in to an opponent.

Shortly afterwards, White, watching below, saw: 'A little dark cross . . . drawing a line of white straight down the sky. *He was one of ours.*'[19] This was probably John Jackson, who, outnumbered, was shot down. Cox, a good mate of Jackson's, was killed too. When Les Jackson, then in hospital, was informed that his brother was missing, he insisted on looking at the one known crash site, where a Kitty had hit a mountainside so hard that its engine was embedded six feet down. The dead pilot's remains were identified as John Jackson's by the largest piece recovered, a foot in a size ten boot. Masters, who heard Jackson's last words, wrote a fitting epitaph: 'John's voice has not been heard since but his spirit, dedication, determination and will to survive live on as a banner of true leadership for us all to carry forward forever.'[20]

Members of the squadron later stated categorically that John Jackson had been under pressure from senior officers to eschew the 'cowardly' tactics of avoiding direct combat with Zeros, and to dogfight more aggressively. His death, argued these colleagues, was attributable to a desire to confound his armchair critics. In a post-war interview, Tucker named Wing Commanders Charles Pearce and Bill 'Hoot' Gibson as the two who accused 75 Squadron of being 'dingoes'. These leaders, he said, had called in Jackson, who afterwards assembled the pilots in the mess. Jackson told them that the wing commanders had complained that the squadron pilots were not getting in close enough and dogfighting the Japanese. When the pilots replied that it was impossible to dogfight them, and that Jackson himself had told them not to, 'John F' replied, with words presaging his death: 'Tomorrow I'm going to show you how.'[21] Tucker pointed also to a poem by David Campbell about Bill Pedrina, whose name had become a byword for courage, but had been accused by Pearce of being 'scared'.[22]

Pearce and Gibson had outstanding credentials: both had earned DFCs in Europe with 10 Squadron, which Pearce had commanded, and in which Gibson sank a U-boat—the RAAF's first, and Coastal Command's second. Moreover, Wing Commander Bill Garing argued later that Pearce had done all he could to ensure the squadron was well housed, fed and reinforced, and that its problems were passed on to higher headquarters. Yet Pearce and Gibson's disparagement of their own men seems undeniable, and prefigures the way in which criticisms from ignorant higher headquarters would soon harry Australian Army officers on the ground in the Kokoda campaign.

Tucker later argued that in Australia at the time there was 'absolute panic and defeatism and a lack of leadership', and that in order to prevent the spread of fear in Port Moresby, men were singled out as suffering 'neurasthenia'—the World War II equivalent of 'shell shock'—and sent south. Those left behind were, he felt, more scared of the prospect of such public humiliation than of the Japanese. Tucker says that every time a pilot reported a malfunctioning aircraft he would be blamed, 'very loudly', and suspected of cowardice. He claims that one man who was accused and returned to Australia subsequently committed suicide, while another whom Tucker considered 'a very valiant and proper pilot' was also defamed for years afterwards.[23] Piper later remarked of the squadron that throughout the war, 'everywhere we went people [i.e. members of the unit] used to kill themselves'.[24] Tucker himself was not immune from accusations of ducking battle, but was rebel enough to ignore them, and felt that this is why he survived where less mature pilots did not.

Yet it would be naive to imagine that all pilots could cope with combat and be left to it. Some, for the well-being of their fellow airmen and themselves, had to be sent home. Two fine officers who later commanded the squadron, 'Woof' Arthur and Colin Lindeman, both stated that retaining ineffectual pilots would undermine the unit's morale.[25] Direct accusations of cowardice probably undermined morale in Port Moresby in 1942, too. Despite such harsh criticism and the common feeling, only expressed later, that each man would probably not come out alive, morale remained high enough for pilots to continue risking their lives on a daily basis. According to Tucker and Whetters, this high morale owed nothing to senior commanders, for neither Pearce nor Gibson visited the squadron during the Moresby battles, even when John Jackson went missing. It appears a 'poor show' that they were not prepared to air their criticisms of the pilots to their faces, or more importantly, to encourage them in their momentous labours. The CAS, Sir Charles Burnett, did visit the unit at Seven Mile Strip on 22 April, though no details of the visit seem to have survived.

No. 75 Squadron was now almost spent. When Zeros and bombers appeared over Moresby on 29 April, they were unopposed. Astonished ground crew watched Zeros no more than 12 feet overhead; Saburo Sakai observed their amazed faces from his Zeke.

Les Jackson was in temporary command of the squadron's limited resources. In a letter home, John Jackson had described Les as 'a top notch fighter pilot and a great leader', while Masters also felt that, as 'a dynamic fighter pilot and the most senior operational pilot', Les was his brother's logical successor.[26] A complex character, Les was never as close to his men as John, and on the ground could behave erratically to the point of irresponsibility, for example drawing his revolver to make a point, and driving a jeep into an occupied tent. He could be arrogant but also generous, for instance by arranging morale-boosting beer supplies, but

Tucker saw him as a negative influence, 'a divisive, degenerate, drunken lout without any sense of responsibility whatever'.[27] Whetters was more sympathetic. Acknowledging that Les was 'unusual' and 'did not have the respect of all pilots', he emphasised that the loss of his brother was 'a big blow', and that given the stress all were under at Port Moresby, he led the squadron 'as well as could be expected'.[28] Yet while Les Jackson apparently made a poor impression on many, in the air he dedicated his considerable skills to the destruction of the nation that had killed his brother, even if it meant flying while suffering from malaria.

The last ten days of April were exceptionally difficult, for often Kittyhawks landing or taxiing after meeting the first attacking wave of enemy aircraft were strafed by a second wave. On 30 April, this ordeal ended, as 75 Squadron was relieved from the air defence of Port Moresby. Its Operations Record Book reported that during that month, it had flown 638 hours, 177 of them in 'air fighting'. It finished with just three serviceable and seven unserviceable aircraft, as well as 211 officers and men.[29] For 44 days, since 21 March, it alone had been responsible for the aerial defence of Port Moresby.

Now Airacobras of Nos 35 and 36 Squadrons USAAF were to assume that responsibility. Some of their pilots had been in Moresby to learn from the Australians early in April. They had got on well, and now the Australians cheered the 26 Airacobras that arrived on 30 April. There should have been more, but in transit from Australia nearly a dozen aircraft were lost or delayed in terrible weather. Another four were lost on 1 May, in their first strike against Lae.

The Australians did what they could to help and on 2 May, when enemy raiders approached Moresby, three 75 Squadron Kittyhawks joined seven Airacobras against them. The three Australians—Whetters, Crawford and Sergeant Don Munro—grappled with the Japanese. Soon Crawford saw Munro's aircraft spinning earthwards, burning slightly. Munro, a 19-year-old bank clerk, had only arrived in Moresby on 28 April and was now dead. Another novice airman crashed his Kittyhawk in taking off to look for Munro. This left just one operational aircraft, which on 3 May lasted just seven minutes in the air before its engine overheated.

Les Jackson officially took command of 75 Squadron on 5 May. There was worrying news that night: a Japanese naval invasion force was headed for Moresby via the Coral Sea. The Engineering Officer, Bill Matson, who had continuously performed miracles with the limited means available, told Jackson he could have three Kittyhawks serviceable to fly against this fleet. When Jackson called for volunteers to fly this mission—likely to be a suicide one—all pilots volunteered. Jackson said he would fly one and drew lots for the other two. Butler and Masters 'won'. These three pilots and 27 ground crew, also volunteers, stayed behind when on 7 May, the rest of the squadron embarked for Townsville. The Battle of the Coral Sea was in the balance, and on 8 May there was great uncertainty in Moresby, where 75 Squadron made provisional escape plans. The Coral Sea battle saved Moresby without the assistance of these P-40s, two of which were damaged in an enemy air raid on 9 May. Jackson flew to Cairns, and the other members shortly afterwards. Tucker described the pilots as 'completely dead to it' by this stage. He himself had lost more than 10 kilograms from an already thin frame.[30]

Collie summarised the unit's claims between 21 March and 3 May as: 18 enemy aircraft destroyed in the air, 17 on the ground, with a further four probables in the air, and 47 damaged in the air or on the ground.[31] In turn he said the unit lost 15 in the air and two on the ground. Five others were written off in accidents. Of the 37 pilots who served in the squadron in this period, 11 were killed in aerial combat, as well as Squadron Leader Cresswell, and another was killed in an accident. While the claims of kills were, as in every air force, exaggerated, Japanese figures for Rabaul, Lae and Salamaua between 1 April and 3 May indicate that 34 Japanese aircraft were damaged in air combat, and a further eight hit by anti-aircraft fire. Twelve were lost in the air, with another ten destroyed or badly damaged on the ground. Fifty were less badly damaged. The sole Australian fighter squadron in New Guinea had contributed significantly to these Japanese losses. Theirs was a remarkable effort, especially given that the unit's pilot strength in the period probably averaged between seven and 12, and it rarely had more than five or six aircraft serviceable at any one time. On the other hand, the Japanese bomber strength—about 24 aircraft at Rabaul—may have been insufficient to damage irreparably the facilities at Port Moresby.

The statistics were probably less important than the fact that from 21 March whenever the Japanese came over—often with numerical and height advantage—Australian pilots had almost always opposed them. Sometimes in only a few aircraft, but always aggressively. This ensured casualties among the Australians, but also brought benefits. By attacking upwards they usually scattered the attacking bomber formations, whose bombing accuracy suffered accordingly; their accuracy also suffered because they flew higher than they would have if unopposed. Furthermore, Japanese fighter strength had to be committed to escorting the bombers. Their most famous ace, Sakai, was quoted above on the inferiority of Allied aircraft in that period. He praised the pilots of these aircraft for their willingness to engage the Zeros, for 'regardless of the odds, their fighters were always screaming in to attack'. He emphasised that the Japanese pilots' status as 'skilled air veterans' together with 'the Zero's outstanding performance . . . afforded us a distinct advantage. The men we fought then were among the bravest I have encountered.'[32]

Those courageous RAAF pilots had damaged the myth of Japanese invincibility, had shown that even the wonderful Zero could be beaten, and often did this in sight of Allied troops whose morale needed boosting and who came to idolise the pilots.

One of those idols, Jack Pettett, who was there from the outset and whom Deane-Butcher considered 'quiet, resolute and top quality', reflected on the human fragility of most 75 Squadron pilots. The 44 days were for them 'the most fearful in their lives. A constant threat to one's life in a burning aircraft is hard to live with', especially when they had no idea when the ordeal would end. He summarised life at Moresby in this period as 'horrendous—bad conditions, bad living and a bad situation'.[33]

The pilots endured and completed their job. It would be wrong to see them as a united 'band of brothers', a 'happy few' without the failings or disagreements that afflict every group of people. They tended not to build close friendships. Tucker, who after the war devoted much of his life to helping others, remembered later how little the deaths of other pilots affected them. 'Rather than having squadron cohesion,' Alan Whetters recalled, 'they were more individuals fighting together.'[34] A large dose of individualism was always inherent in fighter squadrons. Flying alone promoted that independence, while in a larger aircraft you were part of a crew, whose fate was linked with yours.

The unit's tactics reinforced this disconnectedness. Tactical coordination of 75 Squadron was minimal, with little or no briefing before operations, and no attempt to draw lessons afterwards. Although John Jackson inspired his men, and while there was general agreement on the stupidity of dogfighting Zeros, in the air it was 'every man for himself'. This ill-advised approach was also typical of the Japanese, who despite the regimentation associated with their militaristic government, emphasised individualism in aerial combat. A 75 Squadron flight sergeant, probably Mark Sheldon, who challenged Les Jackson on the absence of tactics was upbraided for it. The atomised nature of the squadron was exacerbated by the lack of sympathy from senior officers inside and outside the squadron.

The unreasonable macho expectations that had egged John Jackson to sacrifice his life were not confined to officers outside the squadron. A 'cult of toughness' hung about the unit, causing men to fly when too ill to do so effectively.[35] Sick servicemen never want to let their mates down, but here there was pressure from 'rough and tough' senior pilots not to complain of illness. Deane-Butcher noticed an expectation that pilots would press on, even if they doubted the mechanical ability of their Kitty to reach its target; the unpalatable alternative was to risk being accused of cowardice.[36]

Far more important than the intolerance that marred 75 Squadron's experience were the results of the Kittyhawks' defence. They ended Port Moresby's status as a helpless target and gave it time to become a great base from which Allied bombers could strike the Japanese effectively. Because 75 Squadron ensured that Japanese air power could not neutralise Moresby, it became all the more imperative for Japan to launch seaward and landward attacks to secure that port. The Coral Sea battle thwarted the seaborne attack; the landward attacks, at Milne Bay and Kokoda, would bring the RAAF further challenges, and laurels to add to those that Jackson's few had won in those '44 Days'.

An RAAF padre wrote to John Jackson's mother in August 1942, responding to a query about her son's grave. He replied, 'We shall never forget the Kittyhawks of 75, they created a precedent that will always be an inspiration to those who follow'.[37] In November 1942, Seven Mile Drome would be renamed 'Jackson's Strip', and is today called Jackson's International Airport.

Australians over the Coral Sea

The dangerous work of the RAAF Catalinas and Hudsons did not cease while 75 Squadron defended Moresby. On 6 April, when Terry Duigan's

Catalina was flying reconnaissance from Tulagi, in the Solomons, he received a distress signal from a USAAF Marauder that had crash-landed at Woodlark Island after being damaged in a raid on Rabaul. At Woodlark, Duigan's crew spotted a rubber life raft on the bay. He landed between dangerous coral reefs and taxied to the dinghy, in what was reportedly the first open-sea rescue of the Pacific War.

At the beginning of May, the Japanese were clearly manoeuvring to advance further in the South-West Pacific Area. They occupied Tulagi, which RAAF personnel escaped without loss. Using Moresby as a base or staging post, Hudsons, Catalinas, American Mitchells and Flying Fortresses searched for clues to the enemy's moves. On 4 May, 19 enemy transports were spotted at Rabaul. That day Allan Norman's 20 Squadron Catalina signalled that it was under attack south of Bougainville. The plane was never heard from again, though after the war the decapitated bodies of all nine crew members were found at a Japanese execution ground near Rabaul. In the same grave was 75 Squadron's David Brown. Norman's service had been hectic: he had escaped Rabaul and Gasmata just before the Japanese arrived, and had been at Tulagi during the first Japanese air raid. After that raid, he and his Catalina crew sought vainly to catch and fight the raiders. His luck had then run out.

Two Catalinas flying in the same area reported seeing large enemy vessels, one close to the Louisiade Archipelago just east of New Guinea. The danger to Port Moresby was apparent. On 6 May Godfrey Hemsworth, whom we last saw negotiating his damaged Cat through a marathon flight from Rabaul, was reporting seeing enemy vessels south-east of the Louisiades, when he interrupted and stated he was under attack. His 'Cat-boat' fell to enemy fighters. Its crew were captured by a Japanese destroyer, transferred to a transport and never heard of again. Hemsworth, whom Pearce had criticised earlier in the year for his 'Quantas outlook', had been flying a wider reconnaissance than he was required to make.

The invasion fleet turned back, though land-based Allied aircraft from the South-West Pacific Area did not halt it. The USAAF bombers were operating at extreme range, thus making it difficult to search long for the ships. The US carrier-based aircraft from the South Pacific Area were the key to the Japanese strategic defeat in the Coral Sea. Among those aircraft was a Wildcat fighter flown from USS *Yorktown* by Ensign Leslie Knox. The 25-year-old had been born in Brisbane, and moved to the

US at an uncertain date. While hunting enemy aircraft with ten other Wildcats in poor weather and failing light on 7 May, he shot down a Kate torpedo bomber with his first burst, scattering the enemy formation. The subsequent dogfight so harmed the Japanese force that only six of the 27 Japanese aircraft in the attacking formation made it back to their carriers. Knox never made it back to his carrier either, but the magnitude of his achievement was recognised in the award of the Navy Cross and the naming of a destroyer escort, USS *Leslie L.B. Knox*.

The vital role of the US aircraft carriers first became apparent to the Allied Air Force in the South-West Pacific Area when a bomber crew returned to Moresby and reported seeing 'other aircraft' attacking the Japanese ships. This indicated some of the command challenges ahead, though the result of the Coral Sea battle was precious to Australia. That battle epitomised the importance of aircraft to the Pacific War, for though categorised as a great naval battle, neither side's ships actually sighted or fought each other: the attacks were made by aircraft. The Battle of the Coral Sea is sometimes described as a battle that saved Australia. It did preserve Australia from air raids that the supporting Japanese carrier fleet planned on Townsville, Cooktown, Coen and Horn Island, but Japanese Imperial Headquarters had decided that invading Australia was for the foreseeable future beyond their army's resources. The battles of the Coral Sea in May and Midway in June sealed that decision.

Conquering New Guinea, however, remained a high Japanese priority, and a dangerous one for Australia.

11 Trouble at the top

May 1942 brought Darwin welcome relief from air raids. The Battle of the Coral Sea reduced the chance of an invasion of the Northern Territory, so the need diminished for the Hudsons to reconnoitre enemy ports looking for invasion fleets. They did, however, continue hindering Japanese consolidation of their gains on Timor and Ambon.

'Tich' McFarlane, recently appointed CO of No. 2 Squadron, led an eventful shipping raid on Ambon Harbour on 13 May. After just clearing the hills behind the town, each of the five captains in the first flight chose one ship as a target and dropped his four 250-pound (115 kilogram) bombs from mast height. The bombs were fused for an 11-second delay, but as John Venn dropped his bombs there was an immediate explosion within the ship. His aircraft disintegrated in the blast. The squadron diary stated simply: 'It is not thought that P/O Venn or any of his crew survived.'[1] Astonishingly, one crew member did survive: Leonard Omsby was captured, only to be executed by the Japanese the same day. The other aircraft made it home and reported having sunk one ship (Venn's) and hitting two others. The post-war American assessment committee did not confirm that Venn's sacrifice had in fact sunk the enemy ship. It raises the question, which must have occurred to the crews at the time: were their raids worth it? A Japanese source suggests that the attacks had an impact.

A retreat of Japanese bombers from Penfui to Kendari was attributed to 'the enemy's persistent air-raids', while a Japanese senior officer noted that at Koepang, an initial attitude that it was dishonourable to build air-raid shelters collapsed under the bombing, and refuges were built.[2]

The Japanese were rarely surprised as they were on 13 May, for by monitoring Darwin radio traffic and placing listening posts, they generally had some warning of raids. Thus on 22 May, when McFarlane led another Ambon shipping raid, the enemy was expecting him. The ships, on the move, met their attackers with heavy flak, and after the bombers had fruitlessly tried to sink them, Zeros attacked. They picked out two Hudsons which had dived in last against the ships. Phil Brooks and his crew died when their Hudson crashed into the sea. Brooks, 24, had a one-year-old son, Tony, who would spend much of his life trying to come to terms with his loss.[3] Graham Allchin, flying only his sixth mission, was chased by two Zeros and, with one engine alight, he and Laurence Montgomerie baled out. Their two crewmates died before or in the crash. Allchin and Montgomerie were captured and executed. While the separated Hudsons were shot down, the remainder were in a 'V' formation. The Zeros disengaged after one was shot into the sea and others were damaged.

If the Japanese were reasonably efficient at predicting raids from Darwin, that Australian base was developing a vastly superior warning system. Whereas the Japanese had no radar to detect the Hudsons, three new 'radio location stations'—Nos 38, 105 and 109—were formed in the Darwin area in June. No. 38 would be relocated to Bathurst Island in August, thereby giving Darwin an extra 250 kilometres of coverage. Radar has been called the 'single most important factor' in the air war in northern Australia.[4]

In June the Japanese resumed their raids on Darwin, hitting the RAAF aerodrome and the town over four consecutive days. Casualties and damage on the ground were slight, and the USAAF P-40s shot down more aircraft than they lost.

Four Hudsons were attacking enemy barracks on 2 June when two aircraft collided. One, under Robert Gill, crashed with the loss of all on board. Lindsay Trewren managed to coax the other severely damaged Hudson back to base and resume what would become a distinguished air force career. That first week of June brought the single most important battle of the Pacific War. At Midway, US forces sank the four Japanese aircraft carriers that had delivered the blow on Darwin. Japan's ability to project significant air power into Australia and other major Allied bases had been shattered, probably for good.

When after five weeks the Japanese resumed their raids on Darwin in late July, they attacked at night, setting a pattern for most of 1942. They tended now to attack in small groups, usually of three. When they tried a daylight raid with more than 40 aircraft on 31 July, they lost up to 20, to the Americans' one.

'Bloody, Bloody Darwin'

Few of the thousands of RAAF personnel serving in the Northern Territory liked it. The main town was often described as 'Bloody, Bloody Darwin'.[5] For aircrew, there was no clearly defined 'operational tour' in the Territory, but they had a reasonable chance of being posted out soon. For RAAF non-aircrew, the prospect was more like 18 months, or even longer for essential or forgotten personnel.

LAC Ted Wardley arrived in the Territory full of enthusiasm, but this was dampened first by the 'Gestapo methods' he endured on arriving at Birdum, where, in preparation for a medical examination, all men were forced to strip naked and queue for a long time in 106 degree (41°C) heat. A seven-month posting to Millingimbi—the mere name of which drew sympathy from other airmen—further tested his optimism.[6] There was a good deal of prejudice against the Territory, and those who fell in love with it, like A.F. Howells, were unusual. One of his mates once asked him pityingly, 'What the hell are you always looking at?' Howells replied, 'The country you mug', to which his stunned cobber responded: 'That ain't bloody country you're looking at, mate . . . it's bloody desert!'[7] After five months in Darwin, LAC David Howdle, a driver, wrote this glowing praise: 'Darwin is a very pretty place, lots of coast line with some beaut sights, good winter climate . . . marvellous how everything is so green, lots of Wallabys and coloured birds, good roads from Darwin to Alice Springs.'[8] The outlook of a bomber crewman who returned there in 1944 was more typical: '. . . so here I am . . . back on Australian soil but what soil. It's too barren for me.'[9]

Naturally a shortage of lush vegetation was not the only deficiency that discouraged airmen. Another was beer. The RAAF had a beer ration, which North-Western Area AOC Frank Bladin recalled as 'one bottle, per man, per month, perhaps'.[10] The 'perhaps' was apposite, but in fact it seems officially to have been two bottles per man per week. Bladin also recalls that every mess knew which of its members were teetotallers and thus possible sources of an extra bottle.

The other deficiency was of women. Allan Brayne, of 31 Radar Station, was in the Territory from December 1942 to June 1944, and in that time saw 'a few nurses in the distance at the Adelaide River races in June 1943 and the wives of a couple of our aboriginal neighbours at Peron Island. That was it.'[11] Howdle was in the Territory for 13 months before he spoke to a woman there. There were about a dozen sisters in the RAAF's No. 1 Medical Receiving Station. Bladin observed them 'rout an AIF company of infantry' when, on being driven north from Daly Waters to Batchelor, they contemplated a hundred soldiers in makeshift showers served by the main pipeline along the roadway. 'The men', said Bladin, 'simply could not stand the soprano cheers and shrieks of laughter' emanating from the women.[12] There was a different reaction when the Tivoli Show brought female dancers to Darwin. Howdle, who drove airmen to the show and thoroughly enjoyed it himself, 'never saw such a crowd of men'.[13]

Entertainment for airmen was very limited. Fishing and swimming were classic forms of relaxation wherever possible in the Territory, while sunbaking was a common practice. In the first Darwin raid, 13 Squadron lost all its phonograph records except one: Vera Lynn singing 'It's a lovely day tomorrow'. At first this may have seemed prophetic, but the song was played so often that when someone eventually smashed it there was enormous relief. At Hughes Field there were no movies throughout 1942. However, Peter Finch, at that time a well-known radio and stage personality in southern states, was serving there as a gunner. He starred in fortnightly shows at the base, where his pièce de résistance was a hilarious send-up of Flight Lieutenant Dalkin: Finch wore a fake long moustache, an oversize cardboard DFC and bottle tops on his shoulders as rank insignia. The shows ceased when Finch went south to star in movies. One diarist recorded, tongue in cheek, in April 1943 that 'cricketophilia'—obsession with cricket—had struck one-third of 452 Squadron.[14] Before 31 Squadron arrived, its members sent two pianos for entertainment, in boxes marked 'Aircraft parts. Handle very carefully.' These pianos were arguably as important to sustaining morale in the unit as any spare parts would have been. Even so, for many of that squadron, life at their base 'was just an existence'.[15]

One famous RAAF airman at home in the Northern Territory was Squadron Leader Clyde Fenton. In the 1930s he had been the well-known Katherine 'flying doctor' in the Northern Territory Medical Service. When war broke out he joined the RAAF, and in April 1942 returned to Darwin with the newly formed No. 34 Squadron. This was one of four transport squadrons, Nos 33 to 36, created in February–March and allocated, one each, to North-Eastern, North-Western, Western and Southern Areas. Like all the Allied transport squadrons in the South-West Pacific Area at the time, 34 Squadron's aircraft were largely obsolete: Tiger Moths, Ansons and DH84s. In August 1942, a new RAAF unit, 6 Communications Flight (later 6 Communications Unit) took over and extended the work of 34 Squadron, under Fenton's command. Based at Batchelor, it found and rescued lost servicemen, civilians and aircraft, made emergency medical flights, transported VIPs, towed targets and carried mail and fresh food to isolated posts across the entire Territory coast. It undertook these varied activities in 'probably the strangest assortment of aircraft ever allocated to a R.A.A.F. squadron'.[16] By war's end it had employed DH82s, DH84s, DH90s, Tiger Moths, Ansons, Vultee Vengeances, Hudsons, Beauforts, Catalinas and Walrus amphibians. By then it had grown to 230 personnel and 29 aircraft. Fenton and his squadron formed a philanthropic flying circus, its extrovert and daring fliers inspired by their leader.

Townsville—big base, elusive target

In July, Japanese bombers hit not only the Northern Territory but also Western Australia and Queensland. Their target in Western Australia was Port Hedland, an advanced operational base, which was not heavily damaged.

A more significant objective was Townsville. In February 1942 worried Army generals had considered abandoning it with the rest of Queensland north of Brisbane. Thousands of civilians had left Townsville in the wake of the Japanese landings in New Guinea in March. However, it rapidly developed into the biggest and most important Allied airbase in Australia. It was the largest aircraft depot in northern Australia, the location of North-Eastern Area Headquarters, site of four operational aerodromes (with many more on the way), and a staging point through which aircraft travelled to New Guinea.

The Coral Sea battle had stymied Japanese plans to use their carrier planes to bomb Townsville, but shortly before midnight on 25 July, Townsville had its first air-raid warning. At 12.40 a.m. three Emily flying-boats flew over and dropped six bombs, which fell harmlessly into the sea. A single Emily dropped eight bombs outside the town early on 28 July, and the following day another flying-boat dropped seven bombs, breaking a few windows and dodging two Airacobras that managed to achieve hits. The last raid in the area occurred at Mossman near Cairns on 31 July, when a lone aircraft dropped a single bomb, which landed 20 metres from a house and, by injuring a child, caused the first civilian air-raid casualty on the east coast. These were mere nuisance raids.

A mission against Horn Island on 7 June was more destructive. Japanese bombers dropped about 200 bombs on the RAAF station, damaging buildings and equipment and wounding three. Seven other raids followed in 1942. Consequently, when Sergeant John Clark stayed there overnight in January 1943, he noticed that his hut was 'riddled with shrapnel holes'.[17] Yet Horn Island remained a valuable base and staging post. Even without the enemy's attention, it was a rough posting, short of water and diversions.

Growing strength

Townsville's growth reflected a broader trend in mid-1942: America's burgeoning air strength in the South-West Pacific Area. The Allies would not achieve numerical parity with the Japanese in the area until the end of the year, but it was a year in which America sent more aircraft to the Pacific than to Europe. Finding meaningful figures for respective air strength is notoriously difficult, but even by May 1942 the numbers were probably close.

However, the situation was not as rosy as the bare figures suggest. The unserviceability rate among the available Allied planes was worryingly high, primarily because of dry and dusty airfields. Not only was wastage high, but replacing aircraft from the US was slow and costly. Moreover, the only fighters then available to the Allied Air Forces—the Kittyhawk and Airacobra—were inferior to the Zero. The determination of the British and American governments to 'Beat Hitler First' meant that the South-

West Pacific would not suddenly become flush with top-quality aircraft, so the Allied Air Forces were not yet ready to launch a major offensive.

General Douglas MacArthur, who argued that defeating Japan should be the Allies' strategic priority, consistently asked for more resources from the US. So did the other senior American commander in the Pacific, Admiral Nimitz, who controlled forces in the Pacific Ocean Area. His ships and aircraft had so far achieved the greatest American successes against Japan: the Doolittle Raid, the Battle of the Coral Sea and the Battle of Midway. As well as appealing directly to American leaders, MacArthur urged the Curtin government in Australia to ask Britain for sufficient aircraft to re-equip or bring up to strength all existing squadrons, and to create five more fighter squadrons. This would require 616 more aircraft. Dr Evatt, Curtin's special emissary in London, could not get most of this, though in late May Churchill agreed to send Australia three Spitfire squadrons, two of them Australian. The Spitfires were en route to Australia in June when Rommel captured Tobruk, so Britain asked that the Spitfires be diverted to North Africa. Curtin, with MacArthur's backing, refused, but was ignored. The three promised squadrons would make no impact in the North-Western Area until early 1943.

A more satisfactory result concerned the first 90 Australian-made Beauforts, which Britain had ordered, but now allowed Australia to retain. From January 1942 the Department of Aircraft Production was responsible for Beaufort manufacture. The first Australian-built Beauforts went to 100 Squadron, formed as a torpedo-bomber unit in February 1942. It was named in honour of the RAF 100 Squadron which had lost most of its Vildebeests and crews fighting in Malaya, and which formed the personnel nucleus of the new squadron. The Beaufort became a workhorse of the RAAF, serving with ten operational squadrons and even more communications and training units.

It was a controversial aircraft, particularly before technical deficiencies were overcome in 1944. Nearly 300 Beauforts would be lost, more than half of them in accidents in Australia. There were 467 RAAF Beaufort fatalities—more than 500 if one includes Australians with RAF Beaufort units—and this represented more than 20 per cent of trained Beaufort aircrew. Herb Plenty, who won a DFC in the Hudson and a Bar to it in the Beaufort, felt that although the Beaufort was faster than the Hudson, it had a nasty swing on take-off, many protruding edges to inflict knocks, inadequate little red lights rather than illuminated gauges for night flying, no automatic pilot and was generally 'not as pleasant to fly'.[18] Wing Commander Geoff Nicoll, DFC, another outstanding Beaufort pilot, asserted in a 1944 interview that the Beaufort was very suitable as a medium bomber, but:

> . . . the general opinion of the Beaufort was that it was a good aeroplane but was obsolete in design . . . It was unpleasant to fly for long periods particularly at night, was generally uncomfortable for the crew and was rather too big to enable rapid manoeuvrability.[19]

The Commonwealth Aircraft Corporation engendered hopes of more local production by proposing a new interceptor fighter, eventually called the Boomerang. The War Cabinet, looking at this possibility in February, decided to accept this much improved version of the Wirraway for three reasons: it would provide employment for the 2000 skilled workers who had now completed the Wirraway program; Wirraway parts and materials, which would contribute substantially to the new fighter, were readily available; and, perhaps most importantly, if American fighter availability fell or disappeared, the Boomerang would provide some insurance.

The fact that the Boomerang was unofficially called 'the panic fighter' reflects the fear of Japanese invasion and great uncertainty about the supply of aircraft from Britain and America. An impressive array was on order, as Table 2 suggests. It shows the supply situation of the main types on 8 May 1942.[20]

Table 2 indicates that supply was still far from meeting demand, yet it also hints at the phenomenal growth of the wartime RAAF. By May 1942 the force was 22 times its size on the eve of war. More than 79,000 men and women had joined the RAAF, although just 43,000 were directly involved in home defence units. The remainder were in the EATS (33,000) or EATS squadrons (2000). In early 1942, the Air Staff and War Cabinet mulled over the appropriate goal for the expansion of the RAAF. The Air Staff suggested 73 squadrons, and the War Cabinet approved, subject to the availability of aircraft. When, and if, it reached its full size, this 73-squadron force would comprise 1314 aircraft ranging from flying-boats to fighters, and heavy bombers to army cooperation planes. No fewer than 24 fighter squadrons were planned, thus showing

TABLE 2 AIRCRAFT ON ORDER, 8 MAY 1942

Type	No. on order	Source	Delivery details
Beaufort	180	DAP*	80 by end July
Catalina	119	US	27 received
Hudson	246	—	All received or en route
Kittyhawk	771	—	50 received, 69 en route
Beaufighter	362	UK	54 received or shipped
Vultee Vengeance	367	US	12 possibly en route
Boston	—	US	27 received from NEI**
Boomerang	100	DAP*	10 a month from June 1942
Transports	90	US	Indefinite wait
Flying Fortress	143	US	Indefinite wait

* Department of Aircraft Production

** Netherlands East Indies

that the lessons of Malaya and Darwin had been learned. The War Cabinet's caveat proved sensible: lack of aircraft rendered impractical a plan to have 45 of these squadrons assembled by the end of the year.

American aid was fundamental to the expansion of the RAAF. The generous Lend-Lease program—by which the US lent or leased material to Allied nations, with no payment required until after the war—benefited Australia from the time of Pearl Harbor. Aircraft and aviation supplies were central to the Lend-Lease program in Australia. In return for this vital material, from September 1942, a reciprocal aid agreement had Australia providing food, transport and military stores to the US. By this means, during the war Australia paid more than 80 per cent of the approximately $US 1.4 billion it received in aid. The accounts were settled by 1946.

The government and senior RAAF officers remained committed to the EATS, and by the time George Jones took over as CAS in May, the scheme that he had so efficiently directed in Australia was again fully operational, turning out 800 airmen per month. The needs of the USAAF in Australia put added pressure on existing training facilities, so that, for example, six EATS schools were vacated for USAAF formations, thus requiring the remaining schools to take on more staff and students.

The RAAF and the Allied Air Forces in the South-West Pacific Area had a great need of airfields. In March, General George Brett was seriously concerned about the lack of bases in northern Australia. The following month, the United States Army Air Services was created, and would construct many new airfields in the South-West Pacific Area. On 19 March, a new RAAF unit, No. 1 Mobile Works Squadron, was also formed for this vital work. When it began operations in July, it comprised 27 officers and more than 1000 airmen, with tasks including surveying, planning, camouflage, engineering, camp construction, and repair and maintenance. Its function was to perform all these tasks in forward areas, under threat of air attack. The squadron had enough work, according to one calculation, to keep it fully occupied for five years in the Northern Territory alone. It was the forerunner of many more such units, which came to be called airfield construction squadrons. These units did essential work and their performance everywhere was, as one senior RAAF officer put it, 'absolutely first class'.[21] By the end of 1942 there would be a dozen airfields along the road to Katherine. By the end of 1943, there would be almost 50 in the Territory. General Arnold, Commanding General of the USAAF, concluded in a visit to the South-West Pacific Area in September 1942 that the availability of airfields—rather than the availability of aircraft—would decide the outcome of the air war. He was barely exaggerating, for it was an area in which the Japanese, with a dependence on manual labour rather than machines for airfield construction, lagged far behind.

During his visit, Arnold spoke to General MacArthur in Brisbane, which was from 20 July the headquarters of the Allied Air Forces, and General Headquarters of the South-West Pacific Area. Arnold wrote in his diary that 'everyone' was critical of the Australians and their methods. MacArthur informed him, in the light of recent experience in New Guinea, that 'Australians will not fight', that the typical Australian was neither a 'bushman' nor 'a field soldier', but just 'a city slum dweller. The Massachusetts soldiers knew more about the New Guinea jungle in two days than the Australians in two years.'[22] These slanders would soon be revealed to be well wide of the mark. They are indicative, however, of a widespread attitude towards Australians among MacArthur's leadership group. They were particularly harsh judgements, given the generous willingness of the Australian government and people to accommodate MacArthur's military and economic demands.

MacArthur harboured prejudices against some Americans too. General Brett, the air force officer who until MacArthur's arrival had been the senior commander in the south-west Pacific, was snubbed by MacArthur, who on deigning to speak to him after eight days in Australia, launched into a tirade against the American air force. Brett interpreted this as sour grapes from MacArthur's own failure in the Philippines. The interview ended cordially, but in July MacArthur sought a replacement for Brett. He fixed on Major-General George Churchill Kenney. Short, with close-cropped grey hair and dark blue eyes, Kenney had been highly decorated in World War I, when he shot down two enemy aircraft. He was deeply interested in aeronautical development, mounting the first Browning machine guns in an aeroplane wing and devising the parachute bomb for low-level attacks. In 1939 he commanded the Air Corps Experimental Division and Engineering School. He was commanding a training force on America's west coast when Arnold told him of his new appointment in the South-West Pacific Area.

The day after arriving in Australia on 28 July, Kenney had an interview with MacArthur, who repeated his diatribe against the American air force. Kenney shrewdly replied that he intended to justify the confidence MacArthur had placed in him. He added that he knew how to run an air force, would fix whatever was wrong and produce results. After he assured MacArthur that he and his men would be loyal, the big general walked over to Kenney, put his arm round his shoulder and said he thought they were going to 'get along together all right'.[23]

He was correct. Like MacArthur, Kenney was an egotist and a chauvinist, but also a great leader. Officially appointed in August, Kenney was dynamic, cheerful, innovative and confident in his knowledge of air operations. A senior Australian airman who came to know him well described him as 'invariably full of fire and avid for ideas'.[24] Those ideas included a reorganisation of the Allied Air Forces. Kenney later claimed that he decided to separate the Australians and Americans, but in fact the US War Department had already resolved to form a distinct American air force—numbered, at MacArthur's suggestion, the Fifth—in the South-West Pacific Area, and thus end the irritating say that the RAAF had in American air force matters there. As for the RAAF, it would have its own organisation, from 21 September entitled 'RAAF Command'. The new name that MacArthur had initially announced for most of the RAAF, without consulting the Australians, was 'Coastal Defence Command'. Prime Minister Curtin recognised that this term seemed to denote a purely defensive force, not likely to take the leading role and receive the top aircraft he and the RAAF were anticipating. The change to 'RAAF Command' came only after Curtin and others made representations to the Americans.

As to who would head RAAF Command, Kenney fixed on Bill Bostock, General Brett's Chief of Staff, whose competence and bluntness appealed to him. The CAS, George Jones, was not even consulted. This naturally had implications for relations within the RAAF. Now there were two new organisations under Allied Air Forces Headquarters, both of them operating almost independently: namely, Fifth Air Force and RAAF Command. Fifth Air Force would effectively be under the day-to-day command of Kenney's capable deputy, Major-General Ennis Whitehead, while RAAF Command would be under Bostock, who Kenney replaced as Chief of Staff, Allied Air Forces with an American. The new arrangement could have benefited the RAAF, for although it was ultimately under Kenney, it could plan and conduct operations independently. However if, as American strength in the area grew, Australia wanted to be involved at the forefront of the action, it would have to maintain its ally's respect and support. That would require good relationships between the men at the top of the two air forces. It was promising that Bostock, Air Commodore Joe Hewitt, Group Captain Fred Scherger and Group Captain Bill Garing all got on well with the Americans.

One RAAF unit that Kenney admired so much he wanted it duplicated, was the humble-sounding '1 Wireless Unit'. Formed in April 1942, it was based on a nucleus of just eight airmen, whom Royal Navy personnel had trained to read the unique Japanese 'kana' code. The unit, shrouded in secrecy and initially based in Darwin, had reportedly given more than two hours' warning of the 19 February raid. Expanded after Pearl Harbor, the RAAF interceptor unit became MacArthur's main intelligence gatherer. It moved to Townsville, where in September it occupied a purpose-built bomb-proof air-conditioned operations building, and was fed information from two direction-finding stations in north Queensland. The intelligence its personnel were producing on enemy aerial activity was so valuable that in December Kenney urged the Australian government to create five more such 'wireless units'. The time involved in training operators made this virtually impossible, but two were soon established and sent to Darwin and Moresby. By war's end there would be six, with 1000 RAAF and WAAAF personnel. Detachments would by then have been sent all over New Guinea and Borneo, and have intercepted and decoded tens of thousands of messages.

Kenney demonstrated his energy by making inspection tours in Australia and New Guinea. He was unimpressed, using descriptions such as 'chaotic and 'the goddamest mess you ever saw'. After witnessing a Japanese raid on Moresby and the failure of the P-39s to intercept, he concluded, 'No matter what I accomplished, it would be an improvement.'[25]

Kenney demanded a statement of US aircraft strength. On paper, the 10 August total of 481 looked impressive, but he was appalled to find that only 151 were airworthy. He added 70 RAAF aircraft to this strength, though taking into account Beaufighters and Bostons just coming on strength, the RAAF total was actually more than twice that, 215 on strength and 149 serviceable.

Kenney's underestimate of RAAF strength foreshadowed the way in which he would count it out of the main game in future. He did set about improving the serviceability of American aircraft, sending home incompetent officers and demanding and obtaining improvements in maintenance. He calculated that the Japanese had five times as many aircraft available as the Allies, with more on call. This was an exaggeration, but clearly he faced a massive struggle to achieve the goal he had reported to MacArthur—to 'own' the air over New Guinea.

Moving the experienced 49th Fighter Group from Darwin to New Guinea in September was one response, but Australian squadrons were also about to contribute abundantly to that task.

12 Codename 'Fall River'

The Battle of the Coral Sea saved Port Moresby from amphibious invasion, but its survival was still far from assured, and in Australia a sense of seaborne threat persisted. An enemy naval force was reported, mistakenly, off the Queensland coast on 10 May, after two Hudson crews each spotted and attacked a Japanese submarine near Townsville. Japanese submarines attacked at least 16 ships, sinking seven, off the east coast between May and July 1942. The true extent of the Japanese menace became shockingly apparent at the end of May, when three midget submarines were launched into Sydney Harbour. As preliminaries to these attacks, the Japanese launched float-planes from submarines. Thanks to the still inadequate state of air defences, the first flight was undetected, and US fighters failed to intercept the second. Allied aircraft were unable to find the submarines over subsequent months.

Yet the greatest strategic threat to Australia in mid-late 1942 lay not off the east coast, but in Papua. Given General MacArthur's criticisms of Australian soldiers, it is interesting to note the comparison that the official RAAF historian makes of Australian and American airmen in Papua in this period. Douglas Gillison says that whereas in Darwin the high morale of the American fighter pilots invigorated the depressed Australians, in Papua American morale was relatively low. Although both allies were flying inferior aircraft, and bemoaning that fact, the RAAF was 'virile, well-trained and proud', its men close to home and more experienced than the Americans, whom they tended to see as softer. For example, the Australians suspected that American bomber crews dropped their bombs from too high through fear of coming lower. On the other hand, they also acknowledged the bravery demonstrated by some American aircrews, and 'virtually idolised' American commanders who proved themselves, such as the fighter leaders Paul B. Wurtsmith and Boyd 'Buzz' Wagner, and bomber commander Richard H. Carmichael.[1] In his memoir, George Jones glibly criticises the Americans, too, saying their early aircrews had poor morale and 'would not wash or shave'.[2]

Port Moresby endured 21 air raids in May, and early in June Nos 11 and 20 Squadrons moved to the greater security of Bowen, south of Townsville. Around the same time, their Catalinas attacked their old base at Tulagi. They did so zealously, first dropping their bombs and then coming back with machine guns. A member of Frank Chapman's crew reportedly even fired a Tommy gun at the Japanese, whose losses on 25–26 June were allegedly an incredible 600 killed.

On coming in to land at the American-held island of Efate after the 26 June attack, one Catalina came under 'friendly fire'. Seeing the red circle in the Australian blue, white and red roundels on the wings, an American fighter pilot had opened fire. No one was killed, though the Catalina was damaged. The main repercussion was that the RAAF soon issued orders to remove the large red circles on its wing roundels. By the end of 1942, front-line units generally used just the blue and white national markings, and by July 1943 this was official policy.

The Catalinas carried a variety of bombs. Typically, each would take about eight conventional 500-pound (225 kilogram) bombs, and perhaps twenty 20- or 30-pound incendiaries or anti-personnel bombs, held in the side blister compartment or on the hull floor for crew to throw out. In 1942, Catalinas dropped more than 4300 of these bombs, totalling more than 35 tons, and in 1943 the figures would rise to 6200 and 60 tons. The crew sometimes complemented the small bombs with beer bottles, like the four dozen that two Cats deposited over Lae and Salamaua in one four-hour raid. The justification was that the sound—a mixture of a scream and a shrill whistle—would disturb the enemy's sleep and thus his morale. RAAF Catalinas, like American and Japanese bombers, also began using a powerful bomb fused to detonate six to 12 hours after falling.

'Attie' Wearne used his conventional bombs to great effect in a night raid on Rabaul in August. Within seconds of the call 'Bombs away', there came, in his words, 'the most God awful explosions underneath'. He felt that he had hit several fully fuelled and armed aircraft on the Lakunai airstrip. He was halfway across the harbour, the light bright enough for reading a newspaper, and flak opening up everywhere, when a crew member told him one of the bombs was 'hung up'. Rather than trying to jettison it immediately, Wearne flew on to Vunakanau and used it to start another fire. He considered this sortie the greatest thrill of his life. Vindication of his estimate came later from a diary captured at Buna, in which a Japanese seaman wrote that on that night at Rabaul 'Terrific explosions heard in the direction of the aerodrome ... Fire and smoke filled the air.' Next day the sailor wrote that a bomber and two fighters had been destroyed in this bombing. In an unwitting tribute to the RAAF Cats, he asserted that 'An immediate capture of Port Moresby is necessary because present enemy air operations are hindering our advance. There are night raids every time we enter Rabaul.'[3]

Days later, Wearne landed near Buna and waited more than eight hours for the American crew of a crashed Marauder to be brought out of the jungle so he could fly them to safety. These bright points fell into shadow in September, when Wearne lost his leg to a shark attack near Cairns. 'Attie' would return to operations, commanding 20 Squadron in 1944–45.

No. 100 Squadron's Beauforts first saw combat in June 1942. Their original commander was Wing Commander 'Sam' Balmer, founding commander of 13 Squadron and 'one of the RAAF's most brilliant pilots'.[4] Before the war, Balmer and Dallas Scott had together driven an open sports car in races across the continent. Scott was now dead, and Balmer would eventually die flying a bomber over Belgium. On 25 June Balmer led five planes to Moresby, where after anti-aircraft batteries briefly fired at their unfamiliar shapes, they joined two Beauforts already there for shipping escort, under Squadron Leader Charles Sage and Flight Lieutenant 'Smoky' Douglas. That night Sage and Douglas took off to make a diversionary attack on Salamaua, while Balmer led the remainder to Lae. Balmer's crew included Scotty Jansen, who had shot down a Zero on the first day of the war. Sage and Douglas bombed and strafed Salamaua before heading home. Douglas made it, but Sage was last heard asking Moresby to display searchlights to aid him. Not until 1987 was his aircraft discovered north-west of Port Moresby, with the bodies of 27-year-old regular air force officer Sage and his crew. Theirs was the first Beaufort lost in New Guinea.

While Sage fought to bring his aircraft home, Balmer led his flight to find a 4000-ton ship. He guessed that when the ship heard of the raid on Salamaua it might move east of Lae, and, calculating its probable speed, plotted a course. When the Beaufort came out over the vast moonlit Huon Gulf, the ship was visible steaming east. Using the moon path as a guide to the target, Balmer flew overhead three times and, after two malfunctions, dropped all his bombs from just 100 feet. The rear-gunner saw two flashes as the bombs hit. The second and third Beauforts braved flak to score hits on the now stationary vessel too, and as they left, the ship appeared to be sinking. There is uncertainty as to whether it did sink. After this exciting interlude, 100 Squadron moved south to Laverton, Victoria, and resumed the necessary but thankless work of anti-submarine patrols.

No. 32 Squadron's Hudsons were also undertaking essential work, from Horn Island: 52 reconnaissance and patrol flights in June alone, as well as many shipping escort sorties. Uneventful flights were interspersed with occasional dangerous exploits. For example, on 11 June Bill Pedrina evacuated personnel from Wau, the northernmost Allied airfield in New Guinea, and Lex Halliday shot down a 'Japanese four engined flying boat' during a patrol south of New Britain.

Milne Bay and Kokoda—opening moves

Port Moresby, still the great Japanese objective on New Guinea, was a large and fast-growing base for fighters such as the Kittyhawks that had defended it, bombers such as American Mitchells that attacked from it, and also for transport and supply aircraft, which would prove vital to the coming land battles. Allied headquarters were keen to establish another base further east on the island. This would pre-empt any Japanese plans to establish bases there, and would allow Allied aircraft easier access to New Britain and the Solomon Sea, with its many islands.

A survey party sent to the eastern tip of the island in June fixed on Milne Bay, which had a deep harbour and enough flat land to accommodate airstrips. Coconut planters had cleared 1600 acres (647 hectares) in an area known as Gili Gili. Orders to construct the base followed quickly. American engineers arrived at the end of June, followed by Australian militia. Milne Bay, codename 'Fall River', was a tough area in which to live: annual rainfall of 269 *centimetres*, great humidity, swarms of malarial mosquitoes, and often closed in with cloud. Its rain, heat, mud and pervading sense of menace embodied the 'bastard of a place' that New Guinea was for most who served there. The first RAAF parties included No. 37 Radar Station. When the unit arrived by ship on 26 June, everything had to be floated ashore on makeshift rafts. After much difficulty 'scrounging' the right materials, the station's 27 personnel had it operating by 8 August. It would be on air almost continuously for the remainder of the war.

The first USAAF P-38 Lockheed Lightning in the South-West Pacific Area, a photo-reconnaissance version, was employed to find land suitable for more bases in Papua. An area near Buna was chosen, and plans set in motion to occupy it on 10–12 August. However, the Japanese, who had been expanding their hold over northern New Guinea, now intended also to land in the Buna–Gona area.

An enemy convoy was discovered near Rabaul on 19 July. Two days later it was nearing Buna. USAAF bombers struck that day and the next, sinking one transport, but not really disrupting the landing. Just one RAAF aircraft, Pilot Officer Warren Cowan's 32 Squadron Hudson, participated on 22 July. Ordered to shadow the enemy cruiser force, he inflicted little or no bombing damage, but made an impression on the nine enemy Zero pilots who chased him off.

Among them was Saburo Sakai, who on catching up to Cowan's Hudson, was astonished to see it stop trying to flee and instead turn to tackle its pursuers. Taking advantage of the Zeros' crowding in for the kill, Cowan repeatedly evaded their fire with extraordinary manoeuvres. One involved pulling the power off one engine and simultaneously applying full power to the other, which allowed Cowan to execute fast turns that amazed his attackers. Sakai alone made four ineffective head-on passes. Eventually, though, he managed to knock out the rear-gunner, and thus Cowan's source of information about the Hudson's tail. The enemies then closed in and set the plane alight. They watched as Cowan tried to land the stricken plane, but treetops tore off the wings and it exploded in flame.

For weeks afterwards, the Zero pilots were full of the story of this tenacious Hudson. Cowan, 31, a wool-classing clerk before the war, was married with two children. On receiving a telegram that Warren was 'Missing, believed killed', his wife Betty 'howled [her] eyes out', but clung to hope that he had somehow survived.[5] Near the scattered wreckage, locals discovered and buried the remains of Cowan and his crewmates, David Taylor, Russell Polack and Lauri Sheard. For Sakai, who survived the war, the Hudson pilot of July 1942 remained one of the most memorable of the 200 opponents he faced, and he sought to discover his identity. Sakai's biographer, Henry Sakaida, and two Australian aviation historians, Bob Piper and David Vincent, together identified Cowan. The historians marvelled at the ten-minute length of the dogfight—'an eternity' in dogfighting terms, according to Sakaida, and a period that would have been immensely draining on Cowan.

In motivational speeches he gave after the war, Sakai would often mention this dogfight of 22 July. He stated in a letter, 'I have encountered many brave pilots in my life but Warren F. Cowan stands alone.'[6] He wrote to Cowan's widow and even to the responsible Australian government minister, suggesting that Cowan be awarded the highest possible medal for bravery. However the law prohibits awarding such honours so long after the war.

That July morning the invasion ships sailed home for Rabaul, leaving behind one sunken transport, some 2000 Japanese troops, 1300 conscripted locals and Formosans, and 52 horses. Allied aircraft maintained harassing raids over Buna until the end of July, but these did not markedly affect the Japanese advance towards Port Moresby.

The track they took was the 'Kokoda Track', named for the village that was significant as having the only airfield between Port Moresby and Buna–Gona. Australian aircraft—notably of 32 Squadron—rendered small but important assistance in this early stage by dropping and landing supplies both for the troops opposing this advance and to those around Wau and Salamaua, known as 'Kanga Force'. The USAAF provided most aircraft involved, notably in No. 21 Troop Carrier Squadron, which included two chartered Australian National Airways DC-3s.

When the Japanese brought reinforcements to Buna in late July, American and Australian aircraft attacked again. This time the Fortresses bombed from lower, and were supported by Dauntlesses, RAAF Hudsons and Catalinas. The result was again frustratingly negative, made more painful by the destruction of most of the Dauntlesses.

While MacArthur fumed about these poor outcomes and the Japanese one-upmanship in taking his own proposed base, significant developments were brewing further east. News that the Japanese were building an airstrip on Guadalcanal in the Solomons in July was read correctly by the US Joint Chiefs of Staff as a threat to the line of communications between Australia and the United States. They decided to seize Guadalcanal and nearby Tulagi. The boundary between the South-West Pacific Area and South Pacific Area went through the Solomons, but ultimate responsibility for the campaign fell to Vice-Admiral Ghormley's (later Admiral Halsey's) South Pacific Area, which was in turn part of Admiral Nimitz's Pacific Theater.

The 1st US Marine Division landed at Guadalcanal and Tulagi on 7 August. MacArthur's air forces, including the RAAF, supported the invasion by attacking Rabaul, from which Japanese aircraft could attack the Americans in the Solomons. Consequently the initial American landings went unmolested, but later that afternoon Japanese bombers from Rabaul attacked the beaches. The Guadalcanal campaign would ebb and flow for six months of ferocious land, sea and air fighting. The aerial campaign was not an Australian affair, though five RAAF personnel were killed when HMAS *Canberra* was sunk off Savo Island. These were the pilot, Duncan Murchison, and four maintenance crew of the ship's Walrus aircraft. Pilot Officers Cecil Spencer and Charles Widdy, former residents of the Solomons, provided valuable guidance to the American forces, some of it in the front line.

Guadalcanal profoundly affected the RAAF's own major campaign in New Guinea, for the Japanese were simultaneously trying to win both campaigns. From June 1942 to January 1943 Fifth Air Force's effective strength reportedly fell, but because the Japanese were also occupied in the Solomons, General Kenney's command was able to gain the upper hand in New Guinea.

In mid-August, with Kokoda in Japanese hands and their vanguard just 80 air kilometres away, there was much anxiety in Port Moresby.

The inhabitants' concern increased on 17 August when, after a break of more than a fortnight, the 78th air raid hit Moresby. With just four minutes' warning, the American fighters were unable to intercept the 24 bombers that released 150 bombs. Though the human cost was slight, the loss of aircraft, all parked close together, was severe. Among the five destroyed and 11 severely damaged were seven Dakota transports, two of which were destroyed and the rest put out of commission. Just one transport remained serviceable. These aircraft were, together with 'native carriers', essential to the land campaign on the Kokoda Track. Two dry lake beds at Myola had been selected for flying in and storing supplies, but by the time of the raid a negligible amount had been transported there. There were insufficient 'native carriers' to alter this position significantly. Thus while veteran Australian troops had been rushed to Moresby, they could not yet be moved forward into action. To urgent requests for more transport aircraft, MacArthur replied that nine aircraft would be sent. There were, he explained, just 30 transport aircraft in Australia, of which half were available at any one time. He added that air transport should be seen as 'an emergency rather than a normal means of supply'.[7] Weather, aircrew fatigue, and the need for fighter cover limited the daily flights to Myola to three.

Once the AIF troops reached the Kokoda front in late August, and the most important land battle of Australia's Pacific War began, the air forces found it difficult to provide close support. The proximity of the opposing troops, the small scale of their actions, the sudden changes of fortune and the dense vegetation all prevented pilots finding targets or being directed to them from the ground. Moreover, the 'clouds full of rocks', as the pilots described such terrain, made it dangerous to get close to the action. The Allied combat aircraft, now commanded by General Whitehead, Kenney's shrewd American subordinate, could best contribute to the Kokoda campaign indirectly, north-east of the mountains at the Japanese coastal bases, and on their air units at Lae and Salamaua.

Milne Bay was a different matter.

Milne Bay—the first shots

By 20 July, the first airstrip at Milne Bay was usable. It was called No. 1 Strip or Gurney Field, after Squadron Leader Bob Gurney. A pre-war

Qantas pilot, he had served with 11 Squadron and then commanded 33 Squadron before dying in a Marauder crash when returning from an air raid on Rabaul in May 1942.

When the first Kittyhawks landed on 'Gurney' on 25 July, it was virtually underwater, and would have been impossible to use if not for the ingenious interlocking steel 'Marsden' matting laid over its 1500 by 24 metre area. As it was, when the aircraft landed, they sent up spray like speedboats, and skidded and slithered, sometimes into the mud beyond the matting. 'Buster' Brown, flying with 75 Squadron, considered it 'probably the worst airstrip I've ever operated off'.[8] When not dragging planes out of the morass, the ground staff were busy expanding the territory covered by the matting and building splinter-proof pens into which the aircraft could be dispersed.

The daily rain ensured there was usually ankle-deep mud outside the personnel tents. It could take over an hour to drive—often in vehicles open to rain—just over 2 kilometres from Gurney airstrip to the 75 Squadron camp. It was hot too, temperatures reportedly never falling below 32° Celcius during the coming operations. Rain and gloom alternated with brilliant and burning sunshine. Pilots usually enjoyed excellent visibility in the Pacific, but Milne Bay, with its cloud cover generally no higher than 2000 feet up, and often just a few hundred feet up, was not well suited to dogfighting. While evading an enemy fighter was easy, it was difficult to come to grips with him, finish him off or even determine whether you had hurt him. Importantly, too, the low cloud restricted the Kitty's opportunities to build up height and speed for the dives that were its best chance of hitting enemy aircraft.

By 8 August, more than 6200 Allied personnel of 'Milne Force' had assembled at this rudimentary base to fulfil MacArthur's orders to 'prepare and defend an airdrome'.[9] The force's presence was one indication of the strategic importance placed on the base. Another was the fact that two of Australia's three home-based fighter squadrons were sent there; 75 and 76 Squadrons arrived on 25 July.

While 75 Squadron was now a veteran unit, 'Seventy-Six' had yet to fight as a unit. The squadron had only existed since March, but its members included some accomplished veterans of the European war. Its commander, Squadron Leader Peter Turnbull, not only had 12 kills on the board, but was also a natural leader. A fine rough-rider from a grazier family, he had a great sense of humour too, as became apparent when he was flying Gladiator biplanes in the Middle East. In late 1940 he wrote in the 'Special comments' column of a combat report: 'Father Christmas please give me a Hurricane'. This caused many to laugh, including Air Marshal Tedder, the Air Officer Commanding in the Middle East. Soon afterwards Hurricanes arrived, and Turnbull claimed the credit.[10]

Four other 76 Squadron pilots had flown with 452 Squadron in Europe: Squadron Leader 'Bluey' Truscott, Flight Lieutenant 'Bardie' Wawn, and Flying Officers Eric Tainton and John Elphick. As previously mentioned, this Article XV RAAF fighter squadron had an impressive reputation, and Truscott had become its commander. The 'slim, dark and handsome' Wawn had, as a Spitfire pilot, already shot down two Bf 109s.[11] Truscott's pre-war celebrity and his wartime effort of at least 11 'scalps' made him the best-known RAAF pilot. This was not necessarily an easy burden, for although making exaggerated claims, or 'shooting a line', was part of everyday air force life, pursuing personal glorification was regarded as extremely poor form. Yet Truscott had, according to a wartime publication, 'an infinite capacity for drawing the men of his squadron round him like a family of younger brothers'.[12] An official report said he was 'literally adored by the Pilots and Ground Crew. His devil-may-care swagger, fiery red mop of hair on which a Melbourne Cricket Association Cap was usually perched, and infectious smile just couldn't fail to inspire confidence into others.'[13] Many needed that inspiration, for there were inexperienced men in the squadron too: at least seven accidents occurred during intense training in April and May. To the novices, like the new 75 Squadron pilots, the 'Golden Word' was given: don't dogfight Zeros—dive through, shoot and return.

Relations within 75 Squadron were still not brotherly on the eve of a new battle. In June 15 new pilots, some with experience in the UK, Middle East or Singapore, had joined the squadron. To some of them the Moresby veterans appeared 'bomb happy', and Arthur Tucker admitted that this group were indeed 'keyed up'.[14] Some told the newcomers not to try to tell them how to fight the war. This was a defensive gesture, apparently made before the reinforcements had done any such thing, but it created some ill-feeling. The new pilots were also irritated by the requirement to fly three hours in Wirraways before flying Kittyhawks. Some were not too impressed by the Kitties either: Nat Gould, who had flown with the RAF in England and Russia, found the controls of this 'great big steamroller' sluggish after flying the 'delightful ballerina' that was the Spitfire.[15] He, like others, became much more appreciative in New Guinea, when he saw how much more rugged and enduring the Kitty was than the dainty Spitfire.

Relations between the Moresby veterans and the 'Spitfire pilots' were not helped by the fact that some of the Australians with English experience had acquired English accents and culture, as reflected in their RAF songs. In an attempt to create harmony between the two groups, squadron doctor Deane-Butcher persuaded each to sing the other's songs. At night if the weather permitted there would be group singing, the only light being from fireflies. Some of the songs were dirge-like and sombre, others cheeky, boastful and hilarious. There were traditional RAF songs, like 'The Gremlin Song', with its burden of gremlins creating havoc. Other common topics were beer, women, leave, higher headquarters, and the defiance of death and the enemy. The Wirraway and Beaufort ('The D.A.P.'s Pride') came in for special treatment. The songs could be coarse or obscene, but in singing them even the prudish tended to go all out and let off steam.

Adding the RAF songs doubled the squadron's repertoire and, together with some practical jokes, brought them to a point where the 'nice types' from the war in Europe were generally 'good blokes' like everyone else. Combat would help seal the friendships, although the sense of grievance among some of the new arrivals continued beyond 1945. The ground staff remained much the same as at Moresby, and helped significantly in the maintenance not only of the P-40s, but also of *esprit de corps*. Nevertheless, Tucker later claimed that the squadron, never really united before, entered the Milne Bay battle 'more split up than ever'.[16] He blamed the leadership group for not welding the pilots together through lectures or more informal discussions about past or future experiences and tactics. 'Buster' Brown, a former RAF Spitfire pilot, was not only disappointed at the 'Don't tell us how to fight the war' line, but also the failure of the leaders to show the newcomers how the war against the Japanese should be fought. Tucker blamed the CO—the 'nasty bastard', Les Jackson. Brown also noted that while Jackson was courageous and single-minded in his determination to kill Japanese, he was not a natural leader.[17]

The pilots' lifestyle in the coming weeks included monotonous food: tinned bully beef, spam and 'M and V' (a meat and vegetable product). There was the occasional tropical spread, tinned herrings and tinned bacon, but most airmen, especially those used to eating in English messes and pubs, found these unappetising if not disgusting. Pilots lived four to six men to a tent, others even more, though some buildings, like the 75 Squadron mess, were locally constructed huts. Planks like the duckboards used in the Great War were set down over the mud. While not eating, sleeping or flying, the pilots sat in their tents or, if on standby, in the operations tent with an ear cocked for the words 'It's on!' They read anything they could find, wrote letters or played cards. There was the occasional practical joke too, like putting insects or dead snakes where they would scare the sensitive, or firing a Verey light into the latrines. Throwing coconuts at each other was also fun. There was a record player, which for 75 Squadron played 'Rum Bacardi' interminably.

Effective use of the two squadrons' pilots depended on the availability of runways. On 7 August a battalion of American engineers arrived, thus enabling work to start on two more airstrips. Most laboured on Strip No. 2, south-west of No. 1, which required bridge-building and would eventually prove unusable. Just one company started constructing No. 3, east of No. 1 and later called Turnbull. It would not be operational in time for the coming battle.

A flight of No. 32 Squadron Hudsons soon joined the two RAAF squadrons and support units at Milne Bay. The senior officer at 'Fall River' was Wing Commander Thomas, though he was never formally appointed commander of all RAAF units and left on 5 August.

The Milne Bay garrison faced no enemy air attacks until August, primarily because of strict signals security on the ground and in the air. If the Japanese attacked on the ground, coordination of Allied air and land forces would be crucial. Brigadier Field, commanding Milne Force, ensured that Thomas was appointed air liaison officer at Milne Force Headquarters, and army liaison officers were appointed to the fighter squadrons. After Thomas left, however, the 75 and 76 Squadron commanders, Jackson and Turnbull, had not only to lead their units but also to concern themselves with the other specialist units and wider RAAF involvement at Milne Bay. Still, they and their men remained surprisingly optimistic.

The brief freedom from enemy attack ended on 4 August, when Zeros and a dive-bomber came upon No. 1 Strip. 'War started with strafe by 4 Zeros' wrote Pilot Officer Harry Kerr of 76 Squadron.[18] In fact his squadron's first clash with the enemy had come at Gona on 22 July, when Turnbull and six other pilots fought an inconclusive battle with enemy aircraft they identified as German Focke-Wulfs, but were later declared to have been examples of the new Zero model, the 'Hamp'. However, 4 August would be different. The radar unit was not yet fully operational and thus gave no warning, but eight 76 Squadron Kittyhawks were on patrol. Peter Ash got behind the dive-bomber, apparently a Val, and although he himself was attacked from behind and forced to break off with engine failure, he brought it down. He gained the double distinction of the squadron's first kill and the first Allied victory at Milne Bay. Nevertheless, honours were fairly even after the Zeros attacked the strip, hitting the fuel tank of one P-40, which burnt. Miraculously, the ground crew pushing the Kittyhawk at the time were unhurt.Among the ground staff sheltering from the raiders, one man inspired those around him: Corporal Don 'Donk' Cowper, a 76 Squadron fitter armourer who had served in Malaya. Rather than duck for cover like those around him, this New Zealand-born extrovert took up a rifle and, cursing and challenging, fired back at the Japanese. This gesture and his laughing approach to life invigorated others.

It appears that this raid alerted the Japanese to the existence of the Milne Bay base. Whereas previously their 8th Fleet had intended to attack Allied facilities on the island of Samarai, they now considered the newfound airfield at Milne Bay a direct threat to any seaborne move to Port Moresby and made it their objective.

Radar, however, would warn of every subsequent Japanese air raid. On 7 August enemy aircraft were reported over Samarai, and Kitty-hawks took off to intercept. The result was rather embarrassing, with five pilots running so short of fuel they had to land on an emergency strip on Goodenough Island, further north, clearly exposing the inferior range of Australian fighters. The pilots had to subsist on air-dropped rations until rescued.

The second raid on Milne Bay followed on 11 August. 'Intercepted 12 Zero's over drome' was how 'Bardie' Wawn described the day's duty in his logbook. Twenty-two Kittyhawks of the two squadrons were warned and waiting when the dozen Zeros arrived. Furious dogfighting ensued. Wawn enjoyed some success, recording in his logbook: '5 Squirts. Observed 2 hits.'[19] His tracers entered the cockpit of one Zero.

The numerical odds were with the Australians, who possibly shot down four aircraft. Yet the Japanese fought well: time and again Kittyhawks found Zeros on their tails. Less experienced pilots had a particularly tough time. Kerr was 'jumped' from cloud, as he put it in his logbook, then developed engine trouble and had to land, only for his brakes to fail. He survived the crash, but his logbook adds the forlorn note: 'Mac missing, Inky killed.'[20] Never to return were 75 Squadron's Mark Sheldon—a former Spitfire pilot—and Francis Shelley, as well as 76 Squadron's Albert McLeod and George Inkster. McLeod was last seen flying across the airstrip towards the hills with several Zeros in pursuit.

Deane-Butcher was with an ambulance crew near Gurney when he discerned a Kittyhawk flying low and belching clouds of smoke. On their radio they could hear the pilot talking quickly, agitated as fire took hold. Suddenly he climbed rapidly and, after his plane stalled, leapt out above the ambulance. His parachute was streaming behind him, but before it could open he hit the ground, just a cricket-pitch length from the ambulance. Deane-Butcher's group ran forward to the crumpled body, but George Inkster was beyond help. Deane-Butcher was also sent on a long, difficult journey to Ahioma to investigate news of the discovery of another wreck and body. He found that locals had buried Sheldon and decorated his grave with flowers and shells. Rather than disturb the body, Deane-Butcher carved Sheldon's particulars on a wooden cross before returning to base. As a passenger in a US Tiger Moth later that day, Kerr tried unsuccessfully to find his mate McLeod.

Albert Tucker was very lucky that no one needed to look for his corpse, as that day he had been chased across the bay twice—once by two Zeros, then by three. Clouds proved his salvation, but that night he developed a bad case of the shakes. 'Buster' Brown recalled that after a typical day of flying at Milne Bay, once you got back in the crew room, sitting on a chair or a kerosene tin:

> ... that is when you start to think: what has gone on, what you have been through and if it has been a close shave at any time during a combat, you

> might then get an excitable reaction—the tummy may turn over—and . . . you might have your third cigarette in about three minutes.[21]

In short, Tucker's was a typical post-battle reaction. So was the reaction of his tentmate, Alan Whetters, who laughed heartily at him.

A respite of 12 days without raids followed, primarily because the Japanese were preoccupied with the American landings at Guadalcanal. This preoccupation delayed an attack on 'Rabi' (Milne Bay) that the Japanese had planned for 7 August. Had this attack proceeded—27 Bettys were bombed-up and ready to fly under escort to Milne Bay when orders came to attack Guadalcanal—it may well have been devastating. Instead, the Bettys flew to the Solomons with an escort of elite Tainan Air Group fighters. Four Bettys were shot down, others damaged, two Tainan pilots killed, and Saburo Sakai, their top ace, was so grievously wounded that he would not return to combat until 1944.

The Milne Bay garrison became stronger when the 18th Brigade, veterans of Tobruk, arrived on 12 August, followed by Major-General Clowes, who would command Milne Force. By 22 August there were 8824 soldiers in that force, including 1365 Americans.

General Headquarters had warned on 17 August of an imminent major Japanese attack somewhere: perhaps Port Moresby, Guadalcanal, Goodenough Island or Milne Bay. Despite the distraction of the burgeoning operations at Guadalcanal, the Japanese still planned to take Milne Bay as a means of opening a coastal route for supplying Port Moresby once they occupied it. Air patrols from Milne Bay were increased, and the Kittyhawks were hurriedly modified for a fighter-bomber role. The need for longer-range reconnaissance prompted the arrival of No. 6 Squadron at Horn Island and detachment of one flight to Milne Bay. The Hudson crews had an unenviable task, flying solo six-hour missions in terrible flying conditions, vulnerable to enemy aircraft and looking for convoys that could readily destroy them. More observers were sent to outlying islands to provide visual warning of any invasion force.

A warning came on 24 August, when an observer spotted seven Japanese barges at the entrance to Ward Hunt Strait. They were heading towards Milne Bay. Japanese aircraft were headed there too. Corporal Walmsley of 76 Squadron was driving three men from the canteen to the airstrip when suddenly:

> ... brrrrrp. The Zeros were here again. I stopped the car with a jolt nearly [threw] the blokes through the windscreen shut the engine off and dived into the bush before the other blokes were even out of the bus.

Walmsley and his mates had not heard the alert and now lay on the ground. They could not see the fight above but could hear: 'the Ack-Ack was hammering away and the Kittys was firing like hell'. P-40s had intercepted the Japanese fighters, and played hide-and-seek in the clouds. The Japanese formation split up and a series of inconclusive combats ensued. Walmsley later drove to the strip and counted the Kittyhawks as they came in, including one that 'was riddled with holes a 75 sqn pilot in it how he got it down beat me'.[22] When it was over, neither side sustained any losses, but Zeros had strafed No. 1 Strip.

The next day brought a report that the barges had come ashore on the west coast of Goodenough Island. Nine 75 Squadron Kittyhawks took off in response. Covered by a top flight, a second flight fired 10,000 rounds into the barges and, after six passes, had set all of them alight. These 'Daihatsu barges' were 15 metres long and 3 metres wide, laden with equipment and green-clad soldiers. John Piper got a rare sight of enemy troops, who were 'skedaddling' from the barges across the beach.[23] When the Kitties headed home, a column of smoke 1000 feet high was rising from the blazing craft. A Japanese who was not among the eight killed and nearly 50 wounded in the onslaught wrote, 'We fought back, but what could we do against fighter planes?'[24] The Kittyhawks had frustrated an attempt to land 350 troops from these barges at Taupota, whence they would have moved overland to attack 'Rabi' from the rear.

The main agent of the Japanese plan was a force of seven warships and two transports. As these approached Normanby Island, Milne Force was placed on alert and Clowes took command of all Allied land and air forces in the area. He had to decide how best to deploy these resources to defend the bay, which was about 32 kilometres long and 11 kilometres wide and, with its deep water, offered many good sites for amphibious landings. He chose to protect the airfields, putting his inexperienced militia troops on the bay's north-east coast, and his three veteran AIF battalions at or west of the main base at Gili Gili, near Gurney. Allied bombers were mustered in Queensland and Moresby to repel the attack, but bad weather prevented them finding the invasion fleet.

Early on 25 August, the enemy convoy was sighted from the air and by spotters on Kitava Island. The 75 and 76 Squadron Kittyhawks were bombed-up and ready to strike as soon as the invaders came within range. One of 75's ground staff noted that Les Jackson was 'raring to go and settle a few scores with the Japs for killing his brother at Moresby'.[25] That moment was deemed to have come at 3 p.m. on 25 August, when the fleet was reported to be just south of Normanby Island. It 'was on'. Twelve Kitties, divided equally between the two squadrons, took off. So did Henry 'Robbie' Robertson of 6 Squadron, flying the only serviceable Hudson. A veteran of 8 Squadron in Malaya, 'Robbie' worked himself almost to collapse in this campaign. He now led the way, and the aircraft found the convoy, though the cloud cover was ten-tenths at 1300 feet, rendering high-level bombing impossible. Unaccustomed to dropping bombs, the Kittyhawk pilots missed. Fred Carden, rear turret-gunner in Robertson's crew, had a grandstand view of the enemy convoy forming defensive circles as the attackers approached. Black puffs from enemy anti-aircraft fire hung in the sky around them as they dived towards a troop transport. Painted black underneath, the Hudson made a good target against the grey cloud. Robertson achieved a near miss and strafed the transport, then went round again. At mast height, his crew dropped their remaining bombs and strafed the decks. Robertson's aircraft was hit too but, like the ship, it survived. The same outcome occurred at 6 p.m. when two Hudsons braved what one participant called a 'hose-pipe of ack-ack fire', to drop their bombs from just 100 feet up.[26]

In between the Hudsons' efforts, more Kittyhawks attacked with 250- and 300-pound bombs. Amidst further near misses they reportedly hit one ship. A Japanese diary, captured later, revealed that on at least one of the ships the RAAF attacks inflicted 13 casualties.

Getting back from these raids was difficult in the darkness, after 5 p.m. Alan 'Grandad' Whetters was a voice of moderation within the unit, but had a disagreement with other pilots—not including the absent Les Jackson—about the wisdom of the Kitties' second attack on the ships. Hurt by the implication that he was afraid of going, he insisted on flying it alone. Bad weather forced him to ditch on Sideia Island that night. His breakfast of eggs and tomatoes served by an attractive topless local girl contrasted favourably to the lifestyle at Milne Bay!

The crew of a patrolling RAAF crash tender saw the Japanese convoy entering the bay. Soon after midnight on 25/26 August, General Clowes and Group Captain Bill Garing—now controlling all air operations over New Guinea—knew of it. From 1.30 a.m. patrols reported that Japanese troops were coming ashore near Ahioma, east of the easternmost Australian defences. Naval gunfire soon reinforced the news, thundering at the end of a day in which airmen of all ranks had worked intensely. 'All night you could not sleep for the booming and shelling by the Jap Battleships,' wrote Walmsley.[27]

For many, the uncertainty as to what would follow prompted great anxiety. RAAF ground staff and aircrew toiled for much of the night to prepare Kittyhawks for action at daylight. Truscott, impatient for battle, moved through the mud between each aircraft's ground crew and pilot, joking and revving up the men with the notion that the Japanese were there to be defeated. Even before dawn, the pilots were in their cockpits, aware of what was expected. Most of the pilots resolved not to shave during the coming operation—and by battle's end there would be many hairy faces. They and the muddy state of the aircraft undermined 75 Squadron's nickname, 'the Immaculates'.[28] Would their flying justify the name?

13 Milne Bay: The decisive factor

Dawn reconnaissance on 26 August could not find the enemy ships, which had dropped their charges and departed the bay in the darkness. Some vessels remained though: about 15 steel barges, moored on the beaches where, without opposition, they had landed their now vanished troops. Japanese drums of petrol were floating just offshore. If the Japanese were to conquer Milne Bay, and especially its precious airfields, they would have to advance westwards along a narrow strip of land bound on one side by water and on the other by steep mountains. A rough dirt—or rather mud—road ran through jungle from Ahioma, via KB Mission and Rabi to Gili Gili and more level land. The orders issued to Japanese troops for the operation exhorted the attackers to 'smash to pieces the enemy lines and take the aerodrome by storm'.[1]

Broadly aware of the Japanese dispositions and intentions, Kittyhawks of 75 Squadron and Hudsons set out just after dawn to disrupt them. So close were their targets to the airfield that the ground crews could hear their squadrons' aircraft firing and bombing. First they machine-gunned and bombed the barges until every one of these vital but vulnerable craft had sunk. Later Bob Yeowart, of Truk fame, brought his Hudson in low and bombed the floating oil drums. A huge conflagration resulted. His crew loosed 2000 rounds at the enemy, and received none in reply. John

Piper also made an impression, diving towards a Japanese truck on shore and strafing it until it and its load of ammunition blew sky high. Several Japanese troops fell on the foreshore too. 'Bluey' Truscott 'came out with a cricket cap on and went into battle with same', wrote an admiring member of the ground crew.[2] 'Bluey' led an early strike, which set fire to a landing craft and tank carrier. A Japanese paymaster, Lieutenant Moji, blamed an over-eager anti-aircraft gunner for attracting the fighters' attention to the stores dump. The successive aerial attacks gave him stomach cramps, and undermined his confidence in victory. He and others around him sat on fallen trees, reflecting in silence. He only recovered his composure and confidence at nightfall.

Throughout the day the RAAF's 'flying artillery' could be heard around the bay, but the results of its deadly work were visible only to the executioners and their victims. In the pilots' vernacular, they were going 'full bore': each aircraft in 75 Squadron fired 1400 to 1500 rounds every time it sortied to attack, and there were 26 sorties through the day. No. 76 Squadron reportedly used 35,000 rounds that day.

The destruction of the barges denied the Japanese an opportunity to use the tactics, so effective in Malaya, of bypassing enemy defence lines and landing behind them. The barges would have been useful too for bringing men and materials from ship to shore. The RAAF had destroyed Japanese ammunition, provisions and fuel before these could be distributed to the troops. 'Good results' was 'Bardie' Wawn's conclusion on the day's strafing of marines, vessels, supply dumps and fuel.[3] No aircraft or crews had been lost. But that night the slow Japanese advance pushed back the Australian infantry. There was more naval shelling too, of which Walmsley wrote: 'through the night it was bedlam . . . we had no hope of sleeping'.[4]

Early the following day, 27 August, Peter Turnbull led six Kittyhawks over the barges and stores. One pilot caught a glimpse of two Japanese tanks, a sighting that would have consequences later in the day. Shortly afterwards came a warning that 12 Zeros and eight dive-bombers were approaching. They headed for No. 1 Strip which, if the invasion had gone to plan, would by then have been in Japanese hands—but now, instead of landing on it, the Japanese had to attack it. After briefly swapping rounds with some American bombers, they were over Gurney. Allied anti-aircraft fire drove them off, and the dive-bombers dropped their loads on

Australian troops at KB Mission. The Zeros quickly returned to the strip. Walmsley recorded that:

> ... the battle royal was on ... the noise of Ack Ack Bofors machine guns the rack of cannon fire from the Zeros the booming of bombs it was deafening one chap in the trench with me shook that much that I thought he would never survive the ordeal.[5]

During this raid, Turnbull jumped into an anti-aircraft pit and helped the gunners. Another pilot, John Ollivier, sustained a shoulder wound as he tried to fight back with a revolver.

The strafing Zeros set fire to a grounded US Liberator bomber, winning Les Jackson a bet with the Liberator pilot that the plane would be strafed and burnt. At about this time, one Zero crashed into the sea and another, flown by air ace Petty Officer Kakimoto, ditched into the bay. Jackson and six Kittyhawks now appeared, having been recalled from a patrol. Jackson and his number two, Roy Riddel, came upon two Zeros strafing Kakimoto's aircraft, presumably to prevent it falling into Allied hands. This gesture cost them their lives, for while they concentrated on the derelict Zeke, Jackson and Riddel caught them unawares and shot them down. Riddel let out a yell of pent-up excitement as he pressed the firing button. Kakimoto survived, was captured by locals and brought into camp, trussed to a pole. Desolated by his capture, he would become a leader of the breakout attempt from New South Wales' Cowra prison camp in 1944, during which he committed suicide.

Above this dogfight, two 75 Kittyhawks, flown by Bruce Watson and Peter Jones, tackled three dive-bombers. After chasing them down the bay, they shared the claim for a dive-bomber that 'went in', and claimed a 'probable' and damage on a third. A 75 Squadron intelligence report of the time indicated the difficulty of being certain about kills obtained on Japanese aircraft. It pointed out that two dive-bombers and two Zeros in this action appeared to be hit by anti-aircraft fire, but after going into a spin or trailing smoke, had continued operating. Japanese pilots were apparently using smoke cartridges to mislead the enemy. Stuart Munro of 75 Squadron was last seen heading away from the field with a Zero tailing him. The remains of his aircraft were discovered 13 months later, scattered across a wide area.

Conscious that enemy tanks were proving troublesome, Turnbull took off at about 5 p.m. to see if he could find and hammer them. He was supposed to be resting due to 'Operational Tiredness', but after a day on the ground was pleased to be in the air again. He cheerfully told his wingman, Ron Kerville, that if his engine failed, 'Hop out old boy and swim for it.'[6] Flying low over the enemy positions, with Kerville providing top cover, he looked for openings that might reveal armoured vehicles. At one point they saw enemy troops, possibly supported by a tank, and Turnbull dived towards them with guns blazing. Suddenly, from low altitude the ace's Kittyhawk plunged to the ground, clipping trees on the way down, apparently after a high-speed stall. Turnbull died instantly. Why he crashed remains uncertain. Possible explanations include misjudgement due to fatigue, mud on the wings affecting their lift, and ground fire. One of the ground staff called Turnbull a mystery man, whom they seldom saw, but Walmsley expressed a more common view in labelling him 'a white man' and 'the best leader you could wish to get'.[7] An intelligence officer who worked with Turnbull in the Middle East and at Milne Bay wrote in a report that Turnbull's 'continual cheerfulness, zest for combat, and outstanding leadership [were] an inspiration to those who served under or with him'.[8] Squadron members, including Truscott, had to be dissuaded from going to get him. The loss of such an iconic leader could have been catastrophic to 76 Squadron's morale, but in fact it seems to have bolstered their determination. The unit was spoilt for choice in potential successors, but in the midst of battle the most experienced combat pilot was Truscott, who took command.

Thanks to the P-40s, the Japanese at Milne Bay were short of food and ammunition. Nevertheless they were pushing back the tiring militiamen, whom General Clowes reinforced with the 2/10th Battalion. The airmen did all they could to help too, bombarding the enemy's positions from first light, though rain and low cloud did not help; at one point a 2/10th officer reported that the Kittyhawks had strafed his battalion as well as the enemy.

Ground staff were feeling the strain of working almost non-stop—whether they were armourers or drivers, engineers or mess staff—to load the Kitties' ammunition belts and manhandle bombs and fuel drums. The ammunition rounds and the belts into which they were loaded were provided separately, and on several occasions the ground crew were up all night loading. The Hudsons' ground staff, numbering just 12, had to deal with the heavier bomb and fuel loads for their aircraft, and the fuel drums and bombs were often in dumps in 15 centimetres of water. Fifteen centimetres of rain were said to have fallen in one day during the operation, followed by 10 centimetres the following day. The ground staffs were grimy—their clothes remained unwashed throughout the battle—and wet with rain and sweat, and they also ate in the rain. They were working 14-hour days, at the end of which they had to walk a mile back to camp. The cooks served meals and tea to aircrew from dawn to dusk, even while it poured with rain. As Truscott said of his squadron, 'We were all in it together.'[9]

The strain was more than physical, for the noise of the Kitties' weapons, and of the soldiers' weapons, was getting ever closer. Indeed, the threat to the squadrons' camps was so real that their 200 personnel were moved west of Gurney and adjacent to the main Army camp. With minimal transport and labour this was a difficult task, especially for the sick, and forced the men to live an even more makeshift existence. Nerves were stretched tighter by the enemy's naval gunfire, still interrupting the little sleep on offer.

At dawn on 28 August, Lieutenant Moji and the Japanese around him were downcast when they heard the Australian aircraft engines starting up. Their prospects of taking the airfield now looked poor. At about the same time, 2/10th Battalion infantrymen trudging towards No. 3 Strip looked up and saw a Kittyhawk zooming overhead. As the pilot rolled his aircraft on its side to look at them, they stood, waved and looked hard back at him. His hair and beard were red, but he wore no shirt or headgear. Within minutes they heard the comforting sound of him strafing their mutual opponents. The Australian Army and RAAF were now working side by side. Army liaison officers briefed pilots just before take-off; ground troops used flares to indicate firstly their own location and in what direction they needed support and then, with coloured smoke, the distance between the Australian troops and the target. The pilots were happiest if smoke rounds could be fired astride the target. Inevitably the Kitties were sometimes dangerously inaccurate, but the soldiers were especially appreciative of the P-40s' countermeasures against snipers, an insidious menace that worried infantrymen wherever they fought the Japanese. The latter would send snipers into palm trees, so the Kittyhawk pilots were asked to rake certain patches of jungle with fire. They could not observe the results, but were assured that 'palm fronds, bullets and dead Japanese snipers were pouring down with the rain'.[10] So were the Kitties' bullets. One estimate said they fired 85,000 rounds on 27 August, another that 100,000 rounds had been fired over 26–28 August. Fortunately a Flying Fortress landed on Gurney, loaded with .50 calibre explosive ammunition supplies. Ian Loudon, of 76 Squadron, told his logbook that he 'caught large party of J's on beach'.[11] He saw men stagger, reel, grope and crawl as he pounded the life out of them.

By late afternoon on 28 August, Japanese troops were reportedly less than five kilometres from No. 1 Strip. General Clowes and Group Captain Garing decided that the aircraft based at Milne Bay should fly to the greater safety of Port Moresby, at least for the night. It was a difficult decision, for the move was bound to affect the morale of those left behind. On the other hand, to lose these aircraft in a night attack would have been disastrous, and at least in Moresby the aircraft could receive some much-needed advanced servicing, including replacement of rapidly wearing gun barrels. One of the 30 Kitties that took off for Moresby never made it: Bill Cowe's aircraft struck rock in the clouds near Seven Mile Strip and he was killed. Most pilots left, either flying a P-40 or as passengers in an overloaded Hudson, though Truscott decided to stay.

'Buster' Brown and other pilots went to the 'Officers Club' in Port Moresby, where their beards, bedraggled clothing and 'Gili Gili hats'—slouch hats with both sides turned up cowboy-style—raised some eyebrows. So did their revolvers, which came out when someone tried to close the bar. In between, Jackson brought General Kenney around to meet his men.

Next day the surviving Kittyhawks returned to Milne Bay, though Jackson's tired machine, which he had flown almost without respite since the Japanese arrived, developed engine trouble and he had to crash-land on the coast. He stayed at a mission overnight and reportedly persuaded 20 Papuan women to row him to a point where he could be picked up by boat and returned to Port Moresby. Dire threats were supposedly issued against anyone else making a forced landing in this unique and desirable location.

In the meantime, the RAAF personnel still at Milne Bay faced a nerve-racking night. A Japanese breakthrough seemed imminent. Nearby explosions suggested they were approaching, until someone deduced that cows had wandered into a minefield. When a guard fired a shot, someone panicked and blew up the canteen. Accounts vary as to the consequences, but free beer became available, either because it was lying around after the explosion or it was distributed by sympathetic soldiers.

A welcome RAAF reinforcement arrived by air at Milne Bay on 29 August. Group Captain Bill Garing decided to come from Port Moresby and direct the air battle, which had been without a coordinating commander since 5 August. The energetic and able Garing seemed to relish the uncomfortable and tense situation. He toured forward areas in a Bren carrier, assuring personnel that the fighters would return and telling them there would be no retreat from Milne Bay. Such talks were necessary, for he said of the condition of the forces on his arrival: 'Fighter squadrons okay but other units in a hell of a mess.'[12]

That day Dave Colquhoun, piloting a Hudson, was flying over low, thick cloud when a break allowed him to spot a Japanese cruiser and eight destroyers heading southwards. If it reminded him of spotting the invasion fleet headed for Endau in Malaya, it did not deter him: he dived towards one of the destroyers and, despite heavy flak, managed to drop a bomb before re-entering the low cloud. After seeing the bomb explode under the ship's stern, Colquhoun's crew believed they had sunk it, but post-war records denied it. Truscott and six P-40s tried to stay with the Hudson, but could not find the convoy in bad weather. The frustrating episode finished disastrously, for as the aircraft came in to land at Gurney, guided only by a rudimentary flare path, 'Dizzy' Davis crashed on the wrong side of the path. He had flown a replacement Kittyhawk to the squadron that day and volunteered to go on this mission. Between morning and night the flares were moved across the airfield so as always to be on the pilot's left, but Davis was apparently unaware of this. His injuries proved fatal.

On 28 August, one 76 Squadron pilot wrote in his logbook, 'Too much shelling!!!'—but it went on.[13] On 29 August the shells missed anything significant ashore, but a Japanese warship's searchlight found an RAAF crash launch in the harbour. Its gunfire sank the launch and killed three of its complement of five. One of the two survivors, a soldier, swam ashore, while the other, LAC John Donegan, drifted across the bay wounded and barely conscious, until after 18 hours locals found him behind enemy lines. A mission-trained nurse, Maiogaru Taulebona, sheltered him under an upturned canoe until he could be returned to safety. After the battle the RAAF held a ceremony to present her with gifts as thanks.

The relative quiet of 30 August struck the Australians as ominous. The Japanese were even more anxious, as a reinforcement officer's diary entry showed: 'We have to take constant cover in the jungle. We cannot send up any smoke at all, for if detected by the enemy, we can't escape bombing and machine gun strafing'.[14]

On the morning of 31 August, the Japanese sought to capture No. 3 Strip. Australian infantrymen repulsed three attacks, inflicting heavy losses on opponents endeavouring to cross open ground en masse. That afternoon Clowes asked for RAAF help in silencing a mountain gun—a small but deadly artillery piece—which was inflicting damage from high ground. 'Bluey' Truscott and Ivan Crossing found and then silenced the gun with accurate fire.

On 2 September, the Japanese were still feeling the effects of strafing, Moji seeing red tracers flash past as he lay on a hut floor. After putting out a fire in the roof, he and his comrades scattered. On 4 September Australian infantrymen found Turnbull's aircraft, with his body still strapped in. He was reverently lifted out and buried on the shore, alongside Australian infantrymen. John Clark of 6 Squadron visited the living among the fighter squadrons that day. He met several old friends, and commented in his diary, 'The fighter boys are a wonderful mad mob, all sporting a huge variety of beards and goatees.'[15]

Turnbull's quiet funeral contrasted sharply to the bombardment the Australians poured on the Japanese defences on 5 September. The Kittyhawks joined Australian artillery and mortars in striking the coast road back to where the Japanese had landed. There was even time for a laugh at the Army's expense. A report said:

> An incident that greatly amused Air Force personnel was advice tendered the army when Flight Lt. Winten who had been on a straffing mission and noticed quite a few 25-pounder shells falling in the water instead of the target, suggested that to save wear on the gun barrels the shells should be taken out by boat and dumped in the sea.[16]

Whether or not the Army's 25-pounder gun barrels were worn, the P-40s' certainly were. Nat Gould's armourer gave a graphic demonstration when, after removing one of the guns, he was able to drop a new .5 round straight through the barrel—the rifling had been worn smooth! By 2 September, 75 Squadron alone had fired 91,000 rounds in five days. Replacement barrels were unavailable, and the pilots were concerned as to how they would fare if required to dogfight. No. 75 Squadron seems to have preferred strafing Milne Bay to defending Port Moresby. As one pilot recalled, attacking ground targets was easier and more comfortable than flying at 18,000 feet and wondering where the Zeros were. Ground fire hit many P-40s, but apparently none were lost to it at Milne Bay. That night the forward troops found evidence of a Japanese retreat, and boats were heard moving to and from ships.

Next day, 6 September, Australian troops entered the deserted enemy base. Only after dark was the enemy really active, as the Japanese warships, searchlights flashing and guns blasting, made two frightening visits. The only RAAF casualties were frayed nerves.

September 7 was symbolic for the RAAF, which launched an unprecedented attack from Milne Bay. In the previous two days, six No. 100 Squadron Beauforts under 'Sam' Balmer, and three Beaufighters of 30 Squadron, had arrived and were a sign of changing times. Corporal Walmsley counted 62 Allied aircraft on Gurney airstrip. The Beaufighters were an exciting addition to the RAAF's arsenal, and we shall look closely at them in the next chapter. No. 30 Squadron, the first to receive them, had been formed earlier that year and was about to be blooded in a search for enemy warships. The force seeking the enemy cruiser and destroyer also included Kittyhawks, Hudsons and Beauforts. The operation was not a success. One Beaufighter crashed on take-off, and the Hudsons that led the way achieved only near misses. The torpedoes fired in the Beauforts' first effort with this weapon all ran wide. The Kitties' strafing did not inflict any serious damage either. The failure of the torpedo attack was disappointing, but not surprising. Torpedo sights were not fitted in the Beauforts, so the crews had to employ makeshift ones scratched on their windscreens, against fast vessels that opened an intense fire when the attackers were still five kilometres away. The American-made torpedoes were also unreliable. However, there would be other chances for the Beauforts and Beaufighters to shine.

That night Walmsley and others in his trench shook as the ground trembled, shells whistled overhead and shrapnel fell around. After a quarter of an hour of firing the two warships departed, with the last of the Japanese troops, and this time for good. Nine Japanese bombers joined in the nasty farewells on 8 September, by attacking No. 1 Strip. Their dozens of bombs were inaccurate, but two 75 Squadron airmen, 18-year-old Leonard Rose and 20-year-old Allen Dowton, were fatally wounded.

Milne Bay was a great Allied victory. Americans—including engineers, ack-ack gunners and bomber aircrew—had contributed to the outcome, but the battle had been won predominantly by Australian troops and airmen. The RAAF's destruction of the enemy barges and supplies was critical. So was their ability, apparent from captured documents, to pin down Japanese troops during daylight, restricting them to moving through thick jungle and depriving them of rest and the self-confidence that comes with aerial superiority.

Yet General MacArthur was critical of the Australians, and his poisonous comments to General Arnold, quoted previously, were made in the light of the Milne Bay battle. He told General Marshall, US Army Chief of Staff, that the victory did not reflect the relative fighting capacity of the two sides. 'The decisive factor', he asserted, 'was the complete surprise obtained over him by our preliminary concentration of superior forces.' By contrast, Australian General Rowell said 'the decisive factor' was probably 'the action of 75 and 76 Squadrons R.A.A.F. on the first day'. General Clowes used the same phrase in saying that the Kittyhawk squadrons' 'incessant attacks over three successive days proved the decisive factor'.[17] He spoke too of 'the magnificent efforts on the part of our RAAF comrades'.[18] These generous judgements by senior Army officers in New Guinea spoke volumes about MacArthur, and the Americans on the spot were more generous than the Americans in Australia. An anti-aircraft gunner from Georgia sent Truscott some new clothes and a note saying: 'This is only part of what we think of your squadrons.' And, as if he knew what MacArthur had been saying, he continued: 'You deserve more praise than you will ever get.'[19]

The praise that Rowell and Clowes gave the RAAF reflected the new mutual admiration between the Australian services. AIF troops had been poorly supported in the air in most of their campaigns to this point, and this was the first battle in which Australian ground forces in the

Pacific received powerful assistance from their own air force. 'The A.I.F. are as happy as anyone could be,' wrote Walmsley as early as 26 August, 'for it is really the first time that they have had plenty of air backing.' On 29 August he said 'the AIF are boosting the RAAF to the sky now for the co-operation given to them'.[20] Each service depended on the other for survival. One notable gesture of thanks occurred after the battle when Australian troops presented to Truscott the mountain gun that he and Crossing had destroyed. It was unusual for airmen to see at first hand the results of their destructive work. After the battle, however, they were able to look at the piles of rotting Japanese dead being buried at Turnbull airfield. It was a sickening sight, though one member of 75 Squadron horrified others by pulling gold teeth from corpses.

The absence of air support for the Japanese had contributed to their defeat, just as its presence had been essential to their victories over Australian forces since Malaya. Its non-appearance was partly explicable by bad weather, Allied attacks on the Japanese airstrip at Buna, and especially events at Guadalcanal. The Japanese headquarters in Rabaul were trying to coordinate forces simultaneously at Guadalcanal, Milne Bay, over the Owen Stanleys and in the Lae–Salamaua areas. If the relative lack of Japanese bombers and fighters was noticeable, so was the ineffective Japanese reconnaissance. Walmsley was a member of a party that on 21 August, after a long trek, found a downed Japanese reconnaissance plane containing detailed plans a crewman had apparently drawn of Milne Bay. This news never made it back to the Japanese, and their underestimates of what the Allies had at Milne Bay probably contributed to their undoing. By contrast, Hudsons appear to have detected and reported Japanese convoys every time they came into the bay, despite weather that was often appalling. The Japanese did not exploit their naval superiority to the full either. For all these reasons the Milne Bay battle led Allied forces to realise that their enemy was fallible.

The Kittyhawks had performed remarkably well. No. 75 Squadron's aircraft were new ones, issued shortly before it flew to New Guinea, while 76 Squadron's Kittyhawks had done much flying training. Working from 4.30 a.m., the ground staff had on average maintained an impressive average of 28 fighters available for operations each day, and between them the two squadrons' aircraft fired 196,000 rounds and wore out 300 barrels during the battle. The wear on tyres using the steel matting, and on flaps repeatedly struck by mud thrown up from the undercarriage, required constant attention. The accumulated mud on wings and elsewhere allegedly reduced the P-40s' speed by 'at least 20 miles an hour'.[21] After each sortie, the service ground staff would scoop water into buckets and throw it over the aircraft before checking for damage on flaps and machine guns. An unusually high burden fell on 75 Squadron's Bill Matson, whose ingenuity and dynamism contributed mightily to both squadrons' success. The rain, mud and absence of proper tools did not even deter him and 'his blokes' from replacing an entire Kittyhawk mainplane. Whenever a damaged Kitty came in, he walked around it and examined it 'like an Irish horse doctor' and, after a few minutes' reflection, concluded, 'She'll do—have her serviceable by 3 o'clock.'[22] He was as good as his word. Les Jackson paid the ground crews this compliment: 'The ground staff did a magnificent job and to them the main credit is due.'[23] Jackson himself, 'tough, unafraid and eternally cheerful', and loving the 'rugged life around him and the recurring challenge and danger of combat', deserved much credit too, as did Truscott.[24]

There was more flying—especially patrols—to do. Malaria also began to sweep through all at Milne May, where the disease was endemic and where authorities had taken pathetically inadequate precautions to prevent an epidemic. Malaria would be a constant threat in most places where Australians battled the Japanese, and the Allies fought it off much more effectively. Milne Bay was a sad exception. More than one-third of 76 Squadron's personnel had reported sick by the end of the first month at Milne Bay, most with malaria. Gould, flying his first operations since leaving the RAF, contracted both malaria and dysentery and was, as he put it, 'going off at both ends'. On at least one occasion, squadron doctor Deane-Butcher had just left the tent, telling him 'Don't you get out of that bed', when the CO entered and gave the order 'Right, get airborne'. For the next hour, Gould would be sitting on a wet seat, with muck running down the back of his legs or taking off his oxygen mask to vomit.[25] Flying while suffering diarrhoea or shivering from malaria was considered reasonable when victims were contributing to a desperate battle.

The tireless crews of the Hudson flight spent an enormous 1211 hours on operational sorties in September. The pride all members took in that unit was exemplified when one of the gunners was wounded and six ground crew competed eagerly to take his place. Colquhoun gave each a turn. The Hudsons were relied upon to 'find out what was cookin'', and on 11 September a group of them found two Japanese destroyers, apparently headed for Milne Bay. A Flying Fortress hit and sank one destroyer. Apparently deterred, the surviving destroyer did not disturb the sleep of those at Milne Bay that night, though John Clark, whose Hudson had come under fire, was suffering from 'nervous reaction' and took a long time to nod off. The Hudsons' patrolling, so essential to the Milne Bay garrison, was 'just a hard nerve-racking job', Clark wrote by the light of a torch on another night, with insects literally swarming on him, 'done continually over the sea, through storms and over high, mountainous islands'.[26]

On 21 September, 75 and 76 Squadrons were relieved at Milne Bay by the same two USAAF squadrons that had relieved 75 Squadron after the 44 Days. 'Had Milne Bay, now on way to Darwin,' was one 76 pilot's logbook entry.[27] While 76 Squadron did indeed go to North-Western Area, No. 75 went to Horn Island, until its inadequate facilities for treating the numerous malaria cases helped prompt a move to Cairns. The experience had left them 'ragged' and 'strained'.[28]

However, Walmsley had well caught the mood on the night of 31 August when, with victory almost certain, the men of 76 Squadron and some soldiers gathered around the pilots' tent listening to the BBC news on the radio, which mentioned 'the great victory' at Milne Bay. An infantryman said to Walmsley that he would never forget 76 Squadron for the way it backed them up in the front lines. 'I can see Bluey Truscott sitting in the mess,' wrote Walmsley, who could also observe Wawn and others whose 'glory is famed now'.[29]

14 From Kokoda to the beaches

While the Australians at Milne Bay were winning, those on the Kokoda Track were being forced back. They fought hard, but by 17 September had retreated to Imita Ridge, perilously close to Port Moresby. In conversations with General MacArthur, General Kenney fuelled the Supreme Commander's low estimate of the ability of the Australians on the Track. Kenney wrongly assumed the ground fighting to be dependent on manoeuvres around the so-called Kokoda 'Gap', a V-shaped opening in the Owen Stanley Range that allowed aircraft to fly between the mountains at 7500 feet, rather than over them at 12–13,000 feet. His comments reflected ignorance and contempt for the Australian ground troops.

By the time the front line had reached Imita Ridge the Australians had been reinforced, and the supply problems that had hampered them around Kokoda were instead biting deeply into the Japanese effort. To the Allies, the Japanese Army looked like a massive snake slithering along the narrow track, but it was now actually more like a starving man stretching despairingly for food that lay beyond his grasp. On 26 September the Australians began forcing the Japanese back. The primary defensive task of New Guinea Force, defined as 'the retention of Port Moresby as an *air operational base*', had been achieved.[1]

Halting the Japanese advance was one thing, but driving them back and taking their bases at Buna, Gona and Sananada was quite another. Supply-dropping transport aircraft were essential to any such offensives. In mid-September Kenney had only 41 transports available, 15 of them unserviceable. It was late November before more arrived.

Meanwhile Kenney developed an audacious plan for a new advanced airstrip, based on Australian reconnaissance. While patrolling from Horn Island in June, 32 Squadron's Lex Halliday had to make a forced landing near Wanigela Mission, midway between Milne Bay and Buna. Locals cut a runway through the tall native grass, a second Hudson flew in, and after Halliday's plane was repaired, both flew on to Port Moresby. Group Captain Garing was interested in hearing of this natural landing ground and, after inspecting it, reported it to Kenney. The American was excited by the possibility of developing this base, which he flew over in August. On the same flight he examined the coast to the north-east, and was impressed by the possibilities of the Dobodura plain south of Buna. He envisaged a great base there, from which his aircraft could avoid the hard climb over the Owen Stanley Range and its obstructive weather, and could strike further than ever before. By November he was urging on MacArthur a vision of Milne Bay, Goodenough Island and Buna as fighter and bomber bases from which to launch the 'flying artillery' he considered had rendered tanks and field artillery obsolete in this theatre. He needed to be able to capture Buna first, and he put to MacArthur the possibility of flying in advance parties to Wanigela, employing locals to cut the runways, and airlifting in thousands of troops. MacArthur liked the idea, but felt it was too risky. He changed his mind when in September Kenney demonstrated the possibilities by moving part of the US 32nd Division from Queensland to Moresby, partly with Australian civil airliners. MacArthur then agreed to the Wanigela project, codenamed 'Hatrack'.

Kenney's air transport was now really stretched, for it needed to provide 102,000 pounds (46,250 kilograms) of supplies daily to maintain 'Hatrack', 'Kanga Force' around Wau, a 32nd Division battalion marching to outflank the Japanese, and the thousands of Australian troops now advancing northward across the Kokoda Track. In October the quantity dropped to the last-named force had to be increased. It was, and on 2 November the Australians reoccupied Kokoda. Three days later the first Dakota aircraft landed there. Meanwhile project 'Hatrack' proceeded flawlessly, and American engineers began developing further airstrips between Wanigela and the coast.

The Australian aerial contribution to these operations was limited. Nos 6, 32 and 33 Squadrons and No. 1 Rescue and Communication Flight all helped, but the Americans did nearly all of the vast aerial transport required in New Guinea until December 1942. On the other hand, many Australian aircrew served in American transport squadrons and bomber units, owing to early deficiencies in the training of American aircrew, notably in navigation and instrument flying.

The RAAF was striking the enemy on the ground and damaging its already fragile supply line. The main targets were base areas. The predominance of American air power was becoming increasingly apparent, but the Australian arsenal received a great boon when, on 12 September, No. 30 Squadron arrived in Port Moresby. It came armed with the best aircraft yet received by the RAAF in this war: the Bristol Beaufighter. The 'Beau' was the first aircraft really worthy of the Australians recruited to fly in the Pacific War. The Hudson, Kittyhawk and Catalina were all fine planes, but not at the cutting edge of technology. 'To see those Beaufighters, that was a marvellous experience,' remembered Ralph Nelson, who had served in 21 Squadron at Singapore. He told himself, 'I'm going to get my own back on these buggers now.'[2]

Despite its name, the Beaufighter was not intended for dogfighting. Instead it was perfect for the ground-attack work that would henceforth be fundamental to the Pacific War. A Beaufighter jumped by enemy fighters would go to 'the deck' and escape by pushing the throttles to maximum speed. It would rarely fly above 10,000 feet, and was sluggish at 20,000. It was more attractive than its close relative, the Beaufort, with which it had 75 per cent of its parts and production techniques in common. It was much more powerful too, with its two 1725 horsepower engines as opposed to the Beaufort's twin 1200 horsepower engines. Sometimes described as 'two large engines followed by an aeroplane', the Beaufighter could be very hard to keep straight on takeoff due to the torque of its mighty Bristol Hercules radial engines.[3] Similarly, after landing the pilot needed to use his rudder skilfully to prevent the powerful 'Beau' from veering off dangerously. A wartime publication noted grimly that 'more requiems than reputations have been won by pilots getting too fresh with Beaufighters'.[4] Even when airborne it was notoriously unstable while in the pitching or vertical plane, and this inherent instability meant the pilot could never level it out and let it fly itself. There was no 'George', or automatic pilot, to carry some of the load, as in aircraft like the Catalina.

The Beaufighter's power extended to its weapons, which typically comprised four 20 mm cannon and six machine guns, all firing forward and all capable of firing together. Beaufighters could cut small craft in half and sink 800-ton vessels. Some onlookers described 'Beaus' as giving off so much firepower that the aircraft seemed to be halted in mid-air by the recoil. Later in the war, bombs and rockets would be added to their arsenal. The cannon, which ran close to the pilot's legs, made 'one hell of a "bang, bang"', and the acrid smoke made the eyes water.[5] The 'Beau' had a crew of two, comprising a pilot and an observer (later re-classified as navigator), who was required to 'navigate, operate the wireless equipment, take photographs, load the cannon and be general "lookout"'.[6] These pairs often formed close professional teams and personal friendships.

While 30 Squadron's first operational sortie, at Milne Bay, was anti-climactic, better hunting was inevitable. The Japanese in New Guinea first sampled the Beaufighter's wrath on 17 September, when No. 30 Squadron aircraft attacked enemy barges, bunched together without camouflage, at Sananandia Point and Buna beach. Three vessels were left burning fiercely, with others on fire and cargoes erupting. On approaching from seaward, the Beaufighters' cannons had sawed down coconut trees 'as if they were made of butter'.[7]

Even MacArthur was impressed by the news, calling the raid 'a honey!' in a congratulatory telegram to the squadron.[8] Later that year Kenney dressed down some 30 Squadron pilots for inadvertently strafing American barges, but generally the Americans continued to regard the Beaufighter squadrons as top-notch units. The squadron included at least six pilots who had flown Beaufighters in England. One of them, Warrant Officer Gwynne Hughes, felt shunned by the Australian-based pilots, including squadron legends 'Black Jack' Walker, Ross Little and 'Torchy' Uren. He was not alone in singling out these brilliant pilots as having 'tickets on themselves' and treating others as lesser mortals. Hughes also thought that this and the officers' tendency to eat well at the Moresby

Officers Club, rather than badly with the NCOs in camp, counteracted any feeling of camaraderie in these early days.[9]

The Beaufighters were now let loose on enemy targets including supply lines, troops, artillery, buildings, wharves and vessels from Lae to the Kokoda Track and Buna. Naturally Beaufighters were not invincible, and on 23 September ground fire brought one of them down. The pilot of this aircraft, A19-1, which he had christened 'Upya!', was George Sayer, whom we last saw sailing to safety from Java. The ending of his charmed life, which had seen him complete 48 operational flights in six campaigns, was a shock to the squadron that admired him and enjoyed his gregarious, warlike and confident air.

One 30 Squadron flight was using Gurney, but the main base was at the new Ward's Drome, in Port Moresby, developed by No. 5 Mobile Works Squadron RAAF. One member of the latter, LAC Edwin Spencer, kept a diary after arriving in August. His first day was a six-hour afternoon shift—'quite enough in this heat'—and was marked by an air raid. He was impressed by the Japanese—'they fly wonderful formation' and 'are not the mugs that we thought'—but not by the American defenders. On 9 September he wrote happily:

> First three planes landed on our strip today, some of our own boys. We feel proud of our effort, planes landing 3 weeks after starting the job, everyone pleased about it. Pilots say the best strip on the island, a lot better than the yanks.

He acknowledged, though, that there was 'a lot more work to do yet'. He was excited when Beaufighters arrived a few days later—they and the Beauforts were 'the goods', he felt, and the Beaufighter pilots, with their Middle East experience, were 'a great mob'.[10]

The 'Dirty Thirty' Squadron was the first of many based at Ward's, which although they praised it to Spencer and others, at the time still had primitive facilities. There were no buildings, so the crews lived in tents and soon moved their camp to nearby June Valley, which had fewer mosquitoes. Kerosene lamps provided the only light, and bully beef and biscuits were served for 69 successive meals. The squadron's first operational commander was Wing Commander Brian 'Black Jack' Walker, so named for his black hair. Walker won the confidence of some aircrew for his lack of 'bullshit', his swashbuckling earthy style and his willingness to let his hair down, as at Wagga Wagga, New South Wales, in the early days when, while tipsy, he had once used a Luger to turn off the lights. While all admired his piloting skill, others—like Hughes—found him overbearing and prejudiced. Some ground crew felt that Walker had little time for anyone but the aircrew and their aircraft. Joe Hewitt, a senior airman, considered him an exhibitionist, whose powers of command were weakened by a tendency to be a loner. Walker's memoirs give the impression of a man who loved flying above all else, and who was a rather self-centred and juvenile show-off: for example he refers laughingly to the occasions on which he was court-martialled, and in his conclusion nominates as his only regret that he did not make more money out of flying.

The Beaufighter's excellence was some consolation for the conditions. It was well demonstrated on 1 October when Bill Willard and observer Ralph Nelson attacked enemy positions at Salamaua. Nelson was looking at Japanese crews on an anti-aircraft gun below when the starboard motor suddenly went dead, transfixed by a shell that did not explode. As Willard took the crippled aircraft out to sea, every gun on the well-defended Salamaua isthmus seemed to open up on them. That Willard got his 'Beau' over the Owen Stanleys and home was extraordinary flying, as the early Beaufighters did not have full feathering propellers, and the loss of one engine almost invariably meant a crash-landing.

Attacks on Lae airfield were picturesque and hair-raisingly exciting. After the long flight, as they approached Lae down the Ramu River, Beaufighters crossed in front, behind, above and below each other at high speed, all weapons blazing. The Japanese answered, and tracers from both sides were intermixed with exploding flak puffs. Enemy troops could be seen firing from their gun emplacements or darting around. Even more threateningly, Japanese aircraft were always in attendance, and a Beaufighter that returned from Lae without at least a few bullet holes was lucky indeed. Even 'Black Jack' admitted that Lae was a target he did not like attacking, 'because boy! was it heavily defended!'.[11] Airmen who crashed north of the Owen Stanleys were unlikely to survive.

Spencer recorded his awe as he heard of how the Beaufighters 'played hell with the Japs'. This 'dare devil lot' looked, he thought, 'like a mob of tramps, some have a weeks beard on and dirty clothes but they don't care a hang'.[12] In fact, the Beau crews lived stressful lives. The line between survival and death was thin, and on 13 October Sergeants Butterfield and Wilson were killed when, while strafing, their aircraft crashed into a hill and burst into flames near Kokoda. The dangers were apparent too in the crash of Beaufighter A19-14 at Ward's. The squadron stood by helplessly as Bruce Stephens and Stuart Cameron burnt to death. It was a haunting spectacle. Removing their dead bodies and putting them in an ambulance was distressing to their friends on the medical staff.

While the Beaufighters continued sweeping low over the Japanese bases, American aircraft provided direct support to Australian infantrymen in the Oivi–Gorari battle, which clinched victory in the Kokoda campaign on 9–10 November. The Japanese base area, Buna–Gona–Sananada, would soon become the front line.

Command of RAAF units in New Guinea was, from 1 September, exercised by No. 9 Operational Group, under Garing. All operational units in New Guinea came under American, not Australian, command. RAAF Command, the organisation set up under Kenney's aegis and directed by Bill Bostock, comprised all other RAAF operational units in the South-West Pacific Area. George Jones, CAS of the RAAF, had no operational control over any RAAF units. So while 9 Operational Group was directed in matters of discipline and administration by the RAAF, it was under American operational control, led in October by General Whitehead as commander of Advanced Echelon, Fifth Air Force. Convoluted as this scheme appears, 9 Operational Group was a highly effective force, which under the dynamic and perceptive Garing achieved cohesion and purpose in supporting troops at the front.

Garing's command was augmented when General Blamey insisted that No. 4 Squadron be sent to New Guinea to support Army operations by low-flying tactical reconnaissance. General Headquarters had hesitated to send it, given that its Wirraways were likely to take high casualties in any aerial combat. Blamey got his way, urging that Boomerangs could replace the Wirraways when available. The squadron would in fact render Herculean service. Based at Berry airstrip outside Moresby, its 18 Wirraways were soon fulfilling tasks as varied as reconnaissance, artillery spotting, weather reporting, photography, dive-bombing, strafing, and dropping messages, supplies and propaganda leaflets.

No. 30 Squadron surprised the enemy at Lae on 17 November, leaving a Sally and Zero on fire, with others thoroughly strafed and about half a dozen running Japanese troops cut down. A raid next day in conjunction with American A-20s was welcomed with fire from what the squadron diarist estimated as up to 60 machine guns, as well as barking anti-aircraft guns. One of several hundred flak bursts hit the tail of Walker's Beaufighter, but he made a safe belly-landing at Ward's. He later acknowledged that he had sent the other aircraft in ahead of him on this raid so he could check on any 'duck-shovers', or waverers.[13] It sounds like the search for 'cowards' in the 44 Days.

Zeros sought to intercept subsequent raids. On 22 November Cummins' Beaufighter shot down a Zero that had barely taken off. Ross Little turned towards a Zero that was harassing two other Beaufighters, and on firing saw the 'orange flash of high explosive hitting [the] enemy', which disappeared from sight with smoke pouring from its engine.[14] Other Beaufighters drew away from the chasing Zeros, but Hughes received a lesson in the Zeke's dogfighting brilliance. He attacked one which was annoying a fellow Beaufighter and was amazed when, far from disintegrating as the Australian expected, the Zeke looped up and got onto Hughes' tail. A long chase many kilometres out to sea ensued, and though Hughes got back to base, he left behind many bullet-hole-sized bits of his aircraft. Flak had also hit his Beau, cutting him around the knee and eye. It was his second crash-landing in a week, and his wounds and the effects of tropical illness left him so weak he had to be pulled from the aircraft. One of the squadron's armourers wrote in his diary that day: 'My crate, A19-54, got a bullet through the landing wheel and thus a flat tyre. On landing it skidded into the bush and ran into a tree. The bullet also pierced Ralph Nelson's shorts.' Nelson remembered the bullet being red-hot, even after ricocheting around the fuselage.[15]

Two days later, the armourer was happier to report on the squadron's raid on Buna: 'Today our planes delivered to Nippon 7000 of 20mm rounds and about 40,000 rounds of .303. Hoped he liked it all! We don't mind giving it to them.'[16]

No. 30 Squadron was frequently operating alongside Douglas A-20 bombers of 89 Squadron USAAF. Designed in 1938 as a twin-engined attack bomber, the Douglas DB-7 was the first military aircraft to receive a nosewheel-type landing gear; it and its descendants, including the A-20, which were called the 'Boston' in British Commonwealth service, constituted 'one of the great combat aircraft of all time'.[17] An RAAF Boston squadron, No. 22, had by now also begun operating in New Guinea. The A-20C models given to the squadron from April 1942 had initially been ordered by France, then, after it fell, transferred to the Netherlands East Indies. The fall of Java saw them diverted to Melbourne and a grateful RAAF.

No. 22 Squadron moved to Ward's in October. A series of mishaps blighted its early days there. On 10 November, Vern Morgan's Boston suddenly exploded during a practice bombing mission. All three crew members were killed, as were those in Squadron Leader Ken McDonald's Boston when it exploded while beginning a bombing run over Buna on 26 November. McDonald was an experienced instructor and test pilot. Squadron Leader Charles Learmonth, who would become one of the RAAF's outstanding combat pilots, was lucky to survive his first operational flight that day: when McDonald's aircraft disintegrated into fragments, Learmonth was just 300 metres behind him. Enemy anti-aircraft guns inflicted more than 70 hits on Learmonth's Boston and broke the arm of Robert Hatherley, one of his two gunners. At the time flak was blamed for McDonald's death, but alarm bells rang when, on 29 November, 'Jimmy' Bullmore's Boston blew up in similar circumstances while initiating a bombing run over Gona. Bullmore had been one of the first 12 airmen called up to the EATS, and had flown Havocs—the night-fighter version of the Boston—with the RAF in Europe. Harry Craig, flying another Boston, saw his good mate Bullmore thrown clear of the explosion, still trapped in his seat and arcing down towards the jungle. On observing Bullmore's fatal disaster, Craig immediately broke the usual radio silence to warn other pilots not to bomb. It was subsequently deduced that their own bombs had killed the crews. The three aircraft had carried 20-pound fragmentation bombs, so light that when released into the slipstream one or more would be blown back against the others and, by concussion, all would explode in a detonation fatal to the aircraft and its crew. These bomb-loads were discontinued and there were no repeat occurrences. Kenney introduced the use of parachutes attached to fragmentation bombs, which proved effective.

The Bostons were allocated virtually identical missions to the Beaufighters, and perhaps inevitably these missions were dubbed 'Boston

Tea Parties'. Unlike Beaufighters, Bostons could carry an internal bomb-load, and their tricycle landing gear prevented the swing that troubled Beaufighter pilots. On the other hand, several accidents were caused by Boston pilots not realising just how hard they had to pull back on the control column on take-off. Moreover, the Bostons had less firepower, and unlike the Beaufighters, do not seem to have shot down any Japanese aircraft in the South-West Pacific Area. They were still formidable once modified like the local American ones, with four extra .50 calibre machine guns in the nose, supplementing the original four .30 calibre guns. In these converted Bostons, the transparent sections of the nose, originally designed for a bomb-aimer or navigator, were covered with painted aluminium. The bomb-aimer became redundant, leaving a crew of three; the pilot now released the bombs. One American serviceman at Buna recalled the frightening sound of the Allied 'A-20s', so loud they could be heard from a mile away, and how he made himself thin when their bullets thumped into nearby trees.

The RAAF was responsible from 1 October for maintaining reconnaissance of all 'hostile sea approaches to New Guinea within range', for preserving the Allied sea lanes to New Guinea, and for 'effecting the maximum possible dislocation of Japanese shipping'.[18] Nos 6 and 100 Squadrons carried the brunt of this heavy responsibility. It was demanding to remain airborne for many hours on searches and anti-submarine patrols, often in rain and cloud and over enemy territory. Occasionally the sighting of an enemy ship brought feverish activity. On the moonlit night of 3–4 October, 'Sam' Balmer led ten Beauforts of 100 Squadron to launch a torpedo attack against enemy ships off the Shortland Islands. At least four of the torpedoes seemed to be running straight, but they achieved no hits. Moreover, the crew of Don Stumm, who had flown Hudsons at Kota Bharu and Sumatra, disappeared without trace. It was a sad end to a journey of nearly 1800 kilometres. Defects in the torpedoes were blamed, and indeed an American historian describes the type of US aerial torpedo given to Australia as 'a miserable weapon'.[19]

The danger inherent in the ceaseless vigils was exemplified on 10 November, when David Hersey's Hudson crashed into the sea soon after taking off for an anti-submarine patrol in heavy rain from Gurney. Searchers found only the dead body of Hersey's observer. The National Archives of Australia holds a poignant letter from Hersey's mother, written several months later. She had already endured earlier telegrams telling her that her son was wounded in Malaya—as we have seen—and then, falsely, that he had been captured in Java. Now, with news that David was missing, presumed dead, she asked earnestly whether his Hudson could be recovered with the bodies of the crew and, if so, to tell her the cost.[20]

On 2 December, Reg Green in a 100 Squadron Beaufort spotted four Japanese destroyers heading for Buna. He was ordered to shadow them and then attack. After two hours of shadowing, and just as Green commenced a run in to bomb, Frank Nolan heard on the wireless a mayday call from a Flying Fortress, which was under attack by enemy fighters. The B-17 was shot down, and soon afterwards, before they could attack the ships, Norm Mann in Green's turret reported three Zeros approaching to port. Nolan manned the beam machine gun and thought he saw a look of amazement on the face of one of the enemy pilots, just 40 metres away and passing in front of them. He later felt that the Japanese had mistaken the Beaufort for a Japanese bomber. If so, they quickly realised their mistake, for as Green headed for cloud, the fighters banked and attacked from front-on. They missed, as did Peter May from the nose and Mann in the turret. Then the Zeros returned, attacking from both flanks. Mann's Vickers sent one diving away sharply, while Nolan's fire smashed part of the wing and fuselage off another before it spun out of control. The third fighter departed rapidly. Low on fuel, the Beaufort returned home. Amazingly, on reaching Gurney from its seven hours-plus flight, it was found that all the enemy projectiles fired in that frantic eight minutes had missed. Their effort of besting three enemy aircraft gave a tremendous boost to the squadron's morale. Japanese records later confirmed that the two Zeros they hit were destroyed. All crew members were Mentioned in Despatches, while Green later received the rare distinction of a Conspicuous Gallantry Medal. As Green later reflected, had the crew been able to attack the heavily defended four destroyers, it probably would not have survived.

That night RAAF Bostons, Beaufighters and Beauforts attacked the ships, but obtained no definite hits. The destroyers did go off course, disembarking their troops in barges at the mouth of the Kumusi River. There the Beaufighters gained some solace for the night's failure when, catching the barges still heading for the beach, they pulverised several vessels and killed up to 300 enemy soldiers. More Allied frustration followed on

14 December when, despite attacks on a similar convoy of destroyers and the intense strafing of numerous aircraft, 800 enemy troops made it ashore without losing much more than some equipment and barges.

Nevertheless, these Japanese voyages to their contiguous beachheads at Gona, Sananda and Buna were hazardous. They were also virtually the sole Japanese source of supply and reinforcement, for since late September Allied bombing had rendered Buna's airfield unusable. While the Allies used the dangerous coastal route to supply forces at Buna too, they had the immeasurable advantage of also being able to bring troops and supplies to the front by air. From late November, new airstrips were being cut at Popondetta and Dobodura, just 15 kilometres from the enemy's defences. Within days, one troop of Australian 25-pounder guns was flown to each of these strips in Dakotas and was soon giving fire support that was more accurate than the Allied aircraft could give. The American No. 374 Carrier Group flew most of the supplies to this front, but a large number of its pilots were Australian. There was always a need for more aircraft to join the 30 or so making the 35-minute flight from Moresby to Dobodura up to five times daily. No. 6 Squadron's Hudsons assisted, dropping over 18,000 kilograms of supplies in late November. The transports were unloaded with their engines running and squadrons of fighters operating overhead in relays. The enemy made surprisingly few attempts to interdict this transport with its aircraft, and none with its warships, which could have pounded the Allied strips supporting the beachhead battles. Dobodura's existence virtually ensured that the Allies would capture the beachheads.

Another response to the seemingly insatiable demand for transport was the creation of the RAAF Special Transport Flight. It was a heterogeneous collection of military and civil aviators and aircraft, largely from No. 1 OTU. Its list of pilots read like a who's who of Hudson experts, including Bill Pedrina, David Campbell, Ron Cornfoot, Archie Dunne, Peter Gibbes, Jim Marshall, Jack O'Brien and Ron Widmer. It began flying from Ward's on 14 December, when it dropped supplies at Soputa, on the track to Sananda. The following day Pedrina made four sorties over this area. On the fourth sortie, he and two other pilots took urgently needed ammunition to an AIF unit, even though this required dangerous flying over the Owen Stanleys, and flying at just 200 feet over Soputa. Pedrina's aircraft was on its final run when, in the words of one of his crew, 'the machine shook violently and went into a steep climb'.[21] Struck by flak, it crashed, killing Pedrina and two of his crew. It was an inauspicious start, but fortunately there would be only one more fatality in the unit's six weeks of operations. On 17 December the CO, Squadron Leader Hall, landed successfully on an emergency dropping strip cleared from the kunai grass at Dobodura. It was then decided to land supplies on this strip, rather than drop them and continue losing 30 per cent of provisions on impact. Allied wounded were often evacuated on the return trips.

Squadron Leader Neville Hemsworth, veteran of the Netherlands East Indies and younger brother of Godfrey, had just taken off from Dobodura on 26 December carrying six wounded Australian soldiers when he was attacked by Zeros making their first raid on that base. Like the three accompanying Hudsons, he sought to evade the attackers by flying low. He headed for the coast and the protection of a friendly warship's anti-aircraft defences, but recently arrived American gunners ashore misidentified his Hudson and opened fire. After an incendiary bullet set alight a fuel tank, Hemsworth ditched in the sea. Two wounded soldiers drowned, but small boats rescued the others and the crew. Henry Stephens, a veteran of Singapore and Darwin, fought back with his guns until the last moment, but sustained five severe wounds, which proved fatal. Hemsworth and another crewman were severely burnt. Though damaged, the other Hudsons escaped, and between them shot down at least one Zero.

By mid-January, when the whole unit was permitted to return to Australia, its 15 Hudsons alone had carried nearly 1107 troops and nearly 780 tons of supplies across the Owen Stanleys. Its other aircraft, unsuited to operations over Buna, did valuable service in New Guinea and transporting wounded to Townsville.

In late November, two flights of 4 Squadron Wirraways were sent to the beachhead battlefront. One was based at Dobodura, supporting the Australian and American artillery of Bullforce; the other flight was based at Popondetta, to support the Australian guns of Blackforce. Working in this area was a dangerous proposition, especially considering the fatal consequences when Wirraways had met Zeros over Rabaul. Here though the Wirraway's deficiencies as a fighter were irrelevant. Its slow speed and its second crewman made it well suited to cooperation with ground forces.

To observe personnel and objects in the thick vegetation, they generally had to fly at the minimum (treetop) height over the jungle and even lower over the beach, weaving above features such as rivers and tracks so as to catch any movement. To pinpoint enemy guns, they often purposely exposed themselves to fire. When their own artillery fired at such targets, the 'Wirra' crews reported the results by radio telephone to the artillery commanders and to an Army Liaison Officer (ALO) at Dobodura. ALOs decided when the Wirraways should take off, on what sort of sorties, collated the intelligence they brought back, and maintained contact with both planes and batteries. In air-to-ground liaison the Australians were actually ahead of the Americans, at least temporarily.

The Wirraways' slow, circling form became a familiar, morale-boosting sight to Allied troops. It must have been the opposite to enemy troops, though their tendency to ignore the Wirraways' presence bemused and irritated the crews. 'Sometimes the little swine wouldn't even look up, let alone take cover,' recalled one pilot. 'I used to get incensed and more than once I went down and shot them up.'[22] However, the Wirraways unsettled some enemy commanders, for a Japanese order referred to enemy reconnaissance aircraft 'outrageously reconnoitring at low level'.[23] Some aircrew carried grenades with them to drop on these rude Japanese, until headquarters stopped the practice as potentially too dangerous to the aircraft should someone fumble a grenade.

More conventional bombing was a different matter, for as the only aircraft based in the combat area, the Wirraways were ordered to fly missions against ground targets. On 7 December, for example, eight Wirraways each dropped two 250-pound bombs on enemy troops near Gona mission.

The Wirraways' work was perilous. Enemy fighters were a constant fear, and while flying low helped the Wirraways remain inconspicuous, it made them more vulnerable to Japanese ground fire, even though they were fitted with armour plate. The squadron's first losses, however, were not to the enemy but to nature. Crossing the Owen Stanleys in bad weather was dangerous in a Wirraway, which did not carry oxygen and had an operating ceiling of 10,000 feet. Returning over the Owen Stanleys on 11 December, two became lost in cloud. One, piloted by Albert Smith, disappeared without trace. Smith had been commended by New Guinea Force Headquarters just days earlier for his accurate artillery spotting, which had enabled 25-pounders to destroy three Japanese anti-aircraft positions at Buna. The crew of the other missing Wirraway, Ken Dineen and Lawrence Winter, parachuted from their Wirraway when lost over the mountains. Dineen struggled alone and hungry for five days, the last two after having shot himself in the foot while trying to kill a duck. Locals rescued him, but Winter was unlucky: a local was later charged with his murder.

A more conventional enemy did bring down a Wirraway on 22 December. George Hockings and his passenger, a senior army–air co-operation officer, were killed when a Japanese ack-ack gun sent their Wirraway crashing in flames. Soon afterwards Neil Hutchinson pinpointed this gun based on its attempts to destroy Australian artillery and his own Wirraway. With Hutchinson's enthusiastic encouragement, the 25-pounders knocked out the weapon, a 'pom-pom' gun.

No. 4 Squadron's most famous achievement, and one destined to be recounted as long as stories of the RAAF in the Pacific are told, occurred on Boxing Day 1942. On Christmas Day Jack Archer's Wirraway, A20-103, had received a new fuel tank to replace one holed by ground fire. Next day the squadron Operations Record Book entry says, 'Signal received from R.A.A.F. Popondetta "Confirmed from three sources that P/O. Archer returning from Tac/R [tactical reconnaissance] shot down Zeke this morning."'[24] The message left the headquarters dumbfounded and delighted. Archer and his observer, Les Coulston, had been flying at 1000 feet on a late-morning reconnaissance mission near the so-called 'Gona Wreck', a well-known landmark comprising a stranded Japanese vessel just offshore at Gona. When they suddenly spotted an enemy fighter below them, Archer impulsively dived towards it, looking to take advantage of his superior position. In a 'front quarter attack', he fired a five-second machine-gun burst. The enemy aircraft struck the water and burst into flames. Archer described the incident in unintentionally suggestive terms: 'I put my finger on the tit and down she went.'[25] American aircrews readily mistook Wirraways for Zeros, and Archer thought the Japanese pilot had made the same mistake. Japanese records suggest that Archer's victim may actually have been an Oscar. Soon after this victory, the squadron leader, Wing Commander Charlton, received a message at headquarters requesting six bottles of beer for Archer. Normally this would have been like asking for diamonds, but on this occasion Charlton obliged.

The battles of the beachheads were the Wirraway's finest hour, and Archer's victory was its finest minute, but there were other remarkable feats among the squadron's crews. The observers were courageous and professional: men such as Harold Phillip, killed by anti-aircraft fire over Sananda, and Alan Cole, who won the DFM as a 'calm and most efficient Observer on numerous sorties'.[26] Like Archer, John Mowbray received an American Silver Star. He earned this on 15 December, when he persisted searching at treetop height until he located the source of enemy flak, even though it tore a hole in a wing. Elton Ifould also received a Silver Star. His citation said he 'repeatedly flew at low altitudes to invite anti-aircraft fire that would reveal the location of the guns and, while exposed to fire, directed our fire successfully on these enemy weapons'.[27] On one occasion, Ifould took off at dusk to observe enemy gunflashes more easily. After directing fire onto the weapon, he had to make a perilous landing on a strip illuminated only by two jeep headlights and a few hurricane lanterns. Ifould's brother, Edward, was a highly decorated navigation officer in Europe. Another brother, Frank, died in the RAN, and Elton himself would perish in an air accident in 1944. At Buna, while Elton flew overhead, his first cousin Captain Austen Ifould led men of the 2/10th Battalion in the fighting below, until he was killed at Buna on Christmas Eve. General Eichelberger, the able US commander sent in by MacArthur to take Buna when the inexperienced Americans were floundering, said of the Wirraways: 'I can't say enough. Their work has been so bravely done that all the praise we have ever expressed rolled into one great tribute is due to them.'[28] The 'Wirraway Boys', as the Americans called them, helped Eichelberger lift the morale of his men.

General Blamey complained on 7 December that late each day, when the Allied fighter cover had to return to Moresby, the Japanese could send a message to Lae, summoning Zeros and bombers to attack unmolested. There were indeed occasional sneak raids, like the one that killed 28 servicemen at two Allied medical facilities on 27 November. Yet by 7 December, the Japanese had few remaining aircraft at Lae. When six Beaufighters and five Bostons swept over the airfield on that anniversary there was so much debris that it was difficult to distinguish functional from destroyed aircraft. One pilot, Ron Downing, saw two dozen Japanese running out of a house: searing bullets and shells killed half before they reached cover.

Allied aircraft had many choice targets, as the Japanese were thickly concentrated around their bases at Lae, Salamaua and Buna–Gona–Sanananda. On 2 December, Beaufighters sank two barges loaded with troops before they could reach the Gona shore. The following day, one bitter Japanese told his diary at the beachheads: 'they fly above our position as if they own the sky'.[29] Earlier in the year Australian soldiers had been making similar remarks in Malaya, the Netherlands East Indies and New Guinea.

Gona fell to Australian troops on 9 December. The state of its defences and the number of dead showed that Japanese supplies were not getting through, and although on 10 December a last aerial drop reached Buna's defenders, the Japanese failure to dominate the air space over the beachheads was clearly allowing the Allies to choke them.

A drive on Buna, spearheaded by Australian troops, began on 18 December. Bad weather prevented the Allied Air Forces from contributing to that day's grim tank-versus-bunker battles, but in subsequent days the Beaufighters tore into enemy positions and troops. When in the first week of 1943 the defenders faltered and then collapsed, five Wirraways were in at the death, machine-gunning fugitives who were vainly trying to escape by boat or even by swimming.

The RAAF's contribution to the beachhead victory had been profound. In mid-December a Japanese lieutenant among the Buna garrison wrote an unwitting tribute to the impact Australian aircraft were having on this great Allied triumph:

> Our planes do not appear . . . All aircraft seem to belong to the enemy, so we run for shelter when we hear planes approaching. The only planes we see have white and blue circles. There are no planes with the star insignia . . . At 1200 hours planes with white and blue circles again observed our positions and dropped leaflets. Such impertinence! If and when our infantry arrives, we will annihilate the enemy.[30]

This was not to be. Another Japanese at Buna wrote on the first anniversary of Pearl Harbor: 'We fear aeroplanes most. See several hundreds of enemy aircraft each day.'[31]

While the RAAF was making a real difference to the ground operations in Papua, the balance was shifting in the air. On 27 December,

USAAF P-38 Lightnings made their first substantial offering to the campaign. Twelve Lightnings took on 20 Japanese fighters and seven dive-bombers at Buna and emerged with a stunning victory: nine enemy fighters and two dive-bombers shot down for no loss. A similar outcome five days later led Whitehead to crow, 'We have the Japanese whipped.' Lightnings and other second-generation US aircraft such as the Thunderbolt were superior to Japanese fighters at high altitude, which meant that the Japanese fighter pilot confronting them had to make the horrible choice of either ceding the upper sky to these aircraft, or taking them on at altitudes where he knew his aircraft was inferior. The light frame of the Zero not only made it vulnerable to the battle damage that it was now more likely to suffer, but was also not amenable to much-needed upgrades in armament, armour or engine, though all were tried. Thus the more powerful engine of the 'Hamp', an updated and clipped-winged Zero, meant a loss of range—a critical factor in distant battles such as Guadalcanal.

This changing aerial balance, during a campaign in which the RAAF was excelling, had in it the beginnings of Japanese defeat, but also of Australian disappointment. The Australians were not to receive Lightnings or other advanced fighters that would allow them to participate in the head-to-head battles that would see Allied fighter pilots regularly triumph over the Zeros and Oscars that had previously been their nemesis. Many of the Americans' greatest aces would fly P-38s, which were the aircraft type credited with shooting down most Japanese aircraft.

Another American aircraft, the Boston, was however the pride and joy of No. 22 Squadron. Some squadron members criticised the CO, Keith Hampshire, as too by-the-book and ambitious. Yet he arranged for his brother John to bring beer in his Catalina, and if ambitious at least he had the organising and flying ability to give some justification to his ambition—he would end the war as a Group Captain and air ace. Hewitt considered him 'sincere, intense and determined ... with an emotional regard for his pilots'.[32] Hewitt also regarded those pilots as some of the best that Australia's wartime programs had produced, and attributed much credit for this to Hampshire. On the first day of 1943, Flight Lieutenant Bill Newton, one of Hampshire's newer pilots but already highly popular in the unit, had his first clash with the Japanese. He, Hampshire and Squadron Leader 'Stace' Dillon raided Salamaua and then flew some

250 kilometres south-east to strafe suspected enemy positions near Sananda. In a letter to his mother, Newton likened such operations to 'going in to bat in a cricket match', a natural simile for a young man who had in 1938 been a fast bowler for Victoria's Second XI. At Melbourne Grammar and beyond, he was a fine all-round sportsman. His height, at six feet two or three inches, no doubt helped. The aircraft he usually flew, A28-15, carried a blue shield adorned with a pipe and cigar, a pack of cards, a pin-up girl, a 'noggin' of beer and the words 'Spirit of Sport' written across this symbol of much that appealed to the typical RAAF pilot. A squadron friend considered him 'big' and 'brash', but 'likeable', and noted his ability to attract women and hold liquor.[33] Newton now also told his mother that he was enjoying himself. A fellow pilot, Harold Rowell, recorded that in conversation he and Newton agreed that no airman should be considered for a medal until all of the Australian infantry fighting below them had received two medals each. This respect for the ordeal of the footsloggers was common among operational aircrew. One means of helping the Australians on the ground was preventing Japanese from Buna reaching Sanananda. To this end Learmonth and others found themselves strafing emaciated Japanese in the water: they considered it brutal but necessary.

The Japanese troops in Papua had been reduced to skeletons, largely because of their inability to get supply vessels past Allied aircraft. As an American report said of these last stages of the Papuan campaign, 'without the cooperation of the Fifth Air Force and the RAAF the campaign would have dragged along through many more days of savage combat'.[34] While these starving Japanese fought to the last at Sanananda, almost without air support, General Kenney's attention turned in early January to a threat on the horizon further north. Allied intelligence believed that the Japanese intended to consolidate and expand their hold on the territory around their bases at Lae and Salamaua. At the end of December, Australian Catalinas and American bombers counted 69 merchant ships and 21 warships at Rabaul, and when Japanese floatplanes were spotted near Lae, this was taken as a sign that anti-submarine sweeps were being made before a convoy approached. Sure enough, on 6 January, four days after Buna fell, a convoy was spotted south of New Ireland. Two Catalina pilots, Flight Lieutenant David Vernon of No. 11 Squadron and Squadron Leader Tom Stokes of No. 20 Squadron, were ordered to find and maintain contact with the convoy. They timed their runs from Cairns to arrive over the target area after dusk. Stokes searched for the convoy on his Air to Surface Vessel (ASV) radar, a relatively new and very hush-hush innovation, known colloquially as the 'Jesus Box'. He found the convoy off the south coast of New Britain and attacked. Two of his bombs missed, while the remaining two got 'hung up' and would not drop. Further east, Vernon initially hesitated, unsure whether other aircraft were on the way to bomb the convoy. Eventually he decided to strike out towards the convoy, flying over Gasmata airfield en route. He fired 600 rounds at enemy aircraft parked on the airfield and in three passes dropped, by hand, 30 fragmentation and incendiary bombs. This was routine for Catalinas in the 2000-mile-plus 'milk runs' they flew regularly, from November, over the Japanese shipping routes between New Britain and the Huon Peninsula.

Leaving behind seven fires, Vernon flew south-west towards the convoy. After finding it by radar, and then by sight, he counted eight ships, including five merchant vessels in line astern. One warship was at the front, one on either side. To avoid the warships' ack-ack, he resolved to attack the merchant ships from astern. There was low cloud, but he kept the ships' wakes in sight. More than three hours after sighting the convoy, which had apparently still not seen him, he got a clear enough run to attack. His observer, George Leslie, was able to drop their four remaining bombs towards the second-last merchant vessel. The detonations shook the Catalina, but to the crew's joy, set off explosions along the length of the ship. Three bombs had hit their target. After Vernon headed home, Stokes arrived and confirmed that the vessel, the *Nichiryu Maru*, was listing to port. It subsequently sank, with the loss of 456 Japanese troops killed and 85 missing. Vernon, who arrived back at Cairns after nearly 22 hours aloft, had achieved one of the RAAF's most notable successes in the Pacific War. He later wrote that on the basis of long experience in Europe, he felt that their chances of hitting such a small target had been 'virtually nil', and that their perfectionist bomb aimer, Leslie, deserved the credit.[35]

Bad weather that day protected the convoy, which reached Lae after 52 hours at sea. Raids that night and later could not halt the disembarkation of at least 4000 Japanese troops and equipment. The Japanese lost nearly 70 aircraft in defending the convoy, but Imperial Headquarters rightly congratulated the Japanese fighter planes for safeguarding its arrival. The ships made it back to Rabaul too, despite harassment. When two Beauforts returning to Gurney from an unsuccessful attack crashed in the darkness, eight men were killed. There was small consolation when Vernon's Catalina again found the convoy, and set alight one vessel. However, the Japanese chief of staff at Rabaul reported that the successful arrival of the convoy would 'send chills through our conceited enemy'.[36]

More chills were engendered at Moresby by air raids. On 16 January, a flight mechanic at Ward's told his diary: 'Tojo called and did we shake, they were to [sic] close for my liking.'[37] A week later an armourer in the same squadron recorded '3 raids, and up all night', and then bombing on the two following nights. Several Beaufighters were destroyed on the ground.[38]

As the Papuan campaign drew to a close, General MacArthur commended 'the American Fifth Air Force and the Royal Australian Air Force' for 'outstanding efforts in combat, supply and transportation'. Kenney's daring advocacy of air transport and supply had been vindicated, especially as logistics had clearly been critical to victory in Papua. The Japanese defeats on the beachheads, as on the Kokoda Track, had largely been due to attrition. By emphasising air transport Kenney's forces had, in MacArthur's sententious phrase, 'set up new horizons for air conduct of the war'.[39]

15 'Whispering death'

The two Hudson squadrons in North-Western Area continued through August and September to harass the enemy's island bases and to support the guerrillas in Timor.

When the Japanese landed troops at Beco to destroy the guerrillas, the Hudsons attacked the convoy, hitting several ships. Inevitably, the Dili-based Zeros interfered. On 21 August, two Zeros tackled five Hudsons near Dili. The recent addition of a fifth crew member to Hudsons meant that there were now three gunners rather than two, and that a vulnerable blind spot under the Hudson could be covered by an aft-firing ventral machine gun. Nevertheless, these Zero pilots were highly capable, and though one was shot down, they found weaknesses in the Hudson. Sid Wadey, piloting a Hudson under attack from front-on, felt as if he were viewing events in slow motion as bullets punched star-shaped holes in the instrument panel. When his navigator, Stan Faull, rushed back from the nose into the body of the Hudson, Wadey saw bullets strike him in the back. Some projectiles also hit the internal fuel tank, which exploded in flames near Faull. Wadey was protected by the armour plating behind him, but the rest of his crew had no hope of reaching their parachute packs and escaping. Wadey, who as a pilot wore a parachute fitted for immediate use, jumped through the hatch in the roof. The fuselage brushed him before the stricken Hudson dropped. He saw it emitting flames like a comet tail, but no parachutes. His legs were severely burnt, but locals took him to help from neutral Portuguese officials. Eventually he reached the Australian guerrillas and, more than five weeks after the crash, arrived in Darwin.

The Hudsons' campaign had an ad hoc feeling about it, with operations improvised rather than following any long-term plan; the airmen's operational lives were also full of the makeshift and improvised: inadequate briefings, rough navigation, no radio direction, and not even oxygen in the early Hudsons. Bob Dalkin remembered one incident where a crew, typically underdressed in dirty shorts, a Mae West over their shirtless chests, ignored a group of visiting staff officers and spoke candidly to their Intelligence Officer about their lack of fighter protection and other problems. The staff officers 'were looking at us as if we'd come back from another world and . . . looking back now . . . they were probably right'.[1] By 21 August, No. 2 Squadron alone had lost ten crews since April.

The Japanese bombers and their escorts were sustaining still heavier losses in the Northern Territory. Their 23 August raid occurred, like the previous one, in daylight, this time on Hughes airfield. The 40 or so raiders destroyed fuel, ammunition and two aircraft, but like its predecessor the raid was disastrous for the Japanese: at least nine aircraft—and possibly twice that—were destroyed with the loss of just one USAAF P-40. It was the most successful Allied battle of the whole northern Australian air war. It was also the last Japanese daylight raid in 1942, though there would be another 22 night raids. Most were small scale, involving one to six bombers. The P-40s could not intercept the night bombers, and anti-aircraft fire was ineffectual at night, and while the bombers caused little damage, flying as they did above 20,000 feet, their noisy presence was annoying to sleepy servicemen below.

The 23 August raid was 49th Fighter Group's final battle in the North-Western Area. When it left in September, it had virtually ended the Japanese daylight raids and claimed 79 kills for a loss of just 21 P-40s. Air Commodore Frank Bladin wrote 'I cannot speak too highly of Wurtsmith and his command.' He remarked too that Wurtsmith's command 'were full of admiration for our Hudson squadrons for the way they coped with the Zeros'.[2]

Those Hudsons were being supplemented with other tough RAAF warplanes in late 1942. In August, No. 77 Squadron and its Kittyhawks began arriving at Livingstone. The squadron's young CO, Dick Cresswell, had earlier been an instructor for Australians converting to P-40s, as well as RAAF liaison officer to the American 9th Pursuit Squadron. From that experience Cresswell picked up the importance of emphasising to his air and ground crew the need to develop a profound knowledge of their aircraft, especially in emergencies. Not that all his squadron members needed tuition in such matters: 16 were veterans of Malaya and Singapore, including Daryl Sproule and John Gorton. Cresswell had been an instructor when Gorton was a trainee at Wagga Wagga in 1941, but the facial injuries Gorton sustained in Singapore were such that when Gorton met Cresswell again in 1942, he opened the conversation with the words, 'Sir, you don't recognise me, do you?'[3] Gorton, a man who got on well with men of all ranks, would survive two more life-threatening crashes with 77 Squadron before becoming an instructor in 1944 and Prime Minister in 1968.

For the moment, the Japanese showed a frustrating reluctance to make daylight raids and thus challenge the Australian fighter squadron to prove its quality. Cresswell fired on a night bomber on 25 September, but without luck. That changed on 23 November. LAC Des 'Professor' Dacy, of a radar unit outside Darwin, wrote this vivid diary account of that moonlit night's events:

> 'Here they come again!' and we hear the steady drone once more. We live in an agony of trepidation until they safely pass over us, then bob up to see the display . . . the crash of bombs is heard . . . Here comes another wave! The searchlights have got them again—three silver butterflies on the fringe of a moonlit cloud. This time no ack-ack sounds. We hear the rattle of machine gun fire—our fighters are upon them. Hurrah! They've got one. See the small trail of flame behind him. Yes he's leaving the others and sweeping round in a wide circle. The flames are larger now—he's one big burning inferno. Now he's just above the tops of the trees. A flaming fragment breaks off and floats to earth on its own. That's one of his wings. Hurrah! Hurrah! Hurrah! The shouts resound thru' the scrub—from us, and the rest of our lads across the road, from the army and navy camps surrounding us. Good show! One less you'll have to send over, Tojo![4]

Just after 5 a.m. Cresswell had signalled 'Tally-Ho', meaning 'enemy sighted'. In his P-40E he had intercepted and attacked a flight of three Bettys, which were perfectly silhouetted against the moon. Closing on them from the port rear quarter, he fired a four-second burst from about 200 metres, which hit all three. One of them dropped behind, and Cresswell attacked it again from about 50 metres. Its starboard engine was burning and it was losing height. After a third attack the Betty exploded in mid-air. Bettys were poorly armed, lightly built and almost without armour. Their crews and enemies disparagingly called them 'Flying cigarette lighters'.

Next morning an airman wrote, 'I think everyone in Darwin cheered as that plane came down'.[5] Trevor Woodgate, of 13 Squadron, who just hours before had returned from flying his first night raid, said of Cresswell's effort that he and his mates 'felt honoured at having witnessed such an act'.[6] Amidst the Betty's widely scattered wreckage lay the bodies of nine Japanese aircrew, who to Cresswell's surprise had not been wearing parachutes. The 22-year-old had just achieved two 'firsts' over the Australian mainland: the first confirmed night 'kill' (*'It was the first to be shot down at night in Australia'* wrote Dacy) and the first kill by an Australian pilot.[7] Dick Cresswell, a distant cousin of Barney Cresswell, personified the handsome, courageous, jovial and flamboyant fighter pilot. Like 'Bluey' Truscott, his career had nearly failed to take off, and at Point Cook in 1938 it had been Frank Bladin who had saved him from being 'scrubbed'. Another senior airman, Joe Hewitt, said Cresswell was 'a better leader in the air than on the ground'.[8] Like other fighter pilots, he could misbehave on the ground, as suggested by his 1943 court-martial for 'conduct to the prejudice of good order and air force discipline in that, at the Officers' Mess in Port Pirie . . . he fired a shot from a revolver into the floor of the mess in the immediate vicinity of the foot of [another officer]' who had been supposedly annoying him.[9] On returning from the long flight that culminated in his night victory in Darwin, Cresswell was asked what he felt like. His response was typical of the laconic Australian warrior: 'Breakfast'.[10]

By that time, No. 77 Squadron had been joined by 76 Squadron, which was based at Strauss airfield from October 1942 until February 1943. Corporal Walmsley, who had seen the intense fighting at Milne Bay, commented as the squadron sailed into Darwin harbour with its wrecked ships: 'boy has this place seen some action'.[11] However, lack of action in the Territory became a problem for the squadron's pilots, who once they had recovered from their Milne Bay ordeal became increasingly bored. One highlight occurred on the night of 21/22 January 1943, when 'Bluey' Truscott intercepted three bombers head-on over Darwin and, with just one gun operating effectively, shot down a Betty.

Walmsley remarked in the aftermath of a November raid at Strauss that the 'chaps are pretty shaken', and included himself in that. He described five craters 6 metres wide and 4.5 metres deep, with some 15 others made by the daisy-cutters. Tents were in ribbons.

> We found pieces of shrapnel from the bombs in the form of rivets, old nuts, bolts, pieces of glass and iron and other injurious items. The grass is cut that low in places it looks as though a flock of sheep passed through, some of the gum trees were cut right in two.

The following night came another raid, and the veteran of Papua and Darwin wrote: 'That makes my 17th bombing raid, [plus] 2 dive bombings, 15 straffings, 10 shellings by warships and been in an invasion not to [sic] bad for a lad, but I'm feeling the strain a bit.'[12]

On 25 September, three Hudsons flew to Dili to bomb an enemy ship. The ship had departed, but the raid became celebrated because of the actions of the crew of Flying Officer Ralph James, which in Air Commodore Frank Bladin's words to a radio interviewer, was 'out on its first strike against the Japs'. Engine trouble separated James' Hudson from the other two, which had bombed the town and left by the time he arrived. Two Zeros that had gone up to intercept were still there, and were soon joined by two more from Dili. James headed for the sparse cloud cover, but each time he emerged a Zero seemed to be waiting for him. When at one point he saw one above him, he swung round and Sergeant Pat Reen was able to give the fighter 'a good burst of lead'. The Zero dived and sought to attack from below, but this time Sergeant Hugh Reilly was ready. He recalled for the radio that the Zero 'was an absolute sitter and I think I put enough lead into him to stop any aircraft.' After 30 minutes of dogfighting, the Zero was seen trailing smoke and spinning uncontrollably down. Sergeant Ken Keech warned the gunners of the positions of the various Zeros. He spoke afterwards of being:

> ... so busy jumping from one side of the aircraft to the other, and they seemed so thick I hardly knew which Zero to have a crack at first, but I managed to warn our pilot where the greatest danger seemed to be. The Japs were sending so much tracer our way that it seemed like Guy Fawkes day.[13]

Five minutes after the first went down, Reen sent a second Zero spinning. James wrote to his wife that the danger was still far from over, for:

> ... we had one of our main fuel tanks shot away and had to turn for home which meant crossing Wetar Strait with no cloud . . . we were out of ammunition for the belly gun, and the side gun, and shortly after, the breech block in the port turret gun broke in half and the starboard gun jammed. We were almost a sitter so I dived for the sea at 300 mph and levelled out with our props just clearing the water.

Keech ran to the navigator's guns and collected his ammunition, Reen grabbed a breech block from one of the forward guns and 'the game was on again'. They 'zig zagged to Timor and flew up a river gorge with the Japs almost 3 feet above the river bed'. The Japanese could only follow from dead astern. Though running desperately short of ammunition, Reen managed to obtain sufficient hits on both Zeros to drive them off.

The crew radioed news of their encounter, and on reaching home they were treated to what James called 'a lot of Bally hoo'. For a Hudson to survive a fight with four Zeros—let alone destroy two and possibly three—was, he was told, unprecedented. The story appeared in newspapers and radio broadcasts. James humbly declared to his wife:

> I don't feel proud of myself dear as I didn't fire a shot—merely sat behind the stick and tried some aerobatics. The chaps, especially Pat are to thank that we returned at all. That darling was my first dog-fight and lasted three quarters of an hour.

Little wonder that the Operations Record Book recorded that, this being the crew's first strike, 'it is considered a particularly good show' and even 'a marvellous achievement'.[14] James confidently reassured his wife: 'remember Scamp—I'll never die in an aircraft'.[15]

Sadly this was not to be. On 28 April 1943, with Reen and Keech on board, James was flying on a reconnaissance to the Aru Islands when he reported losing an engine. The aircraft disappeared while trying to return to base. Four Hudsons searched daily for a week, but no trace of the aircraft was ever found. The despairing efforts James' wife made to find out more about her beloved husband's fate are available to read in a War Memorial file, as is a letter from his squadron leader of the time, Wing Commander Jock Whyte, who said he was convinced that her husband was dead, and told her that Ralph was 'an exceptionally brilliant captain and a very good friend of mine'.[16] For the gallant work of men like James, General Kenney sent his congratulations to the Hudson crews in October.

Whyte himself was an outstanding leader. 'As far as we were concerned', wrote one of his cooks, 'that C.O. was a gentleman—Whyte by name and white by nature. Whenever our planes had a successful raid, he'd call a parade to explain the success to us all from top ranks to the bottom, saying we were all responsible for the achievements.'[17] When Whyte was replaced in July, his successor, Squadron Leader Cyril Williams, went missing in terrible weather on his first flight to Timor. Williams was a Sword of Honour winner and experienced regular air force officer whom Charles Learmonth considered 'very brilliant'.[18] He had married just before taking up his new role.

October brought an aircraft type to North-Western Area that would transform the effectiveness of its attacks, supplement the Hudsons and signal the beginning of a new phase. These were the Beaufighters of No. 31 Squadron. Members were initially surprised and disappointed not to be sent to New Guinea, but they would be kept busy.

The Beaufighters were sent on 12 November to a new airfield at Coomalie Creek, about 100 kilometres south of Darwin. Bladin had insisted it be situated there; the engineers who built it dubbed it 'Bladin's Folly', but it sufficed. 'Coomalie Charlie' was the nickname given to the squadron's first commander, Squadron Leader Charles Read, though to his face this natural leader was 'Sir'. An exceptional pilot and administrator, he encouraged the pilots' belief that their new aircraft were the best available. Read and Squadron Leader Bruce Rose were the squadron's only pilots with previous Beaufighter experience, though most had been instructors on Ansons and Oxfords with 2000 hours up.

Operations in North-Western Area offered the Beaufighters different challenges than in New Guinea. For starters, the average sortie was much longer, at six hours in duration. If one ditched it would almost certainly be in the sea, where there was little hope of rescue. Navigation over the huge distances flown was by dead-reckoning, with some assistance from sea markers thrown out of the aircraft. The weather was often frightful, with the heavy tropical rain and towering cumulus cloud unnerving and dangerous. The worst storms could toss the Beaufighters around like the proverbial cork on rough seas. Ken McDonald described one stormy, black night in which, while he tried to keep his Beau level, an updraft 'like a great elevator' lifted it 150 metres.[19] Then, after a hideous jolt, a terrifying downdraft carried the helpless crew towards the sea. With another shock the fall ended and they flew level before reliving the sequence.

A lack of coastwatchers in the area diminished the chance of accurate weather forecasting. Single aircraft depended on instrument flying in the heavy rain. When several aircraft were flying a sortie, visibility during a downpour could be down to 25 metres, and the flight leader stayed low, if possible out of the cloud, with the other aircraft in close attendance. Once over the target, heavy rain affected shooting accuracy, for drops on the windscreen combined with the light illuminating the reflector gunsight to affect visibility. With experience, a routine developed whereby the formation flew just 50 feet up for the last 150 to 250 kilometres.

McDonald, who would win a DFC flying Beaufighters, nominated the weather as one of three great enemies to the aircrews at Coomalie Creek. The other two were the Japanese and 'Gremlins'. 'The reader may be inclined to laugh,' he wrote:

> but who are you, who have not suffered these traumas to dismiss out of hand the existence of Gremlins? Unexplained engine failures, instruments going haywire, compasses that swing round and round—there's no end to the tales of terror told by the aircrews.[20]

Whether or not gremlins were to blame, the squadron's first few operations were disappointing. The first operation was slated for 17 November, when two flights would attack two Japanese-held Timorese villages. McDonald recalls the sleepless night preceding, and then waiting on the strip for the word to go on this, his first mission. Suddenly he was overcome by feelings new to him: 'I started to shake, my mouth went dry, my bladder was suddenly about to burst and I rushed across to the grass verge to empty it. Then it was my bowels, they were almost uncontrollable.'[21] His observer Frank Magee had similar pre-operation fear, which evaporated once the job began.

During the operation, McDonald's flight spotted a Japanese aircraft. As the 26-year-old flight leader, Wing Commander Doug Riding, manoeuvred his aircraft at low level, his wingtip struck the water. He and his observer, Tim Clarke, a pioneer in wartime RAAF navigation improvements, died instantly. The other flight accidentally strafed a friendly village. Australians on the ground there sent a message: 'At 0810 hours four aircraft appeared from the south and strafed effectively. Horses, natives and Aussies in all directions. No casualties but thoroughly recommend for use on enemy.'[22] In subsequent days Beaufighters did strafe and burn enemy-occupied buildings on the island.

Continuing the run of bad luck, on 28 November, another of the squadron's 26-year-olds, Ben Hammat, a farmer who in 1939 had been training for the ministry, died of illness in hospital. Disaster followed again when the Beaufighters supported three Australian warships attempting to evacuate Portuguese civilians and Dutch troops from Timor on 30 November–1 December. The two larger ships, the corvettes *Armidale* and *Castlemaine*, came under air attack three times on 30 November. During one attack Beaufighters drove off a force of eight bombers and six fighters, despite one Beaufighter having its cockpit 'blown off'.[23] The following day, amidst confusion off Timor, *Castlemaine* set out to look for one of its Beaufighter escort that had gone missing on the way to Darwin. It could not find Pilot Officer James Morrison and Sergeant Allan Forrest. The *Castlemaine* made it home, unlike the *Armidale*. After reporting that she was under attack from nine aircraft and complaining twice of 'Absolutely no fighter support', *Armidale* was torpedoed and sunk 560 kilometres from home.[24] Bad weather had prevented the Beaufighters finding the corvettes. Japanese aircraft machine-gunned men in the water for 15 minutes. For another ten days, Hudsons sought the survivors and, on finding various groups, dropped supplies and directed vessels to them. Most disturbingly, a raft carrying 30 survivors was seen intermittently, but then disappeared without trace.

Growing Japanese strength had prompted the Allied forces to leave Timor. The Japanese were doubling their aerial strength there, to 62 aircraft in December. They were also constructing a new airfield at Fuiloro, nearly 100 kilometres closer to Darwin than Dili; hence Fuiloro became a new target for Hudsons and Beaufighters.

In December the Beaufighters came into their own. A wartime account argued that:

> Beaufighters waged a new kind of war against the Japanese. It was aggressive war, war of attack, war of accurate destruction. Hitherto the enemy had been bombed by aircraft which flew at remote heights in the sky. Sometimes they were strafed by low-diving bombers. That kind of attack had given them time to take cover ... Now it was different. Aircraft which skimmed the trees hurtled through the steep valleys of Timor's mountains, the hills screening the noise of their approach. They gave no signs of their coming and their guns' fury destroyed everything in their path.[25]

Wartime propaganda emphasised that the Japanese dubbed the Beaufighter 'whispering death', though there seems to be no hard evidence of this. The story is plausible, as sleeve valves on the engines reduced the noise at the front of the aircraft. Furthermore, any soldier confronted by the Beau's formidable firepower would have felt close to death—and reports from the ground in November suggested that two raids had killed or wounded 250 enemy troops.

An Australian Kittyhawk pilot, Jock Scott, took a chance to fly with a Beaufighter crew on a practice flight in 1945. Standing behind the pilot, he was unimpressed by how noisy the engines were, how the aircraft swung on take-off, how comparatively slow it was to manoeuvre into firing position, and how much longer it would be exposed to ground fire than the faster P-40. To Scott, the bigger flying machine did not appeal, but the Beaufighter captured the imagination of many other fliers and the general public.

For example, Maurice Ball, who became a Beaufighter pilot after doing about 1000 hours in Wirraways, considered the Beaufighter the most beautiful aircraft he had flown. Moreover, he left a fighter squadron to fly it. His reasoning was that a ground-attack aircraft allowed much more initiative than fighters, in which you waited for the enemy to come to you, or bombers, in which you travelled many hours, often at night, and did not see whether you hit the target far below. Moreover, in the Beaufighter, the:

> ... cockpit layout was magnificent—everything had a different colour, a different shape and a different feel. So that if you were flying on instruments or at night you knew exactly where everything was, and you knew what it should feel like—round, square or oblong.

Flying it made him feel like a 'knight of old', really 'achieving something'.[26]

Another view was that of Beaufighter pilot Bob Wemyss. He called the Beau 'a typical British aeroplane; like British motor cars they always seemed to go wrong somewhere. They designed and built them to do the job, and almost as an afterthought it was decided to put a pilot in to fly the thing.' He considered the layout far inferior to that of American aircraft, such as the Boston, which he also flew. He criticised the Beaufighter for insufficient armour plating, an inconvenient cockpit layout, poor performance at 20,000 feet, and a tendency to overheat. He did concede though that 'nothing could beat the Beaufighter as a low-level weapons platform' and that Beaus were 'ideal for the tasks they were given in the Pacific'.[27]

A raid that seemed to confirm the 'whispering death' sobriquet was the Beaufighters' attack on Penfui on 2 December, during one of the longest operational flights ever undertaken by Beaufighters. They had staged overnight, with hordes of mosquitoes, at Drysdale's primitive and scarily short strip, and then refuelled with 44-gallon drums they rolled onto the strip. It was worth the trouble, for the six Beaus took the enemy completely by surprise when they came in low and at full throttle, finding the enemy aircraft all lined up as if for inspection. In their one run, the Beau pilots held down their firing buttons until they had to pull up or crash. As one after another enemy aircraft mushroomed into flames, the Australians received a thrilling demonstration of their own firepower. They claimed to have damaged at least 18 aircraft on the ground.

Bladin was highly impressed by the raid, which Prime Minister Curtin mentioned in Parliament. A newspaper report called the pilots 'Commandos of the Air', which won the squadron the nickname 'Coomalie

Charlie's Commandos'. Bladin asked one of the pilots whether he had obeyed orders and gone in at a low height. The pilot replied, 'Yes sir, if I had been any lower I'd have had to be a Red Indian!' The attack leader confirmed this, noting 'He has some tree leaves in his undercarriage to prove it.'[28]

The squadron was hitting waterborne targets too, such as barges and a sailing vessel—said to be carrying enemy spies—sunk north-east of Timor in mid-December. Five days later, Eric 'Basher' Barnett was pulling up after strafing tents at Fuiloro when he found himself flying directly towards a Nate, which was bearing down on him and firing tracer for all it was worth. Barnett returned the favour with his cannon, and while the Nate missed, Barnett saw part of its engine cowling fall off. After the Nate passed under their wing, Barnett's observer, Patrick Lennon, watched the fighter descending in flames.

Gordon Thomson and his Hudson crew did not survive being shot down on Christmas Eve. Three days later Zeros attacked No. 2 Squadron Hudsons over Timor. Merv Johns could not maintain contact with the formation, and two Zeros eventually caused his Hudson to catch fire, rise out of control and then spiral into the sea. John Robertson's Hudson put a long fatal burst into a Zero and, though four of the five surviving Hudsons were hit, all got home. It was a vindication of the mutual support offered by formation flying and of the introduction of a 'fire control officer', a gunner who controlled the defensive fire of all the formation's Hudsons in any engagement.

December 29 saw two Beaufighters go down. After Glen Gabb made a forced landing off the coast of Timor, he and his observer, David Webb, swam ashore. They dodged Japanese and locals for several days, until a friendly local brought a note from AIF commandos. The airmen spent ten days with the commandos, whom they helped, not least with morale-raising information. They also contracted malaria before returning to Darwin by ship. The second 29 December crash occurred after enemy flak so damaged the Beaufighter's controls that by the time the crew had flown the 725 kilometres back to Bathurst Island, they had to bale out. This was tricky in an unstable Beaufighter, with its escape hatch in the floor behind the pilot—in this case the bulky 'Tiny' Wilkins. The observer, Bill Byrnes, who could not swim, parachuted into the sea. After some five hours afloat, he was rescued by Corporal Alfred Woodnutt of the local RAAF radar station. Woodnutt received the British Empire Medal.

An unusual RAAF unit arriving in Darwin, at McDonald airstrip, was No. 18 (Netherlands East Indies) Squadron. It was formed in April 1942 around a nucleus of Dutch airmen who had escaped from the Netherlands East Indies, and 18 Mitchell bombers the Dutch had ordered before the fall of Java. Dutch airline pilots augmented these personnel, but it was so difficult to find sufficient Dutchmen for a squadron that eventually it was agreed that the RAAF would make up the deficit. This meant that most pilots were Dutch and most other personnel Australian. General Kenney eventually decided that while classified as a Dutch squadron, it would be under RAAF Command's operational control in North-Western Area and, ultimately, under Fifth Air Force. Dutch and Indonesian personnel would be under their squadron commander, while Australian personnel would have their own commander.

In the course of the war, 4000 men of 38 nationalities passed through the unit. At one point its 600 men spoke 13 different languages. Twenty-five RAAF members would be killed, 21 as aircrew. Perhaps inevitably, there was some tension between Dutch and Australian personnel until they became used to each other. One Australian airman wrote home of 'Dutch officers who act like Prussian generals', and asserted that the 'RAAF boys can be led but not pushed'.[29]

The squadron flew the first of many missions in North-Western Area on 18 January 1943, the day it arrived at McDonald. It would bear much of the burden of the bombing in the months ahead—60 missions to the end of April—yet its reputation remained low. Many of the Dutch pilots were reservists, former airline pilots called up for wartime duty and consequently older than the average. Bladin considered them 'best suited for night navigation and night bombing'.[30] Other Australians bluntly said the unit lacked initiative, some calling it 'the fishing fleet' because its aircraft supposedly dropped their bombs too readily at sea before reaching their targets. These prejudices seem to have owed much to personality clashes, mistrust of Dutch imperialism and ignorance of the limitations of early-model Mitchells.

Death stalked 18 Squadron's members, just as it did those of other Allied squadrons. Thus Robert Farnes, a 21-year-old Australian in the squadron, wrote on 5 May:

> We experienced a stroke of bad luck today when we lost another B25. This aircraft took off from Darwin with two others on a reco. flight and almost immediately crashed into the sea. Ron Hill was one of the WAGS and one of the best chaps I have ever met.

With the resigned fatalism typical of young servicemen who risked their lives daily, he concluded, 'These things have to happen though.'[31] They certainly happened to Ron Hill's family: his brother Robert had died in the sinking of HMAS *Sydney*, and their father had been killed in action in Belgium in 1917.

The addition of No. 319 Bombardment Squadron USAAF, with its Liberator bombers, extended the reconnaissance and bombing abilities of the force. This squadron and No. 18 were making an impact by January 1943, the Liberators hitting targets in the distant Celebes and Halmaheras. To extend the range of the Beaufighter, one was modified in January by replacing the six machine guns in the wings with extra fuel tanks. Two more machine guns were installed in the fuselage. These measures extended the range of the modified Beaufighter from 1480 to 1850 kilometres. On this aircraft's first flight, on 28 January 1943, Charles Read strafed and burnt a float-plane at Dobo in the Aru Islands. The Beaufighter pilots saw float-planes as easy meat, although they were more manoeuvrable than the faster Beaus. The Dobo flying-boat base, which the Beaus would often hit, was 708 kilometres from Coomalie, but when a new Allied strip was prepared on the island of Millingimbi, the distance was reduced to about 560 kilometres.

The narrowness of the airstrips in the Territory made taking off and landing the Beaus unusually difficult; the dust on the runways played havoc with the fine tolerances of the cannons, so taxiing was kept to a minimum. Pilots generally chose for the cannon a mixture of 50–50 high-explosive incendiary rounds (popular with pilots on both sides) and ball (standard bullet) ammunition, while four of the machine guns fired armour-piercing rounds, the other two incendiary rounds. Some fired tracer, though certain pilots found it distracting and were loath to warn the enemy that they were a target.

Whichever ammunition they used proved devastating in another raid on Penfui on 30 January. 'Basher' Barnett strafed a building, which the resulting explosion showed to have been an ammunition store. As debris flew 1200 feet skywards, Barnett's aircraft was blown into an inverted position. Debris holed the mainplane and blew out the cockpit escape hatch. Barnett and Lennon saw the building's front door fly past 500 feet up. Barnett, who would receive a DFM for being 'a determined and fearless fighter pilot', continued with the mission, and in his first run over the airfield shot up two bombers standing outside their blast pens. He damaged two more aircraft on a second run—he was reportedly the only pilot ever to make two runs at Penfui—but while looking back to review his successes did not see a radio mast up ahead. This became embedded in the wing, carrying a Japanese flag with it. Barrett relished the thought of this Rising Sun souvenir, but by the time he got home the flag had blown off, leaving just a bit of radio mast in the wing.

Late in February 1943, intercepted Japanese messages suggested that a large formation of aircraft was moving south from the Celebes, either to Timor or New Guinea. The former seemed more likely, to be followed by a major raid on Darwin. Daylight on 28 February was calculated to be the earliest time at which the enemy could launch a raid, and Bladin decided to launch a pre-emptive strike that morning. Beaufighters were sent to Drysdale Mission on the 27th, to await a signal to attack as soon as intercepted wireless signals told of the enemy arrival. The operation caught the Japanese exactly as hoped; 12 aircraft were believed destroyed, with ten more damaged. Zeros and flak met the attackers, and as they left the target, Read asked his observer, John Marr, how many Beaufighters were following him. The answer came: 'There aren't any Beaus, but two Zeros are coming like hell.'[32] The fighters holed Read's aircraft, but eventually he escaped. The encounter lasted 18 minutes, throughout which Read had the Hercules engines running at full power—13 minutes longer than the manufacturer recommended! Read declared this his 'first and last duel in a Beau', for it was 'too unmanoeuvrable against the Jap fighters'.[33] He had no qualms about low-flying attacks against enemy flak, such as that which wounded Marr in the head in June.

The February blow to Japanese offensive power in the North-Western Area was about to be backed up by the arrival among the RAAF of the most famous defensive fighter of the war.

Lockheed Hudsons, with characteristic dorsal turrets, fought in the RAAF's first Pacific War battles, in Malaya. Although not first-rate bombers, they gave stalwart service in that role until replaced from 1943. AWM 006878

Brewster Buffalo fighters of 453 Squadron RAAF at Sembawang airfield, Singapore, 1941. These aircraft were outclassed by the Japanese Zero and Oscar fighters. The 'TD' is the Squadron Code, denoting 453 Squadron, while the 'V' distinguishes this particular aircraft within the unit. AWM 100117

A Catalina of 43 Squadron. This late-war example carries the 'Black Cat' war paint. RAAF Catalinas performed superbly in a great variety of roles. AWM 128022

A Wirraway aircraft of No. 4 Squadron RAAF in New Guinea, in 1942. The observer, Flight Sergeant Ken Davis, would die in an airborne collision of two Beauforts in 1945. AWM P00484.003

Three wartime leaders of the RAAF, photographed in mid-1942. From left, Air Vice-Marshal George Jones, Air Vice-Marshal Bill Bostock and Air Chief Marshal Sir Charles Burnett. Jones had recently taken over as Chief of the Air Staff from Burnett, who had wanted to pass the role to Bostock. The awkwardness of the moment is palpable. AWM 012249

Looking lithe, relaxed and tough, these four veteran 75 Squadron Kittyhawk pilots flew in the squadron's epic air battles of 1942. From left, Lex Winten, Les Jackson, Johnny Piper and Peter Masters. Three are wearing Australian-made, fleece-lined leather flying boots. AWM 150494

The wreckage of Squadron Leader Turnbull's Kittyhawk in the Milne Bay jungle, September 1942. Two Australian infantrymen are resting on the wing. AWM P03766.001

Three Commanding Officers of RAAF squadrons at Milne Bay in September 1942. From left, Wing Commander 'Sam' Balmer (100 Sqn), Squadron Leader 'Bluey' Truscott (76 Sqn) and Squadron Leader Les Jackson (75 Sqn). All three rank highly among Australia's finest ever RAAF pilots. AWM 026643

A No. 4 Squadron RAAF Wirraway flying just above the trees at Buna during the heavy fighting there in December 1942. The Wirraways won high praise from the Australian and American troops below. AWM 013954

Australian soldiers examine a bullet-riddled 'Hamp' at Buna airstrip in January 1943. The 'Hamp' was a square-winged version of the Zero. The photograph gives a good impression of the size of this diminutive, light and attractive aircraft, which in its original version had ruled Pacific skies for much of the previous year. AWM 014042

A smoke ring rises into the air from an exploding Japanese destroyer during the Battle of the Bismarck Sea in March 1943. This scene was photographed from one of the participating Beaufighters. AWM P01275.014

Flight Lieutenant Bill Newton, VC. AWM 100644

A 31 Squadron Beaufighter flying low over a Japanese airfield. The date and place are uncertain. Beaufighters were devastating in such raids, but were also vulnerable to ground fire. AWM P01164.015

The dangers of ground-attack work are apparent on the battle-scarred nose and windscreen of this 31 Squadron Beaufighter. AWM P01164.004

A view through the nose of a No. 100 Squadron Beaufort bomber headed for Lindenhafen, New Britain, on 17 January 1944. Visible too are some of the 31 other Beauforts sent on this mission, which with 73 aircraft was the strongest the RAAF had sent against a single target up to that date. The pilot, Flying Officer Alan Harrison, just visible at left, was killed later that year in a USAAF Liberator near Timor. His navigator, Flying Officer Bob Taylor, would survive. AWM OG0475

Nostalgia for women was one of the strongest emotions among RAAF airmen in the Pacific, and nose art often depicted scantily clad figures like this one. Here Flight Lieutenant David Hopton, 79 Squadron's 'hot shot' pilot, sits in a Spitfire MkVc at Kiriwina in 1943. AWM P02875.384

Wing Commander 'Woof' Arthur, DSO DFC. AWM OG0076

The CAC Boomerang's early nickname, 'Panic Fighter', indicated the circumstances of its introduction. It was an inadequate fighter, but proved an effective army cooperation aircraft. This example, from 5 Squadron, is piloted by Flight Lieutenant Alf Clare, who achieved ace status in Malaya. NEA0413

Pilots of 452 Squadron pose in front of one of their Spitfires at Strauss Airfield, Northern Territory, in April 1943. Dominating the group in his white shirt is Wing Commander Clive R. 'Killer' Caldwell. To the left of him is 'Darky' McDowell, and to the right 'Tim' Goldsmith. Next to Goldsmith is Ted Hall. Kristen Alexander collection

RAAF Warrant Officer Herbert Johnson seated in a Beaufighter in Burma in March 1945. Earlier that month as a member of 89 Squadron RAF he destroyed two Lily bombers in one night. AWM SEA0178

Sergeant Bill Davis of No. 30 Squadron sitting at the navigator's table in his Beaufighter aircraft in 1943. He is in a forward-facing position, but by using a lever, could unlock his seat to rotate 360 degrees. Above his table in front of him, and back to us, are his instruments, including an airspeed indicator and altimeter. AWM OG0086

Vultee Vengeance dive-bombers of 12 Squadron, with their distinctive W-shaped wing, peel off into an attack dive. AWM OG0534

Douglas A-20 Boston bombers of 22 Squadron at Noemfoor in 1944. The Boston at left is one of the unit's first models, with four .50-calibre machine-guns in the nose, and many bomb markings representing its missions. The other Boston is an A-20C, with a characteristic three-gun nose. The best model was the A-20G, which began arriving in mid-1944 and featured a power-operated turret. AWM OG1517

The Douglas Dakota, often called 'Doug' or 'Douglas' by Australians, was one of the war's great aircraft. Here a casualty is being carefully loaded aboard a RAAF Douglas at Nadzab, New Guinea. A senior sister of No. 1 Medical Air Evacuation Unit is marking the patient off on a list. AWM OG3340

Throughout the Pacific War, RAAF airmen acknowledged that Japanese anti-aircraft gunners were accurate and 'game'. The very effective 75 mm Type 88 gun was often encountered. This one, captured at Hansa Bay, New Guinea, in 1944, bears small replicas of Allied aircraft painted on the barrel to denote the planes the crew had destroyed. This gun was used against the Vultee Vengeance raid described in Chapter 21. AWM 075932

Aircrew of 30 Squadron stride in front of a majestic Beaufighter at war-torn Tadji in June 1944. Their smiling, united front belies a more complex reality. AWM OG2762

A classic image of a Beaufighter raid on a Japanese airstrip at Selaru in July 1944. Photographed from the Beaufighter, a Lily—reportedly the Japanese aircraft most often destroyed or damaged on the ground—has been caught in the open after an intercepted wireless message. Attending Japanese personnel are running for their lives. AWM SUK13746

A Beaufort bomber crew pose in front of their No. 100 Squadron aircraft in New Guinea, probably in 1944. From left, Flying Officer Jack Shipman, Flight Lieutenant Jack Fowler, Flying Officer Francis Smith, and Flying Officer Geoff Waite. All were killed by a premature explosion during a bombing run in March 1945. AWM P02067.001

Air Vice-Marshal George Jones, the Chief of Air Staff RAAF (left), and US General George C. Kenney, the Commanding General of Far East Air Forces, each displaying his characteristic demeanour, in mid-1945. AWM VIC1638

This 24 Squadron Liberator crew has just returned to Morotai after spending ten hours in the air in June 1945. Their captain, Squadron Leader John Larkin, is sitting up at far right. Earlier in the year he had received a King's Commendation for Valuable Service in the Air, recognising his 'ability, enthusiasm and devotion' as a flying instructor. AWM OG2988

From the cover of a ridge, Australian infantry watch RAAF Beauforts bombing and strafing Japanese positions on another ridge just 320 metres across the gully in New Guinea, July 1945. AWM 093946

A strikingly beautiful Spitfire Mk VIII at Labuan, Borneo, in 1945. It carries the shark mouth of 457 Squadron, which by this time called itself the 'Grey Nurse Squadron'. The RAAF's experience with the Spitfire was not entirely happy, particularly because of its short range. Nevertheless, if figures from India and Burma are included, Australians appear to have shot down more Japanese planes in Spitfires than in any other aircraft type. AWM P01275.029

16 Wau to the Bismarck Sea

By the end of January 1943 the Japanese had suffered heavy defeats in Papua and Guadalcanal. Yet in New Guinea, they were determined to hang on to their bases at Lae and Salamaua, and make another thrust at Port Moresby. The Allies were equally determined to hold Moresby and to take Lae and Salamaua. Valuable intermediate ground in both sides' planning was a primitive airstrip amidst mountains and rugged terrain at Wau. Before the war, courageous airmen flying Junkers aircraft had carried huge loads of mining machinery between jagged peaks in unpredictable and dangerous weather to Wau. On arriving, they had to land on a grass-covered strip that was one kilometre long and ran disconcertingly uphill. They touched down at a point nearly 100 metres lower than the end of the strip. Just beyond the runway lay mountains, so there could be no second tries. To take off, they had to turn round and fly downhill.

From 15 January 1943, flying into Wau became the top priority of the American No. 374 Carrier Group. That day General Blamey began sending his crack 17th Australian Brigade by air to Wau to become the nucleus of Kanga Force—hitherto a guerrilla force—and block any major Japanese advance towards the airstrip. He estimated correctly that Japanese reinforcements that had just landed at Lae were destined for Wau. Brigadier Moten, commanding 17th Brigade, sent the first of his battalions to arrive, the 2/6th, to defend the two main approaches to Wau, one from Lae via the Bulolo Valley, and the other from Salamaua via Komiatum and Mubo. One battalion could not do the job alone and Moten waited impatiently for the remainder of his force. He was acutely aware that the airstrip was the lifeline for the Australian troops at Wau. Cloud made flying in dangerous and at times impossible: sometimes aircraft had to turn back or flights were cancelled. The issue became pressing when, from 20 January, increasing numbers of Japanese were spotted on the Black Cat Track from Mubo. By the time the 2/5th Battalion arrived, on 27 January, Moten realised that Japanese were approaching Wau from Mubo, along a previously unmapped trail which became known as the 'Jap Track'.

On 28 January the main Japanese force struck unexpectedly at Wandumi, just a few kilometres and hours from Wau. Australian troops under Captain Bill Sherlock gained vital hours by holding them throughout that day, during which bad weather precluded the arrival of any Allied troops or supplies at Wau. Sherlock was eventually killed, and by dawn on 29 January, enemy mortar and small-arms fire was falling on the southeast of the airstrip. At this critical point, the weather cleared. One Allied aircraft landed at 9.15 a.m., to be followed by an unprecedented 59 more that day, bringing 814 soldiers. Further intense fighting ensued, and on the morning of 30 January, the battle of Wau still hung in the balance. In places the opposing troops were just 50 metres apart.

Enemy fire was hitting the airstrip when a C-47 delivered two precious 25-pounders. The gunners soon assembled them and brought them into action that afternoon against a group of up to 400 Japanese heading along a road from buildings known as Leahy's Farm. At about the same time, six Beaufighters from 30 Squadron arrived overhead in answer to an urgent call for support. An Australian Army signaller looked up and saw one Beaufighter open fire: flames that he estimated at 20 feet in length poured from the plane, while empty shell cases rained down on the Australians. The Japanese were on the receiving end of the lethal part of these rounds, with the six Beaus pouring 1400 cannon shells and 20,500 machine-gun bullets into that hapless 400. Either these cannon rounds or artillery shells detonated an ammunition dump at Leahy's Farm, but Army and RAAF both claimed the credit. Some 15 nearby buildings were flattened in the resulting explosion. Ron Downing's Beaufighter was directly overhead when the dump exploded. Ground crew found one large hole in a wing, and counted at least 58 other holes in the aircraft when it returned safely. Some 150 Japanese lay dead after the blast, which dampened the enthusiasm of the survivors. That night Moten was able to report the situation at Wau as 'now well in hand'.[1]

The next day brought another 53 Allied transports to Wau. In the previous 16 days, the number of soldiers there had increased from 403 to 3166, practically all of whom had been moved, with their arms and equipment, by air. While the transport and the fighter protection of these convoys was the fine work of American airmen, the RAAF played a part.

Firstly, the exceptionally complex task of overseeing the airlift—for example the 244 transport sorties into Wau between 29 January and 1 February—was coordinated by No. 4 (RAAF) Fighter Sector at Port Moresby. Its effort in regulating formations of as many as 18 aircraft simultaneously at this crucial time was 'one of the most notable examples of efficient air traffic control in the Pacific war theatre'.[2]

Secondly, Australian Beaufighters and Boston bombers were continuously supporting the Allies at Wau by strafing and bombing Japanese lines of communication and bases, especially around Mubo. Damien Parer, the great war cameraman, accompanied various flights in late January. The airmen impressed this man, whose images of Australian troops in the Kokoda campaign would become etched in the national consciousness. He wrote of one flight, on 4 February, in which the Boston's pilot 'executed a most enthusiastic lot of dives and strafing passes at Japs hidden along the Mubo trail. But I wasn't interested, I had merely reached for an empty ammunition tin to be sick in!'[3] Still, he became a firm friend of the pilot, Charles Learmonth. Parer, whose prodigious courage would cost him his life in 1944, admitted to being 'as windy as hell' during another flight, when CO Keith Hampshire attacked Lae and deliberately banked over for Parer to get a good shot of the anti-aircraft guns that were shooting frantically at them.[4] In fact it was too dark for getting any camera footage then, while another time the 'G' forces involved in pulling out of a dive left him barely able to pull the trigger on the camera. The Beaufighter was more suitable, for Parer discovered that he could stand in a well behind the pilot's seat and film through the windshield. There was some newspaper criticism in Australia when a newsreel showed 'Black

Jack' Walker rubbing his hands before take-off and quoted him saying 'This is a good day for killing'.[5] Walker was just hamming it up, but the destruction Parer filmed him visiting upon enemy barges was real.

Unlike the Allies, the Japanese were strangely reluctant to send air support to their assault on Wau. Interceptions of the Dakotas could have turned the tide of the battle, but only on 6 February, when the outcome was decided, did Japanese aircraft attack the strip. As the bombing began, No. 4 Squadron's Alan Cole, who had distinguished himself at Buna, and his pilot Arthur Rodbourn had just landed in one of the two Wirraways operating over the battlefield. They were only metres from their aircraft when, after throwing themselves to the ground, they saw it catch fire in an explosion. Cole was slightly wounded, but several staff of Army Cooperation Signals were killed when a direct hit destroyed the hut from which they directed the transports. American fighters and anti-aircraft guns brought down at least seven Japanese aircraft. This raid, however, was little more than a gesture, and by 9 February, the battle for Wau was over.

Many targets remained in the area for Allied aircraft. On 21 February seven RAAF Bostons hit three villages reportedly occupied by several hundred Japanese. When Australian troops moved into the villages they faced negligible opposition, and estimated that they found 250 Japanese killed by the Bostons' low-level bombing and strafing. A 2/7th Battalion lieutenant recovering in hospital from the fighting at Wau wrote a tribute to the RAAF's efforts:

> I saw the RAAF in action, and believe me they are the goods. They made a glorious mess of a large body of Japs, not with bombs, but with their machine guns and cannon. It was pretty to watch. I felt very glad that the Japs were on the wrong end of it and not ourselves.[6]

After another Boston mission, the Papuan Infantry Battalion reported simply 'Many Japanese killed in air raid.'[7] Such messages reassured aircrews, who were often frustrated by their inability to see the enemy troops they were attacking.

Despite their setback, the Japanese still had over 20,000 men in New Guinea, with more due to arrive, and airfields spawning along the north coast all the way east to Lae. Allied airfield development was more impressive still. Thanks to American and Australian airfield construction units, even heavy bombers (Liberators and Flying Fortresses) could now base at Port Moresby and Milne Bay. Moresby had six airfields, with dispersal areas and taxiways, while Milne Bay had two. Dobodura was also developing into a major base. General Kenney was still unhappy with the number of aircraft at his disposal for utilising these airfields. His total strength by January 1943 was 537, of which about 200 were always under repair. Of his 330 fighters in New Guinea, only 80 were Lightnings. Japanese strength in the New Britain–New Ireland area was estimated at 50 bombers and 50 to 150 fighters. Kenney had to ration his limited bomber numbers especially carefully.

Twenty Japanese bombers and a similar number of fighters raided Milne Bay on 17 January. John Clark called it 'one of the most frightening experiences I'll ever know'. He and other No. 6 Squadron members 'huddled, shivering in the trench ... After a few anxious moments we climbed out and the smoke and flame of huge petrol fires was already rising from the strip with ammo going off at the same time.' Once it became apparent that no one had been killed, the men laid bets on how many 'kites' had been destroyed. There was some disappointment when they discovered that only one Hudson had been completely wrecked, though five USAAF aircraft, petrol and vehicles had been lost.[8] This and other raids kept those at Milne Bay on edge, but the 17 January raid was unusually successful.

On the night of 20 February, Beauforts attacked Japanese shipping near Gasmata. Two old hands, 'Sam' Balmer and 'Smoky' Douglas, found the ships and tried unsuccessfully to bomb them. Using 'Rooster'—a radio beacon which gave out a continuous signal—the two pilots called to the scene five Beaufort torpedo bombers, which also missed their elusive targets. An enemy shell exploded in the turret of John Smibert's Beaufort, severely damaging the hydraulic system and setting the aircraft alight. Jack Hoskins was severely wounded, but crawled out of his burning turret and smothered the flames with a fire extinguisher. Smibert made a fine belly-landing at Milne Bay. While recovering in hospital, Hoskins learned that he had received a DFM.

No. 75 Squadron returned to Milne Bay in February 1943, and was joined by 77 Squadron from Darwin. Dick Cresswell still commanded 77, but 75 was now under a new regime. Les Jackson had been posted to Allied Air Forces Headquarters, while John Piper, 'Cocky' Brereton, Peter Masters and Jack Pettett had all gone to No. 3 Fighter Sector as controllers. The new CO was Wilfred 'Woof' Arthur. Aged just 23, he was the youngest officer in the squadron, and the third youngest airman—yet on arriving at the unit he had already scored eight destroyed, two probables and six damaged with 3 Squadron in the Middle East. He had achieved kills in Gladiators, Hurricanes and Tomahawks. He had been with 76 Squadron for most of 1942, a year darkened by the death of his younger brother Norman on the Kokoda Track. Soon after taking over 75 Squadron he said, 'I couldn't ask for a better set'.[9] To them he emphasised teamwork, often using the term 'we'. He found the unit disorganised tactically, and stressed the importance of working in fours and especially in pairs, with one pilot more experienced than the other taking the lead. Flying in pairs was routine in 3 Squadron, and indeed in most air forces, though the Japanese tended to work in threes.

'Woof' Arthur used the term 'mister' for all pilots, be they officers or sergeants. In medico Deane-Butcher's words, he was 'correct, polite, observant and strict' and 'led by example'. Arthur was deeply concerned about keeping his pilots alive, and to this end, emphasised intensive training and the need for his pilots to pay attention to details. After one pilot was killed while night-flying at Milne Bay, Arthur went carefully through the man's logbook and was horrified to discover that he had missed the night-flying sessions in his training. The vision of 'this broken, smashed up bloke ... burning' made Arthur resolve to examine the logbook of every man who came to him thereafter.[10] He could not know that he would soon be personally involved in a similar accident. In short, Arthur was very young, but he was also a natural leader. Air Commodore Hewitt and other senior officers were impressed by his courage, modesty and integrity, and were not offended by his independent way of thinking and occasional impatience—at least not yet.

Kenney reasoned that the Japanese would probably attempt to reinforce their troops in New Guinea, especially after their defeat in the Solomons. Intercepted Japanese radio messages showed that part of the Japanese 51st Division was due to arrive in New Guinea on about 6 March, and Kenney wanted no repeat of the failure to halt the convoy that brought part of the same division to Lae in early January. Group Captain Bill Garing knew a good deal about the relationship of aircraft and convoys—he had won a DFC for using his Sunderland flying-boat to protect a ship from five Junkers 88s. He persuaded Kenney that Japanese convoys could be beaten by mass coordinated attacks from differing heights and directions. In the past, bombing from a high and medium level and torpedo bombing had not brought impressive results. Kenney chose to convert some of his Mitchells from largely ineffective medium bombers to deadly low-level attack bombers. Eight additional .50 calibre machine guns were fitted, four in the nose and two pairs on the sides of the fuselage. Firing armour-piercing and incendiary rounds, they could hurt any ship up to cruiser-size. In February 1943, these Mitchells of 90th Squadron began practising against 'the Moresby Wreck', an old hulk outside the harbour. A major coordinated practice occurred on 28 February, with Flying Fortresses bombing from high level, some Mitchells from medium level, then at low level No. 30 Squadron Beaufighters and the modified Mitchells. The Allied fliers were not informed as to the exact purpose of their practices.

Enemy reinforcements were predicted to arrive at Lae, Madang, or a combination of the two between 5 and 12 March, and plans were drawn up for all three possibilities. The one destination that would bring the convoy within range of virtually all the available Allied air strength was Lae, and it was Lae that the Japanese planners chose. They were confident in their navy's ability against any Allied naval forces they might encounter, and in the light of their successful convoy to Lae in January and their superbly executed naval evacuation of more than 10,000 troops from Guadalcanal in February, expected to get through again. Both the naval and army air forces would provide cover with 40 and 60 fighters, respectively, for half a day each. The 51st Division commander said that his formation would reach Lae 'at all costs'.[11]

The four-squadron-strong 3rd Attack Group, designated as the main strike force in the battle ahead, was American, but its 13th and 90th Mitchell squadrons included Australians. Such was the shortage of qualified airmen for its crews that Australians were scattered through every role except commander. The Australians were well treated, and the Allied crews worked together happily.

The Japanese convoy, travelling at just seven knots, left Rabaul late on 28 February. Stormy weather hid it from detection until the afternoon of 1 March, when a US Liberator sighted what it estimated as 14 ships under

Zero escort. Port Moresby was alerted about the convoy's sailing, but as yet the enemy was only in range of heavy bombers, and those sent out later in the day could not find them.

The weather improved only slightly on 2 March. At dawn, six Bostons bombed and strafed Lae airfield, thus preventing it from providing Japanese support that day. At sea, a US Liberator found the convoy, still north of New Britain, early that morning, and two formations of B-17s were sent to attack. During the day's raids they sank a transport and damaged two others. To the Japanese this loss, equivalent to that on the successful January sortie, was acceptable.

Late that day the convoy passed through the Vitiaz Strait between New Guinea and New Britain. The commander, Admiral Kimura, decided not to press on at top speed to Lae, but to time his arrival there for the morning. USAAF aircraft shadowed the convoy until darkness, when Terry Duigan's Catalina took over. Early in the flight his ASV radar detected the convoy west of Umboi Island. He intended to fly overhead in order to release a flare and count the ships, but as a crewman prepared the flare it began a premature ignition and had to be thrown out early. The Catalina was initially illuminated more than the ships, but the crew was soon able to count six vessels, with hints of more; they reacted like ants scattering when their nest is disturbed. Duigan's orders were to stay with the convoy until dawn, though he knew that if he were still there by then, his slow-moving Catalina would quickly be shot down. The night was so dark that the ships were only visible some 2000 feet up, and then merely as blobs trailing white wakes. He dropped a few bombs through the night, then his last four narrowly missed a destroyer. Three 100 Squadron Beauforts found the convoy in the rain and cloud at about 6.15 a.m., well after Duigan had left. One fired a torpedo, which seemed to be running true within 100 metres of a warship, but there was no tell-tale explosion.

By morning on 3 March, the convoy was off the Huon Peninsula and clearly taking the straightest route to Lae. A Japanese soldier on board saw a reconnaissance plane, perhaps Duigan's, and worried that the convoy's course was too obvious. He then reassured himself by considering how easily the ships had dodged the enemy's bombs the previous day. By noon the convoy should be at Lae. The Allied squadrons' training for assaulting a convoy was about to be put into practice, as the enemy ships were coming into range.

Clear weather in Port Moresby that morning allowed more than 90 Allied aircraft to take off as planned for a rendezvous over Cape Ward Hunt, between Gona and Salamaua. The men were excited, though they anticipated heavy losses, and ground crews waved the aircrews farewell with a mixture of grins and anxiety. Thirteen Beaufighters of 30 Squadron met up with 25 Mitchells, in two formations. Above them were 13 Flying Fortresses, and higher still, 28 Lightnings giving fighter cover. American A-20s would also join the attack, while four Bostons again bombed and strafed Lae airfield effectively.

By strafing the decks and anti-aircraft crews, the Beaufighters were to give the Mitchells and A-20s crucial seconds of grace for their low-level attacks. 'Black Jack' Walker ordered his pilots to attack the ships' bridges, thus striking at their control centres. He exhorted his men to prevent an enemy landing, but crews were already excited about the prospect of seeing their target, rather than firing on the blind into jungle. Illness prevented Walker from flying with the squadron, but he sat high above them in a Beaufighter among the Lightnings. Another observer was Damien Parer, who flew with various squadrons in the coming operation. Initially he accompanied one of the flight leaders, 'Torchy' Uren.

Like the aircrews, Parer was mightily impressed when he saw the aerial armada that gathered that sunny morning. He did not film it, as he was saving his stock for the coming action. As the Beaufighters approached the convoy, they flew in two 'V's, one behind the other, and began a shallow dive. Behind them were the low-flying Mitchells.

Down in the convoy, many Japanese were convinced that because they were clear of the narrow waters between New Britain and New Guinea, they were safe. A lieutenant on a transport ship was making that point when his audience spotted approaching B-17s and twin-engine bombers. Only when the attackers were close did the lieutenant notice and give up his pep talk so his audience could go below or man guns. Bombers approached the convoy from all sides, but the experienced naval gunners followed their drills: heavy guns would deal with the four-engined Fortresses, while the smaller guns and evasive manoeuvres would defeat the smaller aircraft. The destroyer crews maintained superb discipline, their shells reportedly bursting within 100 metres of the Beaufighters at nearly 10 kilometres' range. The Beaufighters now descended from

500 feet and attacked side by side. The destroyers, fearing torpedo attack, turned towards the aircraft and away from the transports.

Slightly ahead of the Beaufighters were the Flying Fortresses, which were confronted by 20 to 30 Japanese fighters. However, they in turn were soon tackled by the Lightnings. The latter dropped their fuel tanks, which fell close but harmlessly among the following Beaufighters. It was 10 a.m. and the great air battle was about to commence.

Before the destroyers could get back to their charges, the strafers had made one pass at the transports. George Drury flew his Beau steadily at one vessel, pouring fire into the bridge until he pulled up between its masts. He brought catastrophe to the Japanese on board, for his 20 mm rounds found officers and men changing the ship's watch. Torrents of gunfire struck the bridges, decks and gun crews of other transports too. Under Dick Roe's 20 mm guns, one ship's deck cargo caught fire, then exploded into a fireball which left a huge smoke ring. A crew was swinging its gun around to bear on an approaching Mitchell when Jack 'Sandy' Sandford brought them into his sights and cut them apart. Japanese gunners pointing hands and then weapons at Flying Fortresses did not see a Beaufighter that moments later slaughtered them with thousands of machine-gun and cannon shells. Drury considered the five minutes in which he ran through the convoy more dramatic than anything he had seen in a war movie.

The low-flying Mitchells, coming with and slightly behind the Beaufighters, faced little resistance as they flew in below mast height. A Mitchell pilot, Keith McKee, wrote that 'the Beaufighters came in broadside to the boat and gave me excellent cover, as I was coming in from the bow . . . The A20s and the Beaufighters were doing a superb job.'[12] He was one of several American participants who acknowledged the Beaufighters for destroying or distracting the enemy. From their modified noses, each Mitchell's eight machine guns discharged so much fire that some Japanese thought that the aircraft were alight. Squadron Leader Ross Little, leading the Beaufighters, saw a Zero on a Mitchell's tail, and though firing from 550 metres, tried to distract the enemy. This he did, to a point where the Zero turned its attention to Little. After the Beau had passed under him the Zero dived on Little's tail, rapidly closing to just 275 metres. Little's observer, Alec Spooner, had modified his cockpit to allow a machine gun to fire rearwards, and this weapon probably saved his and Little's life:

he fired over 100 rounds at the Zero, which suddenly lost interest. Fred Cassidy, observer in another Beaufighter, was shocked to look across and see a 500-pound bomb skipping on the water beside them as it bounced towards a ship. This was a tactic American aircraft had developed at Port Moresby. Roe's Beaufighter flew into the blast of one Mitchell's bomb, was flicked skyward and then fell alarmingly down. He straightened out in time, though his fuselage belly had been dented. Many pilots remembered barely escaping flying debris, including George Gibson, who approached one transport just as a bomb exploded amidships. He flew his Beaufighter between the masts and survived. The spectacle of Japanese ships burning, smoking, exploding, firing and sinking amidst aircraft flying, bombing and firing in all directions was unforgettable, even exhilarating to those who participated, though no one person could see it all at once or even sit still to contemplate it. For those who suffered under the onslaught it was also memorable. The Japanese soldier whose earlier sighting of a reconnaissance plane had given him an awful premonition soon found himself pinned down in a cabin, praying and counting 122 hits on the walls from automatic weapons. A bomb soon stopped the destroyer's engine.

By the time the Beaus and low-flying Mitchells had finished their first runs by expending their ammunition and bombs, the convoy was devastated. The Mitchells alone claimed 17 hits in the action, which had taken less than 30 minutes. Indeed, probably within a quarter of an hour of the fight commencing, seven transports were sinking and three destroyers heavily damaged or sinking. The Allied Air Forces had lost just one B-17, three Lightnings and a Mitchell.

The loss of the B-17 occurred under circumstances that quickly circulated among aircrews on returning to Moresby. Woodrow Moore's crew had baled out after a fighter had crippled the B-17. One slipped fatally from his harness, and Japanese fighters machine-gunned the others mercilessly. This event incensed some crews. Zeros tried to intercept the Beaufighters as they departed, but Drury and others dodged their fire, went to sea level and simply outran them. Ron Downing and Danny Box, who had nearly been blown up at Wau, were not so lucky. Opening fire from nearly a kilometre away, a Zero's first burst of 20 mm cannon fire ripped into the Beaufighter, rendering Downing's shoulder 'completely useless' and striking Box's thigh and wrist.[13] Downing had to take the pain and concentrate on evading the fast-closing Zero's subsequent bursts. The Zero came within 30 metres before climbing away. Downing's Beaufighter limped homeward, with one engine stopped, the other damaged, one elevator shot off, and the hydraulic system punctured. The fuselage contained gaping holes and was briefly on fire. He crash-landed at Popondetta.

The hydraulic system was a vulnerable component of the rugged Beaufighter, and was vital to lowering the undercarriage. On one occasion Keith Nicholson's hydraulic system was hit, and although he could get the wheels most of the way down, there was insufficient fluid to allow them to lock into position. After pouring in their water bottles, he and his navigator—a bit desperate anyway after 5 hours aloft—used urine to bring them all the way down. Usually on such long flights, men needing to pee would use a 'relief tube', a funnel clipped under each crewman's seat and attached to a rubber hose that drained out, via gravity, through the aircraft's belly. Nicholson's crew chief was not amused, though probably preferred 'flushing' the hydraulic system to repairing the damage a belly-landing entailed.

After seeing that Downing had landed safely, Bob 'Killer' Cummins flew back to Ward's. As he approached, an hour later than the other returnees, he saw two lonely figures at the end of the strip. They were his two ground crew, Stan Jeffries and Jack Rawlinson, and their relief on seeing Cummins had them at the point of tears.

Bill Blewett, an Australian radio/gunner in a Mitchell, also faced a crash-landing as his aircraft approached the emergency strip at Seven Mile. Flak had heavily damaged the B-25, and the pilot could neither lower its landing gear nor close its bomb doors. All of the crew went to crash positions except the top gunner, who chose to stay in position and watch. As the Mitchell touched down, the front wheel remained in position and caused the aircraft to bounce up and down before it slammed into a ditch at the end of the runway. The top gunner's head struck a gun butt, which killed him. He was the 3rd Attack Group's only fatality that day. Bill Blewett was unconscious for three days, waking up on the fourth in an American hospital and bandaged like a mummy. He was told, erroneously, that only he survived the crash. By the time he arrived in Adelaide, his wife had received a telegram informing her of his death. She had also given birth to their son. Blewett was never able to return to his American squadron, and it would be more than 40 years before he learned that most of his crewmates of 3 March had survived.

While the Mitchell crash began one Australian's ordeal, the torment for the Japanese in the convoy was worsening. The burning transports obviously could not reach Lae, so orders were issued to abandon ship. Those who were able to scrambled into collapsible boats, motorised landing craft or lifeboats. Others clung to planks, rafts, biscuit boxes—anything that would float. Lucky ones were rescued by four surviving destroyers of the convoy. Still, as the afternoon approached, with a second Allied raid inevitable, several thousand Japanese servicemen were floating in the water.

The Allied Air Forces planned to administer the *coup de grâce* in the afternoon, but the weather threatened to prevent this. No. 30 Squadron, for example, had to turn back after an hour attempting to cross the Owen Stanleys from Port Moresby. Squadrons based at Dobodura were able to attack—B-17s, Mitchells, and Lightnings of six American squadrons were accompanied by 22 Squadron's Bostons. The crews had no trouble finding the ships, for there were giant pillars of smoke, and some ships were burning fiercely. They counted two destroyers and four merchant ships, all apparently stopped. Learmonth also saw 'hundreds' of Japanese jumping from the ships, some 'assisted' by explosions.[14] Learmonth later expressed some compassion for these men, but he and his comrades felt the next 15 minutes were 'the time of our lives' as they flew through the bullets and bombs seeking a suitable target. Boston pilots Dick Hunt and Austin Skinner scored direct hits on a stationary destroyer, and were officially credited with its sinking. Enemy fighters, probably Oscars, tried to intercept the five Bostons. Harry Craig turned towards his attacker and drove it off with his four nose machine guns. Skinner was attacked frontally, but took his aircraft down to sea level and escaped. Four fighters chased Learmonth's Boston, but violent evasive manoeuvres, poor Japanese shooting and some timely bursts from Craig all kept him aloft. Every Boston got home. The Mitchells and B-17s wrought further havoc. That night US PT boats sank one crippled ship, while Allied bombers finished off a destroyer next morning. This meant that of the 16 ships that had set out for Lae, four of the eight destroyers and all eight transports had been sunk. By the end of 3 March, the Japanese had also lost up to 34 aircraft.

The convoy's ships had gone, but the fate of the Japanese soldiers and sailors still in the water was yet to be decided. After the bomber formations returned home joyfully on the afternoon of 3 March, individual aircraft arrived and hovered over the wreckage. Their orders were to attack enemy personnel in boats and those clinging to flotsam. Some aircrews tasked to do this then or the following morning were glad to be able to carry the destruction of the convoy to its logical conclusion, particularly as the enemy in the water could otherwise be rescued or make it ashore. Some wanted to kill any Japanese they could in a spirit of revenge for past wrongs, from the Philippines and Malaya to the machine-gunning of Woodrow Moore's crew. Some considered it unpleasant but necessary, while it sickened others. One Japanese soldier estimated that floating in the water near him were 100 victims of four strafings that afternoon. That night Japanese destroyers returned to the scene of devastation and took some survivors north-east. Behind them they left an area, more than 30 kilometres wide, dotted with men clinging to vessels, floating debris and hope of survival. The destroyers would not return—unlike the marauding aircraft.

That night Allied staffs tried to put together a picture of what they had achieved and what remained to finish the job. Clearly they had won a victory, though its magnitude was still uncertain. When, on the morning of 4 March, Kenney rang MacArthur to report on the battle, he exaggerated the numbers of vessels sunk and men killed. MacArthur sent a congratulatory message calling the victory 'magnificent' and 'one of the most complete and annihilating combats of all time'.[15] He would persist in maintaining the overblown early claims of sinkings and killings, but also in his belief that this battle was 'the decisive aerial engagement' of the Pacific War.[16]

At the level of pilots and ground crew, there was still much to do. Flight mechanic Ken Golledge, for example, was up at 4.15 a.m., a time he underlined in his diary. He had been working on Beaufighter A19-87 for much of the previous day, and that morning it and 11 other Beaufighters and A-20s attacked Malahang airfield near Lae. Its pilot, Dick Roe, shot up four camouflaged Zeros on the ground, but as Golledge reported, '87 came back with shell in port motor'.[17] Flak damaged Uren's Beaufighter so severely that he and his navigator were fortunate to survive the resulting crash-landing at Dobodura. Roe and Uren had been especially persistent and effective in their strafing and had nearly paid with their lives.

Golledge's diary also reads: 'Convoy reported smashed'. Walker wrote in his logbook: 'convoy was routed' and 'Bloody good show'. LAC Charles Clegg, on ground crew in Milne Bay, recorded: 'Bismark Sea Battle ends. Sank 22 ships and destroyed 1500 Japs.' And then, with a hint of guilt: 'Followed proceeding like a football match.' Less troubled was the American duty pilot who reportedly shouted as the Beaus returned from the battle: 'Come in, Beaufighters; come in, you beauties.'[18]

Following up on the victory does not seem to have been a preoccupation on 4 March. A Liberator and then three Flying Fortresses flew over the Bismarck Sea battle area (which was primarily in the Huon Gulf rather than the Bismarck Sea), the B-17 crews with orders to attack any signs of life. They did so, but also had to drive off enemy fighters. No RAAF aircraft were sent to attack enemy personnel in that area that day. That night Walker staged a celebration attended by 22 and 30 Squadron crews, with the luxury of a seemingly unlimited supply of beer. Both squadrons would be in action the following day.

The 'Boston Boys' of No. 22 Squadron attacked Lae aerodrome, where Keith Hampshire was a victim of accurate flak. When an enemy shell hit his cockpit, a splinter embedded itself 7 centimetres in his calf. He flew on and dropped his bombs from 50 feet up. Enemy aircraft were burning as he left for home. That evening, when Air Commodore Hewitt visited Hampshire in hospital, the squadron leader 'could talk of nothing but how good his air crews were'.[19]

Five Beaufighters attacked Malahang that morning, but their squadron also had to help destroy the barges and rafts still floating on the water, as well as the bedraggled Japanese afloat on them. Golledge reported, 'Planes operative again on barges, shooting up hundreds of Japs.'[20] This was no exaggeration. In the early afternoon Little led five Beaufighters to attack ten barges reported near the Trobriand Islands. Japanese soldiers stood their ground, firing back with rifles, but the Beaufighters' guns soon revealed that to have been a fatalistic gesture. The bottom of the barges turned blood-red, the sea around them 'a muddy brown reddy colour'.[21] Sharks joined the killing spree. One Beau was hit in the wing, perhaps by a ricochet. Later that afternoon Uren led five Beaufighters, which expended 1250 cannon rounds and 10,000 machine-gun bullets on barges and boats nearly 50 kilometres off Cape Ward Hunt. Again some Japanese fired back, but this time most dived overboard before their vessels were hit by the shattering onslaught. No. 30 Squadron had hit and sunk 24 boats, barges and rafts that day, killing approximately 350 Japanese. Walker observed some men vomit on returning, and did not blame them, though he considered their work a necessity. Group Captain Garing was there too, and when he spoke to one young pilot who had been retching, the pilot referred to all the sharks he had seen in the water. Garing reassured him, telling him that he had saved the lives of Australian soldiers. The official attitude, expressed by one of the flight commanders, was that any of the Japanese soldiers who made it ashore would try to kill Allied troops. Killing them now would thus save Allied lives. This grim logic is hard to deny.

Nearly 200 Japanese were rescued by submarine and returned to Rabaul. These efforts and those of the Allied Air Forces ensured that when four Bostons undertook the day's solitary search of the battle area on 6 March, they found only empty rafts and boats. In the six weeks after the Bismarck Sea battle, 300 Japanese soldiers were killed close to or on the New Guinea coast. For example, a group of about 20 on Nauria Island were seen to be in 'low physical condition', without weapons, and waving flags. At least six died under a Beaufighter's guns. A Beaufort killed 15 Japanese in rafts and rubber dinghies the following day, with 'scores of sharks' milling round.[22] When 305 Radar Station at Kiriwina was informed on 7 March that several boatloads of Japanese had arrived on a nearby beach, the Australians assumed that this was a long-feared Japanese invasion. The intruders were in fact survivors of the Bismarck Sea battle and Australians soon killed or captured 37 of them.

A Japanese estimate said that of the 4357 officers and men of the 51st Division who had set out on the convoy, 1760 had returned to Rabaul. Very few of the remaining 2597 had made it to New Guinea, and the official history gives a Japanese death toll in the battle as 2890. A great deal of material, including equipment for Lae airfield, had been irretrievably lost. In April, more than 2000 men of the Division were transported to New Guinea by other means—submarines, motorised landing craft, and especially fast destroyers. Yet the Bismarck Sea battle had changed the balance of power in New Guinea and contributed markedly to the defeats Japanese forces were to suffer in the Salamaua and Lae areas later in 1943. The Japanese would no longer be able to send such large convoys to New Guinea, which had serious implications for supply of that island. Those troops who were sent to New Guinea could not safely be landed east of Wewak and thus had long marches ahead of them to reach the front. The Japanese Army even considered withdrawing from New Guinea after the Bismarck Sea debacle, but the move was rejected as constricting Japanese naval operations and exposing too many other areas, including other South Pacific islands and the Philippines, to air attack.

In 1941–42 the Japanese had demonstrated the power of land-based aircraft against Allied ships, and now the Allies had delivered their own land-based blow, using more sophisticated techniques. Learmonth declared the attack on the convoy 'the greatest experience I've ever had', as well as 'a major Japanese disaster and an overwhelming victory for the Allied Air Forces'.[23] A diary kept by an unknown Japanese officer in the battle offered some supporting evidence for this view, admitting on 3 March: 'we are unable to cope with the Allied Air Force'.[24]

17 Newton and Yamamoto

The RAAF in New Guinea could not pause for breath after the Bismarck Sea battle. Enemy positions, especially bases and lines of communication, still had to be attacked. The Bostons concentrated on low-level attacks on Salamaua, which was defended by two anti-aircraft units, one naval and one army. Their anti-aircraft cannon—reportedly up to 75 mm calibre—and heavy machine guns were concentrated on the narrow Salamaua Isthmus, especially at a spot called 'McDonald's Junction', near large newly constructed fuel tanks. Those tanks and nearby buildings and stores were the target of seven Bostons under the CO, Keith Hampshire on 16 March 1943. Bill Newton was piloting the same Boston, A28-7, which he had flown on his first mission. With him were his regular upper Wireless Air Gunner, John Lyon, who had flown more than 40 missions with Newton, and 31-year-old lower gunner Sergeant Basil Eastwood, who had arrived at the squadron just four weeks earlier, but whose eagerness had helped him fit in quickly. Newton braved the ack-ack and went straight at the fuel tanks. Several direct hits set the tanks alight, and four fires eventually converged into one, giving off flames several hundred feet high, and a smoke column 3000 feet high. Newton was given the nickname 'Firebug'.

By the time he left the area, Newton's aircraft had taken four direct hits and 98 bullets. One engine was out, the other damaged, as were instruments, hydraulics, electrics, both wings, and his fuel tanks. He chose to avoid the safer option of heading for Dobodura, where there were few repair facilities, and tried for Port Moresby, via 'The Gap'. He made the 290-kilometre flight safely, though A28-7 would not be back in action for some time. Newton would be though, and when he examined the damage, he told fellow pilot Claude Sladen that he would get back at the Japanese responsible. Sladen was a brilliant pilot too: in December, after a Boston crew had made a forced landing in jungle near Wairopi bridge, he had flown to Kokoda, walked to the aircraft, and after several days' preparation managed to get it airborne and home.

On 18 March, No. 22 Squadron tried to repeat the success of two days earlier. Flying in A28-3, Newton approached as usual from the north-north-west, behind 'Stace' Dillon's 'Japanese Ghost Producer'. Newton's target was a building adjacent to anti-aircraft guns, reportedly the ones that damaged his Boston on 16 March. He scored a direct hit on the building, but as he did so flak struck A28-3: the enemy gunners had opened up when the Bostons were still 650 metres away. Newton's Boston was giving off smoke as it left the target, and then caught fire. Though he rapidly lost altitude, Newton had the skill and presence of mind to turn the aircraft away from enemy positions and towards the shoreline. He made a fine landing at speed, skimming across the water and then resting nose-down. As the aircraft sank, between 800 and 1600 metres from the shore and several kilometres from Salamaua, the other five Boston crews saw two figures emerge and swim for shore. In the few seconds before A28-3 sank, the pilot's escape hatch did not open and the inflatable dinghy behind his head failed to appear. The onlookers assumed that the survivors were Lyon and Eastwood. The remaining Bostons circled the swimmers for 35 minutes, until fuel shortage forced them to return home. Another sortie was sent quickly, but by the time it arrived, there was no sign of the swimmers. Bostons continued the search until nightfall, with no luck.

The two men initially seen swimming clear were in fact Lyon and Newton. who made it ashore. Eastwood's remains have never been found. Two friendly locals ushered Newton and Lyon across the coastal road and into the jungle. They initially headed for a coastwatcher, but by mid-afternoon decided to travel back towards the coast, perhaps because a Boston was circling the area. However, a Japanese patrol captured them and took them back to Salamaua. There they were tortured for information. By the following day, the two prisoners had told who they were, their unit and various details about their backgrounds. Newton was identified as 'a person of importance, possessing considerable rank and ability'.[1] The 'ability' bit was correct, but the suggestion that a 23-year-old Flight Lieutenant possessed considerable rank was misplaced. It appears that both airmen were then transported to Lae for further interrogation. About a week later, Lyon was bayoneted to death at Lae in the presence of Rear Admiral Ruitaro Fujita, Commander of the Lae Base Area. The remains of the 26-year-old father of two, whose quieter demeanour contrasted with that of his friend Newton, were buried on the airfield perimeter. They were not discovered for five years. We can only imagine the anguish endured until then by Mrs Lyon, who suffered further after she discovered that an Australian funeral service for her husband was held at Lae in 1948 without her.

Fujita ordered that Newton be returned to Salamaua for execution there. A Japanese document discovered by Allied forces at Salamaua later that year was an eyewitness account of the execution, and read in part as follows:

> Now the time has come, and the prisoner is made to kneel on the bank of a bomb crater filled with water . . . the precaution is taken of surrounding him with guards with fixed bayonets, but he remains calm. He even stretches out his neck, and is very brave. When I put myself in the prisoner's place, and think that in one more minute it will be goodbye to this world, although the daily bombings have filled me with hate, ordinary human feelings make me pity him. The commander has drawn his favourite sword . . . He taps the prisoner's neck lightly with the back of the blade, then raises it above his head with both arms and brings it down with a swoop . . . in that moment I closed my eyes. SSH! . . . It must be the sound of blood spurting from the arteries. With a sound as though something watery had been cut, the body falls forward. It is amazing—he had killed him with one stroke. The onlookers crowd forward. The head, detached from the trunk, rolls in front of it . . . The head is dead white, like a doll.

> The savageness which I felt only a little while ago is gone, and now I feel nothing but the true compassion of Japanese Bushido. A senior Corporal laughs loudly 'Well he will enter Nirvana now!' Then a superior seaman of the medical unit takes the chief medical officer's Japanese sword and, intent on paying off old scores, turns the headless body over on its back, and cuts the abdomen open with one clean stroke.

A slightly abridged version of the gruesome account appeared in an Australian press release on 5 October 1943, and parts of it were reproduced in Australian newspapers.[2] It reinforced the hostility of the public and their government towards the Japanese, though the Japanese sailor's comment about retribution is a reminder that the perpetrators of these horrors had recently been attacked themselves, and that those at Lae had been affected by the Bismarck Sea battle. Yet this is no excuse. The marine who executed Newton, Sub-Lieutenant Komai, was a cold-blooded killer who also acted as executioner in an infamous massacre of Christian Mission workers at Dobodura. He himself was later killed in action in the Philippines in February 1945. Admiral Ruitaro Fujita was of a similar ilk: due to be charged with war crimes, he dodged justice by committing suicide in April 1947. The pilot discussed in the October articles was not publicly identified at the time as Newton, though Australian officials soon determined who he was.

Early in October 1943, at about the same time as the release of the account of Newton's execution, Carl Jacobsen visited Salamaua, which the Australians had recently captured. Jacobsen was an Australian who lived in Lae before the war and began working for American intelligence. He was looking for the body of an 'American' airman locals said had been executed there. Two locals reported hearing and seeing Japanese troops interrogating the tall and athletic airman, who, they said, was 'very proud, held himself erect, and refused to answer questions in spite of threats'. Jacobsen was led to the corpse in a bomb crater. Though none had seen the execution, 'many had seen his body from day to day as they went to work for the Japanese'. On draining the crater, Jacobsen found a headless body in Australian slacks and shirt. It was Newton.[3]

Newton was recommended for the Victoria Cross in June. While emphasising his 'tenacious courage', the recommendation described him as cheerful, well balanced and highly trained. Newton's bravery, exemplified in the fact that 90 per cent of his 52 sorties had been made against heavy anti-aircraft fire, was 'an inspiration' to those around him.[4] By 20 October this recommendation had been approved, and Newton became the first and only member of the RAAF to win a Victoria Cross in the war against Japan. As war cameraman Damien Parer said in a telegram to Newton's mother: 'His magnificent performance will now live on.'[5]

Japan fights back: Operation A

No. 75 Squadron had two victories in early March. Sergeant Max Stirling shot down a Nell in his first combat, with the expenditure of only 100 rounds. Stirling was cool under pressure, and also cool in the fashion stakes. He wore a coloured or white handkerchief round his neck and set a trend by looping the chain from his 'dog tag' under his shirt epaulette, thus allowing the tag to sit in his breast pocket. The second victory fell to 'Woof' Arthur, who overcame repeated gun stoppages to bring down a Betty after a chase that he estimated at 80 miles (130 kilometres), and a battle that left his aircraft with just one bullet hole. He told his wife that it was some compensation for the loss of his brother.

The Japanese were desperate to maintain air supremacy. In the weeks after the Bismarck Sea battle they sent sizeable raiding forces to New Guinea, but destroyed only a few personnel, aircraft, small ships and a wharf. They then launched a more coordinated effort to strengthen their air forces in New Guinea and the Solomons. On 25 March, the Japanese Army and Navy high commands concluded an agreement, whereby a holding operation would be organised in the Solomons and the main effort would be made in New Guinea. Army air forces in New Guinea would be reinforced.

Admiral Yamamoto, the most senior and respected Japanese commander, decided that he must personally orchestrate the destruction of enemy air power in New Guinea and the Solomons in 'Operation A'. He set up an advanced headquarters in Rabaul and arranged to bring in the most powerful force he could muster—350 land and carrier-based aircraft. This was fewer than were used in Pearl Harbor, or the initial attacks on Malaya and the Philippines. His bomber capacity was slightly better than in those campaigns, but the Allied numbers had increased greatly since then. Moreover, owing to wastage in recent battles, many of his aircrews were now inexperienced.

On 11 April, Operation A forces, comprising 45 fighters and dive-bombers, attacked Oro Bay near Buna, hitting three ships, but also losing 16 aircraft to USAAF Lightnings and P-40s. One Zero fell to the guns of John Hodgkinson of No. 77 Squadron, based at Gurney and now flying the improved P-40K. Hodgkinson thereby achieved 77 Squadron's first daylight victory. The following day the Japanese launched their 106th air raid on Port Moresby. They destroyed or damaged 19 aircraft on the ground, cratered runways and killed several men. Overhead, the Americans lost two aircraft, but destroyed at least 24 Japanese planes. The Australian fighter pilots at Milne Bay were terribly disappointed that the Japanese force headed for Moresby and not them. Hewitt, who was with them, said these pilots were 'almost frantic for an opportunity to make a worthwhile killing'.[6] It was coming.

On 14 April, 45 bombers and 20 to 30 weaving fighters were detected approaching Milne Bay for Raid No. 24 on that base. By the time this force arrived, at about 12.30 p.m., both 75 and 77 Squadrons—totalling some 34 Kittyhawks—were running out of fuel as a result of an earlier scramble. No. 75 Squadron's Kittyhawks were at 28,000 feet and made a head-on attack on the enemy's front 'V' of bombers, before breaking left and attacking the second 'V'. Then the enemy fighter escort intervened and, because the Kittyhawks were outclassed at that height, organised Australian attacks ceased, though the Japanese formations became disorganised too.

'Woof' Arthur's guns again proved uncooperative, apparently because of poor maintenance, and became the basis of a famous incident. Arthur intended to land and jump into another aircraft, but as he broke off he found other Kitties following him. He then decided to lead them into an attack—first head-on, then side-on—despite the fact that he was now highly vulnerable to any attacker. This manoeuvre distracted several approaching Vals. He wrote to his wife:

> We had some fun . . . but for me it was the most disappointing day ever. The best chance I've ever had in my life—easy, very easy—and *not a single gun* would fire. So I spent the whole time rushing about at people trying to frighten them but able to do nothing at all. Almost pushed one bird into the sea and that's all. It'll take me days to forget this! Isn't it a pity?[7]

Far from being disappointed, Arthur's superiors praised his 'gallantry, matchless leadership and devotion to duty' in this action and awarded him a DSO.[8] He was anxious to minimise publicity, for he felt that it would damage his reputation within the RAAF at all levels. Yet soon afterwards he was promoted to Wing Commander. 'Polly', the aircraft in which he flew this memorable sortie, is now on display, beautifully preserved, at the Australian War Memorial in Canberra.

On seeing the enemy formation, Arthur's counterpart in 77 Squadron, Dick Cresswell, called out 'Buster' (full throttle) and charged ahead of his squadron. Consequently two Zeros concentrated on him. One of their bullets struck his magneto and deprived his Kittyhawk of power. Before gliding in to land, Cresswell was close enough to the lead bomber to bring it down. Daryl Sproule led the squadron for the rest of the fight. Other Kittyhawks dived and gyrated to evade and attack enemy fighters, or to get a shot in on bombers and dive-bombers. Stirling, who had achieved a kill in his first fight, now brought down another bomber, a Betty, but when he landed his Kitty close to the operations tent, observers saw that his aircraft had been hit. So had he: his leg wound was so serious he had to be evacuated to Australia.

'Ben' Hall saw his tracers enter the wings and cockpit of one target before attacking two 'Hamps'. All three struggled to get into firing positions, though Hall squeezed a burst into one. A second fired at him and missed from just 20 metres before Hall escaped into cloud, from which he saw only one Hamp leave the scene. At 26,500 feet, Hodgkinson blazed at an enemy bomber in a formation coming head-on at roughly 1000 metres and kept firing quick bursts as he closed to 'about 10 yards'. He barely avoided a collision, but before breaking away he saw an engine 'blow up'.[9] He last spied the Betty well alight and diving irrevocably at 10,000 feet.

Sproule downed a bomber, though in return enemy shells tore big holes in his wing and damaged a propeller blade. Norman Houghton wrote home that the odds had been about three to one against the Kitties. When he sought to turn quickly to meet Zeros attacking from behind, he found his Kitty suddenly upside down and then hurtling earthwards with a dead engine. He managed to land on a reef and, as his kite sank, to inflate his Mae West and dinghy. Of the fight still going on overhead, he wrote, in language typical of the day, 'I believe it was a wizard show. I cursed for about five minutes when flopping around in the dinghy.'[10]

Charlie Clegg was among ground crew watching and wrote that he and others were so carried away by the excitement of the 'marvellous' spectacle that they left their trenches to watch, even though incendiary bullets and shrapnel entered their tent lines.[11]

The results of this air-to-air battle were indeed 'wizard'. The enemy bombers achieved negligible results, landing just one bomb on Turnbull Field, while 75 Squadron claimed two Bettys, a Val and two Zeros, and 77 Squadron claimed four bombers and one Zero. Lightnings shot down another two, and all three squadrons claimed probables. Just one RAAF pilot, 77's Lloyd Melrose, was killed. No wonder Cresswell called it 'the great day'.[12] On no other day of the Pacific War did the RAAF destroy so many aircraft—yet in an astonishing oversight, the official histories of the RAAF in World War II do not even mention this encounter.

The Japanese could not afford to maintain the level of attrition experienced so far in Operation A, and it should have been obvious that Allied fighter pilots and aircraft were now generally superior to theirs. This major offensive had achieved nothing. However, Yamamoto received false reports that the four raids had sunk 25 transports and three warships, shot down 134 aircraft and severely damaged four airbases. He decided to make a personal inspection in the Solomons and on 18 April took off from Rabaul for Ballale. After his flight plan was intercepted by American intelligence units and No. 1 Wireless Unit RAAF, Lightnings were sent on the long flight from Guadalcanal to ambush Yamamoto's aircraft. They broke through the defensive fighters and shot him down. The loss of Japan's greatest military leader to American aircraft reflected the decline of Japanese air power and the ever-growing strength of the Allied Air Forces. Japan would probably have been well advised to cut its losses in New Guinea, including New Britain. Instead, throughout 1943 it reinforced both islands with aircraft and troops.

The RAAF was growing too. In January 1943 the government received American assurances of sufficient aircraft for nine new RAAF squadrons. With seven squadrons of locally built aircraft planned, this would allow an expansion to 45 squadrons by the end of 1943, and 51 squadrons by the end of 1944. It also sustained hopes of General Kenney meeting his assurances that the Australians would be with the USAAF 'all the way back to Tokio'.[13]

18 Spitfires at Darwin

Winston Churchill agreed in May 1942 to send three Spitfire squadrons to Australia. Those chosen were No. 54 RAF and two Australian EATS squadrons, Nos 452 and 457. Both RAAF squadrons had been formed in England and had given distinguished service. Though the squadrons' personnel reached Australia in August 1942, their aircraft were delayed as the convoy bringing the Spitfires was diverted to Egypt. Nevertheless, by October 1942 all initial equipment had arrived in Australia. The government was hoping that before the Japanese knew what they were facing, they would suffer great losses to the Spitfires, which to maintain secrecy were termed 'Capstans'. Keeping this secret was difficult while the aircraft trained at Richmond near Sydney and flew over heavily populated areas. There the squadrons were grouped as No. 1 Fighter Wing.

By sea, land and air, more than 70 Spitfires and 700 air and ground crew were moved to Darwin in January 1943. Their commander was Group Captain Allan 'Wally' Walters, a regular air force officer who had commanded No. 1 Squadron and was an outstanding staff officer. Wing leader was 32-year-old Clive 'Killer' Caldwell, who had been the most successful Australian fighter pilot in the Middle East. To be an accomplished fighter pilot, Caldwell considered it essential to attack, and used words such as 'aggressive', 'decisive', 'quick' and 'determined'.[1] Yet he also emphasised the need to stay alive while bringing down the enemy.

Commanding 452 Squadron was 24-year-old Squadron Leader Ray 'Throttle' Thorold-Smith, who had destroyed 6.5 German fighters in 452 Squadron's Spitfires. He and Caldwell were good friends, sharing good looks, an extrovert personality and a sense of humour. Both were big men, and Thorold-Smith, a former first-grade rugby player, liked to use his slight weight advantage to tackle Caldwell to the ground in mock wrestling. No. 457 Squadron was under the command of 22-year-old Squadron Leader Ken James, who had been credited with a shared Focke-Wulf 190. In Europe, rather than fighting defensive battles of the type about to occur over Darwin, the two Australian squadrons had flown across enemy territory, where their chief opponent had been flak instead of fighters. German fighters did come up at times, but even the most experienced 457 pilots, such as Don Maclean, had just 12 combats each before coming back to Australia. The story was similar in 452 Squadron, but not only because of the nature of the post-Battle of Britain air war. Several of its best pilots, including Truscott and Wawn, had left earlier for Australia, so the average number of combats for the squadron's remaining pilots by the time it left England had fallen to just four. Several had single-figure or even no operational hours up. The average combats doubled from four to eight when three very experienced pilots arrived: the 'Malta twins'—aces Adrian 'Tim' Goldsmith and John Bisley—as well as Ken Fox. Goldsmith, like Caldwell and Thorold-Smith an ace, a DFC winner and over six feet tall, had achieved 11 victories when he was transferred from Europe. He had to leave his English bride behind, temporarily. She would follow in 1943, only to die when her ship was sunk en route.

No. 54 Squadron RAF had a proud record, too, but its personnel were mainly newcomers. The flight commanders were Battle of Britain veterans, but the CO, Squadron Leader Gibbs, had no previous experience of fighters, having been in a reconnaissance squadron. Thus although the arrival of the Spitfires brought a great boost to local morale, the pilots were not quite the veterans that many imagined. Moreover, the aircraft were not exactly what they expected either—and not only because they looked like toys compared with the big Kittyhawks.

Clive Caldwell later said that although the Spitfires were considered the most glamorous Allied aircraft, the Mark VCs received in Darwin were designed for use in the desert, with 'performance reducing air intakes and metal airscrews in lieu of the lighter Rotol wooden airscrews'. Moreover, 'the Glycol cooling system had not been properly inhibited before shipment to Australia and the armament was considered inadequate and proved unreliable in service'.[2] The glycol cooling system, which made the Spitfire vulnerable if the engine was struck by any projectile, would be a particular bugbear in Australia, even without enemy action. Before the move to Darwin two accidents, one of them fatal, occurred because the propeller constant speed unit malfunctioned and the propellers went too fast, causing the engine to seize. This problem was far less likely with the wooden-bladed Rotol propellers (airscrews) mentioned by Caldwell. For all that, before the move to Darwin a 'Capstan' shone in a mock combat against the new Boomerang fighter, which although slow had performed well in tests against the Kittyhawk and Airacobra.

Jock Scott, an experienced Kittyhawk pilot, got a chance to fly a Spitfire V later in the war and described it thus:

> The Spitfire was a revelation . . . Rather clumsy and touchy on the ground, with that big, broad Rolls Royce Merlin obscuring the forward view, and a narrow cart [undercarriage] threatening to tip over in any turn, together with a tendency to nose over if you used the poor brakes unwisely, but it blossomed when you opened the throttle and got free of the earth ... The swing was easily controlled, the tail came up in a few yards, and the transformation was complete. Now you had a live, responsive, magnificent creature strapped to your bum. Tail up, accelerating fiercely, responding to light touches, and eager to go.[3]

The Spitfire's shining performance in the test combat may have cost the Boomerang its chance of becoming a front-line fighter. In the test, at No. 2 OTU in Mildura, Victoria, in December 1942, the Capstan was rated 'superior in every way, with the exception of range'.[4] The exception would prove significant.

Apart from potential for disappointment in men and material, there was a certain amount of resentment towards No. 1 Fighter Wing. At Richmond, for example, some regular air force officers made much of the lack of flying hours racked up by certain pilots and criticised the newcomers—probably with some justification—for their supposed arrogance. More importantly, General MacArthur was not entirely happy with the impact of the Spitfires on his patch. He was content to play along with the Curtin government's desire for secrecy, and was initially pleased to have extra fighter squadrons under his command. He was not amused though when the American high command counted this addition against what it might have sent him. He also warned that care should be taken to ensure that veteran airmen who had been fighting for months should not resent attention given to this 'small unit . . . before it had had the opportunity to prove itself in combat'.[5]

The squadrons' members were initially shocked at the conditions they found in Darwin. The tropical setting and primitive if newish facilities were a world away from those of England. There, London had been 30 minutes away by train. When after 18 months in North-Western Area, 457's Jim Grant finally got away from Darwin, it took him nine hours by Douglas DC-3 to get to Brisbane, let alone further south. In the first six months in Darwin he did not see a woman. No. 54 Squadron was based at Darwin, 452 at Strauss and 457 at Livingstone. For most of them, their airstrip and campsite formed a world unto itself: Grant never travelled from Livingstone to Strauss, and only twice visited Darwin.

The squadrons wanted to prove their worth against enemy bombers, but none visited in February. No. 1 Fighter Wing did have its first success that month, when an RAF pilot shot down a Dinah.

Caldwell and the other pilots wondered how the Spitfires would perform against Zeros. He remained sceptical about some of the more imaginative scare stories about Zeros. Depending on the models involved, the Spitfire was generally a little faster than the Zero (and Kittyhawk), but slower in the climb than the Japanese fighter.

No. 1 Fighter Wing's opportunity finally came on 2 March 1943. Radar picked up two groups of Japanese aircraft approaching Darwin and rendezvousing about 100 kilometres west of the town. The defenders were unaware that the 16 Japanese aircraft, all but three of them Zeros, were headed for Coomalie Creek and its tormenting Beaufighters. This 52nd raid was the first daylight one in a long time. Twenty-six Spitfires of 54 and 457 Squadrons were scrambled, led by Wing Commander Caldwell and his No. 2, Group Captain 'Wally' Walters.

The enemy force's exact route was not being plotted by radar or sight, so No. 5 Fighter Sector sent the Spitfire sections to various locations and heights to try to spot the intruders. Eventually six Zeros attacked the Coomalie strip, and within seconds destroyed Beaufighter A19-31—to the intense chagrin of Ken McDonald, for whom it was his pride and joy—and wounded three men. The six Zeros were unopposed, and as they headed for home some Spitfires were still too distant to interfere. However, Caldwell, Walters and four 54 Squadron Spitfires were guided to intercept. By the time Caldwell sighted the enemy aircraft, he had been airborne for some 75 minutes and had enough fuel for at most 20 minutes of the engine performance required for combat. The enemy aircraft were 'stepped up' on either side of the bombers: some flying close cover, others 2000 feet higher, and then the top cover 5000 feet up. Caldwell had insufficient fuel to get above the top cover so, choosing his moment, he dived towards the lowest aircraft, followed by the other Spitfires, and was able to attack them before the diving second tier embroiled the Spitfires in a dogfight.

Caldwell found the enemy pilots poor shots and, although impressed by their manoeuvrability at low speed, managed to lose the Zekes that attacked him. After an eight-minute dogfight, the Spitfires returned home with just Gibbs' aircraft damaged. In return he brought down a Zero, his first kill. Caldwell destroyed a Zero and a Kate. Walters was a conscientious No. 2 to Caldwell, to the point where on landing Caldwell admonished his commanding officer—who was not really supposed to be flying—to look after himself better: 'Wally' had at one point warned Caldwell to duck from fire that was actually directed at him!

In a report on the action, Caldwell criticised the enemy tactics and declared the Spitfire generally superior to the Zero. The secrecy surrounding the Spitfires was officially dropped when Curtin gave a rather exaggerated report on the successes of 2 March, announcing that six enemy aircraft had been destroyed. Other newspaper articles emphasised how 'famous aces' had manned the Spitfires.[6] Churchill cabled that he was pleased 'to learn of the ascendancy they have immediately established over the enemy'.[7] Members of the actual squadrons, however, were 'not amused' at the gushy exaggerations of the newspapers. The inexperience of the pilots whom the papers were calling 'highly trained personnel who fought the Luftwaffe' was apparent in the fact that in the six-week period to 14 March, the three squadrons suffered 17 accidents, in which nine Spitfires were destroyed.[8] Even for experienced pilots, landing on the Livingstone and Strauss airfields—which were mere widenings of the highway, completely surrounded by bush—was a difficult proposition compared with the broad North African and English airstrips.

On 7 March, four 457 Squadron Spitfires were scrambled and found a Dinah headed for its base. The Dinah was one of the war's best reconnaissance aircraft, but two Australians, Don Maclean and 'Darky' McDowell, intercepted it. Allan Brayne of 31 Radar Station recorded a memorable event:

> Witnessed Jap plane being shot down. First a short burst of gunfire overhead, a thin stream of smoke at 20,000 feet heading out to sea and then 10 miles out another burst of fire. The plane fell as a blazing ball into the sea.[9]

When pulled onto the bar of the officer's mess to explain how he did it, 'Darky' said simply, 'I seen me dooty an' I done it.'[10] It was 457 Squadron's first enemy contact since May 1942.

On 15 March, Beaufighters and Mitchells attacked three small but crowded Japanese ships near the Aru Islands. The Mitchells' bombs fell short. The Beaufighters, originally assigned to act as a diversion, became the main executioners, repeatedly strafing the decks of the troop-laden vessels. Squadron Leader Gordon Savage saw Japanese troops 'tumbling overboard as a result of our cannon fire'.[11] Bert Longoni, making his first ever strike, flew over all three ships and was hit. With flames streaming 50 metres behind, his Beau exploded, then fell into the sea.

That day 25 Zeros and 24 Bettys made the 53rd raid on Darwin. Clive Caldwell was having medical attention for old wounds, and on hearing of the raid sent word that Thorold-Smith should lead the wing into action. Thorold-Smith and five other 452 Squadron pilots had flown from Strauss to Darwin on a night-flying exercise the night before, and most were flying back to Strauss when word of the raid came through; 5 Fighter Sector instructed Thorold-Smith to take command and to rendezvous with No. 1 Fighter Wing's remaining 27 aircraft over Hughes airfield. The details of what followed remain mysterious, but the rendezvous was still apparently far from complete when Thorold-Smith was told the compact enemy force was approaching Darwin. He decided to intercept, even without his full force and although he had to climb far towards the enemy formation. No. 54 Squadron was flying cover, but was allegedly in an unsuitable formation and initially too far behind Thorold-Smith. Moreover, the pilots in Thorold-Smith's group were low on oxygen and two had to drop out before the interception was effected. (The oxygen pumps in Darwin were often breaking down, and Thorold-Smith's group had apparently left for the 15-minute flight to Strauss that morning without refilling their oxygen bottles.) This left just 'Tim' Goldsmith and Ted Hall with Thorold-Smith. On intercepting with these two pilots and in line abreast, Thorold-Smith soon fell from the sky, and no one took over command. From Dripstone Caves, Allan Brayne witnessed 'terrific dog fights between Spitfires and Zeros'.[12] The fact that the battle descended into individual dogfights favoured the Zeros, and three more Spitfires were lost. Six Japanese bombers and two fighters were also destroyed, with the amazing Goldsmith destroying one of each. The other Zero fell to an Australian pilot in 54 Squadron, Al Mawer.

Still, the Japanese bombers managed to unload about 100 bombs over Darwin. These wrecked or damaged two oil tanks, and hit the railway line, various buildings and 13 military personnel and civilians. Three Spitfire pilots were killed: two young Englishmen of 54 Squadron, and Thorold-Smith. Though Caldwell searched for his friend's body, it was never found; his aircraft was only discovered 45 years later. Members of the Wing later concluded that lack of oxygen had affected Thorold-Smith's judgement in making the risky attack, or even led to him losing consciousness. Caldwell was understandably reticent about criticising Thorold-Smith in his post-battle report, but he did censure 54 Squadron, and reportedly blamed Gibbs. Regardless of where responsibility lay, these were the first casualties the Japanese had inflicted on No. 1 Fighter Wing.

When news of Thorold-Smith's death reached 76 Squadron at Exmouth Gulf, Western Australia, the CO, Keith 'Bluey' Truscott, walked off for some solitude to mourn. On a recent visit to Darwin, 'Bluey' had reacquainted himself with 'Throttle', his old 452 Squadron comrade, who had let him fly a Spitfire. Truscott greatly missed the Spits, which he much preferred to Kittyhawks. He was frustrated too by the tedious life he and his squadron were enduring in the heat of Exmouth Gulf. Darwin must have seemed preferable, for at least he had shot down a Betty there. That night Truscott swung from the rafters in the mess of another squadron until some sleepy NCOs fired revolver bullets at the roof from outside. He was grabbed, stripped of his clothes and thrown back into his jeep, from which he was heard laughing as he drove off. Now Thorold-Smith was dead, and Truscott was living a boring existence escorting US Catalinas.

On 28 March, he and Ian Loudon were escorting an incoming Cat and, as usual, simultaneously practising attacks. As the Catalina approached to touch down on the water, Truscott flew too low and crashed. Sergeant Charles Walmsley was among those who witnessed the accident. He recorded that when 'the startling news came [that] it was Bluey Truscott our Commanding Officer everyone just about passed out'.[13] Frantic attempts to rescue Truscott were fruitless, and his battered body was discovered the next day. Walmsley noted that 'the chaps are feeling it very much for he was more than C.O. to us, he was a white man, the chaps would have done anything for him'. The language, reminiscent of that used about Turnbull, now sounds strange, but the message is still touching.

Walmsley helped carry Truscott's coffin to an Anson before it was flown to Perth for a funeral with full air force honours. During this slow march to the aircraft, there was 'absolute silence', and Walmsley 'saw some misty looks in a lot of eyes'.[14] In the words of his biographer, 'Thus passed Bluey Truscott, aged twenty-six, brave as few were and loved as few were.'[15] That he was loved not only by fellow pilots but also ground staff was apparent in these words of a 76 Squadron poem:

> He thought as much of the ground staff
> As the aircraft that he flew;
> He loved each one and all of us
> The same as the flying crew.[16]

After 452 Squadron lost its leader, Caldwell moved from Darwin to Strauss and took temporary command. Thorold-Smith's loss was demoralising for the wing, as was the complete absence of action for nearly seven weeks after 15 March. Then, on 2 May, came the long-awaited raid number 54. That morning radar picked up a force approaching from 260 kilometres north-west of Darwin and the three squadrons were scrambled. Some important personnel—including the regular flight leaders of 54 and 457 Squadrons—were missing, down south on leave or duty. Caldwell was leading, with 457's new CO Ron MacDonald as his No. 2.

Pilots of the three squadrons rendezvoused over Hughes airstrip and moved north, climbing towards 30,000 feet so as to be above the Japanese. Each squadron flew line-astern formation. As the Japanese bombers approached Darwin from the west-north-west, their top cover was said to be over 30,000 feet. Caldwell decided that to get above them he would have to keep climbing and forgo any prospect of preventing the bombers dropping their loads. Caldwell was later criticised for this, but with Thorold-Smith's example fresh in his mind, he knew that taking on Zeros while climbing towards them would be risky, if not suicidal. He also knew that there were at the time no major targets on Darwin harbour. Thus, when the Spitfires finally attacked the raiders from above, the Japanese had already dropped 100 bombs on Darwin and were heading home.

Then the gremlins started in the Spitfires. Two 457 pilots had to drop out, one with radio failure, another with faulty oxygen supply. Both MacDonald's cannons malfunctioned, forcing him to retire. Ken Fox took MacDonald's place and almost immediately tangled with a Zero on Caldwell's tail. Fox was hit and had to bale out, though he had done enough to win Caldwell's eternal gratitude. The propeller constant speed units caused engine failure in two other RAAF Spitfires, and Ross Stagg and Bill Hardwick had to bale out and take to their dinghies. Hardwick was rescued that day, but Stagg landed near Point Jenny, became lost in saline coastal flats, and 15 trying days later was discovered more than 60 kilometres inland. He took six months to recover in hospitals and convalescent depots.

Like Stagg on the ground, many of the pilots still in the air were uncertain of their positions, which became significant when during the action, they were told to break off the engagement if low on fuel. As the battle was fought well out to sea, fuel shortage in the Spitfires became a critical issue.

An official report remarked that once the enemy formation broke up, 'a confused melee, very difficult to describe in detail, followed'.[19] It is still not clear what happened in the battle. Afterwards, some RAAF pilots again criticised 54 Squadron, this time for not attacking the enemy top cover, falling back, then being jumped themselves. The official historian says both 54 Squadron, ordered to target the fighters, and 457 Squadron, tasked to hit the bombers, made diving attacks at angles too steep to inflict maximum damage. Fighters intercepted 457 before it reached the Bettys, but Ken

James attacked a formation of four Zeros. One of them did a half-loop and attacked him head-on while flying upside down. James commenced firing at him from 200 metres and 'continued until the enemy filled and overflowed his sights'.[20] Bits flew off the Zero's fuselage. Harry Blake was approaching a bomber from astern when a Zeke came into his sights dead-ahead. He fired at it from 100 metres, closing to 30. The enervated Zero jerked and pulled up slowly, and an explosion threw Blake's Spitty into a spin as he flew overhead. Blake was credited with a probable, James with a 'cert', as was Gibbs. Ultimately the battle turned into a series of dogfights; Caldwell's plan for a coordinated attack misfired.

So did many of the Spitfires' weapons: 16 of the 29 Spitfires that engaged experienced weapons problems. When Caldwell and 452 squadron engaged, one of his cannons malfunctioned, and the other fired just ten shots, slewing the aircraft around and causing him to miss his target. Goldsmith fatally damaged a bomber, but then his controls were shot away and he was thrown from the machine. He parachuted into the sea and survived.

By the end of the action, 14 Spitfires had not returned. Mystery surrounded the death of Sandy McNab of 452 Squadron, last seen pointing down into his cockpit, trying to speak on his radio, and then spiralling, flattening out and crashing without any apparent attempt to jump. He and 'Joe' Gifford of 457 Squadron were the only pilots possibly killed by enemy action, though both appear to have died returning from the air battle.

Gifford was 'a swarthy, tough young man, whose grim exterior was only a façade to a gentleness he was loth to admit'.[21] He was also the unit Transport Officer, initiator of the unit's sporting activities and highly popular, even though men teased him about his devotion to the RAAF. Jim Grant, a member of 357 Squadron who in 1995 wrote an authoritative history of the Spitfires at Darwin, defines the 14 Spitfire losses thus:

- 2 possibly lost to enemy action (both pilots killed)
- 3 definitely lost to enemy action (but all pilots saved)
- 4 lost to mechanical failure (but all pilots saved)
- 5 lost to fuel shortage (but all pilots saved).[22]

Only eight of these 14 Spitfires were destroyed. The Spitfires' mechanical deficiencies had been costly, as had the inexperience of many of their pilots. This time Caldwell acknowledged that the Japanese fighter pilots had done well, flying and shooting with skill and determination, and cooperating effectively. In return the Japanese lost at least four fighters—one to Mawer, now with 452 Squadron—with six other probables, as well as all the relevant crews. Moreover the Japanese bombs inflicted negligible damage, though one Allied soldier was killed, and the bombers got home virtually unscathed.

The enemy side of the ledger was of little interest to the press, which emphasised in succeeding days the 'heavy losses sustained' by the Spitfires.[23] Their reports were based on a communiqué released from MacArthur's headquarters, which though it mentioned the negligible bomb damage, also said 'our own air losses were heavy'.[24] Newspapers noted that this was 'the first occasion that any communiqué issued in this area has reported heavy losses'.[25] The Melbourne *Herald* called for a 'strict examination', the Sydney *Sun* for an 'official inquiry'.[26] Then fictitious explanations were offered in the newspapers, first in terms of the supposed army air aces flying the Japanese aircraft and then poor weather. Nevertheless, the Japanese, who claimed they had shot down 21 Spitfires, found the Australian reports useful propaganda for their own broadcasts.

The pilots resented the way in which the press treated them over this battle. They also disliked the official description of their 'heavy losses' and 'severe reverse', and were justified in that MacArthur's decision to release such a description was ill-judged, even vindictive. The Australian government complained that MacArthur's communiqué had given information to the enemy, a charge he rejected, adding that the newspapers had previously criticised him for presenting too rosy a picture. Curtin then backed MacArthur.

Air Vice-Marshal George Jones did not enhance his reputation among No. 1 Fighter Wing either. When the Advisory War Council asked him to report, especially on the issues of engine failure and petrol shortage, he blamed the former on the inexperience of the crews and the latter on an error of judgement from Caldwell. He did not consult Caldwell, who responded that he had warned about petrol shortages early in the engagement, as Fighter Sector Control had several times afterwards. As all acknowledged, the enthusiasm of some pilots had got the better of them, leading them to keep flying until their fuel ran out. No. 1 Fighter Wing, including Caldwell, considered Jones to have neglected the facts and done too little to protect his own men from criticism. General Kenney was patronising, saying: 'Just what I had feared had happened. The Aussies had tried to outmaneuver the Nip fighters in the air. It couldn't be done, even with the highly maneuverable Spitfire.' He sent Air Vice-Marshal Bill Bostock to Darwin, with instructions to tell the 'kids' that 'if they didn't stop that dogfighting business, I'd send them to New Guinea to serve with the Americans and learn how to fight a Jap properly'.[27]

The recriminations were painful, but probably served a useful purpose. From the time of a conference at Wing Headquarters on the night after the battle, the pilots and leaders thought hard about doing better. Armament and engine problems were identified as part of the problem, as were the need to carry more fuel, to intercept the enemy earlier and to avoid dogfighting the Zeros. The experience undoubtedly made No. 1 Fighter Wing determined to do better next time.

19 'Show of force'

Immediately after the ill-fated 2 May 1943 raid, Air Commodore Frank Bladin ordered a strike on the raiders' base at Penfui before they could withdraw further north. Four Beaufighters flew directly there, rather than via Drysdale, but found that most of the birds had already flown. They hit at least four bombers and Zeros on the ground, before airborne Zekes chased them halfway home.

A strike reconnaissance by two Beaufighters to the Aru Islands a week earlier had a sadder ending. Cyril Greenwood's Beau was tackled by eight aircraft and forced to ditch many kilometres off shore. Greenwood's navigator, Colin Thompson, died as the fighters strafed them in the water, and Greenwood did not make it ashore until the following day. He was captured and tied to a tree for ten days before being transported to Japan, where he was pressured to broadcast propaganda. He refused, despite the unusually brutal regime of the camp: in December 1943, for example, he and an American prisoner who had been caught talking in the lavatory were savagely beaten in front of the whole camp.

Bladin ordered another Beaufighter attack on float-planes spotted near Taberfane. After overnighting at Millingimbi, Gordon Savage led six Beaufighters on the two-hour flight there. They would have 15 minutes over the target before commencing the return journey. Silhouetted against the white sand, the float-planes made perfect targets. Savage led the formation in and set one alight with his cannon. Return fire struck his throttle controls and fuel tank, but its self-sealing properties saved him. The Beaufighters flew back and forth over the float-planes until mechanical faults had stopped all guns. By then nine float-planes had been wrecked. When Savage called the Beaus together again, one failed to respond. Wrinch Budd and Finlay McQueen had been killed in their first operation.

From Millingimbi the Beaufighters could reach most enemy bases in the Arafura Sea. The Japanese recognised this threat, and decided to smash Millingimbi. The radar station on the island, uncomfortable 'home' to No. 59 Operational Base Unit, picked up enemy bombers on 9 May, but could not prevent the seven Sallys from bombing the strip and killing 12 men with daisy-cutters.

Anticipating more raids, Bladin ordered six Spitfires to base at Millingimbi. They were scrambled on 10 May, when radar detected aircraft approaching. It emerged that these were two Beaufighters returning from another raid on Taberfane, so the Spitfires turned back. Just as they were landing, another message arrived of more unidentified aircraft approaching on the same path as the Beaufighters. All but one Spitfire took off. They were still climbing and not yet in formation when the approaching aircraft attacked them. Height and surprise favoured the nine Zeros, but George 'Grumpy' Morse and Rex Watson each shot one down. Watson damaged another, and Bruce Little hit one which flew off stage sounding sick. An explosion in that direction led to Little being credited a probable.

One Spitfire had not taken off. Its pilot, Frank 'Bush' Hamilton, had engine failure, so he decided to use his Spitfire as a transmitting station for relaying messages to the other Spitfires. There was no fighter control at Millingimbi, but the radar station could telephone messages to the signals hut. From there a chain of six men took messages to Hamilton, who relayed them to the airborne pilots. Hamilton's position became perilous when three Zeros that had been flying top cover strafed the airfield. The Beaufighters that flew in before the Zeros were both hit. Little's Spitfire had sustained tail damage in the dogfight, but when he brought it in to land he was unaware of the strafing in progress. On realising what was happening he took off again and, as the Zeros came in low to strafe again, attached himself to the rear one. For ten minutes he and this Zero engaged each other at heights from just 100 to 300 feet. When Little tried a steep turn, his nose ploughed into the island at about 240 kilometres per hour. The Spitfire somersaulted several times and lost both wings, its entire tail, propeller and other pieces. After the Zeros had departed, Little got out and walked the five kilometres back to the airstrip.

A Beaufighter raid on Penfui on 19 May found the enemy fully prepared. The defenders had beefed up their anti-aircraft defences and improved their warning system, for enemy fighters were on patrol. The six Beaufighters destroyed two bombers, but at a high cost. Flak shot down three aircraft, two of which crashed into hills, and the third into the sea. All three crews were killed. Though relative newcomers to the squadron, they were missed. Geoff Coburn, who was killed in the sea crash, was a father of three young daughters. The three remaining Beaufighters escaped the chasing Zeros. Phil Biven, who had led the attack, came home with his cowlings and wing edges dented, but also with tree debris, gathered in low flight, between all the cylinders of both engines. It was amazing that his engines did not overheat.

Eight bombers and five Zeros approached Millingimbi at 20,000 feet on 28 May, but the six Spitfires on duty had received plenty of radar warning and were ready for them. The Bettys managed four runs over the airfield, but it cost them three destroyed. Two Spitfires were lost, together with their veteran pilots, Bruce Beale and Harry Blake. Beale had recently returned from a demanding leave, dealing with his family's distress at the death of his only brother, Herbert, a pilot with the RAF in North Africa. Blake had just lost his closest friend, 'Joe' Gifford, and had been married a few months earlier to a wife he had barely seen since. Referring to these popular men, the squadron diarist wrote: 'It is a difficult task writing to their loved ones.'[1]

General MacArthur was about to begin a major offensive in New Guinea. He wanted the squadrons in the Northern Territory to pin down enemy air forces in the region which might otherwise interfere with this offensive. A diversion was to be effected by a 'show of force' that would keep the Japanese guessing as to whether the Allied offensive would come towards the Netherlands East Indies or New Guinea. General Kenney ordered North-Western Area forces to concentrate on Koepang, Kendari,

Ambon and Babo. Newly arrived USAAF Liberators assisted greatly in this program, as did 31 Squadron's Beaufighters.

On 12 June, for example, Beaufighters destroyed seven float-planes at Taberfane, including one shot down by Mal Forbes, who was on his first operational mission. Ken McDonald was on what turned out to be his last. After destroying three float-planes on the ground, he struggled to bring his Beau home as it lost most of its petrol from a holed fuel line. He also calculated that if not for the five-centimetre thick perspex in his canopy, the location of a bullet mark on it suggested he would have been shot between the eyes. Instead he made it home, and with his navigator Frank Magee was awarded a DFC and posted as an instructor to 5 OTU.

Allied reconnaissance flights, including those in Lightnings of the RAAF's No. 1 Photographic Reconnaissance Unit (PRU), revealed that the Japanese were not only hanging on to Taberfane despite its heavy losses, but also developing further bases. Philip Sinnott of 1 PRU photographed one such base being built on Selaru Island, less than 500 kilometres from Darwin. Bladin decided to destroy this dangerous base with No. 12 Squadron's Vultee Vengeance dive-bombers. The Vengeance had been ordered by the RAF while the Stuka dive-bomber was making an impression on the world. It was to prove of limited value in the tropics, but in 1942 Australia committed itself to obtaining 400 of them. Now, more than a year later, they were to be employed for the first time in their intended role in the South-West Pacific Area, rather than just on escort and search duties. Under Beaufighter escort, 12 Vengeances bombed the villages in which the enemy's construction workers were believed to be living. It was the first of many Allied visits to Selaru, but the Vengeances would fly no more operational sorties in North-Western Area.

The last ten days of June brought a dramatic end to No. 1 Fighter Wing's inactivity. On 20 June came Darwin's 55th raid. Within just minutes the 46 Spitfires of all three squadrons were airborne and headed for a rendezvous at 20,000 feet over Hughes airfield. The speed of this preparation was impressive. The routine was that everyone would run for their aircraft, new boys several hundred metres, squadron leaders far less. Before the pilot reached his kite, the flight mechanic had started the engine, checked the instruments, disconnected the 'trolley-acc' or wheeled box which provided an accumulator and generator when the aircraft was grounded, and jumped onto the starboard wing. The flight rigger removed the covers from the gun camera and pitot head (which measured aircraft speed), and leapt onto the port wing to help the pilot jump up and into the aircraft. The windscreen and perspex canopy were given a quick wipe, and the two crewmen helped the pilot into his harness. The pilot donned his helmet and plugged in the lead to his headphones. From then on he and his crew communicated by signs only, while the pilot waited in the heat for word to taxi out.

On 20 June, 457 Squadron was airborne in six minutes. Caldwell was flying with them, but his radio soon malfunctioned. He gestured to Flight Lieutenant Peter Watson of 457 Squadron to take over, but the Fighter Sector controller ordered Gibbs to do so. Gibbs' engine failed, so he had to return to base. Watson ordered the three squadrons to attack independently. Thanks to Jones' review, Spitfires now carried drop tanks of extra fuel, and after 54 and 452 Squadrons had dropped these they attacked the enemy formation just after it crossed the coast approaching Darwin. No. 54 Squadron destroyed five aircraft, 452 four. With a five-second cannon and machine-gun burst, Mawer made a Zero's wing fold up before the Zeke spun into the sea. Mawer's engine was then hit, and it took considerable skill to land safely. It was the 23-year-old Sydneysider's third and last kill—he would die in a collision with another Spitfire in September.

The surviving Bettys dropped daisy-cutters on Winnellie RAAF station, killing and wounding 14 soldiers. As the bombers headed home, Caldwell, Walters and others tried to intercept. Enemy fighters kept them back, but Caldwell and Walters each destroyed an Oscar. In the meantime low-flying Lilys, undetectable on radar, hit Darwin airfield and Winnellie. One of these was downed, bringing the total Japanese losses to 14 aircraft. In return two Australian pilots were killed. It was a painful introduction to battle for the Japanese Army's 7th Air Division, here making its first attack on Darwin. This was the RAAF's most successful air battle in Darwin to that date.

One RAAF driver in Darwin put it succinctly in his diary: 'Spitfires had a go'.[2] The newspapers returned to their laudatory ways, with headlines such as 'Japs Smashed over Darwin'.[3] MacArthur sent his congratulations, including a personal telegram to Caldwell, who declined to receive it.

The 20 June battle was a personal triumph for Caldwell, who had achieved his fifth kill on Australian soil, and his 25th overall. He had thus become an ace in two theatres of war. Bladin congratulated him on his 'quarter', as well as No. 1 Fighter Wing on its 'decisive win'.[4] Walters recommended Caldwell for a DSO, but this did not succeed. Caldwell later claimed that George Jones rejected the recommendation and insisted that as an EATS trainee, Caldwell was to receive no further awards.

North-Western Area's Hudsons, meanwhile, were fighting on. Don Thomas used his front guns to bring down a Jake, while on Anzac Day, John 'Bunny' Austin, DFC, reportedly brought down a Rufe, the float-plane version of the Zero. His death, from blood poisoning following an insect bite later that year, was a hard blow to 2 Squadron at Hughes. He was commemorated by the naming of an airstrip.

On 28 June, radar detected approaching raiders 240 kilometres north-west of Darwin. The nine bombers dropped their bombs, caused no real damage and skedaddled. Forty-two Spitfires had become airborne within minutes, but 54 and 452 Squadrons could not catch them. No. 457 Squadron engaged and destroyed four fighters, with two 'probables' among the bombers. John 'Snapper' Newton and Thomas Clark together destroyed a Zero, but both suffered damage. Newton was lucky even to have joined the battle: on 20 June he had narrowly escaped death when an armour-piercing bullet struck the plating under his seat. Now bullets penetrated seven potentially fatal points, but he survived. Clark was thrown into an inverted spin and 'redded out', with haemorrhages to his face and eyes. He could not jettison his hood to bale out, but managed to land his battered aircraft, which he was convinced had collided with a Zero.

Raid No. 57, on 30 June, was directed at the USAAF Liberators based at Fenton. The most potent force in the North-Western Area, they had already carried out more than 70 missions and were reinforced by four more squadrons in May–June. The 50 raiders were detected nearly 260 kilometres from the coast. Caldwell ordered 54 and 457 Squadrons to attack the bombers while 452 attacked the fighters, but somehow 452 misunderstood the order and also attacked the bombers. Thus the enemy fighters harassed the Spitfires, cohesion was lost and the bombers reached their target. The consequent pattern-bombing destroyed or damaged ten Liberators. Moreover seven Spitfires were destroyed, two pilots being killed.

Col Duncan was flying a supposedly 'new' replacement Spitfire, which like many others sent to No. 1 Fighter Wing had been used for training at the Mildura OTU. On this first operational flight in the aircraft, his engine developed a glycol leak and caught fire. To release the canopy, the pilot had to pull a golf-ball-sized solid black rubber ball, but this one came away in Duncan's hand. The left wing was tipping dangerously, and fire was licking up beneath the rudder pedals. Eventually by raising the seat as high as possible and pushing with his elbows he slightly opened the canopy, which flew off. He had to sit back in the flames to release the straps holding him in the seat, but then he was out. On landing, he found himself in typical Australian bush. His right arm had suffered second-degree burns from biceps to wrist. A strip of skin hung from his bicep, while his knees were also burnt and painful. Plagued by flies and by mosquitoes that could sting through socks, he decided to wait for rescue rather than try to walk the 80 kilometres to Darwin. On the third day, Clyde Fenton flew over in an Anson, spotted Duncan and dropped a message that an Army search party was on its way. A Beaufighter brought food, cigarettes and a message that Duncan owed the pilot, Frank Gardiner, a beer. On the fourth day the search party arrived and, after a day-long walk and then a drive, Duncan was hospitalised for several weeks. Not until late August did he make it down to Coomalie Creek to meet Frank Gardiner and present him with two bottles of beer. There, however, he discovered that Gardiner was dead: he and his navigator, Lewis Lyne, had collided with another Beaufighter, piloted by former No. 2 Squadron pilot Viv Leithhead, when both had left their top cover positions to strike at a Pete they spotted taking off at Taberfane. Gardiner, Lyne, Leithhead and Robert Graves had died in a collision so violent it tore the mainplanes off both aircraft.

Duncan's ordeal was attributable to the mechanical condition of his Spitfire, as was the fact that in Raid No. 57, the Wing shot down no more than six bombers and two fighters. In other aircraft, freezing armaments and faulty ammunition led to many stoppages. Caldwell's cannon stopped, but with his machine guns he downed a Zero.

Bladin asked for more Spitfires, but replacements had not arrived when a big raiding formation approached Fenton on 6 July. No. 452 Squadron engaged the fighters, downing two Zeros, and diverting others from their escort duties. Three Spitfires were lost, but two pilots baled out safely. The third, Paul Makin, blacked out after a bomber's machine guns hit his Spitfire. When he came to, his engine had overheated, so he prepared to bale out.

His parachute became stuck, so he had to climb back in and make a forced landing. No. 54 Squadron took on the bombers, destroying four and losing two in return. Caldwell sent in his reserve—eight 457 Squadron Spitfires—which downed two more bombers, but three Spits and their pilots were lost. The bombers trundled on and dropped 140 bombs on Fenton, destroying or damaging four Liberators before losing a last Betty.

Among the Spitfire pilots killed was 'Darky' McDowell, who had helped shoot down the Wing's first victim, and 'Bush' Hamilton, who had fought from the ground at Millingimbi. After McDowell's Spitfire was found on 20 July, his remains passed through a guard of honour on the way to a funeral with full military honours at Adelaide River Cemetery. McDowell, who had been the boxing champion of North-Western Area, epitomised the enthusiastic, laconic and inventive Australian serviceman. He would never see the best of his several inventions—a gate operated by remote control from the duty pilot's tower, which prevented road traffic passing while aircraft were taking off. Neither would he see his son, born the following month.

★ ★ ★

Days later, replacement Spitfires at last began arriving, but ironically, the 6 July 1943 raid proved to be the last big one. By August, No. 1 Fighter Wing had in six months of operations lost 44 Spitfires, of which only 17 had fallen to enemy aircraft. The Japanese in turn had lost 63 destroyed and 13 probables.

From 10 August, the Japanese 7th Air Division began moving forces to Wewak. The 23rd Air Flotilla remained on duty. Japanese float-planes had sunk an Australian steamer on 6 August, but when they encountered Allied aircraft, the float-planes were in trouble. That month Millingimbi's Spitfires shot down one, and Beaufighters four more.

The 6 July raid was Bladin's last too, for after 16 months as Air Officer Commanding North-Western Area, he was posted for duty with the RAF in Europe. His replacement, Air Vice-Marshal Adrian 'King' Cole, had experience in the Middle East and Europe in both world wars. A World War I ace, he had recently been Forward Air Controller in the Dieppe raid in northern France, where he had been wounded and earned a DSO.

Not until 13 August did the Japanese dare another raid: an ineffectual night effort. Early on 17 August, a Japanese army unit sent three Dinahs on reconnaissance over the Territory—but 457 Squadron shot down all three. As an RAAF driver told his diary: 'what a day the Spits had'.[5] When a naval Dinah tried the same mission that afternoon, Caldwell was scrambled and sent it crashing into the sea. He counted three bodies in the water from the two-man aircraft. One, wearing an unusual black flying suit, lay spreadeagled and face-up in the water. Caldwell alerted Fighter Sector Control that this man was possibly alive, but as he circled low he saw sharks approach the vessel and felt his own engine sound a bit off. He decided to leave the scene—and was not to know that this was his last confirmed kill of the war.

Another Dinah appeared three weeks later, but with a powerful escort of 20 fighters. By the time the true scale of this intrusion was recognised, the airborne Spitfires were at a height disadvantage, and many were 'jumped' by the Zeros, Oscars and new JAAF Tonys. The Tony's inline engine and cannons were based on German designs, and while it boasted flight characteristics superior to the Oscar and Zero, it was dogged by production and maintenance problems. On this day, however, three Spitfires were lost for one enemy fighter. One RAF pilot died, while MacDonald was badly burnt when a 20 mm shell exploded in his cockpit. After the initial clash, 457 Squadron attacked with a height advantage and destroyed four Zeros, including Philip Watson's fourth kill in Darwin. This former accountant's distinguished fighter pilot career would end in November, with his appointment as an instructor.

In August–September, Air Vice-Marshal Cole sent Beaufighters, Hudsons, Catalinas and Liberators far and wide to harass the enemy, thus drawing attention from MacArthur's imminent New Guinea offensive. The only Japanese response was two ineffectual night raids at Fenton. On 27 September, 21 Lily bombers with a fighter escort attacked Drysdale Mission. There was no fighter defence, but radar detected their approach and everyone took to slit trenches. A direct hit killed Father Thomas of the Drysdale Mission and five Aborigines. Four buildings marked with the Red Cross were destroyed.

From July, 31 Squadron's Beaufighters began carrying bombs, using racks adapted from Mitchells. This added another means of inflicting misery on the Japanese. On 30 August Taberfane, the location of much of that misery, saw three float-planes destroyed or damaged, but also the loss of recently arrived Bill Willard, who had flown so heroically on one engine when damaged at Salamaua.

On 9 October the squadron got its revenge. Squadron Leader Reg 'Butch' Gordon was leading an armed reconnaissance over Selaru when a twin-engined Nick fighter attacked him. He jettisoned his bombs and chased the Nick. Getting to within 25 metres, he shot it down, though his own mainplane and engine were damaged in the exchange. He then turned to strafing barges and, on looking up a few minutes later, saw another Nick attacking a Beaufighter. Using both engines to the maximum, Gordon destroyed this one too, from about 320 metres. On returning home from this eventful flight, one of his engines failed, as did his landing gear, and he had to crash-land at Livingstone. He apologised to Squadron Leader Ken James for not being able to 'park' entirely off the airstrip.

These were the first successes of a brief and brilliant career. Gordon, a regular RAAF officer, had joined 31 Squadron from 5 OTU in July. He had been lucky to survive pilot training, for in July 1939 he had tumbled from the rear cockpit of an Avro trainer while his instructor was demonstrating a slow roll. Gordon's parachute caught on the fuselage and tore, but he landed safely. At 5 OTU, although all saw that he was a skilful and audacious pilot, he was unpopular with the students as a 'hard' man. Indeed some told Gordon's navigator, Ron Jordan, who was to go with him to 31 Squadron, that while they wished no harm to Jordan, they hoped Gordon crashed. At 31 Squadron, too, he could be very critical of those who did not meet his own high standards—or rather low standards, for he expected all to fly at tree-level as he did. He also offended some when, while temporarily commanding the squadron, he nominated NCOs rather than officers to lead flights or elements. However, one 31 Squadron flight sergeant considered Gordon 'a great man', admired and respected for his flying ability, for his consideration for others and for his fearlessness.[6]

Air Vice-Marshals Jones and Cole visited Livingstone in October. Jim Grant comments that for 'the lower levels of air force life', such as himself, seeing high-ranking 'permanent types' was rare and mutually unwelcome. 'Their ideas and ours of how to win a war seemed to be poles apart.'[7]

Death in action was part of both visions of war, and 31 Squadron suffered two such deaths on 19 October. Francis Cridland and his navigator Raymond de Pierres 'went in' after strafing a barge—an official report said they 'were apparently hit by rifle fire'.[8]

The 64th and last Japanese raid on Darwin came on 12 November 1943. For more than three hours after 2.20 a.m., nine bombers flew over Fenton and Darwin and inflicted some wounds and damage. Jack Smithson intercepted three bombers over Darwin and, in a remarkable clash by night, shot down two of them. This won him a DFC and the nickname 'Cat's Eyes'. He had already destroyed two Zeros.

After the November raid, the boredom of duty in the Northern Territory worsened for the Spitfire pilots. The chances of combat became increasingly remote as the Japanese withdrew much of their strength to other areas. Shortages of serviceable Australian aircraft and supply difficulties were also galling to the RAAF in the North-Western Area. Two pilots, Reg Gordon and Donald Ferguson, shot down a Rufe each, but one Beaufighter was lost without trace.

In mid-December, Gordon led 31 Squadron's 100th operation. The unfortunate victim was an escorted convoy of enemy cargo ships north of Timor. Under six Beaufighters' strafing, many crew and soldiers died, while others dived overboard. No. 18 Squadron Mitchells followed up and crippled a ship. Next morning 31 Squadron's CO, Wing Commander Frederick Mann led the Beaufighters back to the struggling vessels. Flying the last 160 kilometres at zero height, their attack began with Mann's bombs hitting a cargo ship. Gordon flew so low that his Beau snapped the wireless aerial between the same ship's masts; his strafing and bombing finished the ship. Gordon then noticed four Nicks approaching. Nicks were easily mistaken for Beaufighters, but Gordon was now accustomed to fighting them. He hit one at close range as it made a stall turn. While it fell into the sea and broke in two, Gordon took on another Nick from head-on. His fire sent bits of the Nick's fuselage careering off, but it escaped.

On 4 January 1944, Gordon would 'do over' a fifth victim, a Betty, thus obtaining ace status in under 150 days. February would see him receive a bar to his DFC, but also his untimely death. He had always been scornful of Japanese shooting ability, though once an enemy flak round had penetrated his Beau's cockpit, knocking out the fuel gauges and spraying both Gordon and Jordan with shrapnel. Gordon's death came more prosaically. While trying to test a faulty propeller, the other propeller feathered and his Beaufighter crashed. Jordan was absent at the time.

An RAAF Public Relations Officer, Ernest Millington, went on a Beaufighter 'bash' with Mann around the end of the year and gave a vivid eyewitness account. Once they reached Timor, the swift movement of Mann's head and eyes reminded Millington of a 'timid lizard'. Flying fast over hills and down valleys recalled Luna Park's Big Dipper. Then when they came upon enemy-occupied buildings, the 'shuddering blast' of the cannon made a uniformed figure astride a horse simply disintegrate. As the Beau roared just feet above a building, the animal bolted and another soldier toppled sideways from the doorway. Mann returned for another strafing run, and caught more troops dashing for sanctuary in the same house. Some fell under his guns, another was crawling. Before the Beau left the scene, two men emerged from the smoking building and dropped dead.[9]

By December 1943 it was safe to move more planes and supplies into Darwin itself and to go fully on the offensive in North-Western Area. As an RAAF publication stated at the end of 1943, in northern Australia in 'a matter of months we have passed from near exhaustion of fighting potential to domination. The enemy is on the run.'[10]

'A magnificent crowd'—Merauke and Horn Island

In the gap between North-Western Area and New Guinea, two squadrons guarded Horn Island, Torres Strait and the port of Merauke on the south coast of Dutch New Guinea. Based on Horn Island, No. 7 Squadron's Beauforts protected convoys, and were joined in April 1943 by No. 84 Squadron's Boomerangs. No. 40 Radar Station operated at Merauke from 1942, and often detected enemy reconnaissance aircraft. On the last day of 1942, 22 Japanese bombers attacked Merauke. MacArthur, concerned about a potential raid or even invasion through the Torres Strait, decided to create a strong air base on Merauke in 1943.

No. 72 Wing was formed to be based there, but before it arrived, Boomerangs undertook their first ever operational role by maintaining a standing patrol over Merauke. Two Boomerangs had one inconclusive tussle with three Bettys before the bombers escaped into cloud. On

18 June, a Beaufort patrolling over Torres Strait detected an enemy aircraft on its radar. The captain, Peter Hopton, found the enemy Jake float-plane. After a ten-minute chase, one five-second burst from the aircraft's four wing guns into the Jake's belly was enough to give the squadron its first victory. Hopton, who after the war would become a church minister, wrote to his mother that 'it was a bit grisly but highly diverting to see him catch alight and crash into the sea'. He told his girlfriend that the subsequent celebrations had given him an 'almost continuous headache for several days'.[11] The squadron would add two more Jakes to its tally, in September and November.

Most of the time Merauke struck its garrison as being a 'hell hole', with its mud and mosquitoes especially obnoxious, and its low cloud a danger to pilots.[12] The Merauke airfield's Marsden matting was completed in June, so in July No. 86 Squadron's Kittyhawks arrived to provide fighter defence. Other elements of 72 Wing arrived through September. On 9 September, when radar detected 16 Bettys and 16 fighters approaching Merauke, 14 Kittyhawks and four Boomerangs took off to intercept. At 25,000 feet they attacked a group of eight fighters following the bombers, but a problem soon emerged. The squadron had recently exchanged its P-40Ms for P-40Ns, and the ground staff had used a new lubricant for the guns. They were not fired before going into action, and ten of the 14 Kittyhawks suffered gun trouble, with no fewer than 41 weapons malfunctioning. Nevertheless the Australians shot down two Zeros and an Oscar for no loss to themselves. Among the victors was former 75 Squadron pilot Arthur Tucker. He and Bill Stuart, who destroyed the Oscar, had both been Queensland schoolteachers before the war. Another victor was Cyril Stark, an outstanding pilot who would by January 1944 be commanding 77 Squadron. Aged 20 and over six feet tall when he enlisted as an air cadet on 4 September 1939, Stark would be awarded an AFC in 1948 and be killed in 1950 while test-flying a Vampire jet in England.

Tucker remembered Merauke as the only operational area where he heard a senior officer speak during the war, when George Jones visited. After drawing diagrams on the sand with a toe, Jones told the men that their mothers would be unhappy with the state of their uniforms. Not inspirational, but Jones' men were doing a fine job there. No. 86 Squadron was commanded by Squadron Leader Jack Meehan, and he, Tucker and Alan Whetters made this squadron far more organised than

75 Squadron had been in 1942. It could get its 16 P-40s airborne within four minutes of the klaxon sounding. Flight Lieutenant Bob Whittle, an air ace twice over, was also a fine leader in the squadron. Flying Tomahawks in North Africa, he had shot down at least 11 aircraft and been officially rated 'an exceptional fighter pilot'.[13] The impact of the universally respected and popular Whittle, as well as Tucker, Whetters and others, made a novice fighter pilot, Flight Sergeant Jack Shaw, reflect after arriving that the squadron 'chappies' were 'really a magnificent crowd'.[14] For example, the pilots addressed each other by Christian names, apart from the CO, who was 'sir'.

After September 1943, enemy activity in the Merauke–Torres Strait area diminished. No. 84 Squadron was re-equipped with Kittyhawks, but it and 86 Squadron had little interesting work to do. However, Stuart managed on 22 January 1944 to intercept and destroy a Betty. The following day in the same area, Whittle shot down one Zero and shared the destruction of another and a Betty. After this 'Battle of Cape Valsch', the Japanese did not intrude at Merauke again. Thus the Horn Island and Merauke squadrons secured the flank of MacArthur's advance.

Wing Commander Donald Thomson was another airman doing important work in Dutch New Guinea. Thomson was an anthropologist and had already led a reconnaissance unit, comprising mostly Aborigines, in Arnhem Land. In late 1943 he and three other airmen were seconded to the Army for patrolling in Dutch New Guinea. A long patrol went into wild territory more than 150 kilometres north-west of Merauke. They gleaned useful information about Japanese movements, but were attacked by locals armed and prompted by the enemy. Thomson and Sergeant Gordon Ritchie were severely wounded, but Thomson led a fighting retreat through deep swamps and dense jungle. They and friendly locals held out at their camp until rescued by a Catalina. Thomson received an Order of the British Empire for this patrol, though his wounds effectively ended his military career.

* * *

While Australian airmen in North-Western Area and Dutch New Guinea were risking all in 1943, their compatriots further east were contributing everything they could to the major offensives there.

20 Breaking the Bismarcks Barrier

By April 1943, Allied forces in the Pacific were ready to take the offensive. In the South-West Pacific the goal was to break 'the Bismarcks Barrier', which extended from Wewak through Madang, Lae and Salamaua in New Guinea, Kavieng in New Ireland, and the Admiralty Islands, to Cape Gloucester, Gasmata and Rabaul on New Britain. The strongest and most important of these posts was Rabaul, with its capacious harbour and five airfields.

In line with a plan to bring Allied forces in both the South-West Pacific Area and South Pacific within close striking range of Rabaul, Admiral Halsey was ordered to move forces from his South Pacific Area up the Solomon Islands chain to Bougainville, while General MacArthur was to create airfields on Kiriwina and Woodlark Islands. From there, Allied air forces could provide cover for ground operations aimed at seizing the Huon Gulf in New Guinea and the western end of New Britain. The RAAF's premier unit, No. 9 Operational Group, now under Air Commodore Hewitt, would provide the right flank cover from bases to be established on Goodenough Island and Kiriwina Island, as well as Milne Bay. Hewitt felt that General Kenney showed great faith in the RAAF by giving it this task.

With planning for offensives now beginning, how was Australia placed to contribute in the air? Of 69 operational squadrons at General Kenney's disposal in April 1943, 31 were Australian. Of these RAAF squadrons, seven were in No. 9 Operational Group: Nos 6, 75, 77 and 100 at Milne Bay, and 4, 22 and 30 at Port Moresby. The RAAF had 1441 aircraft in the Pacific.

MacArthur was urging Curtin's government to continue its program of expanding towards 72 squadrons, but Kenney, who wanted American aircraft for Fifth Air Force, now advised Washington that he doubted Australia could find sufficient personnel to man the 45 squadron target it had set for 1943. When Curtin discovered this he urged Dr Evatt to press hard in Washington for Australia to receive more American aircraft.

In June, Evatt cabled Curtin that President Roosevelt had allocated approximately 475 aircraft for expanding the RAAF between 1943 and 1945, some of which would be sent immediately. Curtin announced triumphantly in Parliament that this would mean a 60 per cent increase in RAAF strength, but in fact the promise was not fulfilled. In 1943, the following were allocated:

- Vultee Vengeance 34
- Kittyhawk 60
- Catalina 12
- Shrike 150
- Mariner 12
- Norseman 14.

As we shall see, Australia's experience with the Vengeance would prove unhappy: one American historian says that in sending Australia this aircraft, 'the Americans had unloaded junk'.[1] The Shrike, another dive-bomber, also proved a dead letter: only ten were delivered by war's end, and were never employed operationally. The Kittyhawks were outmoded. The Mariners and Norseman aircraft were transports, so the addition of these aircraft to the operational strength of the RAAF was in fact puny.

Kenney may appear to have been interfering selfishly, but his views were logical. Australia was not enlisting enough men for its existing RAAF units, thanks largely to conflicting manpower demands for the nation's armed services and war industries. Tropical diseases helped to ensure that RAAF numbers remained well below its establishment strength. In New Guinea, units were 2000 under strength by June, and replacements barely covered the loss of men returned to Australia because their tours of duty—nine months for aircrew, 15–18 months for ground personnel—had expired. Consequently in October 1943, the government decided to revise the 72 squadron plan down to 48 squadrons, although this was later revised up.

The disruptive power relationships within the RAAF and between it and other bodies persisted through 1943. The Australian government was responsible for germinating divisions by separating operational and administrative control of the RAAF, and this was reinforced by the reorganisation of the Allied Air Forces. Everyone involved agreed that the arrangement was unsatisfactory, but could not concur on a solution. In April 1943, George Jones tried replacing Bill Bostock with Hewitt as Air Officer Commanding RAAF Command, but after Kenney opposed this, the postings were cancelled. Soon afterwards, Curtin suggested the creation of a new post, Air Officer Commanding, RAAF, which would unify the operational and administrative aspects of the service. The Minister for Air, Arthur Drakeford, and the Air Board recommended Jones for this post, but MacArthur rejected the proposal, as he did all the other Australian and British airmen proposed as candidates. Curtin would not oppose MacArthur, or force Drakeford to give Bostock the job. The division continued, as did its pernicious effects on issues such as staff for RAAF Command headquarters, advanced operational training and airfield construction. In officers' messes in New Guinea, Hewitt saw the rift promote 'malignant whisperings that exacerbated jealousies and detractions'.[2] When George Jones visited New Guinea in April, Hewitt, who considered the CAS a friend, was struck by his 'washed out' and ungainly appearance. This and his unwillingness to make eye contact or speak his mind contrasted starkly with the smiling directness that met Hewitt in the ball of energy that was George Kenney. Yet on the same visit Hewitt watched the intensely practical 'Jonah' come to life when he saw the construction work going on at Vivigani on Goodenough. Typically, Jones missed an opportunity to congratulate or inspire the earnest young airmen who gathered to greet him at Milne Bay.[3]

The RAAF squadrons at Port Moresby were supporting Allied ground operations around Mubo and Salamaua, often alongside American aircraft. The dangers were apparent when in May, No. 22 Squadron Bostons flew through heavy flak to attack a wrecked ship suspected of being used to store and receive supplies. Flight Lieutenant Harold Rowell did not see the target first time round and returned to make a lone attack. His aircraft was caught in a searchlight and was hit again and again. His stand-in gunner, 20-year-old Arthur Taylor, was killed by a direct hit, and his wireless operator, David Duncan, was seriously wounded. Rowell skilfully brought the badly damaged Boston home. It then fell to him to inform Duncan that his leg had to be amputated, and that his father had died the previous day. Duncan refused permission for the amputation, but still lost most of his foot.

Keith 'Grumpy' Eddison was leading Beaufighters in a raid across Lae airstrip three days later when his aircraft was hit and crashed, killing him and navigator Max Allott. Keith was one of three brothers brought up on their father's soldier-settlement farm near Canberra. Jack Eddison died as a POW in Japan 11 days after Keith, and RAF Squadron Leader Tom Eddison had been killed over Germany in 1941. Allott had been ill for a week before this flight, and only the night before told George Carnegie, who had been filling in for him, that he was ready to fly again.

Even flying above friendly lines could be dangerous. When No. 4 Squadron was re-equipped with Boomerangs, their unfamiliar appearance caused suspicious Allied anti-aircraft gunners to fire at them. In November one of the top American aces, Gerald Johnson, shot down a Boomerang. On discovering his mistake, which was not fatal, he painted an Australian flag on his P-38's nose alongside the Japanese flags that denoted his aerial victories. James Collier was shot down over American positions in July, and though he landed the Boomerang, was mortally wounded when his head struck the gunsight. The squadron and senior officers on the spot had initially advised against replacing the Wirraways with Boomerangs and now reiterated this opinion. Before the changeover was completed, Wirraways carried out many supply drops for the troops.

Japanese aircraft made occasional appearances, but suffered if Lightnings arrived. Although the presence of friendly aircraft near the front was a morale booster, the provision of ground support in the Mubo operations was frustrating for the RAAF and Army alike: it took at least two hours for aircraft called upon for close support to arrive from Dobodura and Moresby and then it was extremely difficult to bomb targets accurately in the jungle. The Army concluded that the best contribution the air force could make was attacking Japanese rear areas. Yet after the war, Japanese officers conceded that Allied air attacks in this area had been painfully effective, pinning many troops in air-raid shelters and killing more than 150 troops at Salamaua. Moreover, relations between the RAAF and Army were generally excellent here. Apart from dropping bombs on the enemy, the Bostons were unofficially also dropping newspapers, magazines, tobacco and even fresh bread to the front-line troops. Those troops gratefully sent the squadron a captured Japanese mortar from Mubo and a Nambu machine gun from Salamaua.

The Beaufighters had an unusual experience in May, when Flight Sergeant Bill Cosgrove spotted a large Japanese submarine, possibly I-122. 'Cossie' wrote soon afterwards that he was:

> ... lucky to see him through the break in the clouds ... Flag was flat out in the breeze, I could see the red stripes on it quite plainly. At 1000ft I opened fire on the hull between the conning tower [and] the stern and could see the HE [high explosive] exploding. Two men ran from the conning tower to a machine gun just forward of the flag. I was then only 50 yds away and saw them stumble as my bullets hit them. At the same time there were four flashes from a heavy gun forward [on the deck], but I did not see where the shots burst. I ran through a rainstorm, turned and swept back to the attack, just as he was submerging.[4]

By the time other Beaufighters arrived, the submarine had gone.

In order to make it easier for No. 9 Operational Group's aircraft to reach Rabaul, Goodenough Island was occupied in May 1943. This mountainous and beautiful island impressed most who went there from New Guinea. Its airfield, Vivigani, became the base for No. 73 Wing, comprising three fighter squadrons: 76 and 77, still flying Kittyhawks, and the recently formed No. 79, with Spitfires. They expected furious air battles above Kiriwina and Woodlark Islands when the scheduled amphibious landings occurred there in June. However, the landings were unopposed—and to the chagrin of the fighter pilots, the aerial resistance never came.

The Australians did see various American aircraft up close. When a USAAF P-38 squadron moved in, many met American personnel for the first time. 'We appreciated their free and easy style,' said Arthur Gately, an Australian armourer, 'their friendliness and generosity.'[5] The Australians were impressed by the Americans' maintenance and mobile workshop facilities, and envious of their beautiful chrome tool kits. Both groups enjoyed a superbly aerobatic mock dogfight between a 'Spitty' and Lightning above the island. Pilots and ground crew shared a mutual love of their allotted Spitfires, which were fastidiously polished and cleaned. When chatting, the many subjects the ground crew discussed included the war, squadron rumours, civilian life, politics, religion and of course women and sex. Homosexuality was a taboo subject. The official attitude towards it is indicated by the treatment of a squadron adjutant convicted of this 'crime': before he was dishonourably discharged, his tunic buttons were publicly torn off as a sign of his disgrace.[6]

An airfield was rapidly constructed at Kiriwina and Nos 76, 77 and 79 Squadrons moved in. Although Kiriwina was the closest Allied base to Rabaul—just 500 kilometres away—the enemy made no serious challenge to these moves, apart from desultory bombing raids. Kiriwina was flat and 'a hell of a place'.[7] Here dense scrub and swamp replaced the many trees, dense vegetation and slopes of Goodenough. Other unhappy features were the constant and stifling heat and humidity, rain, dust, glare from the coral, and huge spiders, whose webs presented an unsettling experience for the unwary walking back to their tents at night. Yet Kiriwina also had well-constructed roads and airstrips, and a beautiful lagoon in which to swim.

Milne Bay was now bigger than in 1942, and more civilised than Kiriwina. Nevertheless the climate and lifestyle there were still awful, with tinned food the staple, and such shortages of clothing supplies that many had to break anti-malarial regulations and wear shorts. Some had to resort to finding footwear from a dump into which the boots of dead Allied servicemen had been thrown. There was also a friendly fire incident here.

When a 100 Squadron Beaufort failed to return to Milne Bay from a long reconnaissance in July, the galling news soon emerged that it had been shot down by a USN Liberator patrolling from the South Pacific. The American crew had realised their mistake when the aircraft crashed, and dropped a raft, flares and food to their victims, who were struggling in the water. Storms grounded search aircraft the following day, and though foul weather persisted in subsequent days, 250 hours were expended unsuccessfully trying to find John Davis's missing crew.

With an influx of men and material in July, No. 9 Operational Group was ready to fulfil its purpose of attacking enemy bases and shipping in and around New Britain. This would prevent the enemy reinforcing their strength in New Guinea and from interfering with the imminent Allied campaign to capture Lae. Sometimes as many as five squadrons participated, as on 22 July when Hewitt ordered out 62 aircraft of Nos 100, 75, 77, 22 and 30 squadrons for the largest mission ever flown by Australian aircraft, a raid on Gasmata. Some aircraft were struck by anti-aircraft fire, but none were lost. The worst injury seems to have been a bullet to the buttocks—and dignity—of one Boston crewman. George Jones, then visiting New Guinea, did not talk with the men who had participated in this unprecedented attack.

In the next big raid on Gasmata, four days later, the Kitties were not just flying escort, but carrying their own bombs. Twenty P-40s each carried four 40-pound general-purpose bombs and two 30-pound incendiary bombs. They bombed accurately and all got home safely, albeit with some holes. To Sergeant Charles Walmsley at Goodenough, 'seeing is believing' a sight as spectacular as the aircraft taking off for that 'marvellous effort'.[8] Kittyhawks were not finding aerial opponents in New Guinea, so to convert them to fighter-bombers and strafers was a sensible means of employing them.

Dick Cresswell led seven strikes on New Britain in July, and was then granted some long-overdue leave: he had commanded 77 Squadron since April 1942. He nominated as his successor Daryl Sproule, who had been flying fighters since Malaya. A takeover ceremony was held on 2 August, followed by a fighter sweep along New Britain's south coast. Cresswell led the first flight, Wilf Arthur a second, and Sproule the third. Sproule was making a low-level attack against enemy positions when he was hit by anti-aircraft fire. He crash-landed successfully on the beach, but had gone when Bostons returned that afternoon. After the war it emerged that just hours after achieving the highly sought-after position of squadron leader, Sproule had been captured and executed by the Japanese. Cresswell had to stay on a little longer.

On 11 August, LAC Harry Tayler of 30 Squadron wrote a longer diary entry than usual. It read: 'Kites went off early morning. A19-74 crashed into sea, F Sgt Cosgrove former Richmond footballer.'[9] Bill Cosgrove had played three matches for Richmond in 1940, and was considered a promising player. He had also flown Blenheims in the Netherlands East Indies with George Sayer, and with George had escaped from Java. Like Sayer, Cosgrove loved a joke. A fellow pilot tells a story of bored aircrew playing 'animal, vegetable, mineral' at Milne Bay. Cosgrove got very close to getting his topic, 'the black mark on the winning post at Randwick Racecourse', but when his 20 questions were up he fulfilled his forfeit with gusto: he ran round the camp stark naked three times, shouting 'I'm a bloody ape'.[10] Now both he and Sayer had died in 30 Squadron Beaufighters, as had Bill's observer, Bernard Le Griffon. Bill was an uncle of General Peter Cosgrove, Chief of Australia's Defence Force from 2002 to 2005.

Flying from Cairns, 11 and 20 Squadron Catalinas were making harassing night attacks in New Britain and Dutch New Guinea. During a September raid, Squadron Leader David Vernon's Catalina became caught in the beams of nine searchlights over Rabaul, but though the crew was dazzled, Vernon skilfully escaped. The RAAF's 'maids-of-all-work' also dropped vital supplies to the coastwatchers still risking their lives in the Solomons, New Britain and New Ireland.

The dangers of that work were exemplified in April when William Clark's Catalina flew the eight-hour trip to northern Bougainville to deliver supplies to a coastwatcher, Jack Read. By then the drops were very accurate, with items released in a series of runs from about 500 feet up into a drop zone marked by fires. This night, with the drops in progress, but before Clark could give the customary farewell waggle of the wings and 'good luck' message on his signal lamp, one of his wings hit some treetops and was sheared off. The aircraft careered on through the trees for another 300 metres. Two of the nine crewmen crawled free, but the rest were trapped inside, dead or injured. Australian commandos and locals found the Cat next morning. Clark and two other crewmen were dead, but another four were freed from the aircraft. Most of the crew were too badly injured to walk, and the rescuers used the Cat's bunks as stretchers to get them to the commandos' camp. An American submarine was due off the coast within a few days, but bad weather prevented the injured men reaching it. Protected by the Australian troops and under Read's supervision, they settled down to recover from their injuries. However, the Japanese were on their trail, and in mid-June made a surprise attack on the camp. Two airmen and three commandos shot their way out, but two injured airmen, Clifton Dunn and John Fenwick, were left behind with a commando, Lieutenant Doug Bedkober, who chose to stay and protect them. All three were captured. Dunn was killed on the spot, Fenwick at Rabaul and Bedkober of illness. The five who had escaped the ambush fared no better. Struggling east across the island, they were eventually betrayed to the Japanese and executed. The last two crewmen, Corporal Wettenhall and Sergeant Thompson, evaded the enemy and were rescued by an American submarine in July 1944, 14 months after being shot down.

In March 1943, Squadron Leader Reg Burrage of 11 Squadron was sent on another challenging rescue mission. Burrage had enormous experience flying Sunderlands, and was a good choice to undertake the hazardous task of rescuing from the New Britain village of Ea Ea an Australian soldier and three American airmen who for many months had been fending for themselves behind enemy lines. He warned his crew that it would be 'a bit of a shaky do, to say the least', but all volunteered. The rescue went off brilliantly, and the Catalina returned to a great welcome at Moresby, where the crew threw out a toilet roll streamer as a 'victory roll'. This rescue boosted air force morale in New Guinea. It was a much-needed fillip to the Catalina crews, for earlier that month Squadron Leader Frank Chapman, 'the most respected, popular and revered Catalina personality at that time' had been lost off Gasmata, to the 'consternation and dismay' of his peers.[18]

On 17 August, Fifth Air Force Liberators and Mitchells launched a surprise attack on Wewak, the principal Japanese Army air base in New Guinea. Its recent reinforcement had been discovered, largely by RAAF wireless units. Over 100 Japanese aircraft were destroyed, leaving the JAAF with approximately 30 aircraft in the area. Devastating American attacks such as this would become common, and crushed Japanese airfields were hereafter often said to have been 'wee-wacked'.[11] The Japanese Navy in the Solomons–New Guinea area still had about 220 aircraft, but the Allied assault on Lae was now much more secure. Fifty per cent of Japanese aircraft losses were now being incurred on the ground, where their inadequate dispersal and protection were attributable to a lack of heavy equipment and maintenance staff.

On 4 September, the 9th Australian Division landed north of Lae. RAAF Bostons and Beauforts attacked Gasmata airfield to prevent

Japanese aircraft there from launching attacks on the troops. John Baker's Beaufort dive-bombed the runway. He recalled, 'I released my bombs at 1500 feet, and dived away to sea level through a barrage of ack-ack. I dodged and weaved all I knew. It was the most thrilling experience of my life.'[12] Though they achieved good hits, one Beaufort, under Tom Allanson, burst into flames amidst the flak, and all on board died.

That day, 76 Japanese aircraft flew from Rabaul to attack Allied shipping in the Huon Gulf. Wing Commander Hugh Conaghan of No. 9 Group had suggested creating fighter-director teams on the beachhead and in vessels offshore, and from one of those vessels, the destroyer USS *Reid*, his team now detected the enemy aircraft. Lightnings shot down many raiders, which nevertheless damaged several landing ships.

Next morning, the Bostons found much of Gasmata airstrip repaired—after they had twice hit it the previous day—and bombed it again. It was vital to keep Gasmata out of action, for that day American paratroops and Australian artillery were to be dropped at Nadzab, north-west of Lae to be followed by transports carrying 7th Division troops as soon as a landing strip was prepared. Thus ten Beauforts of 100 Squadron followed the Bostons to Gasmata. Hewitt had ordered them not to fly lower than 8000 feet during the attack, but they came in low and slow at less than half that altitude. After all, they had done it before with little resistance. Now, however, the fully alert defenders opened up over the airfield with an unexpected 'box barrage', that is, anti-aircraft fire in a box shape. Casualties were inevitable amidst such fire, but the Beauforts gamely flew on. Five were hit. Although Roy Woollacott's aircraft caught fire, he deposited his four bombs on the airstrip before his Beaufort dropped irretrievably. He and his crew died.

Roy Anderson's crew paid the same price for their courage, their Beaufort being blown apart before crashing into the harbour. Clem Wiggins struggled to keep his Beaufort airborne but, wreathed in smoke and flames, it crashed into hills north-east of Gasmata. Chas Walsh got back to Vivigani, though as one tyre had been shot off, his Beaufort ground-looped on landing and was written off. Its crew walked away, but the squadron had lost four crews and five aircraft in two days. Hewitt was remorseful that he had not been more adamant about the correct altitude for the attack. By late September, the squadron would have just five crews for 17 Beauforts.

In September Charles Learmonth reported blowing up a heavy Japanese gun position with his best-ever bomb drop—the resulting explosion sent debris 300 metres into the air. While these small but significant Australian raids occurred on New Britain, the might of American airpower in the South-West Pacific Area was reflected in the sky over Nadzab. More than 300 aircraft took off from eight airstrips in New Guinea, rendezvoused and supported the air-dropping of 1700 soldiers at Nadzab. The next day, an airstrip was prepared and Dakotas landed Australian troops at Nadzab. These Diggers marched on Lae.

Their progress was rapid, but in the interval more RAAF losses followed in New Britain. Flak hit 'Joe' Newman's Beaufighter, which ditched in the sea. Newman was near the end of his tour, but had vowed to get the gun, known as 'Dead Eye Dick', which had earlier hit several other Beaufighters at Palmalmal. Newman, his navigator and an accompanying Army officer were seen to escape into a dinghy. Next day supplies were dropped to them at sea. They waved, but were never seen again. Adding to the poignancy of their deaths, an RAAF Seagull amphibian aircraft was lost without trace during the search for them. The navigator on this flight was Raymond Kelley, who usually flew as navigator to Wing Commander Clarrie Glasscock, 30 Squadron's recently appointed CO. Eight days later Glasscock was leading eight Beaufighters in a raid on Cape Hoskins when, during the final run, he radioed another pilot: 'My port motor is haywire, she's shaking to pieces.' Seconds later he was heard saying, 'I am bailing out, come up front.'[13] The last three words were probably to his new navigator, John Cain. Fellow aircrew saw no parachutes, but only the smouldering wreck of their CO's kite in the jungle. Woof Arthur was upset by this death, for Glasscock had been one of his instructors, and a man 'that no single person seems to have anything but good to say of'.[14] This despite a surname that brought much ribaldry.

Cain and Clive Cooke had tossed a coin as to who would go on this flight, and Cooke 'lost'. He refused thereafter to toss a coin, and would remember this incident every time, as a post-war hockey umpire, he got captains to toss the coin. He was lucky not to have died a week earlier when his Beaufighter suddenly began shaking uncontrollably after a near-miss explosion during a raid. While trying to identify where they had been hit, the pilot called Cooke forward. As Cooke opened the armoured doors between them and stepped forward, he nearly fell to his death, for the pilot's hatch had come open—not a unique event—and affected the Beau's performance. Cooke managed to shut the door, but only by risking a fall into the ocean.

Two Bostons were lost near Gasmata in September, one crew reaching a dinghy, but although Harry Dawkins was captured, neither he nor the other four crewmen survived. Such incidents raised questions about the adequacy of air–sea rescue in the area, though an air–sea rescue Dornier was soon sited at nearby Kiriwina. A third Boston was lost on 12 September, for Harold Rowell had to crash-land his heavily damaged aircraft at Vivigani. Replacements were available, but by November 1943, after one year of operations, No. 22 Squadron had lost 12 aircraft, the equivalent of an entire squadron. Its airmen, of whom 23 were killed or missing, had won a VC, a DSO, four DFCs and a DFM. This was indicative of the quality of their efforts, as is the fact that they had flown 135 operations, with a 99 per cent completion rate, dropping nearly 727,000 pounds (330,000 kilograms) of bombs and firing more than 650,000 rounds.

Kenney called forward the new Vultee Vengeance dive-bombers of No. 24 Squadron, so as to use their ability to make pinpoint attacks. Misidentifications led American vessels to fire on the Vengeances, and American fighters were scrambled to attack the unfamiliar Australian aircraft, though another time Lightnings escorted lost Vengeances back to base, and the USAAF looked after most of their supply and maintenance needs.

During the march on Lae, No. 4 Squadron Boomerangs and Wirraways undertook reconnaissance, supply-dropping, strafing and ferrying missions. A typically dangerous mission was undertaken by Bob Staley, who risked his life to fly captured Japanese plans through appalling weather to Port Moresby. Staley was killed in December while on an artillery reconnaissance flight.

When Lae fell on 16 September, the Allies secured its shipping facilities and an airbase of enormous potential at Nadzab. By December, 80 per cent of personnel in Fifth Air Force USAAF would be in New Guinea, and 60 per cent of these north of the Owen Stanleys, whereas at the beginning of the year, most had still been in Australia. Nadzab would eventually replace Dobodura as Fifth Air Force's main forward base in New Guinea.

After this triumph, new objectives were immediately set in the Markham Valley and at Finschhafen. At a speed of 480 kilometres an hour, the Vengeances dived to within 1500 feet of enemy positions around Finschhafen, and after dropping their 500-pound (225-kilogram) bombs, fired thousands of machine-gun rounds. With six direct hits, they demolished a Japanese radio-location station on an island off 'Finch'. During the final advance on Finschhafen itself, the Vengeances gave support. Their courage could not be faulted—one 'Vultee' flew so low it was hit by a splinter from its own bombs.[15] It was probably that raid that brought this message from the 9th Division: 'Ground troops exhilarated by air attacks, Bostons and Vultees. Bombing and strafing extremely accurate.'[16] One of 24 Squadron's pilots was Bill Hewett, who had narrowly survived the 20 January 1942 battle at Rabaul while flying Wirraways for the same squadron.

During a barge sweep in October, two Beaufighter pilots, Edward Marron and Arthur Thomson, overtook a Betty bomber, and grasped the rare opportunity to shoot down an enemy aircraft. Japanese aircraft numbers rose at Rabaul in September and October, and occasionally its fighters interfered with Australian patrols or raided Goodenough and Kiriwina. Enemy aircraft inflicted 18 casualties at 305 Radar Station on Kiriwina on 5 October.

Salamaua, Lae, the Markham Valley and Finschhafen had all been captured by early October. Many Allied casualties had to be evacuated from these fronts. For the first time, RAAF medical personnel—initially one medical officer and 12 orderlies—were allotted to assist the overworked US Medical Air Evacuation Transport Squadron in this vital task. The experience led to the formation of No. 1 Medical Air Evacuation Transport Unit RAAF. In 1944–45 this unit carried more than 14,000 Allied casualties, without losing a single man in flight. Two more Medical Air Evacuation Transport Units (MAETUs) were formed, with No. 2 operating from Morotai, and No. 3 in and south of Townsville. They used various aircraft but the mainstay was the Dakota, carrying 18 to 24 casualties.

The 15 nurses initially selected for this elite unit had to meet stringent physical and mental standards. The challenges in this job were many. For example, temperatures inside the aircraft changed from intensely hot (up to 65°C) to dangerously cold as the aircraft gained altitude, regularly flying over mountains or bad weather; flights were often bumpy; 15 per cent of patients were psychiatric, many of whom did not travel well, including the American who held a Sister firmly in a headlock until a male orderly freed her; and information on the condition of patients was often inadequate. Margot Scott vividly described the daily experiences of the 'flying nurses':

> We were only young ourselves—all under 30—and we were nursing young men who were about the same ages as ourselves—fine young bodies, smashed or mutilated or with wits all anyhow ... Sometimes we'd have to decide that this group of young men couldn't live, and we'd decide therefore not to emplane them, and move on to those who could live if they were speedily evacuated.

No wonder the sisters 'played hard' at night after such experiences.[17] Their efforts were remarkably successful, and air evacuation proved to be highly efficient, demanding fewer personnel and less time than travel by sea.

General MacArthur was still urging that Rabaul be captured—a task he calculated in February 1943 would require 21 divisions and 1800 aircraft. This may have been an overestimate, but the defences of this 'hot spot' were formidable. In October 1943, there were some 330 Japanese aircraft, mainly fighters, at Rabaul, which was also protected by 367 anti-aircraft guns. Twenty-three of these were 120 mm calibre or higher, and could hit Allied aircraft at any altitude. Allied intelligence estimated the island's garrison as being about 50,000, but in fact it comprised about twice that number. The US Joint Chiefs of Staff rejected MacArthur's urging, insisting that instead he neutralise Rabaul, especially by air attack, and isolate it by occupying the Admiralty Islands. Admiral Halsey would take Kavieng.

General Kenney sent 306 aircraft against Rabaul on 12 October 1943. LAC Clegg saw some flying over Milne Bay, where they made a 'marvellous sight'.[18] Under Wing Commander Gordon Steege, Australian ground crews worked from dawn to dusk on the Lightnings that were continuously staging through Kiriwina. Amidst great noise, the P-38s rendezvoused overhead with the bombers they were to escort. Twelve attackers that day were RAAF Beaufighters. Delayed by dust at Dobodura, they met Mitchells and Lightnings returning from Rabaul, and were briefly fired on. Having survived that, they flew on without escort to Rabaul, and were confronted by 19 fighters. They tried to avoid a dogfight, but got caught up in half an hour's fighting, which saw one Beaufighter destroyed and two Japanese 'probables'. Wing Commander Jim Emerton, who had piloted a Hudson over Singapore, now flew over Rapopo airfield with three Zeros on his tail. Flying at the lowest possible height and at full speed, he strafed the strip and broke away from the enemy fighters at 450 kilometres per hour.

Derrick Stone, who had served in Wirraways at Rabaul, was ecstatic to be headed back there, flying a Beaufighter. However, he never reached it. He and his navigator, Burford Morris-Hadwell, were last seen climbing to take on a Zero that was stalking another Beau. Their bodies would be discovered 57 years later, and the funeral would be attended by Stone's daughter, born days after his death. Just before his death, 30 Squadron had been visited by the CAS, which had special significance for Stone, as George Jones was his brother-in-law.

In the same action in which Stone and Morris-Hadwell died, Alfred Catt was chased by two Zeros. One of them, probably out of ammunition, tried to get in front of Catt and cut him off. For a long time both flew at sea level, wingtip to wingtip. Catt waved to the Japanese pilot, who waved back before eventually giving up on his prey. John McRobbie and Clive Cooke were also being chased by a fighter. Cooke, an experienced gunner, fired several bursts from his Browning 'scatter gun', a local modification fitted to his cupola. The gun came off its mounting and hit Cooke's eye, but the enemy aircraft seemed to take a burst before peeling away. On reaching Goodenough Island, Cooke and McRobbie got an extraordinary reception: the squadron leader's navigator came up and kissed them. He explained that his machine gun had jammed, and an enemy aircraft had been on their tail until McRobbie and Cooke chased it off.

The 12 October raid inflicted heavy losses on the surprised enemy. Yet much more was coming. While escorted USAAF bombers repeatedly attacked during the day, unescorted RAAF Catalinas and Beauforts made nocturnal raids. In late October all three Beaufort squadrons attacked a convoy travelling from Truk to Rabaul. The ships' anti-aircraft fire was intense, but Stephen Hales saw one of his bombs go down a cruiser's funnel, and others observed men entering lifeboats from another blazing vessel. All three squadrons claimed hits on the cruiser, but no ships were ever confirmed sunk in this attack. One Beaufort, under 8 Squadron's Geoffrey Vincent, did not return.

Jack Bailey was Vincent's navigator. On 16 November, his wife

Marjorie wrote to the squadron chaplain that she had not seen her husband for a year, and just three months earlier had borne a third child. 'My heart is just frozen,' she admitted, but she still believed he was alive.[19] When she wrote the letter, her instinct was correct, for Jack was a prisoner in Rabaul. However, on or soon after 25 November, his Japanese guards would behead him. All four crewmen survived the crash, coming ashore on New Ireland, but only Allan Brown would survive captivity. Jack Bailey's body was discovered in a mass grave in 1950 and he was reburied with 14 other Australian and 15 American airmen at Rabaul in a dignified ceremony.

Though Beaufighters ambushed and shot down a Jake off Cape Orford in October, opportunities for the RAAF to dogfight were rare. This was largely because of the Kitties' limited range, and because the Japanese did not send fighters from Rabaul to attack Kiriwina in daylight. Kiriwina was the JAAF's responsibility, but their base at Wewak was suppressed by Fifth Air Force. A JAAF Tony did venture north of Kiriwina on 31 October and was detected by Flight Sergeant Ian Callister in his Spitfire. 'Have you got a bogey?', he signalled base, but when they replied that they had no warning from Fighter Sector, he replied 'Well, I have', and proceeded to pursue. He shot off part of the Tony's mainplane at 730 metres, then, closing to 550 metres, saw it disintegrate under his fire. He had achieved 79 Squadron's first kill, but rather than bask in glory, he declared himself 'a bit lucky'.[20] Callister, still at high school in 1940, was known as 'The Kid' within the squadron. While training in England he had written with childlike excitement about being able to see both sides of the English Channel at the same time.

On the same day that Callister won his first triumph, Wing Commander 'Woof' Arthur added a 'probable' to his list of eight destroyed and one probable. This was a Betty over Jacquinot Bay, New Britain. Just five days after these triumphs, the two pilots' fates became more intertwined when they were involved in a pre-dawn collision at Kiriwina. Each pilot, taking off from opposite ends of the strip and unaware of the other's presence, interpreted an American permission light as signalling him to take off. 'Woof' Arthur recognised the threat just a fraction of a second before impact. In the tremendous smash his Kittyhawk caught fire. Severely burnt, he jumped from his aircraft and rolled in a puddle of oily water. He then rushed to see if he could help 'the Kid'. Callister, whose aircraft had been cut to pieces, was beyond help. One of the ground crew recalled 79 Squadron being afflicted by 'a great sadness for many days'.[21]

Arthur's men were anxious too. They knew more than his mother, to whom the RAAF sent a telegram a few days later, saying that her son's injuries were 'of a very slight nature' and that there was 'no cause for anxiety'. The chaplain wrote to Arthur's wife that 'Woof' was 'burnt but not badly and will be soon over the burns'.[22] In fact Arthur faced weeks of torment. Skin was scraped off his face and hands with a table knife and minimal anaesthetic. He lapsed in and out of consciousness. Then, covered in bandages down to his waist, he spent up to ten days in a bath at Kiriwina. He temporarily went blind. He was not expected to live, but was eventually flown by Beaufighter to Sydney via Townsville for plastic surgery.

Death brought joy rather than sadness to 79 Squadron a few weeks later, for on 28 November Archie Moore was on a test flight in his Spitfire 28,000 feet above Kiriwina when he heard the Kitties being scrambled to intercept a reconnaissance plane. Moore saw the Dinah 2000 feet above him, stalked it and shot it down. He finished the test flight and came in to land.

Another test in November came in the form of a race. Not the Melbourne Cup, but a race between the pride of 22 and 30 Squadrons. The personnel of each squadron had bragged about the respective merits of their Bostons and Beaufighters, and eventually a race was arranged. The Boston won the first race, at Vivigani, but according to 30 Squadron personnel it was an unfair event, because the Boston had been stripped, while the overconfident Beaufighter pilot had not only flown in the standard configuration but had even carried extra passengers to witness the victory. A second race, held on 2 November, and reportedly with a huge amount of money gambled on it, was won by the Beau.

Japanese reinforcement aircraft sent from Truk brought the total at Rabaul to 550 aircraft, but they suffered heavy losses in American raids. Moreover, up to 40 per cent of the garrison was ill, primarily with malaria. The Japanese were taking heavier air losses than the Allies, though MacArthur's headquarters claimed absurdly inflated enemy casualty totals at Rabaul. For the period 10 October–2 November, they asserted that Allied aircraft had destroyed 522 aircraft as well as one cruiser and seven destroyers. We know now that the actual figures were 203 aircraft for Rabaul and the Solomons, and one destroyer. MacArthur's hyperbole made a mockery of the 'real facts' report on the Spitfires at Darwin in June. Journalists at MacArthur's headquarters guffawed at his more absurd claims.

The RAAF leadership became embroiled in a new altercation in November. It revolved around a large-scale torpedo attack that Hewitt, a former naval officer and Fleet Air Arm pilot, was determined to send against shipping at Rabaul. George Jones was urging him to use the torpedo-bombers to justify their expensive facilities, equipment and training. The COs of the three squadrons—6, 8 and 100—were enthusiastic about the prospect. So far RAAF Beauforts had not been successful torpedo-bombers, but if they could achieve a big bang in Rabaul, their reputation might change. Intense preparations were made for 12 Beaufort torpedo-bombers of 8 Squadron to attack shipping at Rabaul on 8 November, aided by a diversion from Beauforts bombing nearby airfields.

The first inkling of gremlins came when a reconnaissance Beaufort returned from a lone sortie to Rabaul. The naval observer on board, Lieutenant Russell Greentree, reported heavy rain in the area and that the Japanese ships had been grouped so as to maximise their anti-aircraft fire against a torpedo run. Any such run would now only be able to approach from a westerly direction, silhouetted against the low moon, and flying over enemy ack-ack batteries on the ground before reaching the combined gunfire of five cruisers and much other naval flak. Greentree and the two torpedo flight commanders, Owen Price and Noel Quinn, recommended against the torpedo attack. Wing Commander Geoff Nicoll, who was to lead the attack, now advised Hewitt that the raid should be called off, and was appalled to be told that it must go ahead. An argument ensued as Nicoll tried to stand his ground. Hewitt later wrote that he was shocked by Nicoll's loud assertion, made without reference to him and based on inadequate reasons. Hewitt felt compassion towards Nicoll, but believed that he had elements of hubris and a tendency to be emotional under stress. Hewitt suppressed his instinct to sack Nicoll on the spot.[23] The senior officers crowded round a map of Rabaul on the moonlit bonnet of a jeep at Kiriwina airfield, and with increasingly frayed tempers, tried to resolve the problem.

Unlike the six torpedo-bomber officers around him, Hewitt wanted the attack to go ahead, and with time running out, suggested that just three aircraft could do the job originally assigned to 12. Hewitt apparently asked Quinn whether he was prepared to proceed with three aircraft, and when the flight lieutenant replied that he was, Nicoll reportedly said that he himself would go if anyone did. Quinn and Price volunteered to accompany him. Hewitt was disappointed that Nicoll did not call for more men—even the whole squadron—to join him. Nicoll had won the Sword of Honour for best cadet at Point Cook in June 1938, and his decision to keep it to three seems to have been a case of 'noblesse oblige'. Before leaving Australia he had told the unit chaplain that he would not permit his highly trained unit to be used as a 'suicide squadron'.[24]

When they took off just after midnight, the three maintained formation through a storm, and as they neared Rabaul, the weather cleared. Nicoll led them over the harbour in line astern, at 100 feet and as fast as they could fly. Intense anti-aircraft fire met them, with dazzling blue, red and orange tracers its visible manifestation. Evading the searchlights, Nicoll dropped his torpedo which, though he could not observe the result, struck a tanker. Relieved of the torpedo's great weight, he flew just above the rooftops of Rabaul's buildings, hoping the enemy would not fire and risk hitting their own accommodation. Nevertheless, as he reached the outskirts, an explosion caved in a bomb-bay door. He evaded small-arms fire and possibly two enemy night fighters by violent diving, climbing and weaving.

Price flew towards the middle of the main source of the flak barrage, a line of cruisers. No trace of his aircraft was ever found: it was apparently blown apart. Quinn manoeuvred wildly to avoid the flak and searchlights and was guided towards a lone cruiser by Greentree, who had bravely agreed to replace Quinn's sick navigator. After dropping his torpedo while blinded by searchlights, Quinn took the Beaufort just over the superstructure and masts of the cruiser, followed by the fire of every gun onboard. Cordite fumes from the flak filled the aircraft, and when the Beaufort suddenly began moving erratically, Greentree looked back from the nose towards the pilot, who was throwing up. Greentree joined him and they negotiated the danger area before Quinn flew home, and like Hewitt, who had watched from further up, made it back to base. Quinn and Nicoll received DFCs, Greentree a Distinguished Service Cross. Price was recommended for the VC, but was only Mentioned in Despatches.

The mother of Tom Hooper, a member of Price's crew, wrote to the squadron chaplain that they 'thought the world of their skipper'. She also thanked the chaplain for sending a comforting letter; by contrast, the matter-of-fact official communications had been 'like a douche of cold water after the fearful shock one is dealt by the shattering news of the loss of one's son'.[25] It was a shock to the squadron too, as was apparent in the diary of 8 Squadron armourer Edward Hubbard, who called this day 'very bad and sorry for us'. He had heard that the ack-ack was so strong it was 'a miracle' any survived, that 'it was very senseless to go', but that 'Hewitt ordered them out and so this was the result and very little damage was caused'.[26]

Hewitt ordered Nicoll to be posted away two days after the raid. Hubbard recorded how 'very sorry' 8 Squadron were to hear this, and that in farewelling them Nicoll was clearly 'cut up about it'. Hubbard reported that most of the squadron put in a request to be posted to Nicoll's new unit.[27] That proved unnecessary, for RAAF Headquarters cancelled Hewitt's order and, on the basis of a negative report on morale and discipline among senior officers in No. 9 Operational Group, transferred not Nicoll but Hewitt. The latter returned to his job as Director of Allied Air Intelligence at Allied Air Force Headquarters.

Thus the commander of the most prestigious, significant and active group of RAAF squadrons had been sacked. Looking back, Hewitt felt that he had made the RAAF in New Guinea 'a dynamic entity'—largely true—which had matched the USAAF proportionately to its resources—which is debatable.[28] Hewitt had proved divisive as a leader, and seems not to have been popular, although it was impossible to win over all players in the RAAF hierarchy. Senior officers generally disliked his aggressive—even cocky—manner, and his tendency to make what they considered hasty and contradictory decisions. On the other hand, Middle East veterans who worked closely with Hewitt at No. 9 Group rated him an excellent operational commander. Perhaps most significantly, General Ennis Whitehead of the USAAF described him as doing an 'excellent job', and when Hewitt was sacked, General Kenney declared it 'bad news'.[29] Hewitt got on so well with the Americans that he could actually influence discussion on policy for the whole Allied Air Forces. That influence ended with his replacement by Air Commodore Lukis, who the Americans did not rate so highly and who was unable to prevent Australian forces being allocated more mundane tasks. Thus while Hewitt could not have ensured that the RAAF would accompany the USAAF all the way to Japan, the manner in which he was sacked served to reinforce American feelings that the RAAF was an organisational mess: he was, after all, the man who in April George Jones had recommended to take over RAAF Command!

Hewitt believed a smear campaign from a staff officer was responsible for his sacking, but also blamed Jones. In his memoir he castigated Bill Bostock's vindictiveness and ambition, too, but at the time refused to press for an inquiry into his dismissal. Hewitt had often flown unofficially with his men on missions, and he so enjoyed flying as a gunner in Learmonth's Boston that he later reflected, understandably, that he would have preferred being in an aircrew to commanding 9 Operational Group.

At 8 Squadron's Christmas Eve concert, Nicoll was grateful for the card he received addressed to 'Old Nic', and wished his men well for Christmas. In preparation, a Beaufort with its turret removed had on 22 December returned from the mainland 'loaded with beer'.[30] First, though, ten of the squadron's Beauforts had to negotiate a bombing raid to New Britain. All returned, but as Theo Kleinig landed, a single 250-pound rod extension bomb that had got 'hung up' exploded, killing all four aboard. One of them was Stan Miller. His mother had expected a telegram from him for Christmas, but instead:

> When the door bell rang just on midnight on the 27th ... I answered the door to receive what turned out to be the sad news. What a shock, a blow I will never forget as Stan and I had been life long pals ... He and I have been alone together since he was a tiny babe but now what beautiful memories.[31]

The convoy that Nicoll, Quinn and Price had attacked had been sent from Truk to Rabaul in response to an American landing at Empress Augusta Bay on Bougainville. The noose around Rabaul tightened further when US Marines landed at Cape Gloucester on 26 December, following a diversionary landing on the south coast at Arawe. Among those going ashore at Arawe were 28 Australians of 335 Radar Station, who helped to capture Pilelo Island. Heavy Japanese air attacks on the Cape Gloucester beachhead and supporting task force were ineffectual. When, in January 1944, American troops landed at Saidor, New Guinea, the Allies controlled both sides of the Vitiaz Strait.

No. 9 Group supported these moves, with the Bostons, Beaufighters and 78 Squadron P-40s jumping forward to Kiriwina, and 6 and 100 Squadrons going to Goodenough Island. All three Beaufort squadrons executed a night raid on Rabaul on 4 December. Squadron Leader Quinn, a hero of the charge of the light bombers in November, led six torpedo bombers into the harbour. After Ralph Finlay's torpedo struck a ship, Quinn was dropping another when his aircraft ran into something—perhaps a mast or steel cable. Quinn sustained a broken nose and was thrown into the water with his observer, Ross O'Loghlen.

Next day Hubbard wrote that Quinn was missing believed killed, probably shot down by night fighters. In fact, when Quinn and O'Loghlen were hurled from their aircraft, they reached their self-inflating dinghy, although both were only semi-conscious. There was no sign of their two crewmates. Japanese motorboats were searching the harbour with searchlights for fellow Japanese who had jumped overboard from a bombed ship, but eventually their lights played on the wretched Australians. The dinghy was towed ashore and the airmen put in the custody of naval staff. The Japanese mistreatment of the Australians included beating O'Loghlen with a baseball bat, and, after pummelling Quinn, carrying out a mock execution that concluded with him being knocked unconscious. After four days of harsh interrogation, Quinn and two American airmen were tied up, blindfolded and loaded into a bomber which took them to Japan for further questioning. O'Loghlen was put on a transport ship, and drowned when it was torpedoed. Quinn survived captivity, and achieved the rare distinction of winning the DFC three times: twice in this war, and once more in the Malayan Emergency in 1954. Hewitt recalls that not only Quinn's squadron, but also Hewitt and other RAAF leaders in New Guinea, were 'unbelievably shaken by the loss of Quinn'.[32]

Quinn's was the 19th and last raid by RAAF Beaufort torpedo planes. The reasons for the failure of this weapons system included deficiencies in the training of the aircrew involved, the unsuitability of torpedoes against the shallow-draft, small Japanese vessels typical in the theatre, the inadequacies of the Beaufort, and the lack of facilities for the use of these sensitive weapons in New Guinea. Most important, though, were deficiencies in the torpedoes. The American torpedoes—used because purpose-built British ones were unavailable—were unreliable, and so wide they could only be carried if the Beaufort's bomb doors were left open in flight, thus degrading the aircraft's already unspectacular performance. The Australian government committed itself in 1941 to producing its own torpedoes, but none were delivered until September 1943.

Raids from more effective weapons systems now hit New Britain from all sides. Aircraft of 13 RAAF squadrons joined the pounding of that island's bases and New Ireland. For example, 63 Kittyhawks struck Gasmata with 500-pound bombs on 6 December. In a rare reprisal, a daring Japanese aircraft followed No. 100 Beauforts unobserved all the way back to Goodenough, where it strafed and bombed as the Beauforts landed. After an explosion next to Barry Fuller's Beaufort, ground staff rushed to help. Fuller emerged dazed from a fuselage that resembled the proverbial colander. The navigator, Wilf Jackson, was found dead at his desk. The other two crewmen lay on the ground. One of them, Jack Walsh, had sustained a wound which necessitated the amputation of his left leg.

In one big raid on Rabaul airfields in January, 46 Beauforts dropped 32 tons of bombs for the loss of one aircraft. That aircraft, A9-313, was Jack Goodwin's, which one moment was seen caught in searchlights, and then after an explosion was lost to sight forever. Edward Hubbard, of Goodwin's ground crew, wrote in his diary:

> It was a terrible thing as I was on his kite ever since Canberra and they were a great crew. One thing is thankful and that is that [they] went quickly and that is what they wanted. Good Bye 313 and crew![33]

The father of one of Goodwin's crew, Flight Sergeant Keith 'Sinker' Sinclair, wrote to the chaplain, and said of their deaths: 'I only hope that his and all his cobbers have not made their sacrifices in vain as it seems we did last time.' He said he would always remember that his son had told him that he and his mates were doing what they did so that his nephew and niece 'and thousands like them could play in the sand in peace'.[34]

21 Nuisance raids and bloody good shows

Despite the horrible individual cost, Australian forces were making a small contribution compared with the Americans. The first two weeks of December 1943 brought 263 victory claims for Fifth Air Force in New Britain and New Guinea, the most in any two-week period. In the same fortnight, the RAAF brought down no aircraft, though on 16 December Gordon destroyed one at Timor.

A fairer comparison might be of bomb-loads dropped. Between 21 November and 26 December, the RAAF dropped 205 tons of bombs, while the Fifth Air Force dropped 3296 tons: 16 times as heavy a load. Moreover, from mid-January the RAAF was no longer bombing Rabaul. The establishment of airfields at Augusta Bay brought Rabaul within close range of Admiral Halsey's bombers, so the South Pacific forces concentrated on Rabaul, while 9 Operational Group was confined to the central area of New Britain. Air Commodore Lukis, now commanding No. 9 Group, complained to General Whitehead that there his fighters would not contact enemy aircraft, just as they were not meeting any resistance over Kiriwina. This, he said, was unsettling them. No wonder Australians joked sarcastically that their force was the 'Non-Ops Group'.

The RAAF was impressing in some ways. On 17 January, Lukis was able to send out the strongest RAAF force yet committed against a single target. Seventy-three aircraft—Beauforts, Kittyhawks and Spitfires—attacked enemy facilities near Lindenhafen, New Britain. Similar raids, opposed only by flak, were repeated through January and February. Ian Loudon, commanding 76 Squadron, destroyed an Oscar on the ground at Cape Hoskins in January, but the defenders soon had their revenge. On 22 January, anti-aircraft fire damaged his Kitty in three places. Though oil pressure was nil, and oil covered his windscreen, the Kitty kept going. At one point he was heard to exclaim on his radio: 'I don't know why this bloody thing keeps flying!'[1] Eventually he had to bale out 130 kilometres from Kiriwina, but was rescued by a US PT boat directed to the scene by a Beaufighter.

Just one day after this ordeal Loudon was flying again, escorting Beauforts to Lindenhafen. On 25 January he was buoyant enough to write 'smooth show!!' after he had led another bombing raid. Steege, the very capable commander of No. 73 Fighter Wing, rated Loudon 'exceptional' as a pilot and an 'excellent leader'.[2] Loudon, who was running a rubber plantation with his father in Port Moresby in 1939, was now just 22, but was rather intimidating to less experienced pilots.

No. 22 Squadron fought a series of deadly battles with Japanese guns at a mission house on the Kabu River, near Gasmata. On 22 January two Bostons were lucky to survive dangerous hits there. The following day two more Bostons took on the same 'ack-ack'. While one flew top cover, Chris Sugden made three runs at the target. The intense fire wounded his rear-gunner, Harry Hughes, in both arms. Sugden had to crash-land at base.

A week later the squadron CO, Jim Emerton, made a sortie to photograph the Japanese guns. That afternoon, Steege was walking to a church service with Padre Powell and said: 'Did you know that Wing-Commander Emerton went in to-day?' Powell's heart sank, for he had been singularly impressed by Emerton's 'unusually noble soul'.[3] The 22 Squadron commander's kindness had been apparent after the death of Sergeant Roy Henkel, a transport man of the squadron who died of burns sustained in an accident, just after his tour of duty had officially ended. Emerton, whose squadron raised £150 for Henkel's bereaved family, personally arranged tropical flowers on Henkel's casket. As a pilot he had flown 1800 hours in 24 different types of aircraft. Hewitt considered the quiet but determined Emerton 'as fine an officer as I have served with', and a worthy successor to Learmonth.[4] But the dead-eye gunners had shot him down. Killed also was his observer, Terence Gawne, who had earlier flown with the USAAF's 90 Squadron.

In April, when US Marines captured the gun positions at Kabu, the defenders fought to the last man. The Marines found the whole area pitted with bomb craters.

RAAF Catalinas made 'nuisance raids' on Kavieng between December 1943 and February 1944. Damien Miller's was one of five Cats that raided on 29 December. After 'stooging' about for half an hour above the target, waiting for the other four to drop their bombs, he twice tried to make his attack, but was caught in searchlights that blinded and disoriented the navigator. They were determined to drop their bombs on a third run, but then flak put the starboard motor out of action. So far from home, they knew they were in trouble. Miller feathered the propeller and ordered all excess weight to be thrown overboard. After this they needed to navigate by compass, and, in the dark and a severe electrical storm, became lost. They thought they were over New Britain, but when dawn came, they realised it was another island—another hostile one. With the aircraft at just 500 feet, heavy enemy fire suddenly opened up at point-blank range. 'Shit—we are gone this time' said Miller, neatly expressing the fears of everyone on board.[5] Yet they got away, and were able to fly on, barely above stalling speed and just 500 feet up. Eventually, with the fuel gauge on nil, they landed at Langemak Bay, near friendly troops around Finschhafen. Surviving this ten-hour 40-minute trip on one engine inspired Miller to make a comment that entered Catalina folklore: 'I have made two friends for life, Mr Pratt and Mr Whitney.'[6] The crew used scrounged bits of metal, parts of a wrecked Liberator and components sent from Port Moresby to get the motor going again and return to base, where their efforts were celebrated in the officer's mess as 'a bloody good show'.[7]

A tragic accident cost lives when a flare in a Catalina returning from another raid exploded and set the aircraft alight. The pilot, Squadron Leader John Todd, made a forced landing at Jacquinot Bay, New Britain. The crew of ten made it ashore, where Japanese troops challenged them. Four airmen escaped into the jungle and were later rescued. The remaining six were captured, and all but one—Brian Stacy—died in captivity. Todd died of illness, four others allegedly in a bombing raid.

Air interceptions even from Rabaul were now rare, and by mid-February 1944 the few serviceable Japanese aircraft at Rabaul had been withdrawn to Truk, leaving air supremacy to the Allies. Rabaul had been a graveyard for more than 800 Japanese aircraft—one estimate puts it at nearly twice that—many of them sent there over recent months. The RAAF, especially its Beauforts, had played a modest but material part in that victory. Their night raids had also maintained psychological pressure on the garrison. Rabaul was still strongly held on the ground, but its offensive ability had gone. A sign of the garrison's necessarily defensive thinking was the great tunnel complex the Japanese now proceeded to build there. Their isolation was reflected too in the fact that after a cargo-carrying submarine docked there in April 1944, no sizeable vessel reached Rabaul.

On 29 February 1944, MacArthur's forces landed at Los Negros in the Admiralty Islands. This completed the isolation of Rabaul. The RAAF again provided indirect support for this operation, while the three squadrons of No. 73 Wing gave fighter cover. Lukis protested unavailingly against the allocation of this wing, believing rightly that its fighters would have little to do. Japanese ground forces defended the island vigorously, and when the ground party of 77 Squadron arrived in a convoy bringing reinforcements, the ships became entangled in a shooting match with Japanese forces not 300 metres away. When one of the first Australians to come ashore asked an American where the front line was, the reply came: 'Boy, you're right in it!'[8] As the Australians began unloading 600 tons of squadron equipment, Mitchell bombers struck enemy positions just 300 metres distant. Three days later Momote airfield had been repaired so as to allow the first RAAF Kittyhawks to arrive.

Throughout the month of the Admiralties campaign, the Australians encountered no enemy aircraft, which indicated the complete Allied air supremacy in the New Guinea–New Britain area. The RAAF aircraft did provide valuable direct support to American ground forces in destroying the enemy garrison, but the short strip, created by the Japanese for their lighter aircraft, was not well suited to Kittyhawks.

No. 79 Squadron found Los Negros cooler and shadier than Kiriwina, but on 16 April suffered one of their worst days. The CO, Squadron Leader Max Bott, was due to return to Australia, but as he and his replacement made to take off in their Spitfires for a familiarisation flight, there was a collision: Bott was killed, Squadron Leader Pilcher injured, and both aircraft destroyed. Amidst driving rain Bott was buried that afternoon in a moving ceremony attended by the whole squadron. It was Bott's 30th birthday. That same day, 16 April, was also 'Black Sunday' for the Fifth Air Force, as 32 airmen were killed when caught in a frightful weather front when returning from a raid.

Five RAAF radar stations were sent to the Admiralty Islands. No. 340 had the misfortune to be sent to tiny Bat Island, where seagulls, rats and wild pigs produced a fetid environment. Before the station was withdrawn, two Australians and four Americans died of the dreaded scrub typhus there, while others contracted it. The Admiralty Island base looked precariously placed, but its safety was assured when the Japanese withdrew their fleet from Truk in February 1944.

In response to a request from General Kenney, the RAAF created a mobile 'air task force' of three fighter squadrons and three Vultee Vengeance squadrons. The force was designated No. 10 Operational Group and assigned to the outstanding Group Captain Scherger. No. 10 Group's purpose was to keep up with the Allied advance, while No. 9 Group would stay in eastern New Guinea as a garrison and communication force. Scherger had orders to maintain good relations with the Americans, and to keep this part of the RAAF up with the advance towards Japan.

By January 1944, No. 10 Group was at Nadzab. RAAF works squadrons, labouring round the clock for 27 days, had constructed for the group No. 4 Airfield, soon to be known as 'Newton Field' after Bill Newton. They also created dispersal facilities for up to 200 aircraft. No. 4 Squadron was still there, leading in attacks by American squadrons in support of Australian Army units. For a few weeks, No. 10 Group also attacked Japanese ground forces. Over a nine-day period, Vengeances made accurate dive-bombing attacks in support of Australian troops fighting for the formidable Shaggy Ridge–Kankiryo Saddle features. Perhaps the Vultees' most notable achievement came on 31 January when Richard Lewis, who had been an RAF Spitfire pilot in the Battle of Britain and would one day command 24 Squadron, led three Vengeances through enemy flak to destroy a significant Japanese bridge at Bogadjim.

Kittyhawks of No. 78 Wing—Nos 75, 78 and 80 Squadrons—escorted USAAF bombers and patrolled the Markham Valley. Australian fighter pilots resented the American command for assigning them such mundane tasks, although Scherger argued that all American squadrons initially did the same. In late January, No. 10 Group suffered its first fatalities. Max Stirling, stylish victor over two aircraft early the previous year, collided with Stan Hunt's Kittyhawk as both dived to strafe an enemy-held island. Neither survived the mid-air explosion.

Twenty-three Vengeances were ordered to attack enemy anti-aircraft positions at Hansa Bay in late February. Howard James-Martin and his observer Alec Boxall were flying one of their first operations, in a 23 Squadron Vengeance. After bad weather threatened to scotch the flight, eventually some ten crewmen got aboard a single jeep, which was needed to take them to their widely dispersed aircraft. Boxall remembered seeing Norm Burnell, a pilot, sitting in front of him. Climbing aboard the 'Vultee' was not easy for the observers, who had to clamber up a searingly hot metal fuselage, but it was nothing compared to what was to follow.

James-Martin was told that there was just one enemy anti-aircraft gun, but that it was camouflaged and accurate. On approaching the target the attackers quickly realised that there were actually three anti-aircraft positions, all within 500 metres of each other. Heavy flak greeted the attackers with 'box barrages'. The explosions were jet black, giving off acrid smoke. The Vengeances dived from about 10–12,000 feet at two-second intervals. James-Martin's aircraft, the third in, turned on its back in regulation fashion and then pulled away and dived as close as possible to the vertical. He used his gunsight to drop his two 500-pound bombs at about 2000 feet. Then, pulling up the nose and retracting his dive brakes, he and Boxall received a jolt in the back as the speed rose suddenly from 650 to an astonishing 925 kilometres per hour. As they pulled out of the dive, the 'Gs' or 'g-force' affected Boxall drastically for a few seconds—pulling his hands down from the guns, draining the blood from his face and making him feel as if his chin was on his knees. Then he strafed for all he was worth. Almost directly underneath them they saw Burnell and the Army Liaison Officer with him crash into the water. Heading off, James-Martin flew 'right across this damn bay with every Jap around firing at us'.[9] Boxall saw ack-ack rounds, which he likened to big oranges, curling towards them and then whooshing past at incredible speed. He ducked instinctively, for the shells looked to be headed for the centre of their aircraft. This was the only time James-Martin ever pushed the throttle 'through the gate', that is, past a flap which signalled that the engine was being thrashed to a point it could theoretically only take for five minutes. He also used every trick and ounce of energy he could muster to move the Vengeance up, down and sideways.

As they left the bay, James-Martin saw another Vengeance, crewed by 'the two Macs'—McDonald and McAllister—trailing black smoke for hundreds of metres, and he edged in close alongside. Boxall wanted to help, but could only make sign language to the crew of the stricken Vengeance, which lost engine power, then dropped into cloud. When the aircraft crashed, McAllister was killed instantly. Frank McDonald survived, but broke his leg on striking a tree in the descent. He was cared for by friendly locals, but was then betrayed and taken to a Japanese headquarters, where he was killed with a pistol. Shot with him was a fellow Vengeance pilot, Leslie Stewart, who had survived ditching his aircraft in the sea.

When 62 Vengeances and Kittyhawks struck enemy airfields at Alexishafen and Madang on 28 February, they must have made a spectacular sight. Up close, though, the airfields appeared to the Vengeance crews to be already disabled. That month 78 Squadron was the busiest in No. 10 Group, racking up 1007 hours, as opposed to the 600 that was typical of RAAF fighter squadrons. That 600-hour figure was based on RAF standards, whereas General Whitehead demanded up to 1500 hours per month for his Fifth Air Force squadrons. He required the RAAF squadrons to vastly increase their flying hours too, if they wanted a share of the confined airfield space in New Guinea. Scherger obliged: the number of pilots and aircraft per squadron were increased to 30 and 24 respectively.

No. 78 Squadron suffered its first fatality on 2 March. Eugene Weber was flying hard at an anti-aircraft position when his Kittyhawk caught fire, lost a wing and then exploded in mid-air. A member of the ground staff lamented the loss of 'one of our best pilots'.[10]

Flak put holes in four Vengeances during a big raid on Rempi village, on 8 March, but the raid was noteworthy as the last mission flown by RAAF Vengeances. General MacArthur's headquarters that day ordered all Vengeance squadrons back to Australia to convert to Liberators, and for the three Kittyhawk squadrons of 10 Group to move to Cape Gloucester. This sudden and surprising move, made after enormous effort had been exerted to make No. 10 Group operational, occurred for several reasons. One was the expansion of the USAAF in the South-West Pacific Area.

Between March 1943 and March 1944, the RAAF there had grown from 34 to 45 squadrons, while the Fifth Air Force had grown from 36 to 82 squadrons. Furthermore, the American aircraft were largely modern types such as Lightnings, well suited to operations Kenney was planning in the Wewak–Hollandia area. The forward airfields in New Guinea were congested, so someone had to move. Scherger acknowledged that had the Vengeance squadrons been American units, they still would have gone. He said the Vengeances were proving mechanically unreliable, had a short range, and were inferior to Kittyhawks, which could carry the same load but also strafe and operate without an escort.

Logical though Kenney's thinking may have been, his rejection of the 'Vultee' was a blow to Australian prestige. Australia had ordered 400 Vengeances from America, and had paid a great deal for the 344 it had received when it cancelled the order. By the time Vengeances began arriving in numbers, they were obsolete. On the other hand, the promise of Liberator heavy bombers on the RAAF order of battle represented the fulfilment of a dream. Both the air force and government had wanted such bombers throughout the war, partly to create a 'balanced', state-of-the art and world-class force. In 1940, the government had raised the possibility of obtaining Flying Fortresses, but Sir Charles Burnett had replied that the B-17 was too expensive and too vulnerable. The fact that they were not British was probably relevant too. Now heavy bombers were considered desirable, not only for doctrinal reasons but also as a means of allowing Australia to participate in the coming offensives towards Japan, in which long-range aircraft would be essential. These hopes were misplaced, for while Australians believed the B-24s would increase RAAF participation in the drive on Japan, they had the opposite purpose. Kenney intended to send them to Darwin, thereby releasing the American bombers based there for more important work further north.

By mid-March, No. 78 Wing's Kittyhawks had moved to New Britain, flying ground-support missions for the 1st US Marine Division, striking ground targets and barges and assisting friendly patrol boats. For Group Captain Brookes, commanding the wing, it was a sweet reversal of fortune, for in January 1942 he had commanded the Wirraways at Rabaul when Japanese marines were landing. The Australians liked their base at Cape Gloucester, and were grateful to be enjoying American rations, cigarettes and toilet goods. A Warrant Officer of 78 Wing wrote that 'The Marines are extra good guys and have made the boys feel at home very smartly.'[11] Major-General Rupertus, commanding the Marines on New Britain, complimented the Kittyhawks on their accurate dive-bombing and strafing after accompanying them on a strike.

The friendship was tested on 27 March when Kittyhawks mistakenly attacked two US patrol boats, leaving 11 killed, missing or wounded. In April, the hard-working wing was ordered to prepare for another move, to support an American amphibious invasion at Hollandia. The promise of air combat made it bearable to be leaving their tropical paradise.

From Kiriwina, Bostons were able to wreak low-flying havoc. For example, two Bostons intercepted Japanese boats fleeing after US Marines landed at Talasea. Strafing at a characteristic height of just 50 feet, the Bostons sent more than 30 Japanese to their doom in water reportedly 'stained red with blood'.[12] At this height, 22 Squadron could often see its victims up close: one was shot dead off a bicycle, another while fishing from a prahu.

More operational RAAF squadrons were in April 1943 committed to anti-submarine and other defensive work in Australia than at the front. On 5 May 1943, an impressive 46 aircraft patrolled the east coast between Port Phillip Bay in Victoria and Thursday Island in the Torres Strait. Nine days later, none of these aircraft spotted survivors of the sinking of the Australian hospital ship *Centaur*, which had been torpedoed by a Japanese submarine off Queensland. No survivors were observed until 34 hours after the sinking. The press questioned this long time lag, and measures were taken to improve anti-submarine patrolling. Nevertheless, for all their efforts, the Beauforts, Ansons, Wirraways, Beaufighters and Catalinas were unable to achieve any confirmed submarine kills, and the unexpectedly high losses of Beauforts posed logistical problems. Curtin pointed out in May that only 121 of the 303 Beauforts so far delivered to the RAAF were still fit for service. By 1943 there was a public image of the 'Bogey Beaufort': so many Beauforts were lost in accidents in Australia that a judicial inquiry was held into their manufacture. No single cause was found to be responsible.

From their base in Cairns in April 1943, the Catalinas began sowing mines in enemy waters. These were landmines—magnetic, acoustic or pressure—rather than floating mines. They weighed more than 1000 pounds

(453 kilograms) each and were carried under the wings, so the armourers who attached them from unsteady barges had a difficult job. US submarines had been doing this mining, but hated it because it necessitated entering shallow water, where they were vulnerable. Once mines were sown in shallow water, Japanese vessels had to enter deeper waters, where the submarines could hunt them. Nos 11 and 20 Squadrons were allotted to this additional activity. Though slow, they were ideal for the task in that they could carry heavy loads—up to four mines—and fly more than 3200 kilometres. It was dangerous work, though, not least because to drop the mines accurately the Cats had to fly just 300 or 400 feet up. They also had to fly level and straight, and thus predictably for enemy gunners, on a predetermined flight path, because accurately dropping the mines on and around a datum point was considered essential. If at this low altitude the aircraft was seriously damaged, the crew's parachutes would not have time to open. And serious damage was a real prospect—flying at a height where even small-arms fire could hurt them, and close to well-armed and alert enemy naval vessels in the harbours that were common targets for mine-laying.

Led by David Vernon, eight Cats flew the first raid, on Silver Sound, near Kavieng. The raid, following a ten-hour flight from Cairns via Milne Bay, occurred in full moonlight. This was done so as to avoid collisions, but it also left the Black Cats—so-called because of the black 'war paint' they now bore—beautifully silhouetted for the enemy gunners. Each dropped its two mines and got home safely, but as Vernon flew over a Japanese ship, anti-aircraft guns tore five holes in the starboard float and four large holes in the port wing. It was soon decided that moonless nights gave the Cats more safety from flak and night fighters, and made little difference to navigation.

Vernon flew a more traditional but even more dramatic flight in June 1943. The task was to bomb Babo. As they made their second run over Babo's T-shaped strip, an anti-aircraft shell entered the Cat just above the second pilot's feet, and left via a fresh hole above Vernon's head. All the aircraft lights, including those on the instrument panel, went out. Still under fire, Vernon managed to get the aircraft away. Fluid running down Vernon's neck turned out not to be blood, but was nearly as bad: oil from the automatic pilot system, which was thus defunct. They now faced a ten-hour trip to Horn Island in complete darkness apart from the navigator's torch. The navigator, Arthur Cleland, had to identify a star above the horizon, to which Vernon had to steer directly. Once that star was no longer on the required line, Cleland would point to another star for Vernon to follow. Normally Vernon would have had two co-pilots to call upon. However, one was absent as he had slept in, and Vernon had gone through with a threat to leave him behind if he did so. The other was on his first operational flight and was not yet up to this difficult task. When Vernon reached Horn Island and got out of his seat for the first time in 11 hours, his legs gave way.

By September 1943, when the first Cat was lost on mine-laying missions, the RAAF had laid 235 mines. At the end of September, three Catalinas twice mined Pomelaa harbour in the Celebes. Denis Lawrence's Cat had sustained many hits there in two visits, the second time from a warship. Wing Commander Gordon Stilling, CO of 20 Squadron, set out to sink this vessel in a Catalina armed with torpedoes, a top-secret application at the time. Accompanying him as a passenger was Lieutenant-Commander 'Pally' Carr of the RAN, who had played a leading part in directing RAAF mine-laying operations. Carr later gave a sober but chilling account of this mission:

> We arrived over Pomala about midnight on Friday 1st October, picked out the ship and made our approach to drop the first torpedo, height about 120 feet, and about 1200 yards from the ship which was only about ½ mile from the shore. We dropped our torpedo, which unfortunately did not run properly. Just as we were about to turn to do another run, the ship and shore opened fire on us with light AA and we were hit straight away, the main tanks caught fire and we hit the water. It all happened very quickly—I remember very little from the moment of fire being opened to finding myself on the bottom of the sea. I came to the surface and found one other floating—Pilot Officer McDiarmed, who was badly wounded. There was no one else in sight though the tail of the Cat was sticking up out of the water—the main tanks were still burning beneath the surface and there were plenty of flames on the water. Later I did see one body, but whoever it was, was already dead. We were picked up by the Japanese after about ½ an hour . . . The only reason that I got away with it was that I was leaning right out of the gun blister in the rear part of the hull of the aircraft and was thrown out when we hit the water ... all those inside the aircraft would have been

> killed instantly when the aircraft hit. McDiarmed was in the gunner's position in the nose, which was open. He was badly wounded in the legs and after having one amputated by the Japanese, he died during the night. I was given a pretty rough time for a while and spent about a fortnight at Kendari nearby, before being taken to Sourabaya and then to Japan.[13]

Another attempt to use the Catalina for torpedo attacks ended badly, with the pilot severely wounded and the aircraft heavily damaged, so the concept was abandoned.

Despite the loss of Carr, the mine-laying program was paying dividends. The mining of Silver Sound twice led the Japanese to close Kavieng in late 1943, while Australian mines sank three ships in that port in September and November. The wheel was turning inexorably towards an Allied victory, even though by the end of 1943, the Japanese home islands were still a huge distance away from Allied bases. The cold hard statistics of aircraft production said that Japan must lose the air war. In 1943 Japan manufactured 16,295 aircraft; by November 1943 the US was producing 8800 aircraft per *month*. By the end of 1943, the Allies would probably have a numerical superiority of planes of at least two to one. Japan's aircraft production would nearly double in 1944, but its aircraft losses would be ruinous. As to Australian production, in December 1943 this constituted just 52 aircraft—all Beauforts, Boomerangs and Wirraways. However, more advanced locally built Beaufighters and Mosquitos were coming.

The passing of the threat from Rabaul gave General MacArthur more freedom of movement, and the success of his audacious move into the Admiralties encouraged him to make daring leaps to fulfil his promised return to the Philippines. Australian airmen and politicians wondered whether the RAAF would jump with him.

22 Burma and India

Burma was critical to the war with Japan. It constituted the Allies' only ground-supply route to China and was a buffer protecting India. That buffer looked thin in December 1941, when Japanese forces entered Burma from Thailand. The minuscule air force in their way consisted mainly of an RAF Buffalo squadron, No. 67, and a P-40 Tomahawk squadron of Colonel Claire Chennault's American Volunteer Group, the famous 'Flying Tigers'. All were based at Mingaladon, and 67 Squadron included some Australians, as did the other RAF Squadron in Burma, No. 60, which was armed with Blenheims. When 80 JAAF aircraft attacked Rangoon on 23 December, they inflicted 2000 casualties on the civilian population, but the defending Buffaloes and Tomahawks shot down 27 aircraft for the loss of just six. The Buffalo pilots included Australian Geoff Norton.

British air reinforcements rushed to Burma from the Middle East included two Blenheim bomber squadrons, Nos 113 and 45. Both were crewed predominantly by Australians, and within hours of arriving in January 1942 took off for a night raid on Bangkok harbour. They bombed individually, each negotiating heavy anti-aircraft fire and many search-lights, but all returned safely with news of explosions and fires. Among them was an all-Australian crew: George Bassingthwaite, Deuchar Gordon and Walter McKerracher. All three would be decorated for bravery in this campaign. One of their notable missions occurred in May 1942 when, despite flak so fierce that they 'were nearly blasted out of the sky', they dropped supplies to Allied troops on the Chindwin River, gathered vital intelligence, and photographed enemy shipping.[1]

No. 45 Squadron's first leader in Burma, a British wing commander, was, according to Australian Flight Lieutenant Wal McLellan, 'hated by No. 45 crews and he made no secret of the fact that he detested Australians'.[2] McLellan transferred to No. 113 Squadron, which in under two months flew 174 bombing sorties plus many reconnaissance flights. Sid Lee, of Adelaide, flew with Nos 45 and 113 Squadrons. A wartime account made the 26-year-old sound like an Arthurian knight: 'always cheerful, always ready with a sympathetic word. He was intelligent, quiet-spoken, courageous, good-looking, tolerant.' He was said also to be modest, and to be nursing an 'intense, seldom-voiced desire' to beat the Germans and Japanese.[3] He was close friends with his crewmen, observer 'Schnoz' Brett of the RNZAF, and WAG 'Yorkie' Walker. With them he flew a high-ranking RAF officer over large tracts of Free China, guided only by a rudimentary Chinese map. On 4 March his Blenheim was bringing up the rear of four Blenheims flying line astern and striking enemy defences along the Sittang River, when four Nakajima 'Tojo' fighters appeared. All concentrated on Lee's aircraft. A bullet struck him in the jaw, blowing much of it away, and the aircraft crash-landed. Brett was thrown through the nose glass and killed. As Lee and Walker staggered from the burning aircraft, the four fighters roared in and strafed. Lee was hit again and fell into the flames, dead. Only Walker escaped.

The Middle East reinforcement of Burma also included RAF Hurricanes. Among several Australian Hurricane pilots based at Mingaladon airfield, near Rangoon, was Pilot Officer 'Jack' Storey, who on his first combat sortie, in January 1942, shot down a Nate. Astonished airmen below saw this Nate's pilot aim his spluttering aircraft at a Blenheim on the ground; he just missed. Storey was also accurate in a big dogfight in February. He led four Hurricanes to try to get between numerous enemy fighters and the sun. However, three enemy Nates pre-empted this move and fell upon the Hurricanes. Storey spiralled down before clawing up towards his surprised opponents and catching one with a lethal burst. After seeing that Nate crash, Storey was attacked by two more. Again he spiralled and climbed, and once more downed an enemy. On returning to base he had two confirmed kills and a further two 'probables'. He was soon made flight commander, despite his lowly rank. His British squadron leader described Storey 'not only as a pilot of exceptional ability, but as one of the best leaders of a formation I have ever seen'.[4] Storey and the other Hurricane pilots operated from makeshift 'kutcha' airstrips, cut into the hard but rough paddy fields. His greatest day would be 5 March 1943, when he was credited with destroying three Oscars near Akyab, and received an immediate DFC.

Naturally, not every Australian was as comfortable taking on enemy fighters as Storey. In his first battle 'Barney' Barnett, of 136 Squadron, found himself badly outmanoeuvred by a nimble Oscar near the squadron's base at Chittagong. In a move familiar to Kittyhawk pilots in New Guinea, he put stick and rudder 'in one corner' and dived away in his bullet-riddled Hurricane. 'It was all pretty sproggish,' he later said of his and his fellow-pilots' efforts in this initial engagement.[5] Barnett had another narrow escape in 1943. While escorting Blenheims, he suddenly heard 'sharp explosions, fist size holes appeared in the emergency panel on the right hand side of the cockpit, instruments were shattered, the engine stopped and the aircraft was spinning.'[6] He would bale out over enemy lines, and reach safety after a series of adventures, which included evading Japanese pursuers in dense mangrove swamp and swimming across the wide Mayu River. In 1944, as a veteran pilot, Barnett would destroy a 'Hamp' with his Spitfire.

As Japanese troops bore down on Rangoon in 1942, the Allied air and ground crews worked under intense strain and heat. The 'dry season' sun could render metal too hot to touch, and sometimes ammunition exploded prematurely. Nevertheless, the continuing success of Allied aerial operations over Burma kept morale high.

Japanese aircraft made a major attempt to win air superiority over Rangoon on 24–26 February 1942. Again they were bloodied, losing at least 37 aircraft. One Allied raid caught a group of Nates coming in to land on their strip at Moulmein. Australian Hurricane pilot 'Bush' Cotton fired a one-second burst into a Nate that was about 2000 feet up. This was enough to flip the slow Japanese fighter over and drop it like a stone. Cotton climbed and then came down towards the strip, where he spotted and destroyed another Nate that was just touching down. When a Japanese air raid hit the Allied airfield at Mingaladon later that day, Cotton was among the No. 17 Squadron RAF pilots who took off to intercept. He shot down one bomber and then took on the arriving fighter escort. As he dived towards them, machine-gun fire came up and through the left side of the Hurricane. One bullet broke his left knee, and 129 others hit the aircraft. He still made a perfect landing, though when his Hurricane stopped he collapsed over the controls. Cotton, who had been a member of No. 1 Course of the EATS course in Canada, would eventually command 17 Squadron.

After their reverses over Rangoon, so different to the stunning Japanese air victories in Malaya, Japanese aircraft avoided Rangoon's airspace until the city fell to Japanese ground forces on 8 March. That month, one unescorted Blenheim of 45 Squadron was attacked by 16 fighters within 25 minutes. Kenneth Gardiner, an Australian gunner, shot down one fighter, but was incapacitated when an explosive projectile blasted splinters from his gun into his arm. The Blenheim got home, carrying 57 bullet holes.

Another Blenheim and its all-Australian crew was that of Douglas Smyth, his navigator Denys Golder and gunner Jeffrey Alt. Smyth was such a fine pilot that after he flew Air Vice-Marshal Stevenson, Air Officer Commanding Burma, during the evacuation from Rangoon, he was told that he and his crew were to be allocated to Stevenson whenever possible. This was a blow to Smyth, who wanted operational flying. He complained to the Squadron CO and then to Stevenson himself, who said that when Smyth was not needed to transport him, his crew could go on operations. Smyth was continually asking Stevenson, 'Do you want me today?', and if the answer was negative, seeking an operation with 45 Squadron.

On 11 March, Smyth's crew was not needed, so were sent on a low-level reconnaissance mission, from Magwe to the Nyaunglebin area. They were permitted to strafe any Japanese troops they saw. They observed many, and while making a second run over a large group of Japanese on a road just 50 feet below, Smyth yelled over the intercom: 'I'm hit'. Golder left off strafing and rushed to Smyth, who was slumped over the controls and apparently trying to hold them. Nevertheless, the Blenheim was diving, and Golder pulled back the stick, somehow avoiding a collision with the trees. Alt came forward from his turret and pulled Smyth out. Golder took the controls, trying to recall what to do from the nine hours he had spent as an air cadet in a Moth. They flew due north without navigation. Alt discovered that ground fire had hit Smyth in the heart, killing him. Alt had only flown for one hour, but he and Golder brought the aircraft back to their airfield at Magwe, where they dropped a message saying they proposed to try to land. They asked that a green light be shone if this was approved, a red light if not. The message drifted away from the airfield, and a red flare went up as a signal to delay the landing. Golder and Alt did not know this and decided to bale out. Taking the aircraft up, they put Smyth in a parachute so that his body would not remain in the aircraft, then jumped to safety. General Alexander, commanding the British Army in Burma, had witnessed the baling out and personally commended Alt and Golder. They were transferred to Stevenson's personal crew.[7]

No such luck for the all-Australian crew of No. 113 Squadron's last serviceable Blenheim, captained by Les Connor. They never returned to Magwe from a reconnaissance on 14 March, and were probably killed in a crash near Mingaladon.

Just before Rangoon fell to the Japanese on 8 March, Allied air forces left for India. The Japanese Army had driven all British and Indian ground forces from Burma by 17 May 1942. On 5 April Japan's main aircraft carrier battle group, under Vice Admiral Nagumo, sent 50 bombers and 35 fighters to attack Colombo. The Hurricane squadrons that opposed them numbered Australians among their ranks. One of them, Garth Caswell, was seen by colleagues to dive through the enemy bomber formation three times, shooting down two. He was killed in the third attack. Allan Browne, a pint-sized car salesman from Hay in New South Wales, was observed downing one Zero and then, after tackling another, diving in flames into a paddy field while his doomed opponent crashed in the distance. These were two of 21 Hurricanes lost that day, for seven enemy planes destroyed.

RAAF airmen were in the thick of the fighting when Nagumo struck again, at Trincomalee on 9 April. Lloyd Rawnsley was flying one of three 261 Squadron Hurricanes vectored towards a group of 91 Kates and 41 Zeros. The Hurricanes dived on an unsuspecting group of escorts, with Rawnsley and the flight commander each bringing down a Zero. In the melee that followed, Rawnsley's aircraft was hit by 'friendly' anti-aircraft fire, but he contrived to pour a five-second burst into another Zero before a cannon shell forced him to crash-land at China Bay airfield. He had been wounded in the ankle and an enemy fighter was strafing him, but an English pilot, Eric Edsall, risked his life by running to the Hurricane and pulling Rawnsley clear.

Another Australian in 261 Squadron, Sergeant K.A.S. 'Kas' Mann, had been preparing for this day. He had infuriated the RAF Station Commander by damaging the wheel of a Hurricane when practising, but now managed to claim a probable—a Zero flying off with fuel leaking from both bullet-ridden wing tanks—before himself being shot into the sea. While swimming for shore, Mann saw another Hurricane tackling six Zeros: the pilot, Sydneysider Bill Pearce, was killed. Almost exactly a year later, Mann's fortunes had changed and Sir Richard Peirse, the Air Officer Commanding-in-Chief in India, referred to him in a 'Command Mention'. The term 'superb flying' was used in describing his achievement of two 'destroyed' and one 'probable' in a tussle with three Oscars.[8] Mann's own irretrievably damaged aircraft received 70 bullet holes.

The bravery of Commonwealth aircrew was never clearer than in an attack by No. 11 RAF Squadron's Blenheims against Nagumo's fleet on that 9 April. The ten aircraft found the target, comprising 40 ships, and were battered by torrential anti-aircraft fire and 50 fighters. Five Blenheims were soon shot down, and the remainder somehow got away. Nine RAAF men died in this hopeless charge.

Beaufighters arrived in India in late 1942, and were allotted to the newly reformed 27 Squadron RAF. The unit's first commander was an Australian, Wing Commander Harry Daish, who led the Beaus in their first operation. Within six months the unit had destroyed 50 locomotives. In one notably destructive raid, Flight Sergeant Ernest Trigwell, a Western Australian, hit ten railway trucks and 11 wagons with cannon and machine-gun fire. One of this 'train busting' unit's flight commanders was Australian 'Snowy' Swift, DFC, who on one occasion came through cloud to find Japanese troops holding a ceremonial parade. They ignored him, but when he flew over a second time and let fly with cannons and machine guns, the survivors ran for their lives.

In January 1943 an Australian Beaufighter pilot, Charles Crombie of 176 Squadron, showed unusual determination and courage over Calcutta. As previously mentioned, Crombie was already an ace in the Middle East. On this evening he approached a group of enemy bombers, which fired from close range, setting fire to one of his motors. He continued towards them, shooting one down and, after ordering his observer to bale out, pursued the others. When his petrol tank blew up, he too baled out. His clothing was now alight, but he made it to safety. He believed he had taken on four Sallys and shot down at least two, but Japanese records suggest that there were three bombers, all Lilys, of which he destroyed just one.[9] The DSO that he received for this and other night fighting operations was well deserved. Short and light, Crombie was well suited to flying in a cramped fighter cockpit. A squadron leader by 1945, he would die in a Beaufighter accident at Williamtown, New South Wales, 11 days after the war ended. His one-year-old son would not grow up to hear his father tell him his remarkable war stories.

Outdated Blenheim bombers continued working into 1943. Wing Commander Pennington-Legh's crew died in an extraordinary incident in June. After surviving a crash-landing induced by flak, they were killed by the inhabitants of a nearby village. Pennington-Legh's crew included two Australians, Bernard Burnley and Bob Ingram, who had received DFCs for distinguished work in the Middle East, Ceylon and Burma. In a bitter postscript, 16 aircraft bombed and strafed the village in reprisal.

A more orthodox 11 Squadron raid hit the major Japanese base at Meiktila on 5 April 1943. For mutual protection the Blenheims stayed close together—too close, as RAAF Flight Sergeant Harvey Besley recorded:

> ... the section leader behind us let his aircraft rise a little too high. I saw the plane a split second before it made contact with the belly of my plane. His propeller cut into the right side of my cockpit. It must have killed my navigator almost on impact ... The sleeve was completely torn off my jacket, and my right arm badly gashed ...[10]

The propeller also hit Besley's fuel tank, which blew up. As the aircraft broke into three pieces, Besley slipped his seat harness and jumped. He could not find his ripcord but, fighting back shock and panic, realised it would be behind him. He pulled it, felt the jerk of the opening canopy and floated down 12,000 feet—towards the enemy airfield. On landing in a paddy field, he quickly hid his parachute and tore strips off his singlet to bandage his bleeding arm. This 'bandage' would remain in place for weeks. He made for a village, but Japanese troops captured him. Though mistreated, he survived.

Only one Japanese fighter, an Oscar, had tried to intercept the Meiktila raiders. Its pilot died of wounds sustained in a dogfight with RAAF Flying Officer Russ Bowes, flying an escorting Hurricane. After this success Bowes was awarded a DFC, promoted and made flight commander. His citation called this his fourth victory, but it is now known that it was his sixth, and that he was an ace. Educated at Geelong and Melbourne Grammar schools, Bowes had travelled widely and looked destined to become an accountant when war brought more exciting prospects. By March 1942 he had trained in Australia, Canada and the UK, and was in India. In December he shot down a Lily, and in March 1943 three Oscars and a Lily. On 21 May, a week after his promotion, he led six aircraft to intercept Japanese raiders over Cox's Bazaar airfield. When the Hurricanes sought to engage the raiding party, they were suddenly 'bounced' by a much larger force. Bowes tried to protect his No. 2, a new pilot, but both were shot down and killed. Fellow pilots believed Bowes downed two more Oscars in this last fight. Although he was Australia's third highest-scoring ace against Japan, he is not mentioned in the RAAF official history. A window does commemorate Bowes' name at Geelong Grammar, as does an economics prize at Melbourne Grammar.

Between June and November, the monsoon weather prohibited land offensives, and the Japanese virtually discontinued air operations. Yet the Allies, operating from nearly 300 all-weather airfields which were viable unless underwater, flew whenever they could. A rare dogfight occurred on 22 September, when several Zeros intercepted a Liberator flying reconnaissance over Car Nicobar Island. The pilot was RAAF Pilot Officer Joseph Cohen, whose enlistment details show him to have been a very short handbag manufacturer of East Melbourne, born in Tel Aviv in 1922. He was also an exceptional pilot, who had been selected the previous month to fly Sir Richard Peirse to the Quebec planning conference. Now he was shot down, though his crew took a Zero with them.

By November 1943, the Allies enjoyed air superiority in the India–Burma theatre. However, the Japanese regularly sent 50 or more fighters over on individual raids, and mounted a series of bombing raids, on Calcutta and the Arakan (Burma) in December 1943. This coincided with the arrival of Spitfire Vs in Bengal. The Spitfires soon shot down four Dinahs, which had previously been reconnoitring with relative impunity. The first fell to an Australian of 615 Squadron, Kevin Gannon. Two Australian pilots, Robert MacDonald and Ron Patterson, made the first interception by No. 152 Squadron, in new Spitfire VIIIs. From its tail, the intercepted Dinah fired a rocket, which exploded in a white flak-like burst 100 metres in front of MacDonald. His aircraft sustained small holes, whereas the Dinah crashed in flames.

On Boxing Day 1943, RAAF Spitfire pilots Bill Andrews and Harry Chatfield were scrambled with orders to intercept a lone enemy aircraft near Chittagong. Soon the number of bogies rose to six, then 20, then 50. While waiting for the rest of the squadron to join them, they saw 20 bombers and an escort of more than 30 fighters. Rather than retreat or wait for assistance, which thanks to a vectoring error never came, they gave battle. Using what Andrews' diary called 'lashings of speed', he and Chatfield repeatedly dived out of the sun on their enemies, whose return fire was plentiful but ineffective.[11] Chatfield dispatched two Sally bombers, Andrews an Oscar and a Sally. Andrews was impressed by the appearance of the Oscars, painted and turned out like 'beautiful oversized toys'; one had to remember, however, that they could out-turn even the Spitfire, and so should only be tackled with a height and speed advantage.[12]

Five days later Spitfires intercepted a large Japanese force returning from a raid on shipping near Akyab. Australian Denis Garvan entered the fight by splitting up two Oscars that were harassing another Spit. As they departed he came upon three Sallys. His first burst struck one's engine, cockpit and wing. As he closed in, driving more bullets into the unprotected bomber, it fell apart and big pieces flew back towards him. Then Oscars threatened, and after a 65-kilometre chase he got home, damaged but triumphant. He had destroyed one Sally, with one probable and two Oscars damaged. In the next 20 days this 'jackeroo' of fashionable Bellevue Hill would be credited with shooting down three more fighters, and two probables. During the dogfights, sometimes against superior numbers, he was once shot down and once wounded. Garvan's CO at 136 Squadron was Noel Alexander, an Australian in the RAF, who destroyed at least three Oscars.

Australians in India–Burma flew Wellington bombers, which gradually replaced the Blenheims until in turn replaced by Liberators. No. 215 Squadron's Wellingtons were under renowned Australian Wing Commander Dereck French, DFC and Bar. Another of the unit's 59 Australians was Neville Brady, who in April 1944 brought his Wellington safely through an attack from two enemy fighters, which badly damaged the 'Wimpy' and wounded one of the crew. Soon afterwards he was commissioned and awarded a DFC. He and his Australian navigator, Henry Deester, were flying a Dakota for 62 Squadron in June when it crashed, killing them and 26 others on board.

Australians in this theatre flew Vultee Vengeance dive-bombers, which did not suffer the same ignominious fate as in the South-West Pacific Area. Wal McLellan converted to them from Blenheims. He was impressed by the reliability of the 'V' and its accuracy as a dive-bomber, was excited by the adrenaline rush it gave in the dive, but not so impressed by the way its engine obstructed visibility in level flight, its 'pure WWI' rear machine-gun equipment and its lack of range. He called it a 'brute'.[13] James 'Sandy' Sandilands, a grazier from Uralla in New South Wales, won a DFC flying Vengeances with 82 Squadron. In April 1944, he was about to practise a new shallow dive and airtest a new wing. Several British ground staff jockeyed for the chance to go up with him: it proved a death wish, for the 'winner' and Sandilands were killed in a crash. One can only imagine the reaction of Sandilands' parents when they heard of his death, for they had already lost another son, John, in an aircraft accident in North Africa, and would lose a third, Geoffrey, to the same cause in the UK later that year.

Australians also flew air transports. One of the finest hours of this group came after the Japanese launched an offensive designed to sweep through Burma to New Delhi in February 1944. British and Indian troops cut off by this advance at Kohima depended on air transport for supplies. Three Australian airmen were said to be the first to move cattle by air into Burma, and until proper carrying arrangements were made, the Australians, led by grazier Frank Austin, had to 'throw' the cattle; that is, cast them to the floor and restrain them. Some RAAF airmen, including Squadron Leaders Geoffrey Furmage and William McLean, manned transports and provided ground support for Brigadier Orde Wingate's 'Chindit' special forces, behind enemy lines in Burma. The great Japanese offensives towards Imphal and Kohima brought them close to airfields, including Palel, where Australian Hurricane pilot Max Cann recalled Japanese mortaring the strip and killing several patients during a raid on the hospital. His squadron, No. 42, bombed and strafed Japanese barely outside the circuit area for taking-off and landing at Palel.

Among those offering effective cover during these operations was RAAF Spitfire pilot Larry Cronin of 81 Squadron. Before arriving in Burma, he had shot down three German fighters in Italy. He soon added a Dinah. On 10 March he landed on one of the Chindits' airstrips, 'Broadway', which was to become a base for eight Spitfires. The strip belied its name, for it was a tiny, rough runway surrounded by trees and with wrecked gliders lying everywhere—but at least it was difficult for the enemy to pinpoint. On 13 March, though, they found it and sent in a big air raid. The garrison received just five minutes' warning, and by the time Cronin got airborne some 30 enemy fighters were overhead. He told his diary he was:

> bounced by eight Japs as soon as I was airborne. Bloody near got killed too. Saw them when they were 80 yards dead behind me firing like mad. Got away from them eventually, they never hit me once—lousy bastards! Got one destroyed—nearly blew him out of the cockpit.[14]

With this kill Cronin achieved ace status.

No. 607 Squadron was the first unit converted to Spitfires in India. A young Australian member, Wilf Goold, performed brilliantly with this squadron. He destroyed an Oscar in December 1942, fighting back after it damaged his Hurricane. In January he surprised two Oscars, and was so close to one he saw his bullets enter the cockpit. When he last saw this aircraft, before the other Oscar got on his tail and he sped off, it was on its back dropping towards the jungle just 50 feet below: it was counted as a 'probable'. By 18 May Goold had added four confirmed Oscars to his tally, bringing him to 'ace' status.

By June 1944 the Japanese were retreating from India and Burma, and the RAF harassed their ragged columns. The pilots' main obstacle was the monsoon season's dense cloud layer, sometimes extending from the ground to nearly 30,000 feet above. For example, on 10 August, of a group of 16 No. 615 Squadron Spitfires which took off towards a base near Calcutta, only eight survived a journey through 'a huge black wall of cloud' which buffeted them mercilessly.[15] Three of the four pilots killed were Australians, including the outstanding CO, Dave McCormack, DFC and Bar. Another Australian victim of frightful weather was 353 Squadron's David Forman, an experienced Hudson and Dakota pilot who had flown over The Hump to China, only to be killed when his aircraft ran into a monsoon in August.

From September 1944, Australian pilots of 261 Squadron enjoyed flying Thunderbolt fighters. These magnificent aircraft, with the most powerful piston engine of any World War II fighter, would have been a wonderful replacement for the P-40s the RAAF was flying in the South-West Pacific Area. They had a much longer range, flew faster and higher, had more firepower and carried more bombs and rockets. Australian 'T-Bolt' pilots in India and Burma helped launch powerful strikes on enemy supply dumps and gave effective ground support. Naturally they were not invulnerable: Thomas Cambridge died on one such strafing raid after his Thunderbolt, fatally damaged by ground fire, burst into flames on crashing. Two Australians given the unusual distinction of commanding RAF Squadrons, Donald McDonald and Roy 'Gatty' May, had Thunderbolt squadrons. At six foot three, McDonald was aptly nicknamed 'Big Mac', and when originally posted to a Spitfire squadron, was too tall to fit. He flew Hurricanes and, from May 1944, Thunderbolts. In 1945 he and May received DSOs.

Australians flew Sunderlands and Mosquitos in the Burma–India theatre too. Wing Commander Harley Stumm was killed with Flight Lieutenant McKerracher, DFM, in an accident during No. 45 Squadron's conversion from Vultee Vengeances to Mosquitos. Stumm was a Rhodes Scholar, a popular leader and one of the outstanding Australian pilots in this theatre.

Another exceptional Australian pilot, Lionel Hudson, arrived in India in 1942 as an EATS graduate. By 1944 he had risen from Sergeant Pilot to Wing Commander, leading a Mosquito Squadron, No. 82. On 19 December 1944 he and his wingman, fellow Australian Alfred McKenzie, made a 'rhubarb'—low-level attack over enemy territory—but as Hudson approached enemy river craft on the Irrawaddy River his aircraft touched the water. Forced to crash-land, he and his British navigator suffered concussion and lacerations. They were captured. On the journey to Kempeitai (military police) headquarters at Myingyan, they were at one point thrown on to the road, their hands tied behind their backs. For up to four hours, passing Japanese soldiers vented their spleen on the two, kicking them and raining down blows with sticks and the flats of their swords. When Hudson was numb with pain a Japanese medical officer half-heartedly bound their wounds—now septic—and their hands, and then punched them into unconsciousness. Once at the Kempeitai headquarters, interrogations began, with much face-slapping and threatening. Eventually taken to cells, they were helped by the local police who, ignoring Japanese orders, fed them. After more brutal interrogations the two pretended to crack and gave false information before being sent to a POW camp in Rangoon.

While No. 45 Squadron's Mosquitos were being modified for tropical conditions in November 1944, the pilots were assigned to undertake casualty evacuation from the Arakan. They were given Tiger Moths, capable of carrying one stretcher case in a coffin-like structure in the rear cockpit. Wal McLellan flew into an area where Allied troops were surrounded by the Japanese. On the first trip, he spotted the short strip on which he had to land, at the bottom of a ravine, 'like a small wound in the dark green jungle'. Even landing at the lowest speed possible on the 'incredibly rough surface,' he would not have been able to pull up before the trees, had not Allied soldiers rushed to the aircraft from all sides and, in a well-practised drill, gripped the wings and tail.[16] They turned the Tiger to face the way it came. While an officer warned him to get away as quickly as he could to avoid Japanese mortaring, the coffin lid was raised and a body on a stretcher placed inside. McLellan pitied his patient, cut off from the world apart from a small perspex panel, and thrown about as the light plane negotiated the thermals.

Soon afterwards, the unit received Stinson Sentinel light aircraft to complement the Tigers. Everyone wanted these superior aircraft, in which a stretcher could lie behind the two front seats, all encased within perspex. On his first flight in a Sentinel, McLellan's load was a fairly senior captured Japanese officer, who had been badly wounded, and was to be returned to base for interrogation. During the flight, McLellan suddenly felt two hands choking him. The Japanese officer had escaped his bonds and seemed determined to take McLellan with him to the grave. McLellan carried a heavy stick with him in case he crashed in the jungle, and used it to silence his recalcitrant passenger. On arrival at base, waiting British officers were unimpressed that McLellan had killed his captive. One of them threatened disciplinary action, until McLellan defiantly stated that if punished he would take it up with the Australian liaison office in India and his own Member of Parliament.

By the beginning of 1945 there were still 923 Australians serving in the Burma–India theatre, down from a high of 1091 the previous July. All but 61 were trained aircrew, with Liberators the most common aircraft type flown, followed by Dakotas. Only 590 were assigned to operational duties, but were spread over 60 operational squadrons. This made a mockery of the RAF's stated intention to follow Australia's wish that RAAF personnel be concentrated in a few squadrons. Although it was decided early in 1945 to repatriate all Australians in the theatre, they continued to be in the thick of the fighting in February and March.

On 11 February a huge Allied raid on Rangoon included Superfortresses as well as Liberators escorted by Lightnings and Thunderbolts. Australians flew in the Liberators and Thunderbolts. The RAAF's last victories in Burma came on 4 March, when Herbert Johnson used his night-fighter Beaufighter to shoot down two Lilys within three hours.

The dozen Australian Thunderbolt pilots supported British infantry in March, flying 'cab-rank patrols', whereby aircraft stayed overhead to be called. The alternative—waiting at their airstrip to be called—was a recipe for a time-lag, which hampered air support in the South-West Pacific Area.

The Japanese abandoned Rangoon on 25 April 1945. Among the 100 Allied airmen POWs liberated were Lionel Hudson and eight other Australians.

The end of the war in Europe in May 1945 created an enormous surplus of RAF members there who could replace Australians in Burma and India. The Australian government recalled all Australians serving in the RAF, and those in India and Burma were either repatriated or posted for service in the RAAF in the South-West Pacific Area, where the last operations were pending. This scheme began in June 1945.

On 16 July Queenslander Brian Bohane completed his second tour of operations with No. 607 Squadron, in which he had shot down one Zero. With the end of his long service in India and Burma in sight, he died in a jeep accident at Mingaladon airfield. He was among the last of more than 200 Australian airmen killed in this campaign.

23 Island hopping

In December 1943 the Allied Combined Chiefs of Staff decided to launch two great simultaneous drives against Japan. One thrust would be across the Central Pacific, the other via New Guinea and the Philippines. MacArthur was ordered to invade Hollandia, on the north coast of Dutch New Guinea, in April 1944, to be followed by the Philippines in November.

Valuable information on Hollandia came from No. 3 Wireless Unit RAAF, which from Darwin monitored the area's wireless traffic. From their three airfields on this distant target, the Japanese were bound to intercept Allied bombers sent against it. However, General Kenney had long-range Lightnings capable of flying to Hollandia and staying overhead for an hour before returning to Nadzab in New Guinea. These P-38s escorted 65 Liberators to Hollandia on 30 March 1944, and more again the following day.

Among the Liberator crews on the second raid were Australian airmen learning to fly B-24s in preparation for the creation of RAAF Liberator squadrons. Flying them was not easy, especially above 20,000 feet. For example, manipulating the rudder was physically difficult. This 'flying boxcar' was doubly hard to manoeuvre if damaged, and although the B-24 was far better armed and armoured than the Betty, it was less robust than the B-17. The Australian pilots included 'Mickey' Jaques, a veteran of 13 Squadron's Hudsons, who had won praise from American onlookers two weeks earlier when, after flak had damaged a landing wheel over Wewak, he brought the immensely heavy aircraft down safely at Nadzab.

Squadron Leader Jack O'Brien, who had flown over the Netherlands East Indies in desperate times, led an entire RAAF flight in the 31 March raid. The RAAF crews had mixed feelings about the raid. Though due to return to Australia to become instructional staff, they were also keen to attack the almost 'virgin' territory that Hollandia represented, in contrast to the devastated targets to which they were usually sent.[1] Just days earlier the Japanese Fourth Air Army had withdrawn from its shattered Wewak base to Hollandia, which had long been untroubled by heavy air attack. This led to careless dispersal among many other Japanese aircraft grounded there because of lack of spares or maintenance. Consequently General Kenney's raids were pulverising. When the Allies captured Hollandia, they counted 340 aircraft wrecks on its three airstrips.

On 22 April American forces landed at Hollandia and, 160 kilometres east, at Aitape. Resistance was light, but the RAAF contributed substantially to the Aitape landings. Because of the long distance of these bases from the nearest Allied airfields, it was imperative to make Aitape's strip, at Tadji, operational quickly. The officer appointed to supervise this task was Wing Commander Bill Dale, commander of No. 62 Works Wing RAAF. Tall and taciturn, Dale was a civil engineer who had been transferred from the Citizen Air Force to become full-time assistant director of works and buildings in October 1939. Dale had proved an exceptional leader during the demanding construction of engineering works at Milne Bay, Goodenough Island, Kiriwina and Nadzab. These works included constructing buildings—250 at Nadzab alone—runways, taxiways, revetments and supply dumps. He had also volunteered to participate in the landings at Guadalcanal and the Admiralties. Little wonder, then, that Dale was appointed to lead the 2500 Australian and American engineers at Aitape.

LAC William Burns was in one of the landing ships at Hollandia and saw a dramatic tableau of events typical of Allied amphibious landings: the preparatory bombardment tearing apart palm trees, American dive-bombers arriving from supporting carriers, the winkle of enemy guns firing back, and Alligator amphibious vehicles ploughing forward and firing rapidly. After their LST (Landing Ship, Tank) hit the beach, they found a Japanese cookhouse there, so recently abandoned that the fish and rice were still warm. There were recently killed Japanese soldiers too. Tense hours lay ahead, especially at night after the ships left the engineers to it. Dale commanded from the front, personally leading his wing ashore and reconnoitring the enemy-held airstrip. He found it overgrown with kunai grass, roughly graded and not long enough for Allied fighters. Burns dubbed it 'a goat track'.[2] Then the construction work began, to a schedule that required the airfield to be ready for use by fighter aircraft the following day. Two of Dale's RAAF construction squadrons, Nos 5 and 6, had been in the tropics for an unbroken 16 months, but were considered indispensable. Fifty hours after Dale came ashore, Allied fighters were flying from the 1188 metre-long steel matting on Tadji airfield to give cover to the American ground forces on Hollandia. First to land was a Beaufort carrying Group Captain Pearce, while the first fighter was flown by a fellow Port Moresby veteran, Squadron Leader Les Jackson.

The fighters basing at Aitape were 78 Wing's three Kittyhawk squadrons, whose pilots and ground staff welcomed the possibility of returning to intense action. The ground crews went in with the airfield construction squadrons, immediately behind the assault forces. Credit for the Kitties' ability to fly at Aitape was due to No. 11 Repair and Salvage Unit (RSU). When the possibility of No. 78 Wing being sent there from Cape Gloucester and Nadzab arose in late March, many of the Kittyhawks desperately needed servicing. The 400 men of 11 RSU, under Squadron Leader Rex Taylor, worked exceptionally hard, including two daily shifts of 12 hours, to ready the Kittyhawks. Their unit had left Australia equipped primarily for servicing Beauforts and Vengeances, but proved flexible and innovative enough to recondition the necessary 28 aircraft in one month. Brigadier-General Wurtsmith, now leading Fifth Air Force Fighter Command, provided 12 Allison engines. No. 11 RSU's effort here was the epitome of the unsung but vital work done by RAAF salvage and repair units in the South-West Pacific Area. According to George Jones, the dearth of new aircraft at the war's outset had forced Australia to develop 'a massive repair system', far superior to that of the Japanese.[3]

Working from Tadji proved difficult, though RAAF personnel toiled to improve it. Burns wrote of working through the night under lights and in deep mud. Two Kitties crash-landed there on the first day and weather prevented its use for some days. The pressed metal sheets laid on the strip were even less suitable for twin-engine aircraft such as Beaufighters. On 30 April a USAAF Lightning making a crash-landing there swung towards a Kittyhawk and decapitated one of the 78 Squadron ground crew who was directing the Kitty from the wing. It then careered into an RAAF staff car, narrowly missing its fast-moving former driver.

Tadji remained crowded and a hive of disease. One compensation was the area's fine surf beaches, which offered much-needed relaxation. The airstrip's value was apparent on 1 May when advancing American troops reached Kamti village. Five Kittyhawks had attacked enemy positions there the previous day, and the Americans found all but two huts destroyed and 75 dead Japanese. Most of the Kitties' work comprised patrols and escort missions for air transports to Hollandia.

The 13 Allied squadrons based in the Northern Territory supported the Hollandia–Aitape operations by bombing, mining and strafing Japanese forces in the vicinity. Beaufighters wrought havoc among enemy vessels, though one Beau was lost with its crew after it struck the mast of a prahu. Not hitting civilians must have been difficult, though usually locals in the vessels would 'wave white or Dutch flags or their arms or stand up and salute'.[4] Civilians must have died under Australian bombs and bullets in the war with Japan, but they are not discussed in the official or unofficial literature. Area bombing, which killed immense numbers of civilians in Europe and Japan, was not practised by the RAAF in the Pacific.

Catalinas go mine-laying

Catalinas of 11, 20 and 43 Squadrons laid mines in the Carolines, but also closer to the Hollandia–Aitape operations. No. 43 was assigned exclusively to the task of laying mines.

May brought a heavy blow to 11 Squadron. Its experienced and able CO, Squadron Leader Geoff Coventry, took on the job of flying a large pump to a ship that was sinking near Milne Bay. After a hard landing next to the ship, the heavy pump was taken aboard, but on a second attempt to take off, the Cat reached no more than 100 feet before crashing down. There were some terrible injuries. When Ken Towns came to he was underwater, doubled up and unable to straighten. He had started breathing in water to hasten his end when he realised he still had a seatbelt on. He released it, and though injured, reached a dinghy. Keith Paris was also stuck when the aircraft began to sink. As he held his breath he saw a large fiery orange ball and waited for the end. Some time later he found himself swimming towards the surface. His injuries included a broken nose, which made his accent even harder to understand for the American tugboat crew who rescued him. The rest of the Cat crew survived, except Coventry, whose chest was reportedly smashed on his control column, and went down with his ship.

Balikpapan had been a target of 11 Australian Catalina sorties since February. Based at Cygnet Bay in Western Australia, the experienced 11 and 20 Squadron crews carried 2000-pound (910-kilogram) loads of mines over more than 1700 kilometres, and made it back with barely 100 gallons of fuel remaining. Allied mine-laying in the Netherlands East Indies worried the Japanese, who were losing ships carrying vital oil and other resources, and also having to delay convoys while sweeping for mines. They allotted 30 ships and 1500 men to mining countermeasures in the area. By September 1944, 25 ships were credited as sunk or damaged in the Netherlands East Indies, for the loss of just six Catalinas and four crews: one Cat per 95 sorties. The sinking totals were later found to be exaggerated, but results were clearly pleasing. From that month Nos 20, 43 and the newly operational 42 Squadron were allocated purely to mine-laying. No. 11 moved to Rathmines to concentrate on anti-submarine patrols and training.

A Catalina crew was lost to flak over Macassar in October 1944. Three other Cats narrowly survived direct hits at Macassar, and Cliff Hull was forced to ditch in the open sea after losing an engine to its flak. No. 43 Squadron's Armand Etienne rescued the crew in waters perilously close to four Japanese airfields and a radar station. The squadron's Operations Record Book asserted that this rescue 'constituted the longest daylight Air Sea Rescue operation carried out by Catalina aircraft in the South West Pacific Area, involving a round trip of 1800 miles'.[5] Russian-born Etienne received a DFC for his efforts.

In 1945 dangerous mine-laying missions would be flown from Morotai and the Philippines to Surabaya in Java, Formosa, Hong Kong and the China coast. An operation to Wenchow, at 28° North, in May represented the RAAF's most northerly operation in the Pacific War.

One Catalina captain, when asked to name his most enduring memory of the war, nominated his first sighting of the coast of China, a land much more mysterious to Australians then than now.[6] Operations were severely restricted after June 1945, when a northerly limit was set for RAAF activity.

Lieutenant-Commander Carr, who before his capture had played a leading role in the mine-laying, claimed that the results of the RAAF mine-laying were 'the equivalent of those that would have been obtained by over *100* Liberator *Squadrons* doing continuous bombing over the same period'. Even more striking perhaps was Carr's claim that Bill Bostock told him 'that the minelaying carried out by the R.A.A.F. Catalinas was easily the most successful and important effort of the whole of the R.A.A.F. in the Pacific War'.[7] No wonder the morale of the Catalina squadrons remained high when that of other units was declining.

How accurate were these claims? After the war, the US Joint Army–Navy Assessment Committee concluded that mines laid by RAAF Catalinas sank nine ships, totalling 21,033 tons. The RAAF claimed 23 sunk and 27 damaged. The US figures probably underestimated the Australian contribution, but even had the Australian estimate been correct, that total was small. Of 3032 Japanese vessels sunk during the war, 266 were lost to mines, mostly ones dropped by Superfortresses near Japan.

Yet the effectiveness of RAAF mining cannot be measured solely by tonnage sunk. Time lost to ships trapped in harbours or forced to take roundabout routes was important too—as were diverted Japanese resources. Part of its purpose was to keep ships out of harbours and thus make them vulnerable to American submarines, the success of which was a key factor in Allied victory over Japan.

'We whack Wewak'

Nos 8 and 100 Squadrons moved to Nadzab in May, so that their Beauforts could contribute to the Allied bombing of Wewak. That month flak hit Lyle MacLaren's Beaufort. With one engine alight, he brought the aircraft down in the sea, only 20 metres from enemy-held But plantation. The crew, injured in the crash, had just paddled their dinghy clear of the aircraft when Japanese machine guns opened up from the shore. MacLaren and his navigator, Syd Anderson, a three-time VFL premiership winner with

Melbourne, were killed, and Ray Graetz, one of two wireless air-gunners, had an ear lobe shot away. The dinghy sank, and as Graetz swam for shore he last saw the other WAG, Francis Maloney, swimming seaward.

Graetz was carried out of view from the beach, and managed to crawl ashore while the lone sentry in his area was looking the other way. Exhausted and weakened by constant bleeding, from under a bush Graetz saw sentries taking position along the beach, then nodded off. He slept for most of the next day, then headed for Tadji via a coastal track used by the Japanese. Having lost his flying boots on getting ashore, he walked barefoot the whole way and drank from water-filled craters. Graetz narrowly avoided several Japanese parties, but was able to wander around the wrecks on But airfield. He disabled some Japanese trucks by lifting the bonnets and removing distributor wires. Finding an unattended anti-aircraft gun—a source of his misfortune—he poured sand down its barrel and into its firing mechanism. While he avoided large parties of fresh-looking enemy troops, he walked straight past various groups of weary Japanese, who ignored him or grunted to him and received a grunt in return. Eventually his waving figure was spotted by an Airacobra and a PT boat rescued him. His eight-day adventure brought him a Military Cross, most unusual for an airman.

In June, 8 and 100 Squadrons moved again, to Aitape, as did 30 Squadron's Beaufighters. All equipment and supplies for this No. 71 Wing had to be carried there by air, so were minimal even when supplemented by generous Americans. Though constrained by a shortage of spare parts, Beaufighters destroyed 18 barges in three weeks.

The day after 30 Squadron's arrival, they lost their new CO, Wing Commander Philip Gibson, killed with his navigator when his Beau hit a bulldozer while taking off on a test flight. Flying Officer Raynor Barber partly blamed himself for Gibson's death. When Gibson had taken over the squadron he had lectured the experienced Barber, warning him not to be overconfident. He had then allegedly rebuked Barber in front of others when Barber missed an attempted take-off on Tadji's narrow strip. Soon afterwards, when Gibson himself was taking off from the strip, he noticed that Barber was watching. Gibson got into a poor take-off position, but chose to try to take off. Barber felt he did so rather than embarrass himself by trying again. Instead, he died.

Barber lost sleep and had nightmares for weeks afterwards. As he notes, in those days Australian men were expected not to show grief, especially in the armed forces. Losses were felt but not discussed, or at least not beyond the 'Poor old John' level. It was a case of maintaining a 'stiff upper lip'.[8] Barber's memoir is a useful corrective to the idea that 1944 and 1945 provided easy work for men in the attack squadrons. So distressing was his dread of not returning to his young family that nearly 60 years after the events, he found it hard to talk about being sent on his first operations back in 1944.

Charles Learmonth had similarly heart-rending emotions when, before travelling to New Guinea, he visited his wife in a Sydney hospital after their hopes for a child were dashed in a miscarriage. They knew each visit could be his last, and eventually he was indeed killed in a Beaufort crash.

Barber's experience in New Guinea was immensely stressful. After returning from missions, he would report to the Intelligence Officer, then lie down for an hour 'to alleviate the shaking'.[9] His anxiety came in part from the expectation that the flak would eventually bring him down, the loss of a string of tentmates, the fear of Japanese soldiers raiding the base, but also from a series of incidents that scarred him mentally. One was ditching his aircraft in the sea near the Celebes. A Catalina rescued the crew after about three hours, but in the interval up to 60 sharks menaced them. This experience gave Barber nightmares for years to come. He was also deeply troubled by an incident in which he was leading a flight of aircraft in take-off when one Beau swung into a ditch and broke in half. When Barber reached the plane, one engine was alight and the pilot's legs had become completely jammed in the pedals. Barber could not pull him out or reach his boots. After fire entered the cockpit, Barber stayed until the heat was damaging his eyes, but then had to give up and let his mate burn to death. Even beyond these horrors, he counted as his 'worst moment' learning of the death of a good friend, Flight Lieutenant Roy MacPherson. Though he was about to return to his beloved family in Australia, MacPherson pleaded to be allowed one last sortie, and Barber let him go, against his better judgement and an unwritten rule within the squadron that aircrews did not fly once they had been told they were going on leave. Informing MacPherson's wife 'tore him apart'.[10]

Pilot Officer Geoff Hiller arrived at 30 Squadron just days before Gibson's death. On the night of the accident, he told his diary that there were 'arguments galore' in his tent, though he did not specify the topics.[11] In the aftermath, he had a rough introduction to operational life. On a familiarisation flight, he not surprisingly found taking off from Tadji 'a bit hairy'. He struggled in landing, too, so a pilot was detailed to show him the ropes. Hiller was 'not particularly impressed by his manner'. He was even less impressed the following day when, on his first operational flight, the other three aircraft on the strafing mission left him behind. 'They just went off and said b– him,' he told his diary. He was late to take off, briefly lost the leader, did not drop his bomb on the first run and then did not catch up on the way back. He was told he would be given a week off flying as a punishment. 'Altogether a bad day', was his mournful diary comment, though he determined to learn from his mistakes.[12] He did so, but would be unhappy until a long interview with the CO in late August led to assurances of more flying. By war's end Hiller was a Flight Lieutenant with a DFC. Still, being a reinforcement was tough.

Bob Wemyss, another new arrival to the squadron, was anxious when he went to the CO's tent after his first operational flight. He had misjudged the weight of the aircraft fully loaded and, as flak threatened him on the run in to But, had kept so low while firing full-bore that he left insufficient space to clear the trees. He went through a clump of them, striking their topmost metre, and to his horror both engines cut out. After what seemed an eternity of waiting for a crash, both engines suddenly returned to life and Wemyss got home. The engine nacelles (covers) were badly damaged, and Wemyss feared that he would be banished to Australia. When he apologised to the CO, he was told not to worry about it—that in fact until you had hit the trees three times you were not considered operationally experienced! This CO was Jack Sandford, who on Gibson's death was promoted to Squadron Leader, and took over the unit with which he had already done one tour. Wemyss came good, but he noticed such fear in some members in the squadron that they tried intentionally to avoid being given flying time. He recalled one pilot deliberately spending hours on end staring at blindingly white coral, until he had to be sent south for his self-induced eyesight problems.

Japanese troops, who numbered in the tens of thousands in the Wewak area, launched an offensive to recapture Aitape in July 1944, but were repulsed. In sorties of just 30 minutes' duration from Tadji, Beauforts and Beaufighters helped to smash this desperate operation. A lone Japanese got close enough to the strip to shoot an RAAF guard, Snowy Milne, in the chest, though the Australian survived. At the height of the operation, Beaufort crews were each flying four sorties a day, which although each might last only 30–40 minutes, put great strain on them and their armourers.

The Beaufighters began seeking enemy barges at night, the prime time for enemy movement. Night raids were dangerous, even though Sandford had experienced night flying with the RAF. On 13 July, his was one of two Beaufighters attacking a barge near But when he saw Cliff Satchwell's Beau hit by flashing tracer rounds. 'I think I'm on fire,' came Satchwell's call on the radio, and then his Beaufighter hit the water.[13] Harry Baldock of the same squadron took off an hour later. On returning from a sortie on 4 July, he had claimed to have killed ten Japanese soldiers crossing a creek, but from this latest flight he never returned. A third Beaufighter that took off in daylight, flown by Squadron Leader Gordon Fenton, was shot down on that disastrous 13 July. The usually matter-of-fact diary of LAC Kaye called it the 'Worst day we have had.'[14]

The results of the Beauforts' and Beaufighters' attacks were rarely visible in the thick jungle, but a captured soldier reported that a July raid on a village killed 70 Japanese. The raiders were No. 100 Squadron Beauforts, under Squadron Leader Herb Plenty, who had witnessed the destruction of 'Force Z' three long years earlier. The Beaufort squadrons were competitive as to the record number of daily sorties. No. 8 Squadron clinched the record on 7 August, when it flew 64 sorties in one day and dropped nearly 400 bombs on enemy troops. One diarist claimed that the two squadrons had killed 2000 Japanese 'observed'.[15]

When in September the Japanese seemed to be repairing Wewak airstrip, 100 Squadron was ordered to render it unserviceable. Squadron Leader John Kessey heightened his crews' enthusiasm by making a competition of it. They called it the 'Wewak Welter' and offered prizes, ranging from a watch and chain for the winner, to a baby's dummy for last place. In the Operations Room, a board was set up with a map of the course, race poster, list of starters and starting times. On 11 September the squadron flew 40 strikes on that well-protected target, with ten aircraft each dropping 2000 pounds (910 kilograms) of bombs. Two other crews acted as observers, and results were broadcast over the squadron PA system. The key result was 80 hits on the now disabled airstrip, with the winning score of 24 achieved by Eric 'Poppa' Crisp's crew. It may have been macabre, especially as more than half the contestants would not survive the campaign, but it achieved its military and morale-boosting purposes.

General MacArthur could now have destroyed the sizeable Japanese forces in New Guinea, which were without air support or shipping supplies. Instead he chose to bypass all locations except those he wanted for bases that would facilitate his drive on the Philippines. This 'island hopping' strategy probably shortened the war. Advances now tended to outrun supply, which affected the RAAF, especially given its low position in the pecking order. General Kenney intended to abandon Port Moresby and Dobodura as operational bases, while the capture of the Admiralties rendered superfluous Milne Bay, Kiriwina, Woodlark and Goodenough. Wakde, Biak, Noemfoor and Sansapor (on the Vogelkop Peninsula) were seized in quick succession, all because of the airfields they offered. Nos 75, 78 and 80 Squadrons supported all these moves, averaging 1400 hours monthly.

On 4 March 1944, 14 No. 75 Squadron Kittyhawks under 'Congo' Kinninmont left Nadzab to escort USAAF Liberators to Wewak. Oscars sought twice to intercept the attackers. The Kitties fought them off, Squadron Leader Colin Lindeman leaving one falling fast and trailing blue smoke. This was 75 Squadron's last aerial combat of the war.

The Kitty squadrons' work in this period was rarely spectacular, but often valuable. For example, after four No. 80 Squadron Kittyhawks dropped bombs to aid American ground forces fighting Japanese attackers, the US commander reported 'Close support mission early this date tremendous success. Air strike broke up Jap counter-attack on our bridgehead.'[16] A week earlier, Squadron Leader Dick McKenny had died after flak struck his Kittyhawk. McKenny, who had flown Buffalos in Malaya, was a popular leader, and one diarist described the day of his death as 'one of the most tragic … in the history of the Wing'.[17]

By contrast, a high point came on 3 June 1944, when a rare flying battle occurred over Biak. Enemy aircraft had been making desultory raids against the Americans, but until that day RAAF patrols had not encountered them. Flight Lieutenant Robert Osment was leading 16 Kittyhawks of No. 78 Squadron on patrol when suddenly Geoff Gadsden, Osment's No. 2, reported two 'bogies'. The Kittyhawks dropped their belly tanks and made a climbing turn. Attacking out of the sun, Osment poured fire into a Kate, which dived fast and flaming into the sea. Richard Cowley damaged one Oscar and then hit another from just 100 metres, closing to 50. Osment, unable to direct his flight because there was too much radio traffic, saw that Oscar catch fire and crash into the sea. William 'Happy' Harnden, following Cowley and being pursued by two enemy aircraft, baled out. His comrades believed he was rescued by an American destroyer, but the warship had been picking up a Japanese airman. It later emerged that Harnden had died because his parachute failed to open; he was the only Australian lost in this battle. Flight Lieutenant Gordon White scattered two Oscars that were harassing another pilot in his flight of four. When White emerged from cloud, he found himself directly astern of an Oscar, which he promptly set smoking. Another burst blasted off its wing and sent the burning fighter plummeting. White then chased and hit a Kate, which crashed on its back into the ocean.

After 40–45 minutes of furious dogfighting, in which the Australians expended 6600 rounds, the Japanese had lost seven Oscars and two Kates. 'Good show 78', wrote a member of 80 Squadron, 'but are our boys envious.'[18] His squadron would not get a chance to match 78's effort, for that unit's first aerial battle was the RAAF's last major flying battle in the Pacific. On the other hand, many more pilots would die, including 22-year-old Gordon White, who would crash into the sea on a barge sweep in August. Before his successes over Biak, he had shot down one and damaged three enemy aircraft in the Middle East. Locals found his body on the beach in Dutch New Guinea, but when they took cover from approaching Japanese troops it was washed back out to sea forever.

The Japanese had withdrawn all their naval aircraft to defend the Mariana Islands, and just a few JAAF aircraft remained to defend New Guinea. The last enemy aircraft shot down over New Guinea fell a week after the Biak dogfight, when eight Kittyhawks of No. 78 Squadron spotted a Tony some eight kilometres away. Two pilots gave chase and Denis Baker, who had shot down an Oscar over Biak, caught up with it. He scored many hits on the Tony before it crashed into the sea.

General Whitehead's requirement that RAAF operational squadrons lift their flying effort was having a marked effect, with 78 Wing's Kittyhawks clocking up more hours than similar American units in May and June. The three squadrons, 75, 78 and 80, each averaged 1406 hours flying on operations in those months. Most of this work comprised bombing and strafing. The P-40s were now often carrying three 500-pound bombs, one in the belly-tank position and one under each wing. They could fly with this heavy load nearly 300 kilometres out. To enable these and other operational squadrons to maintain such a high rate of effort, aircraft and equipment were taken from Nos 86 and 84 Squadrons, which were disbanded. An unusually terrible event was the death of four ground staff in one day, all killed by enemy sniper fire on Biak on 15 July.

North-Western Area supported the Wakde–Biak campaigns, primarily through the USAAF Liberators. The Japanese were abandoning air defence within 800 kilometres of Darwin, but still believed that a major Allied ground offensive through Ambon and Merauke was imminent. Consequently they kept 300,000 troops stationed in the Netherlands East Indies.

A welcome arrival in North-Western Area in May was a Mosquito aircraft to serve with the previously ill-equipped No. 1 Photographic Reconnaissance Unit (PRU). This one aircraft could do the work of six Liberators: when B-24s went on reconnaissance six were sent for mutual defence, but the Mosquito could fly so fast and high that it did not need defensive armament. Piloted by Kenneth Boss-Walker, with Jeffrey Love in the rather uncomfortable navigator position, the aircraft was used to the fullest on nine missions in June. On one occasion one of its engines failed, but Boss-Walker kept taking photographs until his film was finished, then returned the 1450 kilometres to Broome on one engine. This aircraft would make enormous flights with 1 PRU, including 3600 kilometres to Balikpapan and back, and a 3700 kilometre return trip from Broome to central Java.

In June, 452 Squadron shot down a Dinah, but the men of the Spitfire squadrons were desperate for a move to the firing war. They now had a Spitfire model worthy of any action: the superlative Mark VIII, which 452 Squadron began receiving in January 1944, and 457 Squadron in July. Its 46 per cent higher internal fuel capacity and 30 gallon drop tank meant it could remain airborne longer than the Mark V, though it was still a short-range aircraft. It could reach 40,000 feet, was designed to cope with the tropics, and would be a match for any Japanese aircraft. Unfortunately, in North-Western Area there was almost nowhere to use it. No. 457 Squadron painted impressive shark mouths on the noses of its Mark VIIIs, and nicknamed itself the 'Grey Nurse Squadron'.

In June 1944, No. 2 Squadron began using Mitchells, arguably the best bombers employed in the South-West Pacific. Though terribly noisy for the crews, the B-25 was tough, reliable and faster than the B-24s.

Noemfoor—perspiration and inpiration

No. 10 Group moved to Noemfoor in July. Wing Commander Dale's Australian works squadrons were assigned to extending one of the island's airfields. By working without a break, his men lengthened it from 100 to 1830 metres in just a week. On the eighth day a squadron of USAAF Thunderbolts flew in. Before work began on the airfields, RAAF bomb disposal squads cleared enemy mines and defused many unexploded American bombs dropped before the invasion.

Prominent among the bomb squad were 77 Squadron's Fred O'Keefe and Theo Kirk. Though lacking specialised equipment and expertise, they defused at least three 1000-pound bombs that the Japanese had embedded in earth so that a slight knock would detonate them. Both men were Mentioned in Despatches, though O'Keefe's award was posthumous: he was killed by an explosion while conducting an experiment to improve the effectiveness of Kittyhawk belly-tank bombs. Apart from O'Keefe and Kirk, a 77 Squadron report singles out for praise its chief cook on Noemfoor, George Bubb. Within half an hour of the landing ship's arrival he had provided the squadron's personnel with hot tea and biscuits; within three hours they had a hot lunch prepared on an open-air cooker. In the following days, the men got hot meals every time, as well as scones and special dishes. The nearby Americans, living on their 'K rations', were for once said to be 'green with envy', and grateful when the Aussies fed quite a number of them.[19]

So complete was Allied air domination in the region that the day before the Noemfoor landing, aircraft flew over the invasion area to spray DDT: flying insects were more troublesome here than flying Japanese.

From early August, No. 10 Group was commanded by Air Commodore Harry Cobby, World War I air ace. He replaced Group Captain Fred Scherger, who had been seriously injured in a road accident. Cobby had shown that he could still lead by example when a Catalina in which he was a passenger crashed at Townsville in December 1943. He escaped, but others were trapped inside and one of several depth-charges had exploded. Despite being injured he re-entered the submerged hull three times and rescued two injured men. He was subsequently awarded the George Medal.

Now located in western New Guinea, No. 10 Group remained under Fifth Air Force Command. While forward airfields were being hastily constructed in the area, leave was granted to many Fifth Air Force airmen in Australia. The Aussies of No. 78 Wing, on the other hand, were kept exceptionally busy, with the three Kittyhawk squadrons patrolling Sansapor daily. Four pilots were killed in three days in early August—two crashing after strafing attacks, two dying in a collision during a patrol.

No. 77 Wing, including Nos 22 and 30 Squadrons with their Bostons and Beaufighters, also arrived at Noemfoor. Geoff Hiller's comment on the day of arrival was: 'First impressions of camp make your heart sink. Dirty brown coral and filthy mud. Why did we leave Tadji?' Steamy humidity, dense vegetation and heavy rain were other drawbacks. Once settled, Hiller's outlook improved, partly due to the 'inspiring' sight of formations of Kittyhawks, Thunderbolts and Black Widows streaming overhead.[20]

The Beaufighters soon recommenced their aggressive ground-attack work. Dramatic events enveloped Flight Lieutenant Ken Smith on 17 August, when a storm forced him off course. With his fuel low, he force-landed on a little island. Only by ground-looping did he avoid a coral outcrop, though the plane's tail was damaged. Uninjured but unaware of where they were, he and Flight Sergeant John Gleeson explored another little island just 350 metres distant and found a house, desolate but for a medicine bottle with the unhelpful label 'Mrs Brown'.

They radioed Noemfoor with this cryptic information and were eventually told they were on Mapia Island, some 160 kilometres north of Noemfoor. Hiller wrote at the time: 'Smithy ... is irrepressible. Some say that he will have scrounged some petrol from the Japs, others say send his refrigerator. What a story he will have to tell.'[21] A PT boat came to rescue them, dropping three sailors to look for them on Pegun Island, the biggest in the group. Before the sailors found them, the airmen found the PT boat; the boat then sought the rescuers. Ominous shots rang out, and Smith volunteered to go with a party to locate the lost rescuers. They had barely reached the beach when one of the original search party staggered from the trees warning them that there were Japanese behind them. He then fell under a volley of shots. Smith and his party returned to the PT boat and safety. On the night of 22 August nine RAAF men accompanied American troops in a PT boat back to Mapia. Among them were Smith and 30 Squadron's Engineer Officer Flight Lieutenant Ray Wheatley, whom we last saw winning the George Medal in Sumatra. While the Americans fought Japanese troops on Pegun, the RAAF men repaired the Beaufighter. Although he could barely get the aircraft above stalling speed, Smith cleared the rocks and became airborne. Another Beaufighter supported the American troops by harassing some of the 350 Japanese on the island. Eventually the Americans and Australians got away.

On 23 August, 30 Squadron flew 25 sorties, its highest daily number to that point. It was Squadron Leader Sandford's 62nd operational flight in this tour—a record for the unit, which he would extend to 80 flights. The 23 August raids on Dutch New Guinea were part of an all-out three-day offensive by Cobby's Beaufighters, Bostons and Kittyhawks against viable if generally unused Japanese airfields in the Netherlands East Indies. Squadron Leader Neville Rooke, who had barely escaped from Ambon in the last Hudson out in 1942, now took 'great satisfaction' as Operations Controller of No. 10 Group, directing attacks to 'bash' the Japanese on that island.[22]

More than 700 sorties from North-Western Area supported the Noemfoor landing. Four 31 Squadron Beaufighters flying a very long-distance raid enjoyed a rare chance to dogfight on 16 July. Flying from their new airstrip at Truscott, Western Australia, to a Flores Island airfield, they destroyed two aircraft that were about to take off. Squadron Leader 'Pat' Boyd wiped out one on the ground and then after strafing vessels in the harbour, saw and climbed towards four airborne Nicks. Firing at close range, he brought one down and damaged another. He then turned his attention to a ship in the harbour, despite the distraction of flak that his navigator described as worse than in the Bismarck Sea battle. Boyd, a member of a famous artistic family and a fine artist himself, received an immediate award of the DFC. The Spitfires' only clash in July occurred when three Spits intercepted and destroyed another poor Dinah. After that, not even Dinahs came.

August saw the first RAAF Liberator go into action, from Manbulloo, near Katherine. Piloted by Mason Frecker, it attacked an enemy vessel near Banda Island. Frecker had already won the DFM for sorties over Germany, as had his tail-gunner, Bert Middleton. Frecker and Middleton were two of many Australian veterans of bomber squadrons in the European war who had joined the RAAF Liberator squadrons. The bombs missed, and though Frecker's crew strafed the vessel, the return fire killed Middleton. Despite this inauspicious start, the B-24 would become one of the RAAF's most important aircraft. General Kenney, now able to draw on bountiful American production, planned to arm seven RAAF squadrons with Liberators and send them to the Northern Territory so that he could relieve his No. 380 Bombardment Group for use elsewhere.

Australia's first heavy bomber squadrons in the Pacific War were costly. Liberators, being so much bigger than other operational aircraft, needed more spare parts, much larger bomb-loads and more fuel. For example, it took four standard fuel trucks to carry the 16,000 litres of fuel required by just one B-24. RAAF squadrons usually had just three such trucks; the Liberator squadron had six. The squadron was bigger too, with over 650 personnel. Furthermore, the ground staff had to be highly capable, servicing aircraft in which more could go wrong and more men would die if it did.

Crewing a heavy bomber was especially dangerous considering its long flights and the big target it represented. For the US and Britain the costs were worth it, as the rewards in hitting-power over huge distances were great. Whether they were so great for the Australians, in their supporting role, is debatable—but their crews loved them.

24 The rise of 'TAF-RAAF'

North-Western Area's No. 79 Wing lost 26 Mitchell and Beaufighter crewmen in September 1944, mainly in crashes. Among the dead was Squadron Leader Wilbur Wackett, victor of 75 Squadron's first day at Moresby. His and another Beaufighter crashed with no survivors after becoming lost at night. Smoke haze from bushfires had obscured their airfield.

Australian-built Beaufighters had replaced British-built ones in Nos 30 and 31 Squadrons by November 1944. Beaus were also fitted with rockets, four under each wing. The rockets' shrapnel was effective within 300 metres, but they were not as accurate as machine guns or cannon. Raynor Barber felt that they made the Beaufighter even more formidable and gave the crews an incentive to attack. When these destructive rockets flew towards enemy anti-aircraft positions, Barber caught the unprecedented sight of Japanese gunners abandoning their weapons.

September was difficult for 30 Squadron. Barber himself was wounded over the Kai Islands, and barely made it home. While he was recuperating in hospital, another pilot, Bert Moody, took out his Beaufighter, which malfunctioned and crashed as he returned from an operation over Dutch New Guinea. Moody and his navigator, Allan Aitcheson, survived the crash, but were captured and executed. Another Beaufighter crashed into the sea after an engine caught fire, and its pilot, Ken Plowman, was killed. At a dinner celebrating 30 Squadron's second anniversary in New Guinea, the men were understandably 'a bit under and spoke there [sic] minds'. Some home truths came out in a 'proper showdown' with old hands in the unit, including one of its most experienced pilots, who later apologised to several of the complainants.[1] September proved costly for 22 Squadron too. Eleven of its personnel died, mainly in action.

On 20 October came the long-awaited invasion of the Philippines, at Leyte. A battle off Leyte, combined with an earlier one in the Marianas, virtually finished Japanese naval power, even though it was here that the Japanese introduced the fearful 'kamikaze' suicide aircraft attacks. No. 6 Wireless Unit RAAF landed at Leyte too, but with the exception of a few strikes, RAAF aerial support of the invasion was only indirect, through bombing and patrolling in rear areas—yet it was still demanding work. For example P-40s flew more than 300 sorties on and around the Vogelkop Peninsula between 20 and 27 October. From early 1944 the P-40N, the final operational variant and most common version of the P-40 in the RAAF, equipped virtually all Kittyhawk squadrons.

October was better for the Boston squadron, whose monthly report described 'considerable backslapping among the aircrews as the result of some outstanding bombing and strafing'.[2] Vincent Hunt, of the ground staff, was conscious of the 'bitter' cost of success, and had to stop himself from unsettling new crews by telling them about impressive things other fliers of the squadron had said and done before they 'went in'. On the other hand he acknowledged that: 'Day after day the sky throbs to the drone of Aircraft, I cannot say how many but I can say here and now "I cannot count them."' Much of this constant noise came from American aircraft preparing for involvement in the invasion of the Philippines. Hunt continued, 'My Squadron ... is on most of the "Bashes or Does" [raids]. We have had successes and winning knock-outs at enemy targets.'[3] That month No. 77 Wing Bostons and Beaufighters sank 24 vessels.

A unique account of one of these raids came from an Australian eyewitness on the ground. Private Walter Hicks of the 2/21st Battalion had been captured on Ambon in 1942. On 4 October 1944 he was a POW at Tan Toey camp, working in the Japanese cookhouse, when late in the morning he heard ack ack a few kilometres further east. Rushing outside with the Japanese cook, Hicks saw several twin-engined aircraft flying down Ambon Bay, just 50 feet above the water, under fire from anti-aircraft guns on the opposite bank. One aircraft headed towards the camp. Hicks initially thought it was a Lily, but as it approached the cookhouse he identified it as a Boston. It released a bomb, which detonated harmlessly nearby. The Japanese cook hid in a drain, but Hicks stood rooted to the spot, even when the aircraft passed so close that he could see the startled look on the rear-gunner's face. Hicks then turned to see a long pointy yellow object with writing stencilled on the side cartwheeling 10 metres in the air towards the Japanese barracks. It cleared those and exploded in vegetable gardens. Then the Bostons were gone. The cook emerged from his hiding place and asked whether Hicks was crazy and wanted to die. It brought home to Hicks that, as a prisoner of the Japanese, he had already resigned himself to death and he replied that he thought of himself as already dead. Back in the cookhouse the cook poured them each a bowl of Japanese whisky. Hicks reflected that had the raid killed any of the Japanese garrison, reprisals against the prisoners would have been savage.

The 22 Squadron diarist wrote up this raid on Ambon Bay in glowing terms, talking of how one sizeable enemy transport, a 'Sugar Charlie', had been left listing, with several smaller vessels hit or sunk. A tower and three buildings had been hit, and tracers had entered anti-aircraft gun pits. The intensity of the light, medium and heavy-calibre flak was acknowledged, as was the fact that Squadron Leader Woodman's aircraft was 'badly holed' and that Flight Lieutenant McMillan's aircraft—the one that flew over Hicks—had been severely hit and limped home on one motor.[4]

Hicks, on the other hand, thought the operation a waste of the more than five hours each aircraft spent flying from and back to Noemfoor. He may have been unaware of the successes claimed by the Bostons, but believed anyway that the benefits of a low-level flight down a bay with heavy anti-aircraft fire on both sides could never match the potential losses, as the Japanese 'Ambon Island garrison had absolutely zero ... offensive capability'.[5] Moreover, he noted that the flak gunners, probably like Japanese ack-ack gunners throughout the islands, had honed their skills firing in this area, to the point where they could ricochet shells off the water in front of approaching aircraft!

While enemy ack-ack guns were abundant in the Netherlands East Indies, Japanese aircraft numbers were falling. The Japanese were desperately reinforcing their air forces in the Philippines, denuding areas such as the Netherlands East Indies, so that some 200 to 400 Allied aircraft could range from New Guinea to Borneo and Morotai to Java with no aerial opposition as they destroyed targets at will. Arguably they were pinning down 40,000 Japanese troops in Halmahera, Dutch New Guinea and the Celebes alone.

RAAF airfield construction engineers contributed directly to the Philippines campaign at Mindoro Island, near Manila. General MacArthur wanted Mindoro, from where land-based aircraft could support operations at Luzon. No. 3 Airfield Construction Squadron RAAF was included in the operation, and travelled there in LSTs. There was a significant danger of enemy naval and air attack, including kamikaze attacks, and the Australians went in with the first wave. Once ashore they toiled to get all their equipment and supplies dispersed inland so that the landing ships could leave and escape the air attacks that were coming in every 30 minutes. One of several kamikazes tried to crash through the open door of an LST. Several Australians were badly burnt and one, LAC William Barham, was killed. Aged just 17, Barham had put his age up two years on enlistment. The air raids did not halt the procession of Australian bulldozers, trucks, tractors, graders and generating sets. The airmen had first to man a two-kilometre perimeter against possible Japanese attack, then provide personnel to run and maintain railway yards and engine sheds, as well as the electricity and water services in the nearby town. Most importantly, by 19 December No. 3 Squadron had, with an American engineer battalion, constructed the first airfield on Mindoro, 24 hours ahead of schedule. US transport and fighter aircraft arrived the next day, to the delight of the troops.

The ordeal of No. 3 was still not over, however. On Boxing Day, a Japanese naval force bombarded Mindoro, including Australian positions. Nevertheless, Australian volunteers drove truckloads of infantry and ammunition through the fire. An American account tells of an unnamed RAAF airman who coolly approached a senior American officer during the bombardment and offered to help with his bulldozer. The offer was accepted and 'the airman, who was hatless, proceeded to fill in the shell holes on the strip and remove crashed aircraft while shells were falling around him. He was thus instrumental in saving numbers of aircraft from crashing on the strip.'[6] By 24 December, the squadron was enduring another tribulation. Members were falling ill with fever, aching limbs, harsh coughs, skin rashes and gastrointestinal problems. Eventually they were diagnosed with schistosomiasis, a tropical disease usually transmitted by flukes via water snails. This curse was still afflicting the unit when it returned to Australia, in June 1945.

1st TAF and American plans

In mid-1944, Admiral Halsey's South Pacific command was disbanded and most of its resources, including the US Thirteenth Air Force, were assigned to MacArthur. Together with the Fifth Air Force, the Thirteenth formed the Far East Air Force (FEAF) in June 1944. Kenny commanded this new organisation as well as the Australian and Dutch air forces, some US Marine and naval air units and RNZAF units. The 'Allied Air Forces' would now comprise just the RAAF, RNZAF and Netherlands East Indies units, with any American forces Kenney chose to attach. No. 10 Operational Group was transferred from the operational control of the Fifth Air Force to that of the Thirteenth. Kenney decided that Fifth Air Force would be the vanguard in the drive on Japan, with the smaller Thirteenth—and by implication No. 10 Operational Group—playing a supporting role.

No. 10 Group was by October a large force, including two fighter wings (Nos 78 and 81) totalling six squadrons, an attack wing (No.77) comprising 22 and 30 Squadrons, and two airfield construction wings. To impress the Americans with the size and ambitions of that group, on 25 October it was renamed 1st Tactical Air Force (1st TAF, or in rhyming slang, 'Taf-RAAF').[7] This move did not work, for the creation of the FEAF marked the definitive relegation of the Allied Air Forces, and thus the RAAF, to 'Second XI' status. Prime Minister Curtin's government still hoped against hope, so that as late as March 1945, the War Cabinet was thinking that the arrival of 100 Lincoln bombers—the latest version of the superb Lancaster—would together with the Liberator squadrons allow Australia 'to offer a substantial force in the final bombing of Japan'.[8] Yet with the tide turning in Europe, vast stores of arms and equipment were available to the Pacific—so much, in fact, that it became difficult to give meaningful work to all the forces on hand. The RAAF, with its mainly second- and third-rate aircraft, was not an American priority.

The American command intended that 1st TAF should stay behind in New Guinea to support Australian Army operations. In September MacArthur had ordered Australian forces to relieve six American divisions earmarked for the Philippines. Australian troops would take over the role of fighting bypassed Japanese garrisons in New Guinea, New Britain and Bougainville. The RAAF forces supporting them would include Nos 31, 452 and 457 Squadrons, which would leave North-Western Area and join 1st TAF by February 1945.

Bostock, like Curtin, wanted the RAAF not only to support Australian ground operations but to participate in the main American advance towards Japan. Whether MacArthur ever intended for Australians to do that is doubtful. Senior Australian officers believed that Kenney did share this vision until the end of 1943. The best that Bostock could hang on to now was American advice that 1st TAF would be given an important role in forthcoming operations in the Netherlands East Indies.

The in-fighting at the top of the RAAF had a new chapter, but a depressingly familiar outcome. In June 1944 Curtin again suggested to MacArthur the need to create an RAAF position senior to those of both George Jones and Bill Bostock. When MacArthur replied that this was up to the Australian Government, the War Cabinet approved the appointment of RAF Air Marshal Sir Keith Park to the new position. However, in September MacArthur withdrew his approval, saying it was too late and that previous differences at the top of the RAAF were now 'quiet'.[9] MacArthur did not want any additional senior officer trying to encroach on his own, American-dominated turf. Yet if he truly believed that the problems were quiet he was wrong.

Morotai—a base and its raids

In November 1944, 1st TAF's headquarters moved to Morotai, an island midway between New Guinea and the Philippines. The rest of 1st TAF gradually followed. Fifth and Thirteenth Air Forces were garrisoning Morotai, but now the Fifth was moving to the Philippines, with the Thirteenth due to follow. Under the direction of the Thirteenth Air Force, 1st TAF attacked enemy airfields and other targets in the Celebes, Vogelkop Peninsula, Ambon–Ceram, Halmahera, Mindanao and Borneo. Aerial combat was rare and the JAAF was reduced to replying with generally ineffectual small-scale night raids.

An exception came on 22 and 23 November 1944. On the 22nd, eight Bostons had made the first Australian strike on the Philippines, leaving fires rising to 1500 feet on Mindanao. Eight Beaufighters raided Davao Gulf, too, though these Australian numbers were dwarfed by the 517 USAAF aircraft over the Philippines that day. That night nine Japanese bombers headed towards Morotai, seeking revenge. No. 22 Squadron's Vincent Hunt was at the pictures, watching the comedy *Theodora Goes Wild*. 'Right in the middle of the picture', he told his diary, 'the Japs went wild.' The raid unfolded around the cinema audience, with flares, tracers and explosions lighting the sky. 'I dare say I shall never forget the sight,' wrote Hunt, 'Pretty But Deadly'. When the raid ended, more than two hours later, the audience simply returned to the movie.

Having witnessed about 40 air raids in the last 12 months, Hunt may have been a bit blasé, but soon discovered that this raid was unusually destructive. 'Little did I realise', he wrote later, 'that 22 Squadron was going up in smoke and bomb bursts.'[10] For the loss of just one Japanese aircraft, the raiders left 29 Allied aircraft damaged and 15 destroyed, as well as 11 men killed or wounded. Two Australian ground staff risked their lives putting out fires among Bostons loaded with 500-pound bombs, but 22 Squadron lost nine of its precious A-20s. The squadron now had too few serviceable aircraft to keep operating. Cobby had it withdrawn to Noemfoor, where because Australia had insufficient replacement Bostons, the aggrieved crews would be retrained and rearmed with Beaufighters. The galling losses at Morotai were due to the congestion on the airstrips, and the lack of engineers available to build more dispersal facilities.

There were Japanese troops on Morotai too, and Australian airmen lost much sleep from air and ground raids and from anticipating an enemy offensive that never came. Australian aircrews flying from Morotai were still suffering losses from mechanical faults, bad weather and anti-aircraft fire—like the two 77 Squadron Kittyhawk pilots shot down on 23 November. Long flights took a physical toll too. On that costly 23 November, 77 Squadron's Jock Scott recorded that he had a 'sore behind'—a common problem among pilots sitting and sweating, strapped in, for hours directly on top of a rubber dinghy, a parachute, and sometimes on a compressed air bottle. In fact, 'Saw nothing, sore behind' seems to have been a stock description of late-war Kittyhawk sorties. The resulting condition even had a name: 'Dinghy Ding'.[11]

In December, US Major-General Streett directed his Thirteenth Air Force and 1st TAF squadrons to hit enemy installations on Halmahera intensively for four days. Cobby sent in 384 Kittyhawk and 129 Beaufighter sorties. So many aircraft were attacking that each pilot had to get in and out quickly. Allied aircraft dropped 250 tons of bombs, together with napalm and rockets, on an area of just 10 square kilometres. Despite such bombardments, the Japanese still slipped nocturnal raiders over Morotai. Arthur Brealey, who arrived with No. 452 Squadron ground staff on 12 December, saw them the following night. He had already had a rough day: rain had soaked everything inside and outside the newly erected tents, an American B-25 had crashed not 100 metres from him, and 50 or more returning B-24s had roared overhead, one just metres away. Brealey and his mates were at last sleeping when at 4.30 a.m. came three warning shots signalling an enemy raid. His feet were in his boots before the third shot. After five minutes' waiting came the distinctive 'roll' of Japanese engines. Lights went on, anti-aircraft guns were fired, but 'the nip was too high'.[12]

Brealey's writing was unorthodox but evocative, and on 23 December, he used it to describe a proud day for No. 452:

> At noon the Spits arrived and was there some excitement our lads were all pleased to see them … I had to laugh at the Yanks all those who had never seen on[e] before were verry surprised to see them so small and said God damn a little thing like that won't hurt much but when we told them she had 2–20 m.m. cannons and 4–.303 they were astounded and said damnit she packs an awful punch buddy.[13]

The Spitfire further impressed the Americans when in a mock dogfight it shone against a P-40, a Lightning, a Thunderbolt and even a Mustang. Christmas Eve brought still more excitement when two raiders came over at about 10 p.m. The first evaded flak and dropped its bombs. It was closely followed by a second raider, a Nick. When the Red Alert went Brealey was on the strip, too far away to reach his truck. From under a falling tree he watched what followed:

> … he dropped his eggs at the middle of our strip and got a B24 and 25 hell did it shake the ground and did I dig in it was only 400 yds from where we were the flack was flying all round us. He got away out of A.A. range and was still in the light.

But then Brealey and thousands of others heard a Spitfire, 'howling like I never heard before and we started yelling'. Americans and Australians urged on the pilot. The first they actually saw of the 'Spit' was fire from its machine guns, which hit the Nick's port motor. The Japanese returned fire, but the Spitfire 'barrel looped him and came in at the starboard side and gave him 170 rounds … well up went the nip in flames it was a beautifull [sic] sight for us'. The Nick exploded out to sea, with 'a devil of a bang'.[14]

Thousands of Australian and American troops witnessed and applauded this effort of 452 Squadron's Jack Pretty. 'I would have loved the outside world to have heard that cheer that went up,' wrote Vincent Hunt, 'because it was heart felt … we were as Aussies very proud and a little boastfull [sic].'[15]

There would be more raids on Morotai, but they were about to diminish. Hunt caught the mood: 'Thank God and the Spitfires'.[16]

25 'Brothers in arms' and 'mutineers'

Bougainville, New Britain, Aitape-Wewak

Nineteen forty-five promised to be a year of victory, but the RAAF's role, and the human cost of its contribution, remained mysterious. What was certain was that some Australian airmen would pay with their lives, in a variety of places. Though undermanned and underequipped, No. 84 Wing backed Australian troops effectively on Bougainville from November 1944. The cutting edge of the Allied air force in Bougainville was provided by the RNZAF, especially the beautiful and powerful Corsair fighter-bombers the New Zealanders acquired from the US Navy in April 1944. The Corsairs were very destructive, carrying 500-pound bombs and naval depth-charges. During the first Australian infantry fighting of the campaign, on 7 December, their naval depth-charges completely flattened a broad area. Yet from the outset, Australian aircraft were there too. Boomerang pilots of No. 5 Squadron led the Corsairs in on this strike, and marked the target for them, by dropping smoke bombs, firing their cannons or calling in ground fire. The Australians could also direct the Corsairs by radio-telephone. Nicknamed 'the eyes of the Army', No. 5 Squadron's Boomerangs and Wirraways supported the ground forces by identifying and photographing enemy positions, calling in mortar shoots, strafing and dropping supplies. Outstanding among them was a 76 Squadron veteran, Ross Glassop.

Walter Vernon, a radio actor and commentator before the war, was another fine 5 Squadron Boomerang pilot. In January 1945, while leading a strike of Corsairs on a village, he dropped a smoke bomb directly onto the target at Mawaraka. In dropping another he crashed into the target area and was killed. Once Mawaraka was captured, a new airstrip there was named for him. From there, Austers—light observation aircraft—flew reconnaissance to guide artillery and, most valuably, to maintain contact with Australian patrols in the difficult country of southern Bougainville. Elsewhere on Bougainville, RAAF Beauforts and Dakotas dropped supplies and used DDT for anti-malarial spraying.

Over New Britain, Beauforts and Boomerangs supported the 5th Australian Division's operations against an enemy who vastly outnumbered them, while Beauforts, especially of No. 6 Squadron, kept up attacks on Rabaul.

The veteran 6th Division took over garrison duties from American troops at Aitape from late 1944. As it became increasingly apparent that General MacArthur would not employ the division in the Philippines, the Australians' goal in the area developed from protecting Aitape to taking Wewak, the main Japanese base in northern New Guinea. Capturing this and other bases would, it soon emerged, best be done by twin advances, along the coast and inland. Air supply would be essential, especially in supporting the inland drive. Nos 7, 8 and 100 Squadrons' Beauforts were allocated to supporting the combat operations, together with a flight of No. 4 Squadron and miscellaneous American aircraft of the US Combat Replacement and Training Center.

Between November 1944 and January 1945, the Beauforts flew about 500 ground-support sorties per month. Alan Wailes, gunner in a No. 8 Squadron Beaufort crew that was sent into its first operations at Aitape, was struck by how challenging the country was for pilots and navigators: 'apart from a narrow coastal strip there is mountain range after mountain range separated by deep valleys which from the air all look alike and the native villages dotted along many ridges likewise all appear the same'.[1]

Attacking Wewak was perilous, especially as an anti-aircraft gun known as 'Dead-Eye Dick' to the Australians and 'One Shot Charlie' to the Americans repeatedly vindicated its nickname. On 30 January 1945 Wing Commander John Kessey, CO of 100 Squadron, led a formation against this gun and the nest of which it was part. As he flew in low to drop a smoke bomb, flak struck his starboard motor. He dropped more bombs on nearby Muschu Island, then made the long journey home on one engine. Kessey would be an advocate for the Beaufort thereafter. Dead-Eye Dick's crew seem to have survived, though no doubt they were unsettled that day by the 36 bombs that landed around them, each with a screaming beer bottle attached.

No. 71 Wing's crew strengths were by January at two-thirds of establishment, and stocks of fuel and bombs were low too, thanks to a lack of shipping to bring supplies. However, when in February a critical land battle developed over Nambut Hill, the Beauforts and Boomerangs contributed massively. Late in the three-week struggle the Beauforts were dropping 500-pound bombs onto mortar smoke markers just 150 metres in front of the Diggers. This became a standard distance. Rod extensions on the bombs enabled them to explode above ground, as daisy-cutters, rather than penetrate deep in the mud before exploding. Fourteen Beauforts that struck on 17 February broke the last major group of the hill's Japanese defenders, who ran, leaving 14 dead. This paved the way for a rapid coastal advance.

On the inland advance, from a small airfield constructed at Balif, Austers were able to evacuate wounded to Aitape, one casualty at a time. Japanese troops tried using hoax indicators to direct Allied transport aircraft onto their own troops, but the Australians cottoned on: Wailes' diary says Beauforts 'knocked [the Japanese] signals and troops to hell'. Another time the Beauforts hit enemy positions so close to the Diggers that the explosions sprayed the soldiers with dirt. In Wailes' words, 'we were with the A.I.F. all the way'. He was able to see the effectiveness of his bombing up close when on occasion his crew was escorted forward to bombed areas. Several hours of trekking made him appreciate the difficulty of the terrain the AIF were encountering. He saw at least one crushed and dismembered Japanese body at a bunker, and a leg complete with boot. He said he was hardened to the outcomes of war, and felt nothing on seeing such grisly sights, just as strafing left him feeling neither remorse, nor joy, just satisfaction at doing his job within his crew.[2]

The main objective of the inland advance was Maprik, the site of an airfield, and in March it became 71 Wing's main target. Low cloud regularly forced the Beauforts to drop their bombs from as low as 900 feet. One pilot noted that on five of the eight occasions when his Beaufort was holed by shrapnel during his tour in this region, the source was his own bombs. During the advance, Australian commandos captured Milak, a village two days' march from the nearest Australians, but close to Maprik. The Japanese were determined to recapture it, and for five days besieged 40 commandos there. Directed by the commandos' wireless, five Beauforts dropped bombs and strafed to within 15 metres of the hard-pressed defenders' weapon pits on 13 March. During this raid, the horrified troopers saw Jack Fowler's Beaufort disintegrate in a ball of fire when its bombs detonated prematurely on release. Some aircrew had gone on patrol with the commandos several weeks earlier, to witness air–ground communication methods, and the troops had come to see this RAAF squadron as 'true brothers in arms'.[3]

Among Fowler's crew was Geoff Waite, who had been Mentioned in Despatches for 'distinguished services' in North-Western Area. The former policeman had left England 11 years earlier with his wife. The widows' badge she received as acknowledgement of her loss is now in the Australian War Memorial. So are a few of the loving letters that Jack Shipman, of the same crew, wrote about five times a week to his mother.[4] He had made his 100th operational sortie just days earlier, and with the rest of the crew was close to finishing his tour.

When Squadron Leader Phil Dey and his crew were destroyed in another mid-air explosion on 16 March, 100 Squadron had lost eight men in three days. The new CO, Wing Commander Hugh Conaghan, who had led both fatal missions, arranged for an Army concert party to put on a show to divert the unit's thoughts on the evening of Dey's loss. It must have been a subdued show. Bombing missions were cancelled until further notice, and Conaghan and Group Captain Valston Hancock, who had witnessed both fatal detonations, proceeded to Melbourne to report. Hancock was a regular air force officer and fine administrator, but preferred flying and had recently secured a position with No. 100 Squadron. Now he designed an experiment to solve the mystery of the fatal explosions. Two old Beauforts were fitted with bombs, on the wing and in the bomb bay, at Werribee bombing range in Victoria. After each bomb was detonated, Hancock discovered that the wing bomb created the fireball he had seen on Fowler's and Dey's aircraft. Further tests at Tadji identified faulty tail fuses in the wing bombs as responsible for the premature explosions. The Beauforts resumed bombing on 23 March. After the war, Hancock would ultimately assume the leadership of the

RAAF as CAS. He took over No. 71 Wing in April, though he continued to fly with 100 Squadron whenever he could.

More tragedy awaited that unit. On 2 April, two Beauforts touched wings, 'oh so gently it seemed' to one eyewitness, but hard enough for both wings to come off and send the aircraft crashing into the sea.[5] There were no survivors. Eric Crisp and his experienced crew, winners of the 'Wewak Welter', had died just before completing their operational tour.

The coastal advance was meeting little opposition, for although the enemy outnumbered the Australians in the area, Allied aerial dominance had reduced the Japanese to a parlous state even before the campaign. No ships could reach them, and though they grew much of their own food, air raids on Wewak destroyed many supply depots. The Japanese were dying from malnutrition and disease, and their morale was falling.

In April and May Beauforts, including detachments from Nos 6 and 15 Squadrons, daily hit defences blocking the Australian advance on Wewak. Allied aircraft also had an uncanny knack of hitting Japanese headquarters. No. 71 Wing's effort peaked at 109 bombing and strafing sorties on 9 May. The following day, 65 Beauforts reportedly knocked out five artillery pieces. By the end of the month the RAAF had dropped 1236 tons of bombs in support of the 6th Division, but the longstanding shortage of bombs had become acute. The wing had to use captured Japanese bombs in large numbers, though about 40 per cent of these were duds. At least their targets were fairly concentrated, as the Japanese were being forced into an ever-smaller area on the coast and inland. The Beauforts were in the Aitape–Wewak area for more than 12 months, and reportedly accounted for half the total bomb-load dropped by the RAAF in the South-West Pacific Area in that period. In return they received a unique but well-deserved perk: a ration of bourbon whiskey per man after every operational flight. Getting the whiskey to the men was a logistical problem they worked strenuously to overcome.

'Muddy bloody Morotai'

Large-scale logistical problems handicapped the RAAF at Morotai. A chronic lack of transport badly affected life for the 3000 TAF personnel on the island by January 1945. Moving from living to working areas on 'muddy bloody Morotai' was slow, and there was no way of transporting timber needed for accommodation.[6] The diet was meagre, in contrast to Noemfoor, though the gradual introduction of 'choofers'—ingenious contraptions for boiling water—improved life for the many who rigged them up in their tents. No. 31 Squadron's diary spoke of 'general disgust' at the state of their camp and of 'considerable frustration and bewilderment' shared by all ranks at 'the lack of cooperation and appreciation of difficulties'.[7]

Air Commodore Cobby warned that lack of transport was jeopardising 1st TAF's future deployment. Whereas Fifth and Thirteenth Air Forces had their own transport, none of the RAAF's eight transport squadrons had been allotted to 1st TAF or even General MacArthur's command: all were controlled by RAAF Headquarters in Melbourne. In November Cobby requested at least one of these squadrons, for how could he plan any further movements forward without them? A courier service in which RAAF aircrew flew Lockheed Lodestars more than 3000 kilometres from Laverton in Victoria to Noemfoor was instituted, but this was not Cobby's key demand. Fortunately for him, developments in the Philippines had delayed the Fifth Air Force advance.

Still, when General Kenney told George Jones that 1st TAF would early in 1945 need to support Australian ground operations in the Netherlands East Indies, Jones sent just one transport squadron. Admittedly, air transport was at a premium in Australia, and was being used for the Army and Navy as well as the RAAF. Moreover, shipping space was also pathetically inadequate: there were in December 1944 more than 7400 RAAF members and 56,000 tons of equipment awaiting shipment to forward areas.

Shipping was in demand everywhere in the Pacific, with the Philippines taking priority. There the Fifth Air Force was wreaking havoc. Of 243 Japanese aircraft spotted on their main base, Clark Field, on 13 December, by 11 January 1945 just 34 remained serviceable! The Japanese had seen the impossibility of halting the USAAF in the region and had withdrawn their air forces north. By January the once-vaunted Japanese Fourth Air Army virtually ceased to exist, so even the Fifth Air Force had few opportunities for air-to-air fighting. Manila fell to the Allies in February, capping a 3700-kilometre advance by MacArthur's forces in just 12 months.

The 1st TAF was well to the rear of this advance, attacking or keeping an eye on bypassed targets. One notable addition to their arsenal was napalm—jellied petrol carried in 100-pound belly tanks with an igniting fuse attached. The tanks were dropped about 25 metres short of the target from a low height. As the tank broke, the mixture ignited and produced a sheet of intense flame, clinging to all it touched and penetrating openings. A propaganda poster dropped on Japanese forces demonstrated the stunning impact of napalm: before-and-after photos showed a North Borneo village, Likoepang, that Beaufighters transformed from dozens of buildings with a road grid into a flat grey expanse. Jock Scott detested using napalm in his Kittyhawk, partly because it was so nasty, and partly because it was so hard to hit a target with it.

The Australians' casualties kept rising. On 13 January a Spitfire pilot, Edmond Stevenson, crash-landed in shallow water off Ternate. Arthur Brealey called it 'an unlucky day' for the squadron, but reported that 'Stevo', who was due to go home at the end of the month, was 'a prisoner and safe'.[8] This description was an oxymoron where Japanese were the captors. After being tortured, Stevenson died as a POW. That same day four 80 Squadron pilots—Francis Hann, Peter Waters, Ronald Parry and Leon King—flying from Noemfoor to Morotai did not arrive and could not be found. Their Kittyhawks had overshot Morotai and, when their limited fuel ran out, come down off the Talaud Islands. The Japanese soon captured all but Parry, who is believed to have died trying to land. The three airmen were bayoneted to death on 23 March 1945. An RAAF search party found their remains in 1947. Four Japanese officers were executed for ordering or being complicit in what the RAAF Casualty Section called 'an affront to civilisation'.[9] The six soldiers who executed the Australians—supposedly selected because they had not previously had a chance to kill anyone—were sentenced to five years' imprisonment.

The lack of significant targets for their operations and the slow attrition their efforts entailed promoted a feeling within 1st TAF that its members were wasting time and lives. The maximising of sorties and flying hours that the USAAF demanded of the Australians in early 1944 was continuing at the end of that year, even though the broader context had changed. Then the Kittyhawk squadrons had been at the forefront of the New Guinea advance, and had to fight for a place on the limited airstrips. Now the RAAF was far behind the main game, yet the pilots were still being asked to risk their lives in missions with patently little value. The targets were often airstrips, dangerous objectives as they were likely to be defended by flak. Jock Scott remarks pointedly:

> All we did was to make the Japs use up their endless supply of anti-aircraft ammo and improve their shooting. They were isolated, unsupplied, ineffectual and without an effective role to play in the war. —Except to shoot at stupid buggers in Kittyhawks.[10]

In December 1944, a commander arrived at Noemfoor who would eventually seek to address this malaise. Having recovered from the terrible injuries he suffered on Kiriwina, Group Captain 'Woof' Arthur had been appointed to command No. 81 Wing. He flew his first operation on 22 December 1944 and wrote home that although he sustained a 'sore tail' in the long trip, 'it was quite good fun and we should have done quite a lot of damage and killed quite a number'.[11] This optimism did not last. His letters at this time reveal a thoughtful and perhaps restless man, grappling with political and religious issues. Arthur was often considering and discussing the future, for himself, his family—his wife was pregnant—and for Australia. The well-being of his men continued to be important to him.

The waste and unnecessary danger in the campaign from Noemfoor quickly unsettled Arthur. He cancelled scheduled operations for three days in December. When 1st TAF queried this he replied, bravely and cheekily, that 'more suitable and less expensive targets were available'.[12] To support his contention he drew up an 'operational balance sheet', weighing gains and losses in the two previous months. His conclusion was that in October–November, the wing had lost 11 pilots and 15 aircraft, and had in turn destroyed a mere 12 barges and six motor transport vehicles.

Arthur obtained an interview with Cobby, who was sympathetic, but who drew up his own statistics. He concluded that the pilots were wrong in thinking that ack-ack was causing heavy casualties: in fact, he showed, the numbers of aircraft destroyed by flak was one in 862 sorties in November 1944, two in 2249 in December, and five in 2037 sorties in January. This failed to address Arthur's point, that the losses were not balanced by substantial gains. 'Killer' Caldwell of 80 Wing shared this feeling, telling George Jones that his pilots were 'brassed off' with their inactivity, as was he. Dick Cresswell of 81 Wing felt the same. Other pilots had different complaints: the exaggeration and 'glamorisation' of their efforts in the Australian press, insufficient flying hours, and the disjointed and disorganised nature of their lives, especially on Morotai.

The RAAF was of course much better off than the Japanese air forces. Japanese airmen were resorting to suicide attacks to slow the enemy advance. When 1200 US carrier aircraft raided Tokyo on 16 February, they destroyed 300 Japanese planes for the loss of just 29. Moreover, Japan's navy was devastated and its merchant fleet almost eradicated. From March 1945 Japan sent no supplies to troops beyond the home islands. Japanese air strength in the South-West Pacific Area was estimated at 161 aircraft—the lowest in the war, and far fewer than the 663 RAAF aircraft, let alone the 2791 US FEAF planes.

Boxcar battles

In January 1945, No. 82 (Heavy Bomber) Wing, under Group Captain Kingwell, and including Nos 21 and 24 Squadrons began operating in North-Western Area. Aged 27, Kingwell was one of the RAAF's youngest-ever Group Captains. He was also a great enthusiast for the Liberator, which he considered the best of the many wartime aircraft he flew. On the wing's second day of operations, Roger Court scored its first victory when his 24 Squadron Liberator set an enemy vessel aflame from stem to stern. Just 12 days later, though, the squadron lost the first Australian Liberator to enemy action. While flying reconnaissance over Timor, Ken Richards and his crew were killed by typically accurate fire from the Cape Chater anti-aircraft guns, which never seemed to be cloud-covered. Richards had recently been promoted and offered leave that would culminate in a ceremony to receive his DFC. Instead he chose to stay with his crew and undertake this fatal mission.

No. 24 Squadron raided Japanese power installations in Java. These January–February raids, flown at low altitude and casting up great showers of debris, required real courage. They also inflicted irretrievable damage. There was always enemy ack-ack, and on one of these raids, Roger Court's Liberator even had the unusual and unsettling experience of enemy fighter attack. Many RAAF B-24 crewmen never saw an enemy fighter during their operational tour, but when they did, their four turrets and two waist-gun positions made their 'Lib' a daunting opponent. If a fighter was spotted, a long-range burst was often sufficient to warn him off.

When attacks did come in, the typical Japanese fighter approached heavy bombers frontally, so as to minimise the return gunfire. One of the two Oscars that attacked Court employed an unusual tactic, first lowering its undercarriage so as to reduce its speed to the Liberator's, then dropping two phosphorus bombs towards Court's aircraft. The bombs burst 500 feet overhead and sent dangerous white smoke in all directions. The second Oscar attacked more conventionally, but scored no hits in three passes. Court got home. An enemy fighter later dropped a phosphorus bomb over each of three Liberators of No. 25 Squadron, again to no effect.

The Japanese were now trying to withdraw troops from bypassed islands in the Netherlands East Indies, but Allied interdiction sank 29 ships in February alone. From March Japanese fighters operated over some convoys, but achieved no kills in more than 15 interceptions of Australian aircraft that month. A Zero and an Oscar made an extraordinary attack on Kingwell's Liberator. Instead of firing at the B-24, the Zero dropped four cylinders, all of which just missed. The Oscar then attacked from above, achieving numerous hits. One shell cut the main electrical lines and exploded near the rudder pedals. Kingwell and his bombardier were wounded. On the Oscar's third pass something astonishing happened. In the words of the official report, 'the Liberator was hit on the nose by a METAL CHAIN approximately four feet long, which smashed the front turret perspex and hydraulic system, putting the turret out of action, then hit and damaged the port tailplane and fin'.[13] The chain left the marks of its large links on the Liberator's thin aluminium skin. Had it hit a propeller, it would probably have put out an engine. After a 40-minute tussle, the Liberator escaped in cloud cover. Landing was a major challenge, with one wheel leg not locking down. Kingwell made it, and was rewarded with a DSO.

April brought a major clash when the Japanese sent to Timor a convoy including the cruiser *Isuzu*. Plans were made to strike the convoy with all aircraft available in North-Western Area. Mosquitos of 87 Photographic Reconnaissance Flight and Catalinas of 43 Squadron maintained contact with the convoy. When two fighters tried to intercept a shadowing unarmed Mosquito, it easily sped away at 640 kilometres per hour. On 6 April, 20 Mitchells of Nos 2 and 18 Squadrons and nine Liberators of Nos 21 and 24 Squadrons were sent to bomb the convoy. The Mitchells arrived first, and although the Netherlands East Indies squadron claimed two hits, the bombers, Japanese fighters and ships all failed to land killing blows. Twenty minutes later the Liberators arrived and ran into more accurate flak. The fighters closed in too. One came within a few metres of Court's aircraft, but neither was brought down. Two fighters attacked Syd McDonald's Liberator from as close as 15 metres. Cannon shells set fire to the B-24, hitting the flight deck from underneath near the nose wheel. With the fire spreading, McDonald ordered the crew to abandon the aircraft. As the surviving Liberators made a second run over the convoy, an enemy fighter set alight one of Eric Ford's engines. When Ford gave the order to bale out, flames were licking round the feet of his second pilot, Colin Vickers. Ford held the Liberator on a level course long enough for five of the crew to jump out. Then the huge aircraft rolled over and exploded as it hit the sea, taking Ford with it.

Keith Shilling was in McDonald's aircraft when it caught fire. After other crewmen jumped through the bomb bay, one without a parachute, Shilling dived out and pulled his release cord. It took an agonisingly long time to descend. Shilling never saw anyone from his own crew again, but observed six members of Ford's crew floating down. Japanese fighters left them alone, but their ordeal in the heavy seas now began. The enemy cruiser soon passed within 100–200 metres, so close that Shilling could see the troops and their tarpaulin-covered equipment. They could see him too, and he deflated his Mae West and ducked as machine-gun bullets hit the water not two metres away. Once the cruiser had passed, a smaller vessel came so close that its bow wave threw him sideways, and he could hear voices from the deck. Within minutes a Liberator dropped a dinghy nearby. Eventually Charles Bulman's Catalina of No. 112 Air–Sea Rescue Flight picked up a cold and exhausted Shilling. Vickers and Walter Sayer from Ford's crew were there too and, about 30 minutes after taking off, Bulman landed again to pick up a third member. As he did so, a Zero attacked and set the helpless Catalina on fire. Shilling was rushing back through the Cat when a fuel line burst, spraying him with burning fuel. After Sayer extinguished the flames with a sleeping bag, Shilling escaped the now downed aircraft, but was naked, dog-tired and without a life-jacket. He briefly lost consciousness, and on coming to found that Bulman and Arthur Scholes had kept him afloat. After a time their Mae Wests came undone, and they had to pass the job on to Raymond Becke, who helped Shilling for 45 minutes. An air–sea rescue Liberator had dropped more dinghies and a supply canister. The survivors took an hour to reach a dinghy, and then it was another half hour before a rescue Catalina, under Robin Corrie, arrived on the rough sea. The last of the nine survivors had just got aboard when an approaching 'Irving' was spotted. As the Cat took off, the Japanese fighter scored hits. Thus commenced a 20-minute running fight. At the very end of a long day—the operation having begun in early-morning darkness—the Cat reached Darwin. As to the target of the operation, the convoy continued on its hurried way. That night and the following day, US submarines sank a minesweeper and then the damaged *Isuzu* itself. Just three of the 22 crewmen in the two lost Libs survived the action.

One of the most active and effective RAAF Liberator units was 200 Flight, a unit of six modified aircraft established in February 1945 in Queensland. Its task was to drop operatives of 'Z' Special Force behind enemy lines, especially in Borneo, and then to keep them and other clandestine forces supplied. In an escape hatch in the B-24 fuselage, an iron ramp like a child's slippery dip was fitted, down which agents would slide into the air before parachuting. The ball turrets were removed, so the gunner could dispatch free-fall packages and propaganda leaflets. The bombardier released not bombs but 'storpedoes', six-foot-long tough cardboard containers holding weapons, radios and supplies. It was dangerous work. The CO, Squadron Leader Graham Pockley, DFC and Bar, was lost without trace over Borneo on the first mission. In its six months of operations the unit suffered 22 killed and three aircraft lost behind enemy lines.

In February 1945, while the Fifth and Thirteenth Air Forces supported landings in the southern Philippines, 1st TAF was ordered to continue its existing effort in the Netherlands East Indies. When flak hit Billy McGuigan's Beaufighter over the Celebes on 1 February, the burning aircraft came down near a village and his navigator, 19-year-old Alan Lewis, was killed. McGuigan had brought a passenger, fellow Western Australian, Sick Berth Attendant Alec Hill of HMAS *Manoora*. Both were captured and taken to a Menado prison. A local policeman saw them boarding a truck with four others in June. After the war he was able to recognise their clothing when six bodies were exhumed in the presence of Hill's uncle, an RAAF Chaplain. It emerged that all six had been bayoneted to death on 19 June. An Australian captain investigating the case visited the Menado prison, where on one of the cell walls was a drawing of a heart. It was pierced and inverted, and inside were the names of Hill and McGuigan.

★★★

In mid-February about 60 Kittyhawks and 28 Beaufighters hit Tondano, where there was a large concentration of Japanese troops. The Beaus included nine from No. 22 Squadron, flying its first operation since it lost its Bostons. It was the first time the three Beaufighter squadrons had worked together, and they unloaded 26 tons of depth-charges, napalm, fragmentation and HE bombs in one of the largest RAAF attacks of the war.

Many Beaufighters were being lost or damaged in accidents, which were attributed to the changeover from British-built to Australian-built Beaus. The non-locking tail wheels fitted to Australian Beaufighters allegedly led them to swing dangerously to one side on landing. No. 22 Squadron suffered a bitter accidental loss on 27 February. Its newly arrived CO, Squadron Leader Jack Holloway, was leading an attack on a bridge when his wingtip struck some trees, half rolled and crashed. Wreckage was scattered some 300 metres. Locals buried Holloway, but the Japanese removed the body from this temporary grave and, as a mark of respect to someone they apparently considered had died a soldier's death, gave him an honourable burial near the grave of a Japanese pilot. His navigator, David Genders, did not fare so well. He broke his leg during the crash and Japanese witnesses after the war suggested that he developed septicaemia and died of illness on 10 May. The Japanese claimed to have treated his injuries, but he was 'questioned' by the Kempeitai.[14] The last humane gesture he ever received was probably from two local girls who, on seeing him lying on the floor of a stationary Japanese truck, gave him food.

No. 78 Squadron included among its pilots at this time Len Waters, the only Aboriginal fighter pilot to serve in the RAAF during the war. While growing up in Queensland, he was inspired by the feats of Kingsford Smith and other aviation pioneers, and in 1942, aged 18, he enlisted in the RAAF. He was proud of his Aboriginal heritage, and believed that each man created his own destiny. He aimed high, for although he joined as a trainee flight mechanic, he was desperate to fly. He worried that his aptitude at morse code might consign him to being a wireless operator, but he got his way, and after training on Tiger Moths, Wirraways and Kittyhawks found himself at Noemfoor. Gaunt, amiable and modest, he flew 95 sorties, most in a P-40N he inherited called 'Black Magic'. His most memorable flight occurred when an unexploded enemy anti-aircraft shell lodged behind his seat. As he flew the two-hour trip home, hoping the shell would not explode, he felt as if a loaded gun were at his head. Waters could fight on the ground too, winning an RAAF middleweight boxing title.

In March the RAAF's action was largely monotonous, but Jock Scott flew a thrilling sortie. He was selected to fly No. 2 to the 'Winker'—Wing Commander Cresswell—on a mission from Morotai to Roemberpon Island. Cresswell's instructions were brief and simple: in their P-40s they would fly low and each drop a 100-pound bomb casing enclosing money, valuables and instructions for the locals. Scott saw the funny side of what followed:

> We flew the 50 or so miles . . . with the Winker pulling spray off the wave tops all the way. Lord knows if my 100 pounder skipped off the water onto the beach or not but the Winker's certainly did, and disappeared into the boondoo [jungle] at an estimated 300 M.P.H. Maybe it stopped against a coconut palm before it reached the other side of the little island, or it just kept going. The Intelligence Pooh-Bahs never got round to telling me ... if our novel method of delivering the booty worked out for the New Guinean recipients—I hope they were good at dodging 300 mph presents.

The excitement did not end there. As they looked around, Cresswell soon shouted something unintelligible to Scott over the intercom and kept his transmit button down while letting go with his machine guns. Scott climbed to join him and arrived in time to see Cresswell immolating a Japanese motorcycle–sidecar combination. Before Scott opened fire, Cresswell had also finished off a truck and trailer. Both pilots peppered a bulldozer, but to Scott's annoyance even hundreds of incendiaries and tracers could not set it alight. Now the enemy, recovering from what Scott called 'nature study in the surrounding scrub', began to fire back.[15] Scott noticed the red winking of a machine gun trying to hit Cresswell, and accordingly headed for the source. The gunners diverted their murderous attention to him, but Scott ensured that the red winking stopped abruptly. He later wrote sympathetically of these outgunned and stationary Japanese.

After Scott silenced a second gun, the two pilots incinerated another truck. They headed for home, Scott weaving and jinking to avoid the machine-gunners he now feared lay under every bush. Cresswell flew level and straight.

On 31 March Wally Mills was piloting a Catalina over the Macassar Strait, providing air–sea rescue cover for an RAAF Liberator mission. Suddenly his wireless operator, Ron Francis, heard an agitated Beaufighter pilot telling Morotai that his No. 2 had 'bought it', and was ditching. It was, he said, 'a real hot shop', with 'dozens of Nips' on the beach. Mills, who half an hour earlier had seen two Beaufighters fly past, assumed they were the ones involved. He called Morotai and received permission to leave the Liberators and head towards the ditched plane. He was surprised to learn that its position was nearly 500 kilometres away, near Ambon, so he opened up the throttles for the maximum speed he could induce from the Cat-boat. The Beaufighter pilot Francis had heard was Ken Sounness, and his No. 2 Ross Roberts, whose engines had stopped suddenly after being hit by flak. Roberts ditched what an official report called his 'SNAFU Beaufighter' in Haruku Strait east of Ambon, and although the aircraft sank in the regulation 15 seconds, he and his navigator, Basil Phillips, made it into their dinghy.[16] Sounness decided to wait and protect his mate until help arrived, even though this may force him to ditch too. Within an hour, two more Beaufighters arrived and, with one of them as escort, Sounness flew home after more than seven hours aloft. The plain language transmissions the Catalina and the two Beaus made across the airwaves were followed by a growing audience at Morotai. The Japanese ashore had so far not interfered in proceedings, but Roberts and Phillips would almost certainly have been spotted and were probably being left as decoys. They sent away a local who brought out a canoe and offered to help them.

Mills eventually arrived, and swept low towards the two airmen, now positioned some 275 metres offshore. Flak puffs were bursting near the airborne Beaufighter, as were splashes of gunfire near the airmen's dinghy. Their heads were barely visible in the water nearby. Mills overshot the dinghy the first time, and had to come round again. Desperate to slow down the Cat's forward momentum, he lowered the landing gear and stopped his engines before landing safely on the rough water. From the cockpit he shouted to the two exhausted airmen to hurry. Enemy rifles, machine guns and mortars sought to sink him, while a cacophony of noise came from the low-flying Beaufighter strafing the shore, and Mills' own blister machine guns. His gunnery officer, Bill Hastie, took on the enemy from the unprotected gun blister until severely wounded in the stomach. Robert Ballinghall took over the gun while an American medical orderly in the crew bandaged Hastie under fire. There was a big hole in the Cat's hull, too, but Mills got her airborne after a few minutes, even though the rough water inflicted more structural damage. Tom 'Jungle' Ellis, flying the Beaufighter overhead, had done all he could to harass and distract the Japanese. He lost an engine to flak after his third run, but made a fourth to cover the Catalina's bumpy take-off. With his good engine faltering he finally departed. Ellis, Mills, Hastie and Sounness all received DFCs for their efforts. Hastie was in an American hospital on Morotai three hours after the battle.

Prior to enlisting in Sydney in 1941, Mills, a New Zealander, had been training to become a vet. He had since flown as a second pilot and captain in 20 Squadron, worked as an instructor at Rathmines and made two ferry delivery flights from California. He commanded the first crew of No. 113 Air–Sea Rescue Flight, formed in January 1945.

It was a great comfort to the combat fliers, with their numerous flights over great stretches of water and terribly dangerous enemy territory, to know that if they crashed or had to ditch, there was a rescue organisation with aircraft manned by crews like those of Mills, Bulman and Corrie, who were prepared to risk everything to save them. Mills' flight performed more than just rescues: they covered numerous missions, delivered medical supplies to guerrillas, and transported personnel and locals. Mills clocked up an impressive 202 operational missions, 160 in his final tour, when he also rescued 15 pilots. RAAF Catalina crews generally logged more hours than airmen in any other aircraft, because of the great length of their flights. Many logged over 2000 hours; Squadron Leader Bryan Monkton logged a phenomenal 6000.

These rescues were Allied efforts. Australian Cats saved American crews and vice versa. For example Denis Lawrence received an American DFC for rescuing the crew of a US Liberator, even though heavy seas damaged his Cat. An American Catalina rescued Neil Redfern and James Collison, who had ditched their flak-ridden Beaufighter. The Cat co-pilot risked his life by diving into the water to save Collison, a non-swimmer.

Of course, not all rescue stories could have happy endings. John 'Mac' MacLeod's 76 Squadron Kittyhawk was hit by debris from an explosion in Maccleur Gulf in December 1944, and he had to ditch. Three other P-40s with MacLeod protected him as long as they could, twice sinking enemy boatloads of infantry sent to grab the Australian from his dinghy. The only available Catalina was an American one, but it failed to find MacLeod in a mix-up over message codes that engendered bitterness in 76 Squadron. MacLeod was captured and beheaded.

Yet this disaster was exceptional. One estimate says that Catalinas rescued 540 Allied pilots during the war. A senior Japanese commander later noted that Japanese pilots respected the Catalina crews' bravery, and regretted that Japan had not provided such help for its own personnel.[17]

Jones vs Bostock reprised

While Catalina crews put themselves in danger to save other airmen who were risking their lives, the petty struggles at the top of the RAAF dragged on. A nasty exchange between the two Australian Air Vice-Marshals from January 1945 nicely illustrates the point. Jones sent Bostock this signal concerning a staff policy directive: 'I take strong exception to the insubordinate tone of your signal and your repeated attempts to usurp authority of this Headquarters. Communications couched in terms such as the one under reply are to cease forthwith.' To which Bostock replied, with equal testiness:

> Secret, for C.A.S. from A.O.C. I also have responsibilities. You do not understand current Allied air and R.A.A.F. Higher Organisation in accordance with which I am responsible to Commander, Allied Air Forces, and not, repeat not, subordinate to you for the discharge of duties incumbent upon my appointment. I do, and will continue to take the strongest exception to your unwarranted and uninformed interference.[18]

Within days of this vitriolic exchange, the Minister for Air, Arthur Drakeford, sought to have RAAF Command move from Brisbane to New Guinea, or some other forward base, where it would take over both operational *and* administrative control of all RAAF formations outside Australia. Jones, meanwhile, would have administrative *and* operational control of all formations within Australia.

Curtin put this suggestion to MacArthur in late February 1945. Bostock complained bitterly, saying that introducing such a change on the eve of the Borneo offensives might well result in higher command being 'inefficient to a degree which may cause unnecessary casualties and even result in defeat'.[19] This self-important analysis was accepted in the War Cabinet, which with MacArthur's approval shelved the issue—again.

A nasty tiff arose when General Kenney issued an order on Anzac Day 1945 designating Bostock 'Air Officer Commander-in-Chief, RAAF Command'. Bostock passed on details of this virtually self-proclaimed new title to subordinate commanders, but Jones, who had power over such administrative matters, signalled to RAAF Command that the title was 'not approved'. The Australian government backed him, but Kenney seems not to have responded. Perhaps he thought it all too childish and insignificant.

The RAAF Command scandal continued until the end of the war, never resolved by an Australian government too worried about upsetting its American allies. As the official RAAF historian of the period, George Odgers says, this division 'had an unsettling effect on the force'.[20] On the other hand it was unknown at the time to many of the rank and file, who had more pressing worries.

Staying sane

Amidst the stress and horror of war in the operational areas humour helped keep men sane. This could even arise in the tense atmosphere of a court martial, as described in 77 Squadron's Operations Record Book in March 1945:

> . . . F/S Gingell was called quite unexpectedly to give evidence. This NCO was on the volley ball court adjacent to the Court clad in underpants and boots only, covered in sawdust; as time was precious he was put on immediate call and appeared and gave evidence so dressed; a hat was loaned to him which, to make things still more humorous, was 4 to 5 sizes too small.[21]

On the same page of the squadron's operations book, the other extreme of service life is recorded: the story of a fitter, Ron Hunter, killed when he stepped back into a revolving airscrew.

The numbers of RAAF personnel on Morotai continued to climb, as did their frustration. At one time, 700 men of No. 78 Wing were sleeping in the open, and 'Woof' Arthur complained about the lack of tents. When just one week's notice was given of the arrival of the Australian Liberator squadrons from Darwin, there were no tents for the 500–600 men involved.

American and Australian aircraft—one airman counted 31 different types—were taking off constantly from the four crowded airstrips: from Wama alone, Australian flying control personnel handled as many as 400 aircraft a day, sometimes landing at intervals of one every 15 seconds. One airman's first impression of the island was 'Hell of a lot of aircraft.'[22]

The monotonous diet worsened after I Australian Corps arrived in April, when Australian Army rations replaced American ones. Largely because of the maddening lack of transport, Cobby was unable to replace airmen whose normal 15-month tour of duty had expired. Consequently, many were retained for up to 20 months. This proved especially trying on a cramped equatorial island far from civilisation and with few amenities. Many also felt a deep nostalgia for the sight and companionship of white women. One of the sisters of the MAETU had an illuminating experience when she flew to New Britain in the same period. Servicemen in the region had heard that a nurse was coming and when the aircraft door opened, she was confronted by 'a huge semicircle of men, black and white, just looking. Not a smile, not a word, just looking!'[23] This level of attention may have been unusual, but another sister talked of men in the islands invariably stealing a moment from their work to look if a white girl appeared. Just occasionally those on Morotai saw nursing sisters.

A second source of relief—alcohol—was available, in small quantities, at Morotai and Noemfoor. The men received beer, the officers beer and spirits. Despite the enervating heat, increasing numbers were prepared to swap or sell their beer to American servicemen, and something of a racket developed among business-minded Australian airmen, including officers. Flying in beer supplies had always been a tempting challenge for squadrons: it was, for example, the practice in 1942–43 that

Beaufighters and Bostons coming from the mainland to New Guinea, which was officially dry, would bring grog. When Joe Hewitt commanded 9 Operational Group in 1943, he had openly permitted men to fly up alcohol from the mainland, as long as aircraft were not flown specifically for this purpose and that it was always given as a gift, and never used for money or trade. One pilot gleefully described a practice of flying four No. 81 Wing Kittyhawks from Noemfoor to Manus Island, and there obtaining many cans of beer from the US Navy PX (Post Exchange). These were loaded onto the aircraft, especially in the wheel wells, so that the undercarriages of the returning P-40s were partly down on the return flights. The record was 400 cans in one Kitty.

Cobby tried unavailingly to stop the illicit trading in alcohol. However, quite apart from that trade, locally improvised 'jungle juice' was always brewing among servicemen in the islands.

Mutiny at Morotai

'Woof' Arthur was so disappointed by Cobby's failure to correct the RAAF's wasteful policy towards its flying squadrons' aircrews and aircraft that he decided to take decisive action himself. He was prepared to put his own career on the line. In March he went to Morotai and sounded out other senior officers. He found like-minded thinking in Group Captain Caldwell (No. 80 Wing), Wing Commander 'Bobby' Gibbes (an air ace in the Middle East, now No. 80 Wing), Wing Commander Ken Ranger (staff officer), Squadron Leader John Waddy (No. 80 Squadron, one of Australia's top aces in the Middle East), Squadron Leader Grace (No. 82 Squadron), Squadron Leader Vanderfield (110 Mobile Fighter Control Unit) and Squadron Leader Stuart Harpham (60 Operational Base Unit).

When they were on the point of taking action, two of the group became embroiled in controversy about alcohol. Arthur wrote home early in April: 'Clive [Caldwell] and Bobby [Gibbes] have "blotted their copy-books". Both charged with "trading"—in a big way. Clive may be caught on straight out "stealing".'

According to Arthur, Gibbes had been drawn into it, while 'Clive has caused lots of trouble … in lots of ways and has hardly a friend in the place. It's a pity, he has so much ability if he wanted to use it in the right way. He is completely and utterly selfish.'[24]

With the liquor-trading issue hanging above two heads, on 19 April Arthur and the other seven like-minded senior 1st TAF officers mentioned above tried to resign their commissions over the unstated issue of the wastefulness of operations. Their applications said simply: 'I hereby respectfully make application that I be permitted to resign my commission as an officer in the Royal Australian Air Force, forthwith.'[25] Cobby tried but could not get them, either individually or as a group, to explain further.

Bostock came to Morotai and interviewed the eight officers, whom he found 'respectful but bitter and unrelenting'. He offered to take the matter no further if they tore up their resignations. They would not, but agreed to change 'forthwith' to 'at the end of current operations'. Bostock found the morale of 1st TAF at a 'dangerously low level', whereas Cobby said there was discontent, but not low morale.[26]

General Kenney, who was visiting Morotai to discuss air support for the coming Borneo operations, told Jones—who had also flown to Morotai—that he wanted to speak to the eight officers. Kenney found Jones' response so unhelpful and sullen that he threatened to approach Curtin to have him replaced. Kenney spoke to the eight officers, and although he could not change their determination to resign, he felt that they were acting in good faith and with just cause. When Jones considered taking disciplinary action against them, Kenney warned him off, saying that he would speak in their defence and tell the press the causes of the problem—by implication, RAAF leadership. Jones later wrote that Kenney's anger arose partly from his own presence at the interview, but also because the American had no answer to the mutineers' repeated question—which does not appear in other sources—'Why aren't we being taken on to the Philippines?'[27]

Rather than accept the resignations of the rebels, Bostock asked RAAF Headquarters to relieve of their commands three other senior officers: Cobby, Group Captain Gibson—who had been in charge at Port Moresby during the 44 Days—and Group Captain Simms. Jones agreed, and all three were soon replaced. On Jones' recommendation, the government sent Mr Justice Barry to investigate this 'Morotai Mutiny', as it later came to be called. Jones and the government emphasised the issue of alleged illegal trading in liquor rather than the more important issues: the operations of nearly 17,000 men in 1st TAF, and why those on Morotai were so disaffected.

Barry found that disquiet about the operations on which 1st TAF was being sent was a major source of discontent, as were the attitudes of the three senior officers who had since been removed. He found that expenditure on operations far outweighed the return, as did an RAAF Operational Research section report of the time. He also mentioned concern at the continued divisions within the high command of the RAAF, although to most airmen these were either old news, unknown or irrelevant. Moreover, although living conditions at Morotai were trying, those in New Guinea in 1942 had been worse and the flying squadrons' morale had been high. The key reason for the mutiny was the conviction of young leaders that they were engaged in operations with no military justification. Ineffective leadership was another, with senior officers setting a poor example and doing too little to keep their bored men engaged. Cobby and the other leaders involved felt they had been doing the right thing—Cobby arguing, for example, that he was not wasting resources, but instead operating at about one-third capacity, which was all that was needed to neutralise the enemy in their theatre. How best to approach the enemy in areas bypassed in the main advance was a problem everywhere in the South-West Pacific Area, including the Philippines. Because it involved such senior commanders, the 'Morotai Mutiny' affected the atmosphere in 1st TAF. Many airmen of lower rank probably knew little or nothing about it, but one pilot recalled later that afterwards men in 30 Squadron became increasingly moody, introspective and preoccupied with personal survival.

Meanwhile, 1st TAF supported the Australian amphibious landings in Borneo, and at least one group of airmen arriving at Morotai in May were eager to be there. These were the Liberator crews of 82 Wing, arriving from Darwin. 'The war at last!' wrote the 23 Squadron diarist when, from their American Liberty ship, the squadron saw Morotai on the horizon.[28]

26 The final battles

Borneo landings

The Borneo landings, codenamed 'Oboe', were major undertakings for the Australian armed forces. They would supposedly deny the enemy the Netherlands East Indies' oil, but the Japanese had no means of transporting this from Borneo anyway, so the campaigns served little strategic purpose. Some 20 squadrons of 1st TAF supported the landings at Tarakan, North Borneo and Balikpapan. So did squadrons based at Darwin and Western Australia. The RAAF was essentially able to plan its involvement independently, because from early 1945 all operations south of the Philippines were made the responsibility of RAAF Command.

Tarakan, off the north-east coast of Borneo, was the first objective. Its airfield was considered a choice prize, from which aircraft could support the subsequent operations, in North Borneo and Balikpapan. Ominously, though, the planners knew that the western end of the strip was swampy and would require work to make it usable. Having the necessary run of clear weather would be tricky on an island with an annual rainfall of 370 centimetres. General Kenney delegated the planning of the operation's air support to Bill Bostock, putting at his disposal not only 1st TAF, but also the Thirteenth and Fifth Air Forces. RAAF heavy bomber squadrons based in the Northern Territory and Western Australia would be available too. The 1st TAF would attack targets on the island and cover the convoy's voyage to Tarakan, which was unlikely to be disrupted by an enemy air force constituting just 69 aircraft in the Netherlands East Indies. Once the airfield at Tarakan was open, No. 78 Wing (75, 78, 80 and 452 Squadrons), with No. 77 Wing's Beaufighters and four Austers of No. 83 Wing, were to provide an air garrison. Air Commodore Cobby and 'Woof' Arthur, now commanding 78 Wing, would oversee air operations at Tarakan.

For 20 days before the invasion of Tarakan, RAAF Liberators from Morotai, Western Australia and Darwin struck targets in the Netherlands East Indies. It must have been gratifying for Arch Dunne, who had flown Hudsons over the Indies in the war's most terrifying days, and who now commanded 23 Squadron. The Australian Liberators had a demanding schedule, but the more numerous American bombers did most of the pre-invasion bombing. Raids on Tarakan itself built into great intensity. Every visible target was strafed and bombed, including huge oil tanks, which it was feared the enemy might use to send a flow of burning oil against the invaders. Australian Liberators were prominent in destroying these tanks.

Disaster struck when eight 25 Squadron Liberators were caught in bad weather during a raid on Java. Squadron Leader Jack Wawn sent the message 'Aircraft vibrating badly', and said he was heading for Truscott. His next message, the word 'Ditching', showed he did not make it.[1] He and his crew survived the landing, but were captured almost immediately near Sumba Island. They were beaten and tortured, especially Wawn, but survived the war.

In the official historian's words, 'an atmosphere of doubt and confusion' prevailed among RAAF forces preparing to sail for Tarakan.[2] The 'Morotai Mutiny' and the liquor episode contributed to this unsettled atmosphere. Cobby discovered just days before the operation that Bostock had recommended his removal: it was the same kind of change that Bostock had suggested might bring defeat if it happened to him. Moreover, wholesale changes had to be made just as 1st TAF forces were boarding ship, for it was announced that the North Borneo invasion would take place before, rather than after, the Balikpapan landings.

The invasion convoy sailed on 26 April, with American and Australian aircraft providing aerial cover. Embarrassingly, this cover was poorly organised. Matters got worse on the day of the landing, 1 May, while MacArthur and other senior officers were watching the landings from a warship. The aerial formations that arrived for the preliminary bombardment unexpectedly included only USAAF bombers. Bostock felt intensely embarrassed, and soon learned the reason: while the fleet was sailing, and radio silence was in force, his nemesis Jones had sent a message to the RAAF squadrons telling them they were grounded as they had completed their allotted monthly flying hours! When Bostock explained this to General Kenney, the American offered his sympathy. Alan Stephens calls this episode, which jeopardised the lives of Australian soldiers, 'the most shameful example of the depths to which the feud sank'.[3] The same ruling held back an RAAF Liberator from a scheduled air observation flight over Tarakan the next day, but thereafter normal operations resumed. Men closer to the sharp end of the battle were not aware of the machinations at the top.

After the landings the RAAF were, in Odgers' words, 'in trouble at Tarakan from the start'.[4] Faulty loading in Morotai delayed operations on the island. Air-warning facilities, crucial to detecting enemy air attacks, took 34 hours to bring into operation, with different parts loaded in two ships.

'Woof' Arthur had escaped punishment for sticking to his guns throughout the 'Morotai Mutiny', but now found himself among heavy gunfire, albeit friendly, on Tarakan. He described it as 'a rowdy hole', where his headquarters shook constantly and the humidity saturated clothes in minutes. He could have been sweating too because he had to work closely with Cobby, yet he told his wife that 'Cob' had been 'most friendly and cheerful. Can't understand it! He's the same with all the boys and has been all the time. He knows that what we've done will affect him adversely and very considerably too.'[5] Arthur was unaware that Cobby had already experienced some of those adverse effects.

Meanwhile, the Diggers ground their way forward against tough resistance. They took the Tarakan airfield, which had been heavily mined, on 5 May. Four Austers of No. 16 Observation Post Flight were brought ashore to direct artillery fire and provide reconnaissance. Army engineers constructed a makeshift runway, but when Flying Officer James McIntyre tried it on 2 May, he hit a log at the end of the tiny strip and his Auster swung into an anti-tank ditch and caught fire. His passenger, Army Captain Ket, was burning when pulled from the wreckage. He died, and McIntyre was evacuated injured. The Austers moved to the Tarakan airstrip on 6 May.

Army and air force officers on Tarakan looked askance at each other's efforts. Cobby was blamed for his men's poor state of training, and his replacement by Fred Scherger on 10 May pleased Army commanders. Scherger himself appears not to have reciprocated these feelings. He said after the Borneo operations that the Army were 'not only amateurs, but … also work solely, wholly and completely on the selfish idea that they come first'.[6]

The initial plan was that RAAF fighters would provide air cover from the Tarakan airstrip from 7 May, but with the airfield still non-operational by then, Thirteenth Air Force provided the patrols until mid-May, when RAAF Kittyhawks and Beaufighters based at Sanga Sanga Island took over this monotonous task. Two well-equipped airfield construction squadrons (Nos 1 and 8) went ashore on 1 May to help complete the airfield. The Austers were able to operate from one firm narrow section, but most of the strip, needed for transport aircraft and bombers, contained bomb craters inflicted by Allied bombing and was waterlogged. Filling the holes proved an immense task, into which went the labour of hundreds of airmen and locals, thousands of feet of Marsden matting, and 50,000 cubic metres of 'fill' comprising items as diverse as timber, concrete, old machines and sand-filled oil drums. Because the airfield lay below the high water level, stinking liquid filled its lower half when the tide rose. Aircrew laughed at this strip that rose and fell with the tide.

Other problems slowed the reconstruction. The Japanese shelled the strip—though to little effect—and sent in raiding parties. Two airmen, LAC Thomas Irvine and Sergeant Keith Bradshaw, died in these raids, and others were wounded, but the Japanese lost many more. RAAF bomb-disposal experts defused 114 mines on the airstrip and dispersal areas in just two days. Disposal of mines and bombs on Tarakan was a tremendous task, to which No. 5 Bomb Disposal Unit RAAF contributed. It had been kept busy in the Admiralty Islands and in the Philippines, but on Tarakan encountered more mines than anywhere else. For some time the unit operated from 5 a.m. until midnight clearing the airfield and the tracks in front of advancing tanks. This unit suffered no fatalities, though its casualties included two men who each lost an eye and one man wounded by a sniper on Tarakan.

Heavy and persistent rain inhibited work at the airstrip too. The whole episode reflected poorly on the RAAF's intelligence personnel, who paid too little heed to the water-filled bomb craters that appeared in many of their pre-invasion photographs. Why they planned for bombers to damage the airfield that was the objective of the whole campaign is also mystifying. Clive Monk, then Senior Mechanical Engineer Officer of No. 1 Airfield Construction Squadron, later recalled his disgust at the inadequacy of the machinery provided, at the lack of defence training for personnel suddenly in the firing line, and at the inaccuracy of the preliminary 'Engineer Intelligence Report' which said that sandstone and other construction materials would be found on Tarakan. He was deeply suspicious that the motives for the campaign related to Dutch oil, and not Australian air support. Clive Caldwell appears to have been offered the position of Air Task Force Commander for the Oboe operations, but seems to have refused it because of his reservations about Tarakan and its airstrip.

The repeated delays in finishing the strip brought more tension with the AIF, who were fighting and dying in the pointless campaign. It also forced most of the 1st TAF force intended for Tarakan to stay behind at Morotai. Finally, it seems to have led to deception on the part of the RAAF authorities. Jones told the Advisory War Council on 23 May that 'RAAF fighter aircraft were now operating from Tarakan'.[7] In fact it would be another month before that happened. Day after day in that period, LAC Bill Collins summarised the day's activities on the island with references to his losses at cards and the words 'Work strip'.[8] On 30 May, LAC Brealey told his diary: 'if the strip is ready by the 6th [June] the AIF say 3 days with the Spits and they would clean the whole lot up, they (AIF) are badly in need of our Air cover'.[9]

Scherger, who was on the scene, was willing to concede that Oboe 1, the Tarakan operation, was a failure, but stated fairly that the RAAF had been set an impossible task, for which some 900 Australians were killed or wounded. Whereas Tarakan was a 'shemozzle' for the RAAF, its support of the later Borneo operations would be far better planned and executed.

Enemy air activity during the Tarakan campaign was puny. Twice small formations of Jakes ineffectually dropped bombs at night. Collins counted at least five individual raids. The first Beaufighter contact with an enemy aircraft in 18 months occurred in May: two Beaus encountered and hit two Dinahs over North Borneo, but lost them in cloud after the Beaufighters' cannons failed.

The second Borneo operation was the seizure of the Brunei Bay area in North Borneo. The 1st TAF allotted to the operation three Kittyhawk squadrons, one Spitfire squadron, an army-cooperation wing, an attack wing of Beaufighters and Mosquitos, and newly arrived No. 13 Squadron's Venturas.

The unavailability of Tarakan airfield delayed the contribution of Beaufighters to softening up operations before the Brunei Bay landings, but on 3 June Beaus strafed oil installations in Borneo, killing one Japanese in the tower of an oil derrick and sending others scurrying into the trees. More than 3000 sorties were flown in the five days before the landings, but RAAF aircraft flew only a small proportion of them.

When the invasion convoy left Morotai on 4 June, it included not only most of the 9th Australian Division but also 6000 RAAF personnel. Tropical rainstorms soaked men and equipment on a rough voyage. RAAF Liberators bombarded the enemy beaches on the day of the assault, 10 June. They constituted about one-quarter of the bombers involved, and bombed accurately. An RAAF observation Liberator was then sent in to fly low and check for enemy activity on the beaches. After it gave the all-clear the landing craft went in, unopposed.

The following day was terrible for the RAAF based at Sanga Sanga. In unrelated incidents three Beaufighters crashed into the sea, as did a 'Beaufreighter', a light transport version of the Beaufort. Seven aircrew were killed. No doubt the RAAF on Sanga Sanga were not too upset when ordered to return to Morotai and make way for USAAF Lightnings. With Tarakan still unusable, the Australians had to wait until the airstrip on Labuan Island was captured. On 17 June, two 76 Squadron Kittyhawks, flown by the CO, Squadron Leader Peter Jones, and Mervyn Furze landed on Labuan's rough strip, and the following day used it for operational sorties. They quickly discovered and destroyed two enemy aircraft on the ground at nearby Keningau airfield.

Two 457 Squadron Spitfires, based at Labuan, intercepted and destroyed a Dinah on 20 June, in the squadron's first aerial combat since 1943. No. 76 lost a Kittyhawk pilot in strafing Keningau, but on 29 June surprised a Dinah preparing for take-off at the same strip. The five Kittyhawks, led by Jones, destroyed the Dinah and killed the crew who were in it and on the wing. On 4–6 July Kittyhawks, Spitfires, Wirraways and Austers flew 230 sorties in support of ground operations. No. 77 Squadron's pilots alone claimed to have killed 100 Japanese on the ground and 30 swimming on 5 July.

On 6 July, Squadron Leader Jones' luck seemed to have run out. Jones, who had noticed that one sharpshooting Japanese machine-gunner had hit no fewer than four Kittyhawks around him, was flying at 450 feet when he heard a loud bang. Initially he considered it a hot round exploding in his guns, but when his motor would not respond, realised that the same machine gun had hit his oil line. He tried to gain height and bale out, but the engine would not cooperate and he 'squashed' into nearby trees without sustaining major damage. Though near a Japanese-held road, Jones managed to find a tiny fast-flowing stream, which carried him to open water on his dinghy. By flashing a mirror he attracted a friendly aircraft's attention, and was rescued by a Catalina the following day.

Another pilot from Jones' squadron went down over enemy territory on 13 July. William George disappeared from view and contact on a strafing mission over Sarawak. Much energy was expended looking for him. Eventually Australian patrols sent a message that on 19 July locals had located George, who, according to the dry but telling language of an official report:

> … had apparently been wandering through the jungle and when found was in a serious condition. Four fingers of one hand had been broken, his left eye was out of its socket and his right eye was practically closed. He apparently received those injuries when his aircraft crashed. Very shortly after being discovered by the natives he died.[10]

No. 86 Wing's Mosquitos (No. 1 Squadron) and Beaufighters (93 Squadron) were due to operate from Labuan from June, but movement delays and problems with the short runway meant that they only arrived in late July, and shared just three operations between them. No. 93 Beaufighters destroyed an 800-ton vessel with rockets on 7 August, but lost one aircraft in the jungle. Its pilot, Vernon Sims, and navigator, Reginald Farrant, were presumed dead, but made their way towards the coast. Friendly locals took the Australians in a sampan, bluffing their way past suspicious Japanese troops by telling them they were going to catch the soldiers some fish. They reached friendly troops on 20 August, after the war had ended.

No. 1 Squadron's Mosquitos, trained for low-level intruder work, also strafed barges, at Kuching on 8 August, but Squadron Leader Richard Browne and Richard Gregson were killed when they crashed over the target. A photo of Browne's wife, taken from the dead man's wallet, was found at Kuching after the war, pinned up somewhere with what the officer commanding the squadron called 'the usual caustic Japanese remarks'.[11] Squadron Leader Frank Schaaf led his squadron, No. 82, to Kuching too, more than 700 kilometres from their base at Labuan. The Kittyhawks were airborne for 4 hours and 40 minutes, a time outside their accepted duration. They not only made it, but achieved great success, destroying three Oscars which were preparing to take off. Howard James-Martin, who had transferred from Vengeances, flew number two to Schaaf, whom he saw hit a Japanese 'with a burst of machine-gun fire that lifted him about twenty feet into the air from where he fell, splat'.[12]

Balikpapan, the final Oboe target, had been one of Japan's main sources of aviation fuel. Kenney wanted it, and had launched massive raids on it since these became practicable in September 1944. The RAAF had raided it too. Kenney delegated the detailed invasion planning to Bostock, but offered him any FEAF resources he wanted.

Bostock would use Liberators operating from Australia. He planned also to employ Beaufighters and Kittyhawks, but the delays at Tarakan forced him to depend instead on Lightnings based at Sanga Sanga and fighters from three American escort carriers. At his disposal were some 300 aircraft in 40 squadrons. The Japanese were estimated to have only 17 fighters, 17 bombers and a few float-planes, and one can only imagine the outlook of their crews. The operations were primarily an American affair: of 123 Liberators that bombed Balikpapan on 27 June, just six were Australian.

On 28 June LAC Collins on Tarakan began his entry in the usual way: '52 days Tarakan, work strip.' But then came a long-awaited corollary: 'Kittyhawks, Beaufighters, Doug [Dakotas], Lightning landed on st[r]ip'.[13] The airfield had indeed taken its first RAAF warplane that day, when Wing Commander Read landed a Beaufighter. The runway was still lousy: three of the 14 aircraft that landed that afternoon crashed. Although henceforward 78 Wing's Spitfires and Kittyhawks operated from Tarakan, it was found impossible for Beaufighters to use the strip, and their war was effectively over.

The Balikpapan landings took place on 1 July. Twenty of the 82 Liberators that participated were RAAF. Trev Quirk was in one of them, and told his diary:

> Balik is just about in ruins … Our bombs crashed through the area allotted us and as we swung away over the sea a new fire lit up. Flames rose thousands of feet into the air topped by a huge pillar of smoke which rose to about 10,000 ft … It was a pretty sight; a background for the many ships of the invasion force standing off shore … As we turned for home, we could see the first boats of the landing setting out for the shore … I was glad then that I am in the airforce.

In fact, the Australian 'Libs', USAAF Mitchells and naval bombardment so hammered the beach defences that none of the 17 assault waves of infantry suffered casualties in the landing. Thus Quirk was entitled to conclude his diary entry for the day: 'We arrived home proud of our job well done.'[14]

Wing Commander Arthur Davies, captaining a Liberator over the beachhead, reported progress to the command ship, USS *Wasatch*. He also strafed a retreating enemy column, and was fired on by some of the many enemy anti-aircraft guns that survived the bombardment. Davies' air observation aircraft was unharmed, but the Liberator that relieved him was hit. Its commander, Group Captain Donald McLean, No. 82 Wing's CO, decided he had to ditch in the sea. Most of the crew baled out and were rescued, but four, including McLean, were killed. Much as their crews liked the 'dear old Lib', which once airborne 'flew like a bird', the B-24 had a terrible record when ditching in the sea.[15] It tended to flood in seconds, for when belly-landed or heavily ditched, Liberators often fell apart at the forward bomb-bay bulkhead, and the insubstantial bomb-bay doors regularly collapsed. The crew in the rear of the fuselage rarely escaped alive. An RAF study of 16 ditched Liberators showed that only eight of 131 crewmen survived, and only one of them was in the rear. Australian Liberators spent most of their time over water, but the RAAF did not follow an RAF modification, which reinforced the fuselage. If a Liberator had to ditch, baling out was advisable.

On the ground at Balikpapan, RAAF air liaison and support parties accompanied the troops and relayed many calls for air support to headquarters ships. US Liberators made most of the subsequent attacks. A problem arose that first afternoon, as the Australian infantry commander, Major-General Milford, asked for an air strike when the Liberators were due to leave for base. Against Bostock's advice, Milford urged that US Navy dive-bombers be employed for the task. Milford got his way, but the naval aircraft missed the target and instead hit Australian positions, killing or wounding 17.

Observation sorties continued to be perilous. The day after the landing Roy Beattie, DFM, was flying below 1000 feet when flak struck his Liberator. Out of control, it crashed in enemy territory, killing all 14 aboard. 'Gloom pervades the camp,' wrote Trev Quirk. '"What, who" they say "will be the third catastrophe". There are always 3 prangs in a row.'[16] This old aviation superstition came true: three days later, Squadron Leader John Redman was on observation duty at just 200 feet when ack-ack set one of his engines aflame. The aircraft exploded in mid-air and the wreck landed behind enemy lines. Again, everyone on board—11 crew and one Army officer—were killed.

Squadron Leader Barclay led Spitfires on to Sepinggang airfield, Balikpapan, on 15 July. That day they flew a mission to strafe Japanese positions holding up the advance; Arthur Brealey reported that the soldiers called it their best-ever support. Kittyhawks and Spitfires now ran riot at Balikpapan. 'Army elated with support given,' wrote an airman at 78 Wing HQ.[17]

One of 11 barges sunk or burnt at Balikpapan that day was hit by Flight Lieutenant Alexander Blumer, whose arm and Spitfire airscrew were singed in an explosion set off by his gunfire. Brealey saw Blumer on his return 'covered with soot and oil and he couldn't see, we cleaned up his cabin and off he went again'. Brealey concluded from this episode that 'the Jap has good reason to hate these Spitfire boys'. Not knowing Blumer's name, Brealey described him in his diary as 'a DFC chap'. Blumer had won the DFC in Italy, where he had shot down a Stuka and a Messerschmitt Bf 109. During the dogfight with the latter, six other Messerschmitt Bf 109s had attacked him. Blumer baled out from his crippled kite, but two fingers had to be amputated from his wounded left hand.

Twin-engined Japanese aircraft dropped 25 bombs on Balikpapan early on 24 July, in their biggest air attack since the Borneo campaign began. A stand-by Spitfire, flown by 452's Jeffrey King, was directed towards the enemy aircraft. After an inconclusive tussle with one aircraft, which nearly collided with him, King saw a second twin-engined aircraft's exhausts and shot it down.

Misfortune struck the Liberators again three days later. Kenneth Hanson was flying a photographic mission over the Celebes when flak hit his Liberator, which caught fire and exploded against a hillside. Four airmen jumped from the plane before impact. One, Charles Nichol, had no parachute and was killed instantly, as were the eight who did not get out. Of the three who parachuted, John Orgill landed in the garden of a Chinese family. They urged him to make good his escape, but he waited to ascertain the fate of his mates and was captured. On arrival at a Japanese prison he grabbed a bayonet from the scabbard of an indigenous guard and tried to make a fight of it. Four Japanese soldiers disarmed him and beat him for half an hour. He died that night. The other two airmen, Arnold Lockyer and George Lindley, had been injured in baling out. Both were now brutally interrogated, with some of the questioning reportedly concerning the atomic bomb. Even the prosaic wording of the official report on their ultimate fate makes shocking reading: 'In the early hours of the morning of the 21st August, 1945, they were chloroformed and buried, probably alive, at Kasten.'[18] Note the date: six days after hostilities officially ended.

By then yet another Liberator crew had died in action. Jack Faviell's B-24 was lost over the fateful Celebes, in another mission of dubious value. The five Liberators destroyed in July could be replaced, unlike the lives of 48 RAAF personnel, and of several AIF and American men who flew with them.

On 2 August, 79 Squadron suffered its last fatality. After strafing two huts in Halmahera, Barney Newman lost part of a wing and crashed into trees. In a confidential report on Newman just weeks before, his CO, Ken James, described him as 'a definite asset to any squadron'.[19] His many fine qualities were lost to Australia on the eve of its victory. The last RAAF airman to die over Borneo was 80 Squadron's Eldred Quinn. After ground fire hit his P-40 on 9 August, he sought to crash-land, but had no chance when his kite struck an oil field pumping plant.

Kittyhawks and Spitfires flew an impressive 877 sorties from Tarakan and Sepinggang in July. They virtually obliterated the town of Sandakan, harassing the Japanese there, but were not yet aware that this town would forever be linked to an atrocious 'Death March'.

War over

While 877 1st TAF sorties in the month of July seemed remarkable, the Americans sent more than 10,000 such sorties against Japan in just one week of July. The Japanese could only manage 235 sorties. With 80 per cent of Japan's cities destroyed by US air power, the war's ultimate aerial weapon—atomic bombs—sealed its fate.

At the war's end, on 15 August, the RAAF was flying support missions for Australian ground forces still fighting in Borneo, New Britain, Bougainville and the Aitape–Wewak area. Shortly before a message came through to cancel all missions, 30 Beauforts of 100, 8 and 7 Squadrons completed a strike against a village in the Prince Alexander Ranges. Those Beaufort crews may have carried out the war's last bombing raid.

At the time, 137,208 Australians were serving in the RAAF in the Pacific theatre. The force's 54 operational squadrons and 3187 aircraft—1800 of them front-line types—stood in stark contrast to the 12 incomplete squadrons and 250 obsolescent aircraft of 1939. Moreover, the front-line airmen and the commanders who manned this versatile force were combat veterans with an efficient infrastructure to back them.

Edward White's B-25 crew were desperately unlucky, crashing over New Guinea after being lost in cloud on the way to Sepinggang on 14 August: eight men lost their lives. Surviving Australian airmen could think now of home and peace. In many squadrons there was rejoicing, but 452 Squadron's diary said the 'news was received without excitement or demonstration'. No doubt their joy and relief were tempered by the news of the death that morning of Flying Officer Edmund Lee. While taking off to search for lost Kittyhawks 11 days earlier, he had been injured in a collision with a truck, and on 15 August he succumbed to his injuries. His squadron Operations Record Book recorded that 'the loss of this popular member of the Squadron is felt by all ranks'.[20] Thoughts of those who had not made it this far came to RAAF airmen everywhere.

There was still much work to do, for the RAAF was to take a leading role in aiding and repatriating thousands of Allied prisoners, many of them desperately ill. Already on 16 August, an Australian aircraft flew from Labuan to Kuching, delivering the good news that the war was over. Medical supplies, food and clothing were flown to Singapore. In September, RAAF Dakotas, Catalinas, Liberators and Mitchells evacuated former POWs from Singapore.

RAAF aircraft repatriated Australian airmen in the South-West Pacific Area and South-East Asia. It could be a long wait. LAC Collins kept counting in his diary each day he was on Tarakan, even after the 52nd day brought the airfield into commission. His departure for home, on 2 December 1945, was his 208th day on that inhospitable little island.

Many other RAAF personnel had to wait into early 1946 to return from the islands, and this created much ill-feeling.

Some 2020 members of the RAAF would never return from the war against Japan.

Conclusion

The first that many Japanese soldiers on Bougainville knew of their emperor's surrender came via the RAAF. A Beaufort flew over their lines with the astounding message 'Japan surrenders' written in Japanese on the underside of the wings. This practical measure was also symbolic, for air power had been decisive in defeating Japan. How important *Australian* air power had been in that outcome is debatable. The RAAF had been locked in conflict with Japanese forces from the first day of the Pacific War to the last. But in war, as in sport, Australians tend not to be so interested in whether they participate in the match as in whether they win, and especially whether they 'punch above their weight'.

The RAAF in the Pacific War was like a boxer with one hand tied behind his back. In an appeal to Roosevelt, Churchill said famously in 1941, 'Give us the tools and we will finish the job.' Throughout the war the Australian government gave the same message to both Churchill and Roosevelt, especially concerning aircraft. For an air force, the quality of the tools of its trade is exceptionally important. Britain and the US responded with many aircraft, but for reasons that are understandable, these were generally inferior tools and this affected the RAAF's ability to punch, shoot or bomb effectively. One RAAF pilot reflecting on the 'clapped out' condition of Australia's Kittyhawks in 1945 was not far from the truth when he said, 'The RAAF went through the war on the scrap heap of the Yanks.'[1] John Harrison, an RAAF photographer, recalled that Americans he met during the war tended to praise the Beaufighters, but to say of the RAAF, 'You, Aussies, you can fly alright, if you only had some ships to fly.'[2]

Another factor affecting Australia's punching ability was that, for nearly the whole Pacific War, the way in which the Australians used their aircraft was at the direction of a more powerful ally. The defeats in Malaya, Singapore and the Netherlands East Indies were all endured under Allied supervision, whereas from March to September 1942, the fine victories at Port Moresby and Milne Bay were primarily Australian affairs. Nevertheless, once the tide turned in late 1942, the American commanders directing the war employed their own large, ever-growing and concentrated air force to achieve the main objectives, while employing the RAAF and its inferior aircraft on the flanks and for anti-submarine operations. There was no shame in the Australians' efforts here. In the North-Western Area the RAAF played a key part in what was entirely an air war, though the Americans alone defended Darwin's airspace for most of 1942. The RAAF launched most of the attacks from Darwin, and helped fool a large Japanese army into expecting a land invasion from there. Flying from New Guinea, Australians contributed to the beachhead battles, the breaking of the Bismarcks Barrier and the destruction of Japanese air resources at Rabaul. They thereby helped to ensure that by the end of 1943 New Guinea was under air blockade, with the consequence that disease and starvation virtually eradicated entire Japanese units.

The Americans had by mid-1943 developed aircraft superior to the best Japanese counterparts, integrated them in a balanced team, and begun introducing them in great numbers in the USAAF only. By comparison the RAAF could be termed, in 'Woof' Arthur's evocative phrase, 'a toothless poodle'.[3] Other senior RAAF airmen used the sporting metaphor of 'a Second XI'.[4] The RAAF was performing its allotted tasks well, but by 1944 its role was so subordinate as to affect its morale. Its opponents in New Guinea, Bougainville, New Britain and Borneo were virtually prisoners, so attacking them brought Japan no closer to defeat, while being risky to the attackers. Harassing these Japanese allowed them to contribute to Japan's war effort by using up some of Australia's resources—a policy that was illogical and arguably immoral. Although the Tarakan experience was a blemish, the RAAF supported the AIF effectively in achieving victory in the last campaigns at minimal cost. In India and Burma, too, Australians did superbly, but were not allowed to fly in integrated units, and thus made a contribution that was hard to quantify, yet was not decisive.

Wars require antagonists, and one of the factors that made the last year or more of the war so frustrating for Australians was that Japan's air forces ceased to punch above *their* weight. Air power was the spearhead of Japan's stunning early conquests, but strategically and tactically Japan seemed to lose the plot in aerial warfare in the South-West Pacific from late 1942. Their failure, for example, to support their land forces in critical battles at Milne Bay, the Papuan beachheads and Wau contributed substantially to their country's ultimate loss of tens of thousands of Japanese soldiers to starvation and disease in New Guinea.

So did their neglect of air transport, so vital to Kenney's success. Japan's relative hitting power was at its peak in December 1941, and weaknesses—some inherent, others new—became apparent over subsequent years. For example, the Japanese failure to create well-equipped engineer units capable of developing and maintaining airfields and air power in the disease-ridden, wet and jungle-clad areas from which many of their aircraft had to operate proved a major disadvantage, as did a growing inability to obtain the spare parts, fuel and replacement aircraft needed to keep bases viable. 'Victory disease'—the complacency that arose after the initial easy victories—contributed to an inability to keep pace with their fast-learning and ever-growing enemy. Aircraft design that emphasised light construction to maximise range and manoeuvrability worked effectively in China and in the early Pacific War days when the Allies were caught unawares. However, the older Japanese aircraft always struggled to bring down the well-armed Allied bombers or to beat fast-diving Allied fighters, and from mid-1943, once better Allied aircraft and powerful anti-aircraft defences appeared, Japanese aircraft became death-traps. Japan failed to produce reliable and numerous successors to the Zero, Oscar and Betty, so these types remained in service long beyond their use-by date, and in falling numbers. The experienced cadre of elite pilots with which Japan began the war also evaporated quickly from mid-1943, not helped by the failure to provide a 'tour of duty' system. Japan's inadequate replacement system could not produce airmen to match the experienced Allied pilots now facing them. An emphasis on aerial combat units to the virtual exclusion of invaluable assets such as rescue units cost valuable lives. This contributed to the fact that the available figures suggest that over 80 per cent of Japanese naval fighter pilots were killed. Lack of central operational direction—either for all Japanese air power or within the JAAF and JNAF—also proved damaging, as did the inadequate communications equipment available to connect Japanese aircraft with each other and their bases.

As Japanese air resources dwindled, what they did have was thrown not at the Australians but against the Americans on key fronts such as the Philippines. By July 1945, Fifth Air Force units were based on Okinawa in Japan. The foremost Australian squadrons were still closer to Australia than to Japan: the closest RAAF flags to Tokyo at war's end were probably those of three Wireless Units at San Miguel in the Philippines, though Australian Catalinas and Liberators based in the Philippines ran them close. This distance made it hard for Australian airmen to show what they could do. Between 30 November 1944 and 1 July 1945, there were just nine Japanese air attacks recorded in the entire South-West Pacific Area, made by only 17 aircraft. In the war's last nine months, the 1st TAF had just five contacts with airborne enemy aircraft. Had there been more contacts, there would have been more Australian kills, not least because many of the top RAAF fighter aces had come from the European theatre to the Pacific from 1942. Aces such as Vic Curtis, 'Bobby' Gibbes, 'Jock' Perrin, Ron Rankin, Alan Rawlinson, Len Reid, 'Jock' Sanderson, Don Smith, Gordon Steege and John Waddy never got a chance to paint Rising Sun kill badges on their aircraft.

All this meant that although Japan for a time punched above its weight against the American and British heavyweights, Australia's airmen never had a chance of landing a knockout blow against Nippon. They never fought an extended campaign on their own against the Japanese. One American estimate said Australia contributed eight per cent of the Allied effort in the victory against Japan, and this may be generous. Calculating the RAAF's contribution to this modest proportion would be contentious, but surely could not be over 50 per cent. Hewitt's description of his 9 Operational Group's contribution to MacArthur's offensives of 1943 as 'a small but not insignificant part' might be applied to the RAAF's effort within the entire Pacific War.[5] For example, in terms of shooting down enemy aircraft, the RAAF's effort against Japan was modest. Astonishingly, no official count of victories seems ever to have been made. The approximate number, shown in Appendix C, was 250–300, including victories in India and Malaya. This total is small when one considers American estimates. The USAAF 49th Fighter Group alone—counterpart of an RAAF Wing—was credited with 664 victories. The Japanese Navy lost nearly 4500 fighters, 2000 tactical bombers and 1500 multi-engine bombers in the war, most in the South and South-West Pacific, while the Japanese Army lost the best part of 800 aircraft in New Guinea. Like the kill numbers, the tonnage dropped by the RAAF's bombers, bravely and tirelessly though they worked, was relatively small. The relative tonnage totals for the 5th Air Force (later FEAF) and RAAF were:

- 1942 FEAF 2633, RAAF 659
- 1943 FEAF 29,705, RAAF 1404
- 1944 (Jan. to July) FEAF 57,146, RAAF 4336.[6]

Figures are not available for the RAAF for late 1944 and 1945, but the US figure in 1945 was huge: 107,988 tons.

On the other hand, Eric Bergerud, an American historian who pulls no punches in assessing who did what in the Pacific, offers a positive estimate. He acknowledges that the RAAF's significance fell from 1944, when it was 'understandably' required to support the Australian Army in mopping-up operations. He says they did not miss much in the Philippines, where most of the aerial action revolved around aircraft carrier forces. He emphasises that in 1943, when the air war was still fierce and close, the RAAF played a 'crucial role' in helping to destroy Japan's position in the 'South Pacific'.[7] This too, may be American generosity, but it is a salutary call to remember the epic qualities of much of the RAAF's efforts against Japan, especially when all was still in the balance. The Japanese Army had a saying that 'Nobody returns alive from New Guinea', and the RAAF did much to ensure the truth of that grim statement. Or at least its partial truth, for many of the hundreds of thousands of Japanese in New Guinea, the Bismarcks and Timor eventually made it off the islands, but only after the war—too late to contribute as they might have to vital battles such as Saipan, Iwo Jima and Okinawa. The RAAF deserves some of the credit for this.

Blaming its tools, its Allies and the rapid decline of its foe for its inability to punch far above its weight cannot hide the fact that the RAAF had flaws. To function effectively, modern societies with populations of millions—even the modest seven million of 1939 Australia—need large-scale organisations such as government bureaucracies, schools, police, churches and armed forces. These structures are never perfect, just like the people who create and operate them. The RAAF in World War II was especially likely to be flawed, as its expansion was both huge and rapid. By August 1944 the Australian government's wartime expenditure on the RAAF had reached £350 million, as compared to the £2.2 million that comprised the total Australian budget for military and civil aviation in 1937–38. Inevitably there was tension between the members of the small pre-war permanent air force and the vastly larger group who enlisted for the war's duration. A sketch of 'RAAF Types' in one of the wartime Air Force annuals has as its central figure—who would have been familiar to all—an arrogant, mustachioed pilot, with hands on hips, simply titled 'Permanent'.[8] Hewitt felt that experienced officers were spread so thin in the expanding force that discipline suffered: he argued there were too few tough commanders to keep their men in line. He asserted that Australians are difficult to command anyway, as they expect their leaders to provide for their welfare and to lead by example, and they want explanations of operations in which they are ordered to risk their lives. This attitude, exemplified in the 'Morotai Mutiny', was especially likely among aircrew, who were intelligent, well-educated and confident members of the social elite. They had plenty to complain about, but most took the line of Sergeant John Clark at Milne Bay in 1942, who told his diary that he would try to ignore 'the mal-administration and class-distinction of the RAAF'.[9] The need to fit the expanding RAAF into the even larger organisation of an Allied air force was also bound to lead to problems.

Yet the organisational story was in many ways impressive. The wartime RAAF grew into a generally efficient organisation that was able to send thousands of its best men to the European conflict and still fight effectively at home. Moreover, in the South-West Pacific Area the RAAF was a fully integrated organisation with its own senior commanders, rather than simply a holding base providing cannon fodder for the European front.

A large degree of credit for that goes to George Jones, who may have been colourless, self-centred and resentful, but was the RAAF's organiser of victory. Moreover, for Bostock to win the support of a man as able as Kenney, he too must have had ability. This raises the point that not all blame lies with Jones and Bostock, damaging as their public brawl undoubtedly was to the RAAF. Both had support from powerful people. The weight of Kenney and MacArthur backed Bostock, as did Australia's director of munitions Essington Lewis and the Governor General, Lord Gowrie. However, the not inconsiderable support of Arthur Drakeford, a close ally of Prime Minister Curtin, strongly opposed Bostock and backed Jones. These men shared the blame for the command crisis. The government's culpability was also great: it was at fault in mishandling the appointment of Jones, in allowing the unworkable organisational split to persist, and in its failure to nip the damaging and embarrassing feud in the bud by sacking or promoting one of the contenders. Its indecisiveness made a damagingly bad impression on the Americans.

Even if Jones and Bostock had not been at loggerheads, the alternative leaders were, given their ambitious personalities, unlikely to have shown the goodwill needed in such a post—'Dicky' Williams got on poorly with Bostock and 'Jimmy' Goble, while it is improbable that the intelligent but acerbic Hewitt would have promoted harmony. Ironically, there were many superb leaders at lower levels, including Charles Learmonth, 'Woof' Arthur, John Jackson, Frank Chapman and Peter Turnbull. In telling his wife not to talk to the newspapers about him, 'Woof' once explained the secret of his ability to maintain high *esprit de corps*, and the reason that his officers automatically came to attention when speaking to their 23-year-old squadron leader: 'What big thing have I done that should make them this way? Nothing! It is just, all the little things:—they like that I work hard; they like that I am not frightened of anything (i.e. *Pretends* not to be) and above those, they like that I don't boast.'[10] Too few of Arthur's superiors observed a similar ethic.

The hard reality, largely an upshot of the RAAF's inadequate leadership and organisation, is that in late 1944 the Secretary of Defence, Sir Frederick Shedden, could prophesy that one day there would be 'an outcry about the relatively poor RAAF effort in the Southwest Pacific Area'. Shedden put the blame squarely on the organisational set-up, and not what he called the 'magnificent' men of the squadrons.[11] The focus of this book has not been the men at the top of the RAAF organisation, or indeed the many thousands of armourers, fitters, cooks and so on, but those 'magnificent' young aircrew flying in operations against the Japanese. What conclusions can we draw about them?

If we accept the point that they were generally working with inferior machines, like drivers of racing cars too slow to win any race, we should acknowledge that the human material in the RAAF was outstanding. It should have been 'magnificent', because recruits had to meet the highest standards just to become aircrew. If Australia's army punched further above its weight than did its air force, it was not because the soldiers were better. The intellectual gifts in the RAAF were higher. As numerous examples in this book have shown, the courage, skill and self-sacrifice of Australian aircrew were also extraordinary. Only a hard-hearted person would not be moved by the stories of Johnny Lockwood in Malaya, Dallas Scott at Ambon, Arch Tindal at Darwin, John Jackson at Moresby, Peter Turnbull at Milne Bay, Bill Newton at Salamaua, and Donald McLean in the Celebes. Of course these relatively famous and often senior airmen were not alone. Every crew member in the Hudsons, Catalinas, Buffaloes and Wirraways knew each time they flew operational sorties that contact with enemy aircraft would probably be fatal. Indeed, because the tools were so ineffective—despite the prodigious efforts of Australia's aircraft industry—one has to admire the men using them and drawing so much out of them. Even Australia's best machines—the Beaufighters, Liberators, and Spitfires—were dangerous aircraft to fly. The men who joined the air force were not only able but also among the most daring members of the population. They enlisted in many cases because they wanted the adventure and sheer fun of flying. The father of Hugh Pitman, a flight sergeant killed in New Guinea, wrote to the chaplain of 8 Squadron that just before the boy joined the RAAF, Hugh's mother had warned him that an airman's life was short. The boy, like a classical hero, answered 'that it was better to die young and accomplish something, than to live long and accomplish nothing'.[12] Jock Scott took a less morbid view, but one inspired by the same urge to fly. He described his flying days as 'glorious, unfettered, inspiring, soaring, fulfilling'. Looking back on his years in the service, including flying Kittyhawks in action, Scott came to this simple but sincere judgement: 'Lots of pros and cons but dominating all was the ready availability of a fully maintained, fuelled, serviced, updated, free flying machine with capabilities far beyond any super sports car I or my Dad could possibly have provided.'[13]

Wing Commander Athol Wearne, a permanent air force officer who had won a DSO and DFC, reflected that 'it was a bloody good war; they shouldn't have stopped it'.[14] He was referring to his wonderful experiences, but also to the close friendships he had formed, especially in Catalinas.

Many other airmen expressed more problematic feelings once the war ended. Clive Monk was in a field hospital on Tarakan when news of the surrender came. The young airman in the next bed sat up and said, 'Christ, I'm out of a job.' A squadron leader complained within Monk's hearing that his pay would suddenly plunge to 'goodness knows what'. As an engineer, Monk himself was offered a permanent commission in the RAAF. He refused, partly because he felt the life would be too dull, but also because he believed that in the RAAF anyone not wearing wings, signifying membership of aircrew, was 'a second class citizen'.[15]

The end of the war had long been in sight, and thoughts of what would happen afterwards had been there almost from the beginning. For example, in between aerial combats at Milne Bay, Woof Arthur wrote home in 1943: 'In the vacant moments of life in these places one spends many useless hours dreaming of that "after-the-war" time.'[16] In 1939 he had been a student; by war's end he was a Group Captain, but with no prospect or intention of continuing in that role. He still had no other qualifications and little money. After the war he had a stint in the Repatriation Department, where he earned less than £400 per annum, but in 1950 he was appointed Registrar of the Australian School of Pacific Administration in Sydney. The increase in his salary to £1050 made page 2 of the *Canberra Times*, although his distinguished war record was not mentioned.

This book should have dispelled any illusions that either the RAAF or its individual squadrons were one big happy family. Mateship and *esprit de corps* were major factors in the RAAF's success, but the tensions that exist wherever people are in each other's company had many reasons to be magnified in the air force: death was constantly at everyone's shoulder on operational bases, more time was spent waiting around than flying or fighting, and intelligent and ambitious young men were living in unnatural, primitive and claustrophobic environments without safety valves such as family, women and entertainment. Add in the prejudices, resentments and arrogance associated with distinctions between permanent and wartime air force, reinforcements and veterans, officers and NCOs, well-publicised and lesser known squadrons, Australian-based and European-experienced, private school and other education, aircrew and ground staff, and there are many more reasons for arguments or rivalries. Arthur Tucker, whose jaundiced but well-informed perspective we have often heard, felt that such factors as these, as well as the constant turnover of personnel, ensured that in RAAF squadrons 'there was no chance of building up of any *esprit de corps*, ever'.[17] He thought this applied particularly to 75 Squadron. That is unfair, but the truth lies somewhere in between the 'band of brothers' and the 'all airmen were bastards' views.

Alec Boxall believed that his war experiences made him a better person, able to appreciate the value of others despite differences in outlook and to overcome petty obstacles. He initially found it difficult to acclimatise to post-war work and to be accepted by the civilian world, as did Raynor Barber, who had such traumatic experiences as a Beaufighter pilot. Lisa Mariah, who wrote up Barber's memoirs, said that 'Raynor's entire perception of his life pivoted around his nine months in New Guinea from April 1944 to January 1945', and in this he was surely typical.[18] Yet for others, service in the air force was a stepping stone to successful post-war careers. Naturally many became commercial pilots, like John Ryland and Bob Law-Smith, but alternative paths were taken by men such as Bill Stuart and Arthur Tucker, the former Queensland schoolteachers who each brought down Japanese fighters on 9 September 1943. After the war Stuart entered university and became an engineer, chemist and consultant to major companies. Tucker studied medicine and, as a doctor on the Snowy Mountain Scheme, saved lives and pioneered rehabilitation procedures for injured workers. This compassionate, modest and brilliant man ended his professional career as chief scientific officer of the Australian Atomic Energy Commission. In the late 1980s he began airing his feelings about his war experiences. At the end of a 1989 interview he said that, for all his hatred of war-mongering, the war left him with the 'hope that Australia's defence in the future is going to be better—but I doubt it'.[19]

The war's duality as a disturbing time and a highpoint in many airmen's lives seems to have applied to Australia's greatest ace of that conflict, Clive Caldwell. 'Killer', who once seemed indifferent to the pain he inflicted, became increasingly troubled by memories of his victims. One memory that particularly disturbed him was of a Japanese who lay, face upwards and apparently alive, on the water after Caldwell downed a Dinah in August 1943. Caldwell was later haunted by the sight of sharks coming menacingly towards this helpless 'enemy'. When in the early 1990s relatives of the Japanese crew sought to meet him as an act of reconciliation, Caldwell refused and sought to close himself off from the memory. Many other Australian aircrew had material for troubled sleep in their own sorties over water, especially in aircraft more vulnerable than Caldwell's Spitfire.

One such aircraft, a Hudson, was that of Squadron Leader Malcolm Burns and his crew, shot down and killed at Timuka airstrip on 3 April 1943. The Australian War Memorial contains an extract from the diary of an unknown Japanese soldier, written in Dutch New Guinea in 1943. For 23 April, he recounted looking at a two-engine enemy aircraft recently shot down nearby. He said of this crew, almost certainly Burns':

> We felt very sorry for the crew when we saw the tangled wreckage, though they were our enemies. The plane's tail was ripped off, the engine had been torn away and the tyres had come off and were scattered around. The dead enemy soldiers' bodies had already turned to skeletons, with not a piece of flesh left on them. We gathered up the bones that were scattered around, gave them a funeral by burying them, and presented the graves with wild flowers with sincerity in our hearts.[20]

Another chivalrous act occurred at Port Moresby on 28 April 1942. During the raid in which John Jackson was killed, Japanese bombers dropped four packages with white streamers attached. Each package contained about 100 letters that the Japanese had permitted Australian prisoners in Rabaul to write to their loved ones. This act of Japanese humanity seems to have been inspired by an Australian one: the day before the Japanese invasion of Rabaul, the Australian garrison had given a proper burial to the crew of a Japanese reconnaissance aircraft that crashed into a nearby mountain, and this impressed the new Japanese commander. Such generous thoughts and gestures between the antagonists in this air war were all too rare. We have seen how some Australians marvelled at the skill of their opponents early on and how Saburo Sakai respected his adversaries and took that feeling into the post-war period. John Kessey had an unusual postscript to the scrape with 'Dead-Eye Dick' that nearly cost him his life at Wewak. After the war he became a commercial pilot, and while flying with Air Niugini became aware through Japanese acquaintances that the commander of the Wewak flak nest, Taizo Takahashi, was still alive. Kessey visited his old nemesis in Kyoto. Language difficulties looked like being insuperable until Kessey happened to use a pidgin English word, and they discovered that they could both speak the native language of their former battlefield. Together they pored over Takahashi's beautifully preserved silk wartime map of the Wewak area. Although Kessey could never overcome a suspicion of things Japanese, the former antagonists stayed in contact.

Maurice Ball, the Beaufighter pilot who felt like a medieval knight, said he hit targets rather than people, and that he never considered the war a personal affair. However, there was precious little of the 'knights of the air' mentality in this conflict. The barbarous treatment meted out to Australian airmen captured by Japanese ground forces reflected their hostility and also fostered enmity and fear among Australians. Like their Army counterparts, Australian airmen were more racist towards Japanese than their modern compatriots, but their hatred owed more to experience than to prejudice. The same reportedly applied to American airmen, the most hostile of whom were those closest to combat with the Japanese.

Beaufighter pilot Alfred 'Felix' Catt, DFC, did feel that the Japanese pilot he waved to on the way out of Rabaul 'seemed a very nice chap'. Yet generally, he recalled later, 'we regarded the Japanese as animals', and he had no qualms about strafing a group of Japanese he saw swimming.[21] Colin Harvey's maxim concerning Japanese troops, whom he first encountered when they were far advanced on the Kokoda Track, was 'kill the little buggers', which was, he argued, why the RAAF was in New Guinea.[22]

The diary of Alick Makeham, a 20-year-old Kittyhawk pilot in 76 Squadron in 1944–45 gives a rare insight into the way Australian pilots felt about killing Japanese late in the war. Some of the Japanese his squadron annihilated, usually while they tried vainly to hide or escape on rafts around the Vogelkop Peninsula, were so exhausted that Makeham considered it 'mercy killing'. On one occasion, a Kitty was coming in when the lone Japanese survivor of a raft-strafing surfaced: 'Just as Jack pressed the tit he bobbed up and copped the lot. Poor cow couldn't hold his breath long enough.' This entry was darkly humorous, but also empathetic. Other entries are unequivocal: 'Squadron score to date 88 Japs in 11 days. Nice going' and 'saw a stream of blood 10×20 yds where Japs were strafed. Hooray.'[23] Makeham wrote this while not just Japanese but also his compatriots were dying around him. He was himself killed in January 1945.

Beaufighter pilot James Mierisch, on the other hand, enjoyed watching the effects of destructive weapons like napalm and rockets, but at the time it did not even occur to him that individual Japanese were on the receiving end. Killing from an aircraft was not as personal as for an infantryman.

Squadron Leader Charles Learmonth wrote to his wife that for the enemy troops he had killed he 'felt not a whit', but for his friends who had been shot down, in typically stoic manner he confessed only to 'a certain degree of sadness'. He did concede, 'I don't know what effect this will have on us after the war.'[24] For him the question would never be answered.

Alec Boxall felt that much of his four and a half years in the RAAF had been wasted: just six months of operations, and the rest training. He realised later that 'the Air Force didn't have the aircraft' and so had to 'adapt the personnel to fly the sort of aircraft it could get', in his case, the Vultee Vengeance. This problem was a central fact about the RAAF experience. So was one of Boxall's other great regrets. While he acknowledged that he was lucky not to have ended up like some of his close army mates, who went to doomed Rabaul, or to have been thrust into action as much as German dive-bomber crews, he 'always felt that I had trained and reached abilities beyond those that I had the opportunity to use'.[25] This perception sums up much of the RAAF's Pacific War story.

Yet without the RAAF, the dark days of 1942 would have been still more nightmarish and the war in the Pacific even longer. All war wastes life, time and resources, the RAAF's Pacific War especially so. Circumstances prevented many Australian airmen from achieving their full potential, but their presence, endurance and commitment contributed to victory. In 1942, especially over Moresby, Lae, Rabaul, Milne Bay and the beachheads, they had their finest hours, as imperishable as those of Australia's soldiers at Tobruk, Kokoda and Alamein. The more than 2000 airmen who died in the Pacific War numbered among the nation's best and brightest. They died working to defeat a nation that was bent on enslaving its opponents, and which treated not only enemy servicemen but also its own with contempt.

In February 1945 Corporal Vincent Hunt praised the crews of his squadron's Beaufighters as 'game chaps' who could 'stick their necks out and keep smiling'.[26] He was applying his tribute to a few dozen men, but this book shows that it applied to many thousands who flew for Australia. Even those airmen who did not 'stick their necks out', because they worked on the ground, sacrificed much while enduring a lifestyle frequently marked by monotony, an enervating and disease-ridden climate, separation from home and loved ones, and poor food, drink and facilities.

Parts of the complex story of the RAAF's war against Japan were unedifying, gruesome and exasperating, but nearly every member of the RAAF could be proud of temporarily suspending his or her life, and in some cases sacrificing their life, for ensuring that the conflict had a victorious ending for Australia, and for the wider cause of freedom from tyranny.

Appendix A
Aircraft profiles

The scale drawings on the following pages demonstrate the appearance and relative size of the main aircraft mentioned in the text. There was more than one model of most of these types, and the illustrations are only broad representations of their appearance. Scale 1:260.

AUSTRALIAN AIRCRAFT

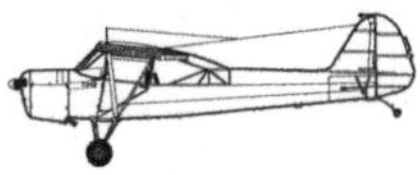

Auster

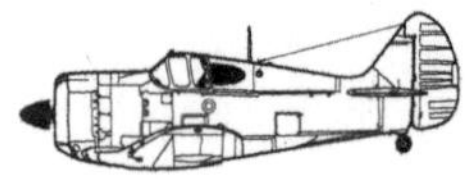

Boomerang

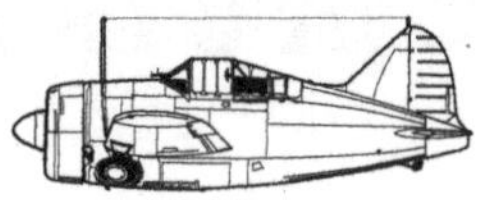

Buffalo

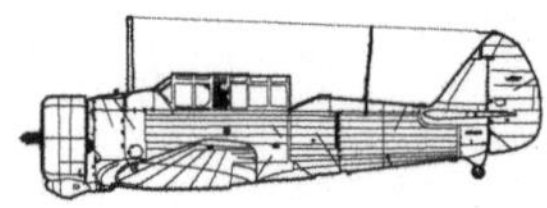

Wirraway

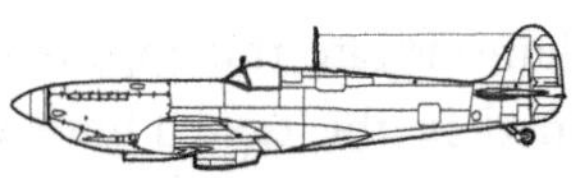

Spitfire

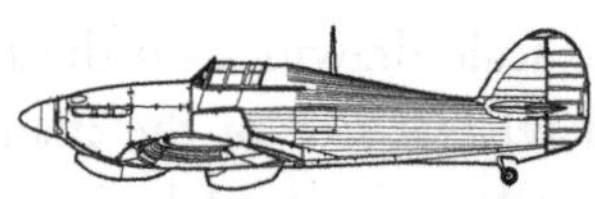

Hurricane

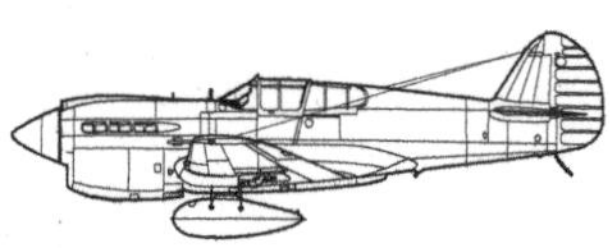

Kittyhawk

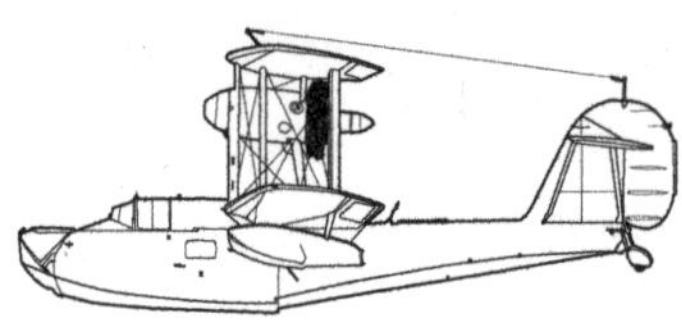

Walrus

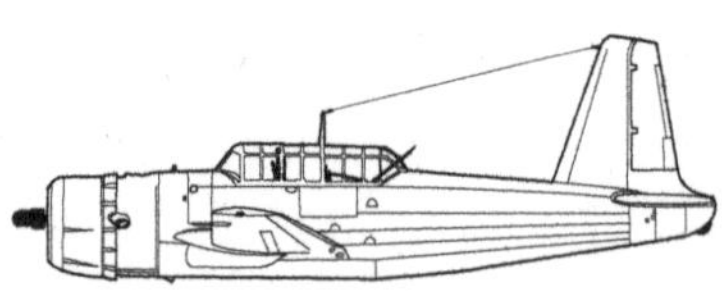

Vengeance

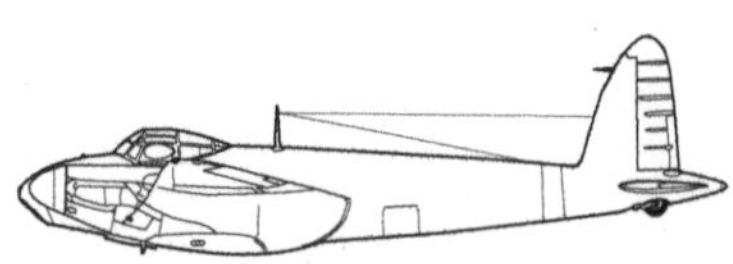

Mosquito

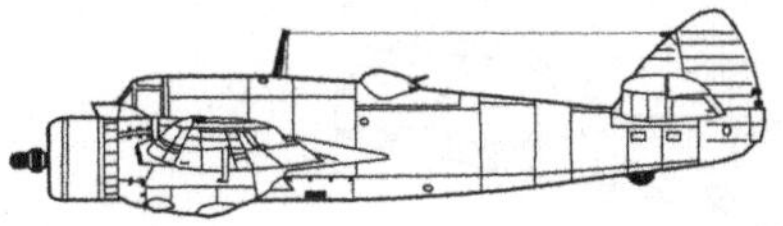

Beaufighter

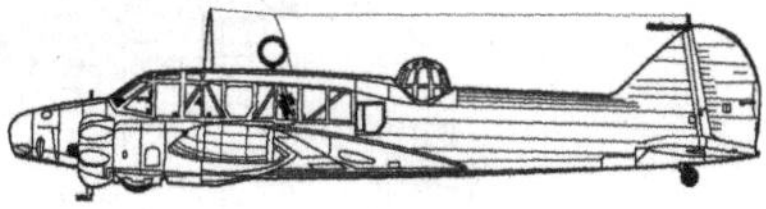

Anson

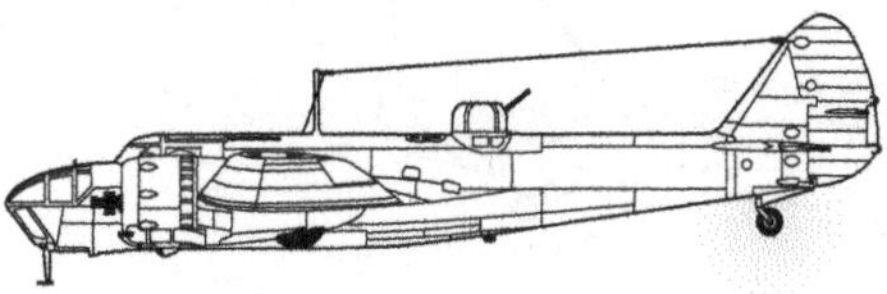

Blenheim

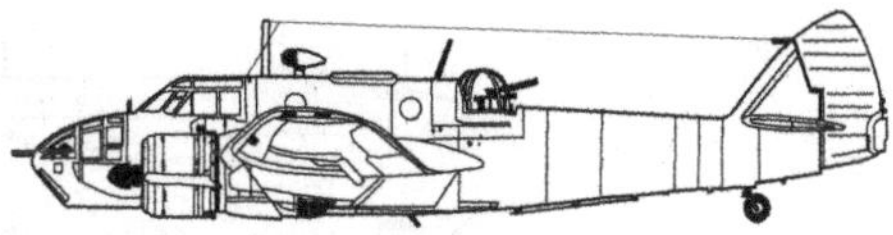

Beaufort

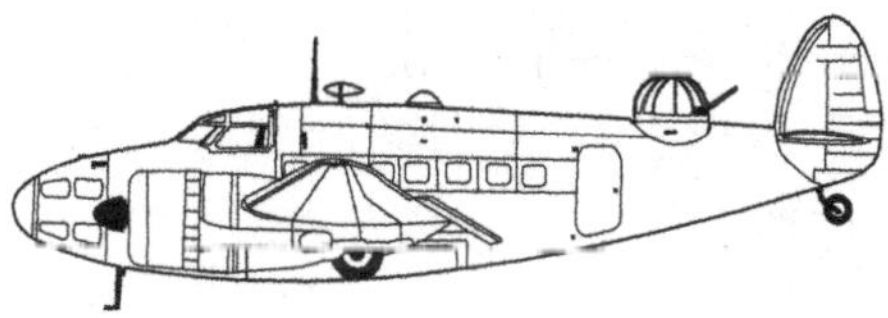

Hudson

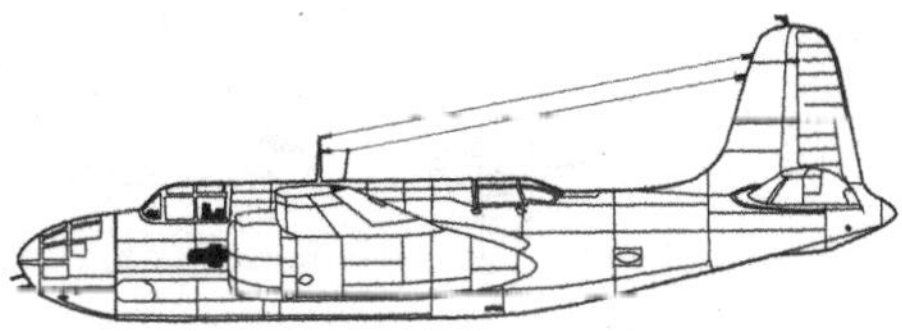

Boston

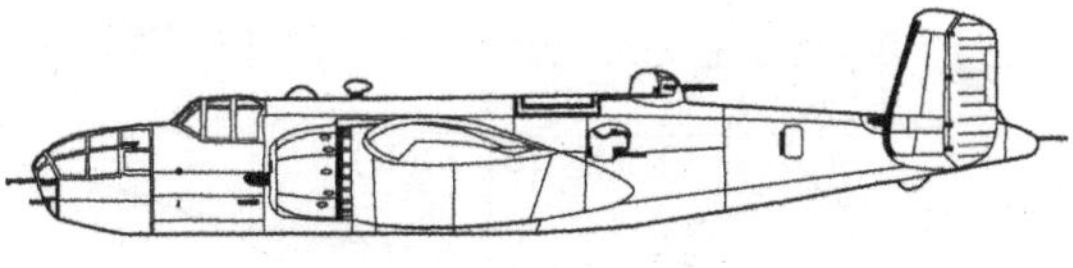

Mitchell

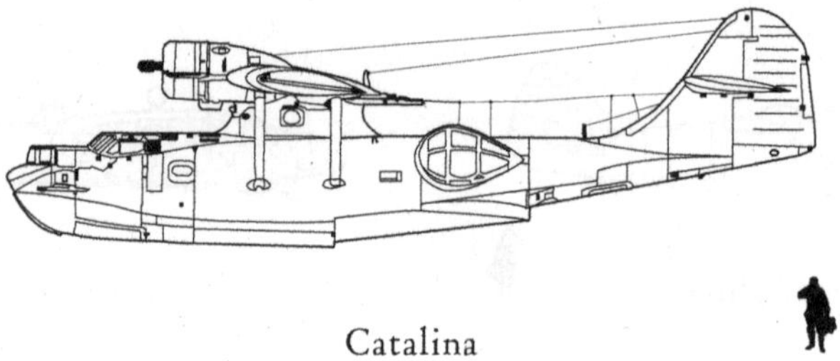

Catalina

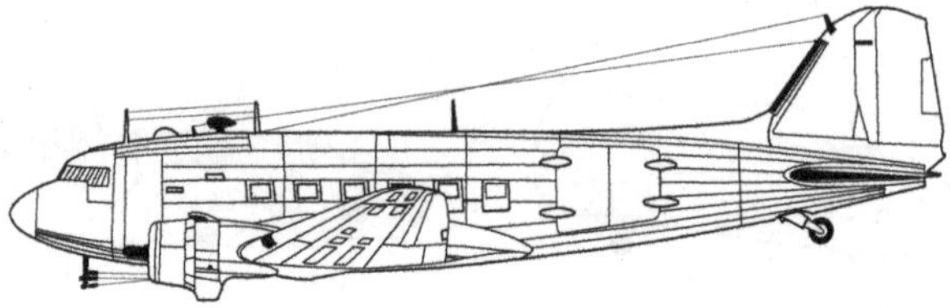

Dakota

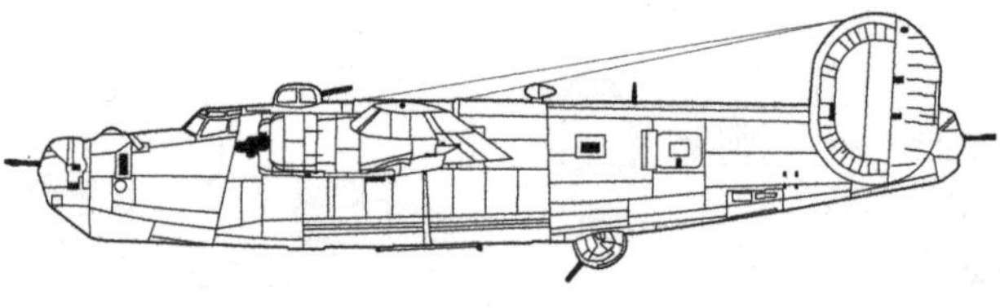

Liberator

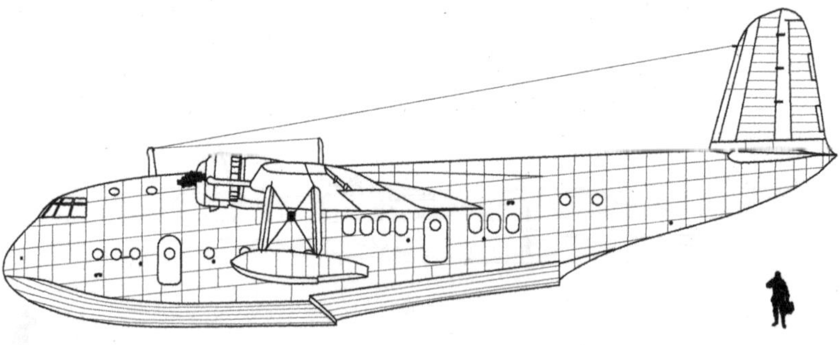

Empire

JAPANESE AIRCRAFT

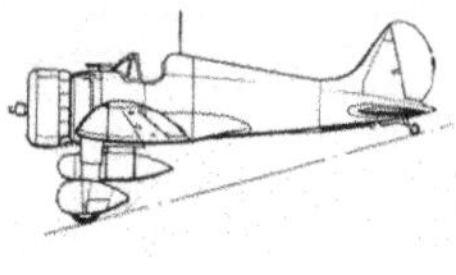

Claude (Mitsubishi A5M)

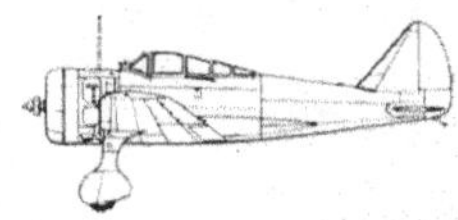

Nate (Nakajima Ki-27)

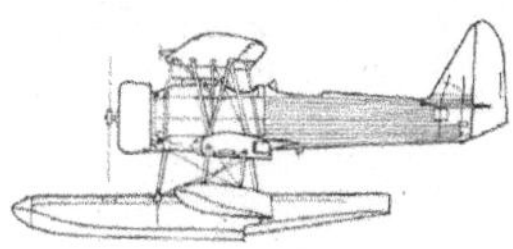

Dave (Nakajima E8N)

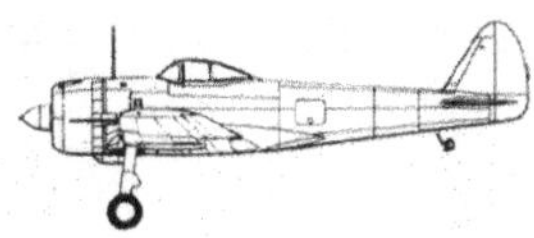

Oscar (Nakajima Ki-43)

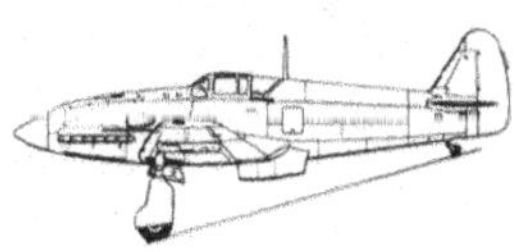

Tony (Kawasaki Ki-61)

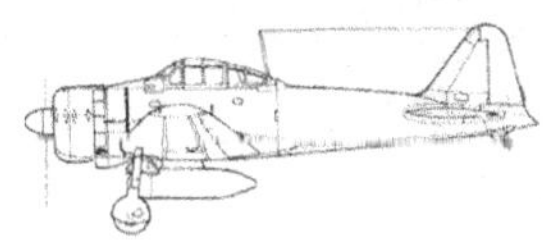

Zero or Zeke (Mitsubishi A6M)

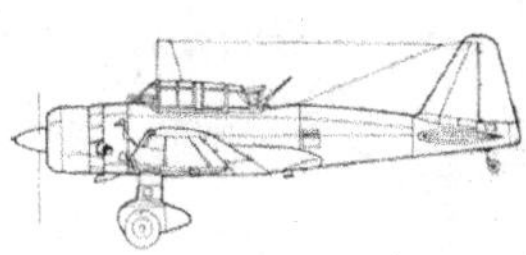

Sonia (Mitsubishi Ki-51)

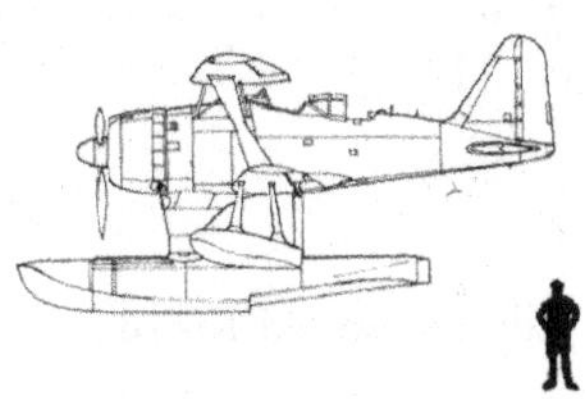

Pete (Mitsubishi F1M)

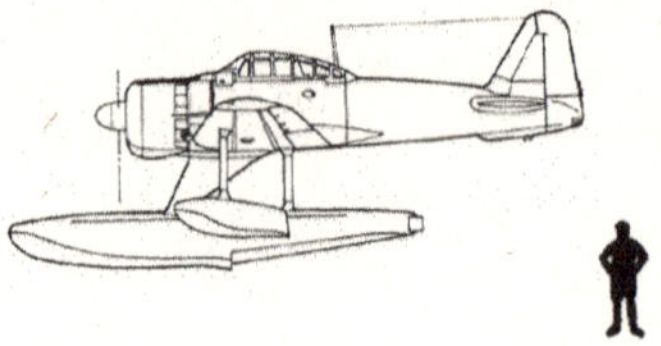

Rufe (Nakajima A6M2-N)

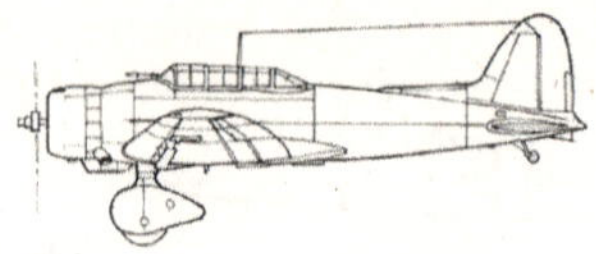

Val (Aichi D3A)

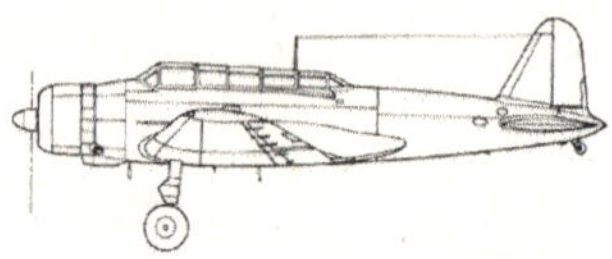

Kate (Nakajima B5N)

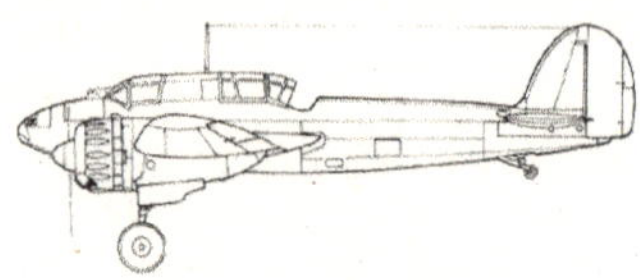

Nick (Kawasaki Ki-45)

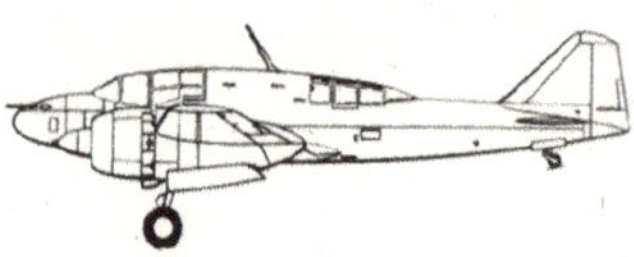

Dinah (Mitsubishi Ki-46)

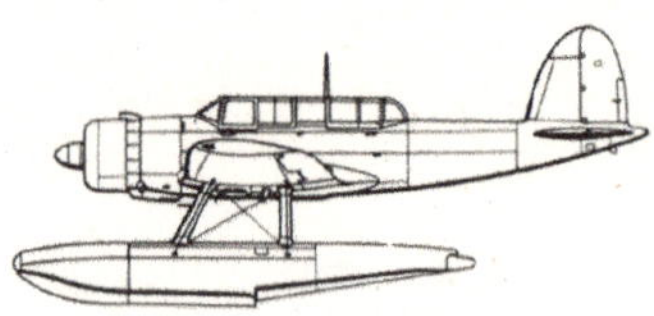

Jake (Aichi E13A1)

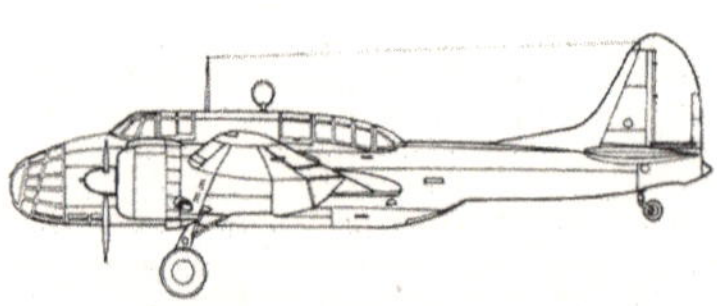

Lily (Kawasaki Ki-48)

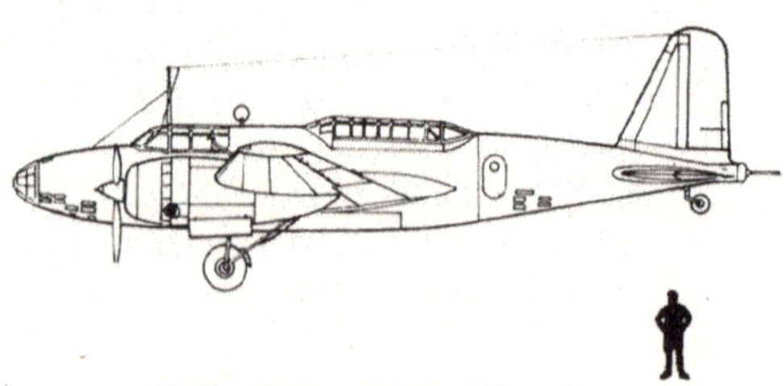

Sally (Mitsubishi Ki-21)

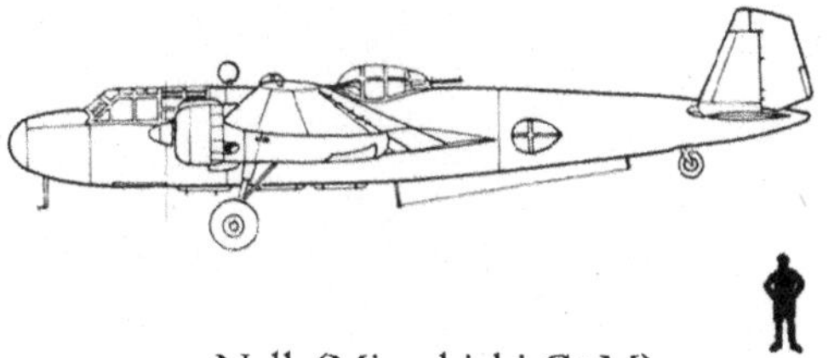

Nell (Mitsubishi G3M)

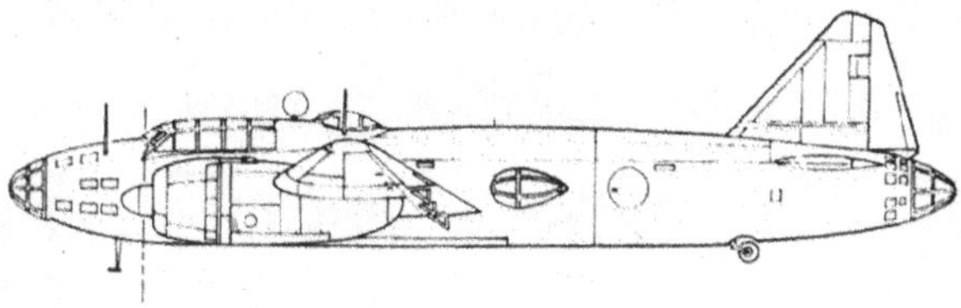

Betty (Mitsubishi G4M)

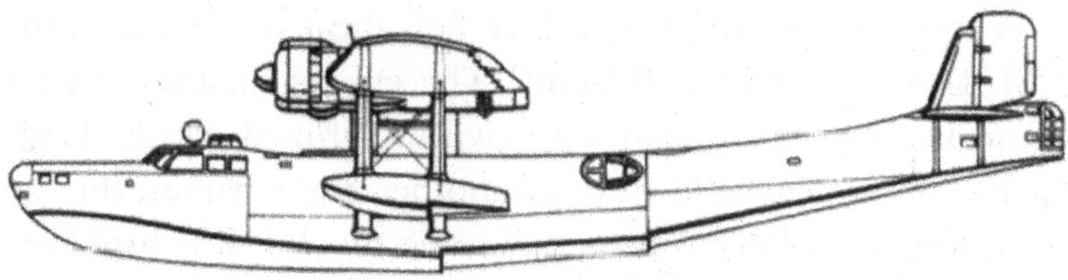

Mavis (Kawanishi H6K)

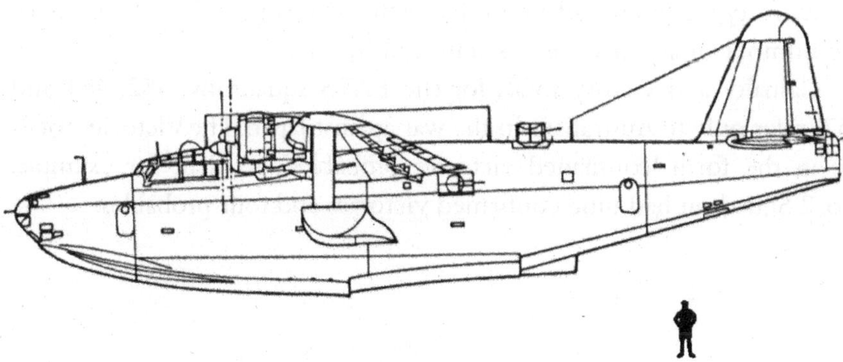

Emily (Kawanishi H8K)

Appendix B
RAAF squadrons and their casualty and victory totals in the Pacific War

At the end of his logbook, Squadron Leader Ian Loudon kept brief notes on 40 pilots he had known in 76 Squadron. At the top of the list were 'SL Turnbull' and 'SL Truscott'. The entries for these two were brief, and in each case ended with two underlined words: 'Had it'.[1] The same phrase appeared next to another eight names, though he missed at least one. Table 3 may miss some too, but it is based on the Australian War Memorial list of deaths in all the main RAAF squadrons that saw action in the South-West Pacific Area. These include accidental deaths, and airmen who were not in aircrew. Also listed are the main types of aircraft flown by each squadron, and an estimate of the number of aerial victories achieved by each.

Casualty and victory totals for the EATS squadrons (452, 453 and 457) refer only to Australians in the war against Japan. The Victories totals are in the form 'confirmed victories/probables', so that, for example, No. 2 Squadron had nine confirmed victories and four probables.

TABLE 3 RAAF DEATH AND VICTORY TALLIES

Sqn	Main aircraft types	Deaths	Victories
1	Hudson, Beaufort, Mosquito	88	0
2	Hudson, Beaufort, Mitchell	176	9/4
4	Wirraway, Boomerang	37	1/0
5	Wirraway, Boomerang	24	0
6	Anson, Hudson, Beaufort	35	0/1
7	Hudson, Beaufort	33	3
8	Hudson, Beaufort	79	1/1
9	Seagull, Walrus	22	0
11	Catalina	102	0/1
12	Wirraway, Vengeance, Liberator	27	0/2
13	Hudson, Beaufort, Ventura	87	0
14	Hudson, Beaufort	35	0
15	Beaufort	15	0
18	Mitchell	25	5/5*
20	Catalina	92	0
21	Buffalo, Vengeance, Liberator	42	5/1**
22	Wirraway, Boston, Beaufighter	65	0
23	Wirraway, Hudson, Vengeance, Liberator	36	0
24	Wirraway, Hudson, Vengeance, Liberator	105	0
25	Wirraway, Liberator	25	0
30	Beaufighter	68	2/3
31	Beaufighter	79	18/1
32	Hudson, Beaufort	78	2
33	DH Dragon, Empire, Anson, Tiger Moth, Dakota	16	0
34	DH Dragon, Tiger Moth, Anson, Dakota	6	0
35	Various, Dakota	7	0
36	Various, Dakota	21	0
37	Lodestar, Dakota	4	0
38	Hudson, Dakota	10	0
40	Sunderland, Mariner	1	0
41	Empire flying boat, Dornier DO24, Mariner	4	0
42	Catalina	12	0
43	Catalina	31	0
67	Anson	6	0
71	Anson, Moth Minor	5	0

Sqn	Main aircraft types	Deaths	Victories
73	Anson, Moth Minor	5	0
75	Kittyhawk	42	29/12
76	Kittyhawk	22	3/1
77	Kittyhawk	18	7/4
78	Wirraway, Kittyhawk	12	10
79	Spitfire	13	2
80	Kittyhawk	24	0
82	Kittyhawk	14	0
83	Moth Minor, Airacobra, Boomerang	4	0
84	Boomerang, Kittyhawk, Mustang	7	0
85	Buffalo, Boomerang, Wirraway, Spitfire	9	0
86	Kittyhawk, Mustang	6	7
87	Buffalo, Lancer, Lightning, Mosquito, Wirraway	5	0
92	Anson, Beaufighter	1	0
93	Beaufighter	13	0
94	Mosquito	0	0
99	Liberator	9	0
100	Beaufort	116	2
102	Liberator	0	0
107	Kingfisher	2	0
452	Spitfire	30	17/2
453	Buffalo, Spitfire	5	25/5***
457	Spitfire	15	27/8

*Probably not piloted by Australians

**All achieved by 21 Sqn pilots in 21/453 Sqn

***Eight of these confirmed victories achieved by 453 Sqn pilots in 21/453 Sqn

Appendix C
RAAF aerial victory claims in the Pacific War

The following seems to be the first attempt to tabulate all Australian aerial victories in the Pacific War. Every air force made exaggerated claims of kills. To give one of many examples, on 15 January 1944 in Burma, RAF Spitfire pilots claimed 16 destroyed, six probables and 17 damaged. Of these, five of the destroyed and one probably destroyed were claimed by Australians. Yet Japanese records suggest they lost just five aircraft in that action. In turn the Japanese claimed eight Spitfires in the same fighting, while the RAF actually lost two.[1] Considering this tendency, no table of RAAF claims in the Pacific will ever be entirely accurate. Some of the claims in this table will be false. I have eliminated some confirmed kills which are now known to be wrong, including three from the 44 Days, but those remaining include doubtful ones. In particular, the claims for Malaya should be treated with scepticism.

There may also be some claims that should be here, but are not. Confirming kills in the rugged terrain of New Guinea was always difficult. For example, in the 44 Days battle, the superior numbers of enemy aircraft made it foolhardy to linger to check that an enemy had hit the ground. Confirmation often depended on observers from the ground, such as soldiers.

Nevertheless, on the whole the RAAF prided itself on being

conservative and severe in its estimates, and the great majority of these claims will be accurate.

Sometimes more than one name appears in the pilot column. Where the victorious aircraft are single-engine, such as P-40s, the names represent those who shared the victory—e.g. Cox and Wackett on 21 March 1942. Victories that RAAF pilots shared with non-Australians in Burma/India are not recorded, though there were probably not many: I have seen references to just three. For Beaufighters, only pilots are listed. Where Hudsons and Beauforts brought down enemy aircraft, I have where possible identified the pilot, then the responsible gunner(s)—e.g. James and Reen on 25 September 1942.

Given the absence of an official list, there is much guesswork with some of these claims. Those of 18 (Netherlands East Indies) Squadron are not included, though it seems to have achieved five confirmed kills and five probables. It would be fascinating to calculate enemy aircraft destroyed on the ground, but it seems impossible to get useful figures on this. The number claimed was well in excess of 100 in the South-West Pacific Area alone.

The sources for Table 4 are numerous, but mainly Gillison's and Odgers' volumes of the official RAAF history, Christopher Shores' and David Wilson's books, squadron Operations Record Books and official combat reports.

TABLE 4 CONFIRMED AND PROBABLE VICTORIES

Confirmed victories: Malaya, Netherlands East Indies and the Pacific

Date	Squadron	Pilot(s)	Aircraft	Opponent	Location
8/12/41	8	Hitchcock	Hudson	Zero	Kuantan
13/12/41	453	Vanderfield	Buffalo	Lily	Penang
13/12/41	453	Vanderfield	Buffalo	Lily	Penang
13/12/41	453	Grace	Buffalo	Nate	Penang
13/12/41	453	Read	Buffalo	Sonia	Penang
13/12/41	453	Read	Buffalo	Sonia	Penang
15/12/41	453	Board	Buffalo	Sonia	Malaya
15/12/41	453	Board/O'Mara	Buffalo	Lily	Malaya
17/12/41	453	Clare	Buffalo	fighter	Ipoh
21/12/41	453	Peterson	Buffalo	Sonia	Kuala Lumpur
22/12/41	453	Clare	Buffalo	Oscar	Kuala Lumpur
22/12/41	453	Clare	Buffalo	Oscar	Kuala Lumpur
22/12/41	453	Clare	Buffalo	Oscar	Kuala Lumpur
22/12/41	453	Board	Buffalo	Lily	Malaya
22/12/41	453	Griffiths	Buffalo	Oscar	Kuala Lumpur
22/12/41	453	Vanderfield	Buffalo	Oscar	Kuala Lumpur
22/12/41	453	Read	Buffalo	Oscar	Kuala Lumpur
22/12/41	453	Gorringe	Buffalo	Oscar	Kuala Lumpur
11/01/42	2	Gorrie	Hudson	float-plane	Namlea
11/01/42	2	Hodge	Hudson	float-plane	Namlea
15/01/42	21/453	Vanderfield	Buffalo	Betty	Singapore
15/01/42	21/453	L. Bowes	Buffalo	bomber	Singapore
17/01/42	21/453	Vanderfield/Grace	Buffalo	Nate	Malacca
17/01/42	21/453	Clare	Buffalo	Nate	Muar River
17/01/42	21/453	Clare	Buffalo	Oscar	Muar River
18/01/42	21/453	Sproule	Buffalo	Nate	Sembawang
19/01/42	21/453	Vanderfield/ Gorringe	Buffalo	Sonia	Batu Paliat
19/01/42	21/453	Kirkman	Buffalo	Sonia	Muar River
19/01/42	21/453	Kinninmont	Buffalo	Oscar	Malacca
19/01/42	21/453	Kinninmont	Buffalo	Sonia	Malacca
23/01/42	232 RAF	Schaffer	Hurricane	Oscar	Singapore
23/01/42	232 RAF	McCulloch	Hurricane	fighter	Singapore

Date	Squadron	Pilot(s)	Aircraft	Opponent	Location
26/01/42	21/453	Sheppard	Buffalo	Nate	Endau
26/01/42	21/453	Grace	Buffalo	Nate	Endau
26/01/42	21/453	Leys	Buffalo	Nate	Endau
20/02/42	232 RAF	Young	Hurricane	Dave	Batavia
21/03/42	75	B. Cox/Wackett	P-40Es	bomber	Port Moresby
22/03/42	75	Turnbull	P-40E	Zero	Lae
22/03/42	75	Pettett	P-40E	Zero	Lae
23/03/42	2	MacAlister	Hudson	Zero	Timor
24/03/42	75	L. Jackson	P-40E	Zero	Port Moresby
24/03/42	75	Piper	P-40E	bomber	Port Moresby
27 or 28/03/42	75	Piper/Bailey	P-40Es	bomber	Port Moresby
31/03/42	32	Kingwell/ Townshend	Hudson	Zero	Salamaua
5/04/42	75	L. Jackson	P-40E	Zero	Port Moresby
10/04/42	75	Atherton	P-40E	Betty	Port Moresby
11/04/42	75	Piper	P-40E	Zero	Lae
11/04/42	75	Piper	P-40E	Zero	Lae
11/04/42	75	Masters	P-40E	Zero	Lae
11/04/42	75	B. Cox	P-40E	Zero	Lae
17/04/42	75	L. Jackson	P-40E	Zero	Port Moresby
17/04/42	75	Tucker/Masters	P-40Es	Zero	Port Moresby
18/04/42	75	L. Jackson	P-40E	Zero	Port Moresby
21/04/42	75	Atherton/Boyd	P-40Es	Zero	Port Moresby
28/04/42	75	J. Jackson	P-40E	Zero	Port Moresby
22/05/42	2	Sharp	Hudson	Zero	Ambon
11/06/42	32	Halliday	Hudson	flying-boat	New Britain
17/07/42	2	Hay/Webster	Hudson	Zero	Koepang
4/08/42	76	Ash	P-40E	Val	Milne Bay
11/08/42	76	Wawn	P-40E	Zero	Milne Bay
11/08/42	75	Atherton	P-40E	Zero	Milne Bay
21/08/42	2	Badger	Hudson	Zero	Maubisse
27/08/42	75	L. Jackson	P-40E	Zero	Milne Bay
27/08/42	75	Riddel/L. Jackson	P-40E	Zero	Milne Bay
27/08/42	75	Jones/B. Watson	P-40Es	dive-bomber	Milne Bay
25/09/42	2	R. James/Reilly	Hudson	Zero	Dili
25/09/42	2	R. James/Reen	Hudson	Zero	Dili

Date	Squadron	Pilot(s)	Aircraft	Opponent	Location
23/11/42	77	Cresswell	P-40E	Betty	Darwin
2/12/42	100	Green/Nolan/ Mann	Beaufort	Zero	Buna
2/12/42	100	Green/Nolan/ Mann	Beaufort	Zero	Buna
23/12/42	31	Barnett	Beaufighter	Nate	Fuiloro
26/12/42	Sp Tpt Flt	O. Hall	Hudson	Zero	Dobodura
26/12/42	4	Archer	Wirraway	Zero	Gona
22/01/43	76	Truscott	P-40E	Betty	Darwin
2/03/43	1 Wing	Caldwell	Spitfire V	Zero	Darwin
2/03/43	1 Wing	Caldwell	Spitfire V	Kate	Darwin
6/03/43	75	Stirling	P-40E	Nell	N Goodenough Is
7/03/43	457	Maclean/ McDowell	Spitfire V	Dinah	Darwin
10/03/43	75	Arthur	P-40E	Betty	Trobriand Is
15/03/43	457	P. Watson	Spitfire V	Zero	Darwin
15/03/43	457	R. Watson	Spitfire V	Zero	Darwin
15/03/43	452	Goldsmith	Spitfire V	Betty	Darwin
15/03/43	452	Goldsmith	Spitfire V	Zero [Hamp]	Darwin
15/03/43	54 RAF	Mawer	Spitfire V	Zero	Darwin
11/04/43	77	Hodgkinson	P-40K	Zero	Oro Bay
14/04/43	75	Brown	P-40E	Val	Milne Bay
14/04/43	75	Atherton	P-40E	Betty	Milne Bay
14/04/43	75	Todd	P-40E	Zero	Milne Bay
14/04/43	75	A. Hall	P-40E	Zero [Hamp]	Milne Bay
14/04/43	75	Stirling	P-40E	Betty	Milne Bay
14/04/43	77	Cresswell	P-40K	Betty	Milne Bay
14/04/43	77	Sproule	P-40K	bomber	Milne Bay
14/04/43	77	Sudlow	P-40K	Zero	Milne Bay
14/04/43	77	Kelly	P-40K	Betty	Milne Bay
14/04/43	77	Hodgkinson	P-40K	Betty	Milne Bay
2/05/43	1 Wing	Caldwell	Spitfire V	Zero	Darwin
2/05/43	1 Wing	Caldwell	Spitfire V	Zero	Darwin
2/05/43	452	Goldsmith	Spitfire V	Betty or Helen	Darwin
2/05/43	452	Mawer	Spitfire V	Zero	Darwin

Date	Squadron	Pilot(s)	Aircraft	Opponent	Location
10/05/43	457	R. Watson	Spitfire V	Zero	Millingimbi
10/05/43	457	Morse	Spitfire V	Zero	Millingimbi
11/05/43	31	Madden	Beaufighter	Jake	Wessell Is
28/05/43	457	Clark	Spitfire V	Betty	Millingimbi
28/05/43	457	Jenkins	Spitfire V	Betty	Millingimbi
28/05/43	457	F. White	Spitfire V	Betty	Millingimbi
12/06/43	31	Forbes	Beaufighter	Pete	Taberfane
13/06/43	75	Atherton	P-40E	Betty	Milne Bay
18/06/43	7	Hopton	Beaufort	Jake	Torres Strait
20/06/43	457	Smithson	Spitfire V	Zero	Darwin
20/06/43	452	Bisley	Spitfire V	Helen	Darwin
20/06/43	452	MacDonald	Spitfire V	Sally	Darwin
20/06/43	452	Evans	Spitfire V	Sally	Darwin
20/06/43	452	Mawer	Spitfire V	Zero	Darwin
20/06/43	457	McDowell	Spitfire V	bomber	Darwin
20/06/43	1 Wing	Caldwell	Spitfire V	Oscar	Darwin
20/06/43	1 Wing	Walters	Spitfire V	Oscar	Darwin
28/06/43	457	MacLean/Halse	Spitfire V	Zero	Darwin
28/06/43	457	Cunningham	Spitfire V	Zero	Darwin
28/06/43	457	Newton/Clark	Spitfire V	Zero	Darwin
30/06/43	452	E. Hall	Spitfire V	Zero	Peron Is
30/06/43	1 Wing	Caldwell	Spitfire V	Zero	Darwin
2/07/43	2	Thomas	Hudson	Jake	Arafura Sea
6/07/43	457	MacKenzie	Spitfire V	Betty	Darwin
6/07/43	457	Batchelor	Spitfire V	Betty	Darwin
6/07/43	457	P. Watson	Spitfire V	Betty	E Perron Is
6/07/43	452	E. Hall	Spitfire V	Zero [Hamp]	Anson Bay
6/07/43	452	MacDonald	Spitfire V	Betty	Darwin
18/07/43	457	K. James	Spitfire V	Dinah	Darwin
10/08/43	452	Young/Coombes	Spitfire V	Pete	Millingimbi
17/08/43	31	Taylor	Beaufighter	Rufe	Taberfane
17/08/43	31	Kilpatrick	Beaufighter	Rufe	Taberfane
17/08/43	31	Unknown	Beaufighter	Rufe	Taberfane
17/08/43	31	Entwistle	Beaufighter	Pete	Taberfane
17/08/43	457	P. Watson	Spitfire V	Dinah	Anson Bay
17/08/43	457	R. Watson/Jenkins	Spitfire V	Dinah	Melville Is

Date	Squadron	Pilot(s)	Aircraft	Opponent	Location
17/08/43	457	K. James	Spitfire V	Dinah	Darwin
17/08/43	452	Caldwell	Spitfire V	Dinah	Darwin
21/08/43	31	McCord	Beaufighter	Rufe	Taberfane
30/08/43	31	Entwistle	Beaufighter	Pete	Taberfane
7/09/43	452	Goldsmith	Spitfire V	Tony	W Strauss
7/09/43	457	P. Watson	Spitfire V	Zero	Darwin
7/09/43	457	MacLean	Spitfire V	Zero	Darwin
7/09/43	457	Smithson	Spitfire V	Zero	Darwin
7/09/43	457	F. White/Gregory	Spitfire V	Zero	Darwin
9/09/43	86	Stark	P-40N	Zero	Merauke
9/09/43	86	Tucker	P-40N	Zero	Merauke
9/09/43	86	Stuart	P-40N	Oscar	Merauke
20/09/43	7	Legge	Beaufort	Jake	Cape Valsch
2/10/43	30	Marron/Thomson	Beaufighters	Betty	SW of New Britain
9/10/43	31	Gordon	Beaufighter	Nick	Selaru Is
9/10/43	31	Gordon	Beaufighter	Nick	Selaru Is
9/10/43	31	McCord	Beaufighter	Sally	Selaru Is
23/10/43	30	Drury/Hastwell/ Fisher/McRobbie	Beaufighters	Jake	New Britain
31/10/43	79	Callister	Spitfire V	Tony	N Kiriwina Is
11/11/43	7	C. Cox	Beaufort	Jake	Horn Is
12/11/43	457	Smithson	Spitfire V	Betty	Darwin
12/11/43	457	Smithson	Spitfire V	Betty	Darwin
21/11/43	31	Gordon	Beaufighter	Rufe	Maikoor Is
21/11/43	31	Ferguson	Beaufighter	Rufe	Maikoor Is
28/11/43	79	Moore	Spitfire V	Dinah	Kiriwina Is
16/12/43	31	Gordon	Beaufighter	Nick	Timor
23/12/43	31	Barnett	Beaufighter	Nate	Timor
4/01/44	31	Gordon	Beaufighter	Betty	Timor
22/01/44	86	Stuart	P-40N	Betty	Cape Valsch
23/01/44	86	Whittle	P-40N	Zero	Cape Valsch
23/01/44	86	Whittle/Kerrison	P-40Ns	Betty	Cape Valsch
23/01/44	86	Whittle/Kerrison	P-40Ns	Zero	Cape Valsch
3/06/44	78	Osment	P-40N	Kate	Biak Is
3/06/44	78	Cowley	P-40N	Oscar	Biak Is
3/06/44	78	G. White	P-40N	Oscar	Biak Is

Date	Squadron	Pilot(s)	Aircraft	Opponent	Location
3/06/44	78	G. White	P-40N	Kate	Biak Is
3/06/44	78	Baker	P-40N	Oscar	Biak Is
3/06/44	78	Smith	P-40N	Oscar	Biak Is
3/06/44	78	Griffiths	P-40N	Oscar	Biak Is
3/06/44	78	Barker	P-40N	Oscar	Biak Is
3/06/44	78	Griffiths/Blesing	P-40Ns	Oscar	Biak Is
10/06/44	78	Baker	P-40N	Tony	Japen Is
12/06/44	452	Gamble/Beaton/ O'Loughlin	Spitfires	Dinah	Darwin
16/07/44	31	P. Boyd	Beaufighter	Nick	Maumore
24/12/44	452	Pretty	Spitfire VIII	Nick	Morotai
20/06/45	457	Campbell/ Scrimgeour	Spitfire VIIIs	Dinah	Labuan
24/07/45	452	King	Spitfire VIII	Helen	Balikpapan

Confirmed victories: Burma/India

Date	Squadron	Pilot(s)	Aircraft	Opponent	Location
29/01/42	135 RAF	Storey	Hurricane	Nate	Mingaladon
6/02/42	135 RAF	Storey	Hurricane	Nate	Mingaladon
6/02/42	135 RAF	Storey	Hurricane	Nate	Mingaladon
23/02/42	135 RAF	Storey	Hurricane	Nate	Rangoon
26/02/42	17 RAF	Cotton	Hurricane	Nate	Moulmein
26/02/42	17 RAF	Cotton	Hurricane	Lily	Moulmein
9/04/42	261 RAF	Rawnsley	Hurricane	Zero	Trincomalee
10/11/42	126 RAF	Haley	Mohawk IV	Oscar	Akyab
15/12/42	79 RAF	R. Bowes	Hurricane	Lily	Chittagong
20/12/42	607 RAF	Goold	Hurricane	Oscar	Magwe
20/01/43	176 RAF	Crombie	Beaufighter	Lily	Calcutta
13/02/43	261 RAF	Mann	Hurricane	Oscar	Arakan
13/02/43	261 RAF	Mann	Hurricane	Oscar	Arakan
5/03/43	135 RAF	Storey	Hurricane	Oscar	Akyab
5/03/43	135 RAF	Storey	Hurricane	Oscar	Akyab
5/03/43	135 RAF	Storey	Hurricane	Oscar	Akyab
5/03/43	79 RAF	R. Bowes	Hurricane	Oscar	Aungdaing
17/03/43	79 RAF	R. Bowes	Hurricane	Oscar	Ramu
17/03/43	79 RAF	R. Bowes	Hurricane	Oscar	Ramu
27/03/43	79 RAF	R. Bowes	Hurricane	Lily	Cox's Bazaar
27/03/43	135 RAF	Crawford	Hurricane	Lily	Ramu

Date	Squadron	Pilot(s)	Aircraft	Opponent	Location
1/04/43	615 RAF	Andrews	Hurricane	Sally	Feni
5/04/43	79 RAF	R. Bowes	Hurricane	Oscar	Thazi
3/05/43	135 RAF	Storey	Hurricane	Oscar	Mt Victoria
22/09/43	160 RAF	Cohen	Liberator	Zero	Nicobar Islands
16/11/43	615 RAF	Gannon	Spitfire V	Dinah	Feni
26/12/43	615 RAF	Andrews	Spitfire V	Oscar	Chittagong
26/12/43	615 RAF	Andrews	Spitfire V	Sally	Chittagong
26/12/43	615 RAF	Chatfield	Spitfire V	Sally	Chittagong
26/12/43	615 RAF	Chatfield	Spitfire V	Sally	Chittagong
31/12/43	136 RAF	Garvan	Spitfire V	Sally	Chittagong
15/01/44	607 RAF	Doudy	Spitfire V	Oscar	Maingaon
15/01/44	136 RAF	Garvan	Spitfire V	Oscar	Teknaf
15/01/44	136 RAF	Garvan	Spitfire V	Oscar	Teknaf
15/01/44	607 RAF	Bohane	Spitfire V	Oscar	Maungdaw
8/02/44	605 RAF	Goold	Spitfire V	Oscar	Mayu Ranges
6/03/44	81 RAF	Cronin	Spitfire VIII	Dinah	Imphal
13/03/44	81 RAF	Cronin	Spitfire VIII	Oscar	'Broadway'
11/05/44	605 RAF	Goold	Spitfire VIII	Oscar	Imphal
18/05/44	605 RAF	Goold	Spitfire VIII	Oscar	Palel
17/06/44	615 RAF	Chatfield	Spitfire V	Oscar	Moirang
17/06/44	615 RAF	Gannon	Spitfire V	Oscar	Moirang
4/02/45	45 RAF	Ewing	Mosquito	Sally	Heho
4/03/45	89 RAF	Johnson	Beaufighter	Lily	Pakokku
4/03/45	89 RAF	Johnson	Beaufighter	Lily	Mandalay

Probable victories: Malaya, Netherlands East Indies, South-West Pacific Area

Date	Squadron	Pilot(s)	Aircraft	Opponent	Location
9/12/41	8	Widmer	Hudson	Nell	Kuantan
13/12/41	453	Collyer/Read	Buffalo	Sonia	Butterfield
13/12/41	453	Collyer/Read	Buffalo	Sonia	Butterfield
13/12/41	453	Collyer/Read	Buffalo	Sonia	Butterfield
21/12/41	453	Peterson	Buffalo	Sonia	Kuala Lumpur
15/01/42	21/453	Kinninmont	Buffalo	Lily	Singapore
21/01/42	11	Hutchinson/Keen	Catalina	Zero	Salamaua
23/01/42	232 RAF	Fairbairn	Hurricane	fighter	Singapore
27/01/42	453	Gorringe	Buffalo	Nell	Sembawang
3/02/42	20	Hemsworth/Dick	Catalina	Claude	Rabaul

Date	Squadron	Pilot(s)	Aircraft	Opponent	Location
9/02/42	232 RAF	Young	Hurricane	Sally	Singapore
28/03/42	75	Woods	P-40E	Zero	Port Moresby
10/04/42	75	Ellerton	P-40E	bomber	New Guinea
13/04/42	2	Cook/Leithhead	Hudson	Zero	Koepang
13/04/42	2	Blanchard/Gitsham	Hudson	Zero	Koepang
26/04/42	75	Atherton	P-40E	Zero	Port Moresby
11/08/42	75	Atherton	P-40E	Zero	Port Moresby
11/08/42	76	Wawn	P-40E	Zero	Milne Bay
11/08/42	75	Whetters/Ollivier	P-40Es	enemy aircraft	Milne Bay
11/08/42	75	Coker	P-40E	enemy aircraft	Milne Bay
27/08/42	75	L. Jackson	P-40E	Zero	Milne Bay
27/08/42	75	Jones/B. Watson	P-40Es	dive-bomber	Milne Bay
22/11/42	30	Cummins	Beaufighter	Zero	Lae
26/12/42	Sp Tpt Flt	O. Hall	Hudson	Zero	Dobodura
27/12/42	2	Robertson	Hudson	Zero	Timor
15/03/43	457	Hamilton	Spitfire V	Zero	Darwin
15/03/43	457	Robinson	Spitfire V	Zero	Darwin
15/03/43	457	Batchelor	Spitfire V	Zero	Darwin
14/04/43	75	J. Morrison	P-40E	fighter	Milne Bay
14/04/43	77	Kinross	P-40K	bomber	Milne Bay
14/04/43	77	J. Cox	P-40K	Sally	Milne Bay
14/04/43	77	Johnstone	P-40K	bomber	Milne Bay
14/04/43	77	A. Morrison	P-40K	bomber	Milne Bay
14/04/43	75	Hall	P-40E	Betty	Milne Bay
14/04/43	75	Jones/Ward	P-40E	Betty	Milne Bay
25/04/43	2	Austin	Hudson	Jake	Maikoor Is
2/05/43	457	Blake	Spitfire V	Zero	Darwin
2/05/43	457	K. James	Spitfire V	Zero	Darwin
2/05/43	452	Evans	Spitfire V	Zero	Darwin
10/05/43	457	Little	Spitfire V	Zero	Millingimbi
4/06/43	31	Entwistle	Beaufighter	Rufe	Taberfane
20/06/43	1 Wing	Caldwell	Spitfire V	Betty	Darwin
28/06/43	1 Wing	Caldwell	Spitfire V	Betty	Darwin
30/06/43	1 Wing	Caldwell	Spitfire V	Betty	Darwin
6/07/43	457	Batchelor	Spitfire V	Betty	Darwin

Date	Squadron	Pilot(s)	Aircraft	Opponent	Location
10/08/43	452	Young/Coombes	Spitfire V	Pete	Millingimbi
7/09/43	457	Mackenzie	Spitfire V	Zero	Darwin
8/10/43	6	Barr	Beaufort	Oscar	Cape St George
11/10/43	30	Unknown	Beaufighter	Zero	Rabaul
11/10/43	30	Unknown	Beaufighter	Zero	Rabaul
31/10/43	75	Arthur	P-40M	Betty	New Britain
16/01/44	20	Cowan	Catalina	fighter	Halmahera

Probable victories: Burma/India

Date	Squadron	Pilot(s)	Aircraft	Opponent	Location
6/02/42	135 RAF	Storey	Hurricane	Nate	Mingaladon
6/02/42	135 RAF	Storey	Hurricane	Nate	Mingaladon
9/04/42	261 RAF	Mann	Hurricane	Zero	Ceylon
13/02/43	261 RAF	Mann	Hurricane	Oscar	Arakan
4/04/43	136 RAF	Goddard	Hurricane	Oscar	Chittagong
31/12/43	136 RAF	Garvan	Spitfire V	Sally	Chittagong
15/01/44	136 RAF	Garvan	Spitfire V	Oscar	Teknaf
15/01/44	136 RAF	Barnett	Spitfire V	Oscar	Teknaf
20/01/44	607 RAF	Goold	Spitfire V	Oscar	Magwe
25/04/44	615 RAF	Gannon	Spitfire V	Oscar	Silchar
26/04/44	615 RAF	Andrews	Spitfire V	Oscar	Imphal

Appendix D
RAAF aces against Japan

As mentioned, victory claims are often uncertain, but it seems that nine RAAF pilots shot down at least five Japanese aircraft, and thus qualified as aces against this enemy alone. Table 5 provides information about the achievements of all nine men. Destroyed and probables refer only to Japanese victims. A '+' denotes that some of the pilot's kills were shared: e.g. Bowes had six destroyed and one shared. Next behind this group were three pilots with four victories: Tim Goldsmith, Jack Smithson and Peter Watson.

TABLE 5 NINE AUSTRALIAN ACES

Rank	Name	Squadron	Aircraft	Destroyed	Probables
S/Ldr	Jack Storey	135 RAF	Hurricane	8	2
Gp Capt	Clive Caldwell	1 Wing	Spitfire	7	3
F/Lt	Russ Bowes	79 RAF	Hurricane	6+1	0
Sqn Ldr	Alf Clare	453	Buffalo	6	0
W/Cdr	Les Jackson	75	Kittyhawk	5+1	1
S/Ldr	Reg Gordon	31	Beaufighter	5	0
S/Ldr	Doug Vanderfield	453	Buffalo	4+2	0
W/Cdr	Geoff Atherton	75	Kittyhawk	4+1	2
F/Lt	Wilf Goold	605, 607 RAF	Spitfire	4 or 5	1

Appendix E
The aircraft: Victors and victims

The main aircraft types in which RAAF pilots achieved victories over Japanese aircraft are shown in Table 6, though there will almost certainly be some inaccuracies.

TABLE 6 SUCCESS RATES FOR RAAF AIRCRAFT TYPES

Aircraft type	Comfirmed/probables
Spitfire	71/17
Kittyhawk	56/17
Buffalo	30/6
Hurricane	25/7
Beaufighter	23/4
Hudson	13/6
Beaufort	5/1

The main Japanese types that were reported as falling victim to RAAF pilots are shown in Table 7, though one must remember that most fighters tended to be called 'Zeros'. Again, numbers refer to confirmed/ probables.

TABLE 7 DOWNED JAPANESE AIRCRAFT, BY TYPE

Aircraft type	Comfirmed/probables
Zero	61/22
Oscar	43/8
Betty	26/7
Nate	14/2
Lily	11/1
Dinah	11/0
Sally	9/3
Sonia	7/4
Jake	6/1
Rufe	6/1
Nick	5/0
Pete	4/1
Kate	3/0
Tony	3/0
Val	2/0
Helen	2/0
Nell	1/2
Dave	1/0
Claude	0/1
'Bomber'	6/4
'Fighter'	2/3
'Float-plane'	2/0
'Dive-bomber'	1/1
'Flying-boat'	1/0

Glossary

A and SD	Administrative and Special Duties
AA	anti-aircraft (also 'ack-ack, flak')
ABDA	American, British, Dutch and Australian Command
AC1	Aircraftman 1st Class
ACH	Area Combined Headquarters
Ack-ack	anti-aircraft
AFC	Australian Flying Corps
AIF	Australian Imperial Force
ASV radar	Air to Surface Vessel radar
AVM	Air Vice-Marshal
AWM	Australian War Memorial, Canberra
Bogey/Bogies	unidentified aircraft
CAS	Chief of Air Staff
CO	Commanding Officer
Cpl	Corporal
DAP	Department of Aircraft Production
DFC	Distinguished Flying Cross
DFM	Distinguished Flying Medal
DSO	Distinguished Service Order
EATS	Empire Air Training Scheme
EFTS	Elementary Flying Training School
FEAF	Far East Air Force

F/Lt	Flight Lieutenant
F/O	Flying Officer
GHQ	General Headquarters
Gp Capt	Group Captain
HQ	Headquarters
JAAF	Japanese Army Air Force
JNAF	Japanese Navy Air Force
LAC	Leading Aircraftman
NAA	National Archives of Australia
NCO	Non-commissioned officer
NEI	Netherlands East Indies
OAFH	Office of Air Force History
OBU	Operational Base Unit
OG	Operational Group
OP	Observation Post
ORB	Operations Record Book—a unit diary
OTU	Operational Training Unit
PO	Pilot Officer
POW	Prisoner of war
PRU	Photographic Reconnaissance Unit
PT boat	Patrol Torpedo boat
RAF	Royal Air Force
RAN	Royal Australian Navy
RFC	Royal Flying Corps
RNZAF	Royal New Zealand Air Force
RSU	Repair and Salvage Unit
S/Ldr	Squadron Leader
SFTS	Service Flying Training School
Sgt	Sergeant
SLV	State Library of Victoria
Sp Tpt Flt	Special Transport Flight
Sqn	Squadron
TAF	Tactical Air Force
USAAF	United States Army Air Forces
VC	Victoria Cross
W/Cdr	Wing Commander
W/O	Warrant Officer
W/T	Wireless Telegraphist, Wireless Telegraphy
WAAAF	Women's Auxiliary Australian Air Force
WAG	Wireless Air-Gunner

Notes

OAFH numbers refer to the Roll and File numbers: thus 460/114 is Roll 460, File 114.

Introduction

1. Sherrod, *On to Westward*, p. 14.
2. Jones, *From Private to Air Marshal*, p. 72.
3. Grantham, *The 13 Squadron Story*, p. 110. Also interview with Charles Roe, 16 October 2010.
4. AWM 3DRL/6732, Cpl V. Hunt, 22 Sqn, diary 20 October 1943.

1 A difficult childhood

1. AWM PR01196, S/Ldr F. X. McMahon, Memoir of Darwin bombing, p. 5.
2. AWM PR01225, Sgt A. Fletcher, 13 Sqn, diary March 1942 re. 19 February 1942.
3. Stephens, *Royal Australian Air Force*, p. 136.
4. Odgers, *RAAF*, p. 43.
5. Gillison, *Royal Australian Air Force*, p. 13.
6. Johnston and Nation, *Australia 1939*, p. 17.
7. 'Goble, Air Vice-Marshal Stanley James', in *Oxford Companion to Military History* (1st edn), p. 270.
8. Stephens, *Power Plus Attitude*, p. 62.
9. AWM Murdoch Sound Archive S00922, Sir Richard Kingsland interview, Tape A Side 1. Intimate club: Stephens, Royal Australian Air Force, p. 37.

10. Long, *Six Years War*, p. 9.
11. Horner, *High Command*, p. 13.
12. Stephens, *Royal Australian Air Force*, pp. 53–4.
13. ibid., p. 55.
14. Odgers, *RAAF*, p. 53.
15. Coulthard-Clark, *The Third Brother*, p. 464.
16. Odgers, *RAAF*, p. 53.
17. Gillison, *Royal Australian Air Force*, p. 22.
18. ibid., p. 48.

2 'They will follow you through hell'

1. Gillison, *Royal Australian Air Force*, p. 60.
2. ibid., p. 81; Stephens, *Royal Australian Air Force*, p. 63.
3. Gillison, *Royal Australian Air Force*, p. 91.
4. AWM PR01563, John O'Keeffe, 'Reminiscences of Second World War', p. 2.
5. RAAF Historical Section, *Units of the Royal Australian Air Force*, vol. 8, Training units, pp. 17, 19, 20, 22. Hereafter cited as '*Units*'.
6. AWM MSS1510, J. Scott, 'World War Two, as seen by one participant', pp. 6–7.
7. Walker, *Black Jack*, p. 39.
8. RAAF Historical Section, *Units*, vol. 8, Training units, p. 107.
9. Walker, *Medical Services of the R.A.N. and R.A.A.F.*, p. 217.
10. AWM MSS1514, Boxall memoir, p. 25.
11. Walker, *Medical Services*, p. 214.
12. Nelson, *Chased by the Sun*, p. 26.
13. Deane-Butcher, *Fighter Squadron Doctor*, pp. 42–3.
14. Sgt-Pilot E. Bannister, in Shelton Smith (ed.), *The Boys Write Home*, pp. 198–9.
15. S00577, Piper interview, Tape 1, Side A; Mariah, *Touched by War*, p. 31; Bergerud, *Fire in the Sky*, p. 118.
16. J. Jackson, letter 22 December 1941, quoted in Patricia and Arthur Jackson (eds), *A Lot to Fight For*, p. 219.
17. Quoted in 'Foreword' to *These Eagles*, p. 7.
18. Garrisson, *Australian Fighter Aces*, p. 77.
19. Quoted in Gillison, *Royal Australian Air Force*, p. 100.
20. ibid.

3 'We may not have much time to spare'

1. Gillison, *Royal Australian Air Force*, p. 138.
2. Kingsland interview, Tape 1, Side B.
3. Gillison, *Royal Australian Air Force*, p. 121.
4. Horner, *High Command*, p. 56.
5. Quoted in Gillison, *Royal Australian Air Force*, p. 161.
6. In Horner, *High Command*, p. 57.
7. Gillison, *Royal Australian Air Force*, pp. 157–8.

8. ibid., p. 155.
9. Bulcock, *Of Death But Once*, pp. 18–19.
10. Cull et al., *Buffaloes Over Singapore*, pp. 33–4.
11. Hewitt, *Adversity in Success*, p. 9.
12. Shores et al., *Bloody Shambles*, Volume 1, p. 69.
13. Bennett, *Defeat to Victory*, p. 5.

4 'We were actually going into action!!'

1. Balfe, *War Without Glory*, p. 36.
2. AWM PR87/109, D. Scott, recollections 1984, p. 13. Emphasis in original.
3. ibid.
4. Nelson, *Prisoners of War*, p. 13.
5. AWM PR91/124, Interview with C.H. Spurgeon, 17 March 1991.
6. Hall, *Glory in Chaos*, p. 91.
7. In Gillison, *Royal Australian Air Force*, p. 222.
8. Hall, *Glory in Chaos*, p. 401.
9. AWM PR00158, Sgt J. Woodward, 27 Sqn RAF, diary 21 January 1942.
10. D. Scott, recollections 1984, p. 14.
11. Bulcock, *Of Death But Once*, p. 43.
12. Woodward, diary 13 December 1941.
13. ibid.
14. AWM 3DRL/6601, LAC J. Shanahan, 453 Sqn, diary 21 December 1941, p. 27.
15. ibid., 22 December 1941.

5 The fight for Singapore

1. Shanahan, diary 25 January 1942.
2. Woodward, diary 21 December 1941.
3. Gillison, *Royal Australian Air Force*, p. 326.
4. ibid., p. 329.
5. Shanahan, diary 17 January 1942.
6. Hall, *Glory in Chaos*, p. 304.
7. F/Lt Sheppard, Report, 1 August 1942, in NAA A705, 163/96/105, Casualty file of Chapman, Norman Richard.
8. Hall, *Glory in Chaos*, p. 304.
9. D. Scott, recollections, p. 16.
10. In Cull et al., *Buffaloes Over Singapore*, p. 154.
11. Shanahan, diary 20 January 1942.
12. Spurgeon interview.
13. AWM PR87/076, W/Cdr R. Davis, 1 Sqn, Narrative of events, p. 17.
14. Woodward, diary 29 January 1942.
15. AWM 3DRL/6601, T. Lamb letter to Shanahan, 1963.
16. Shanahan, diary 4 February 1942.

17. D. Scott, recollections, p. 22.
18. Woodward, diary 17 February 1942.
19. Letter from M. Chapman, 12 March 1949 in NAA 163/96/105, Chapman casualty file.

6 'We who are about to die, salute you!'

1. <www.burleighheadsrsl.com/webpages/NewsArticles/NewsArticle-026.htm> [4 September 2010].
2. McAulay, *We Who Are About to Die*, pp. 53–5.
3. OAFH, 459/0101, 'Operational Complaints and Difficulties Concerning Rabaul.'
4. McAulay, *We Who Are About to Die*, p. 66.
5. OAFH, 460/284, 'Rabaul—Early activities of 24 Squadron', Interview with Group Captain W.D. Brookes, p. 4.
6. AWM PR91/73, Yeowart, Robert, 1943 interview transcript, p. 3.
7. ibid., p. 4.
8. Quotation: Selby, *Hell and High Fever*, p. 27.
9. Brookes interview, p. 6.
10. OAFH, 460/306, '24 Squadron Early Story of Rabaul Based on Experiences of Flight Lieutenant J.V. Tyrell', pp. 5–6.
11. Selby, *Hell and High Fever*, pp. 26–7.
12. Heroism: ibid., p. 28. Ungenerous: McAulay, *We Who Are About to Die*, p. 117.
13. OAFH, 459/87, 'RAAF Operations from Rabaul', Sqn Leader W.D. Brookes, 24 Sqn, Report 24 February 1942.
14. Gillison, *Royal Australian Air Force*, p. 356.
15. This discussion of Lerew's message is based chiefly on my correspondence with Canon John May, September 2008.
16. Tyrell interview, p. 8.
17. AWM PR03185, W/O A. Bates, 11 Sqn, 'Pacific Pilgrimage', wartime reminiscence/diary, 19 February 1942, p. 10.
18. OAFH, 460/29, '20 Squadron Report Corporal Keen 4 February 1942'.
19. Metzler, 'Early Days', in Minty, *Black Cats*, pp. 3–4.
20. Bates, 'Pacific Pilgrimage', 27 January 1942.
21. Kingsland interview, Tape 2, Side A.

7 'Thrilling but terrifying'

1. Grantham, *The 13 Squadron Story*, pp. 36–7.
2. Gillison, *Royal Australian Air Force*, p. 273.
3. Fletcher, diary 6 January 1942.
4. OAFH, 459/1571, 'Interview 13 Squadron Sergeant B. Hack'.
5. Fletcher, diary 7 January 1942.
6. NAA Series 7186, RAAF Unit History sheets, Number 13 Squadron, 6 January 1942.

7. Letter in Grantham, *13 Squadron Story*, Appendix C.
8. Harry Riley, air-gunner quoted in Grantham, *13 Squadron Story*, pp. 143–4.
9. Fletcher, diary 30 January 1942, re 11 January.
10. ibid., re 12 January.
11. Gillison, *Royal Australian Air Force*, p. 310.
12. Fletcher, diary 30 January 1942.
13. Grantham, *13 Squadron Story*, p. 138.
14. Fletcher, diary 30 January, re 22 January 1942.
15. Grantham, *13 Squadron Story*, p. 44.
16. ibid., p. 133.
17. Fletcher, diary 30 January.
18. Grantham, *13 Squadron Story*, p. 52.
19. Gillison, *Royal Australian Air Force*, p. 374; Balfe, *War Without Glory*, p. 169.
20. Fletcher, diary 30 January 1942. My emphasis.
21. Woodward, *Three Times Lucky*, pp. 110–11.
22. Hall, *Glory in Chaos*, p. 189.
23. Davis, notes 14 February 1942.
24. Gillison, *Royal Australian Air Force*, p. 395.
25. AWM PR00646, Sgt W. Cosgrove, 84 Squadron RAF, Letter 17 February 1942.
26. Shores et al., *Bloody Shambles*, Volume 2, p. 116.
27. Cosgrove, letter 17 February 1942.
28. Davis, diary note re February–March 1942.
29. D. Scott, recollections, p. 25.
30. Davis, diary 7 March.

8 Crisis of leadership

1. AWM PR01196, S/Ldr F. McMahon, Memoir, p. 3.
2. Powell, *The Shadow's Edge*, p. 86.
3. McMahon, Memoir, p. 10.
4. Daw, 'Griffith, Sturt de Burgh (1905–1979)', *Australian Dictionary of Biography*, Volume 14.
5. McMahon, Memoir, p. 11.
6. Stephens, *Royal Australian Air Force*, p. 138.
7. McMahon, Memoir, p. 9A.
8. ibid., p. 10.
9. Powell, *Shadow's Edge*, p. 36.
10. Bladin, Memoir (unpublished), p. 6.
11. AWM PR00298, F/Sgt Frank Russell, 11 Squadron, letter 8 March 1942.
12. Quoted in Gillison, *Royal Australian Air Force*, p. 536.
13. Grantham, *13 Squadron Story*, p. 66.
14. Bladin, Memoir, p. 16.
15. ibid., p. 6.
16. McMahon, Memoir, pp. 12–13.

17. Waters, *Valiant Youth*, p. 58.
18. Gillison, *Royal Australian Air Force*, p. 557.
19. Bennett, *Highest Traditions*, p. 157.
20. Gillison, *Royal Australian Air Force*, p. 476.
21. Stephens, *Royal Australian Air Force*, p. 117; Stephens and Isaacs, *High Fliers*, pp. 93–6.
22. Jones, *From Private to Air Marshal*, p. 97.
23. Stephens, *Royal Australian Air Force*, Chapter 6 title; Ashworth, *How Not to Run an Air Force!*

9 The fight over Moresby

1. NAA A9300, Service record of Godfrey Elland Hemsworth, p. 13.
2. OAFH, 460/17, '20 Squadron Interview Wing Commander W.K. Bolitho and Squadron Leader R.M. Seymour'.
3. White, *Green Armour*, p. 73.
4. Campbell, 'Recco over Rabaul', in Bartlett, *Australia at Arms*, p. 181.
5. ibid., p. 183.
6. NAA A9300, Records of Campbell, David Watt Ian, p. 19.
7. Lerew, letter 1943. Courtesy Ian Gould.
8. ibid.
9. White, *Green Armour*, p. 72.
10. AWM PR01751, Ron Munro, 'A resume of my experiences in the RAAF, 1941–45', p. 8.
11. Bates, diary 25 February 1942.
12. ibid., 26 February 1942.
13. ibid., 28 February 1942.
14. ibid., 2 March 1942.
15. White, *Green Armour*, p. 74.
16. Hewitt, *Adversity in Success*, p. 316.
17. Jeffrey, Foreword to Jackson (eds), *A Lot to Fight For*, p. xiii.
18. AWM Murdoch Sound Archive S00701, Arthur Tucker interview, Tape 1, Side 2.
19. AWM Murdoch Sound Archive S00578, Nat Gould, Tape 2, Side A.
20. AWM Murdoch Sound Archive S00583, Bruce Brown, Tape 2, Side A.
21. Masters, *Born Lucky*, p. 27.
22. Jackson, *A Lot to Fight For*, p. 222.
23. Bob Crawford, '44 Days' documentary.
24. Sakai, *Samurai!*, p. 79. There is controversy as to the authorship and accuracy of this book. However, the quotations presented here are consistent with other public statements made by Sakai.
25. White, *Green Armour*, p. 78.
26. Jackson, *A Lot to Fight For*, pp. 224–6.
27. Tucker, 2001 letter quoted in Jackson, *A Lot to Fight For*, p. 255.

28. Deane-Butcher, *Fighter Squadron Doctor*, p. 65.
29. AWM MSS1420, Raymond Neal, '44 Days Plus', 1992, p. 2.
30. ibid. White, *Green Armour*, p. 75.

10 The 44 Days

1. John Piper, '44 Days' documentary.
2. McAulay, *We Who Are About to Die*, p. 191.
3. Deane-Butcher, *Fighter Squadron Doctor*, p. 27.
4. Wilson, *Seek and Strike*, p. 33.
5. S00701, Tucker interview, Tape 2, Side B.
6. AWM Murdoch Sound Archive S00731, Wilfred Arthur interview, Tape 3, Side A.
7. S00583, Bruce Brown interview, Tape 2, Side A.
8. Masters, *Born Lucky*, p. 40.
9. Wilson, *Seek and Strike*, p. 22.
10. White, *Green Armour*, p. 77.
11. Bates, diary 1 April 1942.
12. Masters, *Born Lucky*, p. 31.
13. NAA A705, 166/6/845, Casualty file for David Stuart Brown.
14. S00577, Piper interview, Tape 1, Side B.
15. Jackson's letter is in Jackson, *A Lot to Fight For*, pp. 235–40.
16. S00577, Piper interview, Tape 1, Side B.
17. Gentleman: ibid., Tape 2, Side A.
18. Whetters interview, '44 Days'.
19. White, *Green Armour*, p. 82. White's emphasis.
20. Masters in Appendix C, Jackson, *A Lot to Fight For*, p. 253.
21. S00701, Tucker interview, Tape 3, Side A. See also '44 Days' documentary and Deane-Butcher, *Fighter Squadron Doctor*, pp. 89–90.
22. S00701, Tucker interview, Tape 3, Side A.
23. ibid.
24. S00577, Piper interview, Tape 2, Sides A and B.
25. S00731, Arthur interview, Tape 1, Side B and Tape 3, Side A; S00548, Colin Lindeman interview, Tape 3, Side A.
26. Jackson, *A Lot to Fight For*, p. 241. Masters, *Born Lucky*, p. 38.
27. S00701, Tucker interview, Tape 3, Side B.
28. S00592, Whetters interview, Tape 2, Side B.
29. NAA A9186, 75 Squadron Operations Record Book, April 1942.
30. S00701, Tucker interview, Tape 3, Side A.
31. OAFH, 460/549, '75 Squadron Particulars of Formation and Main Attacks from 21 March–3 May 1942', p. 11.
32. Sakai, *Samurai!*, p. 79.
33. In Deane-Butcher, *Fighter Squadron Doctor*, pp. 37, 68.
34. S00592, Whetters interview, Tape 2, Side A.

35. Deane-Butcher, *Fighter Squadron Doctor*, p. 65.
36. ibid., p. 55.
37. F/Lt the Rev. P. Sands, letter 20 August 1942, in Jackson, *A Lot to Fight For*, p. 243.

11 Trouble at the top

1. NAA A9186, No. 2 Squadron ORB, 13 May 1942.
2. Powell, *Shadow's Edge*, p. 116.
3. In 2004, the television program *George Negus Tonight* presented a segment concerning Brooks and his descendants. A transcript is at: <www.abc.net.au/gnt/history/Transcripts/s1227263.htm> [4 September 2010].
4. Clayton, 'The north Australian air war', p. 41.
5. Sgt T. Quirk, 21 Sqn, diary 11 June 1944. Also poem 'Bloody Darwin' reproduced in Grose, *An Awkward Truth*, pp. xiv–xv.
6. AWM 3DRL/7976, Wardley, Memoir, pp. 3, 4.
7. Powell, *Shadow's Edge*, p. 201.
8. AWM PR00725, LAC D. Howdle, 55 or 52 Operational Base Unit, diary 25 August 1943.
9. Quirk, diary 11 June 1944.
10. Bladin, Memoir, p. 37.
11. AWM PR03202, Sgt A.C. Brayne, 31 Radar Station, diary/reminiscence, p. 16.
12. Bladin, Memoir, p. 37.
13. Howdle, diary 15 September 1943.
14. NAA A9186, 452 Squadron ORB, 29 April 1943.
15. Quoted in McAulay, *Six Aces*, p. 212.
16. Powell, *Shadow's Edge*, p. 207.
17. AWM PR01241, Sgt J. Clark, 6 Sqn, diary 22 January 1943.
18. Herb Plenty, interview with the author, 30 January 2010.
19. OAFH, 459/1381, '8 Squadron Work of Beauforts', p. 3.
20. Adapted from Gillison, *Royal Australian Air Force*, p. 484.
21. Hewitt, *Adversity in Success*, p. 87.
22. Stephens, *Royal Australian Air Force*, p. 149.
23. Kenney, *General Kenney Reports*, pp. 29–30.
24. Hewitt, *Adversity in Success*, p. 83.
25. Kenney, *General Kenney Reports*, pp. 35, 39. Birdsall, *Flying Buccaneers*, p. 7.

12 Codename 'Fall River'

1. Gillison, *Royal Australian Air Force*, pp. 540–1.
2. Jones, *From Private to Air Marshal*, p. 89.
3. OAFH, 459/158, 'Buna Operations: Extract from diary, writer unknown, captured Buna', 9–10, 11 August 1942, p. 3.
4. Odgers, *Mr Double Seven*, p. 11.
5. 'Enemy Lines', *Australian Story*, ABC TV, 1 July 2002.

6. ibid.
7. Gillison, *Royal Australian Air Force*, p. 602.
8. Brown interview, Tape 2, Side A.
9. NAA A11093, RAAF Command Headquarters—South West Pacific Area—Reinforcement of 'Fall River' [Allied Airfield—New Guinea], 2 July 1942, p. 93.
10. NAA A9435, 9 Operational Group Narrative Report, p. 10.
11. Waters, *Valiant Youth*, p. 29.
12. *RAAF Log*, p. 37.
13. 9 Operational Group Narrative Report, p. 7.
14. Wilson, *The Decisive Factor*, p. 98.
15. Gould interview, Tape 2, Side A.
16. S00701, Tucker interview, Tape 3, Side B.
17. ibid. Brown interview, Tape 1, Side B.
18. P/O H. Kerr, 76 Sqn, logbook 4 August 1942, c/o Peter Hunter.
19. F/Lt C. Wawn, 76 Sqn, logbook 11 August 1942, c/o Peter Hunter.
20. Kerr, logbook 11 August 1942.
21. Brown interview, Tape 2, Side A.
22. AWM PR00742, Cpl C. Walmsley, 76 Squadron, diary 24 August 1942.
23. S00577, Piper interview, Tape 2, Side A.
24. Baker and Knight, *Milne Bay*, p. 115.
25. John Koy, in Deane-Butcher, *Fighter Squadron Doctor*, p. 133.
26. AWM Murdoch Sound Archive S00734, Cliff Hull interview, Tape 1, Side B.
27. Walmslcy, diary 25 August 1942.
28. Hairy and 'Immaculates': 9 Operational Group Narrative Report, pp. 7, 9.

13 Milne Bay

1. Gillison, *Royal Australian Air Force*, p. 622.
2. Walmsley, diary 26 August 1942.
3. Wawn logbook, 26 August 1942.
4. Walmsley, diary 26 August 1942.
5. ibid., 27 August 1942.
6. Baker and Knight, *Milne Bay*, p. 168.
7. Walmsley, diary 27 August 1942.
8. 9 Operational Group Narrative Report, p. 10.
9. 'Milne Bay', *RAAF Log*, p. 37.
10. Quoted in Gillison, *Royal Australian Air Force*, p. 613.
11. Loudon, logbook 28 August 1942.
12. Baker and Knight, *Milne Bay*, p. 201.
13. Loudon, logbook 28 August 1942.
14. Baker and Knight, *Milne Bay*, p. 220.
15. Clark, diary 4 September 1942.
16. 9 Operational Group Narrative Report, p. 6.

17. MacArthur, Rowell, Clowes, quoted in Gillison, *Royal Australian Air Force*, p. 617.
18. Wilson, *Decisive Factor*, p. 190.
19. 'Milne Bay', *RAAF Log*, p. 41.
20. Walmsley, diary 26, 29 August 1942.
21. 9 Operational Group Narrative Report, p. 6.
22. Baker and Knight, *Milne Bay*, p. 189.
23. 'Milne Bay', *RAAF Log*, p. 37.
24. Deane-Butcher, *Fighter Squadron Doctor*, p. 161.
25. Gould interview, Tape 2, Side A.
26. Clark, diary 11–12 September 1942.
27. Kerr, logbook 22 September 1942.
28. Deane-Butcher, *Fighter Squadron Doctor*, p. 182.
29. Walmsley, diary 31 August 1942.

14 From Kokoda to the beaches

1. Quoted in Gillison, *Royal Australian Air Force*, p. 623. My italics.
2. McAulay, *Battle of the Bismarck Sea*, p. 33.
3. Parnell, *Whispering Death*, p. 5.
4. 'Test Pilot', *Victory Roll*, p. 24.
5. Mariah, *Touched by War*, p. 33.
6. Parnell, *Whispering Death*, p. 12.
7. AWM PR00646, Colin Harvey interview, p. 244.
8. Gillison, *Royal Australian Air Force*, p. 631.
9. AWM PR00646, Gwynne Hughes interview, pp. 287–8.
10. AWM PR87/041, LAC E. Spencer, 5 Mobile Works Sqn, diary 17, 18 August and 7, 9, 12 September 1942.
11. Walker, *Black Jack*, p. 71.
12. Spencer, diary 17 September 1942.
13. Walker, *Black Jack*, p. 73.
14. NAA A9186, 30 Squadron ORB, November 1942, pp. 105–6.
15. AWM PR00646, LAC L. Crouch, 30 Sqn, diary 22 November 1942. AWM PR00646, Nelson interview, p. 435.
16. Crouch, diary 24 November 1942.
17. Gunston, *Combat Aircraft of World War II*, p. 216.
18. Gillison, *Royal Australian Air Force*, p. 639.
19. Bergerud, *Fire in the Sky*, p. 587.
20. NAA A705, Casualty file, 'Hersey, David', p. 24.
21. In Gillison, *Royal Australian Air Force*, p. 663.
22. 'Army Co-op', *RAAF Log*, p. 56.
23. Crotty, 'One Wirraway's war', *Wartime*, vol. 11, Spring 2000, p. 22.
24. NAA A9186, 4 Squadron ORB, 26 December 1942, p. 142.
25. Quoted in Crotty, 'One Wirraway's war', p. 23.

26. Citation at <www.awm.gov.au/cms_images/awm192/00312/003120420.pdf> [4 September 2010].
27. 'Army Co-op', *RAAF Log*, p. 54.
28. ibid.
29. Gillison, *Royal Australian Air Force*, p. 676.
30. OAFH, 459/158, 'Buna Operations', diary 'presumably of Lt Suganuma', 15 December 1942, pp. 1–2.
31. ibid., 'Diary of unknown persons', 7 December 1942.
32. Hewitt, *Adversity in Success*, p. 61.
33. Quoted in Page, *Wings of Destiny*, p. 151.
34. Watson, *Air Action in the Papuan Campaign*, p. 97.
35. Vernon in Minty, *Black Cats*, p. 34.
36. Bradley, *The Battle for Wau*, p. 84.
37. AWM PR00646, LAC K. Golledge, 30 Sqn, diary 16 January 1943.
38. AWM PR00646, LAC H. Tayler, 30 Sqn, diary 23–25 January 1943.
39. Gillison, *Royal Australian Air Force*, p. 677.

15 'Whispering death'

1. In Powell, *The Shadow's Edge*, p. 119.
2. Bladin, Memoir, p. 17.
3. Odgers, *Mr Double Seven*, p. 24.
4. AWM PR00782, LAC D. Dacy, Group 45 RAAF, diary 23 November 1942.
5. Walmsley, diary 23 November 1942.
6. AWM 3DRL/7554, Sgt T. Woodgate, 13 Sqn, letter 28 November 1942.
7. Dacy, diary 26 November 1942. His emphasis.
8. Hewitt, *Adversity in Success*, p. 79.
9. Stephens and Isaacs, *High Fliers*, p. 127.
10. Odgers, *Mr Double Seven*, p. 32.
11. Walmsley, diary 5 Oct 1942.
12. ibid., 25, 26 November 1942.
13. Transcript in AWM PR00661, F/O Ralph James, 2 Sqn.
14. NAA A9186, No. 2 Squadron ORB, 25 Sep 1942, p. 156.
15. James, letter 26 September 1942.
16. AWM PR00661, Wing Commander J. Whyte, 2 Sqn, letter 12 December 1943.
17. Grantham, *13 Squadron Story*, p. 137.
18. Page, *Wings of Destiny*, p. 267.
19. McDonald, *Coomalie Charlie's Commandos*, p. 49.
20. ibid., p. viii.
21. ibid., p. 13.
22. ibid., p. 15.
23. OAFH, 460/400, '31 Squadron', Interview with Wing Commander Read, p. 10.
24. Gill, *Royal Australian Navy*, pp. 216–17.
25. 'Beaufighters', *RAAF Log*, p. 95.

26. AWM PR00646, Ball interview, pp. 30, 33.
27. AWM PR00646, Wemyss interview, p. 616.
28. Bladin, Memoir, p. 34.
29. G. Wallace, 1943, quoted in Wallace, *Up in Darwin with the Dutch*, p. 124.
30. Bladin, Memoir, p. 36.
31. AWM PR83/108, F/Sgt R. Farnes, 18 Netherlands East Indies Sqn, diary 5 Apr 1943.
32. 'Beaufighters', *RAAF Log*, p. 99.
33. '31 Squadron', Read interview, p. 14.

16 Wau to the Bismarck Sea

1. Bradley, *Battle for Wau*, p. 182.
2. Gillison, *Royal Australian Air Force*, p. 684.
3. Page, *Wings of Destiny*, p. 203.
4. McDonald, *Damien Parer's War*, p. 261.
5. ibid., pp. 261–2.
6. Lt A. Robertson, 2/7 Bn, letter 21 Feb 1943, author's collection.
7. Gillison, *Royal Australian Air Force*, p. 686.
8. Clark, diary 17 January 1943.
9. AWM PR01192, S/Ldr W. Arthur, 75 Sqn, letter 24 February 1943.
10. Arthur interview, Tape 3, Side A.
11. McAulay, *Battle of the Bismarck Sea*, p. 37.
12. OAFH, 459/565, 'Battle of the Bismark [sic] Sea 30 Squadron US Air crew reports'.
13. OAFH, 460/387, '30 Squadron Interview Flying Officer G.R. Downing', p. 1.
14. Page, *Wings of Destiny*, p. 217.
15. McAulay, *Bismarck Sea*, p. 168.
16. Gillison, *Royal Australian Air Force*, p. 695.
17. Golledge, diary 4 March 1943.
18. Walker, *Black Jack*, p. 86. AWM PR89/188, LAC C.E. Clegg, 14 RSU, diary 4 March 1943. Waters, *Valiant Youth*, p. 51.
19. Hewitt, *Adversity in Success*, p. 74.
20. Golledge, diary 5 March 1943.
21. Fred Cassidy, interview in 'The Australians at War Film Archive', Archive No. 0031.
22. OAFH, 459/541, 'Battle of the Bismark Sea. Extracts from 9 OG Operations Record Book', 11–12 March 1943.
23. Page, *Wings of Destiny*, p. 225.
24. OAFH, 459/519, 'Battle of the Bismarck Sea—ATIS Reports', p. 8.

17 Newton and Yamamoto

1. NAA A9300, Service record Newton WE, translation of captured document, p. 143.

2. ibid. This file contains the abridged (pp. 139–40) and lengthier versions (pp. 115–16).
3. ibid., pp. 112–13.
4. Keith Hampshire's recommendation, in Weate, *Bill Newton V.C.*, pp. 73–5.
5. AWM PR83/021, Newton, William E, Telegram from Damien Parer, 21 October 1943.
6. Hewitt, *Adversity in Success*, p. 81.
7. Arthur, letter 17 April 1943. His emphasis.
8. Waters, *Valiant Youth*, p. 63.
9. OAFH, 460/752, 77 Squadron Combat Report F/O J.A.T. Hodgkinson, 14 April 1943.
10. In Wilson, *Seek and Strike*, pp. 93–4.
11. Clegg, diary 14 April 1943.
12. Odgers, *Mr Double Seven*, p. 41.
13. Stephens, *Power Plus Attitude*, p. 68.

18 Spitfires at Darwin

1. Waters, *Valiant Youth*, p. 22.
2. Caldwell, Foreword to Grant, *Spitfires Over Darwin*, p. vii.
3. J. Scott, 'World War Two', p. 49.
4. S. Wilson, *Wirraway, Boomerang & CA-15*, p. 131.
5. Powell, *The Shadow's Edge*, p. 183.
6. Alexander, *Clive Caldwell*, p. 114.
7. Powell, *Shadow's Edge*, p. 183.
8. Quotation from a newspaper in Grant, *Spitfires Over Darwin*, p. 44.
9. Brayne, diary 7 March 1943.
10. NAA A9186, 457 Squadron ORB, 20 July 1943.
11. OAFH, 460/418, Interview with Gp Captain Savage, p. 9.
12. Brayne, diary 15 March 1943.
13. Sgt Walmsley, diary 30 March 1943.
14. ibid., diary 2 April 1943.
15. Southall, *Bluey Truscott*, p. 203.
16. Quoted in PR86/330, L. Woodhouse, 'RAAF memories', p. 11.
17. Clark, diary 31 March 1943.
18. Minty, *Black Cats*, p. 68.
19. OAFH, 462/1320, 'Composite Combat Report 2 May 1943', p. 1.
20. NAA A9186, 457 Squadron ORB, 2 May 1943.
21. ibid.
22. Grant, *Spitfires Over Darwin*, p. 80.
23. 'Heavy Losses Sustained in Raid on Darwin', *Canberra Times*, 4 May 1943.
24. Odgers, *Air War Against Japan*, p. 49.
25. 'Heavy Losses Sustained in Raid on Darwin', *Canberra Times*, 4 May 1943; see also Odgers, *Air War Against Japan*, p. 49.

26. Alexander, *Caldwell*, p. 129.
27. Kenney, *General Kenney Reports*, pp. 239–40.

19 'Show of force'

1. NAA A9186, 457 Squadron ORB, 28 May 1943.
2. AC1 Howdle, diary 20 June 1943.
3. Sydney *Sun*, quoted in Alexander, *Caldwell*, p. 139.
4. ibid., p. 140.
5. Howdle, diary 17 August 1943.
6. McAulay, *Six Aces*, p. 211.
7. Grant, *Spitfires Over Darwin*, p. 148.
8. OAFH, '31 Squadron', p. 4.
9. Millington, 'Beaufighter Bash', *RAAF Saga*, p. 174.
10. 'New Scene', *RAAF Log*, p. 18.
11. AWM PR00587, F/O P. Hopton, 7 Sqn, letters 19 June, 4 July 1943.
12. Howard, *86 Squadron 1943–45*, p. 25.
13. Shores and Williams, *Aces High*, p. 632.
14. F/Sgt J. Shaw, 86 Sqn, diary 21–28 January 1944, c/o Peter Hunter.

20 Breaking the Bismarcks Barrier

1. Bergerud, *Fire in the Sky*, p. 302.
2. Hewitt, *Adversity in Success*, p. 61
3. ibid., pp. 86–7, 160.
4. OAFH, 459/493, 'Chronological Order of Offensive Operations', p. 9.
5. AWM PR00756, A. Gately, 'A Call to Arms', pp. 33–4.
6. Kingsland interview, Tape 2, Side B.
7. Hunt, diary 28 December 1943.
8. Walmsley, diary 26 July 1943.
9. Tayler, diary 11 August 1943.
10. AWM PR00646, Raffen interview, p. 537.
11. Gallagher, *Meatballs and Dead Birds*, p. 35.
12. Quoted in King, *Song of the Beauforts*, p. 108.
13. Parnell, *Beaufighters in the Pacific*, p. 48.
14. Arthur, letter 21 September 1943.
15. Odgers, *Air War Against Japan*, pp. 85–6.
16. OAFH, 459/321, 'Finschhafen Air Operations', p. 7.
17. AWM MSS0702, Len Hall (ed.), 'The Originals', p. 1.
18. Clegg, diary 12–13 October 1943.
19. Letter in AWM PR00218, Chaplain D. Trathen, 8 Squadron, from Mrs Bailey, 16 November 1943.
20. Powell, *Two Steps to Tokyo*, pp. 35–6.
21. Gately, 'A Call to Arms', p. 40.
22. AWM PR01192/235–6, Telegram 8 November 1943. Letter from Chaplain the Rev R.S [surname indecipherable], 5 November 1943.

23. Hewitt, *Adversity in Success*, pp. 171, 194–5.
24. AWM MSS1559, H. Johnson, '8 Squadron RAAF Beaufort Torpedo Bomber World War 2', p. 5.
25. Trathen collection, letter from Mrs E. Hooper, 20 November 1943.
26. AWM PR00239, LAC E. Hubbard, 8 Sqn, diary 8 November 1943.
27. ibid., 14 November 1943.
28. Hewitt, *Adversity in Success*, pp. 208–9.
29. Stephens, *Power Plus Attitude*, p. 67.
30. Hubbard, diary 17 and 22 December 1943.
31. Trathen collection, letter from Mrs L. Miller, 11 January 1944.
32. Hewitt, *Adversity in Success*, p. 211.
33. Hubbard, diary 2 January 1944.
34. Trathen collection, letter from Mr J. Sinclair, 11 March 1944.

21 Nuisance raids and bloody good shows

1. Quoted in Parnell, *Beaufighters in the Pacific*, p. 56.
2. Loudon, logbook 25 January 1944. Steege in Loudon, logbook 7 May 1944.
3. Powell, *Two Steps to Tokyo*, p. 136.
4. Hewitt, *Adversity in Success*, p. 174.
5. OAFH, 460/466, '43 Squadron Interview with Flight Sergeant T.E. Carman', p. 3.
6. Wearne, 'Friends for Life', in Gaunt and Cleworth, *Cats at War*, p. 81.
7. Carman interview, p. 5.
8. Odgers, *Air War Against Japan*, p. 173.
9. AWM MSS1514, James-Martin, memoir, p. 13.
10. AWM PR00023, LAC Burns, 78 Sqn, diary 2 March 1944.
11. PR87/150, WO K. Ellis, 78 Fighter Wing, diary 13 March 1944.
12. 'Attack Aircraft 22 Squadron', p. 5.
13. SLV, La Trobe Collection, MS 11884, Lt Cdr P. Carr, RAN, letter 29 December 1945.

22 Burma and India

1. OAFH, 460/1640, 'Interview Pilot Officer W.J. McKerracher', p. 6.
2. AWM MSS1327, W. McLellan, memoir, p. 5.
3. Gallagher, *Retreat in the East*, pp. 158–160, quoted in NAA A705, 'Lee, Sidney Francis', p. 11.
4. Gillison, *Royal Australian Air Force*, p. 406n.
5. Veitch, *Fly*, p. 173.
6. OAFH, 460/1539, 'Interview Flight Lieutenant D.J. Barnett', p. 1.
7. OAFH, 460/1603, 'Interview Flight Lieutenant D.A. Golder'.
8. OAFH, 460/1622, 'Interview Flight Lieutenant K.A.S. Mann', p. 5.
9. Shores, *Air War for Burma*, pp. 52–3.

10. AWM MSS1056, Besley, 'Six Years in Uniform', p. 63.
11. Franks, *Spitfires over the Arakan*, p. 85.
12. Shores, *Air War for Burma*, p. 140.
13. AWM MSS1327, McLellan, 'Tigers and Sentinels', p. 1.
14. Shores, *Air War for Burma*, p. 180.
15. W/O R. Layfield in Odgers, *Air War Against Japan*, p. 413.
16. McLellan, 'Tigers and Sentinels', pp. 1–5.

23 Island hopping

1. AWM PR01563, O'Keeffe, 'Reminiscences of Second World War', p. 32.
2. Burns, diary 27 April 1944.
3. Jones, *From Private to Air Marshal*, p. 92.
4. AWM PR00646, P/O G. Hiller, 30 Sqn, diary 27 August 1944.
5. NAA, A9186, 43 Squadron Operations Record Book, October 1944.
6. Broughton, 'Slow Boat to China', in ibid., p. 214.
7. Carr, letter 29 December 1945. His emphasis.
8. Mariah, *Touched by War*, p. 52.
9. ibid., p. 54.
10. ibid., p. 82.
11. Hiller, diary 11 June 1944.
12. ibid., 14–16 June 1944.
13. Odgers, *Air War Against Japan*, p. 253.
14. AWM PR00704, LAC A. Kaye, 30 Sqn, diary 13 July 1944.
15. Hubbard, diary 7 August 1944.
16. Odgers, *Air War Against Japan*, p. 223.
17. AWM PR01202, P/O R. Barlow, 80 Sqn, diary 13 May 1944.
18. ibid., 3 June 1944.
19. OAFH, 460/804, 'Admiralties Campaign—77 Squadron Ground Party Interview Flight Lieutenant Irwin'.
20. Hiller, diary 4, 9 August 1944.
21. ibid., 18 August 1944.
22. OAFH, 459/1588, Interview with S/Ldr Rooke, p. 5.

24 The rise of 'TAF–RAAF'

1. Hiller, diary 12 September 1944.
2. NAA A9186, 22 Squadron ORB, October 1944, p. 348.
3. Hunt, diary 2, 11 October 1944.
4. A9186, 22 Squadron ORB, 4 October 1944, p. 351.
5. AWM MSS1547, Hicks, Memoir of 4 October 1944 raid, p. 13.
6. Odgers, *Air War Against Japan*, p. 378.
7. 'Taf-RAAF'—Dacy, diary 28 April 1945.
8. In Stephens, *Power Plus Attitude*, p. 82.
9. Odgers, *Air War Against Japan*, p. 436.

10. Hunt, diary 23 November 1944.
11. J. Scott, 'World War Two', pp. 18, 24. Graham, 'Kittyhawk Victory', *RAAF Saga*, p. 103.
12. AWM PR00346, LAC A. Brealey, 452 Sqn, diary 13 December 1944.
13. ibid., 23 December 1944.
14. ibid., 24 December 1944.
15. Hunt, diary 25 December 1944.
16. ibid., 29–31 December 1944.

25 'Brothers in arms' and 'mutineers'

1. AWM PR03108, Wailes, 'Life in the Armed Services 1942–1945', p. 39.
2. ibid., pp. 45, 57, 59.
3. Quoted in King, *Song of the Beauforts*, pp. 230–1.
4. The badge is AWM REL31197. The letters are at AWM PR01788, Shipman collection.
5. King, *Song of the Beauforts*, pp. 234–5.
6. Hunt, diary 22 December 1944.
7. Odgers, *Air War Against Japan*, p. 381.
8. Brealey, diary 13 January 1945.
9. NAA A705, File 166/17/951, 'Hann, Francis Lawrence', letter on p. 47.
10. J. Scott, 'World War Two', p. 17.
11. Arthur, letter 23 December 1944.
12. Odgers, *Air War Against Japan*, p. 388.
13. Quoted in Nelmes, *Tocumwal to Tarakan*, p. 101. Capitals in original.
14. NAA A705, 166/1/319 PART 3, 'Presumption of Death—Casualties in Royal Australian Air Force Units', p. 105.
15. J. Scott, 'World War Two', pp. 46–8.
16. Minty, *Black Cats*, p. 228.
17. Estimate and commander in Bergerud, *Fire in the Sky*, p. 623.
18. Quoted in Odgers, *Air War Against Japan*, pp. 436–7.
19. ibid., p. 438.
20. ibid., p. 439.
21. NAA A9186, 77 Squadron ORB, 16 March 1945, p. 463.
22. Ellis, diary 19 December 1944.
23. Hunter, 'The Sisters Fly On', *Victory Roll*, p. 43.
24. Arthur, letter 8 April 1945.
25. Odgers, *Air War Against Japan*, p. 444.
26. ibid., p. 445.
27. Jones, *From Private to Air Marshal*, pp. 94–5.
28. Nelmes, *Tocumwal to Tarakan*, p. 110.

26 The final battles

1. Nelmes, *Tocumwal to Tarakan*, p. 127.

2. Odgers, *Air War Against Japan*, p. 456.
3. Stephens, *Royal Australian Air Force*, p. 120.
4. Odgers, *Air War Against Japan*, p. 457.
5. Arthur, letter 3 May 1945.
6. Stanley, *Tarakan*, p. 96.
7. ibid., p. 133.
8. AWM PR03055, LAC W. Collins, RAAF Group 839, Diary May–June 1945.
9. Brealey, diary 20 May 1945.
10. NAA A9845, Kittyhawk A29, Accidents Part 24, pp. 40–1.
11. OAFH, 459/1119, Interview with F/Lt W.E. Richardson.
12. James-Martin, Memoir, p. 25.
13. Collins, diary 28 June 1945.
14. Quirk, diary 30 June 1945.
15. Dear old Lib: Quirk, diary 11 June 1944; Like a bird: Lionel Hogg in O'Keeffe, reminiscences, p. 110.
16. Quirk, diary 2 July 1945. Donor: Judy Foster.
17. Ellis, diary 24 July 1945.
18. NAA A705, Presumption of death, p. 43.
19. NAA 9300, Service record for 'Newman, Benjamin Bernard', p. 30.
20. NAA A9186, 452 Squadron ORB, 4 and 15 August 1945, pp. 370–1.

Conclusion

1. James-Martin, Memoir, p. 27.
2. AWM Murdoch Sound Archive S01504, John Harrison interview 1991, Tape 2, Side A.
3. Arthur interview, Tape 3, Side B.
4. Stephens, *Power Plus Attitude*, p. 57.
5. Hewitt, *Adversity in Success*, p. 154.
6. RAAF figures from *RAAF Saga*, p. 188; US figures from Army Air Forces Statistical Digest World War II, Table 140, <www.usaaf.net/digest/t140.htm> [10 September 2010].
7. Bergerud, *Fire in the Sky*, pp. 381–2.
8. *RAAF Saga*, p. 61.
9. Clark, diary 1–6 October 1942.
10. Arthur, letter 6 June 1943. His emphasis.
11. Quoted in Stephens, *Royal Australian Air Force*, p. 109.
12. Trathen collection, letter from F. Pitman, 22 November 1943.
13. J. Scott, 'World War Two', p. 70.
14. Wearne interview, Tape 2, Side B.
15. Monk, memoir pp. 7–8.
16. Arthur, letter 13 March 1943.
17. Tucker interview, Tape 2, Side A.
18. Mariah, *Touched by War*, p. xi.

19. Tucker interview, Tape 3, Side B.
20. AWM PR00467, Diary of unknown Japanese soldier, 23 April 1943.
21. AWM PR00646, Catt interview, p. 72.
22. AWM PR00646, Harvey interview, p. 245.
23. F/Sgt A. Makeham, 76 Sqn, diary 6, 14, 22 October 1944, in Roe, 'Reminiscences of my time as a Medical Officer', Attchment 2.
24. Page, *Wings of Destiny*, p. 204.
25. Boxall, memoir, p. 24.
26. Hunt, diary 11 February 1945.

Appendix B

1. Ian Loudon, Logbook.

Appendix C

1. Shores, *Air War for Burma*, pp. 148–50.

Bibliography

OFFICIAL RECORDS

National Archives of Australia:

Series A9186, RAAF Unit History Sheets; Forms A50 and A51; Operations Record Books for these squadrons: Nos 2, 4, 6, 11, 13, 22, 30, 31, 32, 43, 75, 76, 77, 79, 452, 457

Series A9845, Beaufighter Accidents Part 7; Kittyhawk Accidents Parts 7, 10, 24; Liberator Accidents Part 2

A705,163/series, Casualty files for Ronald Summerson Bailey, David Stuart Brown, John Joseph Burns, Norman Richard Chapman, William Nicholas Pax Cosgrove, Warren Frank Cowan, David Hersey, Sidney Francis Lee, Francis Charles Marriner, Ronald Reginald Oelrich, Colin Burns Treloar

A705,166/series, Casualty files for John Pretty Bailey, Francis Lawrence Hann, Jack Holloway, John Edward MacLeod, William Roderick McGuigan, Gordon Horace White

A705 File 166/1/319 Part 3, 'Presumption of death—Casualties in Royal Australian Air Force Units'

A9300, Service records for Joseph Cohen, Warren Frank Cowan, John Grey Gorton, Godfrey Ellard Hemsworth, Benjamin Bernard Newman, William Ellis Newton, Ronald Kevin Critchley O'Connor, Cyril William Stark, Donald Ferguson Thomson

A9435, Control Symbol 36, 9 Operational Group Narrative Report in file entitled: 'Commanding Officers' reports—Monthly reports and unit history sheets (A50)—Various Operational Base Units'

A11093, 'RAAF Command Headquarters—South West Pacific Area—Reinforcement of "Fall River" [Allied Airfield—New Guinea]'

Office of Air Force History—see also 'Interviews' (first number refers to Roll 459 or 460, second to File):

'2 Squadron Monthly Scoreboard', 459/1176

'4 Squadron Summary of Operations carried out in Papua', 459/1311

'8 Squadron Work of Beauforts', 459/ 1381

'18 Squadron Précis', 459/1651

'20 Squadron Experience with Fragmentation Bombs and Incendiaries', 460/50

'20 Squadron Report Corporal Keen 4 February 1942', 460/29

'31 Squadron', 460/400

'75 Squadron at Moresby and Milne Bay', 460/539

'75 Squadron Particulars of Formation and Main Attacks from 21 March–3 May 1942', 460/549

'76 Squadron Milne Bay Etc', 460/717

'77 Squadron Combat Report 11 April 1943', 460/734

'77 Squadron Combat Report Flying Officer J.A.T. Hodgkinson, 14 April 1943', 460/752

'78 Squadron Points from Operations Book', 460/855

'Attack Aircraft 22 Squadron History November 1942–September 1944', 460/122

'Battle of the Bismark [sic] Sea 30 Squadron US Air crew reports', 459/565

'Battle of the Bismarck Sea—ATIS Reports', 459/519

'Battle of the Bismark [sic] Sea. Attack by 30 Squadron', 459/547

'Battle of the Bismark [sic] Sea. Extracts from 9 OG Operations Record Book', 459/541

'Brief Sketch of No. 100 Squadron', 460/1068

'Buna Operations', Captured Japanese documents, 459/158

'Chronological Order of Offensive Operations' (30 Squadron), 459/493

'Coastwatchers Flight Lieutenant Leigh G. Vial', 459/429

'Composite Combat Report 2 May 1943', 462/1320

'Finschhafen Air Operations', 459/321

'Japanese Convoy attacked by Allied aircraft in Bismark [sic] Sea', 459/439

'No. 77 Squadron Interception of Raid at Milne Bay, Midday 14/4/1943', 460/799

'Operational Complaints and Difficulties Concerning Rabaul', 459/0101

'RAAF Operations from Rabaul', Sqn Leader W.D. Brookes, 24 Sqn, Report 24 February 1942, 459/87

'Rabaul Catalina Attacks February 1942', 459/77

'Report by S/Leader L. Jackson to G/Capt Garing, 2 September 1942', 460/526

Personal wartime testimonies:

Arthur, W., S/Ldr to Gp Capt. Letters. AWM PR01192

Barlow, R., P/O, 80 Sqn. Diary. AWM PR01202

Bates, A., W/O, 11 Sqn. 'Pacific Pilgrimage'. Diary/reminiscence. AWM PR03185
Brayne, A., Sgt, 31 Radar Station. Diary/reminiscence. AWM PR03202
Brealey, A., LAC, 452 Sqn. Diary. AWM PR00346
Burns, W., LAC, 78 Sqn. Diary. AWM PR00023
Clark, J., Sgt, 6 Sqn. Diaries. AWM PR01241
Clegg, C., LAC, 14 RSU. Diary. AWM PR89/188
Collins, W., LAC, RAAF Group 839. Diary. AWM PR03055
Cosgrove, W., Sgt, 84 Squadron. Letter. AWM PR00646
Crouch, L., LAC, 30 Sqn. Diary. AWM PR00646
Dacy, D., LAC, Group 45 RAAF. Diary. AWM PR00782
Davis, R., W/Cdr, 1 Sqn. Diary and Narrative of events. AWM PR87/076
Ellis, K., W/O, 78 Fighter Wing. Diary. AWM PR87/150
Farnes, R., F/Sgt, 18 Netherlands East Indies Sqn. Diary. AWM PR83/108
Fletcher, A., Sgt, 13 Sqn. Diary. AWM PR01225
Golledge, K., LAC, 30 Sqn. Diary. AWM PR00646
Hiller, G., P/O, 30 Sqn. Diary. AWM PR00646
Hopton, P., F/O, 7 Sqn. Letters, logbook, articles. AWM PR00587
Howdle, D., AC1 to LAC, 55 or 52 Operational Base Unit. Diaries. AWM PR00725
Hubbard, E., LAC, 8 Sqn. Diary. AWM PR00239
Hunt, V., Cpl, 22 Sqn. Diaries. AWM 3DRL/6732
James, R., F/O, 2 Sqn. Letters and other papers. AWM PR00661
Kaye, A., LAC, 30 Sqn. Diary. AWM PR00704
Kerr, H., P/O, 76 Sqn. Logbook. Donor: Harry Kerr via Peter Hunter
Loudon, I., S/Ldr, 76 Sqn. logbook. Donor: Stu Loudon via Peter Hunter
Moline, J., F/O, 20 Sqn. Diary. AWM PR85/385
Quirk, T., Sgt, 21 Sqn. Diary. Donor: Judy Foster
Russell, F., F/Sgt, 11 Squadron. Letter 8 March 1942. AWM PR00298
Shanahan, J., LAC, 453 Sqn. Diary. AWM 3DRL/6601
Shaw, J., F/Sgt, 86 Sqn. Diary. Donor: Jack Shaw via Peter Hunter
Spencer, E., LAC, 5 Mobile Works Sqn. Diary. AWM PR87/041
Tayler, H., LAC, 30 Sqn. Diary. AWM PR00646
Trathen, D., Chaplain, 8 Squadron. Letters. AWM PR00218
Walmsley, C., Cpl to Sgt, 76 Sqn. Diaries. AWM PR00742
Wawn, C., F/Lt, 76 Sqn. Logbook. Donor: Wawn family via Peter Hunter
Whyte, J., W/Cdr, 2 Sqn. Letter. AWM PR00661
Woodgate, T., Sgt, 13 Sqn. Letter. AWM 3DRL/7554
Woodward, J., Sgt, 27 Sqn RAF. Diary. AWM PR00158

Unpublished post-war reminiscences:

Besley, Harvey, 'Six Years in Uniform', n.d., AWM MSS1056
Bladin, Francis, 'Memoir', 1977. Donors: Marnie O'Bryan and Jacqueline Crock
Boxall, Alec, memoir, 1993, AWM MSS1514 (under 'James-Martin')

Bridgman, Max, 'Rabaul', 1992, AWM MSS1429
Carr, Lt Cdr Palgrave, letter, 1945, State Library of Victoria, MS 11884
Day, A., 'The air war over the Arakan 1942–5', AWM MSS1327
Dyer, Alan, 'Anecdotes from the early days of 75 Squadron RAAF', c. 1992, AWM MSS1462
Gately, Arthur, 'A Call to Arms: War Service with the RAAF 1942–1946', AWM PR00756
Hall, Len, 'The Originals', AWM MSS0702
Hicks, W.D., memoir of Ambon air raid, AWM MSS1547
James-Martin, Howard, memoir, 1993, AWM MSS1514
Johnson, H.N., '8 Squadron RAAF Beaufort Torpedo Bomber World War 2', 1995, AWM MSS1559
Lovegrove, John, Sgt, materials relating to escape from Java, AWM PR00443
McLellan, Wal, memoir and 'Tigers and Sentinels', AWM MSS1327
McMahon, S/Ldr F. X., memoir of Darwin bombing, n.d, AWM PR01196
Monk, Clive, reminiscence of Tarakan, AWM PR00719
Munro, Ron, 'A resume of my experiences in the RAAF, 1941–45', 2000, AWM PR01751
Neal, Raymond, '44 Days Plus', 1992, AWM MSS1420
Newton, William E., materials relating to service, AWM PR83/021
Nicholson, Keith, 'Memoirs of World War II', AWM PR00646
O'Keeffe, John, 'Reminiscences of Second World War', n.d., AWM PR01563
Roe, Charles, 'Reminiscences of my time as a Medical Officer in the Royal Australian Air Force From 1943 to 1946', n.d. Donor: Charles Roe
Scott, Douglas, recollections, 1984, AWM PR87/109
Scott (Read), F/O Nancy J., 'A History of the Royal Australian Air Force Medical Air Evacuation Unit', 1989, AWM PR89/018
Scott, J.C.H., 'World War Two, as seen by one participant', n.d., AWM MSS1510
Wailes, Alan, 'Life in the Armed Services 1942–1945', 2001, AWM PR03108
Wardley, E.R., Memoir of Service, n.d., AWM 3DRL/7976
Woodhouse, L., 'RAAF memories', 1986, AWM PR86/330

INTERVIEWS

Australian War Memorial, Keith Murdoch Sound Archive interviews:

Arthur, Wilfred, 1989, S00731
Brown, Bruce, 1989, S00583
Garing, Bill, 1989, S00586
Gould, Nat, 1989, S00578
Harrison, John, 1991, S01504
Hull, Cliff, 1989, S00734
Jeffrey, Peter, 1990, S00951
Kingsland, Sir Richard, 1990, S00922

Lancaster, Alan, 1989, S00953
Lindeman, Colin, 1989, S00548
Piper, John, 1989, S00577
Tucker, Arthur, 1989, S00701
Wearne, Athol, 1989, S00755
Whetters, Alan, 1989, S00592

30 Squadron Beaufighter crew interviews, undertaken by George Dick, and collected in AWM PR00646:
Frederick Anderson; Donald Angus; Maurice Ball; David Beasley; George Carnegie; Frederick Cassidy; Alfred Catt; Clive Cooke; Robert Cummins; Kenneth Delbridge; George Dick; John Farquhar; Charles Harris; Colin Harvey; Leonard Hastwell; Arthur Jaggs; John Mason; James Mierisch; Ralph Nelson; Douglas Raffen; Harold Suthons; Bob Wemyss; Richard Woodgate

Interviews with the author:
Kessey, John, 31 January 2010
Plenty, Herb, 30 January 2010
Roe, Charles, 16 October 2010
Shaw, Jack, 28 September 2008

Office of Air Force History wartime interviews:
Barnett, D.J., F/Lt, 460/1539
Belcher, H., F/Lt, 459/251
Bolitho, W.K., W/Cdr, 460/17
Brookes, W.D., Gp Capt, 460/284
Carman, T.E. F/Sgt, 460/466
Curtis, R.P., S/Ldr, 460/797
Downing, G.R., F/O, 460/387
Golder, D.A., F/Lt, 460/1603
Hack, B., Sgt, 459/1571
Higgs, F.G., F/Lt, 460/236
Irwin, L., F/Lt, 460/804
Law, L.W., S/Ldr, 460/1012
Lindemann, C.W., S/Ldr, 460/519
Mann, K.A.S., F/Lt, 460/1622
Matson, M.I., W/Cdr, 460/539
McKerracher, W.J., P/O, 460/1640
Richardson, W.E., F/Lt, 459/1119
Rooke, N.H.R., S/Ldr, 459/1588
Savage, G.W., Gp Capt, 460/418
Storey, W.J., S/Ldr, 460/1650
Tyrell, J.V., F/Lt, 460/306

Wilson, D.L., S/Ldr, 460/712

Other:

Cassidy, Fred, 'The Australians at War Film Archive', Archive No. 0031, <www.australiansatwarfilmarchive.gov.au/aawfa/interviews/33.aspx> [23 August 2010]

Spurgeon, C.H., 17 March 1991, AWM PR91/124

Wright, John, <www.australiansatwarfilmarchive.gov.au/aawfa/interviews/445.aspx> [23 August 2010]

Yeowart, Robert, 1943, AWM PR91/73

BOOKS

Affleck, James (ed.), *Geelong Grammarians at War*, Geelong Grammarians Inc., Corio, 2002

Alexander, Kristen, *Clive Caldwell, Air Ace*, Allen & Unwin, Crows Nest, 2006

Alford, Bob, *Darwin's Air War, 1942–1945: An illustrated history*, Colemans Printing, Darwin, 1991

Ashworth, Norman, *How Not to Run an Air Force!: The Higher Command of the Royal Australian Air Force during the Second World War*, 2 volumes, Air Power Studies Centre, Canberra, 2000

Australian War Memorial, *The Beaufort Bomber*, Australian War Memorial, Canberra, 2003

Baker, Clive and Knight, Greg, *Milne Bay 1942*, Baker-Knight Publications, Loftus, 1992

Balfe, J.D., *War Without Glory: Australians in the air war with Japan 1941–45*, Macmillan, South Melbourne, 1984

Barnes, Norman, *The RAAF and the Flying Squadrons*, Allen & Unwin, St Leonards, 2000

Bennett, John, *Defeat to Victory: No. 453 Squadron RAAF*, Royal Australian Air Force Museum, Point Cook, 1994

——*Highest Traditions: The History of No. 2 Squadron, RAAF*, AGPS Press, Canberra, 1995

Bergerud, Eric M., *Fire in the Sky: The air war in the South Pacific*, Westview, Boulder, 2001

Birdsall, Steve, *Flying Buccaneers: The illustrated story of Kenney's Fifth Air Force*, Doubleday, New York, 1977

Bradley, Phillip, *The Battle for Wau: New Guinea's frontline 1942–1943*, Cambridge University Press, Port Melbourne, 2008

Brune, Peter, *A Bastard of a Place: The Australians in Papua*, Allen & Unwin, 2003

Bulcock, Roy, *Of Death But Once*, F.W. Cheshire, Melbourne, 1947

Bullard, Steve (translator), *Japanese Army Operations in the South Pacific Area : New Britain and Papua campaigns, 1942–43*, Australian War Memorial, Canberra, 2007

Cassells, Vic, *The Capital Ships: Their battles and their badges*, Kangaroo Press, East

Roseville, 2000

Coulthard-Clark, C.D., *The Third Brother: The Royal Australian Air Force*, Allen & Unwin, Sydney, 1991

Craven, W.F. and Cate, J.L. (eds), *The Army Air Forces in World War II*, Volume I, Plans & Early Operations, January 1939 To August 1942, <www.ibiblio.org/hyperwar/AAF/I/> [10 September 2010]

——Volume IV, The Pacific: Guadalcanal to Saipan, August 1942 to July 1944, University of Chicago Press, Chicago, 1950

Cull, Brian, Sortehaug, Paul and Haselden, Mark, *Buffaloes Over Singapore*, Grub Street, London, 2004

Cutlack, F.M., *The Australian Flying Corps, The Official History of Australia in the War of 1914–1918*, Vol. 8, Angus & Robertson, Sydney, 1941

Deane-Butcher, W., *Fighter Squadron Doctor: 75 Squadron R.A.A.F. New Guinea 1942*, W. Deane-Butcher, Sydney, 1989

Dear, I.C.B. and Foot, M.R.D. (eds), *The Oxford Companion to the Second World War*, Oxford University Press, Oxford, 1995

Dennis, Peter, Grey, Jeffrey, Morris, Ewan and Prior, Robin (eds), *The Oxford Companion to Australian Military History*, Oxford University Press, South Melbourne, 1995 and 2008

Dynes, Phil, *Leyburn's Liberators*, Hinchcliffe, Sandgate, n.d.

Eather, Steve, *Flying Squadrons of the Australian Defence Force*, Aerospace Publications, Canberra, 1995

——*Blue Lightning: The story of 6 Squadron 1917–2005*, Australian Military History Publications, Loftus, 2007

Francillon, René J., *Japanese Aircraft of the Pacific War*, Naval Institute Press, Annapolis, 1990

Franks, Norman, *Spitfires over the Arakan*, William Kimber, London, 1988

Gallagher, James P., *Meatballs and Dead Birds: A photo gallery of destroyed Japanese aircraft in World War II*, Stackpole Books, Mechanicsburg, 2004

Garrisson, A.D., *Australian Fighter Aces 1914–1953*, Air Power Studies Centre and Australian War Memorial, Canberra, 1999

Gaunt, Coral and Cleworth, Robert, *Cats at War: The story of RAAF Catalinas in the Asia–Pacific theatre of war*, J.R. Cleworth, Roseville, 2000

Gill, G. Hermon, *Royal Australian Navy, 1942–1945*, Australian War Memorial, Canberra, 1968

Gillison, Douglas, *Royal Australian Air Force*, Australian War Memorial, Canberra, 1962

Grant, Jim, *Spitfires over Darwin 1943: No. 1 Fighter Wing*, TechWrite Solutions, South Melbourne, 2003

Grantham, Sid, *The 13 Squadron Story*, S.R. Grantham, Dee Why, 1991

Grose, Peter, *An Awkward Truth: The bombing of Darwin, February 1942*, Allen & Unwin, Crows Nest, 2009

Gunston, Bill, *Combat Aircraft of World War II*, Tiger Books, London, 1990

Hall, E.R. (Bon), *Glory in Chaos: The RAAF in the Far East in 1940–42*, Sembawang Association, West Coburg, 1989

Hancock, Valston, *Challenge*, Access Press, Northbridge, 1990

Hasluck, Paul, *The Government and the People, 1939–1941*, Australian War Memorial, Canberra, 1952

Helson, Peter, *The Private Air Marshal: A Biography of Air Marshal Sir George Jones, KBE, CB, DFC*, Air Power Development Centre, Canberra, 2010

Hewitt, Air Vice Marshal J.E., *Adversity in Success*, Langate Publishing, South Yarra, 1980

Horner, David, *High Command: Australia's struggle for an independent war strategy, 1939–45*, Allen & Unwin, Sydney, 1992

Howard, Peter F., *86 Squadron 1943–45: Men, Kittyhawks and Mustangs*, P.F. Howard, Turramurra, 1999

Jackson, Patricia and Arthur (eds), *A Lot to Fight For: The war diaries and letters of S/Ldr J.F. Jackson, DFC*, Church Archivists Press, Virginia, Queensland, 2001

Johnston, Susan and Nation, Lindsay, *Australia 1939*, NSW University Press, Kensington, 1989

Jones, Sir George, *From Private to Air Marshal: The autobiography of Air Marshal Sir George Jones*, Greenhouse Publications, Richmond, 1988

Kelly, Robert H., *Allied Air Transport Operations South West Pacific Area in WWII*, Vol. 1, Robert H. Kelly, Buderim, 2003

Kenney, George C., *General Kenney Reports*, Officer of Air Force History, Washington D.C., 1987

King, Colin M., *Song of the Beauforts: No 100 Squadron RAAF and the Beaufort bomber operations*, Air Power Development Centre, Canberra, 2007

Lockwood, Douglas, *Australia's Pearl Harbour, Darwin 1942*, Penguin Books, Ringwood, 1992

Long, Gavin, *The Six Years War*, Australian War Memorial, Canberra, 1973

Mariah, Lisa, *Touched by War: Memoirs of a Beaufighter pilot*, Australian Military History Publications, Loftus, 2006

Masters, Peter with Turner, Jenny, *Born Lucky*, Seaview Press, Henley Beach, 1998

Mayer, S.L. (ed.), *The Japanese War Machine*, Ure Smith, Sydney, 1976

McAulay, Lex, *Battle of the Bismarck Sea*, Burbank's Books, Blackwood, 1999

——*Blood and Iron: The battle for Kokoda 1942*, Arrow, Milsons Point, 1992

——*Macarthur's Eagles: The U.S. air war over New Guinea 1943–1944*, Naval Institute Press, Annapolis, 2005

——*Six Aces: Australian fighter pilots, 1939–45*, Banner Books, Brunswick, 1991

——*We Who Are About To Die: The story of John Lerew, a hero of Rabaul, 1942*, Banner Books, Maryborough, 2007

McCarthy, Dudley, *South-West Pacific Area—First Year: Kokoda to Wau*, Australian War Memorial, Canberra, 1959

McDonald, Kenneth, *Coomalie Charlie's Commandos: 31 Squadron RAAF Beaufighters at Darwin 1942–43*, Banner Books, Maryborough, 1996

McDonald, Neil, *Damien Parer's War*, Lothian, South Melbourne, 2003

Minty, A.E. (ed.), *Black Cats: The real story of Australia's long range Catalina strike force in the Pacific War*, RAAF Museum, Point Cook, 1994

Moremon, John, *Royal Australian Air Force 1941–1945*, Department of Veterans' Affairs, Canberra, 2005

Nelmes, Michael V., *Tocumwal to Tarakan: Australians and the Consolidated B-24 Liberator*, Banner Books, Belconnen, 1994

Nelson, Hank, *Chased by the Sun: The Australians in Bomber Command in World War II*, Allen & Unwin, Sydney, 2006

——*P.O.W. Prisoners of War: Australians under Nippon*, Australian Broadcasting Corporation, Sydney, 1985

Newton, Dennis, *Australian Air Aces: Australian fighter pilots in combat*, Aerospace Publications, Canberra, 1996

Odgers, George, *Air War Against Japan 1943–45*, Australian War Memorial, Canberra, 1957

—— *RAAF: An illustrated history*, Child and Henry, Brookvale, 1984

——*Mr Double Seven: A biography of Wing Commander Dick Cresswell, DFC*, Air Power Development Centre, Tuggeranong, 2008

Olynyk, Frank, *Stars and Bars: A tribute to the American fighter ace 1920–1973*, Grub Street, London, 1995

Overy, R.J., *The Air War 1939–1945*, Stein and Day, New York, 1981

Page, Charles, *Wings of Destiny: Wing Commander Charles Learmonth DFC and Bar and the air war in New Guinea*, Rosenberg Publishing, Dural, 2008

Parnell, N.M., *Whispering Death: A history of the RAAF's Beaufighter squadrons*, Reed, Sydney, 1980

—— *Beaufighters in the Pacific: A history of the RAAF's Beaufighter Squadrons in the South-West Pacific Area*, N.M. Parnell, Eastwood, 2005

Parnell, N.M. and Lynch, C.A., *Australian Air Force Since 1911*, A.H. & A.W. Reed, Sydney, 1976

Pentland, Geoffrey, *RAAF Camouflage and Markings, 1939–1945*, 2 vols, Kookaburra Technical Publications, Melbourne, 1980 and 1989

Powell, Alan, *The Shadow's Edge: Australia's northern War*, Charles Darwin University Press, Darwin, 2007

Powell, Gordon, *Two Steps to Tokyo: A story of the R.A.A.F. in the Trobriand and Admiralty Islands*, Oxford University Press, London, 1945

RAAF Historical Section, *Units of the Royal Australian Air Force: A concise history*, 10 Volumes, AGPS Press, Canberra, 1995

Robertson, John, *Australia Goes to War 1939–1945*, Doubleday, Sydney, 1984

Ruwoldt, Rex, *Darwin's Battle for Australia: A history of Darwin's role in the defence of Australia in WW-2*, Darwin Defenders, Clifton Springs, 2005

Sakai, Saburo with Caidin, Martin, and Saito, Fred, *Samurai!*, Bantam, New York, 1978

Sakaida, Henry, *Japanese Army Air Force Aces 1937–45*, Osprey, Oxford, 1997

——*Imperial Japanese Navy Aces 1937–45*, Osprey, London, 1998

Selby, David, *Hell and High Fever*, Currawong, Sydney, 1956

Shelton Smith, Adele (ed.), *The Boys Write Home*, Consolidated Press, Sydney, 1944.

Sherrod, Robert, *On to Westward: The Battles of Saipan and Iwo Jima*, The Nautical and Aviation Publishing Company, Baltimore, 1990

Shores, Christopher, *Aces High, Volume 2: A further tribute to the most notable fighter pilots of the British and Commonwealth Air Forces in World War II*, Grub Street, London, 1999

——*Those Other Eagles: A tribute to the British, Commonwealth, and free European fighter pilots who claimed between two and four victories in aerial combat, 1939–1982*, Grub Street, London, 2004

—— *Air War for Burma*, Grub Street, London, 2005

Shores, Christopher, Cull, Brian and Izawa, Yasuho, *Bloody Shambles: Volume 1, The drift to war to the fall of Singapore*, Grub Street, London, 1992

——*Bloody Shambles: Volume 2, The defence of Sumatra to the fall of Burma*, Grub Street, London, 1993

Shores, Christopher and Williams, Clive, *Aces High: A tribute to the most notable fighter pilots of the British and Commonwealth Air Forces in World War II*, Grub Street, London, 1994

Southall, Ivan, *Bluey Truscott*, Angus & Robertson, Sydney, 1958

Stanley, Peter, *Tarakan: An Australian tragedy*, Allen & Unwin, St Leonards, 1997

Stephens, Alan, *Power Plus Attitude: Ideas, strategy and doctrine in the Royal Australian Air Force 1921–1991*, AGPS Press, Canberra, 1992

——*The Royal Australian Air Force*, Oxford University Press, South Melbourne, 2001

Stephens, Alan and Isaacs, Jeff, *High Fliers: Leaders of the Royal Australian Air Force*, AGPS Press, Canberra, 1996

Thomas, Andrew, *Beaufighter Aces of World War 2*, Osprey, Oxford, 2005

——*Spitfire Aces of Burma and the Pacific*, Osprey, Oxford, 2009

Turner, Jim, *The RAAF at War: World War II, Korea, Malaya & Vietnam*, Kangaroo Press, East Roseville, 1999

Various authors, *These Eagles*, Australian War Memorial, Canberra, 1942

——*RAAF Log*, Australian War Memorial, Canberra, 1943

——*RAAF Saga*, Australian War Memorial, Canberra, 1944

——*Victory Roll*, Australian War Memorial, Canberra, 1945

Veitch, Michael, *Fly*, Penguin, Camberwell, 2008

Vincent, David, *The RAAF Hudson Story*, Volume 1, D. Vincent, Highbury, 1999

Walker, Allan S., *Medical Services of the R.A.N. and R.A.A.F.*, Australian War Memorial, Canberra, 1961

Walker, Brian, *Black Jack: 50 years as a pilot; 1935–1985*, Banner Books, Canberra, 1994

Wallace, Gordon, *Up in Darwin with the Dutch: Being the story of 18 Squadron N.E.I.—R.A.A.F. forces from 1942 to 1950*, Gordon Wallace, Surrey Hills, 1984

Waters, J.C., *Valiant Youth: The men of the R.A.A.F.*, F.H. Johnston, Sydney, 1945
Watson, Richard L. Jr, *Air Action in the Papuan Campaign, 21 July 1942 to 23 January 1943*, USAAF Historical Office, Washington, DC, 1944
Weate, Mark, *Bill Newton V.C.: The short life of a RAAF hero*, Australian Military History Publications, Loftus, 1999
White, Osmar, *Green Armour: The story of fighting men in New Guinea*, Wren Publishing, Melbourne, 1972
Williams, E. Kathleen, *The Allied Air Forces in Australia to the Summer of 1942*, Intelligence Historical Division, 1944
Wilson, David, *The Decisive Factor: 75 & 76 Squadrons—Port Moresby and Milne Bay 1942*, Banner Books, Brunswick, 1991
——*Seek and Strike: 75 Squadron RAAF, 1942–2002*, Banner Books, Maryborough, 2002
——*The Brotherhood of Airmen: The men and women of the RAAF in action, 1914–today*, Allen & Unwin, Crows Nest, 2005
Wilson, Stewart, *Wirraway, Boomerang & CA-15 in Australian Service*, Aerospace, Canberra, 1981
——*The Spitfire, Mustang and Kittyhawk in Australian Service*, Aerospace, Sydney, 1988
——*Beaufort, Beaufighter and Mosquito in Australian Service*, Aerospace Publications, Weston Creek, 1990
——*Boston, Mitchell and Liberator in Australian Service*, Aerospace Publications, Weston Creek, 1992
——*Military Aircraft of Australia*, Aerospace Publications, Canberra, 1994
——*Consolidated PBY Catalina in Australian Service*, Notebook Publications, Bungendore, 2004
Winchester, Jim, *Aircraft of World War II*, Grange Books, Rochester 2004
Woodward, Jack K., *Three Times Lucky*, Boolarong Publications, Brisbane, 1991
Zimmerman, John L., *The Guadalcanal Campaign*, Historical Division USMC, Washington, 1949

ARTICLES

Baldwin, Suzy, 'Knight in flying armour', *The Bulletin*, 19 April 1988
Campbell, David, 'Recco over Rabaul', in Bartlett, Norman (ed.), *Australia at Arms*, Australian War Memorial, Canberra, 1955
Clayton, Mark, 'The north Australian air war 1942–44', *Journal of the Australian War Memorial*, vol. 8, 1986, pp. 33–45
Crotty, David, 'Leslie Knox, Australian pilot at Coral Sea', *Wartime*, issue 11, Spring 2000, pp. 16–19
——'One Wirraway's war', *Wartime*, Issue 11, Spring 2000, pp. 20–3
Daw, E.D., 'Griffith, Sturt de Burgh (1905–1979)', *Australian Dictionary of Biography*, vol. 14, Melbourne University Press, 1996, pp. 332–3
Eaton, Cpl Mark, 'Decorated and inspirational, Air Commodore Deryck Kingwell,

CBE, DSO (ret'd)', *Air Force News*, 20 June 2002
Goddard, Chris, 'Piloting a Butcher's Shop', *Wartime*, issue 17, <www.awm.gov.au/wartime/17/butcher.asp> [10 September 2010]
Isaacs, Keith, 'Cobby, Arthur Henry (1894–1955)', *Australian Dictionary of Biography*, vol. 8, Melbourne University Press, 1981, pp. 41–2
Kramer, Leonie, 'Campbell, David Watt Ian (1915–1979)', *Australian Dictionary of Biography*, vol. 13, Melbourne University Press, 1993, pp. 356–7
McAulay, Lex, 'Clisby, Leslie Redford (1914–1940)', *Australian Dictionary of Biography*, vol. 13, Melbourne University Press, 1993, pp. 445–6
Nicholson, Brendan, 'After 66 years, PNG jungle gives up downed aircraft', *The Age*, 27 September 2008
Piper, Bob, 'Zero ace honours his foes', *Panorama*, 14 February 1998
Robertson, Geoffrey, 'War pilot later led in surgery and science', *Sydney Morning Herald*, 12 September 2009
Stephens, Alan, 'Crombie, Charles Arbuthnot (1914–1945)', *Australian Dictionary of Biography*, vol. 13, Melbourne University Press, 1993, pp. 534–5
Sugahara, Kan, 'Chivalry versus Bushido', *Wartime*, issue 52, 2010, pp. 46–9
Wilson, David, 'Jackson, John Francis (1908–1942)', *Australian Dictionary of Biography*, vol. 14, Melbourne University Press, 1996, pp. 545–6

WEBSITES AND WEBSITE ARTICLES

No author, 'Aerial torpedoes—a weapon system failure', *Pathfinder*, vol. 3, July 2004, <http://airpower.airforce.gov.au/admin/ProductFiles/Publication/Materials/252/PF03_Jul04.pdf> [10 September 2010]
No author, <www.pacificwrecks.com> [10 September 2010]
No author, 'Black magic', <www.ww2australia.gov.au/lastbattles/lenwaters.html> [10 September 2010]
No author, 'Military funeral for World War II airmen', <www.defence.gov.au/media/DepartmentalTpl.cfm?CurrentId=439> [10 September 2010]
Shindo, Hiroyuki, *Japanese Air Operations over New Guinea during the Second World War*, <www.awm.gov.au/journal/j34/shindo.asp> [10 September 2010]
White, Peter, 'Memorial to a Brave Airman', *The Whisperer: Newsletter of the Beaufighter and Boston Association of Queensland*, March 2004, pp. 9–10. <www.ozatwar.com/raaf/whisperer/march2004.pdf> [10 September 2010]

DOCUMENTARIES

44 Days, ABC TV, 1992
'Ambon Journey', *George Negus Tonight*, <www.abc.net.au/gnt/history/Transcripts/s1227263.htm> [10 September 2010]
'Enemy Lines', *Australian Story*, ABC TV, 1 July 2002, <www.abc.net.au/austory/transcripts/s590505.htm> [10 September 2010]

Index